The Theology of the Oral Torah
Revealing the Justice of God

The Theology of the Oral Torah demonstrates the cogency and inner rationality of the classical statement of Judaism in the Oral Torah, bringing a theological assessment to bear on the whole of rabbinic literature. Jacob Neusner shows how the proposition that God is One and all-powerful but also merciful and just defines the system and structure of rabbinic Judaism. He argues that in working this proposition out in rich detail the classical texts generate the central rabbinic problem: how can the conflicting traits inherent in the proposition be resolved?

In *The Theology of the Oral Torah* Neusner crafts the central conceptions of rabbinic Judaism into a rigorous, coherent argument by setting forth four cogent principles: that God formed creation in accord with a plan which the Torah reveals; that the perfection of creation is signified by the conformity of human affairs to a few enduring paradigms that transcend change; that Israel's condition, public and personal, is indicative of flaws in creation; and that God will ultimately restore the perfection embodied in his plan for creation. A masterful and original construction of the theology of rabbinic Judaism, Neusner's story of the Oral Torah is also remarkably familiar – the emphasis is still on man's sin and God's response, God's justice and mercy, and the human mirroring of God through the possession of the power of will.

The Theology of the Oral Torah is part of Neusner's ongoing major project – the construction of the theology of rabbinic Judaism – a project which rivals in its scope that of the great Maimonides or, in Christian theology, that of Thomas Aquinas's *Summa*.

JACOB NEUSNER is Distinguished Research Professor of religious studies at the University of South Florida and professor of religion, Bard College, New York.

Volumes in the McGill-Queen's Studies in the History of Religion have been supported by the Jackman Foundation of Toronto.

SERIES ONE
G.A. Rawlyk, Editor

The Theology of
the Oral Torah

Revealing the Justice of God

JACOB NEUSNER

McGill-Queen's University Press
Montreal & Kingston · London · Ithaca

Legal deposit first quarter 1999
Bibliothèque nationale du Québec

Printed in Canada on acid-free paper

McGill-Queen's University Press acknowledges the financial
support of the Government of Canada through the Book
Publishing Industry Development Program Council for its
activities. We also acknowledge the support of the Canada
Council for the Arts for our publishing program.

Canadian Cataloguing in Publication Data

Neusner, Jacob, 1932–
  The theology of the Oral Torah: revealing the justice of God
  (McGill-Queen's studies in the history of religion)
  Includes bibliographical references and index.
  ISBN 0-7735-1802-9
  1. Mishnah–Criticism, interpretation, etc. 2. Judaism–
  Doctrines. 3. God–Righteousness. I. Title. II. Series.
  BM497.8.N49 1999   296.1'2306   C99-900016-0

This book was typeset by Typo Litho Composition Inc. in
10.5/13 Times.

Dedicated to
William S. Green
Manchester, New Hampshire,
on the occasion of his eightieth birthday

Contents

x   Contents

Preface

A religion of numerous gods finds many solutions to one problem, a religion of only one God presents one to many. Life is seldom fair. Rules rarely work. To explain the reason why, polytheisms adduce multiple causes of chaos, a god per anomaly. Diverse gods do various things, so, it stands to reason, ordinarily outcomes conflict. Monotheism by nature explains many things in a single way. One God rules. Life is meant to be fair, and just rules are supposed to describe what is ordinary, all in the name of that one and only God. Thus, in monotheism a simple logic governs to limit ways of making sense of things. But that logic contains its own dialectics. If one true God has done everything, then, since he is God all-powerful and omniscient, all things are credited to, and blamed on, him. In that case he can be either good or bad, just or unjust – but not both.

Responding to the generative dialectics of monotheism, the Oral Torah – the Oral [part of] the Torah revealed by God to Moses at Sinai, to adhere to the language of the documents examined here – systematically reveals the justice of the one and only God of all creation. God is not only God but also good. Appealing to the facts of Scripture, the Written part of the Torah, the sages ("our sages of blessed memory") in the first six centuries of the Common Era constructed, in the documents of the Oral part of the Torah, a coherent theology, to expose the justice of God. Here in detail I show how and with what result. I identify the *logos* of God – the theology seen whole in the Torah, Written and Oral, as set forth by the sages in its originally oral, memorized component.

The theology of the Oral Torah conveys the picture of world order based on God's justice and equity. The categorical structure of the Oral Torah encompasses the components, God and man; the Torah; Israel and the nations. The working system of the Oral Torah finds its dynamic in the struggle between God's plan for creation – to create a perfect world of justice – and man's will. That dialectics embodies in a single paradigm the events contained in the sequences of rebellion, sin, punishment, repentance, and atonement; exile and return; or the disruption of world order and the restoration of world order. None of these categories and propositions is new; anyone familiar with the principal components of the faith and piety of Judaism, the Written Torah, the Oral Torah, and the liturgy of home and synagogue will find them paramount. It is not in identifying but in forming them into a logos – a sustained, rigorous, coherent argument, that can be set forth in narrative-sequential form – that I make my contribution, hence the title of this book.

Let me set forth a somewhat more elaborate synopsis of the same story in these few, still-simple propositions, summarizing the four units of the shank of the book, by which I mean to define the four principles of the theology of the Oral Torah:

1) God formed creation in accord with a plan, which the Torah reveals. World order can be shown by the facts of nature and society set forth in that plan to conform to a pattern of reason based upon justice (chapter 2). Those who possess the Torah – Israel – know God (chapter 3) and those who do not – the gentiles – reject him in favour of idols (chapter 4). What happens to each of the two sectors of humanity, respectively, responds to their relationship with God. Israel in the present age is subordinate to the nations, because God has designated the gentiles as the medium for penalizing Israel's rebellion and, through subordination and exile, provoking it to repent. Private life as much as the public order conforms to the principle that God rules justly in a creation of perfection and stasis (chapter 5).

2) The perfection of creation, realized in the rule of exact justice, is signified by the timelessness of the world of human affairs, their conformity to a few enduring paradigms that transcend change (theology of history). No present, past, or future marks time, but only the recapitulation of those patterns (chapter 6). Perfection is further embodied in the unchanging relationships of the social commonwealth (theology of political economy), which assure that scarce resources, once allocated, remain in stasis (chapter 7). A further indication of perfection lies in the complementarity of the components of creation, on the one side, and, finally, the correspon-

dence between God and man in God's image (theological anthropology), on the other (chapters 8 and 9).

3) Israel's condition, public and personal, marks flaws in creation. What disrupts perfection is the sole power capable of standing on its own against God's power, and that is man's will (chapter 10). What man controls and God cannot coerce is man's capacity to form intention and therefore choose either arrogantly to defy, or humbly to love, God. Because man defies God, the sin that results from man's rebellion flaws creation and disrupts world order (chapter 11, theological theodicy). The paradigm of the rebellion of Adam in Eden governs, the act of arrogant rebellion leading to exile from Eden thus accounting for the condition of humanity. But, as in the original transaction of alienation and consequent exile, God retains the power to encourage repentance through punishing man's arrogance. In mercy, moreover, God exercises the power to respond to repentance with forgiveness, that is, a change of attitude evoking a counterpart change (chapter 12). Since, commanding his own will, man also has the power to initiate the process of reconciliation with God, through repentance, an act of humility, man may restore the perfection of that order that through arrogance he has marred.

4) God ultimately will restore that perfection that embodied his plan for creation. In the work of restoration, death that comes about by reason of sin will die, the dead will be raised and judged for their deeds in this life (chapter 13), and most of them, having been justified, will go on to eternal life in the world to come (chapter 14). In the paradigm of man restored to Eden, Israel's return to the Land of Israel is realized. In that world or age to come, however, that sector of humanity that through the Torah knows God will encompass all of humanity. Idolators will perish, and those who comprise Israel at the end will know the one, true God and spend eternity in his light.

Recorded in this way, the story told by the Oral Torah proves remarkably familiar, with its stress on God's justice (to which his mercy is integral), man's correspondence with God in his possession of the power of will, man's sin, and God's response.

If we translate into the narrative of Israel, from the beginning to the calamity of the destruction of the (first) Temple, what is set forth in both abstract and concrete ways in the Oral Torah, we turn out to state a reprise of the Authorized History laid out in Genesis through Kings and amplified by the principal prophets. Furthermore, the liturgy of synagogue and home recapitulates characteristic modes of thought of the Oral Torah and reworks its distinctive constructions of exemplary figures, events, and conceptions. In defining the religion that the world calls "Judaism" and that calls itself "the Torah," the sages maintained from the very beginning that they possessed the Torah revealed by God to Moses at Mount Sinai ("Moses received Torah at Sinai and handed it on to Joshua, Joshua to elders, and elders to prophets, and prophets handed it on to the men of the great assembly"). By situating the theology of the Oral Torah as the pivot between the Written Torah and the liturgy and piety of the faith, chapter 15 argues that, as a matter of fact, the sages were, and are, right in registering that claim.

To the extent that I expose that integrating logic that holds together each principal component in a single structure and accounts for the working of the system as a whole, this account of the historical theology of the authoritative documents must compel credence. By that criterion its selections of sources will prove representative (a matter explained in chapter 1). Its ordering of matters, *first this, then that*, must be judged integral and necessary. Its result, the presentation of a cogent theology in the logical sequence required by its successive propositions, possessed as they are of their own dialectics, must be confirmed as an accurate and proportionate account of the whole. So everything rests upon the logic that is contained in such simple phrases as "justice of God" and "world order," which recur throughout.

Here, beginning with the integrating basics and encompassing the entire expanse of creation and humanity, from first to last things, are the ideas that impart structure and order to, and sustain, the whole. Starting with the doctrine of a world order that is just and concluding with eternal life, I set out the simple logic that animates all the parts and makes them cohere. The generative categories defined by the thirteen chapters of the shank of the book prove not only imperative and irreducible but, in the context of my narrative, also logically sequential. Each of the four parts of my account of the theology of the Oral Torah – the perfectly just character of world order, indications of its perfection, sources of its imperfection, media for the restoration of world order and their results – belongs in its place and indeed, if set in any other sequence, the four units become incomprehensible. Further, each chapter in order, drawing upon its predecessor, pointing towards its successor, forms part of an unfolding story that can be told in only one direction and in the dictated order and in no other way. Shift the position of a chapter and place it before or after some other, and the entire flow of thought is disrupted. That is the mark of a well-crafted theology, a coherent structure, a compelling system.

But there is yet more – already adumbrated – to be claimed in behalf of the theology of the Oral Torah. In the epilogue, I propose that this theology as set forth here accurately recapitulates the main lines of the paramount theology of the Written Torah, that is, the Hebrew Scriptures of ancient Israel. When the sages insist upon the absolute unity of the two media of revelation, the Written and the Memorized or Oral Torah, calling them "the one whole Torah of Moses, our rabbi," they are right. Their theology is not only linked to verses of Scripture that prove the sages' points, it also is concentric with the principal components of Scripture.

I further maintain that the modes of thought and clusters of intersecting themes that comprise the theology of the Oral Torah are themselves recapitulated by the liturgy of the synagogue set forth in the synagogue documents, the *Siddur*, daily prayer book, and the *Mahzor*, prayer book for the Days of Awe (among the whole of the liturgical life of the faith).

Two facts join. First, the religion, Judaism, meets God through the encounter with him in the one whole Torah of our rabbi Moses, written and oral together. Second, the religion, Judaism, speaks to God in prayer through the *Siddur* and *Mahzor* (and related liturgies). Then the upshot is clear. Out of the resources of the Oral Torah I claim to describe nothing less than Judaism, pure and simple: Scripture, tradition, worship all celebrating the world order created by God's justice. In the present age of chaos and death, that theology defies the norm. But the Torah always has, and so too has holy Israel.

Since this theory of the integrity of the Oral Torah stakes its own claim, its description of the Oral Torah's theology means to offer a vigorous challenge to rigorous learning. To test the theological theses adduced here out of the documents of the Oral Torah, two approaches lie open.

First, one may wish to reject the systematization proposed in these pages in favour of another. In reading the documents all together and all at once and whole, I identify their main focus upon revealing God's justice and allege that all things are so ordered and arranged within the logic of that proposition, but the same documents await the attention of others. Examining them all, drawing upon each, let others realize a competing view. It will have to identify a different category-formation from the one already adumbrated and (I anticipate) found self-evident by the reader, not to mention an alternative dialectics, a wholly-other dynamics. In contemplating the documents whole, I gave thought to other integrating logics than the *logos* I have identified. Others can do the same. When they do, I am sure, they will reject the alternatives as I did. But mere impressions or proof-texts, not emerging from a systematic and logic-based inquiry, will not suffice. Nor will random opinion or mere impression.

Second, one may choose to reject that systematization altogether and maintain that the Oral Torah sustains no such process of rationalization. Many indeed maintain that the documents of the Oral Torah allege everything and its opposite, and that is entirely correct. But studied by their rules, evaluated in accord with the principles of rationality and order that infuse those writings, which are spelled out in chapter 1's discussion of what is normative, representative of the opinions of the sages as a whole, the documents seen whole yield the picture drawn here. Accordingly, allegations of chaos, once order is alleged and made manifest, also bear the burden of demonstration. I claim that the Oral Torah builds all structures upon certain premises and propositions. A single logic infuses the whole.

To establish that not order, but chaos, reigns, others will have to show not only contradictory propositions but conflicting premises as to logic and its rules. As God is one and unique here, let us then be shown how God is multiple and common there. As sin is rebellion here, let us be shown that sin comes about through multiple causes there. That will represent chaos. Isolated and episodic statements that contradict the norm will not serve; demonstration that the documents lack all logic alone will suffice. I do not think that such a demonstration is ever again going to be possible. That is what is at stake in this book.

As learning proceeds, both approaches are to be explored. I express confidence that, whichever route is taken, each road will lead inexorably to the conclusions reached here: first, the Oral Torah is orderly and coherent, wholly possessed of integrity, and second, the rationality of the Oral Torah takes the form I have set forth in these pages – and no other.

The sheer size of this book is commensurate to the dimensions of its claim but can never match the sublimity of its subject. It also responds to the enormous volume of writing that is encompassed by the Oral Torah, a whole library of documents and the near-inaccessibility, even in theological and academic, let alone synagogue, libraries, of most of those documents whether in the original or in translation. That explains why I present illustrations for each point I wish to register, so that readers may judge for themselves, from the actual words of my translations of the documents into English, whether I am providing an accurate account of the meaning of matters.

Indeed, whether what I give is ample for the purpose is a matter of judgment; at every point, I could have multiplied the illustrative materials many times without reproducing more than a tiny proportion of the documents under discussion. If I had alluded to a source and briefly cited its gist, readers would have no way of knowing whether the source says what I say and confirms the conclusion I wish to draw. They also would not encounter the distinctive modes of discourse that characterize the documents – and that convey their message aesthetically, as the actual words do propositionally. That accounts for my provision of compositions, not merely snippets. If I have erred in this regard, it is by giving too little, not too much.

I have made no effort to impose upon the sources "gender-neutral" language, which would violate their character, imputing an originally exclusionary intent that is in fact rarely present. When sages wish to use "Adam" or "he" to refer only to men, they signal that intent in a loud and clear fashion. (That – as everyone knows – an implicit male bias pervades the whole forms a trivial banality.) In any event, in Rabbinic literature, "man/Adam/he" ordinarily stands for male and female, that is, "all of humanity," as "he" and "mankind" in much contemporary usage and in the whole of historical usage of the English and American languages are deemed to encompass both genders. In these pages that usage governs throughout, and "he-or-she" and its persnickety variations and circumlocutions do not occur.

All the translations from the documents of the Oral Torah are my own. Of some of the documents, I was the first translator, for example, Sifra, Tosefta, and the Talmud of the Land of Israel. Of others, I was the second, for instance, the Mishnah and the Talmud of Babylonia. It was necessary to redo the work of others, because I was the first (and to date remain the only) person to conduct systematic form-analysis of the entire literature. The consequent reference system, imposed consistently throughout these translations, is the first ever carried out systematically and uniformly for the entire corpus. Each item signals not only location in a given document but the formal role, within the construction of that document, of a given unit of thought.

It is always a pleasure to acknowledge the support for my research accorded by the academic positions that I am privileged to hold. The University of South Florida, through my distinguished research professorship in religious studies, and Bard College, through my professorship of religion, sustain this work of mine. It is never superfluous to say so and to express thanks to those academic administrators who year by year make decisions that sustain my life-long project of the academic study of the history of Judaism in late antiquity.

A number of historical theologians of Christianity helped me get the work under way in the works that prepared the way for this one. I specify and thank them there. Among them, Dean and Professor Frances Young, University of Birmingham, who sets the standard for thinking about descriptive, historical theology of Christianity and the model for the same work on Rabbinic Judaism, provided not only instruction but inspiration. She writes with the pen of an angel; I envy her imagination, wit, and eloquence.

Here as in many earlier projects I found both learning and inspiration in the writings of my life-long friend and sometime-teacher, Professor Brevard S. Childs, Yale University, whom I consulted in connection with this book. His seminal work supplies the foundation for the first half of chapter 15.

For the entire project, discussions on matters of substance go on constantly with friends and my colleagues in the Department of Religious Studies at the University of South Florida; and with those at Bard College, particularly Professor Bruce D. Chilton.

My work invoking the metaphor of the grammar of a language for the description of the theology of a religion in the *Theological Grammar* heavily depended upon the knowledge and criticism of Professor David Aaron, Wellesley College. He is extensively quoted in the preface and in the introductions to the three volumes of the *Grammar,* but the entire weight of his generous contribution is by no means measured only in those citations. He also discussed with me some of the ideas in the present book, always making interesting observations.

Rabbi Joel Zaiman, Baltimore, Maryland, read the entire manuscript in the first draft and made important comments.

In all of my principal scholarly and other intellectual endeavours, Dean and Professor William Scott Green at the University of Rochester always listens thoughtfully and responds perceptively to the problems I lay out before him and is a constant source of important criticism. He has been a co-worker and conversation-partner for more than thirty years, since he was an undergraduate at Dartmouth College and I was a very green assistant professor, glad to take up the challenges of learning through teaching, to argue with all comers, then as now. So was, and is, he always ready to argue, to negotiate.

My editor at McGill-Queens University Press, the historian Donald H. Akenson, deserves a special word, because he presented the challenge to which my entire theological project – realized in no fewer than five sizable books divided among three projects – responds. First, he approached me to solicit a book; but he wanted a big book, a major project. Since I was then in the midst of my earliest work of a systematic-theological character ("what holds the whole together") in connection with the documents of the Oral Torah, I wrote what I thought would work. But, alas, that turned into the *The Theology of Rabbinic Judaism. A Prolegomenon* (further described in chapter 1). My editor did not want the beginning, he wanted the end. He made me do not only the matter of method by which the work might be done, such as is spelled out in the *Prolegomenon,* but the work itself.

Then I performed a large-scale experiment in method, sifting all the data in response to generative questions, yielding *The Theological Grammar of the*

Oral Torah, an essay in category-formation: native-categories, making connections and constructions, models of analysis, explanation, and anticipation. No, he wanted more, and it was not enough to think it through and establish its categories. So, while I systematically worked matters out in the *Theological Grammar*, I found I had to go back to the drawing board. I did not even trouble him to consider the work, even though it met the criterion of size, reaching three sizable volumes. I knew what his (gentle, loving) response would be.

Rather, by reason of his gentle insistence, I went back to the drawing board. For the actual work had actually to be carried out, not just thought through and sketched. So while I thought – and still think – that the *Grammar* contained the theology, he wanted me to show how it did so, the actual result. He did not think that it would be self-evident to anyone but me. And, of course, he was right at every point. If he also wanted a big fat book, containing a meaningful selection of the evidence, carefully reasoned (in the French sense, *raisonnée*), here he gets it. I wish for all ambitious and productive scholars the advantages of an editor like him and a publisher like his. While I have never worked with an editor in a university press, a religious-academic press, or a secular academic press, who failed to illuminate my work and give me pleasure in doing it, D.H. Akenson has shed the brightest light of them all.

Indeed, I hope all who enjoy the work of learning might enjoy the sustaining resources that I possess, stimulating academic situations at the University of South Florida and Bard College, managed by deans, provosts, and presidents who respect scholarship; colleagues both at home and in distant places ready by the phone to engage in nourishing conversation about new thoughts and in important criticism; ample resources in time and funds for the doing of the work in comfort; publishers ready to find the right audience for the result; and libraries and librarians such as those at the University of South Florida in Tampa and St Petersburg, who are always happy to locate every needed book.

Jacob Neusner
28 July 1997. My sixty-fifth birthday

Bibliography

Childs, Brevard S. *Biblical Theology of the Old and New Testaments*. Minneapolis: Fortress Press 1992.

Friedlander, Gerald, trans. *Pirke deRabbi Eliezer*. London: 1916.

Goldin, Judah, trans. *The Grace after Meals*. New York: The Jewish Theological Seminary of America 1955.

Harlow, Jules, ed. *A Rabbi's Manual*. New York: Rabbinical Assembly 1965.

— *Weekday Prayer Book*, Rabbinical Assembly of America Prayerbook Committee, ed. New York: Rabbinical Assembly 1962.

— *Mahzor*, Jules Harlow, trans. New York: Rabbinical Assembly, rep. 1995.

Mandelbaum, Irving. *A History of the Mishnaic Law of Agriculture: Kilayim. Translation and Exegesis*. Chicago: Scholars Press for Brown Judaic Studies 1982.

Schachter, Lifsa. "Reflections on the Brit Mila Ceremony," *Conservative Judaism*, vol. 38 (1986), 38–41.

JACOB NEUSNER

THE ANALYTICAL WORKS

Judaism: The Evidence of the Mishnah, Chicago: University of Chicago Press 1981. Second edition, Atlanta: Scholars Press for Brown Judaic Studies 1987.

Judaism in Society: The Evidence of the Yerushalmi: Toward the Natural History of a Religion. Chicago: University of Chicago Press 1983. Second printing, with a new preface, Atlanta: Scholars Press for South Florida Studies in the History of Judaism 1991.

Judaism and Scripture: The Evidence of Leviticus Rabbah. Chicago: University of Chicago Press 1986.

Judaism: The Classical Statement. The Evidence of the Bavli. Chicago: University of Chicago Press 1986.

The Making of the Mind of Judaism. Atlanta: Scholars Press for Brown Judaic Studies 1987.

The Formation of the Jewish Intellect: Making Connections and Drawing Conclusions in the Traditional System of Judaism. Atlanta: Scholars Press for Brown Judaic Studies 1988.

The Economics of the Mishnah. Chicago: University of Chicago Press 1989.

Rabbinic Political Theory: Religion and Politics in the Mishnah. Chicago: University of Chicago Press 1991.

Symbol and Theology in Early Judaism. Minneapolis: Fortress Press 1991.

Judaism and Story: The Evidence of the Fathers According to Rabbi Nathan. Chicago: University of Chicago Press 1992.

Androgynous Judaism: Masculine and Feminine in the Dual Torah. Macon, Ga.: Mercer University Press 1993.

THE HISTORICAL CONTEXT IN WHICH THE THEOLOGICAL
SYSTEM TOOK SHAPE

Rabbinic Judaism: The Documentary History of the Formative Age. Bethesda, Md.: CDL Press 1994.

The Presence of the Past, the Pastness of the Present: History, Time, and Paradigm in Rabbinic Judaism. Bethesda, Md.: CDL Press 1996.

Rabbinic Judaism: Structure and System. Minneapolis: Fortress Press 1996.

The Transformation of Judaism: From Philosophy to Religion. Champaign: University of Illinois Press 1992. Second printing, Atlanta: Scholars Press for South Florida Studies in the History of Judaism 1997.

The Emergence of Judaism: Jewish Religion in Response to the Critical issues of the First Six Centuries. Minneapolis: Fortress Press 1998.

THE SYSTEMATIC COMPARISON OF THE TWO TALMUDS

The Talmud of Babylonia: A Complete Outline. Atlanta: Scholars Press for University of South Florida Academic Commentary Series 1995–96.

I.A   *Tractate Berakhot and the Division of Appointed Times. Berakhot, Shabbat, and Erubin.*

I.B   *Tractate Berakhot and the Division of Appointed Times. Pesahim through Hagigah.*

II.A   *The Division of Women. Yebamot through Ketubot.*

II.B   *The Division of Women. Nedarim through Qiddushin.*

III.A   *The Division of Damages. Baba Qamma through Baba Batra.*

III.B   *The Division of Damages. Sanhedrin through Horayot.*

IV.A   *The Division of Holy Things and Tractate Niddah. Zebahim through Hullin.*

IV.B   *The Division of Holy Things and Tractate Niddah. Bekhorot through Niddah.*

The Talmud of The Land of Israel: An Outline of the Second, Third, and Fourth Divisions. Atlanta: Scholars Press for University of South Florida Academic Commentary Series 1995–96.

I.A   *Tractate Berakhot and the Division of Appointed Times. Berakhot and Shabbat.*

I.B   *Tractate Berakhot and the Division of Appointed Times. Erubin, Yoma, and Besah.*

I.C   *Tractate Berakhot and the Division of Appointed Times. Pesahim and Sukkah.*

I.D   *Tractate Berakhot and the Division of Appointed Times. Taanit, Megillah, Rosh Hashanah, Hagigah, and Moed Qatan.*

II.A   *The Division of Women. Yebamot to Nedarim.*

II.B   *The Division of Women. Nazir to Sotah.*

III.A   *The Division of Damages and Tractate Niddah. Baba Qamma, Baba Mesia, Baba Batra, Horayot, and Niddah.*

III.B   *The Division of Damages and Tractate Niddah. Sanhedrin, Makkot, Shebuot, and Abodah Zarah.*

The Two Talmuds Compared. Atlanta: Scholars Press for University of South Florida Academic Commentary Series.

I.A   *Tractate Berakhot and the Division of Appointed Times in the Talmud of the Land of Israel and the Talmud of Babylonia. Yerushalmi Tractate Berakhot.*

I.B   *Tractate Berakhot and the Division of Appointed Times in the Talmud of the Land of Israel and the Talmud of Babylonia. Tractate Shabbat.*

I.C   *Tractate Berakhot and the Division of Appointed Times in the Talmud of the Land of Israel and the Talmud of Babylonia. Tractate Erubin.*

I.D   *Tractate Berakhot and the Division of Appointed Times in the Talmud of the Land of Israel and the Talmud of Babylonia. Tractates Yoma and Sukkah.*

I.E   *Tractate Berakhot and the Division of Appointed Times in the Talmud of the Land of Israel and the Talmud of Babylonia. Tractate Pesahim.*

I.F   *Tractate Berakhot and the Division of Appointed Times in the Talmud of the Land of Israel and the Talmud of Babylonia. Tractates Besah, Taanit, and Megillah.*

I.G   *Tractate Berakhot and the Division of Appointed Times in the Talmud of the Land of Israel and the Talmud of Babylonia. Tractates Rosh Hashanah, Hagigah, and Moed Qatan.*

II.A   *The Division of Women in the Talmud of the Land of Israel and the Talmud of Babylonia. Tractates Yebamot and Ketubot.*

II.B   *The Division of Women in the Talmud of the Land of Israel and the Talmud of Babylonia. Tractates Nedarim, Nazir, and Sotah.*

II.C   *The Division of Women in the Talmud of the Land of Israel and the Talmud of Babylonia. Tractates Qiddushin and Gittin.*

III.A   *The Division of Damages and Tractate Niddah in the Talmud of the Land of Israel and the Talmud of Babylonia. Tractates Baba Qamma and Baba Mesia.*

III.B   *The Division of Damages and Tractate Niddah in the Talmud of the Land of Israel and the Talmud of Babylonia. Baba Batra and Niddah.*

III.C   *The Division of Damages and Tractate Niddah. Sanhedrin and Makkot.*

III.D   *The Division of Damages and Tractate Niddah. Shebuot, Abodah Zarah, and Horayot.*

THE SYSTEMATIC STUDY OF THE CORPUS FOR
THE IDENTIFICATION OF ITS PREMISES:

The Judaism Behind the Texts. The Generative Premises of Rabbinic Literature. Atlanta: Scholars Press for South Florida Studies in the History of Judaism 1993.

I.   *The Mishnah. A. The Division of Agriculture.*

I.   *The Mishnah. B. The Divisions of Appointed Times, Women, and Damages (through Sanhedrin).*

I.   *The Mishnah. C. The Divisions of Damages (from Makkot), Holy Things and Purities.*

II.   *The Tosefta, Tractate Abot, and the Earlier Midrash-Compilations: Sifra, Sifré to Numbers, and Sifré to Deuteronomy.*

III.   *The Later Midrash-Compilations: Genesis Rabbah, Leviticus Rabbah and Pesiqta deRab Kahana.*

IV.   *The Latest Midrash-Compilations: Song of Songs Rabbah, Ruth Rabbah, Esther Rabbah I, and Lamentations Rabbati. And the Fathers According to Rabbi Nathan.*

V.   *The Talmuds of the Land of Israel and Babylonia.*

HISTORICAL-THEOLOGICAL STUDIES COMPLETED
SINCE THIS BOOK WENT TO PRESS

The Halakhah of the Oral Torah: A Religious Commentary. Introduction and vol. I. *Between Israel and God.* Part One. *Thanksgiving: Tractate Berakhot. Enlandisement: Tractates Kilayim, Shebi'it, and 'Orlah.* Atlanta: Scholars Press for South Florida Studies in the History of Judaism 1997.

The Theological Grammar of the Oral Torah. Binghamton, N.Y.: Dowling College Press/Global Publications of Binghamton University [State University of New York]. I. *Vocabulary: Native Categories,* 1998.

The Theological Grammar of the Oral Torah. Binghamton: Dowling College Press/Global Publications of Binghamton University [SUNY]. II. *Syntax: Connections and Constructions,* 1998.

The Theological Grammar of the Oral Torah. Binghamton: Dowling College Press/Global Publications of Binghamton University [SUNY]. III. *Semantics: Models of Analysis, Explanation and Anticipation,* 1998.

The Halakhah of the Oral Torah: A Religious Commentary. Vol. I. *Between Israel and God.* Part Two. *Possession and Partnership. Tractates Ma'aserot and Terumot.* Atlanta: Scholars Press for South Florida Studies in the History of Judaism.

The Halakhah of the Oral Torah: A Religious Commentary. Vol. I. *Between Israel and God.* Part Three. *Possession and Partnership: Tractates Hallah, Ma'aser Sheni, and Bikkurim.* Atlanta: Scholars Press for South Florida Studies in the History of Judaism.

The Halakhah of the Oral Torah: A Religious Commentary. Vol. I. *Between Israel and God.* Part Four. *Possession and Partnership: Tractates Pe'ah and Dema'i.* Atlanta: Scholars Press for South Florida Studies in the History of Judaism.

The Halakhah of the Oral Torah: A Religious Commentary. Vol. I. *Between Israel and God.* Part Five. *Transcendent Transactions: Meeting God without the Land. Tractates Sheqalim, Arakhin, and Ta'anit.* Atlanta: Scholars Press for South Florida Studies in the History of Judaism.

The Halakhah of the Oral Torah: A Religious Commentary. Vol. I. *Between Israel and God.* Part Six. *Transcendent Transactions: Where Heaven and Earth Intersect. Tractate Zebahim.* Atlanta: Scholars Press for South Florida Studies in the History of Judaism.

The Halakhah of the Oral Torah: A Religious Commentary. Vol. I. *Between Israel and God.* Part Seven. *Transcendent Transactions: Where Heaven and Earth Intersect. Tractate Menahot.* Atlanta: Scholars Press for South Florida Studies in the History of Judaism.

The Halakhah of the Oral Torah: A Religious Commentary. Vol. I. *Between Israel and God.* Part Eight. *Transcendent Transactions: Where Heaven and Earth Intersect. Tractates Tamid and Yoma.* Atlanta: Scholars Press for South Florida Studies in the History of Judaism.

The Halakhah of the Oral Torah: A Religious Commentary. Vol. I. *Between Israel and God.* Part Nine. *Transcendent Transactions: Where Heaven and Earth Intersect. Tractates Hagigah, Bekhorot and Me'ilah.* Atlanta: Scholars Press for South Florida Studies in the History of Judaism.

The Halakhah of the Oral Torah: A Religious Commentary. Vol. I. *Between Israel and God.* Part Ten. *Transcendent Transactions: Where Heaven and Earth Intersect. Tractates Temurah, Megillah, and Rosh Hashanah.* Atlanta: Scholars Press for South Florida Studies in the History of Judaism.

The Halakhah of the Oral Torah: A Religious Commentary. Vol. II. *Within Israel's Social Order.* Part One. *Civil Society. Repairing Damage to, Preserving the Perfection of, the Social Order. Tractates Baba Qamma, Baba Mesia, and Baba Batra.* Atlanta: Scholars Press for South Florida Studies in the History of Judaism.

The Halakhah of the Oral Torah. A Religious Commentary. Vol. II. *Within Israel's Social Order.* Part Two. *Protecting the Commonwealth: Idolators, Sinners and Criminals and the Courts. Tractates Sanhedrin-Makkot and Shebuot.* Atlanta: Scholars Press for South Florida Studies in the History of Judaism.

The Halakhah of the Oral Torah. A Religious Commentary. Vol. II. *Within Israel's Social Order.* Part Three. *Protecting the Commonwealth: Idolators, Sinners and Criminals and the Courts Tractates Keritot and Horayot. The Outsider. Tractate Abodah Zarah.* Atlanta: Scholars Press for South Florida Studies in the History of Judaism.

The Halakhah of the Oral Torah: A Religious Commentary. Vol. III. *Inside the Walls of the Israelite Household.* Part One. *At the Meeting of Time and Space. Tractates Shabbat and Erubin.* Atlanta: Scholars Press for South Florida Studies in the History of Judaism.

The Halakhah of the Oral Torah: A Religious Commentary. Vol. III. *Inside the Walls of the Israelite Household.* Part Two. *At the Meeting of Time and Space. Tractates Pesahim, Sukkah, Mo'ed Qatan, and Besah.* Atlanta: Scholars Press for South Florida Studies in the History of Judaism.

The Halakhah of the Oral Torah: A Religious Commentary. Vol. III. *Inside the Walls of the Israelite Household.* Part Three. *Sanctification in the Here and Now. The Table and the Bed. Tractates Hullin, Qiddushin, and Ketubot.* Atlanta: Scholars Press for South Florida Studies in the History of Judaism.

The Halakhah of the Oral Torah: A Religious Commentary. Vol. III. *Inside the Walls of the Israelite Household.* Part Four. *Sanctification and the Marital Bond. Tractates Nedarim, Nazir and Sotah.* Atlanta: Scholars Press for South Florida Studies in the History of Judaism.

The Halakhah of the Oral Torah: A Religious Commentary. Vol. III. *Inside the Walls of the Israelite Household.* Part Five. *The Desacralization of the Household. The Bed. Tractates Gittin and Yebamot.* Atlanta: Scholars Press for South Florida Studies in the History of Judaism.

The Halakhah of the Oral Torah: A Religious Commentary. Vol. III. *Inside the Walls of the Israelite Household.* Part Six. *The Desacralization of the Household. Foci of Uncleanness. The Table. Tractate Kelim.* Atlanta: Scholars Press for South Florida Studies in the History of Judaism.

The Halakhah of the Oral Torah: A Religious Commentary. Vol. III. *Inside the Walls of the Israelite Household.* Part Seven. *The Desacralization of the Household. Foci of Uncleanness. The Table. Tractates Uqsin and Tohorot.* Atlanta: Scholars Press for South Florida Studies in the History of Judaism.

The Halakhah of the Oral Torah: A Religious Commentary. Vol. III. *Inside the Walls of the Israelite Household.* Part Eight. *The Desacralization of the Household. Sources of Uncleanness, Dissemination of Uncleanness. Tractates Ohalot and Makhshirin.* Atlanta: Scholars Press for South Florida Studies in the History of Judaism.

The Halakhah of the Oral Torah: A Religious Commentary. Vol. III. *Inside the Walls of the Israelite Household.* Part Nine. *The Desacralization of the Household. Animate Sources of Uncleanness. Tractates Zabim and Niddah.* Atlanta: Scholars Press for South Florida Studies in the History of Judaism.

The Halakhah of the Oral Torah: A Religious Commentary. Vol. III. *Inside the Walls of the Israelite Household.* Part Ten. *Animate Sources of Uncleanness. Tractates Negaim, Tebul Yom, and Yadayim.* Atlanta: Scholars Press for South Florida Studies in the History of Judaism.

The Halakhah of the Oral Torah: A Religious Commentary. Vol. III. *Inside the Walls of the Israelite Household.* Part Eleven. *Purification from the Pollution of Death. Tractates Parah and Miqvaot.* Atlanta: Scholars Press for South Florida Studies in the History of Judaism.

CURRENTLY UNDER WAY

Eden Restored: The Theology of the Halakhah.

Jewish Law from Moses to the Mishnah. Reading Forward from Scripture to the Generative Premises of the Halakhah.

What, Exactly, Did Our Sages Mean by "the Oral Torah"? An Inductive Answer to the Question of Rabbinic Judaism.

PLANNED IN SUCCESSION

The Integrity of the Oral Torah: The Common Theology of the Aggadah and Halakhah: Ten Cases.

PROLOGUE

1 Imagining Eden and Re-presenting the Result

Imagine Eden as a philosopher would: a world of pure reason, where all things serve their assigned purpose and stand in proper rank. Form a mental image of a world where all things cohere to a single inner logic and so are to be explained in an orderly way. Contemplate a social order in which whatever happens is for good and sufficient cause. Conceive of a kingdom so governed by a moral calculus that an ethical physics describes actuality: each action produces an equal and opposite reaction, a perfect match, a mirror of the deed in the responsive deed. And try to picture a world of peace, in which nothing happens to change the perfect, the acutely just balance of matters.

Contemplate in mind that here, in this perfect world of universal mind and self-evident rationality, is a steady-state world: do this and that will happen, do not do this and that will not happen – measure for measure in all matters. The rational intellect encompasses all, which is why everything is subject to such an exact, reasonable accounting of force and reaction thereto. Among the principles of intellect that inhere in this Eden the most important, the innate sense of justice, ultimately prevails. Fairness and equity rule, and that explains why with thought everything certainly makes sense. Then the task of intellect will be to uncover and reveal how all things are to be justified, meaning, shown to be just to begin with.

Consider how, in this social cosmos conceived by men of reason who take up the task of justification, principles of order describe the final outcome of all transactions, all relationships. Well-ordered nature finds its match in well-construed society of humanity. And at the third dimension of existence, the anthropological, in addition to the natural and the historical, the very traits of man himself correspond to those of nature. The same rule that governs the tree governs me, the orderly mind maintains.

In this world, change defies imagining. In its place is the realization, in full maturity, of what one already is. The *telos*, the ultimate end and goal, of all things, present at the outset, explains and governs what happens, but nothing happens to violate that rational rule. The acorn grown up has not changed but has only realized its end. Teleology, not history, organizes existence. In such a world the future is present even now, the oak in the acorn. Inertia and stasis characterize the teleological universe, in accord with the rules that dictate cause and effect. Proportion and balance, complementarity and commensurability – these traits of the well-ordered world everywhere characterize men and nations, their relationships, and the destiny meted out to each and to all by the purposeful intellect that has made things just so, that philosophers name in diverse ways but, most commonly, God.

That is why, in this imaginary, purposeful world that philosophers alone can conceive (with God in their image, after their likeness), rationality yields compelling explanations for all things and a single integral rationality or *logos* commands. Before the cosmic intellect that has conceived all things in a single reasonable, purposeful way there are no mysteries, neither about the past and what lies hidden, nor about the present and what comes into view, nor even about what lies over the distant horizon of the future. Since rules govern, reason suffices to explain the past, understand the present, and dictate what is going to come about in the future.

Not only public history but private life conforms to the same reasonable laws: do this and that will happen. The well-examined life of persons and their destiny recapitulate those rules of reason, so that, purposeful and properly ranked, private lives embody – and even match item for item – the principles of public order. All things come under the one orderly law of reason: for every thing its place, for every person a calling, for every event a purpose. And that is why those who master the givens of reality and reflect reasonably about them make sense of all being, all doing.

Then in mind – to continue for just a bit longer this exercise in imagining a society situated in utopian eternity – address the question of history, the disruptions of events, and you will understand how reason masters, how logic controls even the chaos of man's remarkable doings, the ones that destroy perfection. In line with the inner logic of the whole, time and change do not – or at least ought not – mar this Eden, where perfection consists in stability in proper balance and proportion. And when change (not just fulfilment of innate *telos*) marks time, change is a problem that requires explanation. And time is subject to the requirement of accountability: how come? If rationality consists in the meting out of measure for measure, so that good is responded to with good, and evil with evil, then that of which history consists – what is remarkable by reason of its sheer illogic – finds no place but must be explained (away). For in this domain of contemplation of what is, or can be made, perfect, men know the rules and how they work and are applied. Consequently, through knowing the regularities of eternity that supersede the random moments of time, the past yields its secrets of how things really work. The present rehearses the rules in the here and the now. The future promises only more of that same regularity and certainty. The categories, past, present, and future, lose all currency.

So to conclude this fantasy constructed six inches above the level plane of the everyday and the here and now, events take place but history does not happen. Events now stand not for that which disrupts, but for that which embodies rules or that actualizes potentials, much as the well-conceived experiment in the laboratory allows the testing of hypotheses. And the same rules govern nations and families, social entities measured in multiples, or even the individual in his or her person and life. Public affairs and private ones match in conforming to the governance of order, purpose, reason. These virtues of the well-constructed intellect not only account for history and the course of nations in the unfolding of time but also prevail in the streets and marketplaces and households. There, in the world of small affairs, fairness and a balanced exchange match in structure and proportion the workings of applied reason and practical logic in the relations of men and nations. In this philosophers' Eden, all things bear reasoned explanation, and there are no mysteries. Here, then, we discern the remarkable, hopeful vision, the fantasy-world of intellectuals who conceive that ideas make all the difference and minds command and reason governs.

Now, if you can imagine such a world perfected by the tastes and aspirations of the rational mind, then you can enter into the world portrayed by the documents of the Oral Torah. These are the writings of "our sages of blessed memory" who set forth the authoritative statement of Rabbinic Judaism in its formative age, the first six centuries of the Common Era. The writings, read all together and all at once as a single coherent statement, portray the reason why things are now as they are. And they show the logic of that reason, revealing its integrity in the working of justice throughout. As the sages portray the Written part of the Torah and set forth the Oral part, the Torah lays heavy emphasis upon the perfection of the timeless, flawless creation that God forms and governs in accord with wholly rational and accessible rules.

If everything fits together and works coherently, it is because, as philosophers maintain in their realm of reflection, a single, unitary logic ("logos"), the logic of monotheism comprised by the one just, therefore reasonable and benevolent, God, prevails.

But for sages there was this difference: while philosophers uncovered the order of nature, employing mathematics abstractly to describe, and natural history comprehensively to organize, and reason to analyse, the facts of the world, it was into the facts of Scripture that sages pursued their comparable analysis. For all that I have asked as a supererogatory act of imagination – a world of pure reason, everything in place and in rank, all things serving an assigned purpose – encompasses the cosmic conception of sages as much as philosophers. To show exactly what it means to treat Scripture as a source of irreducible and irrefutable facts, a single example suffices. Various figures in the Written Torah commence the classification of virtue or vice that they embody:

ESTHER RABBAH VIII:I.I:

I. A. R. Berekhiah commenced by citing the verse, "Who has wrought and done it? He who called the generations from the beginning" (Is. 41:4).

Here is the sages' counterpart to a theory of teleology:

B. "From the beginning of the creation of the world, the Holy One blessed be he designated for every one what was suitable.
C. "Adam was first of all creatures,
D. "Cain was first of murderers,
E. "Abel was first of all victims,
F. "Noah the first of all those who would be saved from disaster."

Now, as always, we turn from humanity to the part of humanity identified with the Torah:

G. "Abraham was the first of all the circumcised,
H. "Isaac the first of all those who were bound for sacrifice,
I. "Jacob the first of all those who were without blemish,
J. "Judah the first of the tribes,
K. "Joseph the first of the pious,
L. "Aaron the first of the priests,
M. "Moses the first of the prophets,
N. "Joshua the first of the conquerors,

O. "Othniel the first of those who divide the spoils,

P. "Samuel the first of those who anoint,

Q. "Saul the first of those who are anointed,

R. "David the first of the singers,

S. "Solomon the first of the builders."

From Israel, we proceed to the gentiles. As is commonly the case in antonymic discourse, once this comes to mind, then the opposite enters:

T. "Nebuchadnezzar the first of the destroyers,

U. "Ahasuerus the first of those who sell [people at a price],

V. "Haman the first of those who buy [people at a price]."

To formulate a theory of the purpose or goal, the sages frame matters in the language of origination, that is, they name the acorn out of which the oak will grow. The question of origins – and even exact definition – of various virtues and vices is answered by appeal to the starting point, Scripture, the sole source of pertinent facts; the sequence of the advent of its exemplary figures then accounts for where and when the various categories originate. But I see no scriptural sequence, rather, the sages' characteristic one (as we shall see in chapters 3 and 4): humanity in general, Israel in particular, and then the antonym for Israel, the gentiles, Israel's enemies. Scripture then provides data for sages, as much as nature and history do for philosophers. The entire classification system of virtue or vice then emerges in the narrative of Scripture, when the data of the narrative are properly systematized.

In the pages that follow, for Chapters 2 through 9, I shall systematically demonstrate how the sages produced a vision of the world comparable in its intellectual traits – the insistence upon the orderly and reasonable and purposeful character of all things, everything subject to a single logic, which is accessible to mind – to that conceived by philosophers. Then, for the following two chapters, 10 and 11, I shall explain how the sages accounted for things as they are and further instructed Israel on how to restore things to the state of grace that Eden had embodied. In the three chapters that succeed, 12, 13, and 14, I spell out the account of moral regeneration and its consequences, set forth in the context of the eschatological theory of the Oral Torah.

What we see is a single, seamless story – and not a very complicated one at that. In these accounts, so far as is possible in their own words, I tell the story of how the sages portrayed the story of the world from start to finish: the rules that account for reality. And that story will strike the reader as remarkably familiar, its cogency sustained by its very commonplace quality: here is the story that we in the West who practise both Judaism and Christianity have been telling ourselves for so long as we have possessed Scripture. And, further, those who practise Judaism will find themselves entirely at home, because in the prayers recited three times a day they encounter the same tale that the sages of the Oral Torah tell. That is because the sages read Scripture – the facts it supplied or oral tradition contributed – as philosophers read nature. They thought philosophically about Scripture. The logic that they uncovered imparted that rationality and coherence to the theological convictions they set forth, to the system they devised to account for the unity of being, the conformity of all reality to the few simple rules of reason that God embodied in his works of creation.

To make this point more concrete: as philosophers sought to generalize out of the facts of nature, so the sages brought system and order to the facts of Scripture, drawing conclusions, setting forth hypotheses, amassing data to them. Analytical principles comparable to those of natural history, specifically, guided them in their reading of the facts that Scripture provided. These involved, in particular, the classification and hierarchization of data in a taxonomical process of comparison and contrast: like followed like rules, unlike, opposite rules. And the rules that classify also hierarchize, for example, what is classified as sanctified or as unclean will then possess the traits that signify sanctification or uncleanness, and these traits will also order themselves, this time at levels of intensity. The classification of matters and their hierarchization – the quest for generalizations, governing rules or principles – are therefore prior to the identification of verses of Scripture that validate said classification.

What is primary is the governing conception of a prevailing logic, a governing reason articulated endlessly out of a few simple propositions of order and coherence. Throughout, a highly articulated system of classification is at work, one that rests on a deep theoretical foundation. The basic method involves a search for abstraction out of concrete data. A variety of cases deriving from Scripture is subjected to generalization, and the whole is then set forth in the form of a generalization sustained by numerous probative cases. The generalization, moreover, is itself elaborated. Cases that validate the generalization are selected not at random but by appeal to common taxonomic traits, and then the generalization not only derives from the cases but from a specific aspect thereof. These cases are all characterized by sudden and supernatural intervention in a crisis, such as the situation under discussion now requires. Or a set of kindred propositions is established through a sequence of cases; no effort is made to order the cases in a compelling sequence. It is adequate to state the generalization and then adduce probative cases out of Scripture.

The whole represents the systematization of Scripture's evidence on a given topic, and it is the systematization of the data that yields a generalization. Let me give a single example, in the framework of *halakhic* discourse, that is, the formulation of norms of behaviour, of how facts of Scripture (and in some details, what is set forth as the oral tradition of Sinai) are dealt with, the way in which sages conduct their inquiry. Then, in the substantive chapters that form the shank of this book, we shall see comparable approaches to *aggadic* or theological discourse. In the present case the sages wish to prove that hierarchization governs the social order, with the several castes related to one another in descending order:

MISHNAH-TRACTATE HORAYOT 3:5, AND TOSEFTA-TRACTATE HORAYOT 2:8:

A. A priest takes precedence over a Levite, a Levite over an Israelite, an Israelite over a mamzer [a person whose parents may not legally ever marry, for example, brother and sister], a mamzer over a Netin [a descendant of the cast of Temple servants], a Netin over a proselyte, a proselyte over a freed slave.
B. Under what circumstances?
C. When all of them are equivalent.

The initial hierarchization having been established out of self-evident facts, the variable is introduced involving the Torah, so making the point that the Torah violates natural hierarchies in favor of God's choice:

D. But if the mamzer was a disciple of a sage and a high priest was an am haares [in context: ignorant of the Torah], the mamzer who is a disciple of a sage takes precedence over a high priest who is an am haares (M. Hor. 3:8).

We now turn to the complementary compilation of laws, the Tosefta, which contains citations and glosses of the Mishnah's rules as well as free-standing statements:

E. A sage takes precedence over a king; a king takes precedence over a high priest; a high priest takes precedence over a prophet; a prophet takes precedence over a priest anointed for war; a priest anointed for war takes precedence over the head of a priestly watch; the head of a priestly watch takes precedence over the head of a household [of priests]; the head of a household of priests takes precedence over the superintendent of the cashiers; the superintendent of the cashiers takes precedence over the Temple treasurer; the Temple treasurer takes precedence over an ordinary priest; an ordinary (T. Hor. 2:10F-H).
F. A priest takes precedence over a Levite; a Levite takes precedence over an Israelite; an Israelite takes precedence over a mamzer; a mamzer takes precedence over a Netin; a Netin takes precedence over a proselyte; a proselyte takes precedence over a

freed slave. Under what circumstances? When all of them are equivalent. But if the mamzer was a disciple of a sage, and a high priest was an ignoramus, the mamzer who is the disciple of a sage takes precedence over a high priest who is an ignoramus.

Matters having been set forth, the Tosefta makes its comment, and it is a harsh one:

G. A sage takes precedence over a king.

H. [For] if a sage dies, we have none who is like him.

I. [If] a king dies, any Israelite is suitable to mount the throne (T. 2:8).

From the sages, the Tosefta's formulation turns to the hierarchy of holy classes in Israel: priests, prophets, messianic priests (anointed ones):

J. [A high priest anointed with oil takes precedence over one dedicated through many garments.]

K. A prophet takes precedence over the high priest anointed for battle,

L. and the high priest anointed for battle takes precedence over the prefect,

M. and the prefect takes precedence over the head of the weekly course [of the priests, who take care of the cult in a given week],

N. and the head of the priestly course takes precedence over the superintendent of the cashiers,

O. and the superintendent of the cashiers takes precedence over the treasurer.

P. And the treasurer takes precedence over an ordinary priest.

Q. And an ordinary priest takes precedence over a Levite (T. Hor. 2:10A–I).

In a well-ordered system, the same principles that govern classes of persons must pertain to classes of objects, that is, the comparison and contrast of the indicative traits. The principle of hierarchization applies to matters of sanctification of objects in place of persons, now a synagogue, an ark, wrappings for a scroll of the Torah, and so on upward or downward, as the passage may require:

MISHNAH-TRACTATE MEGILLAH 3:1:

A. Townsfolk who sold (1) a street of a town buy with its proceeds a synagogue.

B. [If they sold] (2) a synagogue, they buy an ark.

C. [If they sold] (3) an ark, they buy wrappings.

D. [If they sold] (4) wrappings, they buy scrolls [of the prophets or writings].

E. [If they sold] (5) scrolls, they buy a Torah scroll.

What goes up must come down, and a trait of legal formulation – the acutely formal ordering of thought into word-patterns – proves blatant; this is a way in which how things are said conveys the same message as what is said:

F. E But if they sold (5) a Torah scroll, they should not buy scrolls.
G. [If they sold] (4) scrolls, they should not buy wrappings.
H. [If they sold] (3) wrappings, they should not buy an ark.
I. [If they sold] (2) an ark, they should not buy a synagogue.
J. [If they sold] (1) a synagogue, they should not buy a street.
K. And so with the surplus [of the proceeds of any of] these.

By listing in sequence the lesser to the greater, then the greater, to the lesser, levels of sanctification – the categories being givens (synagogue, art, scrolls) – beyond the specific rule that is set forth, the principle is established that matters of sanctification are subject to the rules of hierarchization. The sages rarely find it necessary to spell out the generalization that their array of particulars yields. It is self-evident, and even my supplying ordinals is superfluous.

From what is concrete we turn to abstraction, here involving matters of status. The case is important to show how a single mode of thought, a cogent approach to organizing the data of the everyday world as much as of the Heavens, pertains throughout. Not only so, but, so far as possible, the work of bringing order out of the chaos of facts requires an effort to cover sets of data. These sets, for example, of opposites, may be shown to match or to contrast. The more sets of data one can assemble in a single system, the more one achieves in showing the inner logic and integrity of all creation in all its category-formations. Here we have a protracted example of how the sages match opposites, organizing data in two distinct groups, each group governed by its own indicative traits, and then showing how the two groups form a single coherent complement or match. When, later on, we consider the theological exercises of complementarity and correspondence, which define the modes of thought of the Oral Torah when the work of explaining man and defining God comes to hand, we shall find in play exactly the same large principles. That accounts for the exemplary quality of the rather odd composition of law that we now consider.

Here hierarchization organizes the data of both sanctification and uncleanness in a single structure, even though there is no necessary correspondence of the details of the one to those of the other. The points of differentiation, both as to sanctification and as to uncleanness, however, are the same, arrayed in sets of opposites, a most successful exercise in comparison and contrast to show complementarity and correspondence:

MISHNAH-TRACTATE KELIM 1:5, 6-8

1:5 A. Ten levels of uncleanness pertain to man:

B. (1) He whose atonement [sacrifice] is incomplete [solely in respect to the purificatory sacrifice] is prohibited in regard to Holy Thing(s) but permitted in regard to heave offering and in regard to tithe.

C. (2) He [who] [became unclean so as] to be a tebul-yom [who awaits sunset to complete his purification] is prohibited in regard to Holy Thing(s) and in regard to heave offering but permitted in regard to tithe.

D. (3) He [who] [became unclean so as] to be one who had suffered a pollution is prohibited in regard to all three.

The sages derive all of the governing facts from Scripture, as commentaries to the passage show. The first triplet matches the character of uncleanness that disqualifies a man from eating food in a given level of sanctification with the level of sanctification imputed to foods that have been subject to a given set of rules. Now we proceed to more severe levels of uncleanness and the effect of that uncleanness upon objects, not foods. Here the governing laws are located in Leviticus Chapter 15:

E. (4) He [who] [became unclean so as] to be one who has intercourse with a menstruating woman conveys uncleanness to what lies [far] beneath him [in like degree as he conveys uncleanness to a spread that lies] above [it and directly underneath him].

E. (5) [If] he [became unclean so as] to be a Zab who has suffered two appearances [of flux], he renders the couch and the chair [on which he sits or lies] unclean and needs bathing in running water but is free of the offering.

G. (6) He [who] saw three [appearances of flux] is liable for the offering,

We proceed, at a still more virulent level of cultic contamination, to the uncleanness described in Leviticus Chapters 13 and 14:

H. (7) He [who] [became unclean so as] to be a leper that is shut up [for examination to see whether signs of uncleanness will appear] conveys uncleanness through coming [into a house] but is exempt from loosening [the hair], and tearing [the clothes], and from shaving, and from the bird [offering].

I. (8) And if he was certified [as a leper], he is liable for all of them.

Now comes the most virulent source of uncleanness of all, the corpse:

J. (9) [If] a limb on which there is not an appropriate amount of flesh separated from him, it renders unclean through contact and through carrying but does not render unclean in the tent.

K. (10) And if there is on it [the limb) an appropriate amount of flesh, it renders unclean through contact and through carrying and through the tent.

L. The measure of flesh that is appropriate is sufficient to bring about healing.

The point subject to dispute is a minor detail; the formulation in anonymous terms signals that the law that is set forth is normative:

M. R. Judah says, "If there is in one place enough [flesh] to surround the member with [the thickness of] the thread of the woof, there is sufficient to bring about healing."

Having descended to the lowest layers of uncleanness, we move upward from the initial to the highest levels of sanctification, which is the antonym of uncleanness so far as the sages are concerned:

1:6 A. There are ten [degrees of] holiness(es):
B. (1) The land of Israel is holier than all lands.
C. And what is its holiness? For they bring from it the omer, and the first fruits, and the Two Loaves, which they do not bring (thus) from all lands.

What sanctifies the Land, in this construction, is what originates from the Land for use on the Temple altar. Next comes a level of sanctification indicated not by what is done but by who or what is excluded:

1:7 A. (2) The cities surrounded by a wall are more holy than it [the land].
B. For they send from them the lepers, and they carry around in their midst a corpse so long as they like. [But once] it has gone forth, they do not bring it back.

Our next level of sanctification is marked by what may be done in the designated area:

1:8 A. (3) Within the wall [of Jerusalem] is more holy than they
B. For they eat there lesser sanctities and second tithe.

Here we see the diversity of signifiers, since what marks the next area as more holy is, once more, who may not be permitted to enter the area, and that criterion governs to the end:

C. (4) The Temple mount is more holy than it.

D. For Zabim, and Zabot, menstruating women, and those that have given birth do not enter there.

E. (5) The rampart is more holy than it.

F. For gentiles and he who is made unclean by a corpse do not enter there.

G. (6) The court of women is more holy than it.

H. For a tebul-yom does not enter there, but they are not liable on its account for a sin offering.

I. (7) The court of Israel is more holy than it.

J. For one who [yet] lacks atonement [offerings made in the completion of his purification rite] does not enter there, and they are liable on its account for a sin-offering.

K. (8) The court of the priests is more holy than it.

L. For Israelite(s) do not enter there except in the time of their [cultic] requirements: for laying on of hands, for slaughtering, and for waving.

1:9 A. (9) [The area] between the porch and the altar is more holy than it.

B. For those [priests] who are blemished or whose hair is unloosed do not enter there.

C. (10) The sanctuary is more holy than it.

D. For [a priest] whose hands and feet are not washed does not enter there.

E. (11) The Holy of Holies is more holy than they.

F. For only the high priest on the Day of Atonement at the time of the service enters there.

The pattern for sanctification is clear: a set of available facts – most of them explicit in Scripture, some of them derived by processes of reasoning from Scripture's facts – is organized and laid out in the established pattern of ascension to ever higher levels; but the facts are available, not established through any program of investigation. The single standard pertains: relationship to the same locus of sanctification. If, now, we match the two sets of data, we find that the correspondence is formal, not substantive, but, nonetheless, the effect of the comparison and contrast is clear, transcending the somewhat incongruous details.

So far our consideration of the sages' modes of thought has attended to material culture. What about the abstractions of thought? Hierarchization governs intellectual matters as well. The rules of argument turn out to follow the same principles of organization as the rules of cultic uncleanness. Only the details, the operative criteria, differ as the requirements of the case dictate. We clearly differentiate among types of data, posing what is relevant to the issue and dismissing what is not, in the manner of Meir. Sages maintain that whatever is in the Torah falls into a single classification. Nonetheless, we do give priority to what is relevant, to what is a precedent, to law over exegesis, exegesis over a tale, an argument a fortiori over an analogy, and so on, the whole properly hierarchized:

TOSEFTA-TRACTATE SANHEDRIN 7:7

I. "And in the case in which there is one who asks to the point and another who asks not to the point, they answer the question of the one who asks to the point, and the one who asked not to the point has to state, 'I asked a question not to the point,'" the words of R. Meir.

J. And sages say, "He does not have to do so.

K. "For the entire Torah is deemed a single matter."

Now a sequence of indicators of hierarchy drawn from logical argument is set forth:

L. [If there is] something relevant, and something not relevant, they attend to what is relevant;

M. a precedent and what is not a precedent – they attend to what is a precedent;

N. a law and an exegesis – they attend to the law;

O. an exegesis of Scripture and a tale – they attend to the exegesis of Scripture;

P. an exegesis and an argument a fortiori – they attend to the argument a fortiori;

Q. an argument a fortiori and an analogy – they attend to the argument a fortiori;

From the character of the argument, we turn to the standing of the participant in the debate:

R. a sage and a disciple – they attend to the sage;

S. a disciple and a common person – they attend to the disciple;

T. if both were sages, both disciples, both ordinary folk, both laws, both questions, both answers, both precedents –

U. the speaker has the right from that point [to make his own choices].

The method is consistent throughout. We begin with the premise that species of the same genus are subject to a process of classification, meaning, hierarchization, and then accomplish the work by a systematic ordering of the data by appeal to the pertinent traits of taxonomy and hierarchization. Time and again the process of taxonomy and hierarchization takes over a genus of data and accomplishes both speciation and hierarchization. What forms data into a single class, for example, relationship to what is holy or status as to un-cleanness, also speciates the data of that class (alike in some ways, different in others), and at the same time hierarchizes.

At the same time, hierarchization within one system may be shown to con-flict with hierarchization within another, the latter then disrupting the results of the former. The hierarchization is accomplished by appeal to causation; that which causes but is uncaused takes priority over that which is caused, and the rest follows. A further demonstration derives from the character of penalties, the more severe marking the more consequential deed. In both cases we assess the relative standing of causation, at both the opening and the concluding phases of a sequence of actions (causation, penalties for action or inaction). Hierarchization is accomplished by applying a single, established criterion to two or more classes that are to be ordered; then the result of hier-archization will be subject to exegesis to yield a generalization. Reasoning by a process of comparison and contrast between two distinct classes of being shows how the two correspond, and the evidence is drawn from nature and analysed through a process of pure reason: likeness and unlikeness. Abun-dant details are carefully matched throughout, and the proposition is demon-strated beyond any reasonable doubt.

The upshot is that Scripture's facts are organized and sorted out in such a way as to present a generalization. Generalizations are to be formulated through that same process of collecting kindred facts and identifying the im-plication that all of them bear in common. But Scripture may also be asked to provide illustrative cases for principles that are formulated autonomously, as the result of analytical reasoning distinct from the sorting out of Scriptural precedents. Then Scripture is asked only to define in concrete terms what has been said abstractly. Successive propositions organize and rationalize a vast body of data, all of the facts pointing to the conclusions that are proposed as generalizations. The proof then lies once more in the regularity and order of the data that are collected. The balance and coherence of the opposed laws yield the besought generalizations. The method in no particular will have appeared alien to elementary students of natural history or simple logic in the schools of certain ancient philosophical traditions.

So the sages set forth the rational version of the myths of Scripture: cre-ation and its flaws, Eden and the loss of Eden. But their logic, involving as it did the insistence on perfect and unchanging world, sought out what comple-ments and completes an account, modes of thought that will occupy us later on. Thus, they taught how, also, Eden is to be recovered. Adam and his coun-terpart, Israel, in the cosmic drama acted out every day, here and now, in the humble details of Israel's ordinary life, embodied the simple story of the world: unflawed creation, spoiled by man's act of will, restored by Israel's act of repentance. The rationality of an orderly and balanced world set forth in the Oral Torah comes to full realization in the match of Eden and the Land of Israel, Adam and Israel, the paradise and paradise lost, with one difference. Adam had no Torah, Israel does. Adam could not regain Eden. But Israel can and will regain the Land. The sages' teleology imposed itself on eschatology, so forming a theory of last things corresponding to first things, in a theology of restoration, as we see in chapters 13 and 14.

Private life conformed; it, too, revealed that same flawless character that the world does – when reason takes over, and exception is explained (away). Exchanges of goods – scarce resources – likewise aimed at a perfect balance. Time, for the sages, stood still, history bore no meaning, all things could be shown to exemplify rules and embody regularities. Scripture then conveyed lessons of not history and its admonitions but logic – the logic of creation and its inner tension – and its inexorable result.

Here, we confront the actualization in mythic language of the philosophers' Eden, set forth in abstract terms. The sages in these proportionate, balanced, and measured components revealed a world of rules and exposed a realm of justice and therefore rational explanation. It was the kingdom of Heaven, so the sages called it, meaning the kingdom of God. For that Eden, in the abstraction of natural history that was invented by philosophy, corresponds to the conception of the world and its perfection set forth by the theology of the sages. They accordingly conceived of a philosophical Eden out of Scripture's account – its authorized history of the world from Eden to the return to Zion. What the observed facts of nature taught philosophers, the revealed facts of Scripture taught our sages of blessed memory. Therein theology differs from philosophy – but, in the Oral Torah in particular, the difference is there and there alone and nowhere else.

Working with the facts provided by Scripture and their own observations of nature, the sages cobbled together an account of the world, embedded in the Written part of the Torah itself, that realized the philosophers' ideal of a world of reason and order, balance, and proportion, equity, and reliability. Others emerged from Scripture with quite different visions of the world from Eden onward, different perspectives on different realities. Those who framed the Authoritative History from Genesis through Kings certainly thought in a different way from the sages, in a historical way. And others, who found in Scripture the secret of events to come, not to restore Eden but to transform creation altogether, took yet a third way, the apocalyptic one. We need not catalogue all of the diverse hermeneutics that Scripture was found by various groups to sustain or even require. Among the heirs of Scripture in late antiquity, the sages alone approached Scripture as an exercise in rationality and emerged from Scripture with a world that followed accessible rules and realized a universal logic.

A single statement in detail of that view in general suffices to call attention to the regularities and order, the correspondences, that the sages found linked nature and man in a perfect match. To the sages, stating the matter very simply, man and nature correspond. God created the same matching traits in nature and in man:

ABOT DER. NATAN XXXI:III. I

A. R. Yosé the Galilean says, "Whatever the Holy One, blessed be he, created on earth, he created also in man. To what may the matter be compared? To someone who took a piece of wood and wanted to make many forms on it but had no room to make them, so he was distressed. But someone who draws forms on the earth can go on drawing and can spread them out as far as he likes.

B. "But the Holy One, blessed be he, may his great name be blessed for ever and ever, in his wisdom and understanding created the whole of the world, created the heaven and the earth, above and below, and created in man whatever he created in his world.

C. "In the world he created forests, and in man he created forests: the hairs on his head.

D. "In the world he created wild beasts and in man he created wild beasts: lice.

E. "In the world he created channels and in man he created channels: his ears.

F. "In the world he created wind and in man he created wind: his breath.

G. "In the world he created the sun and in man he created the sun: his forehead.

H. "Stagnant waters in the world, stagnant waters in man: his nose, [namely, rheum].

I. "Salt water in the world, salt water in man: his urine.

J. "Streams in the world, streams in man: man's tears.

K. "Walls in the world, walls in man: his lips.

L. "Doors in the world, doors in man, his teeth.

M. "Firmaments in the world, firmaments in man, his tongue.

N. "Fresh water in the world, fresh water in man: his spit.

O. "Stars in the world, stars in the man: his cheeks.

P. "Towers in the world, towers in man: his neck.

Q. "Masts in the world, masts in man: his arms.

R. "Pins in the world, pins in man: his fingers.

S. "A King in the world, a king in man: his head.

T. "Grape clusters in the world, grape clusters in man: his breasts.

U. "Counsellors in the world, counsellors in man: his kidneys.

V. "Millstones in the world, millstones in man: his intestines [which grind up food].

W. "Mashing mills in the world, and mashing mills in man: the spleen.

X. "Pits in the world, a pit in man: the belly button.

Y. "Flowing streams in the world and a flowing stream in man: his blood.

Z. "Trees in the world and trees in man: his bones.

AA. "Hills in the world and hills in man: his buttocks.

BB. "Pestle and mortar in the world and pestle and mortar in man: the joints.

CC. "Horses in the world and horses in man: the legs.

DD. "The angel of death in the world and the angel of death in man: his heels.

EE. "Mountains and valleys in the world and mountains and valleys in man: when he is standing, he is like a mountain, when he is lying down, he is like a valley.

FF. "Thus you have learned that whatever the Holy One, blessed be he, created on earth, he created also in man."

Shorn of theological and mythic language, the statement says no less than natural philosophy does in its insistence upon the teleology of nature, its hierarchical order. As philosophers follow a procedure of comparison and contrast, resting on the systematic sifting of the data of nature, so too do the sages. But here, nature and Scripture (without differentiation as to source or effect of derivation from nature rather than from Scripture) yield correspondences that are deemed concrete and exact. We begin with a proposition clarified by a parable and then proceed systematically through the parts of nature and their counterparts in the body of man.

So each group working with its chosen source of facts, philosophers and the sages pursue the same issues in much the same way. Intellectuals to their core, confident of the capacity to contemplate, to conceive in mind for speculative analysis a real world that corresponds to the world realized alone in mind, both philosophers and the sages insist upon the primacy of reason. Logic ruled. It was logic that they had the capacity to discern. All things can be made to make sense. Proper analysis transforms the apparent chaos of nature's data into the compelling order of purposeful system and structure: streams in the world, streams in mind, a world of complement and balance. A vast and ordered universe yields its secrets to those who discern regularity in close reading of actualities. Then, in place of mysteries comes reliable knowledge, facts that yield the laws of life. So both philosophers and the sages can have set forth a single conception of the world.

But – I cannot over-stress – when they answered the question, Whence the knowledge of the rules of the ordered society, the world of balance and proportion in all things and of equitable exchange? the sages took their leave of philosophers. Instead of reading nature, they read the Torah. In place of searching for regularities of nature, they found patterns in the Torah. Instead of an abstract, natural teleology, to be defined through systematic work of hierarchical classification, comparison, and contrast, they invoked the will of God. This will they showed to be dependable, regulated by rules man can discern, wholly rational, entirely just. Then, instead of an inquiry into natural history, guided by considerations of hierarchy, order, and ultimate purpose, the sages contemplated the condition of Israel, explaining how those same principles of intent and order governed, the same modes of rational explanation functioned, the same media of reasoned thought in the form of applied reason and practical logic guided thought. That is what distinguished the sages from philosophers and turned them into theologians: the privileged source of truth that the Torah constituted.

How, in concrete terms, did theology takes its leave from philosophy? It was through the appeal to revealed facts of the Torah in place of the discovered facts of nature. Further, the sages' aesthetics required the recasting of those truths from the abstract language of generalization into the concrete myth form of a massive narrative, regularized and ordered into governing rules. Take, for example, the heart of the system of the dual Torah, the conviction of God's rule of a world of order that is to be explained by appeal to the principles of justice. In this view, events serve as the source of moral truth. Destiny is dictated by God, and God's hegemony realizes a morality defined by justice. So justice, not chance, governs Israel, specifically, God's plan. For God has a purpose in what he does with Israel. This point is set forth by reference to exemplary actions, a narrative of what counts. God sent Israel down into Egypt so that he would have occasion to perform miracles, so that the whole world would know that He is God and there is no other:

SIFRÉ TO DEUTERONOMY CCCVI: XXX.2FF.

2. A. "And how on the basis of Scripture do you say that our ancestors went down to Egypt only so that the Holy One, blessed be He, might do wonders and acts of might, and so that his great name might be sanctified in the world?

B. "As it is said, 'And it came to pass in the course of that long time that the king of Egypt died ... and God heard their groaning, and God remembered his covenant' (Ex. 2:23–24).

C. "And it is said, 'For the name of the Lord I proclaim; give glory to our God.' "

The purposeful character of God's actions now is spelled out in further cases:

3. A. "And how on the basis of Scripture do we know that the Omnipresent brought punishments and the ten plagues on Pharaoh and on the Egyptians only so that his great name might be sanctified in the world?

B. "For to begin with it is said, 'Who is the Lord, that I should listen to his voice?' (Ex. 5:2).

C. "But in the end: 'The Lord is righteous, and I and my people are wicked' " (Ex. 9:27).

We move from the punishment of Egypt to the miracles done for Israel, also purposefully:

4. A. "And how on the basis of Scripture do we know that the Omnipresent did wonders and acts of might at the sea and at the Jordan and at the Arnon streams only so that his great name might be sanctified in the world?

B. "As it is said, 'And it came to pass, when all the kings of the Amorites that were beyond the Jordan westward, and all the kings of the Canaanites [that were by the sea, heard how the Lord has dried up the waters of the Jordan from before the children of Israel until they had passed over, their heart melted]' (Josh. 5:1).

C. "And so Rahab says to the messengers of Joshua, 'For we have heard how the Lord dried up the water of the Red Sea before you' (Josh. 2:10).

D. "Scripture says, 'For the name of the Lord I proclaim; give glory to our God.' "

Not only miracles, but suffering and martyrdom serve God's purpose:

5. A. "And how on the basis of Scripture do we know that Daniel went down into the lions' den only so that the Holy One, blessed be He, might have occasion to do wonders and acts of might, and so that his great name might be sanctified in the world?

B. "As it is said, 'For the name of the Lord I proclaim; give glory to our God.'

C. "And Scripture says, 'I make a decree, that in all the dominions of my kingdom men tremble and fear before the God of Daniel ...' (Dan. 6:27–8).

6. A. "And how on the basis of Scripture do you maintain that Hananiah, Mishael, and Azariah went into the fiery oven only so that the Holy One, blessed be He, might have occasion to do for them wonders and acts of might, and so that his great name might be sanctified in the world?

B. "As it is said, 'It seems good to me to declare the signs and wonders that God Most High has done for me ... how great are his signs, and how mighty are his wonders, his kingdom is an everlasting kingdom' " (Dan. 3:32–3).

What is important here is two traits of mind. First, theological truth is discovered in revealed Scripture. But then, second, the facts that are adduced are ordered into generalizations that are subject to the tests of verification or falsification: philosophical modes of thought applied to the data of theology: the search for the logic of God. What philosophers of Judaism accomplished in medieval times, joining Torah to reason, the sages accomplished in the very process of formulating the Torah, Oral and Written, for the ages.

But the sages differed from their philosophical continuators in the Middle Ages. They adapted philosophical modes of thought to their own purpose and dispensed with philosophical doctrines as irrelevant to that purpose. In according privilege to the revealed truth set forth by God's revelation in Scripture, they transcended philosophy. If philosophy found in nature, through the rules of natural history, the logic of the world, the sages studied the origins of nature in the Torah, the account of the program and plan of the Creator of that creation that natural history ordered. So the sages sought the logic of God's mind, to which, through the whole Torah, Oral and Written, and its account of creation, they possessed sole access. They spoke in particular of revealed truth, rather than in general terms (in abstract symbols, for instance) of truth set forth in nature. Accordingly, they pursued a theological program – the logic of God – rather than the philosophical program that addressed the world of universal wisdom. The question of whether theology is philosophy's method applied to God's concerns, or philosophy is theology in a secular mode, need not detain us.

It follows that, when we imagine the world as philosophers conceive it, we find entry into the world as our sages of blessed memory imagine it to work. But if the method is the same, the message that emerges proves fundamentally different. That is because the Torah for the sages takes the place of nature for philosophy. Its narratives, transformed into exemplary cases, replace social thought about mankind in general. The sages' appeal to these examples makes unnecessary historical inquiry, based on sustained narrative, into what men have done. They find a better way to identify the rules that the results yield, whether then or now; to them, history is monumentally irrelevant.

The sages accordingly find in the Torah the account of the balanced and orderly world that God has made. That then serves as counterpart to philosophers' reasoned picture of man's domain and its laws, nature's realm and its regularities. Corresponding to the book of nature that contains the lessons of physics or biology or astronomy that philosophers consult to find the laws of the tangible world for this Eden's philosophers is the Torah. There, and not in nature, concurring with philosophers about teleology yielding a rational and ordered universe, the sages locate the record of God's purpose, God's intent in creating the world:

GENESIS RABBAH I:I.2

A. "In the beginning God created ..." (Gen. I:I):

B. The word ["in the beginning"] means "workman."

C. [In the cited verse] the Torah speaks, "I was the work-plan of the Holy One, blessed be he."

D. In the accepted practice of the world, when a mortal king builds a palace, he does not build it out of his own head, but he follows a work-plan.

E. And [the one who supplies] the work-plan does not build out of his own head, but he has designs and diagrams, so as to know how to situate the rooms and the doorways.

F. Thus the Holy One, blessed be he, consulted the Torah when he created the world.

G. So the Torah stated, "By means of 'the beginning' [that is to say, the Torah] did God create ..." (Gen. 1:1).

H. And the word for "beginning" refers only to the Torah, as Scripture says, "The Lord made me as the beginning of his way" (Prov. 8:22).

In the Torah God wrote out the record of his plans and acts. Read rightly, the laws of the Torah yield law for the wise who can discern regularity and perceive purpose. The facts of nature take second place to the facts of the Torah; there is found the encompassing account of the realm of perfection that Eden promised and that the Torah's social entity, Israel, both man and nation – Israelite man, the kingdom of priests and holy nation of Israel – realize.

Here, therefore, is where philosophers and the sages part company: philosophers turn to the natural world, the sages to the Torah, for the facts that, for both parties, will yield reliable knowledge concerning the regularities and rationality of the orderly world awaiting explanation. In the Oral Torah the facts of nature are subordinated to the facts of the Torah. Facts that derive from other sources, for example, those of nature not set forth in Scripture, or those of history and politics not deriving from the Torah but the ken of Israel, appear only rarely in the discourse of the Oral Torah. When they do, moreover, they turn out to replicate facts of nature, history, or politics that Scripture has already designated as noteworthy. The counterpart of nature for philosophy's natural history, Scripture provides nearly all of the remarkable facts that demand attention. The Torah's are the data demand and yield regularization, comparison, and contrast. The Torah's are the facts that may contradict a hypothesis or demonstrate it, but it is rare that facts deriving from any other source prove a point and, once a hypothesis resting on the Torah's facts is set out, facts deriving from some other source *never* come under consideration at all, except, perhaps, to form exceptions that can be explained by appeal to the rule established in the Torah's facts. To prove a point, it suffices to advance three or more cases from the Torah; these establish a pattern, and the pattern is its own proof.

The world we contemplate encompasses happenings but not history in the conventional sense. The Torah sets forth narrative, but considerations of time and change do not pertain. That is because, as I emphasize, the narrative yields cases that produce generalizations, examples of how things are in general. The narrative yields those rules of the social order that correspond to the laws of physics, biology, or astronomy. Events properly ordered – compared and contrasted and shown to conform to rules – match the regular movement of the stars or the balance and proportion of the imaginary atom. The same calculus, the counterpart-mathematics – these pertain to the affairs of the natural world and those of the world of man portrayed by nature and the Torah, respectively. That is why time and change represent flaws in Eden, where stasis attests to perfection: with all things in place and order, why change anything? Then, if considerations of temporal order do not apply to the Torah's account of affairs, we have to reconstruct, in accord with the rules of natural history, the record of human events set out in the Torah.

How are we to envision this multilayered reality and account for the unity and harmony of things – the cosmic logic of it all? Let us conceive of the description of creation to correspond to the problem of cartographic representation of complex data in different layers. Here is what we may call the geography of creation as the sages' cartography portrayed it. First, contemplate the Torah as a thin translucent overlay over everyday reality, a set of sheets all together joined, with each imposing its lines of structure joined with the lines of the others upon the ordinary and imparting proportionate shape to the workaday world. Seen through the mediating colours and light of these translucent sheets, the ordinary world conforms to the artist's vision of harmonious Eden, man and nature living in perfect peace.

But how are we to conceive in our mind's eye the colours that lend nuance to the ordinary world? To follow that vision we must discern in these sets of translucent sheets the characteristics of each one, not only the joined traits of them all, all together and all at once. For each sheet in visual-outline form contains a portrait of a given moment or event in the Torah: Israel at the sea, Israel at Sinai, Israel in the Land and at the Temple, Israel leaving for exile, Israel returning to the Land – these events are all reproduced in visual tableaux. So, too, are Abraham at Moriah, Isaac blessing Jacob, Jacob wrestling with the angel, Jacob at the well, Jacob and Laban, Joseph in Pharaoh's court, Moses at Sinai, Moses at the rock – great moments, each individually outlined in a few deft strokes. Now, the sheets being separate and translucent, they may be combined and recombined to make designs, to yield patterns, of a different order. Then today's drawing, Israel today, contemplating its condition in exile, at the base, is given structure and balance when the light-bearing sheet is placed on top: Israel going into exile, Israel returning from exile. Similarly, the sheet portraying Jacob wrestling with the angel or Abraham at Moriah may overlay the sheet that conveys the lines of Israel's struggle to endure until redemption.

All of the sheets together then contain and portray whatever happens that matters, whoever makes a difference, in the Scriptural record. Seen all together, the whole set yields a picture of everything, all together, all at once, in a single moment of perfect revelation, that the Torah wishes to portray. For these pages, like the translucent maps in the old geography books, which are formed by differentiated pages and colors, all of them distinct in their own right, but the entire set visible all together and all at once, form a map. But this map portrays, severally by pages and then jointly when bound together, not ranges of mountains and valleys along with places of human settlement, sites of battles, and the locations of industry, mining, and agriculture. Rather, this imaginary map formed by the differentiated layers of the Torah holds together events of time and space, transactions of massive weight in the course of the life of Israel and the nations, happenings in the private life of those persons of enduring memory within Israel that carry consequence, embodying the rules that apply.

Our translucent pages work best – but not only – in sets of two, producing an interesting complication of colour. These sets form binary opposites in the principles of balance, complementarity, proportion, and commensurability that define perfection. Contemplate these pairs in their mixtures of colours: yellow and red, together producing orange; yellow and blue together yielding green, for instance, and so throughout. Envision then translucent sheets, the yellow, Eden, the blue, its match and counterpart in time, the Land of Israel, and the green, the world to come. Or see with your mind's eye these translucent sheets: the yellow, Israel, the red, the nations, the orange, judgment – and so on. The variegated colours of reality all break down into the simple components of which they are comprised; the components of world order and of social order and of historical order all prove susceptible to analysis and division, then also to synthesis and union.

Then what of events and persons? In the kingdom governed by orderly rules formed into balanced opposites, consequential events find their match, persons their counterpart. These prove few and seldom show movement. Eden matched by Land of Israel yields a predictable match: Adam's fall from Eden and Israel's expulsion from the Land of Israel. Yet another page may be superimposed on the page of Adam and Israel, Eden and the Land. Eden's counterpart in time locates itself in the Temple of Jerusalem, in which case Adam's=Israel's counterpart can only be God, who leaves the Temple when Israel leaves Jerusalem. Even God, capable of anything, subjects himself to the analogies of the mortal king, matching in mourning the motifs of ordinary lamentation, in a passage we shall meet again, at greater length, in chapter 9:

PESIQTA DERAB KAHANA XV:III

1. A. Bar Qappara opened discourse by citing the following verse: "In that day the Lord God of hosts called to weeping and mourning, to baldness and girding with sackcloth; [and behold, joy and gladness, slaying oxen and killing sheep, eating meat

and drinking wine. 'Let us eat and drink for tomorrow we die.' The Lord of hosts has revealed himself in my ears: 'Surely this iniquity will not be forgiven you until you die,' says the Lord of hosts]" (Is. 15:12–14).

B. "Said the Holy One, blessed be He, to the ministering angels, 'When a mortal king mourns, what does he do?'

C. "They said to him, 'He puts sack over his door.'

D. "He said to them, 'I too shall do that. 'I will clothe the heavens with blackness [and make sackcloth for their covering]' " (Is. 50:3).

This composition, which we shall read in complete form later on, compares common practice among royalty with verses of Scripture that describe God's state of mind and action. The demonstration is detailed and systematic, and the explanation, in context, compelling. The match of king to The King of the world once more rests on the fundamental conviction of a perfect match, a world we can understand by appeal to governing rules and illuminating analogies.

Two other realms of meaning – other sets of translucent sheets – produce participants of consequence, whose activities require rational explanation by appeal to the principles of balance, complement, and order. These are the people, Israel, and the individual Israelite. The people, Israel, find their counterpart in their progenitors, Abraham, Isaac, and Jacob (rarely: their wives as well). What happens in the life of the people recapitulates what happens in the life of the patriarchs that produced the people. Or Israel matches Adam, as we noticed: the expulsion from the Land is weighed in the balance against the expulsion from Eden. The individual Israelite finds his place within Israel, events of his life their counterpart in what happens to the whole of Israel ("all Israel"). Just as rules of justice and equity govern the whole of Israel, so inexorable justice, meting out true equity for merit, true penalty for sin, rules the life of the individual. This complementary pattern finds its weightiest moment in the match of individual death and resurrection, on the one side, and Israel's exile and ultimate return to the Land, on the second, and God's abandoning of the Temple but restoration of, and return to, the Temple, on the third – and there are no other dimensions.

So in the particular realm formed by Israel we see the working out of those general rules of order and balance that describe the philosophers' Eden. And just as philosophers proposed to show the purpose and order of nature, so the sages pronounced the shape and structure of the future – because, in the timeless world of the permanent present that the sages contemplated, what was, is, and will be is wholly on record in the Torah, properly understood. The future matches and balances the past, and that is why, time and again, the sages speak confidently about what is going to happen. Take the case of the match of beginning and ending, Adam and Israel, Eden and the Land. Creation comes to its natural conclusion with Israel in the Land, the drama of Eden having come to resolution, through the Torah, in the perfection of Adam in Israel. Just as Adam lost Eden, so Israel lost the Land, but creation will come to rest and balance when Israel recovers Eden.

The system invokes the Torah as its dynamic, around which clusters of other key-categories or concepts find their position: Eden-Sinai-Land, Adam-Israel-Land – these define the anticipation that the sages precipitate: a fully systemic construction. So, too, the future in a different perspective: if part of a prophecy is fulfilled, the rest of the prophecy will be realized in due course, a perfectly reasonable and proportionate conception. So, too, the players in the cosmic drama, Israel and the nations, must not lose their sense of proportion; each has his assigned role, including the dimensions of his part. Along these same lines, a simple logic prevails in the conception of Israel's past, present, and future in this logical sequence of action, reaction, resolution: sin, punishment, comfort. That hermeneutics of philosophical perfection produces the exegesis of diverse texts to make the point, with every thing with which the Israelites sinned, they were smitten, and with that same thing they will be comforted.

The analytical inquiry in fact promises to demonstrate a proposition, not merely investigate data that yield one, as in our time we should understand the work. For the generative question that governs throughout, what is going to happen to Israel, and what is Israel supposed to do? derives not from the data, nor even from the problem of ordering the data, nor yet from the proposition that the work in the end yields. It derives rather from the system that calls attention to these data rather than some other, because these data will yield exactly what the system to begin with knows to be true. And that is, that Israel recapitulates the life and teachings of the patriarchs. More to the point, what the patriarchs did governs what Israel now endures. That matters because of what must come: prediction, or, in my language, explanation and anticipation. The system that works out its intellectual disciplines in the identification of what requires analysis and in conducting analysis through a labour of comparison and contrast and generalization therefrom means to set forth the principles that govern what happens to Israel in the future.

This encompassing, enormous, and yet simple theological system, bearing its own principles of reason and order, animates discourse, start to finish. The sage responsible for a cogent statement did not pretend to approach the data in a spirit of mere curiosity; not a philosopher seeking the order of this, the natural world, he was a theologian, intending to set forth the logic of matters having to do with God's actions and intentions in this world, with Israel. The data that he examined presented facts supplied by God in the Torah, and the task he took for himself was to turn those facts into useful knowledge of God's plans and program for Israel in the world. The sage drew upon a model of explanation that itself emerged from an established system, a construction of ideas that formed a given, that sustained all further thought and animated it. Then he knew exactly what he was going to find, which is what he set out to demonstrate.

Now we turn to blunt answers to fundamental questions of systemic description, analysis, and interpretation: if this is what we know, what else do we know? I deal with three questions that require specific answers.

First, what is at stake? It is an explanation of Israel's present condition, and – still more urgent – an identification of the operative reasons that will lead to viable hypotheses concerning Israel's future prospects. Here the systemic subtext shapes articulated thought: the present properly analysed and explained contains within itself the entire past, the whole future, all together, all at once. We turn to Abraham because we wish out of the past to know the future and because we take as fact that Israel's future recapitulates the past of Abraham. God has laid out matters from beginning to end; Scripture not only records the past but provides the key, through patterns we can identify in the present, to the future. The premise of the analysis, then, is that when we understand the facts in hand we also can learn the rules, just as we can in a world created in accord with the requirements of exact balance, proportion, correspondence, complementarity, and commensurability. There are no mysteries, only facts not yet noticed, analyses not yet undertaken, propositions not yet proved.

Second, how to explain the present? The sages' method of explanation will identify the rational principle that is involved. Scripture's facts do not suffice: the patriarchs asked. Reason is demanded: why did they value these experiences? Then rationality is established by appeal not to the given of Scripture but to the conviction that the familiar traits of perfection characterize creation and the Creator. That is to say, the conceptions that in general mark the paramount method of Classical philosophy in its account of nature – teleology joined to order – govern here as well. That is why applied reason and practical logic and not the given and revealed of Scripture alone everywhere sustain thought. The sages do not paraphrase or recapitulate Scripture and its narrative, they transform Scripture into facts to be analysed and reconstructed. The results yield the self-evidently valid doctrines. These prove to be few but paramount: the perfection of creation, the centrality of the Torah as a source of established facts, the subservience of God – therefore creation and history –

to the same reason that animates the mind of man. All things are subject to the rules of logic and order that man's own mind obeys, and explanation in the end must derive from the sources of nature and its laws and the Torah and its regularities, each recapitulating the mind and will of the loving and merciful and reasonable God, in whose image, after whose likeness, man is made.

Third, what of the future? Sages compared themselves to prophets and insisted that their knowledge of the Torah provided a key to the future. Knowing why noteworthy things take place provided them with that key. For a model of anticipation will extrapolate from the results of analysis and explanation those governing rules of an orderly world that define a useful hypothesis concerning the future. Having identified regularities and defined descriptive laws, and then accounted for those rules by spelling out the systemic reasons behind them, the sages had every reason to peer over the beckoning horizon. For their basic conviction affirmed the order and regularity of creation, its perfection. If, therefore, they knew the rules and how they worked (including remissions of the rules), the sages insisted they could predict how the future would take shape as well.

Given what we know about past and present and the signals of Providence that explain the condition of the world, what shall we anticipate for time to come? Like the prophets before them but thinking along quite other lines to reach comparable conclusions, the sages spoke with certainty, therefore, about what Israel may expect in the future. But there was this difference. The prophets invoked God's explicit statements about the future, whereas the sages' message took shape as a result of the analytical soundings the sages made and explained, the data they formed into rules, the rules the logic they set forth by way of explanation. Theirs was the way of the natural historian and the philosopher. But for them the path carried them into Scripture, not nature, and into the logic of God's plan for the world, not the *telos* of nature's impersonal perfection.

That explains why what the sages produced in the manner of philosophers is not philosophy but theology. Philosophy discovered the rules of the natural world, theology, those of the realm of the supernatural; the same principles of reasoned inquiry into factual regularities and rational explanations based on those descriptive laws of how things are governed both inquiries. Analysing nature and Scripture, respectively, philosophy and theology worked in the same way and produced matching results. Because the world is the way we conceive God made it – that is, perfect, therefore, orderly and purposeful for philosophy, rational and ultimately benevolent for the sages' reading of the way the Torah defines it – we can identify anomalies and conduct analyses, explain the results with rational explanations, and extrapolate from the order of the present the shape and structure of the future. That systematic exegesis of the world in accord with the hermeneutics of the Torah defines the theology of the Oral Torah: its focus and the source of its coherence and cogency. Had Aristotle read the Written Torah and chosen the media of law, myth, and exegesis for his discourse, his lectures would have recapitulated the results set forth by the sages. May we claim that the documents of the Oral Torah are what he would have written? Working with the particular facts ordered by the sages, he would have done something quite akin in method and in modes of thought and points of insistence, if not in form let alone in particular doctrine.

But there is this caveat. Had Aristotle compared the Written Torah's theory of Eden and the Land, Adam and Israel, with the everyday world's actualities – whether the conquest of Jerusalem by his own student. Alexander, or scattered Israel's inconsequentiality among the nations – he would have recognized the incongruity of the result. Then he would have abandoned the task of the mythic re-presentation of nature through Scripture, of theological instead of philosophical discourse. Nature sustained Aristotle's philosophy. Israel's actualities contradicted the sages' theology. For the world realized by natural Israel, whether in Aristotle's time, in the fourth century B.C.E., or in the time of our sages of blessed memory, the first six centuries C.E., testified to the absurdity of the vision of rationality and order, within the framework of God's logic, that the Torah portrayed. In no way did the natural world of Israel in actual history ever validate the sages' account of the theological world of mythic, holy Israel. Instead of an imaginary world of balance, match, complementarity, and proportion, Israel lived in a real world of disproportion, where the wicked prospered and the righteous suffered.

Absurdity piled onto absurdity into the ultimate climax of space and time, the Temple mount ploughed over, the only offerings these days the flesh and blood of the Israelite martyrs themselves. That is the everyday world confronted by the second-century sages who produced the Mishnah and its concomitant traditions. A competing, repressed minority competing with Israel over the true message of the shared Scriptures, the Christians, two hundred years later found themselves rulers of the world-empire of Rome. That is the (to them) utter absurdity faced by the fourth- and fifth-century sages who produced the Talmud of the Land of Israel, Genesis Rabbah, and Leviticus Rabbah, among other foundation-documents of Rabbinic Judaism. The world they confronted in no way validated their fiercely held convictions about the ultimate rationality of all things. If everything is subject to a reasonable explanation by appeal to regularities that wisdom may discern, then why are things the way they are?

How, then, did the sages construct this fantasy-world of theirs? It is a world vastly unlike the everyday world in which they lived out the life of Israel. Theirs was a politics of triviality amid kingdoms and empires not called "Israel," one empire, Iran, pagan and, heirs of Ahasuerus, by no means benign, the other, now-Christian Rome, laying claim to the same noble lineage. Specifically, what convictions, resting on what evidence, led them to the conclusions that, in their comprehensive account of theology, they set forth?

The answer is clear from what has already been said: Scripture, the Written Torah, set out a corpus of unassailable and generative facts, out of which all else was to be, and was, discovered and reconstructed (or, in more descriptive language, fabricated). So to understand the theology of the Oral Torah, we must take as our starting point that theology's sources of the conviction of the orderly character of all being. We commence with the starting point of all else: the rule of justice, therefore also of law, that governs all else. How did the sages find in the facts of Scripture that generative principle of their logic? Chapter 1 responds to that question.

From this protracted consideration of problems of philosophical and theological method, let us turn to the book at hand.

Here I maintain that the Oral Torah tells a simple story, the story of how God created the world he pronounced good and sustains creation through the just moral order realized in the people to whom he has made himself known, holy Israel.[1] The theology narrates the unfolding tale of humanity from the creation of the world to the resurrection of the dead to eternal life with God. It is one that sustains complex articulation and extension without losing coherence. That story is told in several distinct forms of discourse, mythic-narrative, exegetical, analytical and argumentative, in media of law and of lore, in statements of a general character and cases examined on their own or treated as exemplary. That sustaining story conveys a cogent logic, self-evident principles of reason and rationality. From a few governing principles or convictions, the entire story spins itself out into the finest details.

That simple story tells of a world governed by the moral order imposed by God's ultimate reason and justice, set forth in the Torah of Sinai, in oral and written media, and realized by God in Israel. Therein I find the governing, integrating theology of the Oral Torah. The generative doctrine of God's perfect justice in his creation and governance of the world is what imparts integrity to

1. Not to be confused with this-worldly and secular meanings attached to the same word, for example, "the State of Israel." In this book, "Israel" bears solely a theological meaning, hence "holy Israel," carefully defined in Chapter 2 out of the documents of the Oral Torah in particular.

the details and proportion to the whole. That story portraying the requirements of justification[2] encompasses the entire tale of humanity in general and its counterpart, Israel in particular. The tale provides a dense record of the reasonable rules that account for what happens in public and, by way of complement and match, at home, to the People and to people. Using the words of the Oral Torah, I tell that sustained story, start to finish, then placing this theology into the larger setting of the history of Judaism and the history of religions. The unfolding of the narrative is exposed on the Contents page and spelled out systematically from beginning to end. The order of the chapters is dictated, also, by that same logic; put one chapter elsewhere than its assigned place in the unfolding of the argument of this book, and the entire construction falls apart.

This book claims, therefore, that, set forth by the initial documents of the Oral Torah, reaching closure in the first six centuries C.E., is a single theological structure and system to sustain Rabbinic Judaism. The Judaism of the dual Torah, Written and Oral, speaks through law and lore, exegesis of received Scripture, and free-standing exposition. Throughout, in *halakhah* as much as in *aggadah* (to invoke the native categories for law and lore respectively), that single system animates the whole. Not only that, but at the end I insist that that structure and system form into a coherent statement exactly what, to begin with, the Written Torah – ancient Israelite Scripture – says.

The four units of the heart of the book therefore show how the Oral Torah advances generative propositions. These are as follows:

1) God formed creation in accord with a plan, which the Torah reveals. It is a world that is perfectly rational and perfectly just. Israel with the Torah knows that plan, the nations with idolatry do not.
2) World order can be shown by the facts of nature and society set out in that plan to conform to a pattern of reason based upon justice. The perfection of creation, realized in the rule of exact justice, is signified by the timelessness of the world and by the unchanging relationships of the social commonwealth. A further indication of perfection lies in the complementarity of the components of creation, on the one side, and, finally, the correspondence between God and man, in God's image, on the other.
3) What disrupts perfection is the sole power capable of standing on its own against God's power, and that is man's will. Because man defies God, the sin that results from man's rebellion flaws creation and disrupts world order.

---

2. Because I propose that the encompassing theology of the Oral Torah works out God's logic of world order framed by the rationality of justice, in these pages I use the word "justify" in a very particular, very exact sense: "to show the justice of …" The theology of the Oral Torah sets forth a systematic and sustained exercise in justification.

4) Responding to the change of will embodied in man's repentance, God ultimately will restore that perfection that embodied his plan for creation.

Expressed baldly, the theology of the Oral Torah takes up the critical theological heritage of the Hebrew Scriptures and to the age to come hands on that
heritage as an ordered, coherent, integrated system, the one that is set forth in
these pages. That is why the religion that the world calls "Judaism" rightly –
and, among all religions, uniquely – calls itself "the Torah" and ubiquitously
identifies the Torah as its central symbol. In the story I lay out in these pages,
I allege, every significant theological conviction that nourishes the documents
of the Oral Torah – the writings of the rabbis, called "our sages of blessed
memory," from the Mishnah of c. 200 C.E. through the Talmud of Babylonia
of c. 600 C.E. – finds its correct order and location.

The sages take as their task the recapitulation of the structure and system that
they identify with the Written Torah and they furthermore encompass within
that theology their own, as we see, very limited amplifications thereto. Indeed,
in behalf of its logic the Oral Torah conveys an apologetics that is implicit and
compelling by every objective measure of well-crafted evidence and sound argument. For the sages implicitly insist that those very ideas, that logic, this
story of theirs – these do recapitulate the ones that the Written Torah sets forth.
Through every available medium of argument, they maintain that the Oral Torah that they set down embodies the ideas, logic, and story presented in the
Written Torah. Their heirs, in early medieval times, saw in the dual Torah,
Written and Oral, a single coherent revelation: "the one whole Torah given by
God to Moses, our rabbi, at Sinai." That apologetics, integral to the theology of
the Oral Torah, takes a critical position in nearly every line of every document.
It defines the form of many documents and the generative energy of all of them.

At the end, in chapter 15, I shall argue that, as a matter of fact and objective,
accurate description, the sages in their way do recapitulate one paramount
story that Scripture tells. In the sense that their theology rests squarely and
symmetrically on scriptural foundations,[3] sages are right in portraying the Oral
part of the Torah as complement and fulfilment of the Written part. In that
factual, descriptive sense, as their act of systematic theology the sages lay out
the one whole Torah given by God to our rabbi, Moses, on Sinai. So I claim in

3. I do not claim that the sages' theology forms the sole correct or possible biblical theology;
to do so would require a systematic confrontation and dialogue with all other accounts of the theology of the Hebrew Scriptures and the demonstration, by some broadly acceptable criterion,
that the sages' is right and all others wrong. A reading of the definitive study of the subject,
Brevard S. Childs, *Biblical Theology of the Old and New Testaments* (Minneapolis: Fortress
Press 1992), leaves no doubt that such an exercise would carry me far afield and lead nowhere.

their behalf, so I demonstrate in these pages – no small venture in the systematic theological study of this religion.

Now that we understand the plan and program of the book, we turn to urgent questions of method. The first is critical. I claim to know what "the rabbis" think everywhere, throughout all their distinctive writings. On what basis do I allege as representative the account that I have offered? Let me explain the criteria that permit me to identify as both representative and also normative a given set of views and to treat as schismatic other opinions, everywhere bypassed in silence.[4] It would make this long book still longer were I to specify at every point why I exclude sayings or stories that may be presented as objections to what I characterize as normative views. It suffices to articulate the general considerations that follow.

My project is to describe theology, and my method then finds its rules and regulations in the analysis of ideas that are presented. I do not know, and I do not think the documents record, what proportion of the sages held which opinion, and that sense of "representative," the political and sociological dimension, does not pertain. And, all the more so, we know very little about what Jews other than the sages and the disciples thought. No one today imagines that the Oral Torah portrays the opinions of those who flourished outside the circles that produced the documents of the Oral Torah and preserved, studied, and proposed to realize them in the common life. That is because, to exaggerate only slightly, every page of the Rabbinic writings of late antiquity attests to the tension and conflict between "our sages of blessed memory" and the rest of that holy Israel that, sages insisted, belongs within the Kingdom of Heaven and under the domain of God, made manifest in the Torah. So on what basis do I portray *the* sages and *their* beliefs and opinions (to allude to the challenge that I laid before my Israeli counterpart when he undertook to accomplish the same theological task carried out here)?[5]

By what is representative I mean not what stands for broadly held opinion, but rather what embodies the ubiquitous and governing modes of rational thought, on the one side, and what sets forth the necessary and sufficient and

4. Since I have studied and translated all of the documents of the Oral Torah set forth here, readers ought to be able to stipulate that a composition or composite that is not dealt within these pages, and that says something to contradict the opinions that are advanced, has not been ignored or neglected or simply missed but rejected as not representative. It is on that basis that I use the language, "the sages thought," and not merely "this document recorded" or "that particular sage said." I claim that little, if anything, has been missed, in a corpus of writings all of which I have systematically translated.

5. See my critique most recently stated in *The Theology of Rabbinic Judaism. A Prolegomenon.*

integral doctrines generated by that rationality, on the other. By that criterion of what is "representative," therefore, the former – the modes of thought – are alleged to define rationality, and the latter – the logically consequent propositions – are claimed to define the *logos*, the principle that pervades the whole. This takes form in the idea that creation reveals God's justice, defined in terms man comprehends, and appears in many forms.

It is within that logic of structure and system that I invoke the claim of normativity. But within that definition, I go to the outer limit of matters. For by what is normative I mean the official position of the rabbis, viewed as a collegium and council in the model of the councils that declared Catholic and Orthodox Christianity. How, then, are we to know what composition or composite represents the whole and was deemed obligatory for all who practised the religion of "the whole Torah of Moses, our rabbi," that the world has long known as Judaism? I owe the reader an account of the criteria by which he or she may form a judgment of whether I am right.

My entire account of the theology of the Oral Torah rests on the claim that what I set forth, and the order in which I lay matters out, beginning to end, encompasses all of the documents that, all together, represent and define that Judaism. I even go so far, in the epilogue, as to maintain that that one whole Torah of Moses, our rabbi, portrayed here encompasses the Hebrew Scriptures of ancient Israel that the sages called "the written Torah" and furthermore defines Judaism as embodied in the piety and worship of the synagogue – thus, here is *Judaism*, pure and simple – no more adjectives, no more qualifiers. So much rests upon the answer to the question, how, other than through subjective impression or personal taste and judgment of an idiosyncratic character, do I claim to define the representative and the normative theology of the Oral Torah? And, to go with that question, how may the reader of this book assess the plausibility of my account of what is representative and normative?

As to what is representative of the entirety of opinion in the documents of the Oral Torah, two approaches strike me as plausible, one of which I have chosen.

The first is to rely upon subjective impressions, buttressed by a broad sample of data. If, for example, we may find expressed in various ways in the diverse documents a given view, we may claim that that view represents the generality of opinion. The position is assigned hither and yon, to many rabbis, in many writings. Many have taken that route in characterizing "the rabbis'" views of this and that, sinking to the treatment of the recurrence of a given saying in several places or versions as "he often used to say ..." But to declare representative a statement that occurs here and there and to treat as idiosyncratic one that occurs fewer times or in only one or two documents strikes me as lazy and uncomprehending – a resort to mere intellectual labour-saving devices. For not much thought goes into counting up occurrences rather than reflecting upon inner arrangements of ideas. A given idea may prove critical to the structure over all, even though it appears only in a document that came to closure early on (then to be taken for granted thereafter) or only very late among documents read in sequence (then to be articulated only long centuries after the initial impact, for example, an event in logic before articulation in a particular case). An ambitious venture requires more thought than is invested in adding up occurrences and finding the common denominator.

The other indicator of what is representative rests on evidence of an entirely different character. In my view, what represents the structure and system that sustains a variety of kindred writings emerges in positions that logically hold together among them all. These positions, whether concerning doctrine or correct modes of thought, will dictate not only what may be said but also what must not be said. And, more consequentially, they will form a tight fabric, of gossamer weight to be sure, spread over the whole, a thin, translucent tent that holds within everything that belongs and keeps out everything that does not. As with philosophy, so here too, consistency with the first-established givens, beginning with the principle of one, sole, omnipotent, just God, opens the way for inclusion, while contradiction among parts, failure to form a seamless whole, excludes.

That inquiry into what represents the logic of the whole, what proves coherent to the principal doctrines of the whole, forms the subtext of my entire account, which claims only that the Oral Torah attests to its own integrity by the common criteria of reasoned thought. The fact that we can make sense of these writings attests to the validity for the writers of the document as much as for us, the readers here and now, of such criteria.[6] By integrity, for example, we mean what they must have meant, because – all learning concurs, wherever

6. Perhaps some hermeneutics of a non-academic, Western order, that is, some other way of reading these writings than the one followed in my translations of them into English, may offer different criteria. There may be some other rationality and hermeneutics to compete with mine. When there is, I shall consider it. Today there is none. Everyone in direct encounter with these documents for the purpose of translation, and the commentary represented thereby, produces exactly the same account of what they say and mean in their own terms. That is shown by the fact that the translations into modern Hebrew, Spanish, and German that I have seen take for granted the same comparability of syntax and grammar and modes of cogent thought and argument that mine do into English. So I am on very firm ground here. When, moreover, I compare my translation of, for example, the Talmud of the Land of Israel, into English, with that of Wewers into German, or of the Talmud of Babylonia with Steinsaltz's into modern Hebrew, thence into English, I find no consequential differences in general or in detail, few occasions to want to correct my rendition, fewer to want to correct those of others, except as to renditions in the American language. When I compare my translations of Midrash-compilations with those now appearing in Spanish, or my translation of the Fathers according to Rabbi Nathan with the great work of Judah Goldin, whom I followed, or of the Talmud of Babylonia with that of the pioneer

that learning takes place – we can understand them. And the rest follows. So by "the logic of the whole" I mean, modes of thought that govern throughout, for instance, analysis through comparison and contrast, on the one side, paradigmatic thinking, on the other. Time and again, in one chapter after another, I point to how conclusions are reached, not only to what they profess. By coherence I mean doctrines that fit in place and do not impose stresses or strains on the structure that encompasses them.

If, to take an obvious example, the one God who created all things is just, then that generative doctrine cannot accommodate cases of structural injustice. So the doctrine that the wicked (nonetheless) prosper cannot on its own find a place. Some solution to anomalies that confront the theologians has to accommodate reality to the system, and the system to reality. And it cannot be a solution that posits two gods or no god or a weak god or an unjust god – that is an obvious instance of systemic coherence.

My account of the Oral Torah seen whole, then, underscores the pervasiveness of specific modes of thought and shows how conclusions reached here, there, and everywhere come about because people are thinking in one way rather than in some other. The dialogue – dialectic, really – between chapter 5 and chapter 13 or between chapters 2 and 3 and chapter 14 suffices to show how this works. I further include only those main beams of doctrine that form a tight fit with other main beams, beginning with the foundations, ending with the roof, in proper sequence of inclusion. Not only so, but – to complete the survey of what I think represents the whole – I allege that a given starting point, the place at which I begin in chapter 2, marks the ground-zero of the structure and system – *the* theology of the Oral Torah viewed whole – and the order of topics, their definition and substantive formulation, must unfold in the sequence in which I present them. Any other order will yield chaos and produce an unintelligible gibberish of random thoughts.

Translating into the characterization of the whole these considerations of logic and consistency and the sole rational and therefore necessary sequence

---

masters, the British rabbis who accomplished the Soncino translation of the 1930s and early 1940s, I find a still more exact identity of representation of meaning. And so throughout. Now, further, with special reference to the Talmud of Babylonia, whether in Israeli Hebrew or British English or American English (and then in many versions), we may say, everyone takes for granted that, without substantial mediation but only with the requisite language required to make sense of matters given in square brackets, we can make good and simple sense of what they are saying in the original. That is because the modes of thought and coherent discourse and persuasive argument that we bring to the text produce intelligible sense out of the text. As I said, if there is some other way of reading these texts, some other hermeneutic than the one that governs here and now, let us see it, how it works, and what it produces.

of thoughts presents no difficulty. I claim that what is representative is that corpus of convictions that fits, logically and doctrinally, and what does not is noted but excluded from the account of representative views. For to describe *theology* is to identify the *logos*, the logic, of religious ideas. This demands thinking philosophically about religion. The result of such thought sets forth in the correct and inexorable order, start to finish, the structure and system that order the whole, even making provision for the preservation of views that do not fit and modes of thought that jar.

As to the inviolable order of ideas, it suffices to say that the problems that are laid out systematically – world order (Parts 1 and 2), sources of disruption (Part 3), means of restoration (Part 4) – become unintelligible in any other sequence than the one I follow. And within each unit, any other presentation of topics would not only disrupt but would corrupt the entire account.

As to modes of thought that pervade, a single example suffices. Chapters 13 and 14, on eschatological components of the theology, pick their way among diverse opinions; where opinion is contradictory, for example, about the character of the world to come or the timing and sequence of the stages en route from here and now to there and then, I make no claim to know what stands for the structure and system, or, in more common language, what represents "the rabbis" as a whole. Where I can explain how conclusions are reached and show the harmony of the result in both correct order – which, readers will discover in chapters 13 and 14, is much laboured over – and integral, harmonious doctrine, I offer that as my account of the theology of eschatology. And so throughout.

But the sages also signify what is normative, so in their behalf a simple response suffices. A fifteen-hundred-year-old tradition of learning, amplified in a few places just now, serves. Several indicators establish the normative view and mark the schismatic one.

First, it is a well-established principle in the legal (*halakhic*) documents that a rule that is not attributed to a named authority stands for all authority, ordinarily setting the norm. One bearing a name may well be, and mostly is, schismatic (with the proviso that certain names carry within themselves signals as to normative status). That hermeneutics is stated explicitly in the earliest documents and is taken for granted in the composition of those that reached closure later on. It forms the premise of much analysis in the two Talmuds.

A further trait of the documents, both of law (*halakhah*) and of lore (*aggadah*), as has been realized more recently but I think was always implicit from the very beginning, requires consideration. It is that the authors of a cogent composition, all the more so the framers of a composite, so set forth their accounts as to give a clear indication of the position they favour. They may announce the besought proposition at the outset and amass evidence to demonstrate it, or they may lead to it at the end, through assembling much evidence, most of it affirmative, some not. I have identified, in my *Theological Grammar of the Oral Torah*, particularly in volumes I and III, a number of composites that set down the coherent judgment of the compilers about a given topic or problem. These composites, as a matter of fact, either prove unique in the entire literature – the sole systematic presentation of a topic – or turn out to be entirely coherent with other composites on the same theme. I have relied heavily, therefore, on the givens of composites. So much for compositions and composites.

Along these same lines, there is the matter of self-evidence, that is to say, indications within the documents of the Oral Torah of principles that are taken for granted and that generate secondary articulation along lines that said principles dictate. The sages have left no doubt about the indicators of self-evidence. These I have spelled out in my *Theological Grammar of the Oral Torah*, volume II, *Connections and Constructions*, the former part of which is based upon *Rationality and Structure: The Bavli's Anomalous Juxtapositions*. Let me briefly explain what I mean. In the Rabbinic writings, particularly but not only in the Talmud of Babylonia, certain points of connection are taken as self-evident, so that compilers of composites simply *know* what native category "obviously" joins with what other one, and what does not. Through what is taken for granted, the system makes its statement of theological givens. For the Bavli, I have shown how odd connections reveal premises as to what is self-evident. This is worked out in rich detail in *Rationality and Structure*. For other documents, the work awaits, but the results sketched in volume II of *Grammar* provide a fine sample of what awaits.

When, therefore, we can outline the principles of constructing groups of categories into intelligible combinations, we find in those principles the main lines of theological order and structure. When we can state what emerges as self-evident when we join two other-wise distinct topics, we gain insight into the established laws of meaning and order that govern a system of coherent thought. So, in examining the rules for joining native categories, we identify those indicators of correct usage that point towards the logic pervading the whole. At many points in my exposition of what I conceive to be the normative theology of the Oral Torah, I introduce evidence of self-evidence in the form of connections that are drawn and conclusions that those connections dictate.

Sages have supplied other signals as well. Even entire documents weigh in, for the compilers of a document have been shown through extensive research to take positions on important questions. This they do by their selection and arrangement of materials, by their juxtapositions of topics beyond the dimensions of composites, and by other subtle editorial means. They leave little doubt as to the positions they deem authoritative. Anyone who has worked through and identified the hermeneutics of, for one example, Genesis Rabbah, or of the Mishnah, for another, will understand that documents seen whole do convey coherent judgments. Most, though not all, of the documents of the Oral Torah set forth coherent statements, which through a systematic labour of comparison and contrast I have already identified. That makes possible the description of the theological system of the writings seen whole. That is because by definition, the statement on a given, fundamental topic that is made by a document within the Oral Torah, not contradicted by the statement made by any other document – and none is! – constitutes a reliable indicator of the theology of the Oral Torah viewed whole.

On the basis of these facts characteristic of compositions, composites, and entire documents, by my presentation of the abstracts and my paraphrase of sources that I have chosen to reconstitute into this coherent tale, I mark as representative of the position of "the rabbis," or the entirety of the Oral Torah, all of the statements I make concerning a given issue. Where the documents contain opinion that contradicts my presentation of matters – and that is seldom and nearly always schismatic in form – I omit it. For a bit of research will show, especially for the interested readers who wish to check, that what I present bears the mark of normative standing within the documents read all together and all at once. That is to say,

1) it will be anonymous or at least entirely unchallenged;
2) it will prove coherent to other statements on the same subject;
3) it will define the premise of making certain connections or it will emerge as a result of making said connection; and/or
4) it will be presented as the regnant opinion when conflicting opinions register, for example, as the opening proposition, or as the climactic statement; or in some other significant way signals will be given to accord privilege to the statement cited or alluded to in these pages as representative of the structure and system of Rabbinic Judaism seen whole, in proportion, as a coherent statement.

When readers check the documents against my use of them, I am confident that they will find that exceptions to these simple rules will prove few and inconsequential.

That is why my picture of the theology of the Oral Torah will be seen to represent our sages of blessed memory as a collegium. Through the media just now outlined, the sages did set forth the orthodox and catholic position of the Torah as they framed matters, the Oral in relationship to the Written Torah. For the work of setting out a coherent logic of the faith, a theological structure and system, they chose the instruments they had available: the instruments of intellect, proposition, evidence, argument, thought and the writing down of thought – consensus attained through persuasion. Like the Jewish people, so the sages had no better options; the people had no politics of consequence, so the sages could not work through political institutions. No emperor confirmed their views, no court enforced their judgments. They met, if at all, only irregularly – except on the field of argument. And, as individuals, to have a say was to deny their own integrity, the logic of their definitive myth – that, after all, is the meaning of claiming to receive and hand on a tradition, as the sages did when they spoke of the oral tradition of Sinai, the Oral part of the Torah.

Their counterparts in the equally complex world of Christianity did two things that the sages did not, and could not do. They held world councils, sponsored by the Roman Empire, from Constantine's time forward, to work out positions to embody Orthodox and Catholic Christianity. And as individuals, they wrote books. No state, as I said, sponsored the sages' ecumenical meetings, and the sages held none. Nor did the logic of the sages permit individuals to write books in their own names, respectively, as did every principal of Christianity beyond the founder himself.

But my claim in writing this book is self-evident: had the sages of the Oral Torah met in world councils, as their counterparts in Christian theology did, these are the positions they would have taken and set forth as normative – every one of them. If we have no counterpart, for Rabbinic Judaism, to the Nicene Creed, we could readily write one out of the Contents page of this book. That claim is what made possible my decision to focus my discussion on the governing logic and to investigate and unpack the principles of coherence and proportion that govern throughout. Each abstract from a source that I present, I claim, speaks for the collegium of the sages, represents the Oral Torah viewed whole, and coheres with all others.

That makes urgent the direct encounter with the sources, in the sages' own words, in English. Because the documents under discussion are not widely accessible, either in the original or in translation, I include a somewhat more generous selection of abstracts than would be required in a work having to do with Scripture, where a mere reference generally suffices. I try to walk the reader through the abstracts, to ease the burden that reading a quite unfamiliar kind of writing imposes.

But the encounter with the sages is the key to all else. For reasons amply spelled out by my translations, I regard the formal and aesthetic context of sayings as integral to the hermeneutics of the documents, all the more so of the theological venture undertaken here. I have shown for many of the documents that the sages make their statement both through how they formulate ideas as well as through what they actually say. That is why I have translated all of the documents, many of them for the first time, the rest for the second. It is in meeting the words of the sages that the reader will assess the aptness of my characterization of the governing logic.

Before proceeding to the body of the work, I have to take up further considerations of context, both the scholarly tradition in which I do this work, and the body of my own work, which, after nearly four decades, accumulates. Here is my bibliographical statement, in two parts, the scholarly tradition and the trajectory of my own work.

First, how to place this account of Rabbinic theology into its scholarly tradition and context? Most books on "Judaism" in the period at hand are ill-informed, disproportionate, lightweight, or just silly. Only two prior, intellectually equally ambitious accounts of the same matter compete with mine, which therefore is to be evaluated in comparison and contrast with them. These are George Foot Moore's and Ephraim E. Urbach's, most recently dealt with by me in my *Prolegomenon*. Studies of special problems, however meritorious – Heschel's study of the theology of revelation comes to mind as exemplary – do not exhibit the requisite intellectual ambition to state the whole in its entirety. But I allege that here is the normative Judaism that Moore (falsely) claimed to set forth. And here is the statement of the entire theological structure and system of the sages, their beliefs and opinions, that Urbach (falsely) claimed to portray. Only one of the three of these vastly different accounts – Moore's, Urbach's, or mine – can fit the evidence of the Oral Torah and, as a practitioner of Judaism, I should add, even aspire to be worthy of that evidence.

Who is right? Readers of their books and this one who wish to pursue the matter should then compare my results with theirs. They ought then to make special reference to whether or not they or I have identified the logic of the whole and plausibly identified what holds the parts together into a single, wholly rational construction. They ought to form a judgment upon whose story fits best both the evidence that is adduced, in balance and proportion, and also encompasses that much larger corpus of evidence that cannot be adduced but only adumbrated.

For that last judgment I refer in the end to what words are meant to embody but cannot exhaustively portray. That is the faith of holy Israel in its life with God through the Torah, the life of piety and worship, as the one whole Torah of our rabbi, Moses, portrays that faith and life. Here, then, I claim to portray, by reading as a coherent statement its authoritative documents, the religion of the Dual Torah that the whole of holy Israel have embodied, and today, in ways more alike than varied, continues to realize in the here and now.

Now, second, comes the context defined by my own prior work. While I provide here all that is needed to follow that story, indeed ample elements of that story as it is told in the sages' own words, still, for me, the study of the theology of the Oral Torah that reaches its culmination here occupied a variety of prior works, first analytical, then synthetic. Much of my earlier work, until the 1990s, undertook the systematic analysis of the documents, read one by one in historical context, and their dismantling into component parts. But that can tell only part of the story, the historical part. For the documents have impressed all who have studied them as cogent, seamless statements of a single law and theology. True, from the Talmud of Babylonia forward, problems of analysis have found their solution in harmonization. But these solutions have tended to favour episodic answers to ad hoc questions. Now, therefore, comes the time to reconstruct the whole, read as an unfolding statement within a single logic, such as I propose in these pages and intend to establish as fact.

The work of synthesis has moved forward for some years. I already have conducted a number of experiments of method and tested a variety of possibilities of how the problem might be solved. First comes the problematic of theology within a large-scale enterprise in the history of religion that I have conducted on Judaism. I asked synthetic questions of system and order of Rabbinic Judaism, seeing everything whole and complete, only after a long period of work of an analytical character. Specifically, I took up the work of describing the theological system that sustains the documents of the Oral Torah when I had completed the systematic description of the inner logic and structure, the system, of each of the constituent documents individually and then had shown how, historically, they took shape in some kind of sequence and determinate political and cultural context. Initially, therefore, I analysed the documents one by one.

Reading the several components of the Oral Torah one by one, document by document, produced results for the history of ideas that defined the challenge of how to frame theological description. It was that work that framed the challenge to descriptive theology to which this work forms a response. The more important items in the analytical corpus are so designated in the bibliography. When this work was well along, I set forth its historical consequences, spelling out what came first and what followed, identifying the large-scale historical setting in which ideas took shape, in works on the developmental history of Rabbinic Judaism in the classical period of its history. The historical context in which the theological structure and system took shape is spelled out in these works, listed as a group in the bibliography.

It was only when the analytical, historical work had come to fruition that the synthetic, theological question demanded a response. The contribution of these and other works to the project at hand is constant, even though only a few of them make a concrete impact upon my discussions in these pages. My initial (and theologically unsuccessful) effort to show how the documents of the Oral Torah read not one by one but all together and all at once is reported in these books, which defined the methodological problem worked out in the foregoing. First I conceived that the answer to the question of a prevailing *logos*, a statement of the whole in proper proportion and balance, would emerge in the final document, because of its perfection in joining into a single, sustained, and utterly coherent statement the several native categories and modes of discourse of all prior writings.

The initial probe, which set forth the entire thesis and explained the purpose of the outline and then the comparison of the two outlines, was *Judaism States Its Theology: The Talmudic Re-Presentation*. That proposal required the comparison and contrast of Talmuds followed by a statement of how I conceive the Bavli to form the ultimate and also the coherent statement of the whole. To accomplish my goal of comparing the Talmuds and so isolating what marks the second one as truly magnificent and compelling, I required a complete statement of the facts of the matter. So I compared the two Talmuds systematically, by outlining each and juxtaposing the outlines of those tractates of the two Talmuds that coincided on the same Mishnah-tractates. I further conducted an ad hoc study of the same problem – comparing the Talmuds – by a systematic review of a rather unfortunate dissertation that purported to solve the same problem but turned out to botch the exercise, start to finish: *Are the Talmuds Interchangeable? Christine Hayes's Blunder*. In that way I was able to conduct a negative experiment by examining an effort to answer the same question with a different result from mine.

This work in hand, I was happy with the answers – how do the Talmuds compare – and the systematic, associated studies, but not satisfied by them. Granting that they were necessary, I did not find the results sufficient. In their nature, they covered only the principal documents, but not the entire corpus. Furthermore, the more I worked along the lines of a literary solution to a theological question, the more I began to realize that the problem was not one of literary analysis, such as I had done for such a long time. Nor was it even one of historical sequences of how documents read individually but in sequence treated a given problem, such as I had already done as well. I had to find a way of crossing documentary lines.

That is why, even as the work was under way, I attempted a separate, "meta-documentary" approach. Goaded by the criticism, in the mid-1980s, of E.P. Sanders and Hyam Maccoby of my *Judaism: The Evidence of the Mishnah,* criticism that posited a vast corpus of ideas and facts that we know a priori [!] and that were taken for granted everywhere, even if we had no evidence whatsoever of that fact, I turned to the evidence of what was taken for granted that we do have. That is to say, I asked about the premises of large-scale compositions and composites and entire documents: what they all took for granted. I thought that there I might find a coherent theological system. The systematic study of the corpus was in the items listed under that rubric in the bibliography. The negative results of the research were set forth in this item, to which, so far as I know, Sanders and Maccoby have remained oblivious: *The Judaism the Rabbis Take for Granted.* There, I pointed out that the premises, the generative convictions, of the several documents yielded nothing I could regard as a *logos,* a system that encompassed the whole and explained all the parts.

From asking the synthetic question in the setting of documentary analysis, I then shifted the grounds of inquiry entirely. I realized that, since my question required crossing documentary lines, I had to identify the evidence that, to begin with, those documentary boundary lines do not affect. That meant reconsideration the category-formation that documentary analysis had imposed upon my work. What is it that pervades all of the documents equally and controls discourse throughout? I required a category-formation congruent to the question of synthesis, yet one that sustained analysis of data.

My answer was to invoke the metaphor of language and to undertake the study of the documents of the Oral Torah as one would study and describe a language-system. This metaphor, in the nature of things, yielded a set of comparisons. The principal vocabulary of a language – "head-nouns," nouns that stand at the head of declarative sentences – finds its counterpart in the paramount native categories of the writings of the Oral Torah; a language's syntax (rules for forming word-clusters) in connections and constructions deemed self-evident in those writings; and semantics in models of analysis, explanation, and anticipation. This last I expressed in the language: "Semantics is to language as models of cogent discourse are to theology." The result of the work was to show that a system, whole and coherent, comes to concrete expression in native categories, in the givens of connections that are deemed self-evident and the constructions that bear inexorable meaning, and in the paradigms of coherence and intelligibility covered by my three types of models of discourse. *The Theological Grammar* led directly to this final work of description of the theological system that governs all of the documents of the Oral Torah.

Accordingly, this book completes a five-part inquiry into the method and message of the theology of the Oral Torah; its predecessors, upon the results of which I draw throughout, are as follows. The first set forth my basic theory of what was to be done: *The Theology of Rabbinic Judaism. A Prolegomenon.* There, I placed my project into relationship with its predecessors. I set forth my extensive critique of Moore and Urbach in the *Prolegomenon*, and specified what I find wrong with their approach. In this protracted dialogue with them and their lesser colleagues, I framed the plan that comes to fruition here. Then came the systematic work itself, yielding the results that would indicate the modes of thought and analysis that govern throughout, *The Theological Grammar of the Oral Torah*, with the details given in the bibliography. The results of that project in hand, I turned to the present one, and the reader now holds what I hope will prove a statement of compelling interest.

So much for historical and descriptive theology. What of the constructive kind? It remains to take note of my one effort at constructive theology, not the historical and descriptive theology such as I undertake in these several studies. My sole constructive theological statement is *Judaism's Theological Voice: The Melody of the Talmud.* To date, I have not found even the correct contemporary starting point for a systematic and also constructive, not merely descriptive, theology for the Judaism of the Dual Torah; most work that people label theology turns out to be nothing more than sociology made urgent by exhortation or mere sloganeering. I have not attempted a systematic, constructive theology, and I have not persuaded myself that I am capable of doing so.

But I should not want readers to suppose that constructive theology of Judaism languishes. Indeed, some others have done commendable systematic work in the theology of Judaism. Contemporary American Judaism encompasses a number of constructive theological systems in the classical idiom of the Torah, such as, for instance, those set forth by Eliezer Berkovits, Abraham J. Heschel, and Eugene Borowitz. Right alongside, major figures in philosophy of religion in the setting of Judaism, such as Mordecai M. Kaplan, have produced a massive systematic oeuvre. It was Heschel's judgment that the bulk of writing on the theology of Judaism was high-class homiletics, and I believe that time has tested that judgment and shown it valid, with the named exclusions.

Still, organized Orthodox Judaism, whether segregationist or integrationist, in the prevailing idiom of the West, has produced no systematic theology worthy of the name. Others will have to set down judgments on the state of the constructive and systematic theology of Judaism in the other languages of Judaism, French, Spanish, and Israeli Hebrew being primary. My limited knowledge leaves the impression that little demands attention to begin with.

In contemporary Judaism overseas, while some with enormous power have done philosophy of religion in a Judaic framework, such as Martin Buber, and, of manifestly less long-term weight, Emmanuel Levinas in Paris and Yishayahu Leibovits in Jerusalem (who produced what might be called a philosophical anti-theology), for the second half of the twentieth century I know of no important theological thinkers at all. For the current age I can point to no counterpart enterprises to Borowitz's, Heschel's, and Berkovits's, and, I hardly need add, certainly none in the Hebrew language of the state of Israel. There, many paraphrase, some recapitulate, few interpret, and fewer still attempt to construct. So far as I can see, theology of Judaism, whether merely constructive or even systematic, in the idiom of the West seems not to have found any native practitioners in the state of Israel. Constructive and weighty (not merely descriptive and episodic) philosophy of religion, drawing upon the resources of Judaism, apart from the commanding presence of the European-North American-Israeli, Emil Fackenheim, receives slight attention.

As to the *yeshiva*-world, whether or not any kind of critical, truly rigorous and systematic thought of a theological (including *halakhic*) character goes on, in the world of the Torah lived outside of the academic idiom of the West, I cannot say. The little I encounter strikes me as at best episodic but mainly little more than shallow, repetitive paraphrase, and much is intellectually coarse and even rhetorically crude and vulgar in any idiom of intellect or expression. But I am inclined to think that, among the authentic continuators of the Oral Torah, creative and rigorous, systematic work goes forward in oral tradition, the natural idiom of the *yeshiva*-world, so that the best of the sages and masters write little if anything. Perhaps the notes that now purport to record their thought are fragmentary and probably incommensurate to the intelligence that animates the great figures of today's Torah. At any rate, I hope that that is so, and my knowledge of the power of the Oral Torah to shape and stimulate thought assures me that it is.

PART I

Sources of World Order

2 The Moral Order:
Reward and Punishment

In the sages' view, which animates every line in the Oral Torah, the will of the one, unique God, made manifest through the Torah, governs, and, further, God's will, for both private life and public activity, is rational. That is to say, within man's understanding of reason, God's will is just. And by "just," the sages understood the commonsense meaning: fair, equitable, proportionate, commensurate. In place of fate or impersonal destiny, chance, or simply irrational, inexplicable chaos, God's plan and purpose everywhere come to realization. So the Oral Torah identifies God's will as the active and causative force in the lives of individuals and nations.

What happens happens by God's will, so, for instance, when it is time for a person to die, nothing will postpone the event, and anything in some way may turn out to carry out God's will. That is stated in so many words and proven on the basis of verses of the Written Torah, and evidence from ordinary events sustains the same view:

I.21 A. R. Alexandri also said in the name of R. Hiyya bar Abba, and some say, said R. Joshua b. Levi, "When the end time of a person has come, everything conquers him: 'And it will be that whosoever finds me will slay me' " (Gen. 4:14).
B. Rab said, "That derives from this verse of Scripture: 'They stand forth this day to receive your judgments, for all are your servants' " (Ps. 119:91).

The humblest creatures serve to accomplish God's purpose at the right moment:

I.22 A. They said to Rabbah bar Shila that a tall man died. He was riding a small mule, and when he came to a bridge, the mule shied and threw the man, and he was killed. To him Rabbah applied this verse: "They stand forth this day to receive your judgments, for all are your servants" (Ps. 119:91).

And coincidence plays its part, so that chance and destiny and intentionality all coalesce, as in the following story:

I.23 A. Samuel saw a scorpion carried across a river by a frog. Then it stung someone who died. He cited this verse: "They stand forth this day to receive your judgments, for all are your servants" (Ps. 119:91).

In these ways the sages go over the fundamental proposition that whatever happens happens by God's will – and therefore must in some way or another be justified, that is, shown to be just and rational.

In that same context, nothing surprises God, for all things conform to his plan even from the very beginning. That is why, the sages maintain, even at the moment of creation, God foresaw the future deeds of righteousness and sin that would be committed, and the day of judgment was prepared at the very outset. What is important in the following statement is the allegation that, built into the very construction of creation is the plan for all things to come. God created man and knew at the outset that, because man exercised freedom of will, the righteous and the wicked would exercise that freedom, each group in its own way. Each component of creation is recapitulated in the here and now, the darkness and the light, by the wicked and the righteous. In the end of time, Eden will be regained and restored, wholly in light, entirely illuminated by God, as we shall see in chapter 14.

GENESIS RABBAH III:VIII.I

1. A. Said R. Yannai, "At the beginning of the creation of the world the Holy One, blessed be he, foresaw the deeds of the righteous and the deeds of the wicked.
B. " 'And the earth was unformed and void' refers to the deeds of the wicked.
C. " 'And God said, "Let there be light" ' refers to the deeds of the righteous.
D. " 'And God saw the light, that it was good,' refers to the deeds of the righteous."

Now the creation-narrative is systematically divided, as indicated, between light and darkness, the righteous and the wicked:

E. " 'And God divided between the light and the darkness' means, [he divided] between the deeds of the righteous and the deeds of the wicked.
F. " 'And God called the light day' refers to the deeds of the righteous.

G. " 'And the darkness he called night' refers to the deeds of the wicked.

H. " 'And there was evening' refers to the deeds of the wicked.

I. " 'And there was morning' refers to the deeds of the righteous.

J. " 'One day,' for the Holy One, blessed be he, gave them one day, [and what day is that]? It is the day of judgment."

I can imagine no more explicit statement that justice, leading to judgment, rules through the very foundations of creation to the end of time. As at many points in the theology of the Oral Torah, we may identify this passage as the starting point and build the entire structure and system on this foundation; nothing that the theology would set forth is lacking.

But the coherence of the theology hardly presents a surprise. The more urgent question is, how do the sages know that God's will is realized in the moral order of justice, involving reward and punishment? For reasons amply spelled out in chapter 1, the sages turned to Scripture for the pertinent facts; that is where God makes himself manifest. But of the various types of scriptural evidence – explicit commandments, stories, prophetic admonitions – that they had available to show how the moral order prevailed in all being, what type did they prefer? The one bearing the greatest probative weight derived from the exact match between sin and punishment. Here is their starting point; from here all else flows smoothly and in orderly fashion. World order is best embodied when sin is punished, merit rewarded.

That body of evidence that Scripture supplied recorded human action and divine reaction, on the one side, and meritorious deed and divine response and reward, on the other. It was comprised by consequential cases, drawn from both private and public life, to underscore the sages' insistence upon the match between the personal and the public, all things subject to the same simple rule. That demonstration of not only the principle but the precision of measure for measure, deriving from Scripture's own record of God's actions, takes priority of place in the examination of the rationality of the sages' universe. That is because it permeates their system and frames its prevailing modes of explanation and argument. The principle that all being conforms to rules, and that these rules embody principles of justice through exact punishment of particular sin and precise reward of singular acts of virtue, defined the starting point of all rational thought and the entire character of the sages' theological structure and system.

That is why, without appeal to that fundamental principle of a just order, no question the sages investigate, no dilemma their inquiry produces, no basic challenge to the absolute given of their world-view makes any sense at all. Whatever they propose to account for the situation of Israel in public or the individual in private, whether the resolution of the historical crisis in the coming of the Messiah and the nations' standing in judgment by the criterion of the Torah or the advent of the world to come and individuals' standing in judgment by the same criterion – all of these massive presences in the sages' thinking about the here and now, the past and the future, rested on the same foundation of conviction. That was that an exact, prevailing justice explained the meaning of all things. Of that principle all thought formed a systematic exegesis, first of Scripture for the explanation – *midrash* is the word the sages might use – of the here and the now, then of the workaday realities to be shaped into a *midrash* upon Scripture. It was a reciprocal process because the same reasonable justice ruled small and great transactions without distinction. Not only so, but for the sages, that conviction required an act not of faith but of rational inquiry into the record of reality, Scripture.

The teleological theory of natural history of philosophy here finds its counterpart. The sages' confidence in the sense, order, and the reasonable, because just, character of all reality matched philosophers' conviction that all things serve, each its assigned purpose. We might conceive that philosophy asked the teleological question of purpose, and theology responded with the revealed answer: to achieve a just world order. The one posited a goal or end, the other defined what that purpose was: all things serve the purpose of taking part in a just and equitable order.

So the sages defined reason and rationality – despite the contrary evidence of everyday reality, beginning with Israel's own situation, subordinated as it was after its loss of great wars to Rome in the first and second centuries. That bedrock certainty identified as the fact of every life and the building block of every society the moral order of a world founded on justice. The sages deemed it a fact that man lived in a world in which good is rewarded and evil punished. Since the world in which they lived knew better, and since the sages framed a system that coheres solely as an explanation of why, though justice is supposed to prevail, present matters are chaotic, we may take for granted that the sages, too, knew better, so far as knowing formed a secular act. It was their theology – the logic of God, systematically expounded – that taught them to see matters as they did.

That is why we seek to identify the sources for their conviction of the order of society, natural and supernatural alike. Since few in the history of humanity have offered as a simple fact of everyday reality such a principle of natural justice, but many have found the opposite, we are forced to ask why our sages conceived matters as they did. Exactly what endowed our sages of blessed memory with certainty that they along with all Israel lived in a trustworthy world of reason and order defined by justice? What we shall see is that their own systematization of the facts of the Written Torah nourished that conviction. Concurring on the teleological character of creation – everything with its goal and end – the sages in Scripture found that pervasive purpose in the rule of justice, resting on reason and on equity. From that generative principle – a fact of revealed Scripture really – all else followed. Then the structure stood firm, the system worked.

What captures our interest therefore is not the conviction but the way in which the sages set forth that conviction. What they found to overcome the doubt that everyday life surely cast upon their belief in the governing of a moral order was the facts of Scripture as they ordered those facts. Now, were we on our own to open Scripture and locate pertinent evidence that God is just and the world he made conforms to rules of equity, we should find that Scripture states it in so many words. It is not merely that when God contemplated the world that he had made, he pronounced it good, as Yannai says, specifically referring to the righteous. That surely represents a subjective judgment that can refer to anything, not only to what Yannai thought self-evident. Scripture leaves no doubt about God's definitive trait of justice, justice understood as man does, in a different context altogether.

It is that when man – Abraham – undertook to dispute God's decision and construct an argument against it, God bound himself by the same rule of common-sense equity that Abraham deemed self-evident: "Will you sweep away the innocent along with the guilty? Far be it from you to do such a thing, to impose death upon the innocent as well as the guilty, so that innocent and guilty fare alike. Far be it from you! Shall not the Judge of all the earth deal justly?" (Gen. 18:23, 25). Then God does not reply, he merely responds by accepting Abraham's premise and proceeding to the negotiation. Silence bears assent: God is not only answerable, but he is answerable on exactly the counts that man deems consequential: justice, reason, commonsense rationality. The sages did not have to search deeply into obscure traditions or difficult passages to uncover the evidence of God's justice. Wherever, in Scripture, they looked, they found ample testimony, especially in the premise of Job's complaint!

Perhaps in that paradigmatic moment before Sodom, the sages identified the principle of the moral order that sustained the world: justice distinguishes the innocent from the guilty and punishes the guilty alone. But that is not how they demonstrated the validity of that principle. They had their own approach, which required them to establish proof through patterning well-analysed facts, compared and contrasted, as I showed in chapter 1. Like natural historians, they assembled evidence of a like kind – in this case, the administration of exact justice through appropriate, proportionate reward and punishment – and they then compared and contrasted the evidence they assembled. The concrete evidence on its own, properly arrayed, then established as fact what to begin with was entered as a postulate or hypothesis to be demonstrated – with no given axiom except the facticity of Scripture.

It is at this point that we turn directly to the method and the message of the governing theology of the Oral Torah in particular. What we want to know is not how *we might find* in Scripture the basis for a position the sages maintained, but how *the sages did find that basis*. What satisfied them as necessary and sufficient demonstration of that fact of world order? While their theology systematically expounded the results of their disciplined study of the written Torah – we might call the process their exegesis of, or *midrash* upon, the Written Torah – the concrete and particular types of proof alone reveal to us the workings of their minds viewed as a single, cogent intellect: the theological system.

To answer the question of the source of probative evidence for the principle that the world is reliable and orderly by reason of justice, we turn to the concrete evidence they held demonstrated their point. When the sages opened Scripture to find out how, in the detail of concrete cases, the judge of all the world bound himself by the rules of justice and systematically does justice, like philosophers in natural history they looked not for the occasional but the enduring: not for the singular moment but the routine pattern. Exegesis without a guiding hermeneutics bore little appeal to them. One-shot proof-texts mattered less than governing paradigms. The sages were theologians before they were exegetes, and they were exegetes because they were theologians. Proof from specific texts emerges from details, but hermeneutics holds details together in a single coherent whole. That is why they composed their account of the workings of the principle of measure for measure – whether for divine punishment or for divine reward – out of cases in which God does not intervene, but in which the very nature of things, the ordinary course of events, showed the workings of the principle.

What would suffice, then, to make a point that – we must assume – people in general deem counter-intuitive? For who from Job onward – no one had to wait for Voltaire's *Candide* – assumed that the ordinary course of everyday events proves the justice (and the goodness) of God? More lost the faith because the here and now violated the rule of justice than gained the faith because it did. So, to begin with, the sages framed for themselves what we might call a null-hypothesis, that is to say, a hypothesis that they would test to prove the opposite of what they sought to show. They asked themselves this question: if justice did not govern, how should we know it? The answer is, we should find not a correlation but a disproportion between sin and consequent result, or penalty, between crime and punishment.

The null-hypothesis framed the question of order through justice in its most palpable, material form. It is not enough to show that sin or crime provoke divine response, that God penalizes them. Justice in the here and now counts. The penalty must fit the crime, measure must match measure, and the more exact the result to the cause, the more compelling the proof of immediate and concrete justice as the building block of world order that the sages would put forth out of Scripture. That is the point at which justice is transformed from a vague generality – a mere sentiment – to a precise and measurable dimension of the actual social order of morality: how things hold together when subject to tension, at the pressure-points of structure, not merely how they are arrayed in general. Here, in fact, is how God made the world and, as Yannai says, what is good about the creation that God pronounced good, as Yannai says.

That is why, when the sages examined the facts of Scripture to establish that principle of rationality and order in conformity to the requirements of justice and equity, what impressed them was not the inevitability but the precision of justice. Scripture portrays the world order as fundamentally just and reasonable, and it does so in countless ways. But Scripture encompasses the complaint of Job and the reflection of Qoheleth. The sages, for their part, identified those cases that transcended generalities and established the facticity of proportionate justice, treating them as not only exemplary but probative. They set out their proposition and amassed evidence in support of it.

Let us turn to a systematic statement of the starting and main point: when God judges and sentences, not only is the judgment fair but the penalty fits the crime with frightening precision. But so too, when God judges and awards a decision of merit, the reward proves equally exact. These two together, the match of sin and penalty, meritorious deed and reward, then are shown to explain the point and purpose of one detail after another, and, all together, they add up to the portrait of a world order that is fundamentally and essentially just – the starting point and foundation of all else.

Here is the sages' account of God's justice, which is always commensurate, both for reward and punishment, in consequence of which the present permits us to peer into the future with certainty of what is going to happen (M. Sot. 1:7ff.). What we note is the sages' identification of the precision of justice, the exact match of action and reaction, each step in the sin, each step in the response, and, above all, the immediacy of God's presence in the entire transaction. They draw general conclusions from the specifics of the law that

Scripture sets forth, and that is about where systematic thinking takes over from exegetical learning about cases, or, in our own categories, philosophy from history:

MISHNAH-TRACTATE SOTAH 1:7

A. By that same measure by which a man metes out [to others], do they mete out to him:

B. She primped herself for sin, the Omnipresent made her repulsive.

C. She exposed herself for sin, the Omnipresent exposed her.

D. With the thigh she began to sin, and afterward with the belly, therefore the thigh suffers the curse first, and afterward the belly.

E. But the rest of the body does not escape [punishment].

We begin with the sages' own general observations based on the facts provided in Scripture. The course of response of the woman accused of adultery to her drinking of the bitter water, which is supposed to produce one result for the guilty, another for the innocent, is described in Scripture in this language: "If no man has lain with you ... be free from this water of bitterness that brings the curse. But if you have gone astray ... then the Lord make you an execration ... when the Lord makes your thigh fall away and your body swell; may this water ... pass into your bowels and make your body swell and your thigh fall away" (Num. 5:20–22). This is amplified and expanded, extended to the entire rite, where the woman is dishevelled; then the order, thigh, belly, shows the perfect precision of the penalty. What Scripture treats as a case, the sages transform into a generalization, so making Scripture yield governing rules.

The same passage proceeds to further cases, which prove the same point: where the sin begins, there the punishment also commences; but also, where an act of virtue takes its place, there divine reward focuses as well. Merely listing the following names, without spelling out details, for the cognoscenti of Scripture support the argument: Samson, Absalom, Miriam, Joseph, and Moses. Knowing how Samson and Absalom match, also Miriam, Joseph, and Moses, then suffice to establish the paired and matched general principles:

MISHNAH-TRACTATE SOTAH 1:8

A. Samson followed his eyes [where they led him], therefore the Philistines put out his eyes, since it is said, "And the Philistines laid hold on him and put out his eyes" (Judges 16:21).

B. Absalom was proud of his hair, therefore he was hung by his hair (II Sam. 14:25–6).

C. And since he had sexual relations with ten concubines of his father, therefore they thrust ten spear heads into his body, since it is said, "And ten young men that carried Jacob's armour surrounded and smote Absalom and killed him" (II Sam. 18:15).

D. And since he stole three hearts – his father's, the court's, and the Israelite's – since it is said, "And Absalom stole the heart of the men of Israel" (II Sam. 15:6) – therefore three darts were thrust into him, since it is said, "And he took three darts in his hand and thrust them through the heart of Absalom" (II Sam. 18:14).

Justice requires not only punishment of the sinner or the guilty but reward of the righteous and the good, and so the sages find ample, systematic evidence in Scripture for both sides of the equation of justice:

MISHNAH-TRACTATE SOTAH 1:9

A. And so is it on the good side:

B. Miriam waited a while for Moses, since it is said, "And his sister stood afar off" (Ex. 2:4), therefore, Israel waited on her seven days in the wilderness, since it is said, "And the people did not travel on until Miriam was brought in again" (Num. 12:15).

MISHNAH-TRACTATE SOTAH 1:10

A. Joseph had the merit of burying his father, and none of his brothers was greater than he, since it is said, "And Joseph went up to bury his father ... and there went up with him both chariots and horsemen" (Gen. 50:7, 9).

B. We have none so great as Joseph, for only Moses took care of his [bones].

C. Moses had the merit of burying the bones of Joseph, and none in Israel was greater than he, since it is said, "And Moses took the bones of Joseph with him" (Ex. 13:19).

D. We have none so great as Moses, for only the Holy One blessed be he took care of his [bones], since it is said, "And he buried him in the valley" (Deut. 34:6).

E. And not of Moses alone have they stated [this rule], but of all righteous people, since it is said, "And your righteousness shall go before you. The glory of the Lord shall gather you [in death]" (Is. 58:8).

Scripture provides the main probative evidence for the anticipation that when God judges, he will match the act of merit with an appropriate reward and the sin with an appropriate punishment. The proposition begins, however, with general observations as to how things are (M. 1:7), and not with specific allusions to proof-texts; the character of the law set forth in Scripture is reflected upon. The accumulated cases yield the generalization.

Beyond the Mishnah two kinds of documents of extension and amplification take up the Mishnah's propositions and strengthen them. One pursues the passages of Scripture important in the Mishnah's exposition, the other carries forward the Mishnah's own method; the one is exegetical, the other propositional, and both take the Mishnah as their starting point. The first type, in the present context, is represented by Sifré to Numbers, a systematic commentary to most of the book of Numbers, frequently (though not invariably) in dialogue with Scripture. Here the Mishnah's statements are brought into alignment with Scripture; verses not cited by the Mishnah are identified and shown to be paraphrased and summarized in the Mishnah. Since I claim to set forth principles uniform throughout the Oral Torah, we are obligated to see how the primary statement is taken up and amplified, so as to assure ourselves that a single, coherent viewpoint governs throughout.

Thus Sifré to Numbers takes up the Mishnah's proposition concerning Numbers 5:23ff., that, when God punishes, he starts with that with which the transgression commenced, which the sages see as a mark of the precision of divine justice:

SIFRÉ TO NUMBERS XVIII:I.I:

I. A. "And when he has made her drink the water, [then, if she has defiled herself and has acted unfaithfully against her husband, the water that brings the curse shall enter into her and cause bitter pain,] and her body shall swell, and her thigh shall fall away, [and the woman shall become an execration among her people. But if the woman has not defiled herself and is clean, then she shall be free and shall conceive children]" (Num. 5:23–8).
B. I know only that her body and thigh are affected. How do I know that that is the case for the rest of her limbs?
C. Scripture states, "… the water that brings the curse shall enter into her."
D. So I take account of the phrase, "… the water that brings the curse shall enter into her."
E. Why [if all the limbs are affected equally] then does Scripture specify her body and her thigh in particular?
F. As to her thigh, the limb with which she began to commit the transgression – from there the punishment begins.

But the sages represented by Sifré to Numbers, exegetes of Scripture and the Mishnah, like the commentators whom we shall meet in the Tosefta that follows, wish to introduce their own cases in support of the same proposition:

G. Along these same lines:

H. "And he blotted out everything that sprouted from the earth, from man to beast" (Gen. 7:23).

I. From the one who began the transgression [namely Adam,] the punishment begins.

Adam sinned first, therefore the flood began with Adam. Now comes a different sort of proportion: the exact match. The Sodomites are smitten with piles:

J. Along these same lines:

K. "... and the men who were at the gate of the house they smote with piles" (Gen. 19:11).

L. From the one who began the transgression the punishment begins.

In the third instance, Pharaoh is in the position of Adam; with him the sin began, with him the punishment starts:

M. Along these same lines:

N. "... and I shall be honored through Pharaoh and through all of his force" (Ex. 14:4).

O. Pharaoh began the transgression, so from him began the punishment.

P. Along these same lines:

Q. "And you will most certainly smite at the edge of the sword the inhabitants of that city" (Deut. 134:15).

R. From the one who began the transgression, the punishment begins.

S. Along these same lines is the present case:

T. the limb with which she began to commit the transgression – from there the punishment begins.

Here comes a point important to the system: God's mercy vastly exceeds his justice, so the measure of reward is far greater than the measure of punishment – and, if possible, still more prompt:

U. Now does this not yield an argument *a fortiori:*

V. If in the case of the attribution of punishment, which is the lesser, from the limb with which she began to commit the transgression – from there the punishment begins,

W. in the case of the attribute of bestowing good, which is the greater, how much the more so!

Punishment is rational in yet a more concrete way: it commences with the very thing that has sinned, or with the person who has sinned. So the principles of reason and good order pervade the world. We know that fact because Scripture's account of all that matters has shown it.

The second response to the Mishnah's treatment comes in the Tosefta, meaning, "supplements," that is to say, supplements to the Mishnah. Like the Mishnah, the Tosefta, sets forth free-standing propositions, not merely exegeses of verses of Scripture. True to its role as the Mishnah's first systematic commentary and amplification in the Mishnah's own order and style (the second and third are the Talmuds of the Land of Israel, c. 400 C.E., and of Babylonia, c. 600 C.E., which take a very different form), the Tosefta contributes further cases illustrating the exact and appropriate character of both divine justice and divine reward. What is important here is what is not made explicit; it concerns a question that the Mishnah does not raise: what about the gentiles? Does the principle of world order of justice apply to them, or are they subject to chaos? The answer given through cases is that the same rules of justice apply to gentiles, not only Israelites such as are listed in the Mishnah's primary statement of the principle.

That point is made through the cases that are selected: Sennacherib, who besieged Jerusalem after destroying the northern tribes in the Kingdom of Israel; and Nebuchadnezzar, who took and destroyed Jerusalem in the time of Jeremiah. Now the sin is the single most important one, arrogance or hubris, and the penalty is swift and appropriate, the humbling of the proud by an act of humiliation:

TOSEFTA TRACTATE SOTAH 3:18

A. Sennacherib took pride before the Omnipresent only through an agent, as it is said, "By your messengers you have mocked the Lord and you have said, 'With my many chariots I have gone up the heights of the mountains ... I dug wells and drank foreign waters, and I dried up with the sole of my foot all the streams of Egypt'" (11 Kings 19:23–4).

B. So the Omnipresent, blessed be He, exacted punishment from him only through an agent, as it is said, "And that night the messenger of the Lord went forth and slew a hundred and eighty-five thousand in the camp of the Assyrians" (2 Kings 19:35).

C. And all of them were kings, with their crowns bound to their heads.

TOSEFTA TRACTATE SOTAH 3:19

A. Nebuchadnezzar said, "The denizens of this earth are not worthy for me to dwell among them. I shall make for myself a little cloud and dwell in it," as it is said, 'I will ascend above the heights of the clouds, I will make myself like the Most High'" (Is. 14:14).

B. Said to him the Omnipresent, blessed be He, "You said in your heart, 'I will ascend to heaven, above the stars of God I will set my throne on high' – I shall bring you down to the depths of the pit" (Is. 14:13, 15).

C. What does it say? "But you are brought down to Sheol, to the depths of the pit" (Is. 14:15).

D. Were you the one who said, "The denizens of this earth are not worthy for me to dwell among them"?

E. The king said, "Is not this great Babylon, which I have built by my mighty power as a royal residence and for the glory of my majesty? While the words were still in the king's mouth, there fell a voice from heaven, O King Nebuchadnezzar, to you it is spoken, The kingdom has departed from you, and you shall be driven from among men, and your dwelling shall be with the beasts of the field, and you shall be made to eat grass like an ox" (Dan. 4:29–32).

F. All this came upon King Nebuchadnezzar at the end of twelve months (Dan. 4:28–29).

As in the Mishnah, so here, too, we wish to prove that justice governs not only to penalize sin but also to reward virtue. To this point we have shown the proportionate character of punishment to sin, the exact measure of justice. The first task in this other context is to establish the proportions, now of reward to punishment.

Is reward measured out with the same precision? Not at all – reward many times exceeds punishment. So, if the measure of retribution is exactly proportionate to the sin, the measure of reward exceeds the contrary measure by a factor of five hundred. Later on we shall see explicit argument that justice without mercy is incomplete; to have justice, mercy is the required complement. Here we address another aspect of the same matter, that if the measure of punishment precisely matches the measure of sin, when it comes to reward for merit or virtue, matters are not that way:

TOSEFTA TRACTATE SOTAH 4:1

A. I know only with regard to the measure of retribution that by that same measure by which a man metes out, they mete out to him [M. Sot. 1:7A]. How do I know that the same is so with the measure of goodness [M. Sot. 1:9A]?

B. Thus do you say:'

C. The measure of goodness is five hundred times greater than the measure of retribution.

D. With regard to the measure of retribution it is written, "Visiting the sin of the fathers on the sons and on the grandsons to the third and fourth generation" (Ex. 20:5).

E. And with regard to the measure of goodness it is written, "And doing mercy for thousands' (Ex. 20:6).

F. You must therefore conclude that the measure of goodness is five hundred times greater than the measure of retribution.

Having made that point, we revert to the specifics of cases involving mortals, not God, and here we wish to show the simple point that reward and punishment meet in the precision of justice.

Before proceeding to the Tosefta's extension of matters in a quite unanticipated direction, let us turn to further amplifications of the basic point concerning the exact character of the punishment for a given sin. The fact is, not only does the sinner lose what he or she wanted, but the sinner also is denied what formerly he or she had possessed, a still more mordant and exact penalty indeed. At T. Sotah 4:16, the statement of the Mishnah, "Just as she is prohibited to her husband, so she is prohibited to her lover" (M. Sot. 5:1) is transformed into a generalization, which is spelled out and then demonstrated by a list lacking all articulation; the items on the list serve to make the point. The illustrative case – the snake and Eve – is given at T. 4:17–18; the list, at T. 4:19.

TOSEFTA SOTAH 4:16

A. Just as she is prohibited to her husband, so she is prohibited to her lover:

B. You turn out to rule in the case of an accused wife who set her eyes on someone who was not available to her:

C. What she wanted is not given to her, and what she had in hand is taken away from her.

TOSEFTA SOTAH 4:17

The poetry of justice is not lost: what the sinner wanted he does not get, and what he had he loses:

A. And so you find in the case of the snake of olden times, who was smarter than all the cattle and wild beasts of the field, as it is said, "Now the serpent was smarter than any other wild creature that the Lord Cod had made" (Gen. 3:1).

B. He wanted to slay Adam and to marry Eve.

C. The Omnipresent said to him, "I said that you should be king over all beasts and wild animals. Now that you did not want things that way, 'You are more cursed than all the beasts and wild animals of the field' (Gen. 3:14).

D. "I said that you should walk straight-up like man. Now that you did not want things that way, 'Upon your belly you shall go' (Gen. 3:14).

E. "I said that you should eat human food and drink human drink. Now: 'And dust you shall eat all the days of your life' (Gen. 3:14).

TOSEFTA SOTAH 4:18

A. "You wanted to kill Adam and marry Eve? 'And I will put enmity between you and the woman'" (Gen. 3:15).
B. You turn out to rule, What he wanted was not given to him, and what he had in hand was taken away from him.

The sages' mode of thought, to uncover patterns through classification and hierarchization, does not require the spelling out of the consequences of the pattern through endless cases. On the contrary, the sages are perfectly happy to list the other examples of the same rule, knowing that we can reconstruct the details if we know the facts of Scripture that have been shown to follow a common paradigm:

TOSEFTA SOTAH 4:19

A. And so you find in the case of Cain, Korah, Balaam, Doeg, Ahitophel, Gahazi, Absalom, Adonijah, Uzziah, and Haman, all of whom set their eyes on what they did not have coming to them.
B. What they wanted was not given to them, and what they had in hand was taken away from them.

Were we given only T. 4:19A, a construction lacking all explanation, we should have been able to reach T. 4:19B! Here is a fine example of how a pattern signals its own details, and how knowing the native categories allows us to elaborate the pattern with little further data. But whether we should have identified as the generative message, What he wanted was not given to him, and what he had in hand was taken away from him, is not equivalently clear, and I am inclined to think that without the fully exposed example, we could not have done what the compositor has instructed us to do: fill out the *et cetera*. What a passage of this kind underscores is the sages' confidence that those who studied their writings would see the paradigm within the case and would possess minds capable of generalization and objective demonstration.

To pursue this proposition about the precise match of punishment to sin being shown, further, in the unfolding of the punishment, we move beyond the limits of the Mishnah and the Tosefta. The same theme is extended in Leviticus Rabbah, a commentary to the book of Leviticus that came to closure in *c.* 450 C.E. Not only does the punishment begin with that with which the sinner has committed the sin, but punishment of sins always comes from the very corpus of the sinner himself:

LEVITICUS RABBAH XVIII:II.1FF.:

1. A. "Dread and terrible are they; their justice and dignity proceed from themselves" (Hab. 1:7).
B. "Dread and terrible" refers to the first Man.

Now we seek matched opposites, pairs that belong together to show how justice is exacted from the wicked and brings reward to the righteous. The first match is Esau and Obadiah, because Esau stands in the sages' sets of matches for Edom, and Obadiah is represented elsewhere as the antonym for Edom:

2. A. Another interpretation: "Dread and terrible" refers to Esau.
B. That is in line with the following verse of Scripture: "And Rebecca took the most coveted garments of Esau, her elder son" (Gen. 27:15).
C. "Their justice and dignity proceed from themselves" (Hab. 1:7).
D. This refers to [the prophet] Obadiah.

The next pair is formed by Sennacherib and his sons, the latter of whom killed the wicked father:

3. A. Another interpretation: "Dread and terrible" refers to Sennacherib.
B. "Who among all the gods of the lands has saved their country from my hand" (Is. 36:20).
C. "Their justice and dignity proceed from themselves" (Hab. 1:7).
D. This refers to his sons: "And it came to pass, as Sennacherib was worshipping in the house of Nisroch, his god, [that Adrammelech and Sarezer, his sons, smote him with the sword]" (2 Kgs. 19:37).

Even the wicked carry out God's justice. Here Nebuchadnezzar does God's work in Tyre, punishing Hiram's arrogance:

4. A. Another interpretation: "Dread and terrible" refers to Hiram, king of Tyre.
B. "Son of man, say to the prince of Tyre, thus says the Lord God, 'Because your heart was lifted up, and you said, I am God ...' " (Ez. 28:2).
C. "Their justice and dignity proceed from themselves" (Hab. 1:7).
D. This refers to Nebuchadnezzar.

Nebuchadnezzar also embodied arrogance, and he, too, was brought down:

5. A. Another interpretation: "Dread and terrible" refers to Nebuchadnezzar: "And you said, I shall go up to heaven" (Is. 14:13).
B. "Their justice and dignity proceed from themselves" (Hab. 1:7).
C. This refers to Evil Merodach.

At the end and climax is Israel, which brings punishment upon itself, from its own body, and this is made explicit:

6. A. Another interpretation: "Dread and terrible" refers to Israel.
B. "I said, You are God [-like beings]" (Ps. 82:6).
C. "Their justice and dignity [or swelling] proceed from themselves" (Hab. 1:7).
D. For Israelites may be smitten with flux and with leprosy [which punishes them for their sins, and comes from their very bodies].
E. Therefore Moses admonished Israel, saying to them, "When any man has a discharge from his body" (Lev. 15:2).

That the punishment is exacted from the sinner himself, and so too the reward, is shown in a sequence of cases, but the emphasis is on cases that show the former, a requirement of the context.

Time and again the sages extended matters by treating the case as exemplary. To them the archetypal sinners are the Generation of the Flood, the Generation of the Dispersion (from the tower of Babel), the Sodomites, the Egyptians, and Samson (in the list that follows, Amnon and Zimri). The cases, turned into a general rule before us, prove of special importance since they clarify, through the very listing, a major issue, the standing of gentiles in world order. Listing these six cases yields a generalization: the same God who exacted punishment from the archetypal sinners will exact punishment from anyone who does as they did. And with Samson, Amnon, and Zimri, we move from the world of gentiles to the world of Israel; justice is equal for all of humanity, both those within, and those beyond, the limits of the Torah defined by Israel:

LEVITICUS RABBAH XXIII:IX

1. A. R. Ishmael taught, " 'You shall not do as they do in the land of Egypt, where you dwelt, and you shall not do as they do in the land of Canaan ... I am the Lord your God' (Lev. 18:3–4).
B. " 'And if not, it is as if I am not the Lord your God.' "

The key point is now introduced: the case supplies a rule, and here, "I am going to exact punishment from anyone who does as they did":

2. A. R. Hiyya taught, "[The text states,] 'I am the Lord your God' two times (Lev. 18:4, 5).
B. "I am the one who exacted punishment from the Generation of the Flood and from the men of Sodom and Gomorrah and from Egypt.
C. " 'I am going to exact punishment from anyone who does as they did.' "

Once more, a list of names with little elaboration serves to prove the proposition at hand:

5. A. "I am the Lord" (Lev. 18:4):
B. "I am he who exacted punishment from Samson, Amnon, and Zimri, and I am going to exact punishment from whoever does as they did.
C. "I am he who rewarded Joseph, Jael, and Palti. I am going to reward whoever does as they did."

I see nothing surprising in this list, until we reach Samson, at which point Israel joins the gentiles in the domain of justice.

Let us now return to Tosefta Sotah 4: 1, which we considered above, because we have come to recognize a striking point. It is that the sages both distinguish the realm of the Torah from the realm of idolatry, Israel from the gentiles, and also treat the two realms as subject to one and the same rule justice. But then what difference does the Torah make for holy Israel, the Torah's sector of humanity? As the Tosefta's passage proceeds, discussion shades over into a response to this very question. The point concerning reward and punishment is made not at random but through the close reading of Scripture's record concerning not only the line of Noah – the Generation of the Flood, the men of Sodom and Gomorrah, the Egyptians – but also the founder of God's line on earth, Abraham. Abraham here, often head of the line with Isaac and Jacob, is deemed the archetype for Israel, his extended family. What he did affects his heirs. His actions form models for the right conduct of his heirs. What happened to him will be recapitulated in the lives and fate of his heirs.

So, from retributive justice and the gentiles the discourse shifts to distributive reward, shared by the founder and his heirs later on. Reward also is governed by exact justice, the precision of the deed matched by the precision of the response:

TOSEFTA TRACTATE SOTAH 4:1

G. And so you find in the case of Abraham that by that same measure by which a man metes out, they mete out to him.

H. He ran before the ministering angels three times, as it is said, "When he saw them, he ran to meet them" (Gen. 18:2), "And Abraham hastened to the tent" (Gen. 18:6), "And Abraham ran to the herd" (Gen. 18:7).

I. So did the Omnipresent, blessed be He, run before his children three times, as it is said, 'The Lord came from Sinai, and dawned from Seir upon us; he shone forth from Mount Paran" (Deut. 33:2).

Justice extends beyond the limits of a single life, when the life is Abraham's. Justice requires that Abraham's heirs participate in the heritage of virtue that he has bequeathed. Point by point, God remembers Abraham's generous actions in favour of Abraham's children into the long future, an intimation of a doctrine involving a heritage of grace that will play a considerable role in the theological system, as we shall see in due course. Here, point by point, what Abraham does brings benefit to his heirs:

TOSEFTA TRACTATE SOTAH 4:2

A. Of Abraham it is said, "He bowed himself to the earth" (Gen. 18:2).

B. So will the Omnipresent, blessed be He, respond graciously to his children in time to come, "Kings will be your foster-fathers, and their queens your nursing mothers. With their faces to the ground they shall bow down to you and lick the dust of your feet" (Is. 49:23).

C. Of Abraham it is said, 'Let a little water be brought" (Gen. 18:4).

D. So did the Omnipresent, blessed be He, respond graciously and give to his children a well in the wilderness, which gushed through the whole camp of Israel, as it is said, "The well which the princes dug, which the nobles of the people delved (Num. 21:18) teaching that it went over the whole south and watered the entire desert, which looks down upon the desert" (Num. 2 1:20).

E. Of Abraham it is said, "And rest yourselves under the tree" (Gen. 18:4).

F. So the Omnipresent gave his children seven glorious clouds in the wilderness, one on their right, one on their left, one before them, one behind them, one above their heads, and one as the Presence among them.

The same theme is expounded in a systematic way through the entire account; it is worth dealing with the complete statement:

TOSEFTA TRACTATE SOTAH 4:3

A. Of Abraham it is said, "While I fetch a morsel of bread that you may refresh yourselves" (Gen. 18:5).

B. So did the Omnipresent, blessed be He, give them manna in the wilderness, as it is said, "The people went about and gathered it … and made cakes of it, and the taste of it was like the taste of cakes baked with oil" (Num. 11:8).

TOSEFTA TRACTATE SOTAH 4:4

A. Of Abraham it is said, "And Abraham ran to the herd and took a calf, tender and good" (Gen. 18:7).

B. So the Omnipresent, blessed be He, rained down quail from the sea for his children, as it is said, "And there went forth a wind from the Lord, and it brought quails from the sea, and let them fall beside the camp" (Num. 11:31).

4:5 A. Of Abraham what does it say? "And Abraham stood over them" (Gen. I 8:8).

B. So the Omnipresent, blessed be He, watched over his children in Egypt, as it is said, "And the Lord passed over the door" (Ex. 12:23).

4:6 A. Of Abraham what does it say? "And Abraham went with them to set them on their way" (Gen. 18:16).

B. So the Omnipresent, blessed be He, accompanied his children for forty years, as it is said, "These forty years the Lord your God has been with you" (Deut. 2:7).

The evidence is of the same character as that adduced in the Mishnah: cases of Scripture. But the power of the Tosefta's treatment of Abraham must be felt: finding an exact counterpart in Israel's later history to each gesture of the progenitor, Abraham, shows the match between the deeds of the patriarchs and the destiny of their family later on. Justice now is given dimensions we should not have anticipated, involving not only the individual but the individual's family, meaning, the entire community of holy Israel. Once more, we note, a systematic effort focuses upon details. Justice is not a generalized expectation but a very particular fact, bread/manna, calf/quail, and so on. There is where the sages find the kind of detailed evidence that corresponds to the sort suitable in natural history.

The focus now shifts shift from how justice applies to the actions of named individuals – Samson, Absalom, Sennacherib, and Nebuchadnezzar – to the future history of Israel, the entire sector of humanity formed by those whom God has chosen and to whom he will give eternal life. It is a jarring initiative. The kinds of instances of justice that are given until that point concern sin and punishment, or the reward of individuals for their own actions. And these cases surely conform to the context: justice as the principle that governs what happens to individuals in an orderly world. But now we find ample evidence of the fundamental position in the sages' system, the generative character in their consideration of all issues that, as the first principle of world order, that justice governs.

For the sages not only accept the burden of proving, against all experience, that goodness goes to the good and evil to the wicked. They have also alleged, and here propose to instantiate, that the holy people Israel itself, its history, its destiny, conform to the principle of justice. And, if the claim that justice governs in the lives and actions of private persons conflicts with experience, the condition of Israel, conquered and scattered, surely calls into question any allegation that Israel's story embodies that same orderly and reasonable principle. Before us the sages take one step forward in their consideration of that very difficult question, how to explain the prosperity of the idolators, the gentiles, and the humiliation of those who serve the one true God, Israel. That step consists only in matching what Abraham does with what happens to his family later on.

The justice of God is shown also in details of Israel's history, to which we return presently, as in the explanation of why Israel went into exile to Babylonia:

TOSEFTA TRACTATE BABA QAMMA 7:3

A. Five matters did Rabban Yohanan ben Zakkai say in the manner of a *homer*:

B. "Why was Israel exiled to Babylonia, rather than to any other country? Because the house of Abraham came from there.

C. "To what may the matter be likened? To a woman who cuckolded her husband.

D. "Now where does he send her?

E. "He sends her back to her father's house."

Yohanan takes as his task the explanation of what is rational about the life of Israel with God:

TOSEFTA TRACTATE BABA QAMMA 7:4

A. "Of the first tablets it is said, And the tablets were the work of God.

B. "But as to the second, the tablets were the work of Moses, as it is said, 'And the writing was the writing of God' (Ex. 32:16).

C. "To what may the matter be likened? To a mortal king who betroths a certain woman. He brings the scribe, ink, quill, document, and witnesses.

D. "But [if] she cuckolded him, she has to supply everything [needed for the writing of the writ of divorce].

E. "It is enough for her if the king merely supplies his signature for recognition [and validation]."

So, too, the details of the law of the Torah have to be shown to conform to the same principle of rationality, measure for measure serving as the criterion of justice once again:

TOSEFTA TRACTATE BABA QAMMA 7:5

B. "And it says, And his master will pierce his ear with an awl (Ex. 21:6).

C. "On what account is the ear among all the limbs designated to be pierced?

D. "Because it heard from Mount Sinai, For unto me are the children of Israel slaves, they are my slaves (Lev. 25:55).

E. "Yet [the ear] broke off itself the yoke of Heaven and took upon itself the rule of the yoke of mortal man.

F. "Therefore Scripture says, 'Let the ear come and be pierced, for it has not observed [the commandment which] it heard.'"

The rules of commensurability and proportion in judgment produce the possibility of predicting as well as explaining what will happen to sinners. Therefore, to know the future and prepare for it, we may appeal to the principle of measure for measure.

If we know how someone has sinned, we also know not only that but exactly how he will be penalized. And the same goes for rewards either in this world, as in the case at hand, or in the world to come. Not only individuals, but classes of sinners and of sins, will be penalized in a manner appropriate to the character of the sin. That accounts for the certainty that justice always prevails and that the one who is punished bears full responsibility for his fate. All the more urgent, then, is the concept of judgment, resurrection and life after death, and the world to come, which in its way addresses the necessary corollary of the perfection of divine justice: the manifest injustice of the workaday fate of perfectly righteous people. In due course, we shall have much more to say about the same matter.

Here, it suffices to take note of a further corollary of the axiom of the exact, proportionate character of punishment. All things match, complementarity governs. But then, having identified Israel as that sector of humanity subject to a different relationship with the just God from that of the idolators, a further point of commensurate response is raised: sin, punishment, but then atonement, repentance, reconciliation, and conciliation. The same principles apply, but the context expands. Let me explain.

When it comes to Israel, the principle of commensurate response to each action extends, also, to God's response to Israel's atonement. Israel is punished for its sin. But when Israel repents (of which we shall hear more later on) and God forgives Israel and restores the holy people's fortunes, then that same principle that all things match takes over. Hence we should not find surprising the logical extension, to the character of God's forgiveness and comfort of Israel, of the principle of measure for measure. When, specifically, Israel sins, it is punished through that with which it sins, but it also is comforted through that with which it has been punished.

What is important to us is not only the logical necessity of the sages' reaching such a position. It also is the character of their demonstration of that fact. Here is a remarkably successful exposition of the way in which sages assemble out of Scripture facts that, all together, demonstrate the moral order of reward and punishment, along with the merciful character of God and his justice. It is a fine case in which a single pervasive logic coordinates a mass of data into a cogent statement of a position that prevails throughout. A passage such as the following can be understood only in light of the insistence at the outset that the sages conduct their inquiries in the manner of natural philosophy, the raw data – the cited verses of Scripture – being recast into a coherent demonstration of the desired proposition:

PESIQTA DERAB KAHANA XVI:XI.I

1. A. "[Comfort, comfort my people, says your God.] Speak tenderly to the heart of Jerusalem and declare to her [that her warfare is ended, that her iniquity is pardoned, that she has received from the Lord's hand double for all her sins]" (Is. 40:1–2).
B. When they sinned with the head, they were smitten at the head, but they were comforted through the head.
C. When they sinned with the head: "Let us make a head and let us return to Egypt" (Num. 14:4).
D. ... they were smitten at the head: "The whole head is sick" (Is. 1:5).
E. ... but they were comforted through the head: "Their king has passed before them and the Lord is at the head of them" (Mic. 2:13).

The construction is pellucid, the triplet of sin, punishment, and comfort applied first to the head, and, predictably, to the other principal parts. Why predictably? Because the sages wish to match nature with supernature, the components of the natural world with the parts of the body, as we saw in the prologue, the components of the body with the paradigmatic actions of Israel through time. All things match in exact balance: the natural world and the body of man, the body of man and the actions of Israel. From the head we now proceed to the eye, the ear, the nose, mouth, tongue, heart, hand, foot – the agencies of the expression of man's will. Once more what is important is not the end-product, which is a tedious and repetitious demonstration, but the way in which the facts of Scripture (proof-texts) are coordinated, selected, and organized to form a pattern that, left on their own, they do not establish at all. The entire passage follows without interruption, because at every point the exposition is clear:

PESIQTA DERAB KAHANA XVI:XI.2FF.

2. A. When they sinned with the eye, they were smitten at the eye, but they were comforted through the eye.

B. When they sinned with the eye: "[The daughters of Zion ... walk] ... with wanton eyes" (Is. 3:16).

C. ... they were smitten at the eye: "My eye, my eye runs down with water" (Lam. 1:16).

D. ... but they were comforted through the eye: "For every eye shall see the Lord returning to Zion" (Is. 52:8).

3. A. When they sinned with the ear, they were smitten at the ear, but they were comforted through the ear.

B. When they sinned with the ear: "They stopped up their ears so as not to hear" (Zech. 7:11).

C. ... they were smitten at the ear: "Their ears shall be deaf" (Mic. 7:16).

D. ... but they were comforted through the ear: "Your ears shall hear a word saying, [This is the way]" (Is. 30:21).

4. A. When they sinned with the nose [spelled "af," which can also mean, "yet" or "also"], they were smitten at the nose, but they were comforted through the nose.

B. When they sinned with the nose: "And lo, they put the branch to their noses" (Ez. 8:17).

C. ... they were smitten at the word af [also]: "I also will do this to you" (Lev. 26:16).

D. ... but they were comforted through the word af [now meaning yet]: "And yet for all that, when they are in the land of their enemies, I will not reject them" (Lev. 26:44).

5. A. When they sinned with the mouth, they were smitten at the mouth, but they were comforted through the mouth.

B. When they sinned with the mouth: "Every mouth speaks wantonness" (Is. 9:16).

C. ... they were smitten at the mouth: "[The Aramaeans and the Philistines] devour Israel with open mouth" (Is. 9:11).

D. ... but they were comforted through the mouth: "Then was our mouth filled with laughter" (Ps. 126:2).

6. A. When they sinned with the tongue, they were smitten at the tongue, but they were comforted through the tongue.

B. When they sinned with the tongue: "They bend their tongue, [their bow of falsehood]" (Jer. 9:2).

C. ... they were smitten at the tongue: "The tongue of the sucking [child cleaves to the roof of his mouth for thirst]" (Lam. 4:4).

D. ... but they were comforted through the tongue: "And our tongue with singing" (Ps. 126:2).

7. A. When they sinned with the heart, they were smitten at the heart, but they were comforted through the heart.

B. When they sinned with the heart: "Yes, they made their hearts as a stubborn stone" (Zech. 7:12).

C. ... they were smitten at the heart: "And the whole heart faints" (Is. 1:5).

D. ... but they were comforted through the heart: "Speak to the heart of Jerusalem" (Is. 40:2).

8. A. When they sinned with the hand, they were smitten at the hand, but they were comforted through the hand.

B. When they sinned with the hand: "Your hands are full of blood" (Is. 1:15).

C. ... they were smitten at the hand: "The hands of women full of compassion have boiled their own children" (Lam. 4:10).

D. ... but they were comforted through the hand: "The Lord will set his hand again the second time [to recover the remnant of his people]" (Is. 11:11).

9. A. When they sinned with the foot, they were smitten at the foot, but they were comforted through the foot.

B. When they sinned with the foot: "The daughters of Zion ... walk ... making a tinkling with their feet" (Is. 3:16).

C. ... they were smitten at the foot: "Your feet will stumble upon the dark mountains" (Jer. 13:16).

D. ... but they were comforted through the foot: "How beautiful upon the mountains are the feet of the messenger of good tidings" (Is. 52:7).

10. A. When they sinned with "this," they were smitten at "this," but they were comforted through "this."

B. When they sinned with "this:" "[The people said ... Go, make us a god], for as for this man Moses ..., [we do not know what has become of him]" (Ex. 32:1).

C. ... they were smitten at "this:" "For this our heart is faint" (Lam. 5:17).

D. ... but they were comforted through "this:" "It shall be said in that day, Lo, this is our God" (Is. 25:9).

11. A. When they sinned with "he," they were smitten at "he", but they were comforted through "he."

B. When they sinned with "he: " "'They have denied the Lord and said, It is not he" (Jer. 5:12).

C. … they were smitten at "he:" "Therefore he has turned to be their enemy, and he himself fought against them" (Is. 63:10).

D. … but they were comforted through "he:" "I even I am he who comforts you" (Is. 51:12).

12. A. When they sinned with fire, they were smitten at fire, but they were comforted through fire.

B. When they sinned with fire: "The children gather wood and the fathers kindle fire" (Jer. 7:18).

C. … they were smitten at fire: "For from on high he has sent fire into my bones' (Lam. 1:13).

D. … but they were comforted through fire: "For I, says the Lord, will be for her a wall of fire round about" (Zech. 2:9).

13. A. When they sinned in double measure, they were smitten in double measure, but they were comforted in double measure.

B. When they sinned in double measure: "Jerusalem has sinned a sin" (Lam. 1:8).

C. … they were smitten in double measure: "that she has received from the Lord's hand double for all her sins" (Is. 40:2).

D. … but they were comforted in double measure: "Comfort, comfort my people, says your God. [Speak tenderly to the heart of Jerusalem and cry to her that her warfare is ended, that her iniquity is pardoned, that she has received from the Lord's hand double for all her sins]" (Is. 40:1–2).

The basic proposition – when they sinned with this, they were smitten at this, but they were comforted through this – maintains that an exact match unites sin and punishment; through that with which one sins, he is punished. But then, that same match links the modes of consolation as well, that is, through that trait through which one is sinned, he also will be comforted. So the conviction of an orderly and appropriate set of correspondences setting forth a world in balance and proportion generates the details. The proofs for the proposition involve an extensive survey of both the media of sin and the character of punishment therefor. But in the restorationist theology that will emerge in chapters 13 and 14 – last things recapitulating first things – a passage such as this plays a typical role. It shows how at stake in world order is not a cataclysmic disruption at the end but rather a serene restoration of the perfection that prevailed at the outset.

Now that we have established the bases in Scripture for the sages' certainty that the creation is governed by a moral order resting on the principle of justice, we have to ask, what was at stake in that conviction? Specifically, we wonder what made urgent the proposition that a rational order, resting on exact justice, governed the world. At stake was making sense of the condition of the world and of Israel now and gaining access to what was going to come about. It was urgent for the sages both to explain the present and also to foresee the future. On what basis? In a world created in accordance with rules of a reasonable character, rules upon which both God and man concur, whatever happens should lend itself to reasonable explanation by appeal to those accessible rules that govern.

My answer derives not from the circumstance of the sages but from the logic implicit in their system. For sociology makes a poor teacher of theology, accounting as it does, in its own way, for who holds what opinion, but unable to explain why one opinion is right, another wrong. By contrast, the sages insisted upon the rationality of all things, meaning, the justice of the everyday. The system the sages put forth promised to explain why things were as they were. And the possibility of explanation carried with it the promise of prediction, a model for anticipating what is going to come about.

It ought, then, to follow that just as a given action will precipitate, on the part of the just God, a predictable reaction, so the sages should find plausible explanations for misfortune and reliable bases for foretelling the future as well. If one suffers such-and-such a penalty for doing so-and-so, then under ordinary circumstances, if one suffers so-and-so, it is because he has committed such-and-such a deed. This is made explicit in an account of why certain calamities befall:

MISHNAH-TRACTATE ABOT 5:8:

A. There are seven forms of punishment which come upon the world for seven kinds of transgression.
B. (1) [If] some people give tithes and some people do not give tithes, there is a famine from drought.
C. So some people are hungry and some have enough.

The match – a pattern of some giving, some not – is that some suffer, some do not. Here someone ought to say, those that do not give tithes will go hungry; that is, in fact, said in other sources. Now comes the match once more: no one gives, so everyone starves.

D. (2) [If] everyone decided not to tithe, there is a famine of unrest and drought.
E. (3) [If all decided] not to remove dough offering, there is a famine of totality.

We move from famine to pestilence, accounting for epidemics in the same reasonable way:

F. (4) Pestilence comes to the world on account of the death penalties which are listed in the Torah but which are not in the hands of the court [to inflict];
G. and because of the produce of the Seventh Year [which people buy and sell].

The sword of justice, which is rational and orderly, is replaced, when justice is delayed, by the sword of war, which is chaotic:

H. (5) A sword comes into the world because of the delaying of justice and perversion of justice, and because of those who teach the Torah not in accord with the law.

5:9 A. (6) A plague of wild animals comes into the world because of vain oaths and desecration of the Divine Name.

Now we move to the level of what happens to all Israel, not only to persons or communities. We invoke what we shall see as the three absolute sins, that is, actions that are sinful in any and all circumstances, idolatry, fornication, and murder; these bring about Israel's exile:

B. (7) Exile comes into the world because of those who worship idols, because of fornication, and because of bloodshed,
C. and because of the neglect of the release of the Land [in the year of release].

We proceed to details, worked out in response to the enumeration of the years of the Seven Year cycle that governs. In specified years, a given category of tithes is required of the farmers. If these are not given in the years that they are required, penalties follow:

D. At four turnings in the years pestilence increases: in the Fourth Year, in the Seventh Year, in the year after the Seventh Year, and at the end of the Festival [of Tabernacles] every year:
E. (1) in the Fourth Year, because of the poor man's tithe of the Third Year [which people have neglected to hand over to the poor];
E. (2) in the Seventh Year, because of the poor man's tithe of the Sixth Year;
G. (3) in the year after the Seventh Year, because of the dealing in produce of the Seventh Year;
H. and (4) at the end of the Festival every year, because of the thievery of the dues [gleanings and the like] owing to the poor [not left for them in the antecedent harvest].

Here the probative evidence derives not from Scripture but from an alleged correspondence of condition and its consequence: so, for example, M. Abot 5:8B-C, where the drought affects some, not others. If all are guilty, the famine is complete.

Again, we see the notion of the complement and match at 5:8H. The sword serves justice, politics standing for the legitimate exercise of violence; or it stands for injustice, which comes through war. Then, if the politics of justice does not bring about justice, the sword of justice becomes the agency of the opposite. At 5:9B the standard list of mortal sins – the triplet, idolatry, fornication, and bloodshed – is invoked to match what the sages deem the insufferable penalty of exile from the Holy Land – but mistreatment of the Land itself finds its match in exile as well, measure for measure. When, at Leviticus 26:34, God through Moses threatens to penalize Israel for neglecting the Sabbatical Year that is owed to the Land through a forcible Sabbatical, Scripture says no less. The insistence upon the perfect match of crime and punishment yields a collection of illustrations; the allegation then is a given, meant to be illustrated, rather than a proposition to be proved. Here, then, we see what it means to maintain an exact correspondence between sin and penalty, crime and punishment.

A similar picture of the match of sin and punishment is at Abot deR. Nathan XXXVIII: II.1: R. Josiah says, "On account of the sin of neglecting the dough offering, a blessing does not come upon the produce, so that people labor but do not suffice. On account of the sin of neglecting the separation of a portion of the crop for the priestly ration and the separation of tithes, the heavens will be closed up so as not to yield dew and rain, and people will be handed over to the government to be sold into slavery for non-payment of their taxes in kind." Along these same lines, Scripture itself yields its own equations, and once more what is important is how the sages regularize discrete data of Scripture into their general propositions:

ABOT DeR. NATHAN XXXVIII:VI.I

A. Exile comes into the world because of those who worship idols, because of fornication, and because of bloodshed, and because of the neglect of the release of the Land [in the year of release].

The proposition having been stated, we proceed to the facts to validate it:

B. On account of idolatry, as it is said: "And I will destroy your high places ... and I will scatter you among the nations" (Lev. 26:30,33).
C. Said the Holy One, blessed be he, to Israel, "Since you lust after idolatry, so I shall send you into exile to a place in which there is idolatry.
D. Therefore it is said, "And I will destroy your high places ... and I will scatter you among the nations."
E. Because of fornication: Said R. Ishmael b. R. Yosé, "So long as the Israelites are lawless in fornication, the Presence of God takes its leave of them,"
F. as it is said, "That he not see an unseemly thing in you and turn away from you" (Deut. 23:15).

G. Because of bloodshed: "So you shall not pollute the land in which you are located, for blood pollutes the land" (Num. 35:33).

From the absolute sins, we proceed to other matters announced in the base-text cited earlier:

H. Because of neglect of the release of the Land in the year of release: how do we know that that is the case?
I. "Then shall the land be paid her Sabbaths" (Lev. 26:34).
J. Said the Holy One, blessed be he, to Israel, "Since you do not propose to give the land its rest, it will give you a rest. For the number of months that you did not give the land rest, it will take a rest on its own.
K. That is why it is said, "Even then shall the land rest and repay her Sabbaths, As long as it lies desolate it shall have rest, even the rest that it did not have on your Sabbaths, when you lived on it" (Lev. 26:35).

The systematic linkage of sin and punishment does not stop there. The sages point to various failures and find in Scripture ample grounds for linking those failures of Israel to Israel's contemporary condition.

Two motifs overspread the theology of the Oral Torah, the destruction of Jerusalem and its Temple and the cessation of its sacrificial service to God, and the fate of the individual; public and private affairs are governed by those same principles of order flowing from justice. When it comes to the manifest punishment represented by the loss of Jerusalem and its medium for divine service, the precision noted in the cases above gives way to a generalized conviction that an entire list of sins found the single punishment. But all of these sins fall into a single category: they are public and for them the community of Israel at large bears responsibility. That accounts for the various specific sins linked to the general ruin of Jerusalem. But there is no distinguishing the sages' explanation of what happens to the individual from what happens to the people or nation. Many times through the pages of this book we shall see how private actions form a charge on the public good, and how a single mode of explanation serves to account for both individual and communal fate.

BAVLI-TRACTATE SHABBAT 16:2 II.42/119B

A. Said Abbayye, "Jerusalem was ruined only because they violated the Sabbath therein: 'And they have hidden their eyes from my Sabbaths, therefore I am profaned among them' " (Ezek. 22:26).

The Sabbath is sanctified both in public and in private. But prayer is personal, and that too shapes the future:

B. Said R. Abbahu, "Jerusalem was ruined only because they stopped reciting the *Shema* morning and evening: 'Woe to them that rise up early in the morning, that they may follow strong drink ... and the harp and the lute, the tabret and the pipe and wine are in their feasts, but they do not regard the works of the Lord,' 'Therefore my people have gone into captivity for lack of knowledge' " (Isa. 5:11–13).

The fate of the Torah governs the destiny of Israel. If the Torah is neglected, if children in particular are not taught, then the entire community suffers:

C. Said R. Hamnuna, "Jerusalem was ruined only because they neglected the children in the schoolmaster's household: 'pour out ... because of the children in the street' (Jer. 6:211). Why pour out? Because the children are in the streets."

Here again, personal conduct affects public life. People sinned openly and shamelessly, so Jerusalem, not only the private home or family, was penalized:

D. Said Ulla, "Jerusalem was ruined only because they were not ashamed on account of one another: 'Were they ashamed when they committed abomination? No, they were not at all ashamed, therefore they shall fall' " (Jer. 6:15).

So too, when the hierarchy of virtue and the authority of learning proved null, then the community as a whole is punished; this affects the failure to accord honour to the great; the failure of people to admonish one another; and the failure to honour disciples of the sages, a set of sins of a single class:

E. Said R. Isaac, "Jerusalem was ruined only because they treated equally the small and the great: 'And it shall be, like people like priest' and then, 'the earth shall be utterly emptied' " (Isa. 24:2–3).
F. Said R. Amram b. R. Simeon bar Abba said R. Simeon bar Abba said R. Hanina, "Jerusalem was ruined only because they did not correct one another: 'Her princes are become like harts that find no pasture' (Lam. 1:6) – just as the hart's head is at the side of the other's tail, so Israel of that generation hid their faces in the earth and didn't correct one another."
G. Said R. Judah, "Jerusalem was ruined only because they humiliated disciples of sages therein: 'But they mocked the messengers of God and despised his words and scoffed at his prophets, until the wrath of the Lord arose against his people till there was no remedy' " (2 Chr. 36:16).

None of the identified sins proves private or particular to one person only, but all require individual action or inaction.

When it comes to the private person, by contrast, the sages aim at a more precise match of sin to punishment. So far as is possible, they match the character of the one with the definition of the other. M. Shab. 2:6 states that on account of three transgressions do women die in childbirth: because they are not meticulous in the laws of (1) menstrual separation, (2) in those covering the dough offering, and (3) in those covering the kindling of a lamp for the Sabbath. The first clearly matches in a particular way, the second and the third are more general. Various specific penalties are incurred for specific sins, and these are to be specified in the Talmud of Babylonia's amplification of that same passage of the Mishnah. As is commonly the case, the sages' exegesis of the received passage involves the provision of facts that, in proper arrangement, validate the proposition that is offered at the outset:

BABYLONIAN TALMUD TRACTATE
SHABBAT 2:6 I.12FF./32B:

I.12 A. It has been taught on Tannaite authority:

B. R. Nathan says, "On account of the sin of a man's unfulfilled vows a man's wife dies: 'If you have not wherewith to pay your vows, why should he take away your bed from under you?' " (Prov. 22:27).

C. Rabbi says, "On account of the sin of a man's unfulfilled vows a man's children die when they are young: 'Suffer not your mouth to cause your flesh to sin, neither say before the angel that it was an error. Wherefore should God be angry at your voice and destroy the work of your hands?' (Qoh. 5:5). What is 'the work of a man's hands'? Say: It is his sons and daughters."

I.13 A. Our rabbis have taught on Tannaite authority:

B. "On account of the sin of unfulfilled vows children die," the words of R. Eleazar b. R. Simeon.

C. R. Judah the Patriarch says, "It is on account of the sin of neglect of the Torah."

In the next item if one preserves a grudge, his own household will be disrupted by discord as well, so what the man has kept going will in the end affect his own home, a principle that has been enunciated in earlier passages; what one wants one does not get, but one loses what one already has:

I.17 A. It has been taught on Tannaite authority:

B. R. Nehemiah says, "For the sin of nursing a grudge [causeless hate], discord grows in someone's house, his wife will miscarry, and his sons and daughters will die young."

The dough-offering, a bit of dough removed before baking the bread, gives back to the priesthood, one of God's surrogates, part of the grain that is used. Since it is a mark of abundance of food, failure to give that offering leads to a scarcity of food:

II.1 A. [The dough-offering:] R. Eleazar b. R. Judah says, "For the sin of neglect of the dough-offering, no blessing comes upon what is in storage, prices are cursed, seed is sown but others eat it up: 'I also will do this to you: I will visit you with terror, even consumption and fever, that shall consume the eyes and make the soul to pine away, and you shall sow your seed in vain, for your enemies shall eat it' (Lev. 26:16). Read the word translated as terror as though it were written, dough-offering.
B. "But if they give it, they are blessed: 'You shall also give to the priest the first of your dough, to cause a blessing to rest on your house' " (Ezek. 44:30).

The gathered crops are liable to the separation of grain for heave-offering and tithes, which represent God's share of the crop; these are given to the surrogates, the priests, Levites, or poor, and some of the tithes also are to be consumed by the farmer in Jerusalem; here, too, God has a claim, and if that is not met, then rain is withheld.

II.2 A. For the sin of neglect of heave-offering and tithes, the heavens are shut up from bringing down dew and rain; prices are high; wages low; people pursue a living but don't catch up to it: "Drought and heat consume the snow waters, so does the grave those who have sinned" (Job 24:19).

Locusts represent thieves of the farmers' crops; for robbery, locusts come up and steal the crops:

II.4 A. For the sin of robbery, locusts come up and famine follows, and people eat the flesh of their sons and daughters: "Hear this word, you cows of Bashan, who are in the mountain of Samaria, who oppress the poor, who crush the needy" (Amos 4:1).
C. And it is written, "I have smitten you with blasting and mildew; the multitude of your gardens and your vineyards and your figs trees and your olive trees has the palmer-worm devoured" (Amos 4:9); and further, "That which the palmer-worm has left has the locust eaten; that which the locust has left the cankerworm has eaten; that which the cankerworm has left the caterpillar has eaten" (Joel 1:4); "And one shall snatch on the right hand and be hungry and he shall eat on the left hand and they shall not be satisfied; they shall eat every man the flesh of his own arm" (Isa. 9:19). Don't read the consonants that yield "the flesh of his own arm" in that way but as though they bore vowels to yield "the flesh of his own seed."

As we have already seen in another context, the failure of the political system – of the just use of the sword for acts of legitimate violence in recompense for violation of the just law – produces political crisis, war and disruption:

II.5 A. For the transgressions of the delay of judgment, perversion of judgment, spoiling judgment, and neglect of the Torah, sword and spoil increase, pestilence and famine come, people eat and are not satisfied, and they measure out the bread that they eat by weight: "And I will bring a sword upon you, that will execute the vengeance of the covenant" (Lev. 26:25). Covenant refers only to the Torah: "But for my covenant of day and night, I had not appointed the ordinances of heaven and earth" (Jer. 33:25), and "When I break your staff of bread, ten women shall bake your bread in one oven and they shall deliver your bread again by weight" (Lev. 26:26), "Because, even because they rejected my judgments" (Lev. 26:43).

Scripture itself precipitated thought along these lines, as a reading of Leviticus Chapter 26 will readily reveal. We should not find surprising that the sages turned directly to that passage to expound in general terms the particular cases set forth there:

II.6 A. For the sin of vain oaths, false oaths, profanation of the Divine Name, and desecration of the Sabbath, wild beasts multiply, domestic ones become few, the population declines, the roads become desolate: "And if by these things you will not be rebuked by me" (Lev. 26:23); Read the letters translated by "these things" as though they bore vowels to yield "by reason of oaths" [that are false]. Further, "and I will send the beast of the field among you" (Lev. 26:22). In regard to false oaths it is written, "And you shall not swear by my name falsely, so that you profane the name of God" (Lev. 19:12), and of the profanation of the Divine Name it is written, "that you do not profane my holy name" (Lev. 22:2), and the profanation of the Sabbath is set forth, "every one who profanes it shall surely be put to death" (Ex. 31:15), and the penalty for profanation derives from the penalty for a false oath. [Freedman: Just as this is punished by the sending of wild beasts, so are the others.]

If the Temple is not kept pure and holy, God's Presence will depart from there:

II.7 A. For the sin of bloodshed the Temple was destroyed and the Presence of God left Israel: "So you shall not pollute the land in which you are, for blood pollutes the land. And you shall not defile the land which you inhabit, in the midst of which I dwell" (Num. 35:33–4). "Lo, if you do make it unclean, you won't live there, and I won't live there."

Public sins against the social order, such as incest, idolatry, and neglect of the Sabbatical Year, are penalized by exile; others, more worthy to live in the Holy Land than Israel, will take over.

II.8 A. For the sin of incest, idolatry, and neglect of the years of release and Jubilee, exile comes into the world, they go into exile, and others come and take their place: "For all these abominations have the men of the land done" (Lev. 18:27), "and the land is defiled, therefore I visit the iniquity thereof upon it" (Lev. 18:25), "that the land vomit you not out also when you defile it" (Lev. 18:28). With regard to idolatry: "And I will cast your carcasses upon the carcasses of your idols" (Lev. 26:30), "and I will make your cities a waste and will bring your sanctuaries into desolation" (Lev. 26:31), "and you will I scatter among the nations" (Lev. 26:33). In regard to the years of release and Jubilee Years: "Then shall the land enjoy her Sabbaths, as long as it lies desolate, and you shall be in your enemies land" (Lev. 26:34), "as long as it lies desolate it shall have rest" (Lev. 26:35).

II.9 A. For the sin of a foul mouth, troubles multiply, evil decrees are renewed, Israel's youth die, and the fatherless and widows cry out and are not answered: "Therefore shall the Lord not rejoice over their young men, neither shall he have compassion over their fatherless and their widows; for every one is profane and an evil doer, and every mouth speaks folly. For all this his anger is not turned away, but his hand is stretched out still" (Isa. 9:16).

So, too, b. Shab. 5:3 XII.12/55a-b adds the more general statement of the governing rule of justice: sin brings on death, transgression, suffering.

As is the manner of the Talmud of Babylonia, the proposition is not only stated but systematically analysed and subjected to provocative challenge. It is not the last word that the Oral Torah has to say about death, suffering, old age, and other particulars of the common life. On the contrary, in due course, in chapter 5, we shall see a quite different view of the same matter. What is important here is not the proposition that death is recompense for sin, suffering for transgression. Rather, we must focus upon the basic principle and – again – how it is validated. Measure for measure accounts for the course of a human life, perfect justice prevails. And that is the point of insistence even in the implacable position taken in the following, with the pertinent factual foundations carefully delineated:

BAVLI-TRACTATE SHABBAT 5:3 XII.12/55A-B

A. Said R. Ammi, "Death comes about only through sin, and suffering only through transgression.

B. "Death comes about only through sin: 'The soul that sins, it shall die; the son shall not bear the iniquity of the father, neither shall the father bear the iniquity of the son; the righteousness of the righteous shall be upon him and the wickedness of the wicked shall be upon him' (Ezek. 18:20).

C. "And suffering only through transgression: 'Then will I visit their transgression with the rod and their iniquity with stripes' " (Ps. 89:33).

Now comes the challenge:

D. [55B] An objection was raised: Said the ministering angels before the Holy One blessed be He, "Lord of the universe, how come you have imposed the penalty of death on the first Adam?"

E. He said to them, "I commanded him one easy commandment, but he violated it."

Surely saints die too. What is to be said of them?

F. They said to him, "But isn't it the fact that Moses and Aaron, who kept the entire Torah, also died?"

G. He said to them, "There is one fate to the righteous and to the wicked, to the good ..." (Qoh. 9:2).

Saints sin, and that is why they too die:

H. [Ammi] concurs with [the view of matters expressed by] the following Tannaite authority, as has been taught on Tannaite authority:

I. R. Simeon b. Eleazar says, "So, too, Moses and Aaron died on account of their sin: 'Because you didn't believe in me ... therefore you shall not bring this assembly into the land that I have given them' (Num. 20:12) – lo, if you had believed in me, your time would not yet have come to take leave of the world."

J. An objection was raised: Four died on account of the snake's machinations [and not on account of their own sin]: Benjamin the son of Jacob, Amram the father of Moses, Jesse the father of David, and Caleb the son of David. But all of them are known by tradition except for Jesse, the father of David, in which case Scripture makes it clear, as it is written, "And Absalom set Amasa over the host instead of Joab. Now Amasa was the son of a man whose name was Itra the Israelite, who went in to Abigail the daughter of Nahash, sister of Zeruiah Joab's mother" (2 Sam. 17:25). Now was she the daughter of Nahash? Surely she was the daughter of Jesse: "And their sisters were Zeruiah and Abigail" (1 Chr. 2:16). But she was the daughter of him who died on account of the machinations of the snake [Nahash]. Now who is the authority here? Shouldn't we say, the Tannaite authority who stands behind the story of the ministering angels?

K. But there were Moses and Aaron, too. So it must be R. Simeon b. Eleazar, and that proves that there can be death without sin, and suffering without transgression. Isn't that a refutation of the position of R. Ammi?

L. It is a solid refutation.

That penalties for not carrying out vows prove extreme, which we have already noted, is shown by appeal to the exemplary precedent set by Jacob or by Abraham. Jacob, too, is shown to have sinned, and that is why even he died, and died for sins particular to the punishment, just as others die for specific sins:

LEVITICUS RABBAH XXXVII:I.3

A. Said R. Samuel bar Nahman, "Whoever takes a vow and delays paying his vow in the end will worship an idol, commit fornication, and spill blood.

B. "From whom do you learn all three possibilities? From our father, Jacob, for, on account of his taking a vow and delaying its fulfillment, he ended up guilty of all three.

C. "How do we know that in the case of idolatry? For it is written, 'And Jacob said to his house and to all those who were with him, "Take away the strange gods" ' (Gen. 38:2).

D. "Fornication? 'And Dinah, the daughter of Leah, went out and Shechem, the son of Hamor, saw her' (Gen. 34:1–2).

E. "As to bloodshed: 'And it came to pass, on the third day, when they were in pain' " (Gen. 34:25).

The sages now generalize and deal with ordinary folk, not saints:

4. A. And rabbis say, "Whoever takes a vow and delays carrying out his vow in the end will bury his wife.

B. "From whom do you learn that fact? From our father, Abraham, for, on account of his taking a vow and delaying fulfilling his vow, he buried his wife,

C. "as it is said, 'And on my account [for late fulfillment of my vow] when I came from Paddan, Rachel died because of me' " (Gen. 48:7).

5. A. Said R. Samuel b. R. Isaac, "Whoever takes a vow and delays fulfilling his vow causes his own death.

B. "What is the proof text? '[When you make a vow to the Lord your God, you shall not be slack to pay it, for the Lord your God will surely require it of you, and it would be sin in you.] But if you refrain from vowing ...' (Deut. 23:21–2). And it is written, 'The soul that sins will die' " (Ez. 18:4).

So we see that the rationality of the system requires not only that sin be punished appropriately, but that the punishment fit the crime in detail. Some trait must join the sin to the penalty, even though the precise trait may not be self-evident. This is clearest in the moral failures that follow a sin of morality, for example, nursing a grudge produces miscarriage, neglecting dough-offering produces famine, and the like. Some of the facts of the matter derive from Scripture, but the principle is systemic and fundamental.

If the sages had to state the logic that imposes order and proportion upon all relationships – the social counterpart to the laws of gravity – they would point to justice: what accords with justice is logical, and what does not is irrational. Ample evidence derives from Scripture's enormous corpus of facts to sustain in the sages' view that the moral order, based on justice, governs the affairs of men and nations. We have now seen that statements of that proposition, together with evidence characteristic of the sages' entire system, come to us from principal documents of the Oral Torah, beginning to end: the Mishnah and Tosefta, Leviticus Rabbah and the Fathers According to R. Nathan, and the Talmud of Babylonia. A more extensive survey will readily turn up still more ample testimony to the prevalence of that same view as the premise of every other document of the Oral Torah.

But I have claimed more than that the principle of justice pervades the entire account of the world that the sages set forth. It is trivial to note that the justice of world order forms a recurrent theme in many documents. Critical to the argument of this book is a different claim altogether. I maintain that that defines the first principle, the governing logic, of the sages' system. By that claim I allege that all else takes its leave from the conviction that by "good" God characterizes creation as just, that an entire system of the social order coheres as amplification and exegesis of that principle, and that justice dictates the primary point of self-evidence: the system's unmoved mover, the point before which there is no appeal, and beyond which, no point unaffected, no refuge for the irrational. How to show that that conviction is not only normative but generative? It is by asking about what the sages deem to require attention and explanation, and what they take for granted as a given.

Let me express the matter of the a priori priority of justice as the first principle of all things in a simple but probative way: *in the sages' discourse, justice never requires explanation but violations of justice always do.* When what happens does not conform to the systemic givens but violates the expectations precipitated by them, then the sages pay close attention and ask why. When what happens does conform, they do not have to: their unarticulated conviction of self-evidence is embodied, therefore, in the character of their discourse: not only the speech but the silence.

Justice therefore defines the rational, and injustice, the irrational. It is now my task to proceed from the self-evidence of justice as the governing logic of all being to the self-evidence of injustice as the challenge to logic: the irrational that requires rationalization in the fullest sense of that word. To the sages, the principal intellectual task is – in the exact sense of the meaning of the word – to *justify* the condition of society by reference to conduct therein, both public and personal. That is, the sages want to explain the sense and meaning, to account for the coherence with justice of what defies the expectations that strict justice would lead us to anticipate. The numerous cases we have considered in this chapter in the end prove episodic. We have now to turn to the systemic data: what do the sages define as the central issues, the critical tensions, when they speak of Israel in its context within all of humanity? And how, further, do they frame the issues of private life? These matching categories now demand attention. Specifically, the same principle now fully spelled out – that everything that happens responds to just cause – has to be shown to define the very problematic of the sages' discourse concerning public and personal Israel. That is, justice must dictate what defines the sages' interest when they speak of Israel and the Israelite.

To begin with, in chapters 3 and 4 we first examine what the sages meant by "Israel" and how the moral order was to come to realization within Israel and then how the sages made sense of "the gentiles" and what sort of justice governed in Israel's relationship with them. Chapter 5 proceeds to the sages' explanation of the irrationality of the personal order, phrased through time in many ways but in a single motif: why do the wicked prosper and the righteous suffer? The premise of the question, whether addressed to Israel and the gentiles, or to the righteous and the wicked, remains the same, namely, the conviction that the moral order of justice governs. That is the conviction that defines the generative question the sages raise at the most profound levels of their discussion of the public order and of the personal situation of households and individuals as well.

3 The Political Order: Israel and the Torah

Politics marks the starting point of this encompassing account of creation ordered by justice that, in my view, the sages systematically formulate through all of their documents. The theory of the political order that is set forth in the documents of the Oral Torah rests on a simple logic of balanced relationships as defined in chapter 2. We begin with the fundamental fact that all humanity is divided into two sectors, the part that knows God through the Torah, and the part that does not but instead worships idols. The former is called Israel, the latter, the gentiles. God rules as sovereign over all mankind, but the two sectors thereof compete and one, the gentiles, currently dominates the other, Israel. It follows that to make sense of, to justify, the political order, the sages had to find the rational principle that accounted for two political entities and their relationships. To spell out the several components of that rationale, the present chapter explains the political theology of Israel, while the following one focuses on the political theology of the gentiles. What that theology says about Israel, *mutatis mutandis*, it says also about the gentiles.

Power-relationships between the two respond to three rules. First, as the prevailing theory of world order maintains in its definition of justice, each action provokes an equal and commensurate reaction. Second, God responds to the attitude as much as to the action of the human actor, especially prizing humility over arrogance. Third, God's special relationship to those who know him through the Torah may require him to use the gentiles to penalize Israel for disobedience, to encourage their return to a proper attitude and consequent action. For the Oral Torah, within those three rules the political order of mankind plays itself out. In combination, they respond to the critical issue of Israel's public life: why do the gentiles prosper while Israel languishes? Where is the justice in the political order of mankind?

The sages' doctrine of the political order of the world is comprised by these convictions. First, because Israel accepted the Torah God loves Israel. The Torah therefore defines Israel's life and governs Israelites' welfare. Second, in genus Israel does not differ from the gentiles, deriving from the same ancestry, sharing the same origin to Abraham. In species, matters are otherwise. Distinguished by the Torah, Israel is alone in its category (*sui generis*), proved by the fact that what is a virtue to Israel is a vice to the nations, life-giving to Israel, poison to the gentiles. Third, Israel's condition of weakness comes about by reason of its own sin, which God justly and reasonably punishes through, among others, political means. Still, fourth, if Israel sins, God forgives that sin, having punished the nation on account of it. Such a process has yet to come to an end, but it will and in time is going to culminate in Israel's complete regeneration and consequently the restoration of Eden, now in Israel's framework. Meanwhile, fifth, Israel's assurance of God's love lies in the many expressions of special concern, in his provision of numerous commandments for Israel to carry out for its own sanctification. This is expressed in the following explicit way:

MISHNAH-TRACTATE 3:16

A. R. Hananiah b. Aqashia says, "The Holy One, blessed be he, wanted to give occasions for attaining merit to Israel.

B. "Therefore he gave them abundant Torah and numerous commandments,

C. "as it is said, 'It pleased the Lord for his righteousness' sake to magnify the Torah and give honour to it" (Is. 42:21).

The media for Israel's sanctification extend to even the humblest and most ordinary aspects of the national life: the food the nation eats, the sexual practices by which it procreates. These life-sustaining, life-transmitting activities draw God's special interest, as a mark of his general love for Israel. Israel then is supposed to achieve its life in conformity with the marks of God's love. That, in theory, forms the moral order that justifies Israel's existence through all time.

Now to the context in which that theory takes shape. The generative problematic of the sages' theory of the political order – what captured attention as irrational and required rationalization – presented itself every day an Israelite in the Land of Israel walked out the gateway of his courtyard and confronted the reality of Roman rule, whether pagan or Christian. If an Israelite in Iranian-ruled Babylonia encountered an agency of the Sasanian state, inclusive of the priests of the established religion of Ohrmazd ("Zoroastrianism"), he, too, had every reason to ask, why them, not us? The gentiles thrive in this world and in this age, and Israel deteriorates, dying a slow, long-term death of dignity: loss of sovereignty and power, loss of the Land, and loss of even the means of serving God as the Torah had specified, through the offerings of the produce of the Land, wheat, wine, grain, oil, and meat. The matter is easily set out in the sages' own language: God passionately loves Israel. The commandments express that passion. Thus, Israel's political condition – its standing in the power-relationships of the nations – defies rationality and disrupts the moral order of the world.

In this protracted argument concerning the theology of the sages, why identify politics as the first occasion for the demonstration that at the heart of the theology is the integrating principle that God governs the world with justice? When the sages addressed issues of the moral order, they turned first to public policy and political order because the Written Torah, Scripture, left them no choice. Its building block of world order is public: acts all together of a community – people, nation, society. As we have already seen in chapter I, the community bore responsibility for the acts of the individual – Israel being represented by every Israelite – so that if private persons sinned, everybody suffered.

That is because no one imagined the construction of world order out of disconnected individuals, a concept that would make its appearance only many centuries later and in a very different world. None conceived as consequential in its own terms the private preserve of the isolated individual, apart from family, household, village, people, or nation. The Torah's imperative of sanctification is phrased in the plural you, and God acts, as recorded in the Torah, upon that plural you. For in the account of the Written Torah God first addressed the community of Israel, only then the individual members thereof. Nearly the whole of the Written Torah's narrative concerns how Israel as a collectivity is to become a kingdom of priests and a holy people, a nation in the image of God, made up of individuals worthy of belonging thereto. As to the individual, Achan, in Joshua, typified the position of everybody: all Israel paid the price of one Israelite's sin against God. But issues of national life – sanctifying God, possessing the Holy Land, preventing individual sin from corrupting the public welfare – take priority.

It is not surprising, therefore, that the systematic exposition of the principle of the moral order of justice should focus upon politics, defined conventionally: who legitimately exercises violence against whom, what ongoing entities control large-scale social aggregates through the regular (institutional) and valid (legitimate) exercise of force. In their consideration of the rationality of the political order, the sages applied to the world of power that principle of rationality which claims that God governs within moral rules. Because of the way in which they organized humanity into hierarchized categories, no component of the larger construction of world order occupied a more central position in their minds. Specifically, they saw the world as comprised of enduring political entities, peoples, or nations that, through enduring institutions, collectively exercised legitimate violence (to review the initial definition). To the sages, it followed logically that the relationships between and among nations ought to take priority in the realization of the moral order of the world. Who legitimately does what to whom should provide probative evidence of God's government.

Then who is the "who" of politics, the head-noun of intelligible sentences? Answering that question requires defining the actor, the subject of the sentence, *who* does what to whom? The political entities that exercised legitimate violence and so were empowered and that also demanded from the sages a place in an account of how things cohere, as I said at the outset, were two: Israel on one scale, all the nations of the world on the other. These are best represented visually: Israel holding to the Torah on the one side, the nations with their idols on the other. For the sages could not imagine either one without its indicative emblem. By "Israel" the sages meant many things, but all definitions concur that Israel is Israel by reason of the Torah. Israel's relationship to the Torah governs all else: God's attitude towards Israel, Israel's understanding of itself, and Israel's conduct of its affairs. And, to turn matters around, to be an Israelite was to know God through the Torah. And the nations were undifferentiated; they were what they were by reason of one indicative trait, which was idolatry, and that is to say, not possessing the Torah. To be a gentile found definition in idolatry. A collectivity defined by a negative trait, the nations' idolatry dictated God's attitude towards them, which, to the sages, was all that mattered.

That definition of political actors then carries with it the principle of logic and order that the prevailing justice should embody. God rules. In a rational world ordered by the principle of justice, therefore, Israel, by reason of knowing God through the Torah, will exercise legitimate violence. The nations, by reason of idolatry, will subordinate themselves. But everyone knew that the nations, and particularly the world-empires, exercised hegemony. I say "particularly" because the sages persistently spoke not of "the nations" so much as the four that mattered, Babylonia, Media, Greece, and Rome, successive world-empires; and the sages in numerous ways insisted that the fifth and last would be Israel, when God's government would commence. In the logic of the sages, therefore, Israel, few in number and scattered in location, took its place in the sequence of, and commensurate with, the four known cosmopolitan empires. So the gentiles' governance of the world, their power and priority, dictated the first and most disruptive fact of the prevailing order. That reality – the rule of God's enemies – marked the starting point for the entire process of making sense of, finding the order in, how things are that the sages made manifest, in their ultimate statement, in the Oral Torah.

How in the sages' theology did Israel and the nations relate? To answer that question, as to deal with all others of a profound character, the sages, like the philosophers, turned to the simple logic of classification: comparison and contrast in a process of hierarchical classification. Israel in no way constituted what we should label a secular category, that is, a people or nation like any or all others – even an empire like Rome. Their understanding of "Israel" as a category would rather correspond to Christianity's "church" (in its various formulations) or Islam's *ummah*. For by "Israel" the sages understood the enchanted Israel of whom Scriptures speak, that is, the supernatural social entity called into being by God. To elect, sanctified Israel, the nations in no way compared except in one: they, too, found definition in their relationship to God. By the nations, which is to say, everyone else, the sages understood idolators, those who come under negative definitions: they do not know and worship the one and only true God, they worship no-gods.

Then why invoke the category of politics at all? While "church" and "ummah" and "Israel" at various times and places sustained this-worldly definitions, all three of them also constituted other-than-worldly entities as well. Certainly, for the first three centuries of Christianity, "church" bore anything but a political meaning; no Christian at the end of the third century could have foreseen the Christian dominance of the Roman world such as was realized by the end of the fourth. But why insist that the politics of Israel and the nations forms the first step in the recapitulation of the sages' theology?

The reason is that, since Scripture's "Israel" constituted a political entity, empowered legitimately to exercise violence to accomplish the common goals that God set for the holy society, the sages naturally regarded the "Israel" of their own time as, by its nature and calling, a political entity. They did not have to take account of the long history of Israel's political autonomy and even independence, down to 70 C.E., to come to such a conception. For it was in the beginning of Israel that Moses had been commissioned to turn a class of powerless slaves into a kingdom of priests and a holy people. He exercised political, not merely cultic or pedagogical or even prophetic functions. In Scripture's account of Moses's activities and the Torah's law, moreover, the government of civil affairs takes priority. Yet, in that regard, the nations, too, manifestly formed political entities that exercised power; indeed, they exercised a great deal more power than Israel did. So, for the sages, the political order of the world was comprised by the political entity unlike all others, Israel, which also formed a social order and a cultic community, on the one side, and by counterpart entities, on the other.

How to justify the comparison and contrast of entities of a single genus but not a common species? In the sages' view, individuals always represented the political entity with which they were identified, for example, idolators with the wicked empire, individual Israelites with God's people Israel. And that helps us to understand why, though Israel was sui generis, it also was to be treated as comparable to the nations. Because the sages did not see Israel as a conglomerate of distinct individuals, but as a social entity that began whole and encompassed the parts, they also did not see the nations as a mass of idolators, counted one by one, but as political entities, collective enterprises. That is why the sages' logic of world order understood "everyone else" to mean not only idolators viewed as individual sinners but idol-worshipping nations that were comparable to, and balanced against, Israel.

Having established the grounds for comparison, in what way Israel and the nations are alike, then, we may ask about the results of the necessary companion of comparison, which is contrast. Let us first take up the contrastive definition, Israel/not gentile. The components already are familiar. In this context Israel is defined both negatively and positively. Israel means not-gentile, and one prominent antonym for Israel, unsurprisingly, is gentile: gentiles worship idols, Israel worships the one, unique God.

But "Israel" in the Oral Torah stands also for the individual Israelite, so another antonym for Israel is Adam. These persons, Israel and Adam, form not individual and particular, but exemplary, categories. Israel is Adam's counterpart, Israel is the other model for Man, the one being without the Torah, the other being with. Adam's failure marked the occasion for the formation of Israel. Israel came into existence in the aftermath of the failure of Creation with the fall of Man and his ultimate near-extinction; in the restoration that followed the Flood, God identified Abraham to found in the Land the new Eden, a supernatural social entity to realize his will in creating the world. Called, variously, a family, a community, a nation, a people, Israel above all embodies God's resting place on earth. I hardly need add that this definition of Israel cannot be confused with any secular meanings attributed to the same word, for example, nation or ethnic entity, counterpart to other nations or ethnic groups.

That explains why, in secular as well as in sacred ways, when viewed as comparable to the nations, Israel emerges as fundamentally different from the nations of the world even – or especially – in practical ways. That is the point of the following passage:

PESIQTA DERAB KAHANA V:V.2

1. A. R. Levi opened discourse by citing the following verse: "And you shall be holy to me [because I the Lord am holy. I have made a clear separation between you and the heathen, that you may belong to me]" (Lev. 20:26).

2. A. Said R. Levi, "In all their deeds the Israelites are different from the nations of the world, in their manner of ploughing, sowing, reaping, making sheaves, threshing, working at the threshing floor and at the wine press, counting and reckoning the calendar:

B. "As to ploughing: 'You will not plough with an ox and and ass together' (Deut. 22:10).

C. "… sowing: 'You will now sow your vineyard with mixed seeds' (Lev. 22:9).

D. "… reaping: 'You will not gather the gleaning of your harvest' (Lev. 19:9).

E. "… making sheaves: 'And the forgotten sheaf in the field you will not recover' (Deut. 24:12).

F. "… threshing: 'You will not muzzle an ox in its threshing' (Deut. 25:4).

G. "… working at the threshing floor and at the wine press: 'You will provide liberally [for the Hebrew servant] out of your threshing floor and wine press' (Deut. 15:14).

H. "… counting and reckoning the calendar: The nations of the world reckon by the sun, and Israel by the moon: 'This month will be for you the first of the months' " (Ex. 12:2).

The points of difference address workaday activities, not matters of ritual or theological difference at all. Israel sustains its natural life in accord with rules that differentiate and sanctify. Israel even tells time by its own clock.

But matters are hardly so simple. For the Scriptural record does place Israel in the same line as all the rest of humanity, from Adam through Noah to Abraham. So does Israel not form part of a common humanity with the gentiles, all deriving from Noah and ultimately from Adam? Three solutions to that problem presented themselves.

First, the sages conceded that Israel and the gentiles form a single genus, as one mankind. But in fact they are are readily speciated as well. Here the process of comparison and contrast, upon which, in chapter 1, I laid heavy emphasis, comes into play. The nations of the world and Israel are both alike and different. They are called by the same name, for instance, but in the case of Israel the name bears a quite different meaning. The points that Israel and the gentiles bear in common also serve to differentiate them, the one for blessing, the other not. Once more, the sages collect and systematize the data of Scripture, forming of the details a single organizing rule, and that accounts for the protracted character of the demonstration of what is, in fact, a very simple proposition:

LEVITICUS RABBAH V:VII.2

A. Said R. Eleazar, "The nations of the world are called a congregation, and Israel is called a congregation.

B. "The nations of the world are called a congregation: 'For the congregation of the godless shall be desolate' (Job 15:34).

C. "And Israel is called a congregation: 'And the elders of the congregation shall lay their hands' (Lev. 4:15).

D. "The nations of the world are called sturdy bulls and Israel is called sturdy bulls.

E. "The nations of the world are called sturdy bulls: 'The congregation of [sturdy] bulls with the calves of the peoples' (Ps. 68:31).

F. "Israel is called sturdy bulls, as it is said, 'Listen to me, you sturdy [bullish] of heart' (Is. 46:13).

G. "The nations of the world are called excellent, and Israel is called excellent.

H. "The nations of the world are called excellent: 'You and the daughters of excellent nations' (Ex. 32:18).

I. "Israel is called excellent: 'They are the excellent, in whom is all my delight' (Ps. 16:4).

J. "The nations of the world are called sages, and Israel is called sages.

K. "The nations of the world are called sages: 'And I shall wipe out sages from Edom' (Ob. 1:8).

L. "And Israel is called sages: 'Sages store up knowledge' (Prov. 10:14).

M. "The nations of the world are called unblemished, and Israel is called unblemished.

N. "The nations of the world are called unblemished: 'Unblemished as are those that go down to the pit' (Prov. 1:12).

O. "And Israel is called unblemished: 'The unblemished will inherit goodness' (Prov. 28:10).

P. "The nations of the world are called men, and Israel is called men.

Q. "The nations of the world are called men: 'And you men who work iniquity' (Ps. 141:4).

R. "And Israel is called men: 'To you who are men I call' (Prov. 8:4).

S. "The nations of the world are called righteous, and Israel is called righteous.

T. "The nations of the world are called righteous: 'And righteous men shall judge them' (Ez. 23:45).

U. "And Israel is called righteous: 'And your people – all of them are righteous' (Is. 60:21).

V. "The nations of the world are called mighty, and Israel is called mighty.

W. "The nations of the world are called mighty: 'Why do you boast of evil, O mighty man' (Ps. 52:3).

X. "And Israel is called mighty: 'Mighty in power, those who do his word' " (Ps. 103:20).

For the sages, the facts of Scripture speak for themselves. At every point at which Israel and the nations intersect, they part company. So when compared and contrasted on the basis of shared traits, Israel and the gentiles are readily differentiated from one another. The processes of classification, entailing as they do judgments as to hierarchization, therefore yield the besought, logical result.

As a second way of solving the problem of classification, the sages introduce an argument based on a metaphor, which is to say, they treat the problem of classification here as they would a problem of classification presented by natural history. Their problem is, the gentiles and Israel stem from a common root. How to distinguish them? The sages invoke the metaphor of the rose on the thorny rose-bush; all draw upon nourishment from one root, but the rose brings pleasure while the thorn causes pain. Israel is like the rose, the nations, the thorns. They may be compared and contrasted by reason of their common point of nourishment, which comparison validates the labor of contrast: here not only is Israel compared to the rose, but the nations are explicitly likened to thorns, and the rest follows. But here, instead of collecting data from Scripture, the sages introduce the qualities of the rose, that is, observed characteristics of nature:

LEVITICUS RABBAH XXIII:VI

1. A. "[And the Lord said to Moses, Say to the people of Israel, I am the Lord your God.] You shall not do as they do in the land of Egypt [where you dwelt, and you shall not do as they do in the land of Canaan, to which I am bringing you]" (Lev. 18:1–3).

B. "As a rose among thorns, [so is my love among maidens]" (Song 2:2):

C. Just as roses are only for occasions of rejoicing,

D. so Israel was created only for carrying out religious duties and doing good deeds.

2. A. Another interpretation of "Like a rose among thorns":

B. Just as a rose is only for the scent, so the righteous were created only for the redemption of Israel.

3. A. Another interpretation of "Like a rose among thorns":

B. Just as a rose is placed on the table of kings at the beginning and end of a meal, so Israel will be in both this world and the world to come.

4. A. Another interpretation of "Like a rose among thorns":

B. Just as a rose is made ready for the Sabbath and festivals, so Israel is made ready for the coming redemption.

5. A. Another interpretation of "Like a rose among thorns":

B. Just as it is easy to tell a rose from the thorns, so it is easy to tell the Israelites from the nations of the world.

C. That is in line with the following verse of Scripture: "All those who see them will recognize them" (Is. 61:9).

6. A. Another interpretation of "Like a rose among thorns":

B. Just as a rose wilts so long as the hot spell persists, but [when the hot spell passes] and dew falls on it, the rose thrives again, so for Israel, so long as the shadow of Esau falls across the world, as it were Israel wilts.

C. But when the shadow of Esau passes from the world, Israel will once more thrive.

D. That is in line with the following verse of Scripture: "I shall be like the dew for Israel. It will blossom like a rose" (Hos. 14:6).

XXIII:VII

1. A. Said R. Berekhiah, "Said the Holy One, blessed be he, to Moses, 'Say to Israel, "My children, when you were in Egypt, you were like a rose among thorns. Now you come into the land of Canaan, you shall be like a rose among thorns.

B. " ' "Be careful not to do deeds like those of this party or that." '

C. "Therefore Moses admonished Israel, saying to them, 'You shall not do as they do in the land of Egypt, where you dwelt, and you shall not do as they do in the land of Canaan, to which I am bringing you. You shall not walk in their statutes' " (Lev. 18:3).

What defines Israel, then, are the religious duties and good deeds that Israel[ites] carry out. That is stated, in the context of law, at Mishnah-tractate Makkot, as we saw at the outset.

Even here, at this preliminary stage of defining Israel within the framework of the Torah, we note what will preoccupy the sages at every point in their discussion of the gentiles and idolatry, the critical problematic that defines what they wish to know about the topic, the gentiles. That is, why Israel is subordinate, the gentiles, superior. Critical to the definition of Israel is the world to come and the resurrection; equally central to the definition of the gentiles, and sinners, is the present age. Israel inherits the world to come, gentiles enjoy this world – and these form the categorical parameters (we cannot call them temporal categories!) of the system.

Third, the sages take account of Israel's origins, meaning, its descent from the patriarchs, whom God called, and who responded with obedience to the commandments even before through the revelation of the Torah Israel came into being. This approach to the problem stands apart from the first two, which respond to the rules of classification, comparison, and contrast. In place of the natural metaphor of the rose, the sages adopt the social metaphor of the family, for Israel. The point of differentiation comes with paternity, hence the enormous weight placed on the election of Abraham in particular. Here we call into service the quite separate conception that, by reason of descent from the patriarchs, Israel forms a distinct entity within the common humanity of Noah's children. In explaining the status and condition of Israel, the conception that Israel inherited a store of unearned grace from the founders, grace accumulated by their supererogatory faith and generosity, came into play. That idea, represented, as we shall see in due course, by the word *zekhut,* roughly to be translated (for the moment) as "an act of divine grace in response to an act of human grace," will take a prominent role in the sages' theology throughout. Abraham's conduct affected Israel's later life with God, because the *zekhut* accruing to Abraham because of his language to God shaped the coming religious duties that God would bestow upon Abraham's children. This is expressed in the sages' comment on the verse, "Abraham answered, Behold, I have taken upon myself to speak to the Lord, I who am but dust and ashes":

BAVLI TRACTATE HULLIN 6:7 1.6/88B-89A

I.6 A. Said Raba, "As a reward for what Abraham our forefather said, '[Abraham answered, Behold, I have taken upon myself to speak to the Lord], I who am but dust and ashes' (Gen. 18:27), his descendants merited two commandments, the ashes of the Red Heifer and the dust given to the woman accused of infidelity."
B. And why do we not include with them [that on his merit they were given the commandment] to cover the blood with dust? For that there it is valid [to eat the animal even if he does not cover the blood. Accordingly] there is a commandment [to cover it]. But there is no benefit [directly derived from the action].

The commandments themselves represent acts of divine grace in response to Abraham's acts of self-abnegation and humility.

C. Said Raba, "As a reward for what Abraham our forefather said, [89a] 'That I would not take a thread or a sandal-thong or anything that is yours, lest you should say, I have make Abram rich' (Gen. 14:23), his descendants merited two commandments, the thread of blue [of the fringes on a garment] and the thong of the tefillin.
D. "Now it makes perfect sense [that there is merit in the commandment to wear] the thong of the tefillin. It is written, 'And all the peoples of the earth shall see that you are called by the name of the Lord; and they shall be afraid of you' (Deut. 28:10). And it was taught on Tannaite authority: R. Eliezer the Elder says, 'These [promises] refer

to the tefillin for the head.' [The peoples will see from the tefillin that you are called by the name of the Lord.]"

Here the systemic idea of *zekhut* is invoked to explain why Israel continues to benefit from, and to be shaped by, the heritage of unearned grace received from Abraham. The commandments distinguish Israel from the gentiles, and some of these even pertained before Sinai.

It follows that Israel at the beginning did not differ from the gentiles. But the election of Israel, starting with God's call to Abraham and Abraham's response, distinguished Israel from the gentiles and so marked gentiles for what they are. If, as we see time and again, Israel is Israel by reason of the Torah, then gentiles are gentiles also by reason of the Torah, that is, not having the Torah, not accepting it. That point, which will form the governing motif of chapter 4 in our inquiry into the theology of the gentiles set forth by the Oral Torah, emerges even now. Israel's special status and relationship to God derive not from intrinsic qualities – though, as we shall see, the sages imputed to Israel palpable qualities that marked them off from the nations and found in the Torah the source of those qualities – but from the record of right attitudes and right deeds.

How were matters before the giving of the Torah to Israel? Gentiles – those who worship idols – had and now have exactly the same opportunities as now are accorded to Israel. In all important ways Israel and the gentiles are constructed in a single, common pattern; they share a category-formation. It is God's selection of Israel that excludes the gentiles. Once a selection has been made as to holiness, what has not been chosen has been excluded. But until a selection is made, all things are equally available for choice, with the result that selection represents an act of sanctification and at the same time exclusion:

MEKHILTA ATTRIBUTED TO R. ISHMAEL I:III.2:

A. Now before the land of Israel was selected, all lands were suitable for acts of speech. But once the land of Israel was selected, all of the other lands were excluded.
B. Before Jerusalem was selected, all of the land of Israel was suitable for altars. Once Jerusalem was selected, the rest of the land of Israel was excluded [for that purpose],
C. as it is said, "Take heed not to offer your burnt offerings in every place that you see but only in the place which the Lord shall choose" (Deut. 12:13–14).
D. Before the eternal house was selected, Jerusalem was suitable for the Divine Presence. Once the eternal house was selected, the rest of Jerusalem was excluded,

E. as it is said, "For the Lord has chosen Zion, he has desired it for his habitation. This is my resting place for ever" (Ps. 132:13–14).

F. Before Aaron was chosen, all Israelites were suitable for acts of priestly service. Once Aaron was chosen, the other Israelites were excluded from performing acts of priestly service,

G. as it is said, "It is an eternal covenant, signified by salt, before the Lord, with you and with your descendants with you" (Num. 18:19; "And it shall belong to him and to his descendants afterward, the covenant of an eternal priesthood" (Num. 2:13).

H. Before David was chosen, all Israelites were suitable to assume the throne. Once David was chosen, the rest of the Israelites were excluded,

I. as it is said, "Should you not know that the Lord, God of Israel, handed the kingdom over Israel to David forever, even to him and his sons by a covenant signified by salt" (2 Chr. 13:5).

What we have in effect is a definition of holiness: that which is exclusively designated as superior out of a sample that, in theory, is available but is rejected. That definition is implicit, and the sequence of cases spells out the point with great clarity. So the act of election makes all the difference. Before that act Israel and the gentiles possessed the same potentialities; afterward, Israel no longer was comparable to the gentiles. It became the rose among the thorns.

On what basis is that special relationship founded? Here again, the nations had every opportunity that was given to Israel. Specifically, they could have received the Torah. (In chapter 4 we shall see how this is worked out in coherent narrative-form.) But God found only Israel truly worthy to receive the Torah. Scripture offers a variety of explanations for the election of Israel, but the Oral Torah presents only one: Israel accepted the Torah, and the nations rejected it. So it was by an act of will on both parties that matters worked out in opposed ways. A function of God's own self-manifestation through the Torah, election is particular to the one that is chosen: God examined all the nations and chose Israel among them, examined all generations and chose the generation of the wilderness to receive the Torah, and so on:

LEVITICUS RABBAH XIII:II.I:

1. A. R. Simeon b. Yohai opened [discourse by citing the following verse:] " 'He stood and measured the earth; he looked and shook [YTR = released] the nations; [then the eternal mountains were scattered as the everlasting hills sank low. His ways were as of old]' [Habakkuk 3:6].

B. "The Holy One, blessed be he, took the measure of all the nations and found no nation but Israel that was truly worthy to receive the Torah.

C. "The Holy One, blessed be he, further took the measure of all generations and found no generation but the generation of the wilderness that was truly worthy to receive the Torah.

D. "The Holy One, blessed be he, further took the measure of all mountains and found no mountain but Mount Moriah that was truly worthy for the Presence of God to come to rest upon it.

E. "The Holy One, blessed be he, further took the measure of all cities and found no city but Jerusalem that was truly worthy in which to have the house of the sanctuary built.

F. "The Holy One, blessed be he, further took the measure of all mountains and found no mountain but Sinai that was truly worthy for the Torah to be given upon it.

G. "The Holy One, blessed be he, further took the measure of all lands and found no land but the Land of Israel that was truly worthy for Israel.

H. "That is in line with the following verse of Scripture: 'He stood and took the measure of the earth.' "

The question that is answered is, why did God choose Israel, the generation that received the Torah, Moriah, Sinai, the Land of Israel, and so on? The answer is, there was no better, more worthy choice, because of Israel's willingness to receive the Torah.

What is at stake at Sinai explains all that follows. At Sinai God announced, "I am the Lord your God who brought you ought of the Land of Egypt, out of the house of bondage. You shall have no other gods before Me." In so stating, and through all that followed, God revealed himself through the Torah. Then, in accepting the Torah, Israel responded as God wanted, but could not coerce, them to do: the act of obedience requires a context of free choice, just as the tragedy of Eden showed. So the Torah joins God to man through Israel by introducing God to man through Israel. That accounts for the election of Israel.

But how did this take place? It was a combination of God's and Israel's actions, the one coercing so far as he dared, the other acceding so far as they had to, both parties in the end satisfied with the outcome – a true negotiation. Specifically, Israel at Sinai was compelled to accept the Torah, but when Israel accepted it and said, "We shall do and we shall obey," Heaven celebrated, for Israel now acted on its own volition:

BABYLONIAN TALMUD TRACTATE
SHABBAT 9:3–4 I.25FF./88A:

I:25 A. "And they stood under the mount" (Ex. 19:17):
B. Actually underneath the mountain.

We start with God's coercion: he held the mountain over Israel and gave them the choice of life or death:

C. Said R. Abdimi bar Hama bar Hasa, "This teaches that the Holy One, blessed be He, held the mountain over Israel like a cask and said to them, 'If you accept the Torah, well and good, and if not, then there is where your grave will be.' "

I.26 A. Said Hezekiah, "What is the meaning of the verse, 'You caused sentence to be heard from Heaven, the earth feared and was tranquil' (Ps. 76:9)? If it feared, why was it tranquil, and if it was tranquil, why did it fear? But to begin with there was fear, but at the end, tranquillity."

B. Why the fear?

At stake was the righting of the catastrophic situation left behind by Adam, who endangered all creation when he was expelled from Eden for his act of disobedience:

C. It is in line with what R. Simeon b. Laqish said, for said R. Simeon b. Laqish, "What is the meaning of the verse of Scripture, 'And there was evening, and there was morning, the sixth day' (Gen. 1:31)? This teaches that the Holy One, blessed be He, made a stipulation with all of the works of creation, saying to them, 'If Israel accepts my Torah, well and good, but if not, I shall return you to chaos and void.' "

Israel for its part still belonged to the seed of Adam, not only accepting the Torah but also sinning against it in building the calf:

I.27 A. Expounded R. Simai, "At the moment that the Israelites first said, 'we shall do,' and then, 'we shall listen,' six hundred thousand ministering angels came to each Israelite and tied on to each of them two crowns, one for the 'we shall do' and the other for the 'we shall listen.' When the Israelites sinned, however, a million two hundred thousand angels of destruction came down and took them away: 'and the children of Israel stripped themselves of their ornaments from Mount Horeb' " (Ex. 33:6).

B. Said R. Hama bar Hanina, "At Horeb they put them on, at Horeb they took them off."

C. "At Horeb they put them on: as we just said.

D. "… at Horeb they took them off: 'and the children of Israel stripped themselves of their ornaments from Mount Horeb' " (Ex. 33:6).

E. Said R. Yohanan, "And Moses had the merit of taking all of them, for nearby it is written, 'And Moses took the tent' " (Ex. 33:7).

F. Said R. Simeon b. Laqish, "The Holy One, blessed be He, is destined to return them to us: 'And the ransomed of the Lord shall return and come with singing unto Zion and everlasting joy shall be upon their heads' (Isa. 35:10) – the joy of old will be on their heads."

Israel's generous response, pledging to do and obey, elicited God's equally generous response, his passionate love for Israel:

I.28 A. Said R. Eliezer, "At the moment that the Israelites first said, 'we shall do,' and then, 'we shall listen,' an echo came forth and proclaimed to them, 'Who has told my children this secret, which the ministering angels take advantage of: 'bless the Lord, you angels of his, you mighty in strength who fulfil his word, who hearken to the voice of his word' (Ps. 103:2) – first they do, then they hear."

I.29 A. Said R. Hama b. R. Hanina, "What is the meaning of the verse of Scripture, 'As the apple tree among trees of the wood, so is my beloved among the sons' (Song 2:3)? Why are the Israelites compared to an apple? To tell you, just as an apple – its fruit appears before the leaves, so the Israelites gave precedence to 'we shall do' over 'we shall hearken.' "

I.38 A. And said R. Joshua b. Levi, "What is the meaning of the following verse of Scripture: 'His cheeks are as a bed of spices' (Song 5:13)? From every word that came forth from the mouth of the Holy One, blessed be He, the world was filled with spices. But since, by the first word, the world was filled, where did the fragrance of the second go? The Holy One, blessed be He, brought forth wind from his treasury and made each pass on in sequence: 'His lips are as lilies dripping myrrh that passes on' (Song 5:13) – read the word for lilies as though it yielded the sense 'that lead step by step.' "

The whole of the story of humanity, start to finish, takes place at Sinai, through judgment and resurrection:

I.39 A. And said R. Joshua b. Levi, "At every word that came forth from the mouth of the Holy One, blessed be He, the souls of the Israelites went forth [they died], as it is said, 'My soul went forth when he spoke' (Song 5:6). But since their souls departed at the first word, how could they receive the next? He brought down dew, with which he will resurrect the dead, and brought them back to life: 'Your God sent a plentiful rain, you confirmed your inheritance when it was weary' " (Ps. 68:10).

I.40 A. And said R. Joshua b. Levi, "At every word that came forth from the mouth of the Holy One, blessed be He, the Israelites retreated for twelve miles, but the ministering angels led them back: 'The hosts of angels march, they march' (Ps. 68:13) – read the word as though its consonants yielded 'they lead.' "

The Torah was not exactly given but rather forced upon Israel. But then, as we see, Israel accepted the Torah and the stipulation of creation was thus met. This is explained by appeal to narrative, which tells how matters took place.

Two further points connected with the election of Israel through their acceptance of God's self-manifestation in the Torah at Sinai are now in order. First, God's special love for Israel responds to God's effort in acquiring

Israel. Second, to adumbrate the sages' statement on the gentiles, the nations proved themselves unworthy of election, so God rejected them. The former view is expressed as follows:

SIFRÉ TO DEUTERONOMY CCCIX:V.I

A. "Is not he the father who has acquired [another meaning for the letters of the word created] you:"
B. Said Moses to the Israelites, "You are precious to him, you are things he has acquired on his own, not merely what he has inherited."

A parable serves to realize the sentiment just now expressed: what one acquires on his own is more highly valued than what comes as a gift:

C. The matter may be compared to the case of someone whose father left him as an inheritance ten fields. The man went and bought a field with his own means, and that field he loved more than all of the fields that his father had left him as an inheritance.
D. And so too, there is the case of someone whose father left him as an inheritance ten palaces. The man went and bought a palace with his own means, and that palace he loved more than all of the palaces that his father had left him as an inheritance.
E. So did Moses say to the Israelites, "You are precious to him, you are things he has acquired on his own, not merely what he has inherited."

Now comes a clustering of God's select acquisitions: Israel, the Torah, and the Temple, all represent foci of his special love:

SIFRÉ TO DEUTERONOMY CCCIX:VI.I

A. "... who acquired you":
B. This is one of the three items that are called acquisitions of the Omnipresent.
C. Torah is called an acquisition of the Omnipresent, for it is said, "The Lord acquired me at the beginning of his way" (Prov. 8:22).
D. Israel is called an acquisition of the Omnipresent, for it is said, "... who acquired you."
E. The house of the sanctuary is called an acquisition of the Omnipresent, for it is said, "This mountain, which his right hand has acquired" (Ps. 78:54).

Thus, the basic conception is elaborated so as to encompass, within the same circle of love, the principal components of the sacred system.

Above all, the right attitude receives the greatest emphasis, a trait we shall see time and again in the theology at hand and work out systematically in chapter 10. God commands, but he commands only man, because man alone enjoys the free will to choose to obey or to choose to rebel. Then the exercise of free will, embodied in proper intentionality, will dictate all else. How does this shape thinking about Israel? Only Israel was suitable to receive the Torah, not because of Israel's intrinsic character but because of Israel's attitude and actions. Specifically, as we shall see time and again, it is the Torah that makes Israel Israel, meaning, Israel's acceptance of the Torah as its meeting place with God makes all the difference:

SIFRÉ TO DEUTERONOMY CCCXI:I.I

A. "... when the Most High gave nations their homes [and set the divisions of man, he fixed the boundaries of peoples in relation to Israel's numbers. For the Lord's portion is his people, Jacob his own allotment]" (Deut. 32:7–9):

B. Before our father Abraham came along, it was as if the Holy One, blessed be He, judged the world in accord with the principle of mere cruelty.

Now comes the familiar trilogy: generation of the flood, people of the tower of Babylon (generation of the dispersion), and men of Sodom:

C. When the generation of the flood sinned, he extinguished them like sparks on water.

D. When the people of the tower of Babylon sinned, he scattered them from one end of the world to the other.

E. When the people of Sodom sinned, he drowned them in brimstone and fire.

Abraham breaks the sequence of sinners:

F. But when our father, Abraham, came into the world, he had the merit of receiving suffering [rather then utter extinction] which began to come along.

G. So it is said, "And there was a famine in the land and Abram went down to Egypt" (Gen. 12:10).

H. Now if you should say, "On what account do sufferings come," it is because of love for Israel:

I. "he fixed the boundaries of peoples in relation to Israel's numbers."

SIFRÉ TO DEUTERONOMY CCCXI:II.I

A. Another teaching concerning the verse, "... when the Most High gave nations their homes":

B. When the Holy One, blessed be He, gave the Torah to Israel, he went and gazed and scrutinized, as it is said, "He stands and shakes the earth, he beholds and makes the nations tremble" (Hab. 3:6).

C. But there was no nation among the nations that was suitable to receive the Torah except for Israel:

D. "... and set the divisions of man, he fixed the boundaries of peoples in relation to Israel's numbers."

Readers may stipulate that passages such as these fill the documents of the Oral Torah: the gentiles were unworthy of receiving the Torah, shown by the fact that they rejected it; Israel was elected because it was worth of election, shown by the fact that they accepted the Torah. In chapter 4 we shall see exactly how the sages represent the gentiles' rejection of the Torah.

The election of Israel on God's part constitutes a statement of love; it is an act of attitude, upon which all else rests. Indeed, God's love for Israel is so intense that it is best represented by metaphors of family devotion:

SONG OF SONGS RABBAH XLIV:II.I:

1. A. "... with the crown with which his mother crowned him":

B. Said R. Yohanan, "R. Simeon b. Yohai asked R. Eleazar b. R. Yosé, saying to him, 'Is it possible that you have heard from your father [Yosé b. R. Halafta] the meaning of the phrase, "with the crown with which his mother crowned him"?'

C. "He said to him, 'Yes.'

D. "He said to him, 'And what was it?'

E. "He said to him, 'The matter may be compared to the case of a king who had an only daughter, whom he loved exceedingly, calling her "My daughter."

F. " 'But he loved her so much that he called her, "My sister," and he loved her so much that he called her, "My mother."

G. " 'So did the Holy One, blessed be He, exceedingly love Israel, calling them, "My daughter." That is shown in this verse: "Listen, O daughter, and consider" (Ps. 45:11).

H. " 'Then he loved them so much that he called them, "My sister," as in this verse, "Open to me, my sister, my love" (Song 5:2).

I. " 'Then he loved them so much that he called them, "My mother," as in this verse, "Listen to me, my people, and give ear to me, my nation" (Isa. 51:4), and the word for "my nation" is written "my mother." ' "

J. R. Simeon b. Yohai stood up and kissed him on his head and said, "If I had come only to hear from your mouth this explanation, it would have sufficed."

The question that is answered is how to explain God's relationship with Israel, and the answer derives from the metaphor that is invoked. The entire Written Torah forms a love-song between God and Israel.

A mark of how much God loves Israel is his intervention into the natural order of things in Israel's behalf. The sages systematize facts of Scripture to demonstrate that, for Israel, God reverses the order of nature:

MEKHILTA ATTRIBUTED TO R. ISHMAEL XXXVIII:I.4

A. Rabban Simeon b. Gamaliel says, "Come and take note of how valued are the Israelites before the One who spoke and brought the world into being.

B. "For because they are so valued to him he altered for them the course of the natural world.

C. "For them he turned the upper region into the lower and the lower into the upper.

D. "Formerly bread would come up from the earth and dew would come down from heaven: 'The earth producing grain and wine, yes, his heavens drop down dew' (Deut. 33:28).

E. "Now things were reversed.

F. "Bread began to come down from heaven, and dew to come up from the earth: 'Behold, I will rain bread;' 'and the layer of dew came up' " (Ex. 16:14).

The Oral Torah many times duplicates statements such as these. It follows that the first question in any account of the moral order of the world is, why Israel? In the exact sense of the word "justify," that is, to show the justice of something, we must ask how the sages account for the rationality and rightness of God's election of Israel and concomitant rejection of the counterparts and opposites, the gentiles. Election occupies us here, rejection in the following chapter, even though the same principle governs the response to both questions.

What about Israel's sin? That question brings us to the center of the structure built upon the election of Israel and carries within itself the answer to the anomaly of Israel's condition among the nations. God's response to Israel's sin produces the probative mark of divine love for Israel, God's capacity to bear with, even to forgive, Israel. Israel tested God ten times, and God forgave them ten times:

BAVLI TRACTATE ARAKHIN 3:5 II.3/15A-B

A. It has been taught on Tannaite authority: Said R. Judah, "Ten trials did our ancestors impose upon the Holy One, blessed be he: two at the shore of the sea, two in the water, two in regard to the manna, two in regard to the quail, one in regard to the [golden] calf, one in the wilderness of Paran."

The systematic collection of facts and analysis and reconstruction of them into probative propositions now commences. Here are the data that when seen all together prove the point:

B. "Two at the sea": one in going down, and one in coming up.

C. In going down, as it is written, "Because there were no graves in Egypt [you have taken us away to die in the wilderness]" (Ex. 14:11).

D. "In coming up": That accords with what R. Huna said.

E. For R. Huna said, "At that time the Israelites were among those of little faith."

M. "Two in the water": at Marah and at Refidim.

N. At Marah, as it is written, "And they came to Marah and could not drink the water" (Ex. 15:23). And it is written, "And the people complained against Moses" (Ex. 17:3).

O. At Refidim, as it is written, "They encamped at Refidim, and there was no water to drink" (Ex. 17:1). And it is written, "And the people struggled with Moses" (Ex. 17:2).

P. "Two in regard to the manna": as it is written, [15B] Do not go out, but they went out, "Do not leave any over," (Ex. 16:19) but they left some over. [The first is not a direct quotation of a verse but summarizes the narrative.]

Q. "Two in regard to the quail": in regard to the first [quail] and in regard to the second quail.

R. In regard to the first: "When we sat by the fleshpots" (Ex. 16:3).

S. In regard to the second: "And the mixed multitude that was among them" (Num. 11:4).

T. "One in regard to the [golden] calf": as the story is told.

U. "One in the wilderness of Paran": as the story is told.

Scripture yields ample evidence of God's unlimited capacity to forgive Israel, so that the relationship between God and Israel is ordered by the principles of love and forbearance, shown by God through all time. So much for the election of Israel and the inner dynamics of that transaction.

But that – Sinai – was then, and this – the world governed by the pagan empire – is now. So it is time to ask, Who and what, exactly *is* Israel in the sages' logic? How about a this-worldly, political definition? First, let me eliminate the most conventional answer. The secular sense of "Israel" and even "the Jews" occurs only very rarely in the Oral Torah. I cannot point to the use of "Israel" to refer solely to the nation in the context of other nations of the same genus, for instance, the comparison of Israel's king and pagan kings; rather, what are compared are Israel's prophets and the pagan prophets. In the Oral Torah "Israel" bears these three meanings, which we have already noted and have now to systematize:

1) holy family, that is, a social entity different from the nations because it is formed by a common genealogy;
2) holy nation among nations but holy among profane, a rose among thorns, sustained by a common root but yielding a different fruit; and
3) unique Israel, *sui generis*, different not in contingent, indicative traits but categorically, that is to say, in its very category from all other nations.

Scripture, to the sages, told the story of "Israel" a man, Jacob. His children therefore are "the children of Jacob." That man's name was also "Israel," and, it followed, "the children of Israel" comprised the extended family of that man. By extension upward, "Israel" formed the family of Abraham and Sarah, Isaac and Rebecca, Jacob and Leah and Rachel. "Israel" thus invoked the metaphor of genealogy to explain the bonds that linked persons unseen into a single social entity; the shared traits were imputed, not empirical. That social metaphor of "Israel" – a simple one, really, and easily grasped – bore consequences in two ways. First, children in general are admonished to follow the good example of their parents. The deeds of the patriarchs and matriarchs taught lessons on how the children were to act. Of greater interest in an account of "Israel" as a social metaphor, "Israel" lived twice, once in the patriarchs and matriarchs, a second time in the life of the heirs as the descendants relived those earlier lives. The stories of the family were carefully reread to provide a picture of the meaning of the latter-day events of the descendants of that same family. Accordingly, the lives of the patriarchs signalled the history of Israel.

While Israel was sufficiently like the gentiles to sustain comparison with them, Rome being treated as a correlative family to Israel but descended from the wrong side, Israel also contrasted with the gentiles. In the end, despite all that has been said about Israel and the nations sharing a common genus, still Israel was to be seen as *sui generis*. Israel also found representation as beyond all metaphor. Seeing "Israel" as *sui generis* yielded a sustained interest in the natural laws governing "Israel" in particular, statements of the rules of the group's history viewed as a unique entity within time. The historical-eschatological formulation of a political teleology in that way moved from an account of illegitimate power to a formulation of the theory of the inappropriate victim, that is to say, of Israel itself. That explains why, as we have already seen, sentences out of the factual a record of the past formed into a cogent statement of the laws of this "Israel"'s destiny, laws unique to the social entity at hand.

Second, the teleology of those laws for an Israel that was *sui generis* focused upon salvation for individual Israelites – resurrection and judgment –

and redemption for all Israel at the end of history, that is, an eschatological teleology formed for a social entity embarked on its own lonely journey through time. Chapters 13 and 14 will show how the gentiles pass from the scene at the last, when the dead are raised, the Land regained, and Eden restored. Then all the living will form one Israel, that is, all mankind will recognize the rule of the one and only God.

The conception of "Israel" as *sui generis*, third, reaches expression in an implicit statement that Israel is subject to its own laws, which are distinct from the laws governing all other social entities. These laws may be discerned in the factual, scriptural record of "Israel"'s past, and that past, by definition, belonged to "Israel" alone. It followed, therefore, that by discerning the regularities in "Israel"'s history, implicitly understood as unique to "Israel," the sages recorded the view that "Israel," like God, was not subject to analogy or comparison. Accordingly, while not labelled a genus unto itself, Israel is treated in that way. The theory of Israel as *sui generis* produced a political theory in which Israel's sole legitimate ruler is God, and whoever legitimately governs does so as God's surrogate. The theory of legitimate sanctions then is recast into a religious statement of God's place in Israel's existence, but it retains its political valence when we recall that the sage, the man most fully "in our image, after our likeness," governs in accord with the law of the Torah. But how do the sages translate into concrete, practical terms the theory of the political order formed by Israel?

This brings us to the theology of politics contained within the image, kingdom of Heaven. Here and now Israel forms the realm of God in this world, where God takes up his presence, in synagogues and in schoolhouses, where prayers are recited and the Torah studied, respectively. God's kingdom, unlike the kingdoms of this world and this age, is not locative, and it is also not tangible. It is a kingdom that one enters by right attitude, through accepting the government and laws of that king and undertaking to obey his rules, the commandments. To be Israel in the sages' model means to live in God's kingdom, wherever one is located and whenever, in the sequence of the ages, one enjoys this-worldly existence. God's kingdom forms the realm of eternity within time. Death marks not an end but an interruption in life with God; the individual is restored to life at the end, within that larger act of restoration of Adam to Eden, meaning Israel to the Land, that Israel's repentance will bring about. Various religious activities represent a taste even now of what is coming, the Sabbath, for example, affording a sixtieth of the taste of the world to come. Embodying God's kingdom by obeying God's will, Israel was created to carry out religious duties and perform good deeds. These are what differentiate Israel from the gentiles-idolators.

What this means, concretely, is that God rules now, and that those who acknowledge and accept his rule, performing his commandments and living by his will, live under God's rule. We recall the observation that, to single out Israel, God sanctified the people by endowing them with numerous commandments. Carrying out these commandments, then, brings Israel into the Kingdom of Heaven, as they acknowledge the dominion of God. That merging of politics and theology emerges in the language of the formula for reciting a blessing before carrying out a commandment or religious duty, "Blessed are you, Lord our God, king of the world, who has sanctified us by his commandments and commanded us to ..." That is the formula that transforms an ordinary deed into an act of sanctification, a gesture of belonging to God's kingdom.

The recitation of a blessing also entails recognition of God's kingship, with the phrase, "... king of the world, who has commanded us ...," and that clause is deemed essential to any blessing:

YERUSHALMI TRACTATE BERAKHOT 9:1 1:3

A. R. Zeira and R. Judah in the name of Rab, "Any blessing which does not include [a reference to] God's kingdom, is not a valid blessing."
B. Said R. Tanhuma, "I will tell you what is the basis [in Scripture for this rule]: 'I will extol thee my God and King'" (Ps. 145:1).

God is addressed in the political metaphor because God's kingdom is at hand not at one moment but at all times; the "us" embodies all Israel even in a single individual, and the critical language then follows: who has given commandments, one of which is going to be carried out. That is how Israel is subject to the dominion of God and, if properly motivated, now lives in the Kingdom of Heaven. The Kingdom of Heaven is a phenomenon of this age as well as the world to come, and it involves tangible actions of everyday life, not only abstract existence. The doctrines in detail hold together in the conviction that God rules here and now, for those who, with a correct act of will and with proper conduct, accept his rule.

This is accomplished in various ways. First of all, it takes place through the declaration of the unity of God in the *Shema*-prayer – "Hear O Israel, the Lord our God, the Lord is one." In so doing, the Israelite accepts God's authority, then the commandments that are entailed by that authority: A person should first accept upon himself the yoke of the kingdom of heaven, that is, recite the *Shema*, and then accept upon himself the yoke of the commandments, for example, the obligation to wear tefillin or phylacteries (Mishnah-tractate

Berakhot 2:2/I) The holy people has accepted God's kingship at Sinai and
does not have the right to serve any other. We recall the statement at Tosefta
tractate Baba Qamma 7:5: "On what account is the ear among all the limbs
designated to be pierced? Because it heard from Mount Sinai, For unto me are
the children of Israel slaves, they are my slaves" (Lev. 25:55). Yet the ear
broke off itself the yoke of Heaven and took upon itself the rule of the yoke of
mortal man. Therefore Scripture says, "Let the ear come and be pierced, for it
has not observed the commandment which it heard." Israel is God's slave and
should be regarded as such. In the following protracted exposition, we see
how the conception of Israel forming God's kingdom plays itself out in the
setting of Israel's current situation. Here we notice, therefore, the way in
which the critical problematic – the anomaly of Israel's subordination to the
idolatrous nations – governs discourse throughout:

SIFRÉ TO NUMBERS CXV:V.4

A. ["I am the Lord your God who brought you out of the land of Egypt to be your
God"]:
B. Why make mention of the Exodus from Egypt in the setting of discourse on each
and every one of the religious duties?

A parable makes the matter transparent:

C. The matter may be compared to the case of a king whose ally was taken captive.
When the king paid the ransom [and so redeemed him], he did not redeem him as a
free man but as a slave, so that if the king made a decree and the other did not accept
it, he might say to him, "You are my slave."
D. When he came into a city, he said to him, "Tie my shoe-latch, carry my clothing
before me and bring them to the bath house." [Doing these services marks a man as
the slave of the one for whom he does them.]
E. The son began to complain. The king produced the bond and said to him, "You are
my slave."
F. So when the Holy One, blessed be he, redeemed the seed of Abraham, his ally, he
redeemed them not as sons but as slaves. When he makes a decree and they do not
accept it, he may say to them, "You are my slaves."
G. When the people had gone forth to the wilderness, he began to make decrees for
them involving part of the lesser religious duties as well as part of the more stringent
religious duties, for example, the Sabbath, the prohibition against consanguineous
marriages, the fringes, and the requirement to don *tefillin*. The Israelites began to

complain. He said to them, "You are my slaves. It was on that stipulation that I redeemed you, on the condition that I may make a decree and you must carry it out."

Israel accepts God's rule as a slave accepts his redeemer's authority; that is, Israel owes God allegiance and obedience. By carrying out God's will through the commandments, Israel enters God's dominion.

As the passage unfolds, the urgent question presents itself: since Israel is governed by the nations of the world, does that not mean that God has given up his dominion over them? If so, Israel no longer is subject to God's authority and need not keep the commandments.

SIFRÉ TO NUMBERS CXV:V.5

A. "[So you shall remember and do [all my commandments and be holy to your God. I am the Lord your God who brought you out of the land of Egypt to be your God.] I am the Lord your God" (Num. 15:37–41):

B. Why repeat the phrase, "I am the Lord your God"?

C. Is it not already stated, "I am the Lord your God who brought you out of the land of Egypt to be your God"?

D. Why then repeat the phrase, "I am the Lord your God"?

E. It is so that the Israelites should not say, "Why has the Omnipresent given us commandments? Let us not do them and not collect a reward."

F. They do not do them, and they shall not collect a reward.

The precedent provided by Scripture shows the governing rule:

G. This is in line with what the Israelites said to Ezekiel: "Some of the elders of Israel came to consult the Lord [and were sitting with me. Then this word came to me from the Lord: 'Man, say to the elders of Israel, This is the word of the Lord God: Do you come to consult me? As I live, I will not be consulted by you. This is the very word of the Lord God]' " (Ez. 20:1–3).

H. They said to Ezekiel, "In the case of a slave whose master has sold him off, has not the slave left the master's dominion?"

I. He said to them, "Yes."

J. They said to him, "Since the Omnipresent has sold us to the nations of the world, we have left his dominion."

K. He said to them, "Lo, in the case of a slave whose master has sold him only on the stipulation that later on the slave will return, has the slave left the dominion of the master? [Surely not.]"

L. "When you say to yourselves, 'Let us become like the nations and tribes of other lands and worship wood and stone,' you are thinking of something that can never be. As I live, says the Lord God, I will reign over you with a strong hand, with arm outstretched and wrath poured out'" (Ez. 20:32–33).

M. "… with a strong hand": this refers to pestilence, as it is said, "Lo the hand of the Lord is upon your cattle in the field" (Ex. 9:3).

N. "… with arm outstretched": this refers to the sword, as it is said, "And his sword is unsheathed in his hand, stretched forth against Jerusalem" (1 Chr. 21:16).

O. "… and wrath poured out": this refers to famine.

P. "After I have brought against you these three forms of punishment, one after the other, then 'I will reign over you' – despite yourselves.

Q. That is why it is said a second time, "I am the Lord your God."

God will not relinquish his rule over Israel, and he enforces his dominion despite Israel's conduct. The moral order, then, plays itself out within the inexorable logic of God's will.

It follows that the Kingdom of God is no abstraction. Within the theory of the sages, the sages' courts govern concrete cases on earth, but only within a larger system in which the Heavenly court exercises jurisdiction over cases of another order (a matter of considerable importance to our study of intentionality in chapter 10). Certain concrete sins or crimes (the system knows no distinction between them) are referred to Heaven for judgment. So Israel forms the this-worldly extension of God's Heavenly kingdom, and that is the fact even now. Not only so, but it is a fact that bears material and tangible consequences in the governance of the social order. That is why the Heavenly court is assigned tasks alongside the earthly one. The sages' court punishes murder when the rules of testimony, which are strict and rigid, permit; when not, there is always Heaven to step in. Or when a man clearly has served as efficient and sufficient cause of death, the earthly court punishes him.

But what are the sorts of concrete actions left over for Heaven to punish – and to penalize as concretely as the earthly court does? These include, for example, the following:

TOSEFTA TRACTATE BABA QAMMA 6:16:

A. He who frightens his fellow to death is exempt from punishment by the laws of man,

B. and his case is handed to Heaven.

C. [If] he shouted into his ear and deafened him, he is exempt.

D. [If] he seized him and shouted into his ear and deafened him, he is liable.

E. He who frightens the ox of his fellow to death is exempt from punishment by the laws of man,

F. and his case is handed over to Heaven.

6:17 A. [If] one force-fed [the ox of his fellow] with assafoetida, creeper-berries, a poisonous ointment, or chicken shit, he is exempt from punishment under the laws of man,

B. and his case is handed over to Heaven.

C. He who performs an extraneous act of labor while preparing purification-water or a cow for purification belonging to his fellow [thus spoiling what has been done] is exempt from punishment by the laws of man,

D. and his case is handed over to Heaven.

E. A court-official who administered a blow by the decision of a court and did injury is exempt from punishment by the laws of man,

F. and his case is handed over to Heaven.

G. He who chops up the foetus in the belly of a woman by the decision of a court and did damage is exempt from punishment by the laws of man,

H. and his case is handed over to Heaven.

I. A seasoned physician who administered a remedy by a decision of a court and did damage is exempt from punishment by the laws of man,

J. and his case is handed over to Heaven.

The Heavenly court alone is asked for a final assessment of the motives behind an action, of the causation embodied in the action when the case is ambiguous, and other imponderables. What the sages' courts cannot discern, the Heavenly court will perceive. What is important in these rules emerges from the concrete character of the cases handed over to Heaven for adjudication. The Kingdom of Heaven embraces the here and now, and the sages took for granted that God and God's agencies would carry out their responsibilities within the larger system of governance of holy Israel that the sages contemplated.

But for all their interest in matters of jurisprudence and politics, the sages believed the Kingdom of Heaven to be realized above all in the ordinary world in which Israel performed the commandments. When an Israelite carried out a positive commandment, or, more important, in obedience to Heaven refrained from a deed prohibited by a negative commandment, that formed the moment of ultimate realization of God's rule on earth. Thus, Israel through Israelites may bring about God's rule on earth. The commandments, originally emerging in small groups, mark the appearance of God's kingdom on earth. But alone among nations Israel finally got all of them, 248 positive ones, matching the bones of the body, 365 negative ones, matching the days of the solar year. So Israel alone within humanity has the possibility, and the power, to bring about God's rule, which, as we shall see, is fully realized in the restoration that marks the last things in the model of first things. Here the gradual delivery of the commandments is spelled out:

PESIQTA DERAB KAHANA XII:I.1FF.:

1. A. R. Judah bar Simon commenced discourse by citing the following verse: "Many daughters show how capable they are, but you excel them all. [Charm is a delusion and beauty fleeting; it is the God-fearing woman who is honored. Extol her for the fruit of her toil and let her labors bring her honor in the city gate]' (Prov. 31:29–31).

We start with the six commandments assigned to Adam, as the facts of Scripture indicate:

B. "The first man was assigned six religious duties, and they are: not worshipping idols, not blaspheming, setting up courts of justice, not murdering, not practising fornication, not stealing.
C. "And all of them derive from a single verse of Scripture: 'And the Lord God commanded the man, saying, 'You may freely eat of every tree of the garden, [but of the tree of the knowledge of good and evil you shall not eat, for in the day that you eat of it you shall die]' (Gen. 2:16).
D. " 'And the Lord God commanded the man, saying': this refers to idolatry, as it is said, 'For Ephraim was happy to walk after the command' (Hos. 5:11).
E. " 'The Lord': this refers to blasphemy, as it is said, 'Whoever curses the name of the Lord will surely die' (Lev. 24:16).
F. " 'God': this refers to setting up courts of justice, as it is said, 'God [in context, the judges] you shall not curse' (Ex. 22:27).
G. " 'the man': this refers to murder, as it is said, 'He who sheds the blood of man by man his blood shall be shed' (Gen. 9:6).
H. " 'saying': this refers to fornication, as it is said, 'Saying, will a man divorce his wife' (Jer. 3:1).
I. " 'You may freely eat of every tree of the garden: 'this refers to the prohibition of stealing, as you say, 'but of the tree of the knowledge of good and evil you shall not eat.'

Noah inherited those six commandments and was given another:

J. "Noah was commanded, in addition, not to cut a limb from a living beast, as it is said, 'But as to meat with its soul – its blood you shall not eat' " (Gen. 9:4).

Abraham got the seven and an eighth (though, elsewhere, it is alleged that Abraham in any event observed all of the commandments):

K. "Abraham was commanded, in addition, concerning circumcision, as it is said, 'And as to you, my covenant you shall keep' (Gen. 17:9).

L. "Isaac was circumcised on the eighth day, as it is said, 'And Abraham circumcised Isaac, his son, on the eighth day' " (Gen. 21:4).

Jacob got a ninth, his son Judah a tenth:

M. "Jacob was commanded not to eat the sciatic nerve, as it is said, 'On that account the children of Israel will not eat the sciatic nerve' (Gen. 32:33).

N. "Judah was commanded concerning marrying the childless brother's widow, as it is said, 'And Judah said to Onen, Go to the wife of your childless brother and exercise the duties of a levir with her' " (Gen. 38:8).

But Israel got them all, matching the bones of the body to the days of the year, the whole of life through all time:

O. "But as to you, at Sinai you received six hundred thirteen religious duties, two hundred forty-eight religious duties of commission [acts to be done], three hundred sixty-five religious duties of omission [acts not to be done],

P. "the former matching the two hundred forty-eight limbs that a human being has.

Q. "Each limb says to a person, 'By your leave, with me do this religious duty.'

R. "Three hundred sixty-five religious duties of omission [acts not to be done] matching the days of the solar calendar.

S. "Each day says to a person, 'By your leave, on me do not carry out that transgression.' "

That Israel got them all is what requires explanation, and the explanation has to do with the union of the days of the solar year with the bones of man: at all time, with all one's being, one obeys God's commandments. The mode of explanation here does not require the introduction of proof-texts, appealing rather to the state of nature – solar calendar, the bone-structure of man – to account for the facts. The Kingdom of Heaven, then, encompasses every day of the year and the components of the human body. The amplification at units R and S cannot be improved upon.

But the concrete realization of God's kingdom required constant encounter with the Torah, and that is not only because the Torah formed the source of the commandments that Israel was to carry out in obedience to its Heavenly Father and King. It also was because, within the words of God's own "I," his self-manifestation was eternally recorded and therefore always to be encountered. Torah-study constituted the occasion for meeting God, because the words of the Torah convey whatever man knows with certainty about God. If

Israel meets God in the Torah, God therefore is present when the Torah is opened and studied; then God is present within Israel:

BAVLI TRACTATE MEGILLAH 4:4 I.14

A. Expounded Raba: What [is meant by what] is written, "Lord, you have been a dwelling place for us" (Ps. 90:1)?
B. These are the synagogues and academies.
C. Said Abbayye, "Initially I used to study at home and pray in the synagogue. After I heard what David said [namely], 'Lord, I loved the place of your house' (Ps. 26:8), I studied in the synagogue."

There the Holy Spirit comes to rest. But that is not at all times or under every circumstance. The following powerful exposition invokes a metaphor to show the connection between Israel and God through the Torah, declaimed in synagogues, studied in schools. The point is this: it is when and where Israel meets God in the Torah that God is present in Israel. To separate God from Israel, the synagogues have to be boarded up, the schools closed. Then the chain forged at Sinai is broken:

YERUSHALMI TRACTATE SANHEDRIN 10:2 II:4

D. R. Honiah in the name of R. Eleazar: "Why is he called 'Ahaz' [seize]?"
E. "Because he seized the synagogues and schools."
F. To what is Ahaz to be compared?
G. To a king who had a son, who handed him over to a governor. He wanted to kill him. He said, "If I kill him, I shall be declared liable to death. But lo, I'll take his wet-nurse from him, and he'll die on his own."

The parable is now applied to the case of Ahaz. His reckoning contains the sages' entire theory of how God and Israel meet:

H. So did Ahaz say, "If there are no lambs, there will be no sheep; if there are no sheep, there will be no flock; if there is no flock, there will be no shepherd; if there is no shepherd, there will be no world, if there is no world – as it were ..."
I. So did Ahaz reckon, saying, "If there are no children, there will be no adults; if there are no adults, there will be no sages; if there are no sages, there will be no prophets; if there are no prophets, there will be no Holy Spirit; if there is no Holy Spirit, there will be no synagogues or schoolhouses – as it were. In that case, as it were, the Holy One, blessed be he, will not let his Presence rest upon Israel."

From the sages come prophets, upon the prophets the Holy Spirit rests, and without the Holy Spirit there are no synagogues or school houses, hence God's presence cannot come to rest in Israel.

The same idea comes to expression in a different way, involving the image of God's hiding his face. That is to say, although Israel is subject to God's rule, God is not always accessible to Israel, because of Israel's own doings. But that is only for a moment. Within the restorationist theology at hand, God may hide his face and make himself inaccessible to Israel by reason of evil, but in the end God will restore his presence to Israel:

J. R. Jacob bar Abayye in the name of R. Aha brings proof of the same proposition from the following verse of Scripture: "I will wait for the Lord, who is hiding his face from the house of Jacob, and I will hope in him" (Is. 8:17).

K. There was never a more difficult hour for the world than that hour at which the Holy One, blessed be he, said to Moses, "And I will surely hide my face in that day [on account of all the evil which they have done, because they have turned to other gods]" (Deut. 31:18).

Now follows the entire theology of restoration: Israel's repentance, God's consoling forgiveness marks the return to perfection as at the beginning:

L. At that hour: "I will wait for the Lord," for thus did he say to him at Sinai, "[And when many evils and troubles have come upon them, this song shall comfort them as a witness,] for it will live unforgotten in the months of their descendants; [for I know the purposes which they are already forming, before I have brought them into the land that I swore to give]" (Deut. 31:21).

M. And to what end?

N. "Behold, I and the children whom the Lord has given me [are the signs and the portents in Israel from the Lord of hosts, who dwells on Mount Sinai]" (Is. 8:18).

O. Now were they really his children? And were they not his disciples?

P. But it teaches that they were as precious to him as his children, so he called them, "My children."

Accordingly, Israel meets God in Torah study, and the more one studies, the more one gains; there is ample occasion to learn by hearing the Torah:

BAVLI-TRACTATE SUKKAH 4:7 IV.4/46A:

M. And R. Zira said, and some say it was R. Hanina bar Papa, "Come and see that the trait of the Holy One, blessed be he, is not like the trait of mortal man.

N. "In the case of mortal man, an empty vessel holds something, but a full vessel does not.

O. "But the trait of the Holy One, blessed be he, [is not like that.] A full utensil will hold [something], but an empty one will not hold something.

P. "For it is said, 'And it shall come to pass, if you will listen diligently' (Deut. 28:1). [One has to learn much and if he does, he will retain his knowledge.]

Q. "The sense is, If you will listen, you will go on listening, and if not, you will not go on listening.

R. "Another matter: If you hear concerning what is already in hand, you will also hear what is new.

S. " 'But if your heart turns away' (Deut. 30:17), you will not hear anything again."

So much for Israel's study of the Torah. It is the propaedeutic of prophecy, which leads to the encounter with the Holy Spirit.

What about prayer, which, alongside practice of the commandments and study of the Torah, forms the focus of the holy life, the métier of Israel? Prayer constitutes the third element in the encounter with God's presence. But on what basis? The sages work through analogies and contrast, referring to the Torah for the governing metaphors. In the case of prayer, they find in Scripture only private prayer, as in Hannah's in 1 Samuel 2, or prayer accompanying public offerings. How then validate synagogue prayer in public, for which Scripture supplies no analogy or precedent? Here Israel's prayers to God in the synagogue are equivalent to offerings in the Temple:

YERUSHALMI TRACTATE BERAKHOT 5:1 I:8:

F. R. Pinhas in the name of R. Yohanan Hoshaia, "He who recites the Prayer in the synagogue is as if he offered a pure meal offering [at the Temple].

G. "What is the basis [in Scripture for this view]? '[They shall declare my glory ... to my holy mountain Jerusalem, says the Lord,] just as the Israelites bring their cereal offerings in a clean vessel to the house of the Lord' " (Isa. 66:19–20).

H. R. Jeremiah in the name of R. Abbahu, " 'Seek the Lord while he may be found' [Isa. 55:6]. Where may he be found? In the synagogues and study halls. 'Call upon him while he is near' [ibid.]. Where is he near? [In the synagogues and study halls.]"

I. Said R. Isaac b. R. Eleazar, "Moreover, it is as if God stands next to those [who are in synagogues and study halls]. What is the basis [in Scripture for this view]? 'God has taken his place in the divine congregation; in the midst of the gods he holds judgment' " (Ps. 82:1).

In this view, prayer is treated as a metaphor for offerings in the cult. Just as God was served, when the Temple stood, through sacrifices of the gifts of the

Land – meat, wine, grain, oil – so, with the Temple in ruins, God receives the surrogate, which is the prayer; all he has left in the world, with the Temple gone, is the four cubits of the law, beginning with its prescription of prayer. Then the Torah's record encompasses all elements of what it means to live in the Kingdom of Heaven: the account of the acts of obedience to the King, the account of the record of the King, his great deeds and his wishes, and the account of the correct mode of service to the King, which is sacrifice when the Temple stands, prayer otherwise.

With what result? The sages had every reason to ask, given Israel's *paideia* or *Bildung* – moral education and formation – in the Torah, what this-worldly traits ought to be instilled through that process of education. In their view, Israel finds its definition not only in its supernatural calling but in its social traits even now. The sages claimed to discern in Israel traits that marked them off, qualities inculcated by the Torah and realized in ordinary life. That is why the sages defined Israel also by ethical traits. They understood that seeking those traits in ordinary folk would produce disappointment, so they wondered about the "genealogy," meaning, in their context, the authenticity *as Israel*, of those who did not exhibit those traits. They certainly did not assume that any Israelite possessed them, only that, to be an authentic Israelite, one would manifest them. In consequence of the Torah, Israel is – or ought to be – a virtuous community, characterized by forbearance, forgiveness, and kindliness. And, more to the point, those who do not show these virtues call into question their own legitimacy within, and as, Israel.

Here is a dramatic formulation of the conviction that to be Israel meant to be merciful and forbearing. To understand the passage, we have to recall the story of the unforgiving Gibeonites, who insisted upon extracting the last ounce of blood from Saul's family in retribution for Saul's actions. This, David found, marked the Gibeonites as outside the framework Israel.

YERUSHALMI TRACTATE QIDDUSHIN 4:I III.2

[M] Now David investigated all his contemporaries and he found not one of them. He turned to inquire of the Urim and Thummim. That is in line with the following verse of Scripture: "[Now there was a great famine in the days of David for three years, year after year;] and David sought the face of the Lord" (2 Sam. 21:1) – through the Urim and Thummim.

[O] "And the Lord said, 'There is blood-guilt on Saul and on his house'" (2 Sam. 21:1).

[P] "In regard to Saul, for you did not behave mercifully with him [for you did not mourn him]."

[Q] "And on his house" because he killed the Gibeonites.

[R] David sent and called them, "What is between you and the house of Saul?"

[S] They said to him, "It was because he killed seven men of us, two hewers of wood, two drawers of water, an instructor, a teacher, and a beadle."

[T] He said to them, "What do you want to do then?"

[U] They said to him, "Let seven of his sons be given to us, that we may hang them up before the Lord at Gibeon on the mountain of the Lord" (2 Sam. 21:6).

[V] He said to them, "What benefit will you have if they are killed? Take silver and gold."

[W] And they said, "We have no claim of silver against Saul and his house."

The Gibeonites want blood for blood. Then they are not authentically Israel, for the facts of Scripture, when assembled into a probative construction, prove the marks of the true Israelite:

[AA] Then David said, "There were three good gifts that the Holy One, blessed be he, gave to Israel: forgiving people, bashful people, and kindly people."

[BB] "Forgiving people," whence [in Scripture]? "[None of the devoted things shall cleave to your hand; that the Lord may turn from the fierceness of his anger] and show you mercy" (Deut. 13:18).

[CC] "Bashful people." whence [in Scripture]? "[And Moses said to the people, 'Do not fear for God has come to prove you,] and that the fear of him may be before your eyes, [that you may not sin]' " (Ex. 20:20). This is a mark of a bashful person, who will not readily sin. And as to whoever is not bashful, it is a matter of absolute certainty that his forefathers did not stand before Mount Sinai.

[DD] "Kindly people," whence [in Scripture]? "[And because you hearken to these ordinances, and keep and do them,] the Lord your God will keep with you the covenant and the steadfast love [which he swore to your fathers to keep]" (Deut. 7:12–13).

[EE] Now as to these, not one of them is master of these virtues. He went and declared them to be put away [from Israel], as it is said, "And the Gibeonites are not members of the children of Israel."

It follows that, in the sages' view, to be an Israelite is defined by possessing the traits that define an Israelite.

What are other such marks? Generosity is a mark of authentic lineage within Israel:

BAVLI TRACTATE BESAH 4:4 III.4/32B

A. And said R. Nathan b. Abba said Rab, "The rich men of Babylonia will go down to Gehenna.

B. "For once Shabbetai b. Marinos came to Babylonia. He asked them for goods to trade for a commission, but they would not provide them. He asked for food. Also they would not provide him any food.

C. "He said, 'These people are [descendants] of the mixed multitude [that left Egypt with the Israelites, Ex. 12:38],

D. " 'as it is written (Deut. 13:17), 'And [God] will bestow on you [the spirit of] mercy and compassion [as he swore to your fathers].'

E. " '[This means that] anyone who has compassion for others is [through his actions] known to be of the progeny of Abraham our father.

F. " 'But anyone who does not show compassion to others is known not to be of the progeny of Abraham our father.' "

The sages' reflection did not extend to the question of whether all those who exhibited the correct social virtues by definition belong to Israel. That is because these virtues were deemed necessary to establish one's belonging to Israel, but not sufficient to validate it.

Virtue does not suffice to gain entry into Israel, and Israel's sin or vice will not in the end estrange God from Israel or permanently exclude an Israelite from God's love:

SIFRÉ TO NUMBERS I:X.I

A. " '[You shall put out both male and female, putting them outside the camp, that they may not defile their camp,] in the midst of which I dwell.' [And the people of Israel did so and drove them outside the camp, as the Lord said to Moses, so the people of Israel did]" (Num. 5:3–4).

B. So beloved is Israel that even though they may become unclean, the Presence of God remains among them.

C. And so Scripture states, "... who dwells with them in the midst of their uncleanness" (Lev. 16:16).

D. And further: "... by making my sanctuary unclean, which [nonetheless] is in their midst" (Lev. 15:31).

E. And it further says: "... that they may not defile their camp, in the midst of which I dwell" (Num. 5:3–4).

F. And it further says, "You shall not defile the land in which you live, in the midst of which I dwell, for I the Lord dwell in the midst of the people of Israel" (Num. 35:34).

God's love is profound and unconditional, the relationship with Israel, eternal. And that fact brings us back to the generative problematic of the sages' thinking about world order: where is justice?

Specifically, how to account for the anomaly of Israel's condition in the world? Embodying virtue, unconditionally loved by God, encountering God through God's own self-revelation in the Torah, forgiven all its sins and faults, Israel ought to enjoy this world while anticipating eternal life. But that expectation conflicts with the sad reality that Israel does not enjoy this world and sees only a long, sad way from now to the end of time. The sages' account of the moral order appealed to justice to explain what is not an anomaly at all: Israel prospers when it does God's will, and it suffers when it does not do God's will. In this simple statement we find that account for reality that shows the prevailing order of all things, beginning with the most disruptive fact of all, Israel's condition:

MEKHILTA ATTRIBUTED TO R. ISHMAEL XXX:I.12

A. Another interpretation of the phrase, "[Your right hand, O Lord,] glorious in power":

B. When the Israelites carry out the will of the Omnipresent, they turn the left into the right: "Your right hand, O Lord, glorious in power, your right hand, O Lord, shatters the enemy."

C. But when the Israelites do not do the will of the Omnipresent, they turn the right hand into the left: "You have drawn back his right hand" (Lam. 2:3).

D. When the Israelites do the will of the Omnipresent, there is no sleep before him: "Behold the one who watches Israel does not slumber or sleep" (Ps. 121:4).

E. But when the Israelites do not do the will of the Omnipresent, then, as it were, sleep comes to him: "Then the Lord awakened as one asleep" (Ps. 78:65).

F. When the Israelites do the will of the Omnipresent, there is no anger before him: "Fury is not in me" (Is. 27:4).

G. But when the Israelites do not do the will of the Omnipresent, then, as it were, anger is before him: "And the anger of the Lord will be kindled" (Deut. 11:17).

H. When the Israelites do the will of the Omnipresent, he does battle for them: "The Lord will fight for you" (Ex. 14:14).

I. But when the Israelites do not do the will of the Omnipresent, then, he fights against them: "Therefore he was turned to be their enemy, the Lord himself fought against them" (Is. 63:10).

J. Not only so, but they make the merciful God into a sadist: "The Lord has become as an enemy" (Lam. 2:5).

The answer appeals to a self-evident principle, which is that God rules and is responsive to Israel; hence, if Israel does God's will, it prospers, and if not, it suffers. Then the condition of Israel itself validates the system's principal convictions.

What Israel must do, then, is to accept God's will, carry out God's commandments, above all, humbly take up its position in the Kingdom of God. Israel's task is to accept its fate as destiny decreed by God, to be humble and accepting, and ultimately to triumph in God's time. Israel is similar to the dust of the earth, which is why Israel, like the dirt, will endure forever:

GENESIS RABBAH XLI:IX.I

A. "I will make your descendants as the dust of the earth" (Gen. 13:16):

B. Just as the dust of the earth is from one end of the world to the other, so your children will be from one end of the world to the other.

C. Just as the dust of the earth is blessed only with water, so your children will be blessed only through the merit attained by study of the Torah, which is compared to water [hence: through water].

D. Just as the dust of the earth wears out metal utensils and yet endures forever, so Israel endures while the nations of the world come to an end.

E. Just as the dust of the world is treated as something on which to trample, so your children are treated as something to be trampled upon by the government.

F. That is in line with this verse: "And I will put it into the hand of them that afflict you" (Is. 51:23), that is to say, those who make your wounds flow ...

G. Nonetheless, it is for your good that they do so, for they cleanse you of guilt, in line with this verse: "You make her soft with showers" (Ps. 65:11).

H. "That have said to your soul, 'Bow down, that we may go over' " (Is. 51:23):

I. What did they do to them? They made them lie down in the streets and drew ploughs over them."

J. R. Azariah in the name of R. Aha: "That is a good sign. Just as the street wears out those who pass over it and endures forever, so your children will wear out all the nations of the world and will live forever."

Israel will show acceptance and humility and so overcome the nations not by power nor by its own might but by means of winning God's help through Torah-study, obedience, and patience.

That brings us, in the end, to the matter of the nations and their idolatry. Just as the Torah teaches Israel to embody certain virtues, and just as an Israelite must be humble and maintain an attitude of forbearance and not arrogance, so Israel must find in its condition as subordinate a reason to hope for God's special favour. For, Scripture demonstrates, God prefers the pursued over the pursuer and favours the persecuted. The following collection of facts is arranged to prove that point, which contains ample consolation for Israel even in the here and now, before the last things have begun the restoration:

LEVITICUS RABBAH XXVII:V.IFF.:

1. A. "God seeks what has been driven away" (Qoh. 3:15).

B. R. Huna in the name of R. Joseph said, "It is always the case that 'God seeks what has been driven away' [favouring the victim].

C. "You find when a righteous man pursues a righteous man, 'God seeks what has been driven away.'

D. "When a wicked man pursues a wicked man, 'God seeks what has been driven away.'

E. "All the more so when a wicked man pursues a righteous man, 'God seeks what has been driven away.'

F. "[The same principle applies] even when you come around to a case in which a righteous man pursues a wicked man, 'God seeks what has been driven away.' "

Now, the general proposition in hand, we turn towards the evidence that establishes its facticity:

2. A. R. Yosé b. R. Yudan in the name of R. Yosé b. R. Nehorai says, "It is always the case that the Holy One, blessed be he, demands an accounting for the blood of those who have been pursued from the hand of the pursuer.

The cluster is formed of familiar players, Abel, Noah, Abraham, Isaac, Jacob, and their enemies, Cain, Noah's contemporaries, Nimrod, Ishmael, Esau, and onward through the sequence, not bound by time, of probative cases, all of them a living presence on that timeless plane on which truth is established:

B. "Abel was pursued by Cain, and God sought (an accounting for) the pursued: 'And the Lord looked (favourably) upon Abel and his meal offering' (Gen. 4:4).

C. "Noah was pursued by his generation, and God sought (an accounting for) the pursued: 'You and all your household shall come into the ark' (Gen. 7:1). And it says, 'For this is like the days of Noah to me, as I swore (that the waters of Noah should no more go over the earth)' (Is. 54:9).

D. "Abraham was pursued by Nimrod, 'and God seeks what has been driven away': 'You are the Lord, the God who chose Abram and brought him out of Ur' (Neh. 9:7).

E. "Isaac was pursued by Ishmael, 'and God seeks what has been driven away': 'For through Isaac will seed be called for you' (Gen. 21:12).

F. "Jacob was pursued by Esau, 'and God seeks what has been driven away': 'For the Lord has chosen Jacob, Israel for his prized possession' (Ps. 135:4).

G. "Moses was pursued by Pharaoh, 'and God seeks what has been driven away': 'Had not Moses His chosen stood in the breach before Him' (Ps. 106:23).

H. "David was pursued by Saul, 'and God seeks what has been driven away': 'And he chose David, his servant' (Ps. 78:70).

I. "Israel was pursued by the nations, 'and God seeks what has been driven away': 'And you has the Lord chosen to be a people to him' (Deut. 14:2).

J. "And the rule applies also to the matter of offerings. A bull is pursued by a lion, a sheep is pursued by a wolf, a goat is pursued by a leopard.

K. "Therefore the Holy One, blessed be he, has said, 'Do not make offerings before me from those animals that pursue, but from those that are pursued: 'When a bull, a sheep, or a goat is born' " (Lev. 22:27).

In each case God explicitly prefers the pursued over the pursuer, and all of the cases together establish that point. What consequence might Israel anticipate from God's favour? Nothing less than eternal life. What in the end made "being Israel" matter so much? The reason is that, at stake in being Israel is life of a particular order, specifically, life beyond the grave. To be Israel means to enjoy the promise of eternal life. Than that there are no higher stakes.

That definition of who and what is Israel emerges in the following, through a simple manipulation of the opening statement: "All Israelites have a share in the world to come," meaning, will be resurrected, stand in judgment, and then live forever. This passage, which will become important in chapter 13, defines who fit into the category of "all Israelites":

MISHNAH-TRACTATE SANHEDRIN 10:1

A. All Israelites have a share in the world to come,

B. as it is said, "Your people also shall be all righteous, they shall inherit the land forever; the branch of my planting, the work of my hands, that I may be glorified" (Is. 60:21).

We may manipulate the opening declaration, reversing the subject and predicate, as follows: all who have a share in the world to come are Israelites. And all who do not cannot fall into the category, "Israelites," as framed in that same sentence.

At the most profound level, therefore, to be "Israel" means to be those destined to rise from the dead and enjoy the world to come. Specifically, the definition of Israel is contained in the identification of "all Israel," as those who maintain that the resurrection of the dead is a teaching of the Torah, and that the Torah comes from heaven. The upshot is, to be "Israel" is to rise from the dead to the world to come. Gentiles, by contrast, are not going to be resurrected when the dead are raised, but those among them who bear no guilt for their sins also will not be judged for eternal damnation, as Yerushalmi Shebiit 4:10 IX explains: "Gentile children who did not act out of free will and Nebuchadnezzar's soldiers who had no choice but to follow the orders of the evil king will not live after the resurrection of the dead but will not be judged for their deeds." If at the end of time Israel is comprised by those who will rise from the dead, in the interim "Israel" finds its definition in those who live the holy life and so imitate God, those who are so far as they can be, "like God." For Israel to be holy means that Israel is to be separate, and if Israel sanctifies itself, it sanctifies God:

SIFRA CXCV:I.2-3

1. A. "And the Lord said to Moses, Say to all the congregation of the people of Israel, You shall be holy, [for I the Lord your God am holy" (Lev. 19:1-4):

2. A. "You shall be holy":

B. "You shall be separate."

3. A. "You shall be holy, for I the Lord your God am holy":

B. That is to say, "if you sanctify yourselves, I shall credit it to you as though you had sanctified me, and if you do not sanctify yourselves, I shall hold that it is as if you have not sanctified me."

C. Or perhaps the sense is this: "If you sanctify me, then lo, I shall be sanctified, and if not, I shall not be sanctified"?

D. Scripture says, "For I … am holy," meaning, "I remain in my state of sanctification, whether or not you sanctify me."

The final trait of God's kingdom – the Kingdom of Heaven – then comes to the fore: its utopian character. To be "Israel" is personal and collective but utopian, not locative. The dead will rise wherever located. While the Land of Israel is elect along with the people of Israel, to be Israel does not mean to live in the Land but to live by the Torah.

Now, we turn to the nations, those who do not imitate the sanctity of God but worship idols and who for that reason will die and not then rise from the grave, but who govern here and now. Where is logic in this state of affairs?

4 The Political Order: The Gentiles and Idolatry

Gentiles are idolators, and Israelites worship the one, true God, who has made himself known in the Torah. In the Oral Torah, that is the difference – the only consequential distinction – between Israel and the gentiles. Still, there is that and one other: Israel stands for life, the gentiles for death. Before proceeding, let us consider a clear statement of why idolatry defines the boundary between Israel and everybody else. The reason is that idolatry – rebellious arrogance against God – encompasses the entire Torah. The religious duty to avoid idolatry is primary; if one violates the religious duties, he breaks the yoke of commandments, and if he violates that single religious duty, he transgresses the entire Torah. Violating the prohibition against idolatry is equivalent to transgressing all Ten Commandments:

SIFRÉ TO NUMBERS CXI:I.1FF.

1. A. "But if you err and do not observe [all these commandments which the Lord has spoken to Moses" (Num. 15:22–6):
2. A. "But if you err and do not observe:"
B. Scripture speaks of idolatry.

Now we test the proposition, as the sages commonly do, by proposing other readings of the evidence that is adduced besides the one offered as normative. Here is a sequence of options:

C. You maintain that Scripture speaks of idolatry. But perhaps Scripture refers to any of the religious duties that are listed in the Torah?

D. Scripture states, "... then if it was done unwittingly without the knowledge of the congregation." Scripture thereby has singled out a particular religious duty unto itself, and what might that be? It is the prohibition against idolatry.

E. You maintain that Scripture speaks of idolatry. But perhaps Scripture refers to any of the religious duties that are listed in the Torah?

F. Scripture states, "But if you err and do not observe," indicating that all of the religious duties come together to give testimony concerning a single religious duty.

G. Just as if someone violates all of the religious duties, he thereby breaks off the yoke [of the commandments] and wipes out the mark of the covenant and so treats the Torah impudently, so if one violates a single religious duty, he thereby breaks off the yoke [of the commandments] and wipes out the mark of the covenant and so treats the Torah impudently.

H. And what might that single religious duty be? It is idolatry, for it is said [in that regard], "... to violate his covenant" (Deut. 17:2). [Thus the covenant refers in particular to the rule against idolatry, which then stands for the whole.]

I. "Covenant" moreover refers only to the Torah, as it is said, "These are the words of the covenant" (Deut. 28:69).

The systematic proof having been completed, we now pursue a different path to the same goal:

J. [Providing a different proof for the same proposition as D-I], Rabbi says, "Here the word 'all' is used, and elsewhere the word 'all' is used. Just as in the word 'all' used elsewhere Scripture refers to idolatry, so in the word 'all' used here Scripture refers to idolatry."

Now we show that idolatry requires the denial of the Ten Commandments:

3. A. "... which the Lord has spoken to Moses:"

B. How do you know that whoever confesses to belief in idolatry denies the Ten Commandments?

C. Scripture says, "... which the Lord has spoken to Moses," and elsewhere, "And God spoke all these words, saying" (Ex. 20:1). "God spoke one word ..." (Ps. 62:12). "Are not my words like fire, says the Lord" (Jer. 23:29). So too in respect to that concerning which Moses was commanded Scripture says, "... all that the Lord God commanded through the hand of Moses."

D. How do we know that that same rule applies also to all matters concerning which the prophets were commanded?

E. Scripture says, "... from the day that the Lord gave commandment [and onward throughout your generations]."

F. And how do we know that that is the case also concerning the commandments entrusted to the patriarchs?

G. Scripture says, "... and onward throughout your generations."

H. And whence did the Holy One, blessed be he, begin to entrust commandments to the patriarchs?

I. As it is said, "And the Lord God commanded Adam" (Gen. 2:16).

J. Scripture thereby indicates that whoever confesses to belief in idolatry denies the Ten Commandments and rejects all of the commandments entrusted to Moses, the prophets, and the patriarchs.

K. And whoever denies idolatry confesses to belief in the entirety of the Torah.

Violating the religious duties in general means breaking the yoke of the commandments, but there is one that carries in its wake the violation of the entire Torah or all Ten Commandments. Idolatry is that one. And that is what defines gentiles, that is, the whole of humanity that does not know God.

To state matters in more general terms: in the theology of the Oral Torah, the category of the gentiles or the nations, without elaborate differentiation, encompasses all who are not-Israelites, that is, who do not belong to Israel and therefore do not know and serve God. That category takes on meaning only as complement and opposite to its generative counterpart, having no standing – self-defining characteristics – on its own. That is, since Israel encompasses the sector of humanity that knows and serves God by reason of God's self-manifestation in the Torah, the gentiles are comprised by every-body else: those placed by their own intention and active decision beyond the limits of God's revelation. Guided by the Torah, Israel worships God; without its illumination, gentiles worship idols. At the outset, therefore, the main point registers: by "gentiles" the sages understand God's enemies, and by "Israel" the sages understand those who know God as God has made himself known, which is, through the Torah. In no way do we deal with secular categories, but with theological ones.

This formulation of matters yields the proposition that those who hate Israel hate God, those who hate God hate Israel, and God will ultimately vanquish Israel's enemies as his own – just as God, too, was redeemed from Egypt. That matter of logic is stated in so many words:

SIFRÉ TO NUMBERS LXXXIV:IV:

1. A. "... and let them that hate you flee before you:"

B. And do those who hate [come before] him who spoke and brought the world into being?

C. The purpose of the verse at hand is to say that whoever hates Israel is as if he hates him who spoke and by his word brought the world into being.

The same proposition is reworked. God can have no adversaries, but gentile enemies of Israel act as though they were his enemies:

D. Along these same lines: "In the greatness of your majesty you overthrow your adversaries" (Ex. 15:7).

E. And are there really adversaries before him who spoke and by his word brought the world into being? But Scripture thus indicates that whoever rose up against Israel is as if he rose up against the Omnipresent.

F. Along these same lines: "Do not forget the clamour of your foes, the uproar of your adversaries, which goes up continually" (Ps. 74:23).

G. "For lo, your enemies, O Lord" (Ps. 92:10).

H. "For those who are far from you shall perish, you put an end to those who are false to you" (Ps. 73:27)

I. "For lo, your enemies are in tumult, those who hate you have raised their heads" (Ps. 83:2). On what account? "They lay crafty plans against your people, they consult together against your protected ones" (Ps. 83:3).

Israel hates God's enemies, and Israel is hated because of its loyalty to God (a matter to which we shall return presently):

J. "Do I not hate those who hate you, O Lord? And do I not loathe them that rise up against you? I hate them with perfect hatred, I count them my enemies" (Ps. 139:21–2)

K. And so too Scripture says, "For whoever lays hands on you is as if he lays hands on the apple of his eye" (Zech. 2:12).

L. R. Judah says, "What is written is not, 'the apple of an eye' but 'the apple of *his* eye,' it is as if Scripture speaks of him above, but Scripture has used an euphemism."

Now the consequences of these propositions are drawn:

V. And whoever gives help to Israel is as if he gives help to him who spoke and by his word brought the world into being, as it is said, "Curse Meroz, says the angel of the Lord, curse bitterly its inhabitants, because they came not to the help of the Lord, to the help of the Lord against the mighty" (Judges 5:23)

W. R. Simeon b. Eleazar says, "You have no more prized part of the body than the eye and Israel has been compared to it. A further comparison: if a man is hit on his head, only his eyes feel it. Accordingly, you have no more prized part of the body than the eye, and Israel has been compared to it."

X. So Scripture says, "What, my son, what, son of my womb? what, son of my vows" (Prov. 31:2).

Y. And it says, "When I was a son with my father, tender, the only one in the sight of my mother, he taught me and said to me, 'Let your heart hold fast my words' " (Prov. 4:3–4).

The propositions just now set forth find proof, also, in the facts of history, which we now assemble and form into a pattern:

Z. R. Yosé b. Eleazar says, "It is like a man who puts his finger into his eye and scratches it. As to Pharaoh, who laid hands on you, what did I do to him? 'The chariots of Pharaoh and his host sank into the sea' (Ex. 15:4).

AA. "As to Sisera, who laid hands on you, what did I do to him? 'The stars in their courses fought against Sisera' (Judges 5:20).

BB. "As to Sennacherib, who laid hands on you, what did I do to him? 'And an angel of the Lord came forth and smote the camp of Assyria' (2 Kgs. 19:35).

CC. "As to Nebuchadnezzar, who laid hands on you, what did I do to him? 'And you shall be made to eat grass like an ox' (Dan. 4:32).

DD. "As to Haman, who laid hands on you, what did I do to him? 'And they hung him on a tree' " (Est. 8:7).

In this same context, when Israel goes into exile, God goes with them, a position to which we shall return in due course:

EE. So you find, furthermore, that so long as Israel is subjugated, it is as if the Presence of God is subjugated with them, as it is said, "And they saw the God of Israel, and there was under his feet as it were a pavement of sapphire stone, like the very heaven for clearness" (Ex. 24:10).

FF. And so Scripture says, "In all their suffering is suffering for him" (Is. 63:9).

The proposition announced at the outset is fully articulated – those who hate Israel hate God, those who are enemies of Israel are enemies of God, those who help Israel help God – and then systematically instantiated by facts set forth in Scripture. The systematic proof extends beyond verses of Scripture, with a catalogue of the archetypal enemies assembled: Pharaoh, Sisera, Sennacherib, Nebuchadnezzar, Haman. So the paradigm reinforces the initial allegation and repertoire of texts. The context, then, of all thought on Israel and the gentiles finds definition in supernatural issues and context in theology. In the Oral Torah, the sages at no point deem as merely secular the category of gentiles.

The gentiles hate Israel and therefore hate God. What accounts for the logic that links the one to the other? The answer to that question fully spells out the doctrine of the gentiles that the Oral Torah constructs, and everything else is commentary. What defines the gentiles – the lack of the Torah – explains also why their very character requires them to hate Israel, the people of the Torah. The gentiles' hatred of Israel came about because of the revelation of the Torah at Sinai:

BAVLI TRACTATE SHABBAT 9:3–4 I.45–6/89A

A. Said one of the rabbis to R. Kahana, "Have you heard the meaning of the words 'Mount Sinai'?"

B. He said to him, "The mountain on which miracles [nissim] were done for Israel."

C. "But then the name should be, Mount Nisai."

D. "Rather, the mountain on which a good omen was done for Israel."

E. "But then the name should be, Mount Simai."

F. He said to him, "So why don't you hang out at the household of R. Pappa and R. Huna b. R. Joshua, for they're the ones who really look into lore."

G. For both of them say, "What is the meaning of the name, Mount Sinai? It is the mountain from which hatred [sinah] descended for the gentiles."

The key to the entire system – the Torah – opens the lock at hand. Israel accepts the Torah, gentiles reject it, and everything follows from that single fact. Israel knows God, gentiles deny him, and relations between the two sectors of humanity are determined by that fact.

What from the late nineteenth century has called itself "anti-Semitism" finds its counterpart in the sages' conviction that the gentiles hate Israel. Whether or not gentile opinion is accurately characterized bears no consequence; the theology itself contains a logic that requires gentiles to hate Israel, and that is the point. If Israel's loyalty to the Torah and commandments accounts for the nations' hostility, then, in concrete ways, history will teach how that worked itself out:

PESIQTA DERAB KAHANA XIX:II.2–3

2. A. "Hear me when I groan, with no one to comfort me. [All my enemies, when they heard of my calamity, rejoiced at what you had done, but hasten the day you have

promised when they shall become like me]" (Lam. 2:21): Rabbis interpreted the cited verse to speak of the nations of the world:

B. "You find that when the sins of Israel made it possible for the gentiles to enter Jerusalem, they made the decree that in every place to which they would flee, they should close [the gates before them].

C. "They tried to flee to the south, but they did not let them: 'Thus says the Lord, for three transgressions of Gaza, yes for four, I will not reverse it [because they permitted an entire captivity to be carried away captive by delivering them up to Edom]' (Amos 1:6).

D. "They wanted to flee to the east, but they did not let them: 'Thus says the Lord, for three transgressions of Damascus, yes for four, I will not reverse it' (Amos 1:3).

E. "They wanted to flee to the north, but they did not let them: 'Thus says the Lord, for three transgressions of Tyre, yes for four, I will not reverse it' (Amos 1:21).

F. "They wanted to flee to the west, but they did not let them: 'The burden upon Arabia' (Is. 21:13).

Now the question arises: why do the nations shut out fleeing Israel? God asks the question, Israel answers it:

G. "Said to them the Holy One, blessed be he, 'Lo, you outraged them.'

Israel now returns the compliment:

H. "They said before Him, 'Lord of the ages, are you not the one who did it? [All my enemies, when they heard of my calamity, rejoiced at what you had done].' "

As proves remarkably common in the theological discourse of the Oral Torah, a parable then is invoked to re-frame matters:

3. A. They drew a parable. To what may the matter be compared?

B. To the case of a king who married a noble lady, and gave her instructions, saying to her: "Do not talk with your neighbours, and do not lend anything to them, and do not borrow anything from them."

C. One time she made him mad, so he drove her out and dismissed her from his palace, and she made the rounds of the households of her neighbours, but there was not a single one who would accept her.

D. The king said to her, "Lo, you outraged them."

E. She said to him, "My lord, king, are you not the one who did it? Did you not give me instructions, say to me, 'Do not talk with your neighbours, and do not lend anything to them, and do not borrow anything from them.' If I had borrowed something from them or had lent something to them, which one of them would have seen me pass through her household and not accept me in her home?"

F. That illustrates the verse: "[All my enemies, when they heard of my calamity, rejoiced] at what you had done."

We now go over the point of the parable:

G. Said Israel before the Holy One, blessed be he, "Lord of the ages, are you not the one who did this: Did you not write for us in the Torah: 'You shall not make marriages with them: your daughter you shall not give to his son, nor his daughter shall you take for your son' (Deut. 7:3).

H. "If we had taken children in marriage from them, or given children in marriage to them, which one of them would have seen a son or daughter standing in trouble and not receive him?"

I. That illustrates the verse: "[All my enemies, when they heard of my calamity, rejoiced[] at what you had done."

Thus, Israel's obedience to the Torah, its refusal to intermarry or to assimilate with the idolators, accounts for gentile hostility. It is a single coherent story that encompasses every important component of Israel's public affairs and reads the whole in a supernatural framework.

Now we return to our exploration of the implications of the logic of monotheism as the sages articulate matters. Why does the chapter of the Oral Torah's theology encompass not only Israel but its antonym? The reason is that, to reveal the justice of God, the sages must devote a considerable account to the challenge to that justice represented by gentile power and prosperity, Israel's subordination and penury. For if the story of the moral order tells about justice that encompasses all creation, the chapter of gentile rule vastly disrupts the account. Like its counterpart, the anomalies represented by the chaos of private life, to which we turn in chapter 5, gentile rule forms the point of tension, the source of conflict, attracting attention and demanding explanation. For the critical problematic inherent in the category, Israel, is that its anti-category, the gentiles, dominate. So what rationality of a world ordered through justice accounts for the world ruled by gentiles represents the urgent question to which the system must respond. And that explains why the systemic problematic focuses upon the question, how can justice be thought to order the world if the gentiles rule? That formulation furthermore forms the public counterpart to the private perplexity: how is it that the wicked prosper and the righteous suffer? The two challenges to the conviction of the rule of moral rationality – gentile hegemony, matched by the prosperity of wicked persons – match. First, let us focus upon explaining the prosperity of the gentiles, defined as idolators, and in the following chapter we take up the counterpart-dilemma provoked by the palpably dubious conviction that by rights and all rationality people get what they deserve.

The initial exposition of how things are, set forth in Genesis, tells how God made the world, recognized his failure in doing so, and corrected it. Through Abraham and Sarah a new humanity came into being, ultimately to meet God at Sinai and to record the meeting in the Torah. But then the question arises, what of the rest of humanity, the children of Noah but not of the sector of the family beginning with Abraham and Sarah, their son and grandson? The simple logic of the story responds: the rest of humanity, outside the holy family and beyond the commanding voice of Sinai, does not know God but worships idols. These are, today, the gentiles. And the gentiles, not Israel, govern the world. And how to resolve that tension imparts dynamism and movement to the story, which then is given an end, therefore also a beginning and a middle. That is Scripture's story, and that also is the story the sages tell in their own idiom and manner. Scripture resorts to a sustained narrative, such as we call "history," that proceeds from beginning to end. That is not how the sages describe and explain the world, for, as we shall see in chapter 6, they think paradigmatically rather than historically. So, to tell the same tale Scripture does, they work out their ideas in a process of category-formation, in this case, the comparison and contrast of categories and their hierarchization, terms familiar from chapter 1.

Who, speaking categorically not historically, indeed are these "non-Israelites," called gentiles ("the nations," "the peoples," and the like)? The answer is dictated by the form of the question: who exactly is a "non-Israelite"? Then the answer concerning the signified is always relative to its signifier, Israel? Within humanity-other-than-Israel, differentiation articulates itself along gross, political lines, always in relationship to Israel. If humanity is differentiated politically, it is a differentiation imposed by what has happened between a differentiated portion of humanity and Israel. It is, therefore, that segment of humanity that under given circumstances has interacted with Israel: Israel arising at the end and climax of the class of world empires, Babylonia, Media, Greece, Rome; or Israel against Egypt; or Israel against Canaan. That is the point at which Babylonia, Media, Greece, Rome, Egypt, or Canaan take a place in the narrative, become actors for the moment, but never givens, never enduring native categories. Then, when politics does not impose its structure of power-relationships, humanity is divided between Israel and everyone else.

In the story of the moral plan for creation, the nations find their proportionate position in relationship to Israel. If the nations acquire importance by reason of their dealings with Israel, the monarchies that enjoy prominence benefit because they ruled Israel:

5. A. "... the mind of Pharaoh and his servants was changed toward the people":
B. This indicates that when the Israelites went out of Egypt, the monarchy of the Egyptians came to an end,
C. as it is said, "Who are our servants?"
6. A. "[and they said, 'What is this that we have done, that we have let Israel go] from serving us?' "
B. "Who are our servants?"] They said, "Now all the nations of the world will be chiming in against us like a bell, saying, 'Now these, who were in their domain, they let go to leave them, how!'
C. "Now how are we going to send to Aram Naharim and Aram Soba officers and task-masters to bring us slave-boys and slave girls?"
D. This indicates that Pharaoh ruled from one end of the world to the other, having governors from one end of the world to the other.
E. This was for the sake of the honour of Israel.
F. Of Pharaoh it is said, "The king sent and loosed him, even the ruler of peoples, and set him free' " (Ps. 105:20).

We now recapitulate the matter, moving through the sequence, Assyria and then the recurring cluster of four, Babylonia, Media, Greece, and Rome, the last four standing for the world-empires to that time, the first six centuries C.E., so far as the sages' memories reconstructed history:

7. A. And so you find that every nation and language that subjugated Israel ruled from one end of the world to the other, for the sake of the honour of Israel.
B. What does Scripture say in connection with Assyria? "And my hand has found as a nest the riches of the peoples, and as one gathers lost eggs have I gathered all the earth, and there was none that moved the wing or opened the mouth or chirped" (Is. 10:14).
C. What does Scripture say of Babylonia? "And it shall come to pass that the nation and kingdom that will not serve this same Nebuchadnezzar, king of Babylonia" (Jer. 27:8).
D. What does Scripture say of Media? "Then king Darius wrote to all the peoples" (Dan. 6:26).
E. What does Scripture say of Greece? "The beast had also four heads and dominion was given to it" (Dan. 7:6).

F. What does Scripture say of the fourth kingdom [Rome]? "And shall devour the whole earth and shall tread it down and break it in pieces" (Dan. 7:23).
G. So you learn that every nation and language that subjugated Israel ruled from one end of the world to the other, for the sake of the honor of Israel.

A nation is distinguished by its interaction with Israel, and that interaction brings about the magnification of the name of that nation. It would be difficult to express with greater power the proposition that Israel forms the centre and heart of humanity, and the gentiles circle in their orbits round about.

What, then, is the difference between the gentile and the Israelite, individually and collectively (there being no distinction between the private person and the public, social and political entity)? A picture in cartographic form of the theological anthropology[1] of the Oral Torah would portray a many-coloured Israel at the centre of the circle, with the perimeter comprised by all-white gentiles, since, in the *halakhah*, gentiles are a source of uncleanness; of the same virulence as corpse-uncleanness, the perimeter would be an undifferentiated white, the colour of death. The law of uncleanness bears its theological counterpart in the lore of death and resurrection, a single theology animating both. As we shall see in chapter 14, gentile-idolators and Israelite worshippers of the one and only God part company at death. Israelites die and rise from the grave, gentiles die and remain there. The roads intersect at the grave, each component of humanity taking its own path beyond. Israelites – meaning those possessed of right conviction – will rise from the grave, stand in judgment (along with some gentiles, as we shall see in a moment), but then enter upon eternal life, to which no one else will enjoy access. So, in substance, humanity viewed whole is divided between those who get a share in the world to come – Israel – and who will stand when subject to divine judgment and those who will not.

These are extreme propositions. How do the sages say what I impute to them, which is, to be Israel is to live forever, and to be gentile is to die once and for all time, so that, at the end of days God will save Israel and destroy idolatry? Here is one such formulation:

BAVLI TRACTATE ABODAH ZARAH I:I I:7–8, 10/4A

I.7 A. R. Hinena bar Pappa contrasted verses of Scripture: "It is written, 'As to the almighty, we do not find him exercising plenteous power' (Job 37:23), but by contrast, 'Great is our Lord and of abundant power' (Ps. 147:5), and further, 'Your right hand, Lord, is glorious in power' (Ex. 15:6).

1. The systematic exposition of theological anthropology comes in chapter 9.

B. "But there is no contradiction between the first and second and third statements, for the former speaks of the time of judgment [when justice is tempered with mercy, so God does not do what he could] and the latter two statements refer to a time of war [of God against his enemies]."

I.8 A. R. Hama bar Hanina contrasted verses of Scripture: "It is written, 'Fury is not in me' (Isa. 27:4) but also 'The Lord revenges and is furious' (Nah. 1:2).

B. "But there is no contradiction between the first and second statements, for the former speaks of Israel, the latter of the gentiles."

C. R. Hinena bar Pappa said, " 'Fury is not in me' (Isa. 27:4), for I have already taken an oath: 'would that I had not so vowed, then as the briars and thorns in flame would I with one step burn it altogether.' "

I.10 A. That is in line with what Raba said, "What is the meaning of the verse, 'Howbeit he will not stretch out a hand for a ruinous heap though they cry in his destruction' (Job 30:24)?

B. "Said the Holy One, blessed be he, to Israel, 'When I judge Israel, I shall not judge them as I do the gentiles, for it is written, "I will overturn, overturn, overturn it" (Ezek. 21:32), rather, I shall exact punishment from them as a hen pecks.'

C. "Another matter: 'Even if the Israelites do not carry out a religious duty before me more than a hen pecking at a rubbish heap, I shall join together [all the little pecks] into a great sum: "although they pick little they are saved" (Job 30:24)

So I cannot over-stress the given on which all else is built: to be a gentile is to practice idolatry and to die, and to be Israel is to serve the one true God and to rise from the grave. That principle governs throughout. Everything else flows from it, and, in due course we shall see, upon that basis the present condition of the world is shown to cohere with the principle of the moral order of justice that prevails.

How does this conviction, already adumbrated in my definition of Israel in Chapter 3, play itself out? That the world to come opens before Israel is explicit, as in the opening statement of the Mishnah-treatise on the subject, Mishnah-tractate Sanhedrin 11:1A: "All Israelites have a share in the world to come, as it is said, 'Your people also shall be all righteous, they shall inherit the land forever; the branch of my planting, the work of my hands, that I may be glorified'" (Is. 60:21). But in that very context, we recall, not even all Israel enters in. The ones who do not find definition in the logic of the Oral Torah viewed whole: those who deny the normative principles of the faith – that the Torah comes from Heaven, that the teaching of the resurrection of the dead derives from the Torah – lose out, for by their own word they do not know God, so, while remaining Israel, join the gentiles before the very gate of the world to come. So too the principle of measure for measure furthermore applies: those who deny resurrection as a principle of the Torah – the sole source of truth so far as the sages are concerned – also do not get it.

This brings us from the principles to the details of the sages' theology of the gentiles. What specifically do we know in the Torah about the gentiles? First, all those prior to Noah simply are wiped out, do not get a share in the world to come, and do not stand in judgment. As to those after the flood, while they have no share in the world to come, they will stand in judgment. Justified, they still do not enter the world to come:

MISHNAH-TRACTATE SANHEDRIN 11:3A–CC

A. The Generation of the Flood has no share in the world to come,

B. and they shall not stand in the judgment,

C. since it is written, "My spirit shall not judge with man forever" (Gen. 6:3)

D. neither judgment nor spirit.

Once the Generation of the Flood enters, it draws in its wake the generation of the dispersion and the men of Sodom:

E. The Generation of the Dispersion has no share in the world to come,

F. since it is said, "So the Lord scattered them abroad from there upon the face of the whole earth" (Gen. 11:8).

G. "So the Lord scattered them abroad" – in this world,

H. "and the Lord scattered them from there" – in the world to come.

I. The men of Sodom have no portion in the world to come,

J. since it is said, "Now the men of Sodom were wicked and sinners against the Lord exceedingly" (Gen. 13:13)

K. "Wicked" – in this world,

L. "And sinners" – in the world to come.

M. But they will stand in judgment.

N. R. Nehemiah says, "Both these and those will not stand in judgment,

O. "for it is said, 'Therefore the wicked shall not stand in judgment [108A], nor sinners in the congregation of the righteous' (Ps. 1:5)

P. 'Therefore the wicked shall not stand in judgment' – this refers to the generation of the flood.

Q. 'Nor sinners in the congregation of the righteous' – this refers to the men of Sodom."

R. They said to him, "They will not stand in the congregation of the righteous, but they will stand in the congregation of the sinners."

Now we shift to Israelite sinners, three classes of persons, with the same result: here too, some stand in judgment but will not enter the world to come. The spies who rejected the Land, the generation of the golden calf, condemned to die in the wilderness, and the party of Korah define the Israelites who lose out. They are those who rejected the restoration to the Land and so do not re-enter the land at the restoration that commences with resurrection, those who opted for an idol instead of God, and those who rejected the Torah of Moses. So these classes of Israelites match the gentiles, for they deny the three principal components of salvation and redemption: restoration, service of one God, and acceptance of the authority of the Torah of Sinai; we note that some opinion differs, but the anonymous opinion represents the consensus of the sages, as always:

S. The spies have no portion in the world to come,

T. as it is said, "Even those men who brought up an evil report of the land died by the plague before the Lord" (Num. 14:37)

U. "Died" – in this world.

V. "By the plague" – in the world to come.

W. "The generation of the wilderness has no portion in the world to come and will not stand in judgment,

X. "for it is written, 'In this wilderness they shall be consumed and there they shall die'" (Num. 14:35), The words of R. Aqiba.

Y. R. Eliezer says, "Concerning them it says, 'Gather my saints together to me, those that have made a covenant with me by sacrifice'" (Ps. 50:5).

Z. "The party of Korah is not destined to rise up,

AA. "for it is written, 'And the earth closed upon them' – in this world.

BB. "'And they perished from among the assembly' – in the world to come," the words of R. Aqiba.

CC. And R. Eliezer says, "Concerning them it says, 'The Lord kills and resurrects, brings down to Sheol and brings up again'" (1 Sam. 2:6).

The Mishnah then takes up special cases of particular classes of gentiles singled out by Scripture.

What about gentiles in general? All depends upon their own actions. Since the point of differentiation is idolatry as against worship of the one God, gentiles may enter into the category of Israel, which is to say, they recognize the one God and come to serve him. That means, whether now or later, some, perhaps many, gentiles will enter Israel, being defined as other Israelites are defined: those who worship the one and only God. The gentiles include many righteous persons. But by the end of days God will bring these to Israel:

YERUSHALMI BERAKHOT 2:8 I:2:

A. When R. Hiyya bar Adda, the nephew of Bar Qappara, died Resh Laqish accepted [condolences] on his account because he [Resh Laqish] had been his teacher. We may say that [this action is justified because] a person's student is as beloved to him as his son.

B. And he [Resh Laqish] expounded concerning him [Hiyya] this verse: "My beloved has gone down to his garden, to the bed of spices, to pasture his flock in the gardens, and to gather lilies" [Song 6:2]. It is not necessary [for the verse to mention, 'To the bed of spices']. [It is redundant if you interpret the verse literally, for most gardens have spice beds.]

C. Rather [interpret the verse as follows:] My beloved – this is God; has gone down to his garden – this is the world; to the beds of spices – this is Israel; to pasture his flock in the gardens – these are the nations of the world; and to gather lilies – these are the righteous whom he takes from their midst.

Now a parable restates the proposition in narrative terms; having chosen a different mode of discourse from the narrative one that dominates in the Authorized History, Genesis through Kings, the sages reintroduce narrative for an other-than-historical purpose, as here:

D. They offer a parable [relevant to this subject]. To what may we compare this matter [of the tragic death of his student]? A king had a son who was very beloved to him. What did the king do? He planted an orchard for him.

E. As long as the son acted according to his father's will, he would search throughout the world to seek the beautiful saplings of the world, and to plant them in his orchard. And when his son angered him he went and cut down all his saplings.

F. Accordingly, so long as Israel acts according to God's will he searches throughout the world to seek the righteous persons of the nations of the world and bring them and join them to Israel, as he did with Jethro and Rahab. And when they [the Israelites] anger him he removes the righteous from their midst.

It follows that Israel bears a heavy burden of responsibility even for the gentiles. When Israel pleases God, the righteous among the gentiles are joined to them, and when not, not. So while gentiles as such cannot inherit the world to come, they, too, can enter the status of Israel, in which case they join Israel in the world to come. And as we shall see in Chapter 14, that is precisely what the sages expect will happen.

This the gentiles will do in exactly the way that Israel attained that status to begin with, which is by knowing God through his self-manifestation in the

Torah, therefore by accepting God's rule as set forth therein. In this way the theology of the Oral Torah maintains its perfect consistency and inner logic: the Torah determines all things. That point is made explicit: If a gentile keeps the Torah, he is saved. But by keeping the Torah, the gentile has ceased to be gentile and become Israelite, worth even of the high priesthood. First comes the definition of how Israel becomes Israel, which is by accepting God's dominion in the Torah:

SIFRA CXCIV:II.I

1. A. "The Lord spoke to Moses saying, Speak to the Israelite people and say to them, I am the Lord your God":

B. R. Simeon b. Yohai says, "That is in line with what is said elsewhere: 'I am the Lord your God [who brought you out of the land of Egypt, out of the house of bondage]' (Ex. 20:2).

C. "'Am I the Lord, whose sovereignty you took upon yourself in Egypt?'

D. "They said to him, 'Indeed.'

E. "'Indeed you have accepted my dominion.'

F. "'They accepted my decrees": You will have no other gods before me.

G. "That is what is said here: 'I am the Lord your God,' meaning, 'Am I the one whose dominion you accepted at Sinai?'

H. "They said to him, 'Indeed.'

I. "'Indeed you have accepted my dominion.'

J. "'They accepted my decrees:' You shall not copy the practices of the land of Egypt where you dwelt, or of the land of Canaan to which I am taking you; nor shall you follow their laws."

I cite the passage to underscore how matters are defined, which is by appeal to the Torah. Then the true state of affairs emerges when the same definition explicitly is brought to bear upon the gentiles. That yields the clear inference that gentiles have the power to join themselves to Israel as fully naturalized Israelites, so the Torah that defines their status also constitutes the ticket of admission to the world to come that Israel will enter in due course. The sages could not be more explicit than they are when they insist that the gentile ceases to be in the status of the gentile when he accepts God's rule in the Torah:

SIFRA CXCIV:II.15

15. A. "... by the pursuit of which man shall live":

B. R. Jeremiah says, "How do I know that even a gentile who keeps the Torah, lo, he is like the high priest?

C. "Scripture says, 'by the pursuit of which man shall live.'"

D. And so he says, "'And this is the Torah of the priests, Levites, and Israelites,' is not what is said here, but rather, 'This is the Torah of the man, O Lord God'" (2 Sam. 7:19).

E. And so he says, "'open the gates and let priests, Levites, and Israelites will enter it' is not what is said, but rather, 'Open the gates and let the righteous nation, who keeps faith, enter it'" (Is. 26:2).

F. And so he says, "'This is the gate of the Lord. Priests, Levites, and Israelites ...' is not what is said, but rather, 'the righteous shall enter into it' (Ps. 118:20).

G. And so he says, "'What is said is not, 'Rejoice, priests, Levites, and Israelites,' but rather, 'Rejoice, O righteous, in the Lord'" (Ps. 33:1).

H. And so he says, "It is not, 'Do good, O Lord, to the priests, Levites, and Israelites,' but rather, 'Do good, O Lord, to the good, to the upright in heart'" (Ps. 125:4).

I. "Thus, even a gentile who keeps the Torah, lo, he is like the high priest."

That is not to suggest God does not rule the gentiles. He does – whether they like it or not, acknowledge him or not. God responds, also, to the acts of merit taken by gentiles, as much as to those of Israel. The upshot is that "gentile" and "Israel" classify through the presence or absence of the same traits; they form taxonomic categories that can in the case of the gentile change when that which is classified requires reclassification.

Here an important qualification is required. Gentiles, to be sure, may become Israel, but while they are accepted when they present themselves properly, ordinarily they are not pressed to enter the Kingdom of Heaven. The motivation must well up from within; Israelites do not encourage gentiles to become Israel, because, in this world, clear penalties attach themselves to those who accept God's rule. It is not easy to be Israel. So a gentile are not encouraged to become part of Israel, because of the rigors of such a commitment and the disadvantages incurred thereby; if he still persists, he is welcomed. This view of how, in the present age, before the time of the resurrection and the judgment, gentiles are to be dealt with is expressed in so many words as follows:

BAVLI-TRACTATE YEBAMOT 4:12 I.37/47A–B

A. Our rabbis have taught on Tannaite authority:

B. A person who comes to convert at this time – they say to him, "How come you have come to convert? Don't you know that at this time the Israelites are forsaken and harassed, despised, baited, and afflictions come upon them?" If he said, "I know full well, and I am not worthy [of sharing their suffering]," they accept him forthwith. And they inform him about some of the lesser religious duties and some of the weightier religious duties. He is informed about the sin of neglecting the religious duties involving gleanings, forgotten sheaf, corner of the field, and poorman's tithe. They further inform him about the penalty for not keeping the commandments.

The gentile has to face the reality of Israel's condition in this world, but also the expectations that the Torah imposes, the matters formerly of no concern that now become occasions for sin, for example. What the gentile thinks makes no difference, presents the gentile with the opportunity to violate God's will in the Torah.

C. They say to him, "You should know that before you came to this lot, if you ate forbidden fat, you would not be penalized by extirpation. If you violated the Sabbath, you would not be put to death through stoning. But now if you eat forbidden fat, you are punished with extirpation. If you violate the Sabbath, you are punished by stoning."

D. And just as they inform him about the penalties for violating religious duties, so they inform him about the rewards for doing them. They say to him, "You should know that the world to come is prepared only for the righteous, and Israel at this time is unable to bear [47B] either too much prosperity or too much penalty."

E. They do not press him too hard, and they do not impose too many details on him.

The door is kept open, and if the gentile accepts the condition of Israel, he is taken into the community and then instructed further:

F. If he accepted all this, they circumcise him immediately. If any shreds that render the circumcision invalid remain, they do it a second time.

G. Once he has healed, they immerse him right away.

H. And two disciples of sages supervise the process and inform him about some [more] of the lesser religious duties and some of the weightier religious duties.

I. He immerses and comes up, and lo, he is an Israelite for all purposes.

J. In the case of a woman, women sit her in the water up to hear neck, and two disciples of sages stand there for her outside, and inform her about some [more] of the lesser religious duties and some of the weightier religious duties.

Slaves are admitted into the covenant, their humanity affirmed, just like proselytes, with exactly the same result: they enter Israel and gain life. So the passage proceeds:

K. All the same are a proselyte and a freed slave.

L. And in a place in which a woman immerses a proselyte and a freed slave immerse.

M. And whatever would be deemed an invalidating interposition in the case of an immersion is deemed an invalidating interposition in the case of a proselyte and a freed slave.

This final detail bears the implication that, at the moment of baptism, all of the laws governing Israel apply to the gentile, so that the baptism itself must conform to the rules of Israelite immersion. In practical terms a door is open before the gentile, but he is not inveigled, let alone pushed, through it. The important point is that the gentiles have every opportunity to become Israel, and, when they take that opportunity, they enter Israel without any discrimination by reason of originating outside Israel.

Clearly, the moral ordering of the world encompasses all humanity. But God does not neglect the gentiles or fail to exercise dominion over them. For even now, gentiles are subject to a number of commandments or religious obligations. God cares for gentiles as for Israel, he wants gentiles as much as Israel to enter the Kingdom of Heaven, and he assigns to gentiles opportunities to evince their acceptance of his rule. One of these commandments is not to curse God's name, thus, b. San. 7:5 I.2/56a says, "Any man who curses his God shall bear his sin" (Lev. 24:15). It would have been clear had the text simply said, "A man." Why does it specify, "Any"? It serves to encompass idolators, who are admonished not to curse the Name, just as Israelites are so admonished. Not cursing God, even while worshipping idols, seems a minimal expectation. But, in fact, there are seven such religious obligations that apply to the children of Noah:

TOSEFTA-TRACTATE ABODAH ZARAH 8:4-6

A. Concerning seven religious requirements were the children of Noah admonished:
B. setting up courts of justice, idolatry, blasphemy [cursing the Name of God], fornication, bloodshed, and thievery.

We now proceed to show how each of these religious obligations is represented as applying to gentiles as much as to Israelites:

C. Concerning setting up courts of justice – how so [how does Scripture or reason validate the claim that gentiles are to set up courts of justice]?
D. Just as Israelites are commanded to call into session in their towns courts of justice.
E. Concerning idolatry and blasphemy – how so? ...
F. Concerning fornication – how so?

G. "On account of any form of prohibited sexual relationship on account of which an Israelite court inflicts the death-penalty, the children of Noah are subject to warning," the words of R. Meir.

H. And sages say, "There are many prohibited relationships, on account of which an Israelite court does not inflict the death-penalty and the children of Noah are [not] warned. In regard to these forbidden relationships the nations are judged in accord with the laws governing the nations.

I. "And you have only the prohibitions of sexual relations with a betrothed maiden alone."

The systemization of Scripture's evidence for the stated proposition continues:

8:5 A. For bloodshed – how so?

B. A gentile [who kills] a gentile and a gentile who kills an Israelite are liable. An Israelite [who kills] a gentile is exempt.

C. Concerning thievery?

D. [If] one has stolen, or robbed, and so too in the case of finding a beautiful captive [woman], and in similar cases:

E. a gentile in regard to a gentile, or a gentile in regard to an Israelite – it is prohibited. And an Israelite in regard to a gentile – it is permitted.

8:6 A. Concerning a limb cut from a living beast – how so?

B. A dangling limb on a beast, [which] is not [so connected] as to bring about healing,

C. is forbidden for use by the children of Noah, and, it goes without saying, for Israelites.

D. But if there is [in the connecting flesh] sufficient [blood supply] to bring about healing,

E. it is permitted to Israelites, and, it goes without saying, to the children of Noah.

As in the case of Israelites, so the death penalty applies to a Noahide. So b. San. 7:5 I.4–5/57a: "On account of violating three religious duties are children of Noah put to death: on account of adultery, murder, and blasphemy." R. Huna, R. Judah, and all the disciples of Rab say, "On account of seven commandments a son of Noah is put to death. The All-Merciful revealed that fact of one of them, and the same rule applies to all of them." But just as Israelites, educated in the Torah, are assumed to exhibit certain uniform virtues, for example, forbearance, so gentiles, lacking that same education, are assumed to conform to a different model.

Just as the sages define Israel in the abstract terms of their relationship to God, but also impute to Israel certain traits they are deemed to hold in common, so they view gentiles. Gentiles, by reason of their condition outside the Torah, are characterized by certain traits natural to their situation, and these are worldly. Not only so, but the sages' theology of gentiles shapes the normative law on how to relate to them. If an Israelite is by nature forbearing and forgiving, the gentile by nature is ferocious. Gentiles are always suspect of the cardinal sins, bestiality, fornication, and bloodshed, as well as constant idolatry. That view of matters is embodied in normative law:

MISHNAH-TRACTATE ABODAH ZARAH 2:1A-F

A. They do not leave cattle in gentiles' inns,
B. because they are suspect in regard to bestiality.
C. And a woman should not be alone with them,
D. because they are suspect in regard to fornication.
E. And a man should not be alone with them,
F. because they are suspect in regard to bloodshed.

The law of the Mishnah corresponds to the lore of scriptural exegesis; the theory of the gentiles governs in both. Beyond the Torah there not only is no salvation from death, there is not even the possibility of a common decency. The upshot may be stated simply. Israel and the gentiles form the two divisions of humanity. The one will die but rise from the grave to eternal life with God. The other will not.

The gentiles thus sustain comparison and contrast with Israel, the point of ultimate division being death for the one, eternal life for the other. If Israel and the gentiles are deemed comparable, the gentiles do not acknowledge or know God, and therefore, while they are like Israelites in sharing a common humanity by reason of mythic genealogy – deriving from Noah – the gentiles do not receive in a meritorious manner the blessings that God bestows upon them. God blesses the gentiles, but they do not respond properly. God gives the gentiles prophets, but the prophets to the gentiles do not measure up. So God favours the gentiles with blessings and with prophets. Not only so, but each party to humanity, Israel and the gentiles, forms its own piety as well. But with what result!

Now let us see how the gentiles are characterized in this-worldly terms, as we have noted how "being Israel" is assumed to mean that a given set of virtues will mark the Israelite individual. When God blesses gentile nations, they do not acknowledge him but blaspheme, but when he blesses Israel, they glorify him and bless him; these judgments elaborate the basic principle that the gentiles do not know God, and Israel does. But what emerges here is that even when the gentiles ought to recognize God's hand in their affairs, even when God blesses them, they still deny him, turning ignorance into willfulness. What is striking is the exact balance of three gentiles as against three Israelites, all of the status of world-rulers, the common cluster, Pharaoh, Sennacherib, Nebuchadnezzar, versus the standard cluster, David, Solomon, and Daniel:

PESIQTA DERAB KAHANA XXVIII:I.I

A. "On the eighth day you shall have a solemn assembly. [You shall do no laborious work, but you shall offer a burnt-offering, an offering by fire, a pleasing odour to the Lord ... These you shall offer to the Lord at your appointed feasts in addition to your votive-offerings and your freewill-offerings, for your burnt-offerings and for your cereal-offerings and for your drink-offerings and for your peace-offerings]" (Numbers 29:35–9):
B. But you have increased the nation, "O Lord, you have increased the nation; [you are glorified; you have enlarged all the borders of the land]" (Is. 17:25).

The proposition having been stated, the composer proceeds to amass evidence for the two contrasting propositions, first gentile rulers:

C. You gave security to the wicked Pharaoh. Did he then call you "Lord"? Was it not with blasphemies and curses that he said, "Who is the Lord, that I should listen to his voice" (Ex. 5:2)!
D. You gave security to the wicked Sennacherib. Did he then call you "Lord"? Was it not with blasphemies and curses that he said, "Who is there among all the gods of the lands ..." (2 Kgs. 18:35).
E. You gave security to the wicked Nebuchadnezzar. Did he then call you "Lord"? Was it not with blasphemies and curses that he said, "And who is God to save you from my power" (Dan. 3:15).

Now, nicely balanced, come Israelite counterparts:

F. "... you have increased the nation; you are glorified":
G. You gave security to David and so he blessed you: "David blessed the Lord before all the congregation" (1 Chr. 29:10).
H. You gave security to his son, Solomon, and so he blessed you: "Blessed is the Lord who has given rest to his people Israel" (1 Kgs. 8:56).
I. You gave security to Daniel and so he blessed you: "Daniel answered and said, Blessed be the name of God" (Dan. 2:20).

Here is another set of opposites – three enemies, three saints, a fair match. In each case, the Israelite responded to God's favour with blessings, and the gentile with blasphemy. In this way the gentiles show the price they pay for not knowing God but serving no-gods instead.

But perhaps gentiles may exculpate themselves by the claim that they have had no access to God's instructions, through the Torah and through prophecy, such as Israel has enjoyed. The sages address that claim and reject it. Gentiles are not deprived of direct communication with God, which, like Israel, takes place through prophets. Both Israel and gentiles are accorded access to God through prophecy. What is the difference between the prophets of Israel and those of the nations? The comparison and contrast, through the same taxonomic categories, of the two classes of prophets yield a clear result:

GENESIS RABBAH LII:V.1FF.=LEVITICUS
RABBAH I:XIII.1

1. A. "But God came to Abimelech in a dream by night [and said to him, 'Behold, you are a dead man, because of the woman whom you have taken, for she is a man's wife']" (Gen. 20:3):

B. What is the difference between the prophets of Israel and those of the nations?

C. R. Hama b. R. Haninah said, "The Holy One, blessed be he, is revealed to the prophets of the nations of the world only in partial speech, in line with the following verse of Scripture: 'And God called Balaam' (Num. 23:16). [Lev. R. I:XIII.1.C adds: On the other hand, he reveals himself to the prophets of Israel in full and complete speech, as it is said, 'And the Lord called (WYR') to Moses'" (Lev. 1:1).]

D. Said R. Issachar of Kepar Mandi, "[Lev. R. I:XIII.1.D adds: Should that prophecy, even in partial form, be paid to them as their wage? Surely not, in fact that is no form of speech to gentile prophets, who are frauds.] The connotation of the language, 'And God called to Balaam' (Num. 23:16) is solely unclean. That is in line with the usage in the following verse of Scripture: 'That is not clean, by that which happens by night' (Deut. 23:11). [So the root is the same, with the result that YQR at Num. 23:16 does not bear the meaning of God's calling to Balaam. God rather declares Balaam unclean.]

E. "But the prophets of Israel are addressed in language of holiness, purity, clarity, in language used by the ministering angels to praise God. That is in line with the following verse of Scripture: 'And they called one to another and said, "Holy, holy, holy is the Lord of hosts"'" (Is. 6:3).

The first comparison yields the point that gentile prophets do not receive a clear vision, Israelite ones do. The second comparison places gentile prophets far from God; their prophecy takes place by night:

2. A. R. Yosé said, " 'The Lord is far from the evil, but the prayer of the righteous does he hear' (Prov. 5:29).

B. " 'The Lord is far from the wicked' refers to the prophets of the nations of the world.

C. " 'But the prayer of the righteous does he hear' refers to the prophets of Israel.

3. A. R. Yosé b. Bibah said, "The Holy One, blessed be he, appears to the prophets of the nations of the world only by night, when people take leave of one another: 'Now a word was secretly brought to me … at the time of leave-taking, from the visions of the night, when deep sleep falls on men' " (Job 4:12–13).

Gentile prophets also do not have the power to pray with good effect, Israelite ones do:

4. A. Said R. Eleazar b. Menahem, " 'The Lord is far from the evil' (Prov. 5:29) refers to the prophets of the nations of the world.

B. " 'But the prayer of the righteous does he hear' (Prov. 5:29) speaks of the prophets of Israel.

C. "You furthermore find that the Holy One, blessed be he, appears to the prophets of the nations of the world only like a man who comes from some distant place. That is in line with the following verse of Scripture: 'From a distant land they have come to me, from Babylonia' (Is. 39:3).

D. "But in the case of the prophets of Israel, he is always near at hand: 'And he appeared [not having come from a great distance]' (Gen. 18:1). 'And the Lord called' (Lev. 1:1).' [These usages bear the sense that he was right nearby.]"

Predictably in theological discourse, a parable then restates the main propositional point but now in narrative form:

5. A. What is the difference between the prophets of Israel and those of the nations?

B. R. Hinena said, "The matter may be compared to a king who, with his friend, was in a hall, with a curtain hanging down between them. When the king speaks to his friend, he turns back the curtain and speaks to his friend."

C. And rabbis say, "The matter may be compared to the case of a king who had a wife and a concubine. When he walks about with his wife, he does so in full public view. When he walks about with his concubine, he does so discreetly. So too, the Holy One, blessed be he, is revealed to the prophets of the nations only at night,

D. "in line with that which is written: 'And God came to Balaam at night' (Num. 22:20). 'And God came to Laban the Aramean in a dream of the night' (Gen. 31:24). 'And God came to Abimelech in a dream by night' " (Gen. 19:3).

Here is a standard mode of analysis: the comparison and contrast of facts, whether those of Scripture or those gained through observation of the everyday world. The comparison between the description of Balaam, the gentiles' prophet, and Moses and his fellows, who stand for Israel, is then systematic and detailed, and the same categories pertain throughout, yielding contrasting results. Then a parable is invoked to go over the same point and convey it in narrative form.

That brings us, finally, to contrasts in the matter of piety. Israel worships God, gentiles serve their idols. Israel's piety pleases God and saves the world, while the gentiles' impiety so outrage him as to make him consider destroying it.

SONG OF SONGS RABBAH CXV:II.3

3. A. "Make haste, my beloved:"

B. Said R. Levi, "The matter may be compared to the case of a king who made a banquet and invited guests. Some of them ate and drank and said a blessing to the king, but some of them ate and drank and cursed the king.

C. "The king realized it and considered making a public display at his banquet and disrupting it. But the matron [queen] came and defended them, saying to him, 'My lord, O king, instead of paying attention to those who ate and drank and cursed you, take note of those who ate and drank and blessed you and praised your name.'

D. "So is the case with Israel: when they eat and drink and say a blessing and praise and adore the Holy One, blessed be he, he listens to their voice and is pleased. But when the nations of the world eat and drink and blaspheme and curse the Holy One, blessed be he, with their fornications of which they make mention, at that moment the Holy One, blessed be he, gives thought even to destroy his world.

E. "But the Torah comes along and defends them, saying, 'Lord of the world, instead of taking note of these, who blaspheme and spite you, take note of Israel, your people, who bless and praise and adore your great name through the Torah and through song and praise.'

F. "And the Holy Spirit cries out, 'Make haste, my beloved: flee from the nations of the world and cleave to the Israelites.' "

Here is yet another way of saying the same simple thing, which is that the division of humanity into two parts yields God's party and the party of God's enemies.

Having seen how the division of humanity into Israelites and gentiles is spelled out in principle, we have now to ask about the basis for the division. Like philosophers, the sages in the documents of the Oral Torah appeal to a single cause to account for diverse phenomena; the same factor that explains Israel has also to account for the opposite, that is, the gentiles; what Israel has, gentiles lack, and that common point has made all the difference. Idolatry is what angers God and turns him against the gentiles, a point stated in so many words at b. A.Z. 1:1 I.23/4b: "That time at which God gets angry comes when the kings put on their crowns on their heads and prostrate themselves to the sun. Forthwith the Holy One, blessed be He, grows angry." That is why it is absolutely forbidden to conduct any sort of commerce with gentiles in connection with occasions of idolatrous worship, such as festivals and the like. So M. A.Z. 1:1 states, "Before the festivals of gentiles for three days it is forbidden to do business with them, (1) to lend anything to them or to borrow anything from them, (2) to lend money to them or to borrow money from them, (3) to repay them or to be repaid by them." Gentiles' deeds – idolatry, rejection of God – and not their genealogy are what define them as non-Israel. Proving that point is critical to this account of the theological anthropology of the Oral Torah.

Nothing intrinsic distinguishes Israel from the gentiles, only their attitudes and actions. Opinion coalesces around the proposition that Israel and the gentiles do form a single genus, speciated by the relationship to God and the Torah. So, in the end, a ferocious Israelite or a forbearing gentile represent mere anomalies, not categorical imperatives. Sufficient proof derives from the explicit statement that, when Israel acts like gentiles, it enters the classification of gentiles; if Israel conducts itself like the gentiles, Israel will be rejected and punished as were the gentiles, with special reference to Egypt and Canaan. This matter is spelled out in another formally-perfect composition:

SIFRA CXCIII:I.1–11

1. B. "The Lord spoke to Moses saying, Speak to the Israelite people and say to them, I am the Lord your God":
C. "I am the Lord," for I spoke and the world came into being.
D. "I am full of mercy."
E. "I am Judge to exact punishment and faithful to pay recompense."
F. "I am the one who exacted punishment from the generation of the Flood and the men of Sodom and Egypt, and I shall exact punishment from you if you act like them."

First comes Egypt:

2. A. And how do we know that there was never any nation among all of the nations that practiced such abominations, more than did the Egyptians?
B. Scripture says, "You shall not copy the practices of the land of Egypt where you dwelt."

C. And how do we know that the last generation did more abhorrent things than all the rest of them?

D. Scripture says, "You shall not copy the practices of the land of Egypt."

E. And how do we know that the people in the last location in which the Israelites dwelt were more abhorrent than all the rest?

F. Scripture says, "... where you dwelt, you shall not do."

G. And how do we know that the fact that the Israelites dwelt there was the cause for all these deeds?

H. Scripture says, "You shall not copy...where you dwelt."

Now we deal with the Canaanites, following the given form:

3. A. How do we know that there was never a nation among all the nations that did more abhorrent things than the Canaanites?

B. Scripture says, "You shall not copy the practices ... of the land of Canaan [to which I am taking you; nor shall you follow their laws]."

C. And how do we know that the last generation did more abhorrent things than all the rest of them?

D. Scripture says, "You shall not copy the practices of the land of Canaan."

E. And how do we know that the people in the place to which the Israelites were coming for conquest were more abhorrent than all the rest?

F. Scripture says, "... to which I am taking you."

G. And how do we know that it is the arrival of the Israelites that caused them to do all these deeds?

H. Scripture says, "or of the land of Canaan to which I am taking you; nor shall you follow their laws."

The two cases are expounded in the same terms, and the specific type of laws that Israel is not to follow is defined:

7. A. If "You shall not copy the practices of the land of Egypt ... or of the land of Canaan ..."

B. might one think that they are not to build their buildings or plant vineyards as they did?

C. Scripture says, "nor shall you follow their laws":

D. "I have referred only to the rules that were made for them and for their fathers and their fathers' fathers."

E. And what would they do?

F. A man would marry a man, and a woman would marry a woman, a man would marry a woman and her daughter, a woman would be married to two men.

G. That is why it is said, "nor shall you follow their laws."

8. A. ["My rules alone shall you observe and faithfully follow my laws":]

B. "my rules": this refers to laws.

C. "... my laws": this refers to the amplifications thereof.

D. "... shall you observe": this refers to repeating traditions.

E. "... and faithfully follow": this refers to concrete deed.

F. "... and faithfully follow my laws": it is not the repetition of traditions that is the important thing but doing them is the important thing.

At stake in differentiating Israel from the gentiles is life in the world to come; the gentiles offer only death:

9. A. "You shall keep my laws and my rules, by the pursuit of which man [shall live]":

B. This formulation of matter serves to make keeping and doing into laws, and keeping and doing into rules.

10. A. "... shall live":

B. in the world to come.

C. And should you wish to claim that the reference is to this world, is it not the fact that in the end one dies?

D. Lo, how am I to explain, "... shall live"?

E. It is with reference to the world to come.

11. A. "I the Lord am your God":

B. faithful to pay a reward.

Here we find the entire doctrine of the gentiles fully exposed. God judges Israel and the gentiles by a single rule of justice; to each is meted out measure for measure. Israel is not elect by reason of privilege; Israel is elect solely because Israel accepts the Torah and so knows God. The same punishment exacted from the generation of the Flood, the Sodomites, the Egyptians, and all others will be exacted from Israel if Israel acts like them. At that point, Israel becomes gentile. It is the Torah that differentiates. And, at the end, the stakes are exactly what the reading of Mishnah-tractate Sanhedrin 10:1–2 sets forth implicitly: entry into the world to come, as we noted earlier.

Since, we note time and again, the generative transaction involves intention and attitude, which form the source of the system's dynamism, as we shall see in chapter 10, we cannot find surprising the focus, here too, upon intention. It is, specifically, upon how the idolator regards matters, rather than upon what he actually has done in making and worshipping the idol. The attitude of the idolator governs God's disposition of matters. God hates idolators more than he hates the idol itself, for, all parties concur, in any case there is no substance in idolatry itself. The idolator rejects God and so makes the idol. So what is at issue in idolatry is the attitude of the idolator, that is, his rejection of the one true God, made manifest in the Torah. The idolator by his attitude and intention confers upon the idol a status that, on its own the idol cannot attain, being inanimate in any event. So the logic that governs distinguishes the actor from the acted upon, the cause from that which is caused, and the rest follows.

What is striking in the formulations to follow is the repeated resort, for probative arguments, to parables. The framer of the compositions in the composite appeals not to proof-texts of Scripture, for Scripture's evidence is not accepted at face value by the idolator who is the debating partner. Hence only evidence in a form that both parties can accept is adduced, and that takes the form of parables, deemed self-evidently valid responses. Then the argument concerns the pertinence of the analogy out of which the parable's narrative is spun.

BAVLI TRACTATE ABODAH ZARAH 4:6 I.2FF./54B-55A:

I.2 A. A philosopher asked Rabban Gamaliel, "It is written in your Torah, 'For the Lord your God is a devouring fire, a jealous God' (Deut. 4:24). How come he is more jealous against the worshippers of the idol than against the idol itself?"

B. He said to him, "I shall give you a parable. To what is the matter to be compared? To a mortal king who had a single son, and this son raised a dog for himself, which he called by his father's name, so that, whenever he took an oath, he exclaimed, 'By the life of this dog, my father!' When the king heard, with whom was he angry? Was he angry with the son, or what he angry with the dog? One has to say it was with the son that he was angry."

At this point the question of the substantiality of the idol emerges; the debate to this point is framed to presuppose the sages' position. Now we ask how one can dismiss the power of idols in their own right:

C. [The philosopher] said to him, "Are you going to call the idol a dog? But there is some substance to it."

D. He said to him, "What makes you say so?"

E. He said to him, "One time a fire broke out in our town and the entire town burned up, but that temple was not burned up."

F. He said to him, "I shall give you a parable. To what is the matter to be compared? To a mortal king against whom one of the provinces rebelled. When he makes war, with whom does he do it? With the living or with the dead? You must say it is with the living he makes war."

G. He said to him, "So you're just calling it names – a dog, a corpse. In that case, then let him just destroy it out of the world."

If God exercises so much power, then why not simply wipe out idolatry? Here we once more ask a fundamental question, which receives a reasonable response:

H. He said to him, "If people worshipped something of which the world had no need, he certainly would wipe it away. But lo, people worship the sun, moon, stars, and planets, brooks and valleys. Now do you think he is going to wipe out his world because of idiots?

I. "And so Scripture says, [55A] 'Am I utterly to consume all things from off the face of the ground, says the Lord, am I to consume man and beast, am I to consume the bird of the heaven and the fish of the sea, even the stumbling blocks of the wicked' (Zeph. 1:2).

J. "Now simply because the wicked stumble on account of these things, is he going to destroy them from the world? Don't they also worship the human being, 'so am I to cut off man from off the face of the ground'?"

Nonetheless, Scripture itself attests to God's own recognition of the substantiality of idolatry. He is jealous of idolatry, and that shows he himself concedes that idols compete. In the same line of questions figures, also, the possibility that idols do some good. As before, the argument is framed through parables.

I.3 A. General Agrippa asked Rabban Gamaliel, "It is written in your Torah, 'For the Lord your God is a devouring fire, a jealous God' (Deut. 4:24). Is there jealousy, except on the part of a sage for another sage, on the part of a great athlete for another great athlete, on the part of a wealthy man for another wealthy man?"

B. He said to him, "I shall give you a parable. To what is the matter to be compared? To a man who married a second wife. If she is more important than she, she will not be jealous of her. If she is less than she, she will be jealous of her."

So much for the matter of gentile idolatry: to be a gentile means to be an idolator.

But cannot idolators point to the great deeds of their gods in their temples? We turn now to concrete cases in which both parties concede something happens in a temple of an idol, whether healing or some other sort of supernatural event. The first of the two cases involves a rather complex parable. In the second, since the sages form the conversation, texts of Scripture are introduced and accepted as self-evident proof.

I.4 A. Zeno asked R. Aqiba, "In my heart and in your heart we both know that there is no substance whatsoever in idolatry. But lo, we see people go into a shrine crippled and come out cured. How come?"

B. He said to him, "I shall give you a parable. To what is the matter to be compared? To a reliable person who was in a town, and all the townsfolk would deposit their money into his care without witnesses. One man came and left a deposit in his charge with witnesses, but once he forgot and left his deposit without witnesses. The wife of the reliable man said to him, 'Come, let us deny it.' He said to her, 'Because this idiot acted improperly, shall we destroy our good name for reliability?' So it is with troubles. When they send them upon a person, they are made to take the oath, 'You shall come upon him only on such-and-such a day, and you shall depart from him only on such-and-such a day, and at such-and-such an hour, through the medium of so-and-so, with such-and-such a remedy.' When it is time for them to take their leave, it just happened that the man went to a temple of an idol. So the afflictions plea, 'It is right and proper that we not leave him and go our way, but because this fool acts as he does, are we going to break our oath?' "

From the parable, we turn to concrete cases in the everyday world:

I.5 A. Raba b. R. Isaac said to R. Judah, "There is a temple to an idol in our locale. When there is need for rain, the idol appears in a dream and says to them, 'Kill someone for me and I shall bring rain.' So they kill someone for her, and she brings rain."

B. He said to him, "If I were dead, no one could tell you this statement which Rab said, 'What is the meaning of the verse of Scripture, "... which the Lord your God has divided to all the peoples under the whole heaven" (Deut. 4:19)? [Since the letters of the word "divided" may be read as "smooth," the verse means this:] this teaches that he made them smooth talkers, so as to banish them from the world."

C. That is in line with what R. Simeon b. Laqish said, "What is the meaning of the verse of Scripture, 'Surely he scorns the scorners, but he gives grace to the lowly' (Prov. 3:34)? If someone comes along to make himself unclean, they open the gate for him. If he comes along to purify himself, they also help him do so."

To summarize: the rationality of God's attitudes requires explanation. He despises idolators more than the idol because the idolators act as though there were substance to the idol. He does not concede any substance to the idol and therefore bears the object no special malice. God does not destroy things gentiles worship, since that would prove disproportionate.

Now to revert to the main thesis concerning the character of the theology of the Oral Torah that I set forth in chapter 1: the world order is defined by rationality, which finds its substance in the rule of justice. Then the moral order of justice enters at just this point. Having established that idolators subject themselves to God's hatred by reason of their attitudes and consequent actions, we ask about the matter of fairness. To explain matters, we turn to an account of how things came about – a reason we should call historical but the sages would classify as paradigmatic. That is, the sages' explanation, framed in terms of a narrative of something that happened, turns out to be a picture of how things now are – a characterization of the established facts as these are realized under all circumstances and at any time, the tenses, past, present, or future, making no difference. So when we ask, why to begin with have gentiles entered the category of death, and why is it just that they should not enjoy life eternal? we take up a tale that casts in mythic-narrative form what constitutes an analysis of characteristic traits. Not only so, but the narrative explicitly points to the enduring traits, not a given action, to explain the enduring condition of the gentiles: that is how they are, because that is how they wish to be.

So now the question becomes urgent: how has this catastrophic differentiation imposed itself between Israel and the gentiles, such that the gentiles, for all their glory in the here and now, win for themselves the grave, while Israel, for all its humiliation in the present age, inherits the world to come? And the answer is self-evident from all that has been said: the gentiles reject God, whom they could and should have known in the Torah. They rejected the Torah, and all else followed. The proposition then moves in these simple steps:

1) Israel differs from the gentiles because Israel possesses the Torah and the gentiles do not;
2) because they do not possess the Torah, the gentiles also worship idols instead of God; and
3) therefore God rejects the gentiles and identifies with Israel.

And where do considerations of justice and fairness enter in? Here, at a critical turning, the system reaches back into its fundamental and generative conception, that the world is ordered by justice. The Oral Torah then has to demonstrate that the same justice that governs Israel and endows Israel with the Torah dictates the fate of the gentiles and denies them the Torah. And, predictably, that demonstration must further underscore the justice of the condition of the gentiles: measure for measure must play itself out especially at this point.

The gentiles deprived themselves of the Torah because they rejected it, and, showing the precision of justice, they rejected the Torah because the Torah deprived them of the very practices or traits that they deemed characteristic, essential to their being. That circularity marks the tale of how things were to begin with in fact describes how things always are; it is not historical but philosophical. The gentiles' own character, the shape of their conscience, then, now, and always, accounts for their condition – which, by an act of will, as we have noted, they can change. What they did not want, that of which they were by their own word unworthy, is denied them. And what they do want condemns them. So when each nation comes under judgment for rejecting the Torah, the indictment of each is spoken out of its own mouth, its own-self-indictment then forms the core of the matter. Given what we know about the definition of Israel as those destined to live and the gentile as those not, we cannot find surprising that the entire account is set in that age to come to which the gentiles are denied entry.

When they protest the injustice of the decision that takes effect just then, they are shown the workings of the moral order, as the following quite systematic account of the governing pattern explains:

BAVLI TRACTATE ABODAH ZARAH I:I I.2/2A-B:

A. R. Hanina bar Pappa, and some say, R. Simlai, gave the following exposition [of the verse, "They that fashion a graven image are all of them vanity, and their delectable things shall not profit, and their own witnesses see not nor know" (Isa. 44:9)]: "In the age to come the Holy One, blessed be he, will bring a scroll of the Torah and hold it in his bosom and say, 'Let him who has kept himself busy with it come and take his reward.' Then all the gentiles will crowd together: 'All of the nations are gathered together' (Isa. 43:9). The Holy One, blessed be he, will say to them, 'Do not crowd together before me in a mob. But let each nation enter together with [2B] its scribes, "and let the peoples be gathered together" (Isa. 43:9), and the word 'people' means 'kingdom': 'and one kingdom shall be stronger than the other' " (Gen. 25:23).

We note that the players are the principal participants in world history: the Romans first and foremost, then the Persians, the other world-rulers of the age:

C. "The kingdom of Rome comes in first."
H. "The Holy One, blessed be He, will say to them, 'How have you defined your chief occupation?'
I. "They will say before him, 'Lord of the world, a vast number of marketplaces have we set up, a vast number of bathhouses we have made, a vast amount of silver and gold have we accumulated. And all of these things we have done only in behalf of Israel, so that they may define as their chief occupation the study of the Torah.'

J. "The Holy One, blessed be he, will say to them, 'You complete idiots! Whatever you have done has been for your own convenience. You have set up a vast number of marketplaces to be sure, but that was so as to set up whorehouses in them. The bathhouses were for your own pleasure. Silver and gold belong to me anyhow: "Mine is the silver and mine is the gold, says the Lord of hosts" (Hag. 2:8). Are there any among you who have been telling of "this," and "this" is only the Torah: "And this is the Torah that Moses set before the children of Israel'" (Deut. 4:44). So they will make their exit, humiliated.

The claim of Rome – to support Israel in Torah-study – is rejected on grounds that the Romans did not exhibit the right attitude, always a dynamic force in the theology. Then the other world-ruler enters in with its claim:

K. "When the kingdom of Rome has made its exit, the kingdom of Persia enters afterward."
M. "The Holy One, blessed be he, will say to them, 'How have you defined your chief occupation?'
N. "They will say before him, 'Lord of the world, We have thrown up a vast number of bridges, we have conquered a vast number of towns, we have made a vast number of wars, and all of them we did only for Israel, so that they may define as their chief occupation the study of the Torah.'
O. "The Holy One, blessed be he, will say to them, 'Whatever you have done has been for your own convenience. You have thrown up a vast number of bridges, to collect tolls, you have conquered a vast number of towns, to collect the corvée, and, as to making a vast number of wars, I am the one who makes wars: "The Lord is a man of war" (Ex. 19:17). Are there any among you who have been telling of "this," and "this" is only the Torah: "And this is the Torah that Moses set before the children of Israel"' (Deut. 4:44). So they will make their exit, humiliated.
R. "And so it will go with each and every nation."

As native categories, Rome and Persia are singled out; "all the other nations" play no role, for reasons with which we are already familiar. Once more the theology reaches into its deepest thought on the power of intentionality, showing that what people want is what they get.

But matters cannot be limited to the two world-empires of the present age, Rome and Iran, standing in judgment at the end of time. The theology values balance, proportion, seeks complementary relationships, and therefore treats beginnings along with endings, the one going over the ground of the other. Accordingly, a recapitulation of the same event – the gentiles' rejection of the Torah – chooses as its setting not the last judgment but the first encounter, that is, the giving of the Torah itself. In the timeless world constructed by the

Oral Torah, what happens at the outset exemplifies how things always happen, and what happens at the end embodies what has always taken place. The basic thesis is identical – the gentiles cannot accept the Torah because to do so they would have to deny their very character. But the exposition retains its interest because it takes its own course.

Now the gentiles are not just Rome and Persia but others; and of special interest, the Torah is embodied in some of the ten commandments – not to murder, not to commit adultery, not to steal; then the gentiles are rejected for not keeping the seven commandments assigned to the children of Noah. The upshot is that the reason that the gentiles rejected the Torah is that the Torah prohibits deeds that the gentiles do by their very nature. The subtext here is already familiar from chapter 3: Israel ultimately is changed by the Torah, so that Israel exhibits traits imparted by their encounter with the Torah. So, too, with the gentiles: by their nature they are what they are; the Torah has not changed their nature.

Once more a single standard applies to both components of humanity, but with opposite effect:

SIFRÉ TO DEUTERONOMY CCCXLIII:IV.1FF.:

1. A. Another teaching concerning the phrase, "He said, 'The Lord came from Sinai' ":
B. When the Omnipresent appeared to give the Torah to Israel, it was not to Israel alone that he revealed himself but to every nation.
C. First of all he came to the children of Esau. He said to them, "Will you accept the Torah?"
D. They said to him, "What is written in it?"
E. He said to them, " 'You shall not murder' " (Ex. 20:13).
F. They said to him, "The very being of 'those men' [namely, us] and of their father is to murder, for it is said, 'But the hands are the hands of Esau' " (Gen. 27:22). 'By your sword you shall live' " (Gen. 27:40).

At this point we cover new ground: other classes of gentiles that reject the Torah. Now the Torah's own narrative takes over, replacing the known facts of world politics, such as the one the earlier account sets forth, and instead supplying evidence out of Scripture as to the character of the gentile group under discussion:

G. So he went to the children of Ammon and Moab and said to them, "Will you accept the Torah?"
H. They said to him, "What is written in it?"
I. He said to them, " 'You shall not commit adultery' " (Ex. 20:13).

J. They said to him, "The very essence of fornication belongs to them [us], for it is said, 'Thus were both the daughters of Lot with child by their fathers'" (Gen. 19:36).

K. So he went to the children of Ishmael and said to them, "Will you accept the Torah?"

L. They said to him, "What is written in it?"

M. He said to them, "'You shall not steal'" (Ex. 20:13).

N. They said to him, "The very essence of their [our] father is thievery, as it is said, 'And he shall be a wild ass of a man'" (Gen. 16:12).

O. And so it went. He went to every nation, asking them, "Will you accept the Torah?"

P. For so it is said, "All the kings of the earth shall give you thanks, O Lord, for they have heard the words of your mouth" (Ps. 138:4).

Q. Might one suppose that they listened and accepted the Torah?

R. Scripture says, "And I will execute vengeance in anger and fury upon the nations, because they did not listen" (Mic. 5:14).

At this point we turn back to the obligations that God has imposed upon the gentiles; these obligations have no bearing upon the acceptance of the Torah; they form part of the ground of being, the condition of existence, of the gentiles. Yet even here, the gentiles do not accept God's authority in matters of natural law:

S. And it is not enough for them that they did not listen, but even the seven religious duties that the children of Noah indeed accepted upon themselves they could not uphold before breaking them.

T. When the Holy One, blessed be he, saw that that is how things were, he gave them to Israel.

Now comes another parable, involving not a king but a common person:

2. A. The matter may be compared to the case of a person who sent his ass and dog to the threshing floor and loaded up a *letekh* of grain on his ass and three *seahs* of grain on his dog. The ass went along, while the dog panted.

B. He took a seah of grain off the dog and put it on the ass, so with the second, so with the third.

C. Thus was Israel: they accepted the Torah, complete with all its secondary amplifications and minor details, even the seven religious duties that the children of Noah could not uphold without breaking them did the Israelites come along and accept.

D. That is why it is said, "The Lord came from Sinai; he shone upon them from Seir."

Along these same lines, the gentiles would like to make a common pact with Israel, but they cannot have a share in God:

SIFRÉ TO DEUTERONOMY CCCXLIII:IX.2:

A. Thus the nations of the world would ask Israel, saying to them, " 'What is your beloved more than another beloved' (Song 5:9)? For you are willing to accept death on his account."

B. For so Scripture says, "Therefore they love you to death" (Song 1:3).

C. And further: "No, but for your sake are we killed all day long" (Ps. 44:23).

Now comes the envy of the gentiles, their desire to amalgamate with Israel, and Israel's insistence upon remaining a holy people, a people apart:

D. [The nations continue,] "All of you are handsome, all of you are strong. Come and let us form a group in common."

E. And the Israelites answer, "We shall report to you part of the praise that is coming to him, and in that way you will discern him:

F. " 'My beloved is white and ruddy ... his head is as the most fine gold ... his eyes are like doves beside the water-brooks ... his cheeks are as a bed of spices ... his hands are as rods of gold ... His legs are as pillars of marble ... His mouth is most sweet, yes, he is altogether sweet' (Song 5:10–16)."

G. When the nations of the world hear about the beauty and praiseworthy quality of the Holy One, blessed be he, they say to them, "Let us come with you."

H. For it is said, "Where has your beloved gone, O you fairest among women? Where has your beloved turned, that we may seek him with you" (Song 5:1).

Israel's is not the task of winning over the gentiles. That is God's task, and it will be done in God's own good time:

I. What do the Israelites answer them? "You have no share in him: " 'I am my beloved's and my beloved is mine, who feeds among the lilies" (Song 6:3).

The various gentile nations rejected the Torah for specific and reasonable considerations, concretely, because the Torah prohibited deeds essential to their being. This point is made in so many words, then amplified through a parable. Israel, by contrast, is prepared to give up life itself for the Torah.

So much for the gentile component of the theological anthropology of the Oral Torah.[2] Now that we have a clear picture of how humanity is constituted, we turn to the urgent question of the contemporary condition of Israel among the nations. The now-routine question, which the system identifies as

---

2. The Israelite component is set forth in chapter 9, in the framework of the correspondence of man and God.

critical, requires no elaboration: why, for all that, do the gentiles rule Israel? The answer is, that is how God has arranged matters, and at every point the divine plan to impose justice is realized. The key-proposition contains two elements: God has decided to do things in just this way, and God's plan accords with the requirements of the just governance of world order. It is the second of the two components that is elaborated, provoking the question natural to this theology: what has Israel done to deserve its punishment? And why this punishment in particular?

When we recall that, within this theology, world history orbits about Israel, we cannot find surprising that the present arrangement of world politics responds to Israel's condition, specifically, its sinfulness. The reason the gentiles rule is that Israel sinned. When Israel repents, they will regain dominion. This simple proposition comes to expression in so many words in the following statement:

ESTHER RABBAH XI:I.11

A. Said R. Aibu, "It is written, 'For the kingdom is the Lord's and he is the ruler over the nations' (Ps. 22:29).

B. "And yet you say here, 'when King Ahasuerus sat on his royal throne'?

C. "In the past dominion resigned in Israel, but when they sinned, its dominion was taken away from them and given to the nations of the world.

D. "That is in line with the following verse of Scripture: 'I will give the land over into the hand of evil men'" (Ez. 30:12).

F. [Continuing D:] "In the future, when the Israelites repent, the Holy One, blessed be he, will take dominion from the nations of the world and restore it to Israel.

G. "When will this come about? 'When saviors will come up on Mount Zion'" (Obadiah 1:21).

Israel controls its own condition, its attitude governs its own fate. Because Israel sinned, gentiles rule; when Israel by an act of will repents, then Israel will regain dominion over itself. The nations serve as instruments of God's wrath; nothing that they do comes about by their own volition, but only by consequence of Israel's. Israel is justly punished for its own sins, and its present condition demonstrates the working of God's justice. All things are foreseen, but free will is accorded to Israel, and within those two principles is located a clear and reasonable explanation for the enormous anomaly that idolators rule God's people. That turns out not anomalous but wholly coherent to the principle of the rule of justice.

But if Israel is in control, why should punishment take the particular form of subjugation to idolators? The reason is that Israel's condition responds not only to its own actions and intentions, which ought to have subjected Israel to the penalty meted out to Adam for his act of rebellion. Israel enjoys also the protection and intervention of the founders of Israel, the patriarchs. They establish the point of difference between Adam and Israel: God's intervention, his identification of the patriarchs as the means by which he will ultimately make himself known to humanity. Hence the very formation of Israel bears within itself the point of differentiation between Adam and Israel. As to the dominion of the gentiles, entailing also exile from the Land of Israel, that penalty for sin represents a choice made by Abraham. Foreseeing all that would come about through time, God set forth the four constituents of Israelite being: the gentiles, Gehenna, the sacrifices, the Torah. They formed a balance: if Israel practices the commandments and studies the Torah, they will be spared gentile rule and Gehenna; that is, they will thrive under the dominion of the Kingdom of Heaven, on the one side, and they will inherit the world to come, on the other. But God knows that Israel will sin, so, to begin with, Abraham is offered the choice of penalties. He chooses the lesser of the two penalties, the dominion of the gentiles, reserving for Israel the greater of the two alternatives, life eternal. The system at each point recapitulates its main principles. Here is how the matter is spelled out.

PESIQTA RABBATI XV [=PESIQTA DERAB KAHANA V]:II.I

1. A. "Great things have you done, O Lord my God; your wonderful purposes and plans are all for our good; [none can compare with you; I would proclaim them and speak of them, but they are more than I can tell]" (Prov. 40:5).

Now begins the process of the justification of subjugation to the nations; whatever happens happens for the good of Israel:

B. R. Hinenah bar Papa says two [teachings in respect to the cited verse]: "All those wonders and plans which you made so that our father, Abraham, would accept the subjugation of Israel to the nations were for our good, for our sake, so that we might endure in the world."
C. Simeon bar Abba in the name of R. Yohanan: "Four things did the Holy One, blessed be he, show to our father, Abraham: the Torah, the sacrifices, Gehenna, and the rule of the kingdoms.
D. "The Torah: '... and a flaming torch passed between these pieces' (Gen. 15:17).

E. "Sacrifices: 'And he said to him, Take for me a heifer divided into three parts' (Gen. 15:9).
F. "Gehenna: 'behold a smoking fire pot.'
G. "The rule of the kingdoms: 'Lo, dread, a great darkness' " (Gen. 15:12).

Here is the principal message: Torah and sacrifice preserve Israel, the subjugation to the nations and Gehenna penalize Israel for failing to maintain Torah-study and sacrifice:

H. "The Holy One, blessed be he, said to our father, Abraham, 'So long as your descendants are occupied with the former two, they will be saved from the latter two. If they abandon the former two of them, they will be judged by the other two.
I. " 'So long as they are occupied with study of the Torah and performance of the sacrifices, they will be saved from Gehenna and from the rule of the kingdoms.' "

Israel's failure is foreseen, if not foreordained, and now Abraham is offered a choice for his descendants' future:

J. " 'But [God says to Abraham] in the future the house of the sanctuary is destined to be destroyed and the sacrifices nullified. What is your preference? Do you want your children to go down into Gehenna or to be subjugated to the four kingdoms?' "

All this conformed to Abraham's wishes:

K. R. Hinena bar Pappa said, "Abraham himself chose the subjugation to the four kingdoms.
L. "What is the scriptural basis for that view? 'How should one chase a thousand and two put ten thousand to flight, except their rock had given them over' (Deut. 32:30). That statement concerning the rock refers only to Abraham, as it is said, 'Look at the rock from which you were hewn' (Is. 51:1).
M. " 'But the Lord delivered them up' (Deut. 32:30) teaches that God then approved what he had chosen."

Once more working out their own narratives in response to Scripture's, the sages now present an account of Abraham's thinking when he made the fateful choice:

2. A. R. Berekhiah in the name of R. Levi: "Now Abraham sat and puzzled all that day, saying, 'Which should I choose, Gehenna or subjugation to the kingdoms? Is the one worse than the other?'

B. "Said the Holy One, blessed be he, to him, 'Abraham, how long are you going to sit in puzzlement? Choose without delay.' That is in line with this verse: 'On that day the Lord made a covenant with Abram saying'" (Gen. 15:18).

C. What is the meaning of, saying?

D. R. Hinena bar Pappa said, "Abraham chose for himself the subjugation to the four kingdoms."

E. We have reached the dispute of R. Yudan and R. Idi and R. Hama bar Haninah said in the name of a certain sage in the name of Rabbi: "The Holy One, blessed be he, [not Abraham] chose the subjugation to the four kingdoms for him, in line with the following verse of Scripture: 'You have caused men to ride over our heads, we have been overcome by fire and water' (Ps. 66:12). That is to say, "you have made ride over our heads various nations, and it is as though we went through fire and through water" (Ps. 66:21).

Since Israel lives out the patterns originally set by the patriarchs, to understand Israel's condition we have to examine the deeds of Abraham and his selected son and grandson. But those deeds embodied the fundamental truths of the system. Torah and sacrifices preserve Israel from Gehenna and the rule of the kingdoms (the one personal, the other communal, in both instances). Faced with the choice of Gehenna or subjugation, Abraham chose the latter.

This brings us to a familiar motif of a system founded on God's perfect justice: how punishment in detail fits the specifics of a crime. If what happens to Israel comes about by reason of Israel's own character, not because of what the nations do, how do concrete calamities respond to specific failures or sins? In the following, we find the counterpart to the specification of the sin that has brought about a given condition of punishment. Accounting for Israel's recent calamities, a sage links specific failures to concrete events:

TOSEFTA TRACTATE MENAHOT 13:22

A. Said R. Yohanan b. Torta, "On what account was Shiloh destroyed? Because of the disgraceful disposition of the Holy Things which were there.

B. "As to Jerusalem's first building, on what account was it destroyed? Because of idolatry and licentiousness and bloodshed which was in it.

C. "But [as to] the latter [building] we know that they devoted themselves to Torah and were meticulous about tithes.

D. "On what account did they go into exile? Because they love money and hate one another.

E. "This teaches you that hatred of one for another is evil before the Omnipresent, and Scripture deems it equivalent to idolatry, licentiousness and bloodshed."

The same position is worked out in other ways. Israel's history, chapter by chapter, is written in terms of its virtue, and the relationship between Israel's vice and Israel's decline is constant:

TOSEFTA-TRACTATE SOTAH 14:3–9

14:3 A. When hedonists became many, fierce wrath came upon the world, and the glory of Torah ceased.

B. When those who went about whispering in judgment multiplied, conduct deteriorated, the laws were perverted, and the Holy Spirit ceased in Israel.

Now we give a series of cases in which the advent of a given form of corruption produced an immediate result in the decline of the social order:

14:4 A. When those who displayed partiality in judgment multiplied, the commandment, "You shall not respect persons in judgment" (Deut. 1:17) was annulled, and "You shall not be afraid of anyone" (Deut. 1:17) ceased.

B. And they removed the yoke of Heaven from themselves, and accepted the authority of the yoke of mortal man.

The decline of Israel continues apace, each sin provoking appropriate punishment:

14:5 A. When they compelled people to be their business agents, bribing became commonplace, and justice was perverted, "And they went backward and not forward" (Jer. 7:24).

B. And about them is said what is said about the sons of Samuel, "Yet his sons did not walk in his ways, but turned aside after gain; they took bribes and perverted justice" (I Sam. 8:3).

The leadership set the standard, the people followed suit:

14:7 A. When there multiplied judges who say,] "I accept your favour," and "I appreciate your favour," there was a multiplication of "Every man did that which was right in his own eyes" (Judges 17:6).

B. And the whole kingdom went rotten, declining more and more.

C. And when there multiplied: "Every man did that which was right in his own eyes," common sorts became exalted, and people of stature became humbled.

D. And the whole kingdom went rotten, declining more and more.

From public we turn to private sin, the improper attitudes that ordinary folk formed for themselves, envy in place of generosity of spirit, for example:

E. When envious men and plunderers multiplied [– they are those who shed blood –] those who hardened their heart multiplied, everybody closed his hand and transgressed that which is written in the Torah, "Take heed lest there be a base thought in your heart ... and your eye be hostile to your poor brother and you give him nothing" (Deut. 15:9).
14:8 A. When those who draw out their spittle multiplied, the disciples became few in number, and the glory of the Torah was annulled.
B. When there were multiplied "Their heart goes after their gain" (Ezek. 33:31), there multiplied "Those who call evil good and good evil" (Is. 5:20).
C. When there multiplied "Those who call evil good and good evil," the whole world was filled with people saying, "Woe, woe."
D. When arrogant people increased, Israelite girls began to marry arrogant people,
E. because in our generation people see only the outward appearance.

Above all, haughtiness and arrogance take the measure of Israel's decline, as we should anticipate given the sages' appreciation for humility and forbearance:

14:9 A. When there multiplied those "who stretched forth necks and wanton eyes" (Is. 3:16), the ordeal of the bitter water became common.
B. But it was suspended.
C. When the haughty of heart became many, contentiousness increased in Israel [– they are those who shed blood].
D. When those who accept gifts became many, days became few, and years were shortened.
E. When disciples of Shammai and Hillel who had not served the masters sufficiently well became many, disputes became many in Israel, and [the Torah was] made into two Torahs.

What is important in the catalogue of sins and their social punishment is the specificity of the list, the correspondence between a given sin and the appropriate punishment that it provoked.

From these specific points of correlation, we turn to the more general, consequential claim of the Oral Torah, that God foresaw all that has come upon Israel. The importance of that conviction comes to the surface when we see the corollary:

1) the Kingdom of Heaven continues to encompass Israel, even while it is ruled by the gentiles; and that

2) the anomaly and injustice of gentile hegemony will ultimately come to an end, by reason of Israel's own act of will.

The prophets called the gentiles the instruments of God's wrath. The sages took the same view. They explained that the gentiles do not act on their own but carry out God's will. What happens to Israel, therefore, reassures Israel that the holy people continues to live in the Kingdom of Heaven, and the very fact of the anomaly of pagan rule turns out to guarantee God's rule and Israel's role. Israel has not lost its position in the unfolding of the story of creation of a just world order set forth in the revelation of Sinai. Israel is now writing, and will continue to write, its own chapter of that story. Not only so, but Israel is not subordinate to the world-empires but their equal, standing in its assigned position at the end and climax of that part of the story of creation that the gentile empires are assigned to write. These convictions are expressed in systematic expositions that utilize the first three of the four principal media of expression of the Oral Torah – exegesis, mythic-narrative (even the symbolization of discourse through list-making and the amplification of lists), and halakhah – to make a systematic statement.

We commence with the main point. The dominance of the gentiles, particularly in the form of the standard cluster of the succession of four world-empires, guarantees that the just pattern that God has foreordained will impose structure and order upon history. That pattern leads inexorably from one gentile kingdom to the next in order but finally to the rule of holy Israel, defined as those who know God. Israel will be the fifth and final monarchy, inaugurating God's rule and the end of Israel as a sector of humanity altogether. The sages maintained that world order is not only just and proportionate but also regular and balanced. Hence they conceived that patterns reproduce themselves, because order governs.

Accordingly, and principally, the four kings marked the beginning and also the end of Israel's history. When the fourth kingdom (Rome) falls, Israel will take over:

GENESIS RABBAH XLII:II.2:

A. Said R. Abin, "Just as [Israel's history] began with the encounter with four kingdoms, so [Israel's history] will conclude with the encounter with the four kingdoms.

B. "'Chedorlaomer, king of Elam, Tidal, king of Goiim, Amraphel, king of Shinar, and Arioch, king of Ellasar, four kings against five' (Gen. 14:9).

C. "So [Israel's history] will conclude with the encounter with the four kingdoms: the kingdom of Babylonia, the kingdom of Medea, the kingdom of Greece, and the kingdom of Edom."

So, too, the following finds the world empires at the end in the first encounter of nascent Israel with the nations, Abraham's in the time of Amraphael. Thus, what happened at the outset will happen at the end. This, then, is spelled out at the final comment, which tells Israel how to tell time – that is, what will signify the advent of the end:

GENESIS RABBAH XLII:IV.4:

A. Another matter: "And it came to pass in the days of Amraphael, king of Shinar" (Gen. 14:1) refers to Babylonia.

B. "Arioch, king of Ellasar" (Gen. 14:1) refers to Greece.

C. "Chedorlaomer, king of Elam" (Gen. 14:1) refers to Media.

D. "And Tidal, king of Goiim [nations]" (Gen. 14:1) refers to the wicked government [Rome], which conscripts troops from all the nations of the world.

E. Said R. Eleazar bar Abina, "If you see that the nations contend with one another, look for the footsteps of the king-messiah. You may know that that is the case, for lo, in the time of Abraham, because the kings struggled with one another, a position of greatness came to Abraham."

The same pattern recurs at Genesis Rabbah LXVI:IX.1:

F. R. Abba bar R. Pappi, R. Joshua of Sikhnin in the name of R. Levi: "Since our father, Abraham, saw the ram get himself out of one thicket only to be trapped in another, the Holy One, blessed be he, said to him, 'So your descendants will be entangled in one kingdom after another, struggling from Babylonia to Media, from Media to Greece, from Greece to Edom. But in the end, they will be redeemed by the horns of a ram: 'And the Lord God will blow the horn ... the Lord of Hosts will defend them' " (Zech. 9:14–15).

What is at stake is evident: a systematic explanation for the workings of history. In a moment we shall also notice how the world-empires signify chaos, with Israel's rule under God coming to re-establish world order. The point is clear throughout.

Now we see how the theme of the four kingdoms is elaborated. Let us first take a case in which the sages deliver their message through the fourth principal medium, *halakhah,* that is, a statement made through a normative action or act of restraint. *Halakhah,* speaking in general terms and avoiding excessive differentiation by cases, by its nature cannot accomplish the differentiation among diverse types of gentiles that to accomplish their purpose the exegesis and myth effect. Even here the statement is made through a detail of law. The law is that Noah's descendants may not eat the meat with its life-blood in it: "But for your own life-blood I will require a reckoning: I will require it of very beast, of man, too, will I require a reckoning for human life, of every man for that of his fellow man: whoever sheds the blood of man by man shall his blood be shed, for in his image did God make man' (Gen. 9:4–6). This verse refers to all of humanity, encompassing the gentiles.

On that basis, the sages demonstrate, the four kingdoms, but especially Rome, are answerable for the murders that they commit:

GENESIS RABBAH XXXIV:XIV.3

A. "At the hand of every beast will I require it" (Gen. 9:5)
B. This refers to the four kingdoms [Babylonia, Media, Greece, and Rome, who are answerable for murders that they commit.]
C. "At the hand of man" (Gen. 9:5):
D. Said R. Levi, "That means, from the hand of the Edomite."
E. "Even at the hand of every man's brother" (Gen. 9:5). "Deliver me, I pray you, from the hand of my brother, from the hand of Esau" (Gen. 32:12).
F. "Will I require the life of man" (Gen. 9:5). This refers to Israel. "And you my sheep, the sheep of my pasture, are men" (Ez. 34:31).

The exegesis encompasses Esau/Edom and Israel, and now the admonition that murder will be published – pertaining to all humanity – is refocused upon the particular conduct of Edom/Esau/Rome. But use of halakhic passages for substantive, not merely symbolic, discourse through list-making is rare in this context.

Let us start with exegesis. What the sages prove on the foundations of Scripture is that God foresaw all that would come about. Having brought Israel into being and given Israel the Torah, God gave Israel free will to obey or to suffer punishment for disobedience. He then realized what would come about and determined an appropriate punishment, one of a different order altogether from that inflicted on the generation of the Flood. It would be a punishment appropriate to the sin. Since Israel did not accept the dominion of God, living in the Land of Israel, Israel would have to suffer the rule of world-empires, and would live in exile from the Land of Israel. Then Israel would repent of its sin, recognize the error of submitting to pagan rule, which was cruel, rather than the rule of God, which is benevolent. And, as we shall see in due course, all the rest would follow.

All of this was foreseen. In response to the participation of the patriarchs, particularly Abraham (as we have seen) and Jacob, God not only chose exile as the penalty for Israel's disobedience of God's will set forth in the Torah. He even identified the particular nations that would subjugate Israel. These nations would be world-rulers, as we already have noted, and thus appropriate in stature to the status of the nation they would rule. They would come in orderly succession, so indicating that a single plan covered all of world politics, and it would be clear to all concerned that the penultimate and greatest of the nations, Rome, would ultimately give way to the ultimate nation, holy Israel itself. Exegesis yielded these propositions. At the same time, numerous stories also served to bear elements of the same tale. But, as is clear, the entire complex of convictions forms a continuous story, beginning with creation, passing by Sinai, and ending up with the end of time as we now know it. These convictions are spelled out in exquisite elaboration, every detail of which warrants examination.

We start with the fundamental point that the world-empires were built into the very structure of creation. Here exegesis links the four kingdoms to the condition of the world at creation:

GENESIS RABBAH II:IV.I

A. ["And the earth was unformed and void. And darkness was upon the face of the deep" (Gen. 1:2)] R. Simeon b. Laqish interpreted the verses at hand to speak of the empires [of the historical age to come].

B. "'The earth was unformed' refers to Babylonia, 'I beheld the earth and lo, it was unformed' (Jer. 4:23).

C. "'And void' refers to Media: 'They hasted [using the letters of the same root as the word for void] to bring Haman' (Est. 6:14).

D. "'Darkness' refers to Greece, which clouded the vision of the Israelites through its decrees, for it said to Israel, 'Write on the horn of an ox [as a public proclamation for all to see] that you have no portion in the God of Israel.'

E. "'... upon the face of the deep' refers to the wicked kingdom [of Rome].

F. "Just as the deep surpasses investigation, so the wicked kingdom surpasses investigation.

G. "'And the spirit of God hovers' refers to the spirit of the Messiah, in line with the following verse of Scripture: 'And the spirit of the Lord shall rest upon him'" (Is. 11:2).

Choosing a verse deemed to refer to the specified world-empire and finding the correct point of intersection with a verse concerning creation, the exegete accomplishes his goal. It is to show that the chaos of creation finds its match in the chaos of the present age, the epoch of gentile domination. And then the point is made explicit: this age will come to an end, the act of creation at the beginning matched and completed by the advent of the Messiah at the end.

We proceed to the presence of the world-empires at a critical turning for Israel. Diverse readings of verses link these four monarchies, leading up to Israel's dominion at the end of days. The passage first of all establishes its context and then proceeds to the main point:

ESTHER RABBAH I I:I.I ON EST. I:3,
AND ESTHER RABBAH II:I.I:

3. A. Rab interpreted the verse to speak of the time of Haman.

B. "'And your life shall hang in doubt before you': this speaks of the twenty-four hours from the removal of the ring.

C. "'night and day you shall be in dread': this speaks of the time that the letters were sent forth.

D. "'and have no assurance of your life': this was when the enemies of the Jews were told to be 'ready against that day'" (Est. 3:14).

That is the context in which the recurrent list occurs, Babylonia-Media-Greece-Rome (the lust also known as Edom). The point of the list, as we see, is to show an orderly sequence, not a disorderly concatenation, of empires, one then the next, yielding a linear view of history; at the end and climax of the line is the empire not listed at all, which can only be Israel; the rhetoric embellishes what is a very simple motif:

E. "In the morning, you shall say, 'Would it were evening!' and at evening you shall say, 'Would it were morning!'"

F. "In the morning," of Babylonia, "you shall say, 'Would it were evening!'"

G. "In the morning," of Media, "you shall say, 'Would it were evening!'"

H. "In the morning," of Greece, "you shall say, 'Would it were evening!'"

I. "In the morning," of Edom, "you shall say, 'Would it were evening!'"

J. Another interpretation of the verse: "In the morning, you shall say, 'Would it were evening!' and at evening you shall say, 'Would it were morning!':"

K. "In the morning" of Babylonia, "you shall say, 'Would it were the evening of Media!'"

L. "In the morning," of Media, "you shall say, 'Would it were evening of Greece!'"

M. "In the morning," of Greece, "you shall say, 'Would it were evening of Edom!'"

N. Why so? "because of the dread which your heart shall fear and the sights which your eyes shall see."

The same list contains within itself many possibilities; in the next version, the list serves to reassure Israel that, whoever rules the world, God remains loyal to Israel. And now the age to come, or the time of Gog and Magog, enters into the picture. Once more we see the working of paradigmatic thinking. When we have established a pattern, the applications of the pattern prove numerous; all kinds of data make sense within the pattern.

4. A. Samuel commenced by citing the following verse of Scripture: "Yet for all that, when they are in the land of their enemies, I will not spurn them, neither will I abhor them so as to destroy them utterly and break my covenant with them, for I am the Lord their God; but I will for their sake remember the covenant with their forefathers, whom I brought forth out of the land of Egypt in the sight of the nations, that I might be their God: I am the Lord" (Lev. 26:44–5).

Samuel applies the paradigm to the standard cluster:

B. " 'I will not spurn them': in Babylonia.
C. " 'neither will I abhor them': in Media.
D. " 'so as to destroy them utterly': under Greek rule.
E. " 'and break my covenant with them': under the wicked kingdom.
F. " 'for I am the Lord their God': in the age to come.

Hiyya asks the paradigm to deal with more contemporary figures of Roman times, mixed together – the past forming a chapter in the present – with those of Persian times past:

G. Taught R. Hiyya, " 'I will not spurn them': in the time of Vespasian.
H. " 'neither will I abhor them': in the time of Trajan.
I. " 'so as to destroy them utterly': in the time of Haman.
J. " 'and break my covenant with them': in the time of the Romans.
K. " 'for I am the Lord their God': in the time of Gog and Magog."

Listing the four kingdoms opens the way to the theme of the fifth and final one, which will be Israel. But that list by itself carries no detailed message, and juxtaposing the four kingdoms hardly even dictates the topics that will be discussed in detail. What we have, rather, is a set-piece list, to be matched with other set-piece lists, as the treatment by Samuel shows with great clarity. But then there is no proposition at all.

The Babylonians and Chaldeans, Medians and Persians, Greeks and Macedonians, Edomites and Ishmaelites, form another, comparable set. But the principal version consists of four entries:

LAMENTATIONS RABBAH XLVIII.I.6:

A. ["They were set upon my neck," reading the word "set" to mean] "knit together:"

B. He brought them against me at intervals.

C. He brought them upon me in pairs: Babylon and the Chaldeans, Media and Persia, Greece and Macedon, Edom and Ishmael.

D. He alternated them as to their behaviour: Babylon was harsh, Media lenient, Greece harsh, Edom lenient, the Chaldeans harsh, Persia lenient, Macedon harsh, Ishmael lenient:

E. "So part of the kingdom shall be strong, and part broken" (Dan. 2:42).

PESIQTA DERAB KAHANA XVII:IV.2

2. A. "Then my anger shall be kindled against them in that day": in Babylonia.

B. "... and I will forsake them": in Media.

C. "... and I will hide my face from them": in Greece.

D. "and they shall be devoured [and many evils and troubles shall come upon them]": in in Edom.

E. That is in line with this verse: "Behold the fourth beast ... devoured and broke in pieces and stamped the residue with its feet" (Dan. 7:7).

So much for list-making as a mode of stating the paradigm of pagan, then Israelite, rule in the sequence of empires. The power of exegesis takes over, showing a vast variety of ways in which the four empires make their appearance. Since, like philosophers, the sages prefer abstract discourse to narrative, they identify in the symbolism of laws, more than in the articulated narrative of "history," the presence of the nations and their place in Israel's existence. An extreme example of their symbolization of hierarchical classification in the present case occurs when the sages maintain that the types of skin ailments of Lev. 13:2 refer to Babylonia, Media, Greece, and Edom/Rome. This huge passage is represented here by one abstract only:

LEVITICUS RABBAH XV:IX.I:

A. "A swelling (lifting up, S'T), [or eruption (SPHT) or a spot (BHRT)]" (Lev. 13:2).

B. "[A swelling] refers to Babylonia."

H. "Eruption" (SPHT) refers to Media, which produced Haman, that wicked man, who inflamed [Media's] people like a snake, on the account of, "On your belly will you go" (Gen 3:14).
I. "Bright spot" (BHRT) refers to Greece, which publicizes (MHBRT) its [harsh] decrees, saying to Israel, "Write on the horn of an ox that you have no portion in the God of Israel."
J. "A spot of leprosy" (Lev. 13:2) refers to Edom, which originated in the strength of the old man [Isaac, who blessed Esau].
K. It was on account of the statement, "And it shall be on the skin of his body" (Lev. 13:2).
2. A. Now in this world, a priest examines spots of leprosy, but in the world to come, the Holy One, blessed be he, has said, "I shall declare you clean."
B. That is in line with the following verse of Scripture: "I shall pour out on you waters that purify, and you will be clean" (Ex. 36:25).

A far more elaborate, and successful, exercise in symbolic discourse demonstrates that various prophets foresaw the domination of the four empires and the ultimate rise of holy Israel. Much of the Thirteenth Parashah of Leviticus Rabbah is devoted to that very matter. I give only the exposition of how Moses conveyed future history when he specified animals that Israel may not eat, the camel, rock badger, hare, and pig. Each one of these represents one of the four pagan empires, and the traits of the respective empires are embodied in the chosen animal. Specifically, the animals forbidden at Dt. 14:7, camel, rock badger, hare, and pig, represent Babylonia, Media, Greece, and Rome:

LEVITICUS RABBAH XIII:V.9FF.:

9. A. Moses foresaw what the evil kingdoms would do [to Israel].
B. "The camel, rock badger, and hare" (Deut. 14:7). [Compare: "Nevertheless, among those that chew the cud or part the hoof, you shall not eat these: the camel, because it chews the cud but does not part the hoof, is unclean to you. The rock badger, because it chews the cud but does not part the hoof, is unclean to you. And the hare, because it chews the cud but does not part the hoof, is unclean to you, and the pig, because it parts the hoof and is cloven-footed, but does not chew the cud, is unclean to you" (Lev. 11:4–8).]

We start with a simple statement of the proposition:

C. The camel (GML) refers to Babylonia, [in line with the following verse of Scripture: "O daughter of Babylonia, you who are to be devastated!] Happy will be he who requites (GML) you, with what you have done to us" (Ps. 147:8).

D. "The rock badger" (Deut. 14:7) – this refers to Media.

I. "The pig" (Deut. 14:7) – this refers to Edom [Rome].

Now we are given reasons for the identification of the four animals with the four empires.

11. A. Another interpretation: "The camel" (Lev. 11:4).

B. This refers to Babylonia.

C. "Because it chews the cud (MLH GRH) [but does not part the hoof]" (Lev. 11:4).

D. For it brings forth praises [(MQLS) with its throat] of the Holy One, blessed be he. [The Hebrew words for "chew the cud" – bring up cud – are now understood to mean "give praise." GRH is connected with GRWN, throat, hence, "bring forth (sounds of praise through) the throat."]

N. "The rock badger" (Lev. 11:5) – this refers to Media.

O. "For it chews the cud" – for it gives praise to the Holy One, blessed be he: "Thus says Cyrus, king of Persia, 'All the kingdoms of the earth has the Lord, the God of the heaven, given me' " (Ezra 1:2).

P. "The hare" – this refers to Greece.

Q. "For it chews the cud" – for it gives praise to the Holy One, blessed be he.

S. "The pig" (Lev. 11:7) – this refers to Edom.

T. "For it does not chew the cud" – for it does not give praise to the Holy One, blessed be he.

U. And it is not enough that it does not give praise, but it blasphemes and swears violently, saying, "Whom do I have in heaven, and with you I want nothing on earth" (Ps. 73:25).

A different set of elaborations now serves the same purpose, in each case showing the reason for the identification of beast with empire.

12. A. Another interpretation [of GRH, cud, now with reference to GR, stranger:]

B. "The camel" (Lev. 11:4) – this refers to Babylonia.

C. "For it chews the cud" [now: brings up the stranger] – for it exalts righteous men: "And Daniel was in the gate of the [Babylonian] king" (Dan. 2:49).

D. "The rock badger" (Lev. 11:5) – this refers to Media.

E. "For it brings up the stranger" – for it exalts righteous men: "Mordecai sat at the gate of the king [of Media]" (Est. 2:19).

F. "The hare" (Lev. 11:6) – this refers to Greece.

G. "For it brings up the stranger" – for it exalts the righteous.

J. "The pig" (Lev. 11:7) – this refers to Rome.

K. "But it does not bring up the stranger" – for it does not exalt the righteous.

L. And it is not enough that it does not exalt them, but it kills them.

M. That is in line with the following verse of Scripture: "I was angry with my people, I profaned my heritage; I gave them into your hand, [you showed them no mercy; on the aged you made your yoke exceedingly heavy]" (Is. 47:6).

N. This refers to R. Aqiba and his colleagues.

Here comes the climax and the point of the construction: a trait that differentiates one beast from another also points towards the resolution of the tension of Israel's history with the nations – the place of Israel on the list of world-empires:

13. A. Another interpretation [now treating "bring up the cud" (GR) as "bring along in its train" (GRR)]:

B. "The camel" (Lev. 11:4) – this refers to Babylonia.

C. "Which brings along in its train" – for it brought along another kingdom after it.

D. "The rock badger" (Lev. 11:5) – this refers to Media.

E. "Which brings along in its train" – for it brought along another kingdom after it.

F. "The hare" (Lev. 11:6) – this refers to Greece.

G. "Which brings along in its train" – for it brought along another kingdom after it.

H. "The pig" (Lev. 11:7) – this refers to Rome.

I. "Which does not bring along in its train" – for it did not bring along another kingdom after it.

J. And why is it then called "pig" (HZYR)? For it restores (MHZRT) the crown to the one who truly should have it [namely, Israel, whose dominion will begin when the rule of Rome ends].

K. That is in line with the following verse of Scripture: "And saviours will come up on Mount Zion to judge the Mountain of Esau [Rome], and the kingdom will then belong to the Lord" (Ob. 1:21).

The key always comes as the climax: Edom/Esau/Rome will give way to Israel; Obadiah 1:21 suffices to make that point explicit. The upshot is that, through the elaboration of the list, the sages make their statement in powerful and compelling form.

That is not to suggest that continuous narrative plays no role; far from it. The sages appeal to the form of a tale – first comes this, then that happens, then, finally, the other thing takes place – to convey their message. In the present instance they take up a narrative of the life of Jacob and translate it into the story of what would happen to his children. For they maintained, that the patriarchs joined God in planning Israel's future history. Here, Israel's history was predetermined by Jacob's conduct at a crucial turning in his life, and all that happened with the four kingdoms followed from that event.

J. R. Berekhiah, R. Helbo, and R. Simeon b. Menassia: "Meir expounded [the following verse:] 'Nonetheless they still sinned and did not believe in his wondrous works' (Ps. 78:32). [This verse] speaks of Jacob, who did not believe and so did not ascend.

K. "Said to him the Holy One, blessed be he, 'Jacob! If you had believed and ascended, you would never again have gone down. Now that you did not believe and did not ascend, lo, your sons will be held fast among the nations and wander aimlessly among the kingdoms, from one to the next, from Babylonia to Media, from Media to Greece, and from Greece to Edom.'

L. "He said before him, 'Lord of the ages, is it forever?'

M. "Said to him the Holy One, blessed be he, 'Then fear not, O Jacob my servant ... nor be dismayed, O Israel, for lo, I will save you from afar' (Jer. 30:10): from Gallia and Aspamea and nearby lands.

N. " 'And your offspring from the land of their captivity': 'Jacob shall return from Babylonia.

O. " 'And have quiet' from Media.

P. " 'And ease' from Greece.

Q. 'And none shall make him afraid' on account of Edom."

With reference to Song 3:1, "Upon my bed by night," the exegete invokes the same pattern:

A. Said R. Levi, "Said the Community of Israel before the Holy One, blessed be he, 'Lord of the world, in the past, you would give light for me between one night and the next night,

B. " 'between the night of Egypt and the night of Babylonia, between the night of Babylonia and the night of Media, between the night of Media and the night of Greece, between the night of Greece and the night of Edom.

C. " 'Now that I have fallen asleep neglectful of the Torah and the religious duties, one night flows into the next.' "

Narrative enters in especially when the stories of the lives of the patriarchs are asked to account for world history. Here is how sages show that Jacob experienced the future history of Israel involving the four monarches:

GENESIS RABBAH XLIV:XVII.4

A. "[And it came to pass, as the sun was going down,] lo, a deep sleep fell on Abram, and lo, a dread and great darkness fell upon him" (Gen. 15:12):

B. "... lo, a dread" refers to Babylonia, as it is written, "Then was Nebuchadnezzar filled with fury" (Gen. 3:19).

C. "... and darkness" refers to Media, which darkened the eyes of Israel by making it necessary for the Israelites to fast and conduct public mourning.

D. "... great ..." refers to Greece.

G. "... fell upon him" refers to Edom, as it is written, "The earth quakes at the noise of their fall" (Jer. 49:21).

The paradigm, independent of history and considerations of temporal order, can work backwards as well as forwards:

H. Some reverse matters:

I. "... fell upon him" refers to Babylonia, since it is written, "Fallen, fallen is Babylonia" (Is. 21:9).

J. "... great ..." refers to Media, in line with this verse: "King Ahasuerus did make great" (Est. 3:1).

K. "... and darkness" refers to Greece, which darkened the eyes of Israel by its harsh decrees.

L. "... lo, a dread" refers to Edom, as it is written, "After this I saw ... a fourth beast, dreadful and terrible" (Dan. 7:7).

The paradigm, moreover, takes command of diverse passages of Scripture and delivers its message in each one. Here is a completely different way of utilizing the one pattern. Isaac prefigured the four kingdoms in asking for venison.

GENESIS RABBAH LXV:XIII.3

A. Another matter: "Now then take your weapons, your quiver and your bow and go out to the field":

B. "Weapons" refers to Babylonia, as it is said, "And the weapons he brought to the treasure house of his god" (Gen. 2:2).

C. "Your quiver" speaks of Media, as it says, "So they suspended Haman on the gallows" (Est. 7:10). [The play on the words is the same as at No. 2.]

D. "And your bow" addresses Greece: "For I bend Judah for me, I fill the bow with Ephraim and I will story up your sons, O Zion, against your sons, O Javan [Greece]" (Zech. 9:13).

E. "and go out to the field" means Edom: "Unto the land of Seir, the field of Edom" (Gen. 32:4).

In these and similar compositions, the sages link verses to make their point, recasting the narratives of Scripture into demonstrations of propositions framed in symbolic language. The main point should not be missed for the rich and dense elaboration: God foresaw Israel's sin and chose the nations as the instrument to punish them. Hence Israel's present situation validates the main principle of the Oral Torah, the justice of the world order that has dictated the very character of creation.

What then does God hope to accomplish through exercising dominion over Israel by means of the nations? It is the medium for re-establishing his rule over Israel through Israel's own intentionality. First of all, Israel will be lead through suffering in exile to repentance, at which point God will forgive them. The sages learn that point from Leviticus Chapter 26, just as they derive most of what they have to say from Scripture:[3]

SIFRA CCLXIX:II.I, 3

A. "But if they confess their iniquity and the iniquity of their fathers [in their treachery which they committed against me, and also in walking contrary to me, so that I walked contrary to them and brought them into the land of their enemies; if then their uncircumcised heart is humbled and they make amends for their iniquity; then I will remember my covenant with Jacob, and I will remember my covenant also with Isaac and my covenant also with Abraham, and I will remember the land. But the land shall be left by them and enjoy its Sabbaths while it lies desolate without them; and they shall make amends for their iniquity, because they spurned my ordinances, and their soul abhorred my statutes. Yet for all that, when they are in the land of their enemies, I will not spurn them, neither will I abhor them so as to destroy them utterly and break my covenant with them; for I am the Lord their God; but I will for their sake remember the covenant with their forefathers whom I brought forth out of the land of Egypt in the sight of the nations, that I might be their God: I am the Lord. These are the statutes and ordinances and laws which the Lord made between him and the people of Israel on Mount Sinai by Moses]" (Lev. 26:40–46):

B. This is how things are as to repentance,

C. for as soon as they confess their sins, I forthwith revert and have mercy on them,

D. as it is said, "But if they confess their iniquity and the iniquity of their fathers in their treachery which they committed against me."

---

3. A point to which we return in chapter 15.

The second point is that God will never permit Israel to remove itself from his dominion; willy-nilly they will remain his kingdom:

3. A. "... and brought them into the land of their enemies":
B. This is a good deal for Israel.
C. For the Israelites are not to say, "Since we have gone into exile among the gentiles, let us act like them."
D. [God speaks:] "I shall not let them, but I shall call forth prophets against them, who will bring them back to the right way under my wings."
E. And how do we know?
F. "What is in your mind shall never happen, the thought, 'Let us be like the nations, like the tribes of the countries, and worship wood and stone.' 'As I live,' says the Lord God, 'surely with a might hand and an outstretched arm and with wrath poured out, I will be king over you. [I will bring you out from the peoples and gather you out of the countries where you are scattered, with a mighty hand and an outstretched arm and with wrath poured out' " (Ez. 20:33–3).
G. Whether you like it or not, with or without your consent, I shall establish my dominion over you."

Israel, subject to the gentiles, then gains the opportunity to repent and reconcile itself with God, and that is the plan that God has devised to overcome the workings of strict justice; exile and subjugation, then, form acts of mercy on God's part, just as Abraham had foreseen when he wisely chose the rule of the nations over Gehenna.

The final question that requires attention returns us to our starting point, the comparison of Israel and the nations, in the present case, the Israelite with the gentile. That is framed in terms of Israel and Adam, meaning, the sector of humanity within, and the part of humanity outside, the circle of the Torah. By reason of disobedience Adam sinned and was justly punished by exile from Eden; that represented an act of mercy, since he was not wiped out, as Eve had said he and she would be. Because of disobedience Israel sinned and was justly punished by exile from the Land of Israel, counterpart to Eden. But, then, is Israel not just another Adam – rebellious and permanently punished on that account? There is a distinction, one that makes all the difference. The Torah, carrying with it the possibility of repentance, changes Israel's condition.

Israel is like Adam, but Israel is the Other, the Last Adam, the opposite of Adam. We shall now systematically compare Adam and Israel, the first man and the last, and show how the story of Adam matches the story of Israel – but with a difference:

2. A. R. Abbahu in the name of R. Yosé bar Haninah: "It is written, 'But they are like a man [Adam], they have transgressed the covenant' (Hos. 6:7).
B. "'They are like a man,' specifically, like the first man. [We shall now compare the story of the first man in Eden with the story of Israel in its land.]

Now the composer identifies an action in regard to Adam with a counterpart action in regard to Israel, in each case matching verse for verse, beginning with Eden and Adam:

C. "'In the case of the first man, I brought him into the garden of Eden, I commanded him, he violated my commandment, I judged him to be sent away and driven out, but I mourned for him, saying "How ..."' [which begins the book of Lamentations, hence stands for a lament, but which, as we just saw, also is written with the consonants that also yield, 'Where are you'].
D. "'I brought him into the garden of Eden,' as it is written, 'And the Lord God took the man and put him into the garden of Eden' (Gen. 2:15).
E. "'I commanded him,' as it is written, 'And the Lord God commanded ...' (Gen. 2:16).
F. "'And he violated my commandment,' as it is written, 'Did you eat from the tree concerning which I commanded you' (Gen. 3:11).
G. "'I judged him to be sent away,' as it is written, "And the Lord God sent him from the garden of Eden' (Gen. 3:23).
H. "'And I judged him to be driven out.' 'And he drove out the man' (Gen. 3:24).
I. "'But I mourned for him, saying, "How ...".' 'And he said to him, "Where are you"' (Gen. 3:9), and the word for 'where are you' is written, 'How ...'

Next comes the systematic comparison of Adam and Eden with Israel and the Land of Israel:

J. "'So too in the case of his descendants, [God continues to speak,] I brought them into the Land of Israel, I commanded them, they violated my commandment, I judged them to be sent out and driven away but I mourned for them, saying, "How ..."'
K. "'I brought them into the Land of Israel.' 'And I brought you into the land of Carmel' (Jer. 2:7).
L. "'I commanded them.' 'And you, command the children of Israel' (Ex. 27:20). 'Command the children of Israel' (Lev. 24:2).

M. " 'They violated my commandment.' 'And all Israel have violated your Torah' (Dan. 9:11).

N. " 'I judged them to be sent out.' 'Send them away, out of my sight and let them go forth' (Jer 15:1).

O. " '… and driven away.' 'From my house I shall drive them' (Hos. 9:15).

P. " 'But I mourned for them, saying, "How …" ' 'How has the city sat solitary, that was full of people' " (Lam. 1:1).

Here we end where we began, Israel in exile from the Land, like Adam in exile from Eden. But the Torah is clear that there is a difference, which we shall address in its proper place: Israel can repent.

So to conclude: the just world order is comprised by the division of humanity into Israel with the Torah, and the gentiles with their idols. The one is destined to life eternal with God, the other to the grave, there to spend eternity. World order then finds its center and focus in Israel, and whatever happens that counts under Heaven's gaze takes place in relationship to Israel. That division yields rich and dense details but only a simple story, easily retold. In a purposeful act of benevolence, the just God created the world in so orderly a way that the principle of justice and equity governs throughout. Fair rules apply equally to all persons and govern all circumstances. God not only created man but made himself known to man through the Torah. But man, possessed of free will, enjoys the choice of accepting and obeying the Torah, therefore living in the kingdom of Heaven, or rejecting the Torah and God in favour of idolatry and idols.

Now we realize the full potentiality contained in the simple doctrines with which we began: that those who accept the Torah are called Israel, and the others are called gentiles. The gentiles hate Israel because of the Torah, and they also hate God. But the world as now constituted is such that the gentiles rule and Israel is subjugated. Where is the justice in that inversion of right, with God's people handed over to the charge of God's enemies? Israel has sinned, so rebelled against God, and the gentiles then form God's instrument for the punishment of Israel. God's justice governs, the world conforms to orderly rules, embedded in the very structure of creation. Israel's own condition stands as the surest testimony of the world's good and just order. That guarantee is for now and all time to come.

So much for the large abstractions: justice worked out in the world-encompassing dimensions of the relationship of the two vast components of humanity, Israel and the gentiles. We now turn from macrocosm to microcosm, to that other dimension of order, the humble one that takes the measure of the workaday world. What logic, what justice, governs a world in which – as the marketplace and household attest – the wicked prosper and righteous suffer and no logic of justice demonstrably governs, but only happy accident for the fortunate, and misery for everybody else?

5 Ordering the Ultimate Anomaly: Private Lives

The same premises that guided the sages' thinking about Israel and the Torah, the gentiles and idolatry, required deep thought indeed on the ultimate anomaly of a logic animated by the principle of God's rational justice: the actualities of everyday life. That God orders the world through justice accessible to human reason confronts the everywhere acknowledged obstacle: justice prevails only now and then. Man's fate rarely accords with the fundamental principle of a just order but mostly discredits it. But if the human condition embodied in Israelites' lives one by one defies the smooth explanations that serve for justifying the condition of Israel in the abstract, then the entire logic of the Oral Torah fails.

How, then, reveal God's justice in the chaotic, scarcely manageable detritus of private lives? It is through articulation of the doctrine of reward and punishment, the insistence on the justice of God in whatever happens. Within the logic at hand, reward and punishment not only precipitate but define the teleology of all thought. In terms of the alternatives set forth in the preface, God is always God, but by no means good to all. This is stated in so many words, as is every critical proposition of the entire theological system animating the Oral Torah:

LAMENTATIONS RABBAH LXXXVII.I.IFF.

I. A. "The Lord is good to those who wait for him, to the soul that seeks him":
B. Might one suppose that God is good to all?
C. Scripture says, "to the soul that seeks him."

May we distinguish Israel from the gentiles? Not at all:

2. A. Along these same lines: "Surely God is good to Israel" (Ps. 73:1).
B. Might one suppose that God is good to all?
C. Scripture says, "Even to those who are pure in heart" (Ps. 73:1).
D. That is, those whose heart is pure and in whose hand is no wickedness.

Then to whom is God good? To those who keep the Torah:

3. A. Along these same lines: "Happy is the one whose strength is in you" (Ps. 84:6).
B. Might one suppose that God is good to all?
C. Scripture says, "In whose heart are the highways" (Ps. 84:6) – those in whose heart the paths of the Torah are kept.

God is good to those who are sincerely upright:

4. A. Along these same lines: "Do good, O Lord, to the God" (Ps. 125:4).
B. Might one suppose that God is good to all?
C. Scripture says, "And to those who are upright in their hearts" (Ps. 125:5).

God is good to those who sincerely seek him:

5. A. Along these same lines: "The Lord is near to all those who call upon him" (Ps. 145:18).
B. Might one suppose that God is good to all?
C. Scripture says, "To all who call upon him in truth" (Ps. 145:18).

God is good to the remnant of Israel, those who are forgiven their sin:

6. A. Along these same lines: "Who is a God like you, who pardons iniquity and passes by transgression" (Mic. 8:18).
B. Might one suppose that God is good to all?
C. Scripture says, "Of the remnant of his heritage" (Mic. 8:18).

God is selective and elects those that ought to be selected, punishes and rewards those that deserve the one or the other. So God's justice is what is explained. God is good to those that deserve it and punishes those that deserve it. Scripture explains the matter through the qualifying language that it uses in context; it is Scripture's cases that are ordered into the governing principle of the whole.

Treating the holy people, Israel, and individual Israelites as one, the sages never for one minute doubted that the world order of justice encompassed those private lives. This they stated in countless ways, the simplest being the representation of Hillel's statement encased in a fragmentary narrative:

TRACTATE ABOT 2:6

[One day he was walking along the river and] he saw a skull floating on the water and said to it, "Because you drowned others, they drowned you, and in the end those who drowned you will be drowned."

Somewhere, somehow, the wicked get their comeuppance. The just God sees to it. But what about the righteous? Is their just reward equally certain? However dubious the former of the two propositions – the ultimate triumph of justice over the wicked when a crime or sin has been committed – that the righteous get their just reward certainly conflicted, then as now, with everyday experience. Indeed, the basic conviction of world order defined by justice violated every intuition, every perception, every reflection upon man's fate, that private lives provoked. Then as now people lived in a world of caprice and, right or wrong, discerned no justice at all.

Indeed, to formulate the problem of evil as a critical issue for their theology, the sages did not have to open the book of Job, or Jeremiah's deep reflections on the prosperity of the wicked, or Qohelet's (Ecclesiastes') morose recognition that the righteous and the wicked come to a single fate. The logic of their generative principle of a just world order established by the the singular Creator left no alternative. For wherever they turned, their claim that the one God, ruler of the world, reliably orders the world with rational justice found slight confirmation. To discern grounds for doubt, the sages had only to walk out of the door of the schoolhouse and consider the condition of their neighbors, indeed, to contemplate their own lives. They devoted themselves to the study of the Torah, ordinarily doing so – their stories take for granted – in conditions of poverty, while round about Israelites who neglected the Torah prospered. How justify the lives of ordinary folk, when the rule of justice does not find validation in even their own lives of Torah study? The good fall, the wicked rise, the ignorant or the arrogant exercise power, the sages can merely rant and cavil – so where is that orderly world of reason infused with justice?

If through their theology of Israel and the gentiles, the sages could account for gentile rule over Israel, explaining private lives required a more complex and diverse construction of thought. The thin, one-dimensional solution to the challenge to the theology of world order posed by gentile rule – the gentiles serve God's will in ruling Israel, thereby punishing Israel for its sin, but will themselves give way to Israel at the last – nicely served. But a much thicker explanation would be required to encompass the diverse cases all bundled together in the phrase: righteous in a bad way, wicked in a good way, or covered by the language, "why do the wicked prosper?" For when it comes to everyday life, the anomaly represented by a random, not a just, fate, encompassed many cases, each with its own special traits, none easily resolved by appeal to a single overriding principle of reward and punishment. And the cases pressed in, near at hand, in the next house, the next room. So the human condition presented its own anomalies to the rule of the just order. Suffering, illness, and death come to all, the wicked and the righteous alike. So, responding to that cliché of everyday life, Qoheleth, among many sages, surely forbade framing easy answers and making facile distinctions.

Not only so, but because the sages constructed a single coherent theology, encompassing every dimension of existence, they had to show the justice of a single principle of explanation for private and public affairs alike. Then how to hold together, within a unitary rule of order, explaining in the same way the abstract situation of an imagined nation and the concrete circumstance of ordinary people near at hand? When the sages reflected upon the complex problem of how a world order of justice governs private lives, three principles set bounds to their speculation. These principles responded, in logical sequence, to three questions:

1) can the individual be at all distinguished from all Israel?
2) if not, then on what basis does the individual matter at all? and
3) can the same explanation that necessarily accounts for the condition of Israel sufficiently serve also for that of Israelites, and if not, what further components does the encompassing rationalization of Israelite existence require?

What we shall now see is that the sages maintained that the category "Israel" covered the holy people as a collectivity and also every individual therein, referring to a private person by the same word as applies to the nation all together. But they did accord to the individual an autonomous standing, apart from the community. And they vastly expanded their thinking beyond the limits of the categories, Israel and the gentiles. Rather, they composed a complex, many-sided theory of the way in which order consisting of justice explained private lives too.

The logic of system-building that covered category-formation offered no alternative but to invoke a single principle to cover the undifferentiated category, "Israel," meaning both the collectivity and the individual. The alternative, one rule for the nation, another for the private person, violated the very premise of all thought within the monotheist framework, which found the ground of all being, the explanation of all things, in one God, the benevolent and just creator of heaven and earth. So the sages' systematic thought insisted that individual Israelites cannot be thought about in a manner separate from all Israel. Consequently, the same rules that apply to all Israel – the rule of justice, the appeal to the self-evident rationality expressed by the equation of measure for measure – explain what happens to individuals.

That principle closed off one possible way of solving the problem of evil confronting monotheism. The sages could not resolve the conflict between faith and personal fate by distinguishing between Israel, which plays out its history in a world of justice and fairness, and the individual Israelite, whose private life has no bearing upon public policy in God's dominion. In fact, the sages took for granted the very opposite: to be an Israelite was to embody Israel in the here and now. The fate of the individual is wrapped up in the destiny of all Israel; the same calculus describes both. That is why monotheism's requirement of systemic coherence by nature produced an endless sequence of anomalous cases.

How did the union of public and private Israel take place? Here the justification of Israel's fate at the hands of the nations, outlined in chapters 3 and 4, serves. Take the case of martyrdom, which represents the ultimate joining of holy Israel and the private person's act of sanctifying God's name. Then the individual gives his life for the Torah shared by all. But even here we differentiate Israel and Israelite. For individuals enjoy the option, which, by definition, the community as a whole does not, of changing their private situation, improving it by joining the idolators. It is at that point that the anomaly of unjust or unfair results emerges most sharply: How long are you going to do good deeds on his account, for him alone, while he pays you back with evil? And so the alternative presented by idolators of good will: join us and we shall treat you well.

Here is how the united faith of Israel and the Israelite recapitulates the problem of evil in one concrete statement:

SONG OF SONGS RABBAH LXXXIX:I.9, 11–12

A. ["Return, return, O Shulammite, return, return that we may look upon you. Why should you look upon the Shulammite, as upon a dance before two armies?" (Song 6:13)]. "Return that we may look upon you":
B. The nations of the world say to Israel, "How long are you going to die for your God and devote yourselves completely to him?"
C. "For thus Scripture says, 'Therefore do they love you beyond death' (Song 1:3).

D. "And how long will you be slaughtered on his account: 'No, but for your sake we are killed all day long' (Ps. 44:23)?

E. " 'How long are you going to do good deeds on his account, for him alone, while he pays you back with bad things?

F. "Come over to us, and we shall make you governors, hyparchs, and generals,

G. " 'That we may look upon you:' and you will be the cynosure of the world: 'And you shall be the look out of all the people' " (Ex. 18:21).

So is set forth the gentile *défi*. Now comes the Israelite response:

H. And the Israelites will answer, " 'Why should you look upon the Shulammite, as upon a dance before two armies:' "

As usual, Scripture's facts are systematized and formed into general rules, as the philosophical sages transform Scripture into natural philosophy:

I. "In your entire lives, have you ever heard that Abraham, Isaac, and Jacob worshipped idols, that their children should do so after them? Our fathers did not worship idols, and we shall not worship idols after them.

J. "But what can you do for us?

K. "Can it be like the dance that was made for Jacob, our father, when he went forth from the house of Laban?"

We now turn to instances of Israel's redemption, at the sea and in the time of Elisha:

11. A. [Continuing 9.K:] "Or can you make a dance for us such as was made for our fathers at the sea? 'And the angel of God removed ...' (Ex. 14:19).

B. "Or can you make a dance for us like the one that was made for Elisha: 'And when the servant of the man of God was risen early and gone forth, behold a host with horses and chariots was round about the city. And his servant said to him, Alas, my master, what shall we do? And he answered, Do not be afraid, for they who are with us are more than those who are with them. Forthwith Elisha prayed and said, Lord, I pray you, open his eyes that he may see. And the Lord opened the eyes of the young man, and he saw, and behold, the mountain was full of horses and chariots of fire around about Elisha' " (2 Kgs. 6:15).

And finally comes the end-time, to which the gentiles will not come anyhow:

C. "Or can you make a dance for us like the one that the Holy One, blessed be he, will make for the righteous in the age to come?"

The passage continues with the exposition of God at the last as lord of the dance, which we shall meet in chapter 14.

The question confronts individuals, for the dance is a most private act: How long are you going to die for your God and give him the last full measure of devotion? And there is no dance without individual dancers. But death is public, and there also is no dance without a shared rhythm and gesture. The problem carries along its own solution: at the end of time the individual Israelite joins all Israel in the eschatological dance to be led by the Lord of the dance, God himself. Here, then, we find a fine metaphor to make the systematic statement of the problem of evil formulated in both communal and individual terms: each dancer dances on his own, but all do the same step, stamping together in the same rhythm – predictably, within this theological system, with God leading the way.

That is why, to be an Israelite individual is to form part of all Israel. Here, too, the public and the private merge. Individual males are (personally) circumcised – but that is into the public community of the covenant. External emblems of belonging to Israel serve, but only contingently. Circumcision defines who is an Israelite male, but only within limits; being an Israelite vastly transcends the mark of circumcision into the covenant of Abraham, which is a contingent indicator, not the decisive denominator that the earliest Christians conceived it to be:

MISHNAH-TRACTATE NEDARIM 3:11

G. [If he said,] "Qonam [forbidden as what is consecrated to the Temple be whatever] I derive as benefit from the uncircumcised," he is permitted [to derive benefit] from uncircumcised Israelites but prohibited [from deriving benefit] from circumcised gentiles.
H. "Qonam [forbidden as what is consecrated to the Temple be whatever] I derive as benefit from the circumcised" – he is prohibited [to derive benefit] from uncircumcised Israelites and permitted [to derive benefit] from circumcised gentiles.
I. For the word "uncircumcised" is used only as a name for gentiles, as it is written, "For all the nations are uncircumcised, and the whole house of Israel is uncircumcised at hear" (Jer. 9:26).
J. And it says, "This uncircumcised Philistine" (1 Sam. 17:36).
K. And it says, "Lest the daughters of the Philistines rejoice, lest the daughters of the uncircumcised triumph" (1 Sam. 1:20).

The rite of circumcision by itself bears no probative value; then to be called "Israel" is what counts; that title is correctly applied by other criteria altogether, as we noted in chapter 3, and the condition of the individual as to even the most personal of rites is subordinate. The upshot is simple: the sages deemed Israel to form a collectivity, the individual to cohere with, and find definition in, the shared traits of the group.

That brings us to the second question: what difference do the state and fate of the individual make, if the individual Israelite finds himself subjected to the same fate as all other Israelites who constitute all Israel? And why do individual persons come under the purview of the theological system at hand? A single explanation, the one governing all Israel, ought to serve for the complaint of private persons at the injustice of what is meted out to them. But that is not the position that the sages' theology adopts. Rather, they find particular purpose in the identification of the category, the free-standing individual, defined in his own terms and in the framework of his own existence, not only within all Israel. The word "Israel" does refer to persons, Israelites one by one, not only to the people. So a dialectic, not to be resolved, takes shape between the public and the private. Each individual enjoys his own justice. But individuals suffer along with all Israel. All Israel designs its own destiny by its attitude and consequent actions. But all Israel is shaped by the actions and attitude of individuals one by one – a complex dialectic indeed, in which justice may well be obscured.

Individuals matter, on their own, not only within the collectivity of Israel. On what basis do the sages construct their doctrine of individual worth? The sages themselves hardly valued for its own sake the perpetuation of the individual's name. As we noted in chapter 1, in their normative statements, the law followed the anonymous, not the assigned ruling. One who wished to make a long-term contribution, therefore, had to seek to submerge his private views within a public consensus. Eternity for one's contribution demanded anonymity for one's person, much as, to save one's child, a parent will willingly give up life itself. But the sages did recognize that for worthy purposes the individual could be distinguished.

The first, and most readily anticipated, way of explaining why a name would last, that is, an individual would enjoy recognition not solely within the framework of all Israel, drew attention to those prepared to give up their lives for God's sake. God will preserve the name of one who is prepared to accept martyrdom to sanctify God's name, that is, for a divine commandment:

PESIQTA RABBATI V:II.I:

A. Another interpretation of the verse, "If I should write for him the larger part of my Torah, then he would have been seen as a stranger" (Hos. 8:12):
B. This is one of the three matters for which Moses was prepared to give his life, on account of which the Holy One, blessed be he, gave them in his name [in line with the sense of the verse, I should write for him, meaning, in his name].

C. The three are the rule of justice, the Torah, and the building of the tabernacle in the wilderness.

Scriptural facts are ordered to sustain the stated general rule:

D. How do we know that that is so of the Torah: "Remember the Torah of Moses, my servant" (Mal. 3:22).

E. The rule of justice: "Moses the lawgiver … maintained the righteous judgments of the Lord and his ordinances among Israel" (Deut. 33:21).

F. How do we know that Moses was prepared to give his life for the sake of the tabernacle:

G. R. Hiyya b. Joseph said, "On each of the seven days of the consecration of the tabernacle, Moses would dismantle the tabernacle twice a day and then set it up again [thus, morning and evening, for the obligatory daily whole-offering done twice a day]."

H. R. Hanina the Elder said, "Three times a day he would dismantle it and then erect it."

I. And should you suppose that someone of the tribe of Levi would give him a hand, our masters have said, "He by himself would dismantle it, and no person of Israel helped him in any way.

Next comes secondary amplification of the point:

J. "How [do we know that Moses did it by himself]? As it is said, 'And it came to pass on the day that Moses completed setting up the Tabernacle, [he anointed and consecrated it; he also anointed and consecrated its equipment, and the altar and its vessels. The chief men of Israel, heads of families, that is, the chiefs of the tribes who had assisted in preparing the detailed lists, came forward and brought their offering before the Lord]' (Num. 7:1–2). [All that the others did was make the lists and then give their own offering. Moses did the rest.]"

The match now is between eternal life – a name endures – and willingness to give up life. That for which one is prepared to give his life secures for him an enduring name. The principle of rational balance – you get what you give – is then established by facts of Scripture. Then, just as the sages insist, "A name made great is a name destroyed" (Tractate Abot 1:13), so they maintain that a life surrendered to God is a life recognized by God.

But that mode of individuation accorded consequence only to the exceptional person in the remarkable circumstance. What about ordinary Israelites, one by one, and, more to the point, ordinary men, whether Israelite or gentile? Here the figure of Adam enters in. The second validation of individuality is that God deliberately created individuals, one by one, in the model of the unique Adam, after whom all who followed are modelled. The individual is not subsumed entirely within that sector of humanity to which he belongs but bears the traits of autonomy and individuality, and this is how God planned matters. A number of explanations coalesce in response to the question of why man was created one by one, alone; of these, the fourth is most germane to our problem, but it should be examined in documentary context:

MISHNAH-TRACTATE SANHEDRIN 4:5:

J. Therefore man was created alone, (1) to teach you that whoever destroys a single Israelite soul is deemed by Scripture as if he had destroyed a whole world.

K. And whoever saves a single Israelite soul is deemed by Scripture as if he had saved a whole world.

L. And (2) it was also for the sake of peace among people, so that someone should not say to his fellow, "My father is greater than your father."

M. And (3) [it was also on account of the heretics,] so that the heretics should not say, "There are many domains in Heaven."

N. And (4) to portray the grandeur of the Holy One, blessed be he. For a person mints many coins with a single seal, and they are all alike one another. But the King of kings of kings, the Holy One, blessed be he, minted all human beings with that seal of his with which he made the first person, yet not one of them is like anyone else. Therefore everyone is obligated to maintain, "On my account the world was created."

Manuscript versions of the passage vary and include those that omit "Israelite" at J and K, leaving the doctrine to pertain to all of the children of Noah, Israelite and gentile alike. However we read the passage, its message for our problem is clear. It is there that we find an explicit doctrine validating recognition of individual difference.

The Talmud of Babylonia's amplification of that point underscores the legitimacy of individuality:

BAVLI TRACTATE SANHEDRIN 4:5 IV:I, V.I/38A

V.I A. To portray the grandeur ... (M. 4:5N):

B. Our rabbis have taught on Tannaite authority:

C. [Tosefta:] Another matter: Why was he created one and alone?

D. To show the grandeur of the king of the kings of kings, blessed be he.

E. For if a man mints many coins with one mold, all are alike.

F. But the Holy One, blessed be he, mints every man with the mold of the first man [Tosefta: for with a single seal, he created the entire world], and not one of them is like another [T. from a single seal all those many diverse seals have come forth],

G. as it is said, "It is changed as clay under the seal, and all this things stand forth as in a garment" (Job 38:14) (M. 4:5N) (Tosefta San. 8:5A-D).

So much for the general principle. But now to details: faces, voices, minds:

H. And on what accounts are faces not like one another?

I. On account of imposters,

J. so no one should see a lovely house or woman and say "It is mine" [Tosefta: jump into his neighbour's field or jump in bed with his neighbour's wife],

K. as it is said, "And from the wicked their light is withheld and the strong arm is broken" (Job. 38:15).

L. It has been taught on Tannaite authority: R. Meir says, "The Omnipresent has varied a man in three ways: appearance, intelligence, and voice

M. intelligence, because of robbers and thieves, and appearance and voice, because of the possibilities of licentiousness" (=Tosefta San. 8:6A-F).

The singularity of Adam – and of all men – finds explanation in a variety of moral considerations.

The premise is that the rationality of creation encompasses self-evident moral rules and theological facts. Individuation, here distinguishing one man from all others, as much as the Israelite from all Israel, serves the purpose of defining the private person as a moral category, a field of moral justice and judgment, distinct from all Israel. The upshot is that a person's fate cannot be accounted for solely within the framework of what happens to collective Israel. Being part of Israel means that the same rules that apply to all Israel apply to the individual. But being autonomous means that the individual has the right personally, in his own terms, to expect justice, the exact meting out of measure for measure. On that basis, the ordering of the ultimate anomaly, what happens in private lives, emerges as a critical problem facing the theological system.

That brings us to the third question: can we invoke the same explanation for private lives that serves in accounting for the public condition of all Israel? The answer is affirmative, but with important qualifications. The fundamental affirmation, pertaining to public Israel and private Israelite alike, maintains that exact justice governs. No anomalies will persist past the resurrection, the last judgment, and the world to come, a subject of which, in chapters 13 and 14, we shall hear much more. But the application of that principle yields much thicker layer of instantiation and application, far more diversity in the range of explanation, than in the case of the condition of Israel subjugated by the nations.

Private matches public. If the nations are responsible for their condition, so is Israel, so are Israelites. So, too, is the rule of justice, and justification, for private lives. Everything begins with the insistence that people are responsible for what they do, therefore for what happens to them, as much as Israel dictates its destiny by its own deeds. Justice reigns, whatever happens. The reason that man (therefore, groups formed by men) is responsible for his own actions is that he enjoys free will. Man is constantly subject to divine judgment; he has free choice, hence may sin (a matter of critical consequence, as we shall see in chapter 11); God judges the world in a generous way; but judgment does take place:

TRACTATE ABOT 3:15

A. R. Aqiba says, "Everything is foreseen, and free choice is given. In goodness the world is judged. And all is in accord with the abundance of deeds."
B. He would say, "(1) All is handed over as a pledge, (2) And a net is cast over all the living. (3) The store is open, (4) the storekeeper gives credit, (5) the account book is open, and (6) the hand is writing.
C. "(1) Whoever wants to borrow may come and borrow. (2) The charity collectors go around every day and collect from man whether he knows it or not. (3) And they have grounds for what they do. (4) And the judgment is a true judgment. (5) And everything is ready for the meal."

God may foresee what is to happen, but man still exercises free will. His attitude and intentionality make all the difference. Because man is not coerced to sin, nor can man be forced to love God or even obey the Torah, an element of uncertainty affects every life. That is the point at which man's will competes with God's. It follows that, where man gives to God what God wants but cannot coerce, or what God wants but cannot command – love, generosity, for instance – there, the theology of the Oral Torah alleges, God responds with an act of uncoerced grace. But in all, one thing is reliable, and that is the working of just recompense for individual action. Expectations of a just reward or punishment, contrasting with actualities, therefore precipitate all thought on the rationality of private life: what happens is supposed to make sense within the governing theology of a just order.

But that expectation rarely is met. How do the sages justify – meaning, "show the justice of" – what happens in private lives? Let us first consider how the sages explained private fate as a consequence of individual behaviour. Their first principle, predictably, is that, as Israel defines its own fate, so individuals bear responsibility for their own condition. A person is responsible for his own character. Even though one is surrounded by wicked people, he may still remain righteous, and vice versa. A measure of righteousness is not to conduct oneself in the manner of one's wicked neighbours. Not only so, but the righteous son of a wicked father enjoys much admiration but bears no burden of responsibility for his ancestry, and so for the contrary circumstance:

SIFRÉ TO NUMBERS CXXXIII:II.I

A. "[Then drew near the daughters of Zelophehad] the son of Hepher son of Gilead son of Machir son of Manasseh":

B. Scripture thus informs [us] that just as Zelophehad was a first-born, so all of them were first-born [daughters] [to their mothers]; that all of them were upright women, daughters of an upright man.

C. For in the case of whoever keeps his [worthy] deeds concealed, and his father's deeds are concealed, Scripture portrays a worthy genealogy, lo, this was a righteous man son of a righteous man.

D. And in the case of whoever keeps his [unworthy] deeds concealed, and his father's deeds concealed, Scripture portrays a disreputable genealogy, lo, this is a wicked man son of a wicked man.

The matter is now subject to amplification, with concrete cases of Scripture linked to the governing generalization:

E. R. Nathan says, "Scripture comes to teach you [about] every righteous man who grew up in the bosom of a wicked man and did not act like him, to tell you how great is his righteousness. For he grew up in the bosom of a wicked man but did not act like him.

F. "And every wicked man who grew up in the bosom of a righteous man but did not act like him – that tells you how great is the wickedness of such a one, who grew up in the bosom of a righteous man but did not act like him.

Next come the cases:

G. "Esau grew up between two righteous persons, Isaac and Rebecca, but he did not act like them. Obadiah grew up between two wicked persons, Ahab and Jezebel, but did not act like them. And he prophesied concerning the wicked Esau, who grew up between two righteous persons, Isaac and Rebecca, but did not act like them, as it is said, 'The vision of Obadiah: thus says the Lord God concerning Edom: we have heard tidings from the Lord and a messenger has been sent among the nations'" (Obadiah 1:1).

As usual, Scripture provides ample facts to be organized into the proposition that each person is responsible for himself. The corollary must follow: what happens to the private person in the end cannot produce an anomaly for the governance of justice but, in some way or other, must accord with the rules of world order.

Not only so, but the principle that man is responsible for what he does is established in the very creation of the First Man. Just as individuation is explained by appeal to the figure of Adam, so man's responsibility for his own deeds is adumbrated and exemplified by Adam. Adam acknowledged that he bore full responsibility for his own fate, and built into the human condition, therefore, is that same recognition:

PESIQTA DERAB KAHANA XIV:V.I

A. It is written, "Thus said the Lord, What wrong did your fathers find in me that they went far from me and went after worthlessness and became worthless?" (Jer. 2:5)

B. Said R. Isaac, "This refers to one who leaves the scroll of the Torah and departs. Concerning him, Scripture says, 'What wrong did your fathers find in me that they went far from me.'

C. "Said the Holy One, blessed be he, to the Israelites, 'My children, your fathers found no wrong with me, but you have found wrong with me.

A case – the archetypal one, man himself – will illustrate the generalization contained within the statement of Isaac. People who violate the Torah do so on their own volition, not by reason of a tradition of rebellion. They therefore bear responsibility for their own sins.

D. " 'The first Man found no wrong with me, but you have found wrong with me.'

E. "To what may the first Man be compared?

F. "To a sick man, to whom the physician came. The physician said to him, 'Eat this, don't eat that.'

G. "When the man violated the instructions of the physician, he brought about his own death.

H. "[As he lay dying,] his relatives came to him and said to him, 'Is it possible that the physician is imposing on you the divine attribute of justice?'

I. "He said to them, 'God forbid. I am the one who brought about my own death. This is what he instructed me, saying to me, 'Eat this, don't eat that,' but when I violated his instructions, I brought about my own death.

Man is the archetype; he brings upon himself his own death:

J. "So too all the generations came to the first Man, saying to him, 'Is it possible that the Holy One, blessed be he, is imposing the attribute of justice on you?'
L. "He said to them, 'God forbid. I am the one who has brought about my own death. Thus did he command me, saying to me, 'Of all the trees of the garden you may eat, but of the tree of the knowledge of good and evil you may not eat' (Gen. 2:17). When I violated his instructions, I brought about my own death, for it is written, 'On the day on which you eat it, you will surely die' " (Gen. 2:17).

God is not at fault for Adam's fall; Adam brought about his own death. So justice governs, and people may appeal to that sense for the fitting penalty for the sin to explain what happens in ordinary, everyday affairs.

But who bears responsibility when an infant dies, or a woman in childbirth, or a man before his appointed time (prior to age sixty in the Talmud's estimation)? And how do the sages reasonably explain the anomalies round about, those manifested by Scripture and embodied in the here and now of everyday life? Several distinct explanations serve, depending on the circumstance. In one the individual's fate is bound up with that of the group, Israel, or of the generation, of which he is part; in the second type of explanation, a specific sort of malady or affliction is bound up to a particular sort of sin, a principle we have already established in chapter 2; and in due course other approaches to the same problem will come before us. Since old age, sickness, suffering, and death come to all, moreover, the sages do not concede that these common mediators of man's fate represent punishment for sin.

Let us take up the first, that individuals suffer as part of Israel. What happens to this one or that one may make sense within the story of what happens to Israel collectively. The sages thereby concede that, in an exact sense, life is not, cannot be, fair; we are not responsible for the fact that we are born into interesting times, though we become responsible for how we respond to those points of interest. But while the sages do accord the moral role to the individual, they never conceive of the individual as utterly isolated, free-standing in any time or place; the individual is not necessarily party to the sin of his generation, but he is always part of the community that God has identified as the principal actor in the drama of human events, Israel. Haman hated

Israel because of Mordecai. Moses was set adrift in the river because Pharaoh feared mighty Israel. It made no difference whether the individual or the group precipitated the crisis. But that meant, once the angel of death unleashed his scythe, everyone would be caught on its blade.

The book of Lamentation provides a sustained exercise in linking public history to private destiny, mourning for both equally, treating the one as definitive of the other. There, the fate of the individual bears within itself proof of Israel's election. The story of a single individual demonstrates that when Israel suffers, it is because of their own sin, and when Israel prospers, it is because of service to God, acceptance of God's will:

BAVLI TRACTATE KETUBOT 6:4 II.4/66B

II.4 A. Our rabbis have taught on Tannaite authority:

B. There was the case of Rabban Yohanan b. Zakkai, who was riding on his ass leaving Jerusalem, and his disciples were following him. He saw a girl who was picking barley seeds from the shit of Arab cattle. When she saw him, she covered herself with her hair, stood before him, and said to him, "My lord, give me some food."

C. He said to her, "My daughter, who are you?"

D. She said to him, "I'm the daughter of Naqdimon b. Gurion."

The sage immediately identified the woman with the fate of her father's household, of which she was an undifferentiated part, not asking what she personally might have done to suffer degradation:

E. He said to her, "My daughter, what ever happened to the money of your father's house?"

F. She said to him, "My lord, doesn't the Jerusalem proverb go, 'The salt [that keeps] money [secure] is distributing it [to the poor]?' "

G. Others say, "… acts of loving kindness [done with the money] …"

H. "And what ever happened to the money of your father-in-law's house [pledged to your marriage contract]?"

I. She said to him, "The [funds were mingled, and] one came and destroyed the other."

J. She said to him, "My lord, do you remember when you signed my marriage contract?"

K. He said to his disciples, "I remember full well, when I signed her marriage contract, I read in it, 'A thousand thousand gold denars from the house of her father, not counting what comes from her father-in-law …' "

So much for the individual. Now the composition proceeds to treat the individual as exemplary of the condition of the holy people, Israel. Today's misery foretells tomorrow's redemption, a position integral to the systemic theodicy being worked out here:

L. Rabban Yohanan ben Zakkai wept and said, "Happy are you, Israel! When you do what the Omnipresent wants, no nation or alien tongue can rule you, and when you don't do what the Omnipresent wants, he hands you over to the most degraded nation, and not only into the power of the most degraded nation, but into the power of their cattle."

At the same time, the individual's fate demands an accounting, so the specific sin that the woman's father has committed, with the result that she is left penurious, is examined in its own terms:

II.5 A. So didn't Naqdimon b. Gurion do acts of philanthropy? And has it not been taught on Tannaite authority: They said concerning Naqdimon b. Gurion that when he went forth from his household to the house of study, they would strew before him [67A] woolen garments, and then the poor would follow after him and roll them up [and take them home]?
B. If you wish, I shall say, it was for his own glory that he did things like that, and if you wish, I shall say, he didn't do it to the full extent that he could have, as people say, "In accord with the strength of the camel is the burden that you load on it."

Public history and private destiny flow together, yet part company. In the first story, the fate of the young girl is explained by reference to Israel's: when Israel adheres to the covenant, no one can rule them; but when not, then an individual finds herself picking for food in the dung of Arab cattle. And in that same context, the girl's father lost his money for just cause, because he did not give to the poor. But the comment calls into question the justification that has been offered: the man did the right thing. Then the elastic causes enter: he had the wrong motive, or he did not carry out philanthropy to the full extent that he ought to have. We thus see how the innocent daughter's situation is explained by reference to what has happened to all Israel, on the one side, and to her father, on the other.

The second approach to justification of what happens to private persons forms a variation on the first. Just as individual Israelites are caught up within the fate of Israel, so they are party to what happens in their own day and age. That involves not so much temporal as circumstantial considerations: it is good to be a contemporary of righteous persons, and it is unfortunate to live in the age or place of wicked ones. Whatever happens comes about by reason of the character of a given generation and the presence of the righteous or the wicked. The righteous bring goodness to the world, and when they die, retribution follows; the wicked bring retribution to the world, and when they die, goodness returns. This is spelled out in so many words:

TOSEFTA-TRACTATE SOTAH 10:1–11:2

10:1 A. When righteous people come into the world, good comes into the world and retribution departs from the world.

B. And when they take their leave from the world, retribution comes into the world, and goodness departs from the world.

10:2 A. When bad people come into the world, retribution comes into the world, and goodness departs from the world.

B. And when they depart from the world, goodness comes back into the world, and retribution departs from the world.

As anticipated, general propositions require demonstration, and in the Oral Torah systematic presentation of probative cases supplied by verses of Scripture serves for that purpose (only the Bavli demands a different kind of logical demonstration altogether from the exemplary one that prevails):

C. How do we know that, when righteous people come into the world, goodness comes into the world, and retribution departs from the world? Since it is said, "And he called him Noah, saying, This one will comfort us in our work and in the toil of our hands" (Gen. 5:29).

D. And how do we know that, when they take their leave of the world, retribution comes into the world and goodness departs from the world? Since it is said, "The righteous man perishes and no one lays it to heart" (Is. 57:1), and it says, "He enters into peace, they rest in their beds who walk in their uprightness" (Is. 57:2) – He goes in peace to the grave. And it says, "But you, draw near hither, sons of the sorceress, offspring of the adulterer and the harlot" (Is. 57:3).

E. And how do we know that when bad people come into the world, retribution comes into the world and goodness departs from the world? Since it is said, "When the wicked comes, then comes also contempt, and with ignominy, reproach" (Prov. 18:3).

F. And how do we know that, when he departs from the world, goodness comes into the world and retribution leaves the world? Since it says, "And when the wicked perish, there is exultation" (Prov. 11:10). And it says, "So that the Lord may turn from the fierceness of his anger and show you mercy and have compassion on you" (Deut. 13:17).

Secondary amplification now takes over, and we show, once more out of the facts established by Scripture, the validity of the generalization:

10:3 A. So long as bad people are in the world, fierce anger is in the world. When they perish from the world, retribution and fierce wrath depart from the world.

B. And it is not that the righteous people support the world when they are alive only, but even after death, as it says, "And after seven days the waters of the flood came upon the earth" (Gen. 7:10).

C. Now what is the meaning of these seven days? These are the seven days of mourning for Methuselah, the righteous man, which held back the retribution from coming upon the world.

D. Therefore it is said, "And after seven days".

We turn to proofs deriving from the lives of the patriarchs, particularly Abraham, Isaac, and Jacob, and then Joseph, Miriam, and Aaron – the principals of redemption, such as will be matched at the end of days – with cases from their lives serving as facts subject to generalization:

10:5 B. All the time that Abraham was alive, there was plenty, since it says, "And Abraham was old, well advanced in years, and the Lord had blessed Abraham in all things" (Gen. 24:1).

C. But once Abraham had died, "There was famine in the land" (Gen. 26:1).

10:6 A. When Isaac came along, there was plenty, as it is said, "And Isaac sowed in that land and reaped in the same year a hundredfold" (Gen. 26:12).

B. So long as Abraham was alive, the wells gushed forth water. When Abraham had died, what does it say? "Now the Philistines had stopped and filled with earth all the wells which his father's servants had dug in the days of Abraham his father" (Gen. 26:15).

C. For they said, "Now that they do not gush forth water, they are only a hazard for travelers." They (therefore) went and stopped them up.

D. Isaac came along, and the wells gushed water, as it is said, "And lsaac dug again the wells of water which had been dug in the days of Abraham his father … And when Isaac's servants dug in the valley and found there a well of springing water …" (Gen. 26:18–19).

10:7 A. Before Jacob went down to Aram Naharaim, the house of Laban the Aramaean had not received a blessing, as it is said, 'For you had little before I came, and it has increased abundantly, and the Lord has blessed you wherever I turned" (Gen. 30:30).

B. Once he came down, what does it say? "And the Lord has blessed you wherever I turned."

C. And it says, "I have learned by divination that the Lord has blessed me because of you" (Gen. 30:27).

Now to the paradigm of redemption, the case of Egypt:

10:8 A. Before Joseph went down to Egypt, the house of Potiphar had not received a blessing. But once he went down, what does it say?

B. "From the time that he made him overseer in his house and over all that he had, the Lord blessed the Egyptian's house for Joseph's sake" (Gen. 30:5).

10:9 A. Before Jacob went down to Egypt, there had been famine, as it is said, "For the famine has been in the land these two years" (Gen. 45:6).

B. Once he came down there, what does it say? "Now here is seed for you, and you shall sow the land" (Gen. 47:23).

C. Said R. Yosé, "When Jacob our patriarch died, the famine came back where it had been, as it is said, 'So do not fear; I will provide for you and for your little ones' (Gen. 50:21).

o. " 'Providing' is stated here, and 'providing' is stated later on. Just as in this context it is a situation of famine, so in the other context, it is a situation of famine."

Next come Joseph, Miriam, and Aaron, and we end with the climactic figure of Moses:

10:10 A. So long as Joseph and the tribes were alive, the Israelites enjoyed greatness and honour, as it is said, "And the children of Israel were fruitful and multiplied" (Ex. 1:7).

B. When Joseph died, what does it say? "And Joseph died ... And a new king arose who knew not Joseph ... And he said to his people ... Come, let us take counsel against him" (Ex. 1:6, 8–10).

11:1 A. So long as Miriam was alive, the well provided ample water for all Israel. Once Miriam had died, what does it say? And Miriam died there, and there was not enough water for the congregation (Num. 20:1–2) – for the well dried up.

B. So long as Aaron was alive, a pillar of cloud led Israel. Once Aaron had died, what does it say? "When the Canaanite, the king of Arad, who dwelt in the Negeb, heard that Israel was coming" (Num. 21:1).

C. That bad man grew strong, and he came and made war against Israel. He said, "Where has their seer gone, who paved the way for them into the land?"

11:2 A. As long as Moses was alive, the manna came down to Israel. When Moses died, what does it say? "And the manna ceased on the morrow" (Josh. 5:12).

The individual forms a moral arena of his own, but he also participates in the life and fate of Israel, on the one side, and his own generation, on the other.

Scripture provides ample evidence of that fact. So it is in the nature of things that the individual cannot claim exact justice in the here and now; circumstances intervene, and, when it comes to God's government, what happens to the holy people or to the community at large takes priority over the fate of the individual. That admission reaffirms the essential rationality of the divine rule, the justice that prevails overall, even while accepting that individuals may present anomalies. But these anomalies will work themselves out in another way, and the program of justification takes account of yet other, available solutions to the problem of evil. The individual may suffer in his generation, but that is only for the moment; at the end of days, when the dead return to life, the individual will be judged on his own and accorded a portion of the world to come commensurate with his virtue in this life, a point that takes on critical important at the end of the story, in chapter 14, as it did at the outset, in chapter 2: measure for measure, throughout.

A third approach addresses the individual in his own terms and framework and states in so many words that, just like the community of Israel, so too individuals suffer by reason of the result of their own deeds. We have already considered penalties for specific actions. The doctrine of reward and punishment is spelled out in close detail. First let us take up the matter of punishment for specific sins or crimes. Here is a clear statement that the individual brings his fate upon his own head, in the context of a specific disaster. The person afflicted with the imaginary ailment described at Leviticus Chapters 13 and 14, here translated as "plagues," or "plague of leprosy," has brought the illness upon himself by gossiping, and Scripture contains ample proof of that fact:

SIFRA CLV:I.8

A. "... saying" (Lev. 14:35) –

B. The priest will say to him words of reproach: "My son, plagues come only because of gossip [T. 6:7], as it is said, 'Take heed of the plague of leprosy to keep very much and to do, remember what the Lord God did to Miriam' (Deut. 24:8o).

C. "And what has one thing to do with the other?

D. "But this teaches that she was punished only because of gossip.

E. "And is it not an argument *a fortiori*?

F. "If Miriam, who did not speak before Moses' presence, suffered so, one who speaks ill of his fellow in his very presence, how much the more so?"

Not only gossip, but other sins bring on specific penalties, arrogance too:

G. R. Simeon b. Eleazar says, "Also because of arrogance do plagues come, for so do we find concerning Uzziah,

H. "as it is said, 'And he rebelled against the Lord his God and he came to the Temple of the Lord to offer on the altar incense and Azariah the Priest came after him and with him priests of the Lord, eighty strong men, and they stood against Uzziah and said to him, It is not for you to do, Uzziah, to offer to the Lord, for only the priests the sons of Aaron who are sanctified do so. So forth from the sanctuary. And Uzziah was angry,' etc. (II Chron. 26:16)" (T. Neg. 6:7H).

Then one who gossips is penalized by an attack of the skin-ailment under discussion here (no one knows what they mean). God has spelled out in the Torah both sins and the penalty attaching to them. So what happens to the individual will naturally be explained as a consequence of what he has done.

Despite their confidence that justice will prevail, the sages by no means turned into a hard science the determination of which sin provoked which penalty. For much that took place they simply appealed to the general explanation that such was the divine decree, responding to good cause. Thus, for example, a person's entire allotment for the year is determined by God between New Year's Day and the Day of Atonement, except for the expenses of celebrating Sabbaths and the expenses of celebrating festivals and the expense of educating his sons in Torah. For if he spends .ess on these things than he should, he is given less. While if he spends more than is expected, he is given more, so Bavli tractate Besah 2:1 I.5/16a.

That final detail reminds us that justice involves not only penalty for sin, but reward for merit. For the sages, it was equally important to account for prosperity as for misfortune. They held that, just as even minor sins provoke penalties, so even small gestures enjoy the appropriate reward, divine justice extending to every deed:

BAVLI TRACTATE BABA QAMMA 4:3 II.6–7/38B

II.6 A. Said R. Hiyya bar Abba said R. Yohanan, "The Holy One, blessed be he, does not hold back from any creature the reward that is coming to it, even the reward for a few appropriate words, for in the case of the elder daughter of Lot, who named her son Moab [= from father] [Gen. 19:30–8], said the Holy One, blessed be he, to Moses, 'Do not distress the Moabites, neither contend with them in battle' (Deut. 2:9). The sense then is, it is war in particular that one is not to make against them, but one may well exact taxes from them. But in the case of the younger daughter of Lot, who named her son Ben Ammi [son of my people], the Holy One, blessed be he, said to Moses, 'And when you come near against the children of Ammon, do not distress them or meddle with them at all' (Deut. 2:19) – not even exacting taxes from them."

Here the reward vastly outweighs the meritorious deed; in this case the daughter's proper naming of her son sufficed to win for her heirs an enduring exemption from taxes. The same point is restated in a still more concrete way in the continuation:

II.7 A.   Said R. Hiyya bar Abba said R. Joshua b. Qorha, "One should always give precedence to a matter involving a religious duty, since, on account of the one night by which the elder daughter of Lot came prior to the younger, she came prior to her by four generations: Obed, Jesse, David, and Solomon [via Ruth]. As to the younger, she had none until Rehoboam: 'And the name of his mother was Naamah the Ammonitess' " (I Kgs. 14:31).

In these ways the sages underscore their conviction that a generous justice takes account of all matters of consequence, everything that Israelites and those within their circle do.

Since the sages regarded early death (before sixty) as a form of penalty inflicted by Heaven, so they regarded long life (beyond seventy) as a mark of divine favour. They had no reason to ask why a wicked person lived a long life; in a moment we shall examine their stock-explanation for the prosperity of evil people. But they deemed the great sages as self-evidently righteous men, and so when some of them lived to a ripe old age, they asked for an explanation. Such an explanation coming from a sage served as proof in the same way that linking a particular sin to a particular punishment specified by Scripture offered probative evidence of facts. Standing in the tradition of Sinai through the Oral Torah, the sage then served as Scripture served to supply specific instantiations of the important theological principle at hand. This provided the occasion for matching reward to virtue or acts of merit, just as they looked for opportunities to show how the principle of measure for measure accounted for misfortune. There is a long sequence of systematic colloquies that spell out the doctrine of reward for merit or virtue, a composite that organizes discrete facts into a compelling demonstration of a proposition of world order:

BAVLI TRACTATE SOTAH 7:6 I.21/28A-B

21. A.   The disciples of R. Eliezer b. Shammua asked him, "On what account have you lived so long?"
B.   He said to them, "I never turned a synagogue into a short cut, I never stepped over the heads of the holy people [when the people were seated before a master]. I never raised my hands [in the priestly benediction] without saying a blessing."

II.6 A. R. Pereidah's students asked him, "On what account have you attained long life?"

B. He said to them, "In my [entire] lifetime, no one ever preceded me at the academy; [28a] and I never recited a blessing before a priest; and I never ate from an animal whose [priestly] gifts were not removed."

Liturgical virtue then is introduced as source of particular reward of long life. But in the next entry, moral virtue takes over:

II.8 A. R. Nehuniah ben HaQaneh's students asked him, "On what account have you attained long life?"

B. He said to them, "In my [entire] lifetime, [1] I was never honoured through my fellow's embarrassment; [2] and my fellow's curse never followed me to bed; [3] and I was generous with my money."

Now come the particular virtues of patience, restraint, humility, and self-abnegation:

II.11 A. R. Zeira's students asked him, "On what account have you attained long life?"

B. He said to them, "In my [entire] lifetime, [1] I never got angry in my house; [2] and I never walked in front of someone greater than myself; [3] and I never thought [holy thoughts] in unclean alleys; [4] and I never walked four cubits without Torah or without Tefillin; [5] and I never slept in the academy, neither soundly nor dozing; [6] and I never rejoiced at the misfortune of my fellow; [7] and I never addressed my fellow by his insulting nickname, some say, not even by his [regular] nickname."

Readers may stipulate that the sequence of explanations moves in its own protracted trajectory. The further cases make the same point. Long life forms Heaven's response to humility and forbearance, virtues that come to the surface time and again. The mixture of liturgical and moral virtues should not obscure the clear premise that, just as misfortune is explained as punishment for sin, so good fortune must find justification as well, and that will turn attention to singular, and specific, virtues.

In accounting for what happens to individuals, the sages had to address two sources of explanation besides individual responsibility for sin or crime and the penalty thereof. Both challenged the purposive principle of applied justice that, in general, the sages invoked. The first source of rational explanation defying justice derived from astrology, the second from sheer accident. The sages took opposed positions on these, denying the one, affirming the other. The stars do not govern Israel, only God does. But God works his will through what man may deem a mere accident, the chance throw of the dice, as Scripture's Oracles (*Urim vethumim*) indicated. That is because the active, just God they encountered could never permit the movements of the stars to limit his acts of justice, for he created the stars and they are subject to his will. But in his wisdom, in accord with his vast design for creation in justice, he could, and in the sages' view did, work his will through what man saw as mere chance as well as through what they deemed destiny.

The former of the two positions, challenging astrology, placed the sages in opposition to the science of their day, which took for granted that the positions of the stars dictated events on earth. The sages could not dismiss such established science, any more than their contemporary continuators can plausibly reject the laws of gravity or Copernican astronomy. But the sages took up a distinctive position on astrology, one consistent with their theology of holy Israel. Specifically, the sages took for granted that astrology governed the gentiles, but, true to their generative convictions about Israel, what most (though not all) of them could and did maintain was that the laws of astrology do not affect holy Israel. Israel is *sui generis*, because God alone, and not determinism in any form, dictates what happens to Israel and to Israelites. What happens to Israel realizes God's will, that alone.

Gentiles, by contrast, live within the ordinary rules of nature that pertain to all but Israel and so are subject to astrology, having rejected a position in God's dominion and chosen not to live under his rules, beyond nature's. That is why God does not choose to overrule the stars, because gentiles do not accept his dominion in the Torah, and that is why they are ruled by impersonal forces of physics. At stake in the logic of an orderly world subject in every detail to the rationality of justice, then, is the working of God's just will. Where God chooses to govern and is so chosen, there the stars affect nothing. So we see once more the working of the doctrine of Israel and the Torah, the gentiles and idolatry. While recognizing the scientific standing of astrology, therefore, most sages represented in the Oral Torah concurred that, when it comes to Israel, God rules, not the stars.

But some did not see matters in that way. Insisting as I do that the theology of the Oral Torah spins out the story told through the simple logic of a just order, I have also to show that, in this important detail, normative opinion responds to the requirements of that governing logic. Opinion that here takes a position in contradiction to that authoritative logic ought to be represented as schismatic, associated with individually named sages, and not normative. Now, as we realize, to determine the normative position, it does not suffice merely to collect random opinion. Rather, since the Oral Torah, particularly the Bavli, sets forth systematic topical expositions, not merely random opinion, and organizes those composites in such a way as to indicate the thrust and direction of opinion, I choose the Bavli's one sustained statement on the subject. That systematic statement is so organized as to yield only a single conclusion. Specifically, I focus upon the single most systematic composite on the subject, which is so framed as to demonstrate that astrology does not apply to Israel:

BAVLI TRACTATE SHABBAT 24:4 III.9/156A-B

A. It has been stated:
B. R. Hanina says, "One's star is what makes one smart, one's star is what gives wealth, and Israel is subject to the stars."
C. R. Yohanan said, "Israel is not subject to the stars."

Clearly, two opinions competed. Two characteristics mark the normative one in a dispute: 1) whose opinion is explored, whose neglected; and 2) whose opinion is complemented with sustaining authorities' views, whose not. In the following, Yohanan's position is analysed, Hanina's ignored:

D. And R. Yohanan is consistent with views expressed elsewhere, for said R. Yohanan, "How on the basis of Scripture do we know that Israel is not subject to the stars? As it is said, 'Thus says the Lord, Do not learn the way of the gentiles, nor be dismayed at the signs of the heavens, for the nations are dismayed at them' (Jer. 10:2). They are dismayed, but the Israelites are not dismayed."

Now begins a long sequence of systematic demonstrations that Israel is not subject to astrology. We begin with exegetical-scriptural proof:

III.10 A. And so Rab takes the view that Israel is not subject to the stars, for said R. Judah said Rab, "How on the basis of Scripture do we know that Israel is not subject to the stars? As it is said, 'And he brought him forth outside' (Gen. 15:5). Said Abraham before the Holy One, blessed be he, 'Lord of the world, Someone born in my household is my heir' (Gen. 15:3). He said to him, 'Not at all. But he who will come forth out of your own loins' (Gen. 1:4). He said before him, 'Lord of the world, I have closely examined my star, and I have seen that I am destined to have no children.' He said to him, 'Abandon this astrology of yours – Israel is not subject to astrology. Now what's your calculation? [156B] Is it that Jupiter stands in the west [and that is your constellation]? I'll turn it back and set it up in the East.' And so it is written, 'Who has raised up Jupiter from the east? He has summoned it for his sake' " (Isa. 41:2).

Scripture, as always, supplies the initial demonstration. Wherever possible, the patriarchs will be asked to show that, even at the very beginning of Israel, the besought principle applied. At the next stage, we are given exemplary cases that show us how and why the sages maintain that Israel is not subject to astrology. The first case pits astrological judgment against divine intervention; the latter sets aside the testimony of the stars.

Not only so, but a specific reason is adduced to account for the special favour shown the man, which is the man's own supererogatory act of generosity, to which Heaven responds with a supererogatory miracle:

B. It is also the position of Samuel that Israel is not subject to the stars.
C. For Samuel and Ablat were in session, and some people going along to a lake. Said Ablat to Samuel, "That man is going but won't come back, a snake will bite him and he'll die."
D. Said to him Samuel, "Yes, well, if he's an Israelite, he will go and come back."
E. While they were in session, he went and came back. Ablat got up and took of the man's knapsack and found in it a snake cut up and lying in two pieces.

So there must be a reason, and the reason has to do with an act of generosity or some other source of merit. The man acted in a way that the law could not require but that God could, and did, much appreciate:

F. Said Samuel to the man, "What did you do [today in particular]?"
G. He said to him, "Every day we tossed our bread into one pot and ate, but today one of us had no bread, and he was shamed. I said to him, 'I will go and collect the bread.' When I came to him, I made as if to go and collect the bread, so he shouldn't be ashamed."
H. He said to him, "You have carried out a religious duty."
I. Samuel went forth and expounded, " 'But charity delivers from death' (Prov. 10:2) – not [merely] from a grotesque death, but from death itself."

In the next case astrology is set aside by a sheer accident, which, we shall see in a moment, the sages identify as a medium of God's will. Here the astrologers ("Chaldaeans") make a flat prediction, and an accident overturns their prognostication; once more, the supererogatory act of generosity accounts for God's personal intervention:

III.11 A. It is also the position of R. Aqiba that Israel is not subject to the stars.

B. For R. Aqiba had a daughter. Chaldaeans [astrologers] told him, "On the day that she goes into the bridal canopy, a snake will bite her and she'll die."

C. This worried him a lot. On that day she took a brooch and stuck it into the wall, and by chance it sank into the eye of a snake. The next day when she took it out, the snake came trailing along after it.

D. Her father said to her, "What did you do [today in particular]?"

E. She said to him, "In the evening a poor man came to the door, and everyone was busy with the banquet so no one could take care of him, so I took some of what was given to me and gave it to him."

F. He said to her, "You have carried out a religious duty."

G. R. Aqiba went forth and expounded, "'But charity delivers from death' (Prov. 10:2) – not from a grotesque death, but from death itself."

If piety on the part of an Israelite overcomes astrology, a lapse in piety for even a moment subjects the man to the influence of the stars. Here, keeping one's head covered serves as a sign of fear of Heaven, and the rest follows:

III.12 A. It is also the position of R. Nahman bar Isaac that Israel is not subject to the stars.

B. For to the mother of R. Nahman bar Isaac the Chaldaean said, "Your son will be a thief." She didn't let him go bareheaded, saying, "Keep your head covered, so fear of Heaven may be upon you, and pray for mercy."

C. He didn't know why she said that to him. One day he was in session, studying under a palm tree. His head covering fell off. He lifted his eyes and saw the palm tree, and was overcome by temptation; he climbed up and bit off a cluster of dates with his teeth.

The proof therefore is positive and negative, and the composite leaves no doubt as to the position taken by the Oral Torah, even while dissenting opinion registers.

  If determinism in the form of astrology conflicts with the logic inherent in the theology of a just God, freely acting in a rational way, then what appears to come about by sheer accident – in other words, what others may deem sheer chaos – coheres with that logic. Chance or accident reveal God's intent and plan; there is no such thing as sheer chance and pure accident. The sages regard what happens by chance as an act of Heavenly intervention, an event in the dominion of the Kingdom of Heaven. In the Oral Torah, casting of lots and other forms of chance yield God's decision. How the lot falls reflects how God wants things, since, to begin with, God commands and fate conforms. Nothing in fact takes place by chance, so by allowing the dice to fall where they will, man discovers God's wishes. That position, explaining events in private life rather than in public affairs – we do not have a single instance in which sheer chance serves to explain an event in the life of Israel or the gentiles in relationship to Israel – is formulated more in halakhic than in aggadic terms. The fact that the identification of chance with God's determinate will forms the premise of entire bodies of the law proves the normative standing of that conviction.

Chance is the preferred mode of identifying that which God desires, for example, within a given batch of produce. When the farmer wishes to designate God's share (the heave-offering or priestly ration) of the crop, so that he may then retain the rest as his own, secular food, he must do so in a random manner. The volume must not be measured; the designation should not be subject to the will of the farmer. For instance, when the householder separates out of the harvested crop the portion that belongs to God and is to be delivered to the priests or other divine surrogates in ownership of the Land of Israel, he cannot designate that portion, called heave-offering, by designation or an act of intention. God must be permitted to choose his share, and that means that sheer accident must intervene.

MISHNAH-TRACTATE TERUMOT I:7
(TRANS. ALAN J. AVERY-PECK)

A. They do not separate heave offering by (i) a measure [of volume], or by (2) weight, or by (3) a count [of the number of pieces of fruit being separated as heave offering].

B. But he separates the heave offering of (1) [produce] which has been measured, of (2) that which has been weighed, and of (3) that which has been counted.

C. They do not separate heave offering in a basket or in a vessel which [hold a known] measure.

D. But he separates heave offering in them [if they are] one-half or one-third part [filled].

E. He may not separate heave offering in [a basket which holds one] seah, [if it is] one-half part [filled], since the half thereof is a [known] measure.

What is to be God's portion must not be deliberately identified but must come about through the working of chance, accompanied by a gesture made in a liberal spirit. Intention must play no role here.

The matter of chance likewise governs the designation of produce for the poor in the form of the forgotten sheaf, an estimate being made of whether or not it is likely that the farmer intended to go back and collect a sheaf that is left in the field. If he intended to leave the sheaf, it is not regarded as a forgotten sheaf that God has assigned to the poor. So the workings of chance in the form of random forgetfulness or unintentional neglect convey God's interest:

MISHNAH-TRACTATE PEAH 6:4 (TRANS. ROGER BROOKS)

A. And these are [the rules which apply to sheaves left at] the ends of rows [in a field]:
B. (1) Two men who began [to harvest a crop] from the middle of a row, one facing north and the other facing south,
C. and they forgot [sheaves] in front of them [toward the edge of the field], and at their backs [in between them] –
D. [a sheaf which they forgot] in front of them is [subject to the restrictions of the] forgotten sheaf, [for it is in clear view while they harvest] –
E. But [a sheaf which they forgot] at their backs is not [subject to the restrictions of the] forgotten sheaf, [for neither of the workers had the sheaf in plain view while they harvested the field].
F. (2) An individual who began [to harvest a field] from the end of a row, and forgot [sheaves] in front of himself and behind himself –
G. [a sheaf which he forgot] in front of himself is not [subject to the restrictions of the] forgotten sheaf, [for he can gather it when he harvests that part of the row] –
H. But [a sheaf which he forgot] behind himself is [subject to the restrictions of the] forgotten sheaf,
I. because it is under [the law], [When you reap your harvest in your field, and have forgotten a sheaf in the field,] you shall not go back [to get id (Deut. 24:19).

Ordinarily, the Mishnah's cases on their own, without further exposition, set forth implicitly the general rule that governs cases not specified. But here, the sages supply a generalization to put together the details into a coherent statement:

J. This is the general [principle]:
K. Whatever [sheaf] is under [the law] 'You shall not go back' is subject [to the law of the] forgotten sheaf.
L. But what is not under [the law] 'You shall not go back' is not subject [to the law of the] forgotten sheaf.

The casting of lots serves along the same lines. That these rules simply recapitulate not only the principles of the Torah's laws, but also the details, is self-evident, a matter to which we return in the concluding chapter of the shank of this book.

If what man sees as sheer accident attests to not chaos but the orderly working of the divine will, then what is to be said of man's fate, that is, the work that occupies the most of a person's life? That certainly reveals God's plan and will. Here the sages are equally explicit: it is God who decides who follows an easy trade and who does the heavy lifting, who prospers and who does not. But the matter of how one makes his living elicits several opinions. While all the sages concede God's role in the matter, some assign man responsibility in the form of sin, others explain man's responsibility for his vocation in quite other terms. The basic principle is shared by them all.

The first, and predictable one, tells us that man proposes, God disposes; one should teach his son a desirable trade, but God will then decide the outcome. As Meir puts it:

MISHNAH-TRACTATE QIDDUSHIN 4:14

E. R. Meir says, "A man should always teach his son a clean and easy trade. And let him pray to him to whom belong riches and possessions.

G. "For there is no trade which does not involve poverty or wealth.

H. "For poverty does not come from one's trade, nor does wealth come from one's trade.

I. "But all is in accord with a man's merit."

As we have seen time again, the matter of merit intervenes, which is to say, God's response to an act of supererogatory generosity with an act of uncoerced grace. The very fact that man has to work for a living is God's will, the penalty for the catastrophe of Eden. To quote Simeon b. Eleazar, recapitulating the story of Genesis:

J. R. Simeon b. Eleazar says, "Have you ever seen a wild beast or a bird who has a trade? Yet they get along without difficulty. And were they not created only to serve me? And I was created to serve my Master. So is it not logical that I should get along without difficulty? But I have done evil and ruined my living."

Now comes the conflict between teaching a trade and teaching the Torah. In the theology of the Oral Torah, Torah-study takes precedence over all else, all other religious duties being weighed in one side of the balance, Torah-study in another, at M. Peah 1:1:

MISHNAH-TRACTATE PEAH 1:1

A. These are things which have no [specified] measure:

B. (1) [the quantity of produce designated as] peah, (2) [the quantity of produce given as] first fruits, (3) [the value of] the appearance offering, (4) [the performance of] righteous deeds, (5) and [time spent in] study of Torah.

C. These are things the benefit of which a person enjoys in this world, while the principal remains for him in the world to come:

D. (1) [deeds in] honour of father and mother, (2) [performance of] righteous deeds, (3) and [acts which] bring peace between a man and his fellow.

E. But the study of Torah is as important as all of them together.

It is in that context (to which we return in chapter 14) that we understand the dispute with which Mishnah-tractate Qiddushin 4:14 continues. Now the issue is, should one teach his son anything but the Torah? One set of opinions maintains that one should do what Meir has said at the outset, teach his son a trade; the premise is, one should also teach his son the Torah, but time must be spent, also, in learning a trade. The contrary opinion holds that it suffices to teach one's son only the Torah, and everything else will work out.

MISHNAH-TRACTATE QIDDUSHIN 4:14

K. Abba Gurion of Sidon says in the name of Abba Gurya, "A man should not teach his son to be an ass driver, a camel driver, a barber, a sailor, a herdsman, or a shopkeeper. For their trade is the trade of thieves."

L. R. Judah says in his name, "Most ass drivers are evil, most camel drivers are decent, most sailors are saintly, the best among physicians is going to Gehenna, and the best of butchers is a partner of Amalek."

The virtues attached to the several callings have to do with faith. Sailors commit their lives to the sea, depending upon God's mercy rather than their own ability. Butchers cheat and, meat not being marked "kosher" or otherwise, sell as kosher what is not suitable. Physicians are charlatans. Shopkeepers buy low and sell high, exceeding the true value that the system imputes to whatever is traded, as we shall see in chapter 7. But this complexity – righteous and wicked callings – is now reduced to a simple choice:

M. R. Nehorai says, "I should lay aside every trade in the world and teach my son only Torah.

N. "For a man eats its fruits in this world, and the principal remains for the world to come.

O. "But other trades are not that way.

P. "When a man gets sick or old or has pains and cannot do his job, lo, he dies of starvation.

Q. "But with Torah it is not that way.

R. "But it keeps him from all evil when he is young, and it gives him a future and a hope when he is old.

S. "Concerning his youth, what does it say? 'They who wait upon the Lord shall renew their strength' (Is. 40:31). And concerning his old age what does it say? 'He shall still bring forth fruit in old age' " (Ps. 92:14).

The sages' dispute should not obscure the shared premise, which is that God has a heavy stake in the conduct of everyday affairs, and that God's just will governs what to the uneducated appears to be the chaos of vocational choices.

But if some are virtuous and some commit sin, everyone dies. The fortunate reach old age. The common folk encounter sickness. How accommodate man's fate to God's benevolent, just providence? Accordingly, from the ordinary and everyday, we turn to other dimensions of the complex corpus of doctrines on how the just world order accounts, also, for what happens in all ordinary lives: death, sickness, old age, suffering, not to mention disappointment in its myriad of forms.

Before proceeding, let us briefly review what we have established to this point. In our examination of how the theology deals with the individual in his own terms, we have demonstrated that destiny is justice, that what happens to individuals in one way or another is susceptible to explanation by appeal to God's just intent. Astrology and impersonal fate dismissed, chance and accident accounted for, what still requires theological justification is man's fate: sickness, suffering, death.

Let us start with premature death. As we have noted along the way, the sages treat death before one's "time" as a divine penalty for certain types of sin or crime. The penalty inflicted by Heaven is extirpation, the premature death of the felon or sinner, which we shall meet once again in chapter 10. That accomplishes the expiation of the felony or the sin. Then the felon or sinner enters that right relationship with Heaven that allows life to go forward "in the world to come." Clearly, then, just as execution by the court corrects matters, so execution by Heaven does the same. The counterpart to the death penalty inflicted by the earthly or by the Heavenly court is one and the same: atonement yielding life eternal. Sin and crime are for the here and the now; but life eternal beyond the grave is for all Israel.

Along these same lines, the sages maintain, it is better for a person to die innocent than guilty, which is why justice may require pre-emptive punishment. Even a youth may die, after all, and in some cases even the earthly court is admonished to address the case of one who must not be permitted to grow old. That is the premise of M. San. 8:5: A rebellious and incorrigible son is tried on account of what he may end up to be. This is explained in the following language: "Let him die while yet innocent, and let him not die when he is guilty." Consequently, some people may be put to death to save them from doing evil:

MISHNAH-TRACTATE SANHEDRIN 8:7

A. And these are those who are to be saved [from doing evil] even at the cost of their lives:

B. he who pursues after his fellow in order to kill him –

C. after a male, or after a betrothed girl;

D. but he who pursues a beast, he who profanes the Sabbath, he who does an act of service to an idol – they do not save them even at the cost of their lives.

The ones put to death pre-emptively all wish to commit rape in violation of the Torah's laws. But both extirpation and pre-emptive punishment deal with very special cases.

But ordinary folk do not commit crime and rarely sin so grievously as to attract Heaven's sustained attention. In more encompassing terms, how do the sages show the justice of suffering? The answer, predictably, will involve the classification and hierarchization of types of suffering. Suffering forms an atonement for sin, which by definition is to be desired. But, among the types of suffering, some are easier to take than others. Some suffering serves to rebuke a sinner and to call him to repentance; some penalizes sin in this world, leaving the sin expiated and facilitating entry into the world to come.

GENESIS RABBAH XCII:I.2

A. Said R. Alexandri, "You have no one without troubles. Happy is the person whose Torah brings about his sufferings [that is, because of his hard work in studying the Torah]."

This leads to the critical distinction, suffering that impedes study of the Torah, suffering that does not prevent it:

B. Said R. Joshua b. Levi, "All sufferings that come upon a person and prevent him from his Torah-study constitute sufferings that serve to rebuke. But all forms of suffering that do not prevent a person from studying the Torah are sufferings that come out of love [that a person may suffer in this world and rejoice all the more the age to come]."

As we should expect, what follows will provide a narrative illustration, whether a parable or a case; here is a case:

3. A. Rabbi saw a blind man who was labouring in Torah-study. He said to him, "Peace to you, free man."
B. He said to him, "Did you hear that I used to be a slave?"
C. He said to him, "No, but you will be a free man in the age to come."

The basis for hierarchizing here is the established point of priority, Torah-study; what is in harmony with Torah-study is an act of love, and what is not is an act of rebuke. So a single criterion serves to hierarchize the classifications at hand.

The second, and more general, type of suffering is that which atones for sin, and to suffer is to enjoy the opportunity for repentance and atonement. First, suffering on its own constitutes a form of expiation and atonement, no less than an offering in the Temple in olden times. Second, suffering alerts man to his having sinned, telling him to find out what sin he has done and to repent for that sin. The prophets said the same thing to all Israel that the sages say to Israelites. This kind of suffering represents an act of benevolence as well and is to be desired; it requires no justification beyond its own purpose.

SIFRÉ TO DEUTERONOMY XXXII:V.5FF.

5. A. And, furthermore, a person should rejoice in suffering more than in good times. For if someone lives in good times his entire life, he will not be forgiven for such sin as may be in his hand.
B. And how shall he attain forgiveness? Through suffering.

Here, we see, suffering serves a just purpose and does not have to be explained further. Now a sequence of statements underscores the benevolence of God, expressed when he brings suffering to the sinner:

6. A. R. Eliezer b. Jacob says, "Lo, Scripture says, 'For whom whom the Lord loves he corrects, even as a father corrects the son in whom he delights' (Prov. 3:12).
B. "What made the son be pleasing to the father? You must say it was suffering [on account of correction]."
7. A. R. Meir says, "Lo, Scripture says, 'And you shall consider in your heart, that as a man chasten his son, so the Lord your God chastens you' (Deut. 8:5).

B. " 'You know in your heart the deeds that you did, and also the suffering that I brought upon you, which was not in accord with the deeds that you did at all.' "

Suffering forms a mark of God's special engagement with the man:

8. A. R. Yosé b. R. Judah says, "Beloved is suffering, for the name of the Omnipresent rests upon the one upon whom suffering comes,
B. "as it is said, 'So the Lord your God chastens you' " (Deut. 8:5).

Suffering forms a covenant with God, no less than the covenant at Sinai or at circumcision:

9. A. R. Nathan b. R. Joseph says, "Just as a covenant is made through the land, so a covenant is made through suffering, as it is said, 'The Lord, your God chastens you' (Deut. 8:7).
B. "And it says, 'For the Lord your God brings you into a good land' " (Deut. 8:7).

That conception broadens the range of discourse. Now the entire repertoire of positive categories contributes, for suffering also serves as the prerequisite of certain gifts that Israel is given, the Torah, the Land of Israel, and the world to come, the three most important components of Israel's public life then depending upon the condition of the Israelite:

10. A. R. Simeon bar Yohai says, "Suffering is precious. For through suffering three good gifts were given to Israel, which the nations of the world desire, and these are they: the Torah, the land of Israel, and the world to come.

As we now expect, to demonstrate the validity of Simeon's proposition, we find proof in facts set forth by Scripture:

B. "How do we know that that is the case for the Torah? As it is said, 'To know wisdom and chastisement' (Prov. 1:2). And it is said, 'Happy is the man whom you chastise O Lord and teach out of your Torah' " (Ps. 94:12).
C. "How do we know that that is the case for the land of Israel? 'The Lord your God chastens you ... for the Lord your God brings you into a good land' (Deut. 8:5, 7).
D. "How do we know that that is the case for the world to come? 'For the commandment is a lamp and the Torah is a light, and reproofs of chastisement are the way of life' (Prov. 6:23). What is the way that brings a person to the world to come? One must say it is suffering."

Another approach to the same matter, also finding that suffering forms an act of divine grace, compares suffering to the offerings on the altar. Suffering now, with the Temple in ruins, forms the counterpart to sacrifices on the altar when the Temple stood. As the latter atoned for sin, so the former atones for sin. That turns suffering into a valued occasion, not to be rejected or explained away but appreciated:

11. A. R. Nehemiah says, "Beloved is suffering, for just as offerings appease, so does suffering appease.

B. "In the case of offerings, Scripture says, 'And it shall be accepted for him to make atonement for him' (Lev. 1:4).

C. "And in the case of suffering: 'And they shall be paid the punishment for their iniquity' (Lev. 26:43).

D. "And not only so, but suffering appeases more than do offerings. For offerings are a matter of property, but suffering, of one's own body.

E. "And so Scripture says, 'Skin for skin, yes, all that a man has will he give for his life' " (Job 2:4).

Suffering by reason of punishment for sin is to be valued, because through suffering one atones. Hence a doctrine of suffering encompasses not only the cause – rebellion – but also what is achieved – humility, yielding repentance. That is a matter of doctrine, as No. 5 shows, but Scripture also represents suffering as divine chastisement and instruction, to be received gratefully. Not only does suffering yield atonement, it also appeases the way offerings do.

We earlier noted that suffering forms the equivalent to a sacrifice, a means of atonement for sin. Why should suffering be valued as a medium of atonement? The reason is that suffering provokes introspection and serves as source of reflection on the sins one has committed, so providing the occasion for repentance, which yields atonement as offerings yielded atonement. Accordingly, the most important reason that suffering is precious is that it changes one's attitude. Through suffering, one is moved to atone for sin, and therefore suffering brings about that atonement that the sages seek, appeasing God through a form of sacrifice as much appreciated as the sacrifice on the altar. That is, the sacrifice of one's own will in favour of God's decree. When suffering comes, it brings about submission to God, a point demonstrated in narrative form but through the substance of the anticipated exegesis:

A. Now when R. Eliezer was sick, four sages, R. Tarfon, R. Joshua, R. Eleazar b. Azariah, and R. Aqiba, came to visit him.

The first responses fail, because they merely commiserate and compliment the sufferer, which hardly addresses the issue of suffering at all:

B. Responded and said to him R. Tarfon, "My lord, you are more precious to Israel than the sun's orb. For the sun's orb gives light to this world, but you give light to us in this world and the world to come."

C. Responded and said to him R. Joshua, "My lord, you are more precious to Israel than the gift of rain, for rain gives life in this world, but you give life to us in this world and the world to come."

D. Responded and said to him R. Eleazar b. Azariah, "My lord, you are more precious to Israel than a father or a mother. For a father or mother bring one into this world, but you bring us into this world and the world to come."

The three miss the point. The fourth hits the bulls-eye:

E. Responded and said to him R. Aqiba, "My lord, suffering is precious."

F. R. Eliezer said to his disciples, "Lift me up."

G. R. Eliezer went into session, saying to him, "Speak, Aqiba."

The proof for the announced proposition derives from a specific case of Scripture:

H. He said to him, "Lo, Scripture says, 'Manasseh was twelve years old when he began to reign, and he reigned for fifty-five years in Jerusalem. And he did what was evil in the eyes of the Lord' (2 Chr. 33:1). And it further says, 'These are the proverbs of Solomon, which the men of Hezekiah, king of Judah, copied out' (Prov. 25:1).

I. "Now can anyone imagine that Hezekiah taught Torah to all Israel, while his son, Manasseh, he did not teach Torah?

J. "But one must conclude that, despite all of the learning that his father taught him, and all the work that he put into him, nothing worked for him except suffering.

K. "For it is said, 'And the Lord spoke to Manasseh and to his people, but they gave no heed. Therefore the Lord brought upon them the captains of the host of the king of Assyria, who took Manasseh with hooks and bound him with fetters and carried him to Babylonia. And when he was in distress, he besought the Lord, his God, and humbled himself greatly before the God of his fathers and prayed to him, and he was entreated of him and heard his supplication and brought him back to Jerusalem into his kingdom' (2 Chr. 33:10–13).

L. "That proves that suffering is precious."

From such a perspective, suffering represents not an anomaly in, but confirmation of, the theological logic that begins all thought with the principle of God's justice and benevolence. Suffering helps man to help himself, returns man to God, precipitates man's repentance. What more can one ask of a just God than the opportunity to shape one's own will to conciliate him?

No wonder, then, that the Oral Torah's framers, focused as they are on the patriarchs as paradigms for their children, Israel, and enduring sources for a heritage of virtue, go so far as to invoke the fathers as the founders of suffering. Here, the patriarchs themselves asked God to bestow old age, suffering, and sickness, because the world needed them. These components of the human condition not only do not form challenges to the logic of God's just governance of the world, but express that very benevolence that infuses justice. So the patriarchs initially beseeched God to bestow on man the blessings of old age, suffering, and sickness, each for its rational purpose. Here the theology transcends itself:

GENESIS RABBAH LXV:IX.I

A. "When Isaac was old, and his eyes were dim, so that he could not see, he called Esau his older son, and said to him, 'My son,' and he answered, 'Here I am'" (Gen. 27:1):

B. Said R. Judah bar Simon, "Abraham sought [the physical traits of] old age [so that from one's appearance, people would know that he was old]. He said before him, 'Lord of all ages, when a man and his son come in somewhere, no one knows whom to honour. If you crown a man with the traits of old age, people will know whom to honour.'

C. "Said to him the Holy One, blessed be he, 'By your life, this is a good thing that you have asked for, and it will begin with you.'

D. "From the beginning of the book of Genesis to this passage, there is no reference to old age. But when Abraham our father came along, the traits of old age were given to him, as it is said, 'And Abraham was old'" (Gen. 24:1).

So much for old age. But what about what goes with it, the suffering of infirmities? Here Isaac makes his contribution, now being credited with that very conception that, as we have seen, explains the justice of human suffering:

E. "Isaac asked God for suffering. He said before him, 'Lord of the age, if someone dies without suffering, the measure of strict justice is stretched out against him. But if you bring suffering on him, the measure of strict justice will not be stretched out against him. [Suffering will help counter the man's sins, and the measure of strict justice will be mitigated through suffering by the measure of mercy.]'

F. "Said to him the Holy One, blessed be he, 'By your life, this is a good thing that you have asked for, and it will begin with you.'

G. "From the beginning of the book of Genesis to this passage, there is no reference to suffering. But when Isaac came along, suffering was given to him: his eyes were dim.'

Finally, what of sickness, the third in the components of man's fate? That is Jacob's contribution, and the wisdom and good will of God come once more to full articulation in suffering:

H. "Jacob asked for sickness. He said before him, 'Lord of all ages, if a person dies without illness, he will not settle his affairs for his children. If he is sick for two or three days, he will settle his affairs with his children.'

I. "Said to him the Holy One, blessed be he, 'By your life, this is a good thing that you have asked for, and it will begin with you.'

J. "That is in line with this verse: 'And someone said to Joseph, "Behold, your father is sick" ' " (Gen. 48:1).

K. Said R. Levi, "Abraham introduced the innovation of old age, Isaac introduced the innovation of suffering, Jacob introduced the innovation of sickness.

We proceed to a further case of the same classification, chronic illness and its origin in the wisdom of the saints, now Hezekiah:

L. "Hezekiah introduced the innovation of chronic illness. He said to him, 'You have kept a man in good condition until the day he dies. But if someone is sick and gets better, is sick and gets better, he will carry out a complete and sincere act of repentance for his sins.'

M. "Said to him the Holy One, blessed be he, 'By your life, this is a good thing that you have asked for, and it will begin with you.'

N. " 'The writing of Hezekiah, king of Judah, when he had been sick and recovered of his sickness' " (Is. 38:9).

O. Said R. Samuel b. Nahman, "On the basis of that verse we know that between one illness and another there was an illness more serious than either one."

Old age, suffering, and sickness do not represent flaws in creation but things to be desired. Each serves a good purpose. All form acts of divine mercy. The mode of explanation appeals to reason and practical considerations attached thereto. Another version has it that Abraham, Jacob, and Elisha brought brought about old age, illness, and healing:

BAVLI TRACTATE BABA MESIA 7:1.IV.19/87A:

A. Until the time of Abraham there was no such thing as old age. One who wanted to speak with Abraham might well speak with Isaac and one who wanted to speak with Isaac might well speak with Abraham. Abraham came along and begged for mercy, and old age came about, as it is said, "And Abraham was old, getting along in years" (Gen. 24:1).

B. Until Jacob, there was no such thing as illness, but Jacob came along and begged for mercy, and illness came about, as it is said, "And someone told Joseph, behold your father is sick" (Gen. 48:1).

C. Until Elisha came along, there was no one who ever got sick and then got well again, but when Elisha came along, [Elijah] begged for mercy and he was healed, as it is written, "Now Elisha had fallen sick of the illness of which he died" (22 Kgs. 13:14), which proves that he had been sick earlier but had recovered.

What is fresh is the initiation of recovery from illness, an extension of the initial tale of how the patriarchs asked for suffering.

Still, matters do not come out even; all die, but not everyone suffers premature death or sickness. Much more galling: sometimes wicked people live long, healthy, and prosperous lives, happily making everyone around them miserable, then die peacefully in their sleep at a ripe old age. And – then or now – one need not visit a cancer ward to find misery afflicting genuinely good and pious people. So while the doctrine of the benevolence expressed by sickness, suffering, and old age serves, it hardly constitutes a universal and sufficient justification. And, however reasonable suffering may be shown to be, in the end reason hardly suffices in the face of the raw agony of incurable illness. That is why, in the sages' view, further responses to Job, Jeremiah, and Qoheleth are called for. One additional effort to bring suffering within the framework of the rational, to show the justice of the matter, is made.

Specifically, the same anomalies in the just order encompassing private life may come about for yet another reason, namely, God's own plan. When the righteous suffer, it is God who is testing them.

GENESIS RABBAH LV:II.1F.

I. A. "The Lord tries the righteous, but the wicked and him who loves violence his soul hates" (Ps. 11:5).

This is now embodied in metaphors drawn from the potter, the flax maker, and the farmer:

B. Said R. Jonathan, "A potter does not test a weak utensil, for if he hits it just once, he will break it. What does the potter test? He tests the strong ones, for even if he strikes them repeatedly, they will not break. So the Holy One, blessed be he, does not try the wicked but the righteous: 'The Lord tries the righteous' " (Ps. 11:5).

C. Said R. Yosé bar Haninah, "When a flax maker knows that the flax is in good shape, then the more he beats it, the more it will improve and glisten. When it is not of good quality, if he beats it just once, he will split it. So the Holy One, blessed be he, does not try the wicked but the righteous: 'The Lord tries the righteous' " (Ps. 11:5).

D. Said R. Eleazar, "The matter may be compared to a farmer [Hebrew: householder] who has two heifers, one strong, one weak. On whom does he place the yoke? It is on the one that is strong. So the Holy One, blessed be he, does not try the wicked but the righteous: 'The Lord tries the righteous' " (Ps. 11:5).

We conclude the exercise with the juxtaposition of the base-verse, Gen. 22:1, and the intersecting-verse, Ps. 11:5, at the meeting of which the point just now stated was triggered:

LV:III.1. A. Another interpretation: "The Lord tries the righteous, but the wicked and him who loves violence his soul hates" (Ps. 11:5):

B. The cited verse speaks of Abraham: "And it came to pass after these things God tested Abraham" (Gen. 22:1).

The suffering of the righteous pays tribute to their strength and is a mark of their virtue. That is shown by appeal to both analogies (potter, flax maker, householder) and Scripture. Suffering shows God's favour for the one who suffers, indicating that such a one is worthy of God's attention and special interest.

That suffering is a valued gift explains the critical importance of the theological principle that a person should accept whatever God metes out to him, even suffering. In a context defined by the conviction that suffering forms a gift from a benevolent, just God, we cannot find surprising that loving God should involve accepting punishment as much as benefit. This is stated in so many words: One is obligated to bless over evil as one blesses over the good, as it is said, "And you shall love the Lord your God with all your heart, with all your soul, and with all your might" (Deut. 6:5). "With all your heart" – with both of your inclinations, with the good inclination and with the evil inclination. "And with all your soul" – even if he takes your soul. "And with all your might" – with all of your money (M. Ber. 9:4A–E). Accordingly, the correct attitude towards suffering entails grateful acknowledgment that what God metes out is just and merciful. The same matter is amplified in the following exegesis of the same verses of Scripture:

SIFRÉ TO DEUTERONOMY XXXII: V. 1–12

1. A. R. Aqiba says, "Since it is said, 'with all your soul,' it is an argument *a fortiori* that we should encompass, 'with all your might.'

B. "Why then does Scripture say, 'with all your might'?

C. "It is to encompass every single measure that God metes out to you, whether the measure of good or the measure of punishment."

Now further verses are shown to deliver the same message:

2. A. So does David say, "[How can I repay the Lord for all his bountiful dealings toward me?] I will lift up the cup of salvation and call upon the name of the Lord" (Ps. 116:12–13).

B. "I found trouble and sorrow but I called upon the name of the Lord" (Ps. 116:3–4).

Job, who formulated the "problem of evil" in its most dramatic statement, takes the same position, so far as the sages are concerned:

3. A. So does Job say, "The Lord gave and the Lord has taken away. Blessed be the name of the Lord" (Job 1:21).

B. If that is the case for the measure of goodness, all the more so for the measure of punishment.

C. What does his wife say to him? "Do you still hold fast your integrity? Blaspheme God and die" (Job 2:9).

D. And what does he say to her? "You speak as one of the impious women speaks. Shall we receive good at the hand of God and shall we not receive evil?" (Job 2:10).

Now we show the contrasting attitude, one that substitutes churlishness for gratitude churlishness, and for acceptance of punishment, which the sages admire, dignity in dumb submission:

4. A. The men of the generation of the flood were churlish as to the good, and when punishment came upon them, they took it willy nilly.

B. And is it not an argument *a fortiori*: if one who was churlish as to the good behaved with dignity in a time of punishment, we who behave with dignity in response to good should surely behave with dignity in a time of trouble.

C. And so did he said to her, "You speak as one of the impious women speaks. Shall we receive good at the hand of God and shall we not receive evil?" (Job 2:10).

Now we turn to the familiar position that, since suffering is a medium of atonement and repentance, people should accept it thankfully:

5. A. And, furthermore, a person should rejoice in suffering more than in good times. For if someone lives in good times his entire life, he will not be forgiven for such sin as may be in his hand.

B. And how shall he attain forgiveness? Through suffering.

6. A. R. Eliezer b. Jacob says, "Lo, Scripture says, 'For whom whom the Lord loves he corrects, even as a father corrects the son in whom he delights' (Prov. 3:12).

B. "What made the son be pleasing to the father? You must say it was suffering [on account of correction].'

God punishes with love and, as we already know, some types of suffering – the ones that permit Torah-study withal – constitute suffering inflicted with love:

7. A. R. Meir says, "Lo, Scripture says, 'And you shall consider in your heart, that as a man chasten his son, so the Lord your God chastens you' (Deut. 8:5).

B. "'You know in your heart the deeds that you did, and also the suffering that I brought upon you, which was not in accord with the deeds that you did at all.'"

8. A. R. Yosé b. R. Judah says, "Beloved is suffering, for the name of the Omnipresent rests upon the one upon whom suffering comes,

B. "as it is said, 'So the Lord your God chastens you'" (Deut. 8:5).

9. A. R. Nathan b. R. Joseph says, "Just as a covenant is made through the land, so a covenant is made through suffering, as it is said, 'The Lord, your God chastens you' (Deut. 8:7).

B. "And it says, 'For the Lord your God brings you into a good land'" (Deut. 8:7).

The composite concludes with the to-us familiar statement of the same matter: suffering is precious, not as exegesis of Scripture but as a narrative of a colloquy among the exemplary sages. This protracted composite shows the normative standing of the conviction that comes to expression in the several media of discourse, didactic, exegetical, and even (pseudo-)narrative. Proof derives from Scripture, from analogy, from the lives and teachings of the exemplary sages. The entire intent is clear: people are expected to accept suffering as a mark of divine favour and love, as an indication that God has special confidence in them, or that God has a particular purpose in dealing with them as he does. Even the patriarchs asked for sickness, old age, and other forms of suffering, all the more reason gratefully to accept as a mark of divine justice the miseries of the human condition.

So the sages mounted argument after argument. They framed and found scriptural bases for doctrine after doctrine. All this was to try to persuade themselves that somehow the world conformed to rationality defined by justice. True, the claim that anguish and illness, premature death, and everyday suffering fit under the rules of reasonable world order; that insistence that when the wicked prosper, justice still may be done – these propositions, necessary to the system, may well have transcended the here and now and conformed to a higher reality. But still, when all is said and the day is done, the doctrine of suffering could not encompass all cases, let alone persuade everybody who raised the question, why me? why now? Nor did the sages so frame matters as to suggest they found theology's panglossean solutions, if necessary, wholly sufficient let alone compelling. True, suffering is to be accepted as a mark of God's grace, a gift, an occasion, a mode of atonement and reconciliation with God. True, the patriarchs found much good in man's fate and asked God to arrange matters as they are. And yet – and yet the fact remains that some folk suffer more than others, and, not uncommonly, the wicked prosper and the righteous do not.

So the doctrine of suffering on its own could not, and did not, complete the Oral Torah's account of the confrontation with the key-dilemma of the sages' theology of world-order, the anomalies that manifestly flaw private lives, viewed in comparison and contrast with one another. Say what they would, the sages in the end had to complete the circle: some do not get what they deserve, whether for good or for ill, and, if their time is replicated in our own, those some were very many. To that protean problem, the sages found in their larger theology a commensurate and predictable response.

The sages identified with the Torah the promise of life eternal, with idolatry the extinction of being. This would come about, as we shall see in chapters 14 and 15, at the last days, which will correspond with, and complete, the first days of creation. Justice will be done only when the world is perfected. With that conviction forming the foundation of their very definition of world order, divided between those who will overcome the grave, Israel with the Torah, and those who will not, the gentiles with idolatry, the sages found in hand a simple solution. The righteous suffer in this world and get their just reward in the world to come, but the wicked enjoy this world and suffer in the world to come. Since the theology of the Oral Torah distinguished the Torah and life from idolatry and death, what happens in this world and in this life does not tell the whole story. And when that entire story is told, the received formulation of the problem of evil no longer pertains and the final anomalies are smoothed out.

That theology further contemplated a world beyond the grave – the world to come, in which individuals would resume the life they knew, but now for eternity. This conviction, critical to the system as a whole, also provided a solution to the problem of the prosperity of the wicked and the misery of the righteous. By insisting that this world does not tell the whole story of a private life, the sages could promise beyond the grave what the here and now denied. The simplest statement of that position is as follows:

BAVLI TRACTATE HORAYOT 3:3 I./11A

6. A. Expounded R. Nahman bar Hisda, "What is the meaning of the verse of Scripture, 'There is a vanity that occurs on the earth, for there are the righteous who receive what is appropriate to the deeds of the wicked, and there are the wicked who receive what is appropriate to the deeds of the righteous' (Qoh. 8:14).
B. "Happy are the righteous, for in this world they undergo what in the world to come is assigned as recompense for the deeds of the wicked, and woe is the wicked, for in this world they enjoy the fruits of what is assigned in the world to come to the deeds of the righteous."

The righteous will enjoy the world to come all the more, and the wicked will suffer in the world to come all the more; the one has saved up his reward for eternity, the other has in this transient world already spent such reward as he may ever get. But that still begs the question:

B. Said Raba, "So if the righteous enjoy both worlds, would that be so bad for them?"

Raba acts in the model of Abraham facing God before Sodom! But he has a better solution, making still more radical claim:

C. Rather, said Raba, "Happy are the righteous, for in this world they get what is set aside for the [meritorious] deeds of the wicked in this world, and woe to the wicked, for in this world they get what is assigned for the deeds of the righteous in this world."

Raba's solution takes account of the theory of atonement through suffering. The righteous atone in the here and now, that is why they suffer. Then the world to come is all the more joyful. Now follows a story that shows how disciples of the sages enjoy in this world such benefit as the wicked ought to have had in the world to come, and the rest follows.

D. R. Pappa and R. Huna b. R. Joshua came before Raba. He said to them, "Have you mastered such and such tractate and such and such tractate?"
E. They said to him, "Yes."
F. "Have you gotten a bit richer?"

G. They said to him, "Yes, because we bought a little piece of land."

H. He recited in their regard, "Happy are the righteous, for in this world they undergo what in the world to come is assigned as recompense for the deeds of the wicked."

To grasp how, in massive detail, ultimate justice pervades the here and now, the premise of this passage should not be missed. It is that of a steady-state moral economy: a finite store of rewards and punishments awaits the righteous and the wicked alike, so what comes to the one is denied the other. In due course – in chapter 7 – we again shall encounter the sages' powerful yearning for a world of stability and hierarchical order, in which fair exchange assures that nothing much changes. There, not surprisingly, we shall once more address the dialectics of Torah versus land-ownership, wealth in the transcendent and mundane planes of reality. Here it suffices to note that world order defined by reasoned justice serves to justify – show God's justice in – even humble, everyday experience. It follows that the rules that govern and account for everyday experience are supposed to make sense of the nonsense of the present age.

But the sages were no fools, and hope for the at-present-intangible future did not dim their dark vision of the ordinary experience of life, its nonsense, its anomalies. While pursuing philosophical modes of thought, in the end the sages valued sagacity beyond reason, however compelling. For all their insistence upon the rule of God through a just order, the sages accepted that beyond the known and reasonable lay the unknowable, the realm of God beyond the part set forth in the revealed Torah. They affirmed, ultimately, their own failure, which makes them plausible and human in their claims to account for much, if not all, of the anguish of which the private lives even of the most holy of men are comprised. In the end we all die, and who knows how long the interval until the resurrection? So the sages' last word on the reasonable rule of the just order consists of a single imperative: humility, the gift of wisdom, not of wit.

Here is a passage that generations of Talmud-students have found sublime, the statement of all things, all in all:

BAVLI TRACTATE MENAHOT 3:7 II.5/29B

5. A. Said R. Judah said Rab, "At the time that Moses went up on high, he found the Holy One in session, affixing crowns to the letters [of the words of the Torah]. He said to him, 'Lord of the universe, who is stopping you [from regarding the document as perfect without these additional crowns on the letters]?'

B. "He said to him, 'There is a man who is going to arrive at the end of many generations, and Aqiba b. Joseph is his name, who is going to interpret on the basis of each point of the crowns heaps and heaps of laws.'

C. "He said to him, 'Lord of the Universe, show him to me.'

D. "He said to him, 'Turn around.'

E. "He went and took a seat at the end of eight rows, but he could not grasp what the people were saying. He felt faint. But when the discourse reached a certain matter, and the disciples said, 'My lord, how do you know this?' and he answered, 'It is a law given to Moses from Sinai,' he regained his composure.

F. "He went and came before the Holy One. He said before him, 'Lord of the Universe, How come you have someone like that and yet you give the Torah through me?'

G. "He said to him, 'Silence! That is how the thought came to me.'

H. "He said to him, 'Lord of the Universe, you have shown me his Torah, now show me his reward.'

I. "He said to him, 'Turn around.'

J. "He turned around and saw his flesh being weighed out at the butcher-stalls in the market.

K. "He said to him, 'Lord of the Universe, 'Such is Torah, such is the reward?'

L. "He said to him, 'Silence! That is how the thought came to me.' "

God rules, and man in the end cannot explain, account for the rationality of, everything God decrees. The sages offer more than reasonable explanations for the perceived violation of justice. They offer also the gift of humility in the form of silence. That forms the barrier before the ultimate terror – not understanding, not making sense of things.

Accordingly, the sages placed humility before God above even the entire theological enterprise with its promise of the explanation, understanding, and justification. But the last word must register: that God's decrees, however inexplicable those decrees to the mind of man, bears the comforting message that God cares. And since the premise of the mystery of suffering is formed by the conviction of God's justice (otherwise why take note of the case at hand as an anomaly?), that God cares also means God loves. And it is a love for man, taken care of one by one, a love so deep as not to leave anybody ever unattended – even Aqiba in his martyrdom, but especially ordinary folk, when they suffer, when they bleed, when they die, as all do. Now to the dream of perfection: the sages' account of how the world ought to be made to conform to God's plan for an orderly, justified creation.

PART II

Perfecting World Order

6   World Beyond Time

In the Oral Torah the sages reveal the perfection of world order through an-other-than historical mode of thought. They organized experience through a mode of thought I call paradigmatic, identifying enduring patterns to account for how things were, are, or will be, rather than appealing to the sequence of happenings – first came this, then came that – to say why the present is what it is. So the sages framed a world beyond time and deemed null the sequence of events, judging as false the illogical proposition that merely because one thing happened before another, therefore the one thing caused the other (*post hoc ergo propter hoc*). Here is the one critical point at which the sages in the Oral Torah part company from the Written Torah, so far as people with rea-son deem the Written Torah to make its statement through historical narra-tive, as conventionally understood. In our terms, the sages were not historians but social philosophers, or, we might say, social scientists.

In the sages' world beyond time as historically understood, we deal with a realm in which the past is ever present, the present a recapitulation and refor-mulation of the past, and the future embedded in the here and now.[1] To under-stand their mode of thought, at least as I represent it, requires a bit of effort, for we have to abandon what, in our time and circumstance, is the given of social explanation: appeal to history. History's time is rigidly differentiated into past, present, and future, and history's events are linear and sequential. History may yield patterns, but history transcends those patterns.

---

1. In chapter 15 we shall observe that the liturgy of home and synagogue recapitulates exactly this mode of thought and is incomprehensible if read as a statement of a historical character.

Now consider the sages' view of time and paradigm. When people recapitulate the past in the present, and when they deem the future to be no different from the remote long-ago and far-away, they organize and interpret
experience in a framework that substitutes patterns of enduring permanence
for models of historical change. Instead of history with its one-time, unique
events to be read in a singular manner, thought proceeds through the explanation of paradigms, events being recast as exemplars, and then interpreted
by the criterion of the likenesses or unlikenesses of things set forth in an
original and generative pattern. That is why the familiar modes of classifying noteworthy events, the long-ago and the here and now, lose currency.
What is lost to us – the children of the Enlightenment – is the gift of memory
as the medium of interpretation of the social order; historical thinking as a
mode of explanation of the social order ceases to serve. Universal paradigms
govern instead, against which all things, now, then, anytime, are compared.
That is why events lose all specificity and particularity.

The Oral Torah formulates its conception of world order in enduring paradigms that admit no distinction between past, present, and future. Its narrative
of the life of its "Israel" and the meaning of that life transcend time and
change. All things take form in a single plane of being; Israel lives not in historical time, moving from a beginning, to a middle, to an end, in a linear plan
through a sequence of unique events. Nor does it form its existence in cyclical time, repeating time and again familiar cycles of events. Those familiar
modes of making sense out of the chaos of change and the passage of time
serve not at all. Appealing to a world of timeless permanence that takes shape
in permanent patterns, the Oral Torah accounts for how things are, not by
appeal to what was and what will be, but by invoking the criterion of what
characterizes the authentic and true being of Israel.

Paradigms respond to the question, if not change in linear sequence of
unique events then what? The pattern that controls recapitulates the paradigmatic lives of the patriarchs and matriarchs, or the tale of Eden and
Adam, or the story of Israel and the Land, or the model of the Temple built,
destroyed, and rebuilt, to take principal sources of paradigmatic construction. Therein, the sages find the models of the perfection of a changeless
world, where a set of established patterns governs. Here history gives way
to not eternity but permanence; the rules of the paradigm tell us, not how to
make sense of what was or how to predict what will be, but only what it is
that counts. It is this conception of a timeless perfection, attained at the
beginning, restored at the end, that accounts for the sages' design for death,
resurrection, judgment, and the world to come, as we shall see in chapters
13 and 14.

Paradigmatic thinking, and the particular paradigms at hand, frame a world order that is fully realized and stable, a world beyond the vagaries of time. The sages, like philosophers, conceived order to require a world at rest. Perfection entailed stasis, all things in place in a timeless realm of stability. So they thought about past, present, and future in a manner different from the familiar historical one. To the sages, then, change marked by linear time signified imperfection, a symptom that things continue in an incomplete process of realization, falling short of realizing their goal. In a completed state of order, the balanced exchanges of justice set the norm. All things in place and proportion, each will have achieved its purpose.

In this world of stasis, governed by propositions of a uniform and ubiquitous reason, men meet in a timeless plane of eternity. They are able to exchange thoughts, conduct debates, without regard to considerations of anachronism. It is a shared logic that makes possible their encounter in debate. We have already found Moses listening to Aqiba, and, more to the point, throughout the Oral Torah the sages construct conversations between people of widely separated periods of history. They fabricate conversations that, by their reason, people ought to have had. Indeed, the formidable proportion of the documents that is taken up by fabricated dialogue attests to one prevailing assumption. Reason is timeless, right thinking transcends circumstance; therefore, whenever or wherever people lived, they can confront one another's ideas and sort out their differences by appeal to a common mode of thought and a shared rationality. Paradigmatic thinking comes to expression every time a sage tells a story with an ample selection of what "he said to him ... he said to him," indeed, at every occasion at which a sage imputes a speech to God himself. All of this forms the consequence of that timeless, perfect world that the sages find in Scripture and propose in their setting to recapitulate as well. That is only possible, only conceivable, when time stands still.

Accordingly, a just order attains perfection – an even and proportionate balance prevailing – and therefore does not change. To the sages, the entire Torah, oral and written, portrayed a world that began in perfection at rest, an eternal Sabbath, but then changed by reason of sin. The world preserved within itself the potentiality of restoration to a state of rest. The truly orderly world, then, is represented by the Sabbath, when God completed creation and sanctified it in its perfection. The weekly Sabbath, celebrating creation perfected and accordingly at rest, affords a foretaste of the world to come, one sixtieth of the Garden of Eden that awaits, the Talmud says.

In the Oral Torah the concept of history, coming to expression in the categories of time and change, along with distinctions between past, present, and future, therefore surrenders to an altogether different way of conceiving time and change as well as the course of noteworthy, even memorable social events. The past takes place in the present. The present embodies the past. And there is no indeterminate future over the horizon, only a clear and present path within a different paradigm, to be chosen if people will it. With distinctions between past, present, and future time found to make no difference, and, in their stead, different categories of meaning and social order deemed self-evident, the Oral Torah transforms ancient Israel's history into the categorical structure of eternal Israel's society, so that past, present, and future meet in the here and now. Two basic propositions defined the sages' doctrine of time and change, one negative, the other positive.

First comes the negative: time, divided into eras or epochs or periods, bears no relationship to paradigms that organize into a single plane of eternity the past, present, and future. To the sages, time is neither linear nor cyclical but unremarkable, that is, not kept. It is a minor detail, a contingency made congruent with the critical paradigms – Israel and the nations being the one we now have in hand on the basis of chapters 3 and 4 – that the theology devises in a single model. Time subject to a paradigm yields a pattern that differentiates one period from some other. Events removed from linear, sequential time bear their own, other-than-time-bound signification of the meaning and consequence of a given period. Thinking through paradigms, with a conception of time that elides past and present and removes all barriers between them, in fact governs the reception of the Written Torah by the Oral Torah. Before proceeding, let me give a single instance of how a paradigm forms the medium for interpreting time as contingent and merely notional:

MISHNAH-TRACTATE ZEBAHIM 14:4–8

14:4 A. Before the tabernacle was set up, (1) the high places were permitted, and (2) [the sacrificial] service [was done by] the first born (Num. 3:12–13, 8:16–18).
B. When the tabernacle was set up, (1) the high places were prohibited, and (2) the [sacrificial] service [was done by] priests.
C. Most Holy Things were eaten within the veils, Lesser Holy Things [were eaten] throughout the camp of Israel.

Now comes the next stage, incidentally sequential, but essentially differentiated not by sequence but by other indicators altogether:

14:5 A. They came to Gilgal.
B. The high places were permitted.
C. Most Holy Things were eaten within the veils, Lesser Holy Things, anywhere,

The paradigmatic indicators remain the same, the details now shift:

14:6 A. They came to Shiloh.
B. The high places were prohibited.
C. (1) There was no roof-beam there, but below was a house of stone, and hangings above it, and (2) it was "the resting place" (Deut. 12:9).
D. Most Holy Things were eaten within the veils, Lesser Holy Things and second tithe [were eaten] in any place within sight [of Shiloh],

The same pattern applies once more, the data of the cult being organized not sequentially but essentially:

14:7 A. They came to Nob and Gibeon.
B. The high places were permitted.
C. Most Holy Things were eaten within the veils, Lesser Holy Things, in all the towns of Israel.

Now comes the last realization of the paradigm, marked as final by its own essential traits:

14:8 A. They came to Jerusalem.
B. The high places were prohibited.
C. And they never again were permitted.
D. And it was "the inheritance" (Deut. 12:9).
E. Most Holy Things were eaten within the veils, Lesser Holy Things and second tithe within the wall.

Here time is divided by the periods of the cult, a correspondence that will bear deep significance in chapter 8 when the consequence of paradigmatic thinking, the quest for complementarity and correspondence, is fully exposed.

The first division is before and after the tabernacle, the second is marked by Gilgal, then Shilo, then Nob-Gibeon, and finally Jerusalem, which is the end-time. The consequence of dividing time concerns the conduct of the sacrificial service and the character of its location, the definition of the officiating authorities, and the like. In this paradigm, as in any other, one-time events bear no consequence on their own; sequences of linear events lead nowhere; and, most important, the radical division of time into past, present, and future simply does not apply. "Past" is before the tabernacle, and "future" is Jerusalem in timeless eternity.

To extend the matter of how a paradigm replaces historical time, we see how the sages recognized no barrier between present and past. To them, the present and past formed a single unit of time, encompassing a single span of experience. That is why the liturgy, too, can say, "In all generations an Israelite is to regard himself as if he too were redeemed from Egypt." Why was that so? It is because, to them, times past take place in the present too, on which account, the present not only encompasses the past (which historical thinking concedes) but take place in the same plane of time as the past (which, to repeat, historical thinking rejects as unintelligible). Why? It is because the sages experienced the past in the present. What happened that mattered had already happened; an event, then, was transformed into a series; events themselves defined paradigms, yielded rules. A simple formulation of this mode of thought is as follows:

MISHNAH-TRACTATE TAANIT 4:6

A. Five events took place for our fathers on the seventeenth of Tammuz, and five on the ninth of Ab.
B. On the seventeenth of Tammuz
   (1) the tablets [of the Torah] were broken,
   (2) the daily whole offering was cancelled,
   (3) the city wall was breached,
   (4) Apostemos burned the Torah, and
   (5) he set up an idol in the Temple.
C. On the ninth of Ab
   (1) the decree was made against our forefathers that they should not enter the land,
   (2) the first Temple and
   (3) the second [Temple] were destroyed,
   (4) Betar was taken, and
   (5) the city was ploughed up [after the war of Hadrian].
D. When Ab comes, rejoicing diminishes.

We mark time by appeal to the phases of the moon; these then may be characterized by traits shared in common – and so the paradigm, from marking time, moves outward to the formation of rules concerning the regularity and order of events.

In the formulation just now given, we see the movement from event to rule. What is important about events is not their singularity but their capacity to generate a pattern, a concrete rule for the here and now. That is the conclusion drawn from the very passage at hand:

MISHNAH-TRACTATE TAANIT 4:7

A. In the week in which the ninth of Ab occurs it is prohibited to get a haircut and to wash one's clothes.

B. But on Thursday of that week these are permitted,

C. because of the honour owing to the Sabbath.

D. On the eve of the ninth of Ab a person should not eat two prepared dishes, nor should one eat meat or drink wine.

E. Rabban Simeon b. Gamaliel says, "He should make some change from ordinary procedures."

F. R. Judah declares people liable to turn over beds.

G. But sages did not concur with him.

Events serve to define paradigms and therefore, also, to yield rules governing the here and now: what we do to recapitulate. Here is how diverse events are shown to fall into a single category, so adhere to the same rule, thus forming a paradigm through the shared indicative traits but then losing that very specificity that history requires for events to make sense.

Thus, when we speak of the presence of the past, we raise not generalities or possibilities but the concrete experience that generations actively mourning the Temple endured. When we speak of the pastness of the present, we describe the consciousness of people who could open Scripture and find themselves right there, in its record. They found themselves present in not only Lamentations but also prophecy and, especially, the books of the Torah. Here we deal not with the spiritualization of Scripture but with the acutely contemporary and immediate realization of Scripture: Scripture in the present day, the present day in Scripture. This is what we mean when later on we shall observe that the sages read from Scripture to the present, while their competition, in Christianity, would read from the present back to Scripture (from the "New" to the "Old" Testament, in their language).[2] That is why it was possible for the sages to formulate out of Scripture a paradigm that imposed structure and order upon the world that they themselves encountered.

To generalize: unlike the mode of telling time familiar in the secular West, for the sages time is not marked off in a sequence of singular, unique, one-time events. Rather, time forms an entity, like space, like food, like classes of persons, like everything, meant to be differentiated and classified, hierarchized. The world perfected and at rest does not tell time through an account of what came first and then what happened, a clock that measures the

2. In chapter 15 this matter will take on weight.

movement of time and change. Therefore, history, with its clear division between past, present, and future, linked through sequences of singular events,
does not apply. Rather, the sages defined the world by ages or periods, with no
link to sequential division of past, present, and future but rather differentiated
by indicative traits. Events exemplify indicative traits of the social order in
relationship to God.

What, then, of the narrative of Scripture, particularly the Authorized
History, Genesis through Kings, which bears the traits of history as defined in
a secular way: past, present, future, the changing aspects of one-time linear
and sequential events teaching lessons of history? Considerations of temporal
sequence play no role in the Dual Torah. That statement, in so many words,
demonstrated by the usual assembly of probative cases, simply dismisses the
historical mode of thought as irrelevant to Scripture as mediated by oral tradition (as philosophers would find it irrelevant to natural history):

MEKHILTA ATTRIBUTED TO R. ISHMAEL XXXII:I.1−7

A. "The enemy said, ['I will pursue, I will overtake, I will divide the spoil, my desire
shall have its fill of them. I will draw my sword, my hand shall destroy them]' ":
B. This [statement was made] at the outset of the sequence of events, and why then
was it stated here?
C. It is because considerations of temporal sequence play no role in the Torah.
2. A. Along these same lines: "And it came to pass on the eighth day that Moses
called" (Lev. 9:1).
B. This [statement was made] at the outset of the sequence of events, and why then
was it stated here?
C. It is because considerations of temporal sequence play no role in the Torah.
3. A. Along these same lines: " "In the year that king Uzziah died" (Is. 6:1).
B. This [statement was made] at the outset of the sequence of events, and why then
was it stated here?
C. It is because considerations of temporal sequence play no role in the Torah.
4. A. Along these same lines: "Son of man, stand on your feet" (Ez. 2:1).
B. Some say, "Son of man, put forth a riddle" (Ez. 17:2).
C. This [statement was made] at the outset of the sequence of events, and why then
was it stated here?
D. It is because considerations of temporal sequence play no role in the Torah.
5. A. Along these same lines: "Go and cry in the ears of Jerusalem" (Jer. 2:2).
B. This [statement was made] at the outset of the sequence of events, and why then
was it stated here?

C. It is because considerations of temporal sequence play no role in the Torah.

6. A. Along these same lines: "Israel was a luxuriant vine" (Hos. 10:1).

B. This [statement was made] at the outset of the sequence of events, and why then was it stated here?

C. It is because considerations of temporal sequence play no role in the Torah.

7. A. Along these same lines: "I, Qoheleth, have been king over Israel in Jerusalem" (Qoh. 1:12).

B. This [statement was made] at the outset of the sequence of events, and why then was it stated here?

C. It is because considerations of temporal sequence play no role in the Torah.

The atemporality of Scripture's narrative is further illustrated in a still more striking statement:

MEKHILTA ATTRIBUTED TO R. ISHMAEL XXII:I.24

A. R. Yosé the Galilean says, "When the Israelites went into the sea, Mount Moriah had already been uprooted from its place, with the altar of Isaac that was built on it, and with the array of wood on it, and Isaac was as if bound and set on the altar, and Abraham as though his hand were stretched out, having taken the knife to sacrifice his son.

B. "Said the Omnipresent to Moses, 'Moses, my children are in trouble, with the sea shutting the way before and the enemy pursuing, and you are standing and protracting your prayer!'

C. "Moses said to him, 'And what am I supposed to do?'

D. "He said to him, 'Lift up your rod [and stretch out your hand over the sea and divide it, that the people of Israel may go on dry ground through the sea].'

E. "'You should now exalt, give glory, and praise, and break out in songs of praise, exaltation, praise and glorification of the One who possesses war.'"

But even if the matter were not made explicit, we should find ample evidence of the sages' ahistorical mode of thought on nearly every page of the documents of the Oral Torah, for every time the sages speak as though Abraham and David were contemporaries of theirs, they announced their conviction that the Torah was timeless.

The only way to validate the striking proposition that temporal considerations do not affect the narrative of Scripture, which pays no attention to the order in which events took place, is through examples of atemporality. The examples of the first composition show that the Torah cites later in its narrative what in fact took place earlier, and these shifts validate the claim made at the outset. The second composition makes the same point in a very different way, by claiming that the binding of Isaac was taking place at the very moment at which Israel was tested at the sea. The events then correspond and take place in the same indeterminate moment. And the third proceeds to another probative example of the same.

To say that the sages rejected historicism imposes upon them the burden of difference from our norm. But what about the positive side of matters, and how does the sages' anti-historicism produce a constructive result? The positive side of the same proposition bears a large burden of hermeneutics. Since historical time does not measure the meaning of Scripture, a philosophical one does, that is to say, that quest for regularity and order that in chapter 1 we considered at some length. That quest for the rules of the social order is advanced when the Torah narrates not history – past, present, future – but rather an enduring paradigm, as I said at the outset. Accordingly, portraying a timeless world in which the past forms a principal part of the present, and the present takes place within an eternity of contemporaneity, yields an intellectually formidable reward.

If Abraham, Aqiba, and Ashi live within the same uniform plane of existence as do you and I, this morning, then we gain access to the orderly unfolding of the rules of a well-ordered world, with special emphasis upon the social rules of Israel's life instead of upon the physical rules of the natural world. That is why it was self-evident for the sages that when the Israelites descended into the sea, Moriah was uprooted from its place, with Isaac bound on the altar and Abraham's hand poised with the knife, lessons are to be learned for their Israel too. No wonder, then, that Moses then recapitulates Abraham's gesture (at Mekhilta XXII:I.24) – and the rest follows. This conception of events as patterned – here the gesture is what joins the one scene to the other – defies the historical notion of events as singular, sequential, linear.

Before we proceed to a systematic presentation of how the sages portrayed the perfection of creation in its timeless present, let us take up an account of how they divided time. In their view, temporal past, present, and future, signified by the neutral and natural passage of time, bore no consequence. Rather, they maintained that all time, whether past, present, and future, is differentiated and classified by the indicative traits of Israel's relationship with God. Time is contingent upon the given, when Israel is at one with God, then world order is attained, and nothing more can happen. But, as a matter of fact, that relationship, marking time, will signify the advent of the world to come, that is to say, the end of time as man knows it altogether:

E. Since it is written, "From the rising of the sun to its setting the name of the Lord is to be praised!" (Ps. 113:3). What do you derive from that verse of Scripture? [The Hallel must be read in proper order.]

F. Said R. Abin, "The matter of reading the Hallel in proper order involves the right order of the various sections thereof, thus:

G. " 'When Israel went forth from Egypt, [the house of Jacob from a people of strange language]' (Ps. 114 – this refers to times past.

H. " 'Not to us, O Lord, not to us, but to thy name give glory, [for the sake of thy steadfast love and thy faithfulness!]' (Ps. 115:1) – this refers to the present generations.

I. " 'I love the Lord, because he has heard my voice and my supplications' (Ps. 116) – this refers to the days of the Messiah.

J. " '[The Lord is God, and he has given us light.] Bind the festal offering with cords [up to the horns of the altar!]' (Ps. 118:27) – this refers to the days of Gog and Magog.

K. " 'Thou art my God, and I will give thanks to thee; [thou art my God, I will extol thee]' (Ps. 118:28) – this refers to the age to come."

Here is a fine example of paradigmatic organization of time, a more accessible one than the organization by appeal to the traits of Israel's sacrificial service that we saw just now. Predictably for the Oral Torah, the differentiation of time responds to the critical component of world history, Israel's relationship with God. It follows that no boundary distinguished past from present; time was understood in a completely different way. Within the conception of time that formed consciousness and culture, the past formed a perpetual presence, the present took place on the plane of the past, and no lines of structure or order distinguished the one from the other.

With the past very present, the present an exercise in recapitulation of an enduring paradigm, therefore, time and change signify nothing but imperfection, as much as permanence beyond time and change signifies perfection. And that carries forward that quest for the perfection of the world order that the sages anticipate will justify – show the justice, meaning, perfection of – God's work. That is why, as I said, time in a system of perfection can be neither linear nor cyclical; time in historical dimensions simply is not a consideration in thinking about what happens and what counts. Instead, paradigms for the formation of the social order of transcendence and permanence govern, so that what was now is, and what will be is what was and is.

It follows that the two conflicting conceptions of social explanation – the historical, the paradigmatic – appeal to two different ways of conceiving of, and evaluating, time. Historical time measures one thing, paradigmatic time, another, though both refer to the same facts of nature and of the social order. For its exposition of the cogency and meaning of Israel's social experience, the Oral Torah possesses no concept of history and therefore produces as its statements of the sense of the life of the people neither sustained historical narrative nor biography. Rather, the Oral Torah presents exemplary moments, significations of paradigm, and exemplary incidents in lives of saints, also indicators of a prevailing pattern. These stories yield chapters, not "lives."

To be "Israel" – God's portion of humanity – therefore means to conform to a pattern of actions and attitudes set forth for all time and without distinction in time. That pattern, or paradigm, comes to definition in the lives of the patriarchs and matriarchs. It is then recapitulated in a social world that knows not change but conformity to paradigm – or non-conformity. Since the paradigm endures, we explain happenings by appeal to its rules, and the event is not what is singular and distinctive but what conforms to the rule: we notice what is like the paradigm, not what diverges from it. To the paradigm, matters of memory and hope prove monumentally irrelevant, because they explain nothing, making distinctions that stand for no important differences at all.

That is why, when in the Oral Torah the sages want to explain what it means to be "Israel," they appeal to not time and change but eternity and permanence. Or rather, the conception of the category, time – what is measured by the passage of the sun and moon in relationship to events here on earth – altogether loses standing. In place of distinguishing happenings through the confluence of time, measured by the passage of the sun and moon, and event, distinguished by specificity and particularity, paradigmatic thinking takes another route. It finds an event in what conforms to the paradigm, what is meaningful in what confirms it. In paradigmatic thinking we examine the norms for an account of how things ought to be, finding the rule that tells us how things really are. Then past, present, future differentiate not at all, the pattern of an eternal present taking over to make sense of the social order.

It follows that in the paradigmatic mode of thinking about the social order, the categories of past, present, and future, singular event and particular life, all prove useless. In their place come the categories defined by the actions and attitudes of paradigmatic persons, Abraham and Sarah, for instance, or paradigmatic places, the Temple, or paradigmatic occasions, holy time, for instance. We identify a happening not by its consequence ("historical") but by its conformity to the appropriate paradigm. We classify events in accord with their paradigms as not past, present, or future, therefore, because to the indicators of eventfulness – what marks a happening as eventful or noteworthy – time and change, by definition, have no bearing at all. Great empires do not make history; they fit a pattern.

What they do does not designate an event, it merely provides a datum for classification within the pattern. We have already seen numerous examples of such a procedure. To this way of thinking, Scripture's apocalypse, with its appeal to symbol to represent vast forces on earth, makes its contribution; but paradigmatic and apocalyptic thinking (as distinct from facts deriving from apocalyptic passages of Scripture) about Israel's social being scarcely intersect. The paradigmatic excludes the historical, the indicative, the categorical pattern, the possibility of noteworthy change. Matters are just the opposite, indeed: paradigmatic thinking accommodates historical thinking not at all, since the beginning of history, in the notion of the pastness of the past, contradicts the generative conception of the paradigm: the very paradigmatic character of the happening that bears meaning.

In that context, therefore, the governing categories speak of not time and change, movement and direction, but the recapitulation of a given pattern, the repetition of the received paradigm. Being then moves from the one-time, the concrete, the linear and accumulative, to the recurrent, the mythic, and the repetitive: from the historical to the paradigmatic. These modes of identifying a happening as consequential and eventful then admit no past or present or future subject to differentiation and prognostication, respectively. Time therefore bears no meaning, nor the passage of time any consequence.

It is one in which shared experience takes on meaning when the received paradigms of behaviour and the interpretation of the consequence of behaviour come to realization once again: the paradigm recapitulated is the paradigm confirmed. What takes place that is identified as noteworthy becomes remarkable because today conforms to yesterday and provokes, too, tomorrow's recapitulation as well. We notice not the unlike – the singular event – but the like, not what calls into question the ancient pattern but what reviews and confirms it. If, then, we wish to make sense of who we are, we ask not where we come from or where we are heading, but whom we resemble, and into which classification of persons or events we fit or what happens appears to repeat. The social order then finds its explanation in its resemblances, the likenesses and the unlikenesses of persons and happenings alike.

Let me make this point concrete. The meaning of shared experience, such as history sets forth in its categories of past, present, future, and teleology through narrative of particular events or through biography of singular lives, emerges in a different way altogether. In the formulation of the social order through paradigm, past, present, future, the conception of time in general, set forth distinctions that by definition make no difference. Events contradict the paradigm; what is particular bears no sense. Then remarkable happenings, formed into teleology through history-writing, or noteworthy persons' lives, formed into memorable cases through biography, no longer serve as the media of making a statement bearing intelligible, cultural consequence.

Paradigmatic thinking is never generalized, only is meant to yield generalizations (a very different thing). Specific paradigms come into play. They define the criteria for the selection as consequential and noteworthy of some happenings but not others. They further dictate the way to think about remarkable happenings, events, so as to yield sense concerning them. They tell people that one thing bears meaning, while another does not, and they further instruct people on the self-evident meaning to be imputed to that which is deemed consequential. The paradigms are fully as social in their dimensions, entirely as encompassing in their outreach, as historical categories. We deal not with the paradigms of universal, individual life, taking the place of those of particular, social existence, such as history, with its unique, one-time, sequential and linear events, posits. The result of paradigmatic thinking is no different from that of the historical kind.

For before us is not a random sequence of entirely personal recapitulations of universal experiences, for instance, birth, maturing, marriage, love, and death; these modes of permanence in change, these personal paradigms that form a counterpoint to one-time, public moments play no role in the formation of what endures, whether past, whether future, in the eternal now. The definition of the consequential, permanent paradigms that replace the conception of history altogether will emerge in due course. At the outset, what is at stake must be clear. The shift from historical to paradigmatic thinking represents a movement from one kind of thinking about the social order to another kind. The particularity of history finds its counterpart in the particularity of the paradigm of thought.

This leads directly to the kind of thinking – paradigmatic, ahistorical, and, I claim, utterly anti-historical and dismissive of particularities of time or circumstance but rather philosophical and generalizing – that characterizes the Oral Torah's theological structure and system. Here the past is present, the present is past, and time contains no delineative future tense at all; eschatological teleology gives way to paradigmatic teleology, and – it goes without saying – biography abdicates in favour of highly selective paradigms of exemplarity in the lives of persons, events to patterns. Sustained narrative is abandoned because it is irrelevant; biography, because it is filled with useless information. The concept of organizing the facts (real or fabricated) of the social world of Israel into history as the story of the life and times of Israel, past, present, and future, is succeeded by the concept of organizing the received and now perceived facts of the social world of Israel into the enduring paradigm in which past, present, and future fuse into an eternal now. The final chapter asks how the two versions of Israel's reality, the historical and the paradigmatic, come together. That question, deriving from the Judaism that is under study here, is necessary to an understanding of the theology of the Judaism of the Dual Torah, which obviously recognized what we for our part see in, and of necessity asked about, the complementarity and cogency of the two parts of the single Torah.

When recapitulative paradigms of meaning obliterate all lines between past, present, and future, so that the past forms a permanent presence among the living, and the present recapitulates the paradigm of the past, the conception of history, with a beginning, middle, and end, a linear and cumulative sequence of distinct and individual events, is lost. And writing, too, changes in character, for with the loss of historical thinking perish three kinds of writing. These are, first, narrative, the tale of a singular past leading to present and pointing towards the future, the concretization therefore of teleology. The second kind of writing is biography, the notion of an individual and particular life, also with its beginning, middle, and end. The third is formulation of events as unique, with close study of the lessons to be derived from happenings of a singular character.

And the loss of these three types of writing, commonplace in the standard history, Genesis through Kings, of the Hebrew Scriptures, signals a shift in categories, from the category of history, resting on the notion of time as a taxonomic indicator, to a different category altogether. For the concept of history generates its conception of time, made concrete through the writing of narrative and biography, the formulation of things that have taken place into the formation of consequential, singular events, comparable to the identification of particular persons as events of consequence, worthy of preservation; time starts somewhere and leads to a goal, and lives begin, come to a climax, and conclude as well.

With the end of linear, cumulative, and teleological-historical thinking, the realization of history in narrative, event, and biography loses currency. Narrative strings together one-time events into meaningful patterns, with a beginning, middle, and end; that is the medium of history, and that medium bears history's self-evident messages (whatever they may be). Biography does for individuals what narrative accomplishes for remarkable moments in the existence of the social entity; the narrative takes its measure in different dimensions, but the mode of thought is identical, and the medium for explanation the same. So, too, the conception of time, that is, a sequence of distinct moments, whether cyclical, following a pattern of recurrence, or linear, pursuing a single line from start to finish, also loses all self-evidence. In place, the passage of the fixed stars and planets, the moon and sun, cease to mark off ages and signify periods in human events – this year, this event, next year, that event – and instead measure something else altogether. Just as the passage of a person's life from birth to death takes place outside historical, that is, public, shared, eventful time, only rarely intersecting with the historical and the consequential, so the paradigms mark off something other than the cumulative passing of public time, or of any time that people ordinarily would measure at all.

This is the context in which we review a statement of the proposition that temporal considerations do not apply to the Torah:

SIFRÉ TO NUMBERS LXIV:I.I

A. "And the Lord spoke to Moses in the wilderness of Sinai in the first month of the second year after they had come out of the land of Egypt, saying, ['Let the people of Israel keep the passover at its appointed time. On the fourteenth day of this month, in the evening, you shall keep it at its appointed time; according to all its statutes and all its ordinances you shall keep it.']" (Num. 9:1–14):
B. Scripture teaches you that considerations of temporal order do not apply to the sequence of scriptural stories.
C. For at the beginning of the present book Scripture states, "The Lord spoke to Moses in the wilderness of Sinai in the tent of meeting on the first day of the second month in the second year after they had come out of the land of Egypt" (Num. 1:1).
D. And here Scripture refers to "the first month," so serving to teach you that considerations of temporal order do not apply to the sequence of scriptural stories.

Here we find a clear statement of the ahistorical character of thought in the Oral Torah. To call other-than-historical thinking merely "ahistorical" tells us only about what is not present, but not about what is, in the mind of those who read Scripture through the paradigmatic prism.

What is at stake in the conception of time within paradigmatic thinking? By a paradigm, time is marked off by indicators that are utterly free-standing, in no way correlated with natural time at all; a paradigm's time is time defined in units that are framed quite independent of the ephemera of time and change as we know it in this life, on the one side, or the cycle of natural events that define and also delineate nature's time, on the other. Paradigms may be formed on a variety of bases, but all paradigmatic formulations of time have in common their autonomy of nature, on the one side, and events beyond their own pattern's definitions (whether by nature or by historical events), on the other. God in creation has defined the paradigms of time. Scripture conveys those paradigms, and humanity discovers, in things large and small, those paradigms that inhere in the very nature of creation itself.

These general definitions should be made still more concrete in the setting of the documents of the Oral Torah. Let me give a single example, among numerous possibilities, of time paradigmatic, in contrast to the conceptions of time that govern in the Hebrew Scriptures. The character of paradigmatic time is captured in the following, which encompasses the entirety of Israel's being (its "history" in conventional language) within the conversation that is portrayed between Boaz and Ruth; I abbreviate the passage to highlight only the critical components:

RUTH RABBAH XL:I.I

A. "And at mealtime Boaz said to her, 'Come here and eat some bread, and dip your morsel in the wine.' So she sat beside the reapers, and he passed to her parched grain; and she ate until she was satisfied, and she had some left over":

B. R. Yohanan interested the phrase "come here" in six ways:

Ruth is the ancestress of David, who takes first place in the exposition of cases of the pattern:

C. "The first speaks of David.

D. " 'Come here': means, to the throne: 'That you have brought me here' (2 Sam. 7:18).

E. " '... and eat some bread': the bread of the throne.

F. " '... and dip your morsel in vinegar': this speaks of his sufferings: 'O Lord, do not rebuke me in your anger' (Ps. 6:2).

G. " 'So she sat beside the reapers': for the throne was taken from him for a time."

I. [Resuming from G:] " 'and he passed to her parched grain': he was restored to the throne: 'Now I know that the Lord saves his anointed' (Ps. 20:7).

J. " '... and she ate and was satisfied and left some over': this indicates that he would eat in this world, in the days of the messiah, and in the age to come.

Second comes Solomon, David's son who built the Temple:

2. A. "The second interpretation refers to Solomon: 'Come here': means, to the throne.

B. " '... and eat some bread': this is the bread of the throne: "And Solomon's provision for one day was thirty measures of fine flour and three score measures of meal' (1 Kgs. 5:2).

C. " '... and dip your morsel in vinegar': this refers to the dirty of the deeds [that he did].

D. " 'So she sat beside the reapers': for the throne was taken from him for a time."

G. [Reverting to D:] " 'and he passed to her parched grain': for he was restored to the throne.

H. " '... and she ate and was satisfied and left some over': this indicates that he would eat in this world, in the days of the Messiah, and in the age to come.

Yet another worthy heir of David is Hezekiah, in the time of the Assyrian invasion from the north, who stood firm and believed that God would protect Israel:

3. A. "The third interpretation speaks of Hezekiah: 'Come here': means, to the throne.

B. " '... and eat some bread': this is the bread of the throne.

C. " '... and dip your morsel in vinegar': this refers to sufferings [Is. 5:1]: 'And Isaiah said, Let them take a cake of figs' (Is. 38:21).

D. " 'So she sat beside the reapers': for the throne was taken from him for a time: 'Thus says Hezekiah, This day is a day of trouble and rebuke' (Is. 37:3).

E. " '... and he passed to her parched grain': for he was restored to the throne: 'So that he was exalted in the sight of all nations from then on' (2 Chr. 32:23).

F. " '... and she ate and was satisfied and left some over': this indicates that he would eat in this world, in the days of the Messiah, and in the age to come.

Manasseh is another embodiment of the paradigm, this time showing how one may lose the throne and regain it, just as Israel has lost Jerusalem and the Temple but will be restored in the last days:

4. A. "The fourth interpretation refers to Manasseh: 'Come here': means, to the throne.

B. " '... and eat some bread': this is the bread of the throne.

C. " '... and dip your morsel in vinegar': for his dirty deeds were like vinegar, on account of wicked actions.

D. " 'So she sat beside the reapers': for the throne was taken from him for a time: 'And the Lord spoke to Manasseh and to his people, but they did not listen. So the Lord brought them the captains of the host of the king of Assyria, who took Manasseh with hooks' " (2 Chr. 33:10–11).

K. [Reverting to D:] " 'and he passed to her parched grain': for he was restored to the throne: 'And brought him back to Jerusalem to his kingdom' (2 Chr. 33:13).

N. " '... and she ate and was satisfied and left some over': this indicates that he would eat in this world, in the days of the messiah, and in the age to come.

From the restoration of the monarch, we come to the Messiah who will restore Israel to the Land, all within the pattern now established:

5. A. "The fifth interpretation refers to the Messiah: 'Come here': means, to the throne.
B. " '... and eat some bread': this is the bread of the throne.
C. " '... and dip your morsel in vinegar': this refers to suffering: 'But he was wounded because of our transgressions' (Is. 53:5).
D. " 'So she sat beside the reapers': for the throne is destined to be taken from him for a time: For I will gather all nations against Jerusalem to battle and the city shall be taken' (Zech. 14:2).
E. " '... and he passed to her parched grain': for he will be restored to the throne: 'And he shall smite the land with the rod of his mouth' " (Is. 11:4).
I. [reverting to G:] "so the last redeemer will be revealed to them and then hidden from them."

The paradigm here may be formed of six units: 1) David's monarchy; 2) Solomon's reign; 3) Hezekiah's reign; 4) Manasseh's reign; 5) the Messiah's reign. So paradigmatic time compresses events to the dimensions of its model. All things happen on a single plane of time. Past, present, future are undifferentiated, and that is why a single action contains within itself an entire account of Israel's social order under the aspect of eternity.

The foundations of the paradigm, of course, rest on the fact that David, Solomon, Hezekiah, and Manasseh, and therefore also the Messiah, all descend from Ruth's and Boaz's union. Then, within the framework of the paradigm, the event that is described here – "And at mealtime Boaz said to her, 'Come here and eat some bread, and dip your morsel in the wine.' So she sat beside the reapers, and he passed to her parched grain; and she ate until she was satisfied, and she had some left over" – forms not an event but a pattern. The pattern transcends time; or more accurately, aggregates of time, the passage of time, the course of events – these are all simply irrelevant to what is in play in Scripture. Rather, we have a tableau, joining persons who lived at widely separated moments, linking them all as presences at this simple exchange between Boaz and Ruth; imputing to them all, whenever they came into existence, the shape and structure of that simple moment: the presence of the past, for David, Solomon, Hezekiah, and so on, but the pastness of the present in which David or Solomon – or the Messiah for that matter – lived or would live (it hardly matters, verb tenses prove hopelessly irrelevant to paradigmatic thinking).

Taking account of both the simple example of B.C. and A.D. and the complex one involving the Israelite monarchy and the Messiah, we ask ourselves how time has been framed within the paradigmatic mode of thought. The negative is now clear. Paradigmatic time has no relationship whatsoever to nature's time. It is time invented, not discovered; time predetermined in accord with a model or pattern, not time negotiated in the interplay between time as defined by nature and time as differentiated by human cognizance and recognition. Here the points of differentiation scarcely intersect with either nature's or history's time; time is not sequential, whether in natural or historical terms; it is not made up of unique events, whether in nature or in the social order; it is not differentiated by indicators of a commonplace character. Divisions between past, present, and future lie beyond all comprehension.

Natural time is simply ignored here; years do not count, months do not register; the passage of time marked by the sun, correlated with, or ignored by, the course of human events, plays no role at all. All flows from that model – in the present instance, the model of time divided into chapters of Davidic dynastic rulers, time before the Messiah but tightly bound to the person of the Messiah; the division of time here, then, can take the form of before Boaz's gesture of offering food to Ruth and afterward; before David and after the Messiah; and the like. A variety of interpretations of the passage may yield a range of paradigms; but the model of paradigmatic time will remain one and the same. Not much imagination is required for the invention of symbols to correspond to B.C. and A.D. as a medium for expressing paradigmatic time.

The case now permits us further to generalize. The paradigm takes its measures quite atemporally, in terms of not historical movements or recurrent cycles but rather a temporal units of experience, those same aggregates of time, such as nature makes available through the movement of the sun and moon and the passing of the seasons, on the one hand, and through the life of the human being, on the other. A model or pattern or paradigm will set forth an account of the life of the social entity (village, kingdom, people, territory) in terms of differentiated events – wars, reigns, for one example, building a given building and destroying it, for another – yet entirely out of phase with sequences of time. The pattern that the cases embody turns out to focus upon the loss and recovery of perfection, here, the throne, which embodies so much more for Israel in exile, either overseas or subject to gentile rule.

Clearly, in paradigmatic existence, time is not differentiated by events, whether natural or social. Time is differentiated in another way altogether, and in that way so recasts what happens on earth as to formulate a view of existence to which any notion of events strung together into sequential history or of time as distinguished by one event rather than some other is not so much irrelevant as beyond all comprehension. To characterize Rabbinic Judaism as atemporal or ahistorical is both accurate and irrelevant. That Judaism sets forth a different conception of existence, besides the historical one that depends upon nature's and humanity's conventions on the definition and division of time.

Existence takes on sense and meaning not by reason of sequence and order, as history maintains in its response to nature's time. Rather, existence takes shape and acquires structure in accord with a paradigm that is independent of nature and the givens of the social order: God's structure, God's paradigm, the sages would call it; but in secular terms, a model or a pattern that in no way responds to the givens of nature or the social order. It is a conception of time that is undifferentiated by event, because time is comprised of components that themselves dictate the character of events: what is noteworthy, chosen out of the variety of things that merely happen. And what is remarkable conforms to the conventions of the paradigm.

In accord with the governance of paradigmatic instead of historical thinking, the rationality of a fixed order of events gives way. Now, events are reversible; no fixed order governs. That is why Abraham and Isaac at Moriah are coincident with Moses at the shore of the Red Sea, the raised hand of Abraham, the raised hand of Moses, forming a single pattern, coinciding in a single result. The logic of sequence – first this, then that, therefore this caused that – plays no role. Had we put Moses's raised hand before Abraham's, there would be no loss of sense or meaning. Here the science of society shades over into the imagination of art.

Under such conditions explaining the world as it is by reference to the past is impossible because, in an exact sense, it is unthinkable: it simply cannot be thought. That is to say, by means of thinking with principles such as we shall now examine, history – a mode of accounting for the social order by appeal to how things have been – in the simplest and most conventional definition cannot be conceived. If history cannot identify that dividing point between past and present, it also cannot project that linear sequence of events, singular and irreversible, that forms its second premise. For if past flows smoothly into present, then the reverse also commands plausibility, the present flowing into the past (as indeed we see in the paradigmatic mode of analysing human events followed by the sages).

In the Oral Torah, therefore, the present flows into the past, the past into the present, and at no point do we discern a trace of consciousness that the past is over and done with. These traits of the data before us cannot present any surprises, since, after all, until modern times, the West projected present onto past, representing the past, also, in the garments of today. So we shall not find it difficult to demonstrate that, for the sages, the past and present formed a single plane of time – and consciousness. A single case suffices to show us how events in Scripture were rewritten:

SIFRÉ TO NUMBERS LII:I

1. A. "On the second day Nethanel the son of Zuar, the leader of Issachar, made an offering" (Num. 7:18):

B. Why does Scripture provide this information?

C. It is because the tribe of Reuben came and entered a complaint, saying, "It is enough that Judah came before me [the elder] in the order of the tribal journeys. Let me give an offering in the sequence of the birth of the tribal ancestors [hence, first]."

D. Moses rebuked him, saying, "It is directly from the mouth of God that the instructions have come to me to present the offerings in accord with the order in which the tribes are arranged for the journeys."

E. So it is said, "... Offer," and that word bears the sole meaning that the Holy One, blessed be he, instructed him for the tribes to make their offerings in accord with the order in which they are arranged for the journeys.

There is a number of stories about events portrayed in Scripture, and, in a history of Israel from the beginnings to the present, stories such as these will have found a place along with the Scriptural narrative itself; in them, there is no pretense at joining the present narrative into the language or thought-patterns of Scripture.

Not only does the present flow into the past, the past is made to flow into the present. In the type of narrative given here, Scripture is updated in every possible way; new speeches are written, and no one pretends these speeches were made long ago; new details are set forth without the slightest interest in formulating matters to conform to the style or discipline of Scripture:

SIFRÉ TO NUMBERS XCV:II

1. A. "So Moses went out and told the people [the words of the Lord, and he gathered seventy men of the elders of the people and placed them round about the tent.] Then the Lord came down in the cloud [and spoke to him, and took some of the spirit that was upon him and put it upon the seventy elders; and when the spirit rested upon them they prophesied, but they did so no more.] Now two men remained in the camp, [one named Eldad, and the other named Medad]" (Num. 11:24–26):

B. Some say that their names had remained in the lottery-box. For the Holy One, blessed be he, had said to Moses to choose seventy men for him. Moses replied, "How shall I do it? Lo, all of the tribes will get six representatives each except for two tribes, which will get only five. [Sixty from each of ten tribes, five from each of the other two.] Which tribe will agree to have only five selected from its midst?"

C. Moses made an arrangement. He took seventy slips of paper and wrote on them the word "elder," and he took two further slips and left them blank and mixed them up and put them all into a lottery-box. He said to them, "Come and pick your slips."

D. To everyone who chose a slip on which was written, "elder," Moses said, "The Omnipresent has already sanctified you."

E. And to those who chose a slip on which was not written, "elder," Moses said, "It's from Heaven [and there is nothing I can do about it], so what can I do for you?"

Procedures attested in the Mishnah, for example, for the division of the priestly sacrifices in Mishnah-tractate Tamid, are now retrojected into the remote past. No effort is invested into citing Scriptural evidence that the practice familiar from contemporary writings prevailed even long ago. That fact is simply taken for granted; past and present exist on the same plane. But more is at stake here than merely the atemporality of time. We shall now see how ancient times are fabricated out of contemporary materials.

Not only do scriptural stories undergo an updating and made to accept a reformulation in acutely contemporary terms, but the sages invent chapters in the life of biblical figures, for example, Abraham. Once more we find no interest in joining the story to Scripture's account; it is told entirely in its own terms, in the manner of a Rabbinic polemic-narrative. A single case suffices to make the point that, just as in the first set of documents, events are invented or totally recast, so in the second as much as in the first, considerations of the pastness of the past do not prevent fabrication of whole chapters in lives of saints. The premise once more is that the present is part of the past, and vice versa.

I have chosen for my illustrative case the matter of David. What is interesting is that, when David is reworked into the model of the sages, the conditions of David's life, as portrayed in Scripture, and those of Torah study that rabbis recognized from day to day, were treated as uniform; here is a fine example of what I mean by obliterating the sense of the pastness of the past, while, at the very same time, insisting on the presence of the past in the time of the sages as well. No lines distinguished one age from the other, even while the account of Scripture, read in its own terms, is scarcely acknowledged as exhibiting points of contrast:

PESIQTA DERAB KAHANA II:I.I

A. "O Lord, how many are my foes! Many are rising against me; many are saying of me, there is no help for him in God. Sela" (Ps. 3:2–3):

B. R. Samuel bar Immi and Rabbis:

C. R. Samuel bar Immi interpreted the verse to speak of Doeg and Ahitophel:

D. " '... many are saying of me,' refers to Doeg and Ahitophel. Why does he refer to them as 'many'?

E. "For they formed a majority in Torah-study.

F. " '... many are saying of me,' – They say to David, 'A man who has seized a ewe-lamb, killed the shepherd, and made Israelites fall by the sword – will he have salvation? 'There is no help for him in God.'

G. "Said David, 'And you, O Lord, have concurred with them, writing in your Torah, saying, 'The adulterer and the adulteress will surely die' (Lev. 20:10).

H. " 'But you, O Lord, are a shield about me' (Ps. 3:4): For you have formed a protection for me through the merit attained by my ancestors.

I. " 'My glory' (Ps. 3:4): For your restored me to the throne.

J. " 'And the lifter of my head' (Ps. 3:4): While I was liable to you to have my head removed, you raised my head through the prophet, Nathan, when he said to me, Also the Lord has removed your sin and you will not die' " (2 Sam. 12:13).

The point hardly requires elaboration. David is now turned into something that Scripture's account does not adumbrate, a disciple of the sages, and the politics of his court followed those of the academy. The flow from present to past is unimpeded.

A still more striking revision of times past into the framework of the rabbis' own times involves the rewriting of the story of Hezekiah and the Babylonians. Now the past forms a palpable component of the present. What is important in this example is the provision of an elaborate, sustained narrative, in which history is invented through a process of invention of anecdotes or events; not a single indicator of the presence of a historical mentality can be located in this historical narrative – not one:

SONG OF SONGS RABBAH XXXVIII:II

34. A. ["At that time Merodach Baladan, the son of Baladan, sent" (Is. 39:1) – Spelling out the story to which allusion has just now been made:] he was a sun-worshipper, and he would ordinarily eat at the sixth hour and sleep to the ninth hour.

B. But, in the time of Hezekiah, king of Judah, when the sun reversed its course, he slept through it and woke up and found it was dawn.

C. He wanted to kill his guards. He accused them, "You let me sleep all day and all night long."

D. They said to him, "It was the day that returned [the sun having reversed its course]."

E. He said to them, "And what god reversed it?"

F. They said to him, "It was the God of Hezekiah who reversed it."

G. He said to them, "Then is there a god greater than mine?"

H. They said to him, "The God of Hezekiah is greater than yours."

I. Forthwith he sent letters and a present to Hezekiah: "At that time Merodach-baladan, son of Baladan, king of Babylonia, sent letters and a present to Hezekiah [for he had heard that he had been sick and recovered]" (Is. 39:1).

J. And what was written in them?

K. He wrote him, "Peace to King Hezekiah, peace to the city of Jerusalem, peace to the Great God!"

L. But when the letters had been sent, his mind was at ease, and he said, "I did not do it right, for I greeted Hezekiah before his God."

M. Forthwith he arose and took three steps and retrieved the letter and wrote another instead, in which he said, "Peace to the great God, peace to the city of Jerusalem, peace to King Hezekiah."

N. Said the Holy One, blessed be he, "You have risen from your throne and taken three steps in order to pay honour to me. By your life, I shall raise up from you three cosmopolitan kings, who will rule from one end of the world to the other."

O. And who are they? Nebuchadnezzar, Evil-Merodach, and Belshazzar.

P. But when they went and blasphemed, the Holy One, blessed be he, crushed their eggs out of the world [exterminated them] and set up others in their place.

The story is made up, beginning to end; Scripture's event is recast in a process of imagination and retrojection, and we discern not the slightest interest in harmonizing the story with Scripture's data. The process of writing history in the model of the present, obliterating all lines of differentiation between past and the present age, may be illustrated by one final case. In the following, the death of the prophet is given a reprise.

Here, the storyteller retrojects the destruction of the second Temple into the events of the first, or, more to the point, finds no point in distinguishing one from the other. As at Mishnah-tractate Zebahim 14:4–9, where we differentiate epochs in the Temple's history in such a way that sequence on its own bears no message, here too patterns homogenize periods and then differentiate them by indicative traits that have no bearing upon sequence at all. Two events conform to a single paradigm, and the second of the two will produce the same outcome as the first, repentance, atonement, forgiveness, and restoration:

LAMENTATIONS RABBATI CXIII.I.I.

A. "This was for the sins of her prophets and the iniquities of her priests, who shed in the midst of her the blood of the righteous":

B. R. Yudan asked R. Aha, "Where did the Israelites kill Zechariah? Was it in the courtyard of women or in the courtyard of the Israelites?"

C. He said to him, "It was neither in the women's courtyard nor in the Israelites' courtyard, but in the priests' courtyard.

D. "But they did not dispose of his blood like the blood of a hind or a ram: 'He shall pour out the blood thereof and cover it with dust' (Lev. 17:13).

E. "But here: 'For the blood she shed is still in her; she set it upon a bare rock; she did not pour it out on the ground to cover it with earth' (Ezek. 24:7).

F. " 'She set her blood upon the bare rock, so that it was not covered, so that it may stir up my fury to take vengeance' " (Ezek. 24:8).

From the initial narrative, we turn to a generalization:

2. A. Seven transgressions did the Israelites commit on that day: they murdered [1] a priest, [2] prophet, [3] judge, [4] they spilled innocent blood, [5] they blasphemed the divine name, [6] they imparted uncleanness to the courtyard, and it was, furthermore, [7] a Day of Atonement that coincided with the Sabbath.

B. When Nebuzaradan came in, he saw the blood of Zechariah begin to drip. He said to them, "What sort of blood is this dripping blood?"

C. They said to him, "It is the blood of oxen, rams, and sheep that we offered on the altar."

D. He forthwith sent and brought oxen, rams, and sheep and slaughtered them in his presence, but the blood continued to drip.

E. He said to them, "If you tell the truth, well and good, but if not, I shall comb your flesh with iron combs."

F. They said to him, "What shall we tell you? He was a prophet who rebuked us. We conspired against him and killed him. And lo, years have passed, but his blood has not stopped seething."

G. He said to them, "I shall appease it."

H. He brought before him the great sanhedrin and the lesser sanhedrin and killed them, [until their blood mingled with that of Zechariah: "Oaths are imposed and broken, they kill and rob, there is nothing but adultery and licence, one deed of blood after another" (Hos. 4:2)].

I. Still the blood seethed. He brought boys and girls and killed them by the blood, but it did not stop seething.

J. He brought youngsters from the school house and killed them over it, but it did not stop seething.

K. Forthwith he took eighty thousand young priests and killed them on his account, until the blood lapped the grave of Zechariah. But the blood did not stop seething.

L. He said, "Zechariah, Zechariah, All the best of them I have destroyed. Do you want me to exterminate them all?"

M. When he said this, the blood forthwith came to rest.

The gentile draws the right conclusion, repents, and accepts the one true God and so becomes one of Israel:

N. Then he considered repenting, saying, "Now if for killing one soul matters are thus, as to that man who has killed all these souls, how much the more so!" [He fled and sent a parting gift and converted.]

O. On the spot the Holy One, blessed be he, was filled with mercy and made a gesture to the blood, which was swallowed up in place.

P. To that Scripture refers when it says, "This was for the sins of her prophets and the iniquities of her priests, who shed in the midst of her the blood of the righteous."

A final instance allows us to follow the sages' bold recasting of the scriptural narrative, inventing dialogue, action, and motive. The following is invented out of whole cloth. No consideration is given to distinguishing the time of Moses from the time of the narrator; we detect not the slightest interest in identifying the sources of the story, for example, in remote antiquity. History fabricated is simply not history; it is something else:

THE FATHERS ACCORDING TO RABBI NATHAN XXXIII:V.I

A. When our fathers stood at the sea, Moses said to them, "Get up and pass through."

B. They said to him, "We are not going to pass through until the sea is turned into passages." Moses took his staff and hit the sea, and the sea was turned into passages, as it is said, "You have hit through with rods, the head of his rulers" (Hab. 3:14).

C. Moses said to them, "Get up and pass through."

D. They said to him, "We are not going to pass through until the sea is turned a valley before us." Moses took his staff and hit the sea, and the sea was turned into a valley before them, as it is said, "He made a valley of the sea and caused them to pass through" (Ps. 78:13), and it is said, "As the cattle that go down into the valley, so did you lead your people" (Is. 63:14).

E. Moses said to them, "Get up and pass through."

F. They said to him, "We are not going to pass through until the sea is cut into two parts before us." Moses took his staff and hit the sea, and the sea was cut into two parts before them, as it is said, "To him who divided the Red Sea into two parts" (Ps. 136:13).

G. Moses said to them, "Get up and pass through."

H. They said to him, "We are not going to pass through until the sea is turned clay for us." Moses took his staff and hit the sea, and the sea was turned into clay, as it is said, "You have trodden on the sea with your horses, through the clay of mighty waters" (Hab. 3:15).

I. Moses said to them, "Get up and pass through."

J. They said to him, "We are not going to pass through until the sea is turned into a wilderness before us." Moses took his staff and hit the sea, and the sea was turned into a wilderness, as it is said, "And he led them through the deep as through a wilderness" (Ps. 106:9).

K. Moses said to them, "Get up and pass through."

L. They said to him, "We are not going to pass through until the sea is turned into pieces before us." Moses took his staff and hit the sea, and the sea was turned into pieces, as it is said, "You broke the sea in pieces by your strength" (Ps. 74:13).

M. Moses said to them, "Get up and pass through."

N. They said to him, "We are not going to pass through until the sea is turned rocks before us." Moses took his staff and hit the sea, and the sea was turned into rocks, as it is said, "You shattered the heads of the sea monsters" (Ps. 74:13). And where does one smash the heads of the sea monsters? One must conclude that they are shattered only on rocks.

O. Moses said to them, "Get up and pass through."

P. They said to him, "We are not going to pass through until the sea is turned into dry land before us." Moses took his staff and hit the sea, and the sea was turned into dry land, as it is said, "He turned the sea into dry land" (Ps. 66:6), and further, "But the children of Israel walked on dry land in the midst of the sea" (Ex. 14:29).

Q. Moses said to them, "Get up and pass through."

R. They said to him, "We are not going to pass through until the sea is turned into walls before us." Moses took his staff and hit the sea, and the sea was turned into walls, as it is said, "And the waters were a wall for them on their right hand and on their left" (Ex. 14:29).

S. Moses said to them, "Get up and pass through."

T. They said to him, "We are not going to pass through until the sea [stands up and is] turned into the shape of a bottle before us." Moses took his staff and hit the sea, and the sea was turned into the shape of a bottle, as it is said, "The water stood up right like a bottle containing liquid" (Ex. 15:8).

The narrative pattern is now fully realized, and the story draws to a conclusion:

U. Fire came down and licked up the water between the parts, as it is said, "When fire caused that which melts to disappear, and the fire lapped up the water, to make your name known to your adversaries" (Is. 64:1).

V. And the bottles let out oil and honey into the mouths of infants, and they sucked from them, as it is said, "And he made them suck honey out of the rock" (Deut. 32:13).

W. And some say, "They produced fresh water from the sea and they drank it in the paths,

Y. "[continuing W] as it is said, 'Flowing streams' (Deut. 32:13), and 'flowing streams' refers only to sweet water, as it is said, 'A well of living water and flowing streams from Lebanon'" (Song 4:15).

The examples just now set forth can be duplicated many times over. They embody the fundamental attitudes towards historical time that characterize the Oral Torah. In all, to the past is imputed no autonomy; between past and present is conceived no dividing line of any kind; vastly transcending the mere flaws of anachronism, the conception that time past and time present flow together yields the principle that events may be ordered in accord with a logic quite autonomous of temporal order. The point at which we started forms a fitting conclusion to this brief experiment in the testing of a null-hypothesis. Not only do we find not a trace of historical thinking, as that mode of thought is defined in the Hebrew Scriptures. We find expressions of a quite different mode of thought altogether.

Now that we recognize a different way of thinking about time past, present, and future, we come to the question: what, exactly are the paradigms through which the sages set forth the world order they proposed to discern. In their view the written part of the Torah defined a set of paradigms that served without regard to circumstance, context, or, for that matter, dimension and scale of happening. A very small number of models emerged from Scripture, captured in the sets of Eden and Adam; Sinai and the Torah; the land and Israel; and the Temple and its building, destruction, rebuilding. Within these paradigms nearly the whole of human experience was organized. These paradigms served severally and jointly, for example, Eden and Adam on its own but also superimposed upon the Land and Israel; Sinai and the Torah on its own but also superimposed upon the Land and Israel, and, of course, the Temple, embodying natural creation and its intersection with national and social history, could stand entirely on its own or be superimposed upon any and all of the other paradigms. In many ways, then, we have the symbolic equivalent of a set of two- and three- or even four-dimensional grids. A given pattern forms a grid on its own, one set of lines being set forth in terms of, for example, Eden, timeless perfection, in contrast against the other set of lines, Adam, temporal disobedience; but upon that grid, a comparable grid can be superimposed, the Land and Israel being an obvious one; and upon the two, yet a third and fourth, Sinai and Torah, Temple and the confluence of nature and history.

By reference to these grids, severally or jointly, the critical issues of exist-ence, whether historical or contemporary, played themselves out in the theology of the Oral Torah. I identify four models by which, out of happenings of various sorts, consequential or meaningful events were selected, and by reference to which these selected events were shown to be connected ("meaningful") and explicable in terms of that available logic of paradigm that governed both the making of connections and the drawing of conclusions.

First, how shall we organize (mere) happenings into events? On the largest scale the question concerns the division into periods of not sequences but mere sets of happenings. Periodization involves explanation, of course, since even in a paradigmatic structure, once matters are set forth as periods, then an element of sequence is admitted into the processes of description and there-fore analysis and explanation.

Second, how does Israel relate to the rest of the world? This involves explaining not what happened this morning in particular, but what always happens, that is, defining the structure of Israel's life in the politics of this world, explaining the order of things in both the social, political structure of the world and also the sequence of actions that may occur and recur over time (the difference, paradigmatically, hardly matters).

Third, how to explain the pattern of events, making connections and draw-ing conclusions from what happens? Paradigmatic thinking, no less than his-torical, explains matters. But the explanation derives from the character of the pattern, rather than the order of events, which governs historical explanation. Connections then are drawn between one thing and something else serve to define a paradigm, rather than to convey a temporal explanation based on sequences, first this, then that, and therefore this explains why that happened. The paradigm bears a different explanation altogether, one that derives from its principle of selection, and thus the kinds of explanations paradigmatic thinking sets out, expressed through its principles of selection in making con-nections and drawing conclusions, will demand rich instantiation.

Fourth, how to anticipate the future history of Israel? That concerns not so much explaining the present as permitting informed speculation about what will happen in the future. And that speculation will appeal to those principles of order, structure, and explanation that the paradigm sets forth at the outset. So future history in historical thinking and writing projects out of past and present a trajectory over time to come, and future history in paradigmatic thinking forms projects along other lines altogether.

Here is how the entire history of Israel, beginning to end, is to be portrayed in a systematic narrative of an other-than-historical character. The exegesis of "remember the days of yore" leads us to a review of God's relationship with the world through Israel. "Remember" here does not precipitate a review of times perceived as past – not at all. Memory is an act that is contemporary, calling up the past as a player in the acutely present tense of today's world. Not only so, but the climax focuses not on the past but on the future. The catalogue is complete, the message clear. The past is now invoked as a model for the messianic future, which is to be anticipated.

I abbreviate the passage to highlight the structure of the paradigm that takes the place of history in the description of the existence of Israel.

SIFRÉ TO DEUTERONOMY CCCXIII:I

1. A. ["He found him in a desert region, in an empty howling waste. He engirded him, watched over him, guarded him as the pupil of his eye. Like an eagle who rouses his nestlings, gliding down to his young, so did he spread his wings and take him, bear him along on his pinions; the Lord alone did guide him, no alien god at his side" (Deut. 32:10–12).]

Abraham is our first exemplary figure, establishing the paradigm:

B. "He found him in a desert region":

C. This refers to Abraham.

2. A. "... He engirded him":

B. In line with this verse: "The Lord said to Abram, 'Go from your land' " (Gen. 12:1).

3. A. "... watched over him":

B. Before Abraham came into the world, it was as if the Holy One, blessed be he, was king only over heaven alone, as it is said, "The Lord, God of heaven, who has taken me ..." (Gen. 24:7).

C. But when Abraham our father came into the world, he made him king over heaven and also over earth, as it is said, "I impose an oath upon you, by the Lord, God of heaven and God of earth" (Gen. 24:2).

4. A. "... guarded him as the pupil of his eye":

B. Even if the Holy One, blessed be he, had asked from our father Abraham the pupil of his eye, he would have given it to him, and not only the pupil of his eye, but even his soul, which was the most precious to him of all things.

C. For it is said, "Take your son, your only son, Isaac" (Gen. 22:2).

D. Now was it not perfectly self-evident to him that it was his son, his only son.

E. But this refers to the soul, which is called "only," as it is said, "Deliver my soul from the sword, my only one from the power of the dog" (Ps. 22:21).

From Abraham we turn for our second exemplary figure to Israel:

1. A. Another teaching concerning, "He found him in a desert region":
B. This refers to Israel, as it is said, "I found Israel like grapes in a desert" (Hos. 9:10).
2. A. "... in an empty howling waste":
B. It was in a difficult situation, a place in which were marauding bands and thugs.
3. A. "He engirded him":
B. Before Mount Sinai, as it is said, "And you shall set a boundary for the people round about" (Ex. 19:12).
4. A. "... watched over him":
B. Through the Ten Commandments.
C. This teaches that when the act of speech went forth from the mouth of the Holy One, blessed be he, the Israelites saw it and understood it and knew how much amplification was contained therein, how much law was contained therein, how many possibilities for lenient rules, for strict rulings, how many analogies were contained therein.
5. A. "... guarded him as the pupil of his eye":
B. They would fall back twelve mils and go forward twelve mils at the sound of each and every act of speech,
C. yet they did not take fright on account of the thunder and lightning.

We have dealt with a particular person, then the entire group, and now, in a category-shift, we move on to a particular epoch, a spell defined by its own enchantment, so to speak:

1. A. Another teaching concerning, "He found him in a desert region":
B. This refers to the age to come.
C. So Scripture says, "Therefore behold, I will seduce her and bring her into the wilderness and speak tenderly to her" (Hos. 2:16).
2. A. "... in an empty howling waste":
B. This refers to the four kingdoms, as it is said, "Who led your through the great and dreadful wilderness" (Deut. 8:15).
3. A. "He engirded him":
B. with elders.
4. A. "... watched over him":
B. With prophets.
5. A. "... guarded him as the pupil of his eye":

B. He guarded them from demons, that they not injure them, in line with this verse: "Surely one who touches you touches the apple of his eye" (Zech. 2:12).

The paradigm then covers Abraham, Israel, and the world to come – person, community, age. It is not a historical paradigm, since it does not organize and classify sequential periods of the same character. What is set into relationship are three modes of being: Abraham, the model; Israel, to conform to the model; the world to come, to mark the fruition of the model.

The urgent question takes up the relationship of Israel and the nations, an issue that occupied us in chapter 4. Elected by God, Israel experienced a this-worldly fate that contradicted its supernatural standing. How is its place in world affairs to be accounted for – if not by reference to history? That question is readily framed in this-worldly, historical terms, and a variety of conventional historical writing did just that. What makes the following important is its demonstration of the way in which paradigmatic thinking takes over historical events. The paradigm defines that which counts, among the variety of events at hand: defines, but then explains:

SIFRÉ TO DEUTERONOMY TO EQEB XLIII:III

7. A. Rabban Gamaliel, R. Joshua, R. Eleazar b. Azariah, and R. Aqiba were going toward Rome. They heard the sound of the city's traffic from as far away as Puteoli, a hundred and twenty *mil* away. They began to cry, while R. Aqiba laughed.
B. They said to him, "Aqiba, why are we crying while you are laughing?"
C. He said to them, "Why are you crying?"
D. They said to him, "Should we not cry, since gentiles, idolators, sacrifice to their idols and bow down to icons, but dwell securely in prosperity, serenely, while the house of the footstool of our God has been put to the torch and left [Hammer:] a lair for beasts of the field?"
E. He said to them, "That is precisely why I was laughing. If this is how he has rewarded those who anger him, all the more so [will he reward] those who do his will."
8. A. Another time they went up to Jerusalem and go to Mount Scopus. They tore their garments.
B. They came to the mountain of the house [of the temple] and saw a fox go forth from the house of the holy of holies. They began to cry, while R. Aqiba laughed.
C. They said to him, "You are always giving surprises. We are crying when you laugh!"
D. He said to them, "But why are you crying?"
E. They said to him, "Should we not cry over the place concerning which it is written, "And the common person who draws near shall be put to death' (Num. 1:51)? Now lo, a fox comes out of it.

F. "In our connection the following verse of Scripture has been carried out: 'For this our heart is faint, for these things our eyes are dim, for the mountain of Zion which is desolate, the foxes walk upon it'" (Lam. 5:17–18).

G. He said to them, "That is the very reason I have laughed. For lo, it is written, 'And I will take for me faithful witnesses to record, Uriah the priest and Zechariah the son of Jeberechiah' (Is. 8:2).

H. "And what has Uriah got to do with Zechariah? What is it that Uriah said? 'Zion shall be plowed as a field and Jerusalem shall become heaps and the mountain of the Lord's house as the high places of a forest' (Jer. 26:18).

I. "What is it that Zechariah said? 'Thus says the Lord of hosts, "Old men and women shall yet sit in the broad places of Jerusalem'" (Zech. 8:4).

J. "Said the Omnipresent, 'Lo, I have these two witnesses. If the words of Uriah have been carried out, then the words of Zechariah will be carried out. If the words of Uriah are nullified, then the words of Zechariah will be nullified.

K. "'Therefore I was happy that the words of Uriah have been carried out, so that in the end the words of Zechariah will come about.'"

L. In this language they replied to him: "Aqiba, you have given us comfort."

Here the paradigm that Aqiba finds in Scripture tells him what data require attention, and what do not. The prosperity of the idolators matters only because the paradigm explains why to begin with we may take account of their situation. The destruction of the Temple matters also because it conforms to an intelligible paradigm. In each case, we both select and also understand events by appeal to the pattern of defined by the working of God's will. The data at hand then yield inferences of a particular order – the prosperity of idolators, the disgrace of Israel in its very cult. We notice both facts because they complement one another and illustrate the workings of the model: validating prophecy, interpreting experience in light of its message.

The passages just now reviewed leave no doubt about the character of the explanations of the paradigms of Israel's experience. Explanation will derive from whether or not Israel obeys the Torah, whether or not Israel studies the Torah, the character of Israel's moral condition, Israel's separating itself from the ways of the gentiles, and the like. None of these explanations will have surprised or even much puzzled the framers of the Authorized History. A single case suffices to show the character of paradigmatic explanation. Here we have quite a remarkable statement, that the great men, and the nation, are punished for their sins in such a way that the punishment derives from them themselves; we move along a rather strange line of people who sinned through their arrogance: Adam, Esau, Sennacherib, Hiram, Nebuchadnezzar, and then Israel. But the part of Israel under discussion is the part punished through the affliction, through natural, internal causes, of leprosy or flux. This then yields a comprehensive theory of Israel's history. I have abbreviated the passage as much as possible:

LEVITICUS RABBAH XVIII:II.I

A. "Dread and terrible are they; their justice and dignity proceed from themselves" (Hab. 1:7).

B. "Dread and terrible" refers to the first Man.

G. "Their justice and dignity proceed from themselves" (Hab. 1:7).

H. This refers to Eve.

I. That is in line with the following verse of Scripture: "The woman whom you gave to be with me is the one who gave me of the tree, and I ate" (Gen. 3:2).

2. A. Another interpretation: "Dread and terrible" refers to Esau.

B. That is in line with the following verse of Scripture: "And Rebecca took the most coveted garments of Esau, her elder son" (Gen. 27:15). [This clothing came from Nimrod, so Esau was more of a hunter than he, hence, "dread and terrible."

C. "Their justice and dignity proceed from themselves" (Hab. 1:7).

D. This refers to [the prophet] Obadiah.

E. Said R. Isaac, "Obadiah was a proselyte of Edomite origin, and he gave a prophecy concerning Edom, 'And there shall not be any remnant of the house of Esau for the mouth of the Lord has spoken it' " (Ob. 1:18).

3. A. Another interpretation: "Dread and terrible" refers to Sennacherib.

B. "Who among all the gods of the lands has saved their country from my hand" (Is. 36:20).

C. "Their justice and dignity proceed from themselves" (Hab. 1:7).

D. This refers to his sons: "And it came to pass, as Sennacherib was worshipping in the house of Nisroch, his god, [that Adrammelech and Sarezer, his sons, smote him with the sword]" (2 Kgs. 19:37).

Once more, we notice that the appeal to one paradigm obliterates lines of structure and order that we should have anticipated, for example, differentiation between the personal and the public, or the social and the natural. As much as lines of differentiation among spells of time (past, present, future) are obscured, so all other indicators of classification are set aside by the ones that are in play here. Indeed, the power of paradigmatic thinking is not only to order what should be classified, but also to treat as lacking all differentiation what does not require classification. What we have is a reordering of all of the lines of existence, nature's and humanity's, as much as an obliteration of conventional points of differentiation, for example, of time or space for that matter.

The purpose of paradigmatic thinking, as much as historical, thus points towards the future. History is important to explain the present, also to help peer into the future; and paradigms serve precisely the same purpose. The choice between the one model and the other, then, rests upon which appeals to the more authentic data. In that competition, Scripture, treated as paradigm, met no competition in linear history, and it was paradigmatic, not historical, thinking that proved compelling for a thousand years or more. The future history of Israel is written in Scripture, and what happened in the beginning is what is going to happen at the end of time. That sense of order and balance prevailed.

The restorationist theology that infuses the sages' expression of paradigmatic thinking with its structure and system comes to expression in a variety of passages, of which a severely truncated selection will have to suffice:

GENESIS RABBAH XLII:II

2. A. Said R. Abin, "Just as [Israel's history] began with the encounter with four kingdoms, so [Israel's history] will conclude with the encounter with the four kingdoms.
B. " 'Chedorlaomer, king of Elam, Tidal, king of Goiim, Amraphel, king of Shinar, and Arioch, king of Ellasar, four kings against five' (Gen. 14:9).
C. "So [Israel's history] will conclude with the encounter with the four kingdoms: the kingdom of Babylonia, the kingdom of Medea, the kingdom of Greece, and the kingdom of Edom."

Another pattern serves as well, resting as it does on the foundations of the former. It is the familiar one that appeals to the deeds of the founders. The lives of the patriarchs stand for the history of Israel; the deeds of the patriarchs cover the future historical periods in Israel's destiny.

A single formulation of matters suffices to show how the entire history of Israel was foreseen at the outset:

PESIQTA DERAB KAHANA XXI:V

1. A. R. Hiyya taught on Tannaite authority, "At the beginning of the creation of the world the Holy One, blessed be he, foresaw that the Temple would be built, destroyed, and rebuilt.

B. " 'In the beginning God created the heaven and the earth' (Gen. 1:1) [refers to the Temple] when it was built, in line with the following verse: 'That I may plant the heavens and lay the foundations of the earth and say to Zion, You are my people' (Is. 51:16).

C. " 'And the earth was unformed' – lo, this refers to the destruction, in line with this verse: 'I saw the earth, and lo, it was unformed' (Jer. 4:23).

D. " 'And God said, Let there be light' – lo, it was built and well constructed in the age to come."

A single specific example of the foregoing proposition suffices. It is drawn from that same mode of paradigmatic thinking that imposes the model of the beginning upon the end. In the present case the yield is consequential: we know what God is going to do to Rome. What God did to the Egyptians foreshadows what God will do to the Romans at the end of time, as we shall see in detail at Pesiqta deRab Kahana VII:XI.3, cited in chapter 14.

We have now to ask why the sages rejected the linear sequence of unique events that Scripture sets forth in the Authorized History in favour of the kind of paradigmatic thinking that has now been amply instantiated. Historical thinking yielded an unintelligible result, paradigmatic thinking, a rational one. The reason is that historical thinking – sequential narrative of one-time events – presupposes order, linearity, distinction between time past and time present, and teleology, among data that – for the sages, struggling with the secular facts of Israel's condition – do not self-evidently sustain such presuppositions. Questions of chaos, disorder, and disproportion naturally intervene; the very possibility of historical narrative meets a challenge in the diversity of storylines, the complexity of events, the bias of the principle of selection of what is eventful, of historical interest, among a broad choice of happenings: why this, not that. Narrative history first posits a gap between past and present, but then bridges the gap; why not entertain the possibility that to begin with there is none? These and similar considerations invite a different way of thinking about how things have been and now are, a different tense structure altogether.

A way of thinking about the experience of humanity, whether past or contemporary, that makes distinctions other than the historical ones between past and present and that eschews linear narrative and so takes account of the chaos that ultimately prevails, now competes with historical thinking. Paradigmatic thinking, a different medium for organizing and explaining things that happen, deals with the same data that occupy historical thinking, and that is why when we refer to paradigmatic thinking, the word "history" gains its quotation marks: it is not a datum of thought, merely a choice; contradicting to its core the character of paradigmatic thinking, the category then joins its opposite, paradigm, only by forming the oxymoron before us: paradigmatic thinking about "history."

What Scripture ("Written Torah," "Old Testament") yields for the Oral Torah, therefore, is not one-time events, arranged in sequence to dictate meaning, but models or patterns of conduct and consequence. These models are defined by the Written Torah. No component of the paradigm we have reviewed emerges from other than the selected experience set forth by Scripture. But the models or paradigms pertain not to one time alone – past time – but to all times equally – past, present and future. Then, "time" no longer forms an organizing category of understanding and interpretation. Nor does nature, except in a subordinated role. The spells marked out by moon and sun and fixed stars bear meaning, to be sure. But that meaning has no bearing upon the designation of one year as past, another as present. The meaning imputed to the lunar and solar marking of time derives from the cult, on the one side, and the calendar of holy time, on the other: seven solar days, a Sabbath; a lunar cycle, a new month to be celebrated, the first new moon after the vernal equinox, the Passover, and after the autumnal, Tabernacles. The Oral Torah tells time the way nature does and only in that way; events deemed worth recording in time take place the way events in nature do. What accounts for the difference, between history's time and paradigmatic time as set forth here, I maintain, is a conception of time quite different from the definition of historical time that operates in Scripture: the confluence of the nature's time and history's way of telling time: two distinct chronographies brought together, the human one then imposed upon the natural one.

Israel kept time with reference to events, whether past or present, that also were not singular, linear, or teleological. These were, rather, reconstitutive in the forever of here and now – not a return to a perfect time but a recapitulation of a model forever present. Israel could treat as comparable the creation of the world and the exodus from Egypt (as the liturgy commonly does, for example, in connection with the Sabbath) because Israel's paradigm (not "history") and nature's time corresponded in character, were consubstantial and not mutually contradictory. And that consubstantiality explains why paradigm and natural time work so well together. Now, "time" bears a different signification. It is here one not limited to the definition assigned by nature – yet also not imposed upon natural time but treated as congruent and complementary with nature's time. How so? Events – things that happen that are deemed consequential – are eventful, meaningful, by a criterion of selection congruent in character with nature's own. To understand why, we must recall the character of the Torah's paradigms:

1) Scripture set forth certain patterns which, applied to the chaos of the moment, selected out of a broad range of candidates some things and omitted reference to others,
2) the selected things then are given their structure and order by appeal to the paradigm, or described without regard to scale;
3) that explains how some events narrated by Scripture emerged as patterns, imposing their lines of order and structure upon happenings of other times; and
4) this yields the basis for the claim of consubstantiality: Scripture's paradigms – Eden, the Land – appealed to nature in another form.

The upshot, then, is that the rhythms of the sun and moon are celebrated in the very forum in which the Land, Israel's Eden, yields its celebration to the Creator. The rhythmic quality of the paradigm compares with the rhythmic quality of natural time: not cyclical, but also not linear. Nature's way of telling time and the Torah's way meet in the Temple: its events are nature's, its story a tale of nature too. Past and present flow together and join in future time too because, as in nature, what is past is what is now and what will be. Out of that presence of eternity in time, the world is ordered in perfection, quietly singing in its perfect orbit a hymn of praise to the Creator.

7 World without Change

The sages maintained that, in a world without change, justice required that each person should emerge from a transaction exactly as he entered it. A perfect world – one beyond time – also is a world wholly at rest, in a steady state so far as wealth is concerned, and for the same reason. Perfection entails stasis, permanence, transcending both time and change alike. That is why, with all things in proper place, hierarchically arrayed, exact justice requires that in all exchanges no one's circumstance should shift upward, no one's downward. All should preserve the status quo, possessing at the end the same value as at the start of the transaction. Since the sages took as their task to reveal the perfection of justice in all dimensions of the world that God made, they naturally turned to questions of a material order. The sages' theology of the commonwealth, of political economy, forms the equivalent of the principle of measure for measure in establishing justice for crime and sin, but it applies to everyday affairs. For in the sages' theology of justice, enduring stability is to characterize the perfection of all relationships in Israel as in Eden.

Not only intellectuals but men of standing and political responsibility – politicians in this world, not only teachers in an intangible heavenly academy – the sages therefore encompassed within their theology a theory of political economy. That is because, as much as the sages to accomplish their theological purpose had to form an account of Israel and the nations, they also could make their theological statement whole and complete only through a doctrine of economics. But, not surprisingly, their theory of the rational disposition of scarce resources – that is, their economics – encompassed transactions of both this-worldly and other-worldly venues. This meant, as we shall see, a theory of both stability in what represents permanent value in this world, meaning, real estate, and also unlimited riches in what is of supernatural worth. This yielded two complementary positions. The sages first held that all transactions among men, to attain the standard of justice, have to preserve the steady state of wealth in concrete terms. But there is value that is not limited to a specific amount or volume – the opposite of a scarce resources – but susceptible of infinite increase, and that is, Torah-learning. So when dealing with what is finite, the law (*halakhah*) that served as the theological medium so arranged matters as to assure the equitable transfer of true value between both parties to an exchange.

At the same time, second, the law treated what was infinite – Torah-learning – as counterpart to what was finite – in context, real estate. So when dealing with what is infinite, the lore (*aggadah*) of the Oral Torah took the position that wealth was freely fungible and infinitely transferable, without regard to balance or proportion, because everyone could make himself rich if he wished.

Accordingly, addressing the stability of the social order, the sages' theology of political economy provided an account of the rules for the rational management of scarce resources, and, as we shall see, also the rational increase of the authentic goods of Heaven. This world was not to change, but Israel lived in an order of being able to sustain unlimited increase. The riches of this world were to be preserved in a steady state, but the wealth of Heaven was there for all to attain without limit. These two matching principles, the one of economics in a conventional sense, the other of a categorical counterpart to economics, together coalesced to portray that world without change but with infinite potential for increase to which the sages aspired. Here is a critical chapter in the demonstration of the justice of God in every dimension of creation and the world of man.

It follows that the sages' theory of political economy expressed in material terms and, as we shall see, in the language of the normative law or *halakhah* the same theology of a just world order that in other components was set forth in exegetical, or narrative, or abstract terms. Given the subject matter, we cannot find surprising that the theology of a steady-state political economy took shape in rules governing how actual transactions are to be conducted. Law as much as lore served as an appropriate medium of theological discourse. The statement the sages set forth through law ensured that, in any given transaction, fairness governed, so that no one emerged the richer, none the poorer, from the exchange. An exact transfer of true value was meant to take place.

Let us first take up the this-worldly economy, consisting of land and exchanges of real property. Then we shall identify the equivalent and counterpart to land, which is Torah-study. Forming a bridge to counterpart economics, a noteworthy passage will tell us that real estate and Torah-study form a single category, the one a scarce resource of uncertain reliability, the other an abundant resource of enduring value. From that point we shall see how a counterpart economics states the other half of the design of that perfect world at rest, subject to the Torah, that the sages portray as God's perfect accomplishment.

The sages set forth a fully articulated and systematic economics, answering questions concerning wealth, money, property, production and the means of production, ownership, control of the means of production, price and ("true") value, and the like. That statement cannot be treated as mere moralizing, for it vastly transcended the requirements of episodic sayings about mercy to the poor, recommendations of right action, fairness, honesty, and so on. These honourable sentiments, commonplaces in religions, do not by themselves add up to an economics. Issues of the rational disposition of scarce resources are treated in a sustained and systematic, internally coherent theory that in an encompassing way explains why this, not that, and defines market in relationship to ownership of the means of production.

To understand the economic principle of the sages' theology of a practical world without change, we must take note of the difference between two economic systems, the market economics with which we are familiar, and distributive economics. In market economics, merchants transfer goods from place to place in response to the working of the market mechanism, which is expressed in price. In distributive economics, by contrast, traders move goods from point to point in response to political or theological or other commands independent of market pressures. In market economics, merchants make the market work by calculations of profit and loss; in distributive economics, there is no risk of loss on a transaction.[1] In market economics, money forms an arbitrary measure of value, a unit of account; in distributive economics, money gives way to barter and bears only intrinsic value, as do the goods for which it is exchanged. It is understood as "something that people accept not for its inherent value in use but because of what it will buy."[2] The idea of money requires the transaction to be complete in the exchange not of goods but of coins. The alternative is the barter transaction, in which, in theory at least, the exchange takes place when goods change hands. In distributive economics money is an instrument of direct exchange between buyers and sellers, not the basic resource in the process of production and distribution that it is in market economics.

1. William I. Davisson and James E. Harper, *European Economic History* (New York: Appleton-Century-Crofts 1972), 130.

2. Ibid., 131.

The sages' this-worldly economics at every point opted for the principles of distributive economics; God in the Torah dictated the principles of distribution. Community, self-sufficiency, and justice – these formed the foci of economic thinking. In the sages' theology, society is neatly organized by households, defined in relationship to the control of the means of production – the farm, for the household is always the agricultural unit. The sages maintained the conception of a simple world of little blocks formed into big ones: households into villages. Community, or village (*polis*), is made up of households, and the household (*bayit/oikos*) constituted the building block of both society or community and also economy. It follows that the household forms the fundamental, irreducible, and, of course, representative unit of the economy, the means of production, the locus and the unit of production. For the sages, therefore, Israel was made up, on earth, of households and villages, the economic unit also framed the social one, and the two together composed, in conglomerates, the political one, hence a political economy (*polis, oekos*), initiated within an economic definition formed out of the elements of production.

In the sages' political economy, the village or *polis* comprising the household or *oikos* is orderly, with all things in relationship and in proper order and proportion. True, the political economy encompassed other economic entities, in particular, craftsmen and traders, both of them necessary for the conduct of the household. But each was placed into relationship with the household, the one as a necessary accessory to its ongoing functioning, the other as a shadowy figure who received the crops in volume and parcelled them out to the market. The relationships between householder and craftsman, or between householder and hired hand, are sorted out in such a way as to accord to all parties a fair share in every transaction. Responsibilities of the one as against the other are spelled out. The craftsman or artisan, to be sure, is culpable should he damage property of the householder, but that judgment simply states the systemic interest in preserving the present division of wealth so that no party to a transaction emerges richer, none poorer, a point that will recur in one topic after another:

MISHNAH-TRACTATE BABA QAMMA 9:3

A. If one gave something to craftsmen to repair, and they spoiled the object, they are liable to pay compensation.

B. If he gave to a joiner a box, chest, or cupboard to repair, and the latter spoiled it, he is liable to pay compensation.

C. A builder who took upon himself to destroy a wall and who smashed the rocks or damaged them is liable to pay compensation.

D. If he was tearing down the wall on one side, and it fell down on the other side, he is exempt. But if it is because of the blow that he gave it, he is liable.

All that is at stake here is the preservation of wealth in its established proportions, so that one party does not emerge richer, another poorer, from any transaction or encounter.

In everyday transactions as the sages sorted them out, they proposed to effect the vision of a steady-state economy, engaged in always equal exchanges of fixed wealth and intrinsic value. Essentially, the law as medium of theology aimed at the fair adjudication of conflict, worked out in such a way that no party gained, none lost, in any transaction. The task of Israelite society, as the sages saw it, is to maintain perfect stasis, the prevailing situation, to secure the stability of not only relationships but status and standing. That in the end reinforces the results of hierarchization, leading upward in the social order from God, the one, at the top, to the many distributed below. That is why, in the interchanges of buying and selling, giving and taking, borrowing and lending, transactions of the market and exchanges with artisans and craftsmen and labourers, it is important to preserve the essential equality, not merely the proximate equity, of exchange.

Fairness alone does not suffice. Status quo ante forms the criterion of the true market, reflecting as it does the exchange of value for value, in perfect balance. That is the way that, in reference to the market, the systemic point of urgency, the steady state of the polity, therefore also of the economy, is stated. The upshot of the sages' economics is simple. No party in the end may have more than what he had at the outset, and none may emerge as the victim of a sizable shift in fortune and circumstance. All parties' rights to and in the stable and unchanging political economy are preserved. When, therefore, the condition of a person is violated, the law will secure the restoration of the antecedent status.

In framing matters in this way, the sages carried forward the conception of the Priestly authorship of Leviticus[3] that the ownership of the land is supposed to be stable, so that, if a family alienates inherited property, it reverts to that family's ownership after a span of time. The conception of steady-state economy dominated, so that, as a matter of fact, in utter stasis, no one would rise above his natural or inherent standing, and no one would fall either. And that is the economy the sages portray and claim to regulate through their legislation. In such an economy, the market did not form the medium of rationing but in fact had no role to play, except one: to ensure equal exchange in all

---

3. Leviticus forms part of the Priestly Code, that strand of the Pentateuch produced by the priesthood in the time before Ezra.

transactions, so that the market formed an arena for transactions of equal value and worth among households each possessed of a steady-state worth. Since, in such a (fictive) market, no one emerged richer or poorer than he was when he came to market, but all remained precisely as rich or as poor as they were at the commencement of a transaction, we can hardly call the Mishnah's market a market mechanism in any sense at all.

This brings us to the centerpiece of the sages' conception of the exchange of goods and services outside the market mechanism, which is the notion of inherent or true worth. In market economics, true value bears no clear meaning. The market mechanism – willing seller, informed buyer – dictates value, without the mediation of other considerations. In distributive economics, people know precisely what true value means. In line with this conception, prices must accord with something akin to true or intrinsic value, so the market simply facilitates the reasonable exchange of goods and services by bringing people together. The market provides no price-setting mechanism that operates on its own, nor is the market conceived as an economic instrument, but rather, as one of (mere) social utility in facilitating barter, encompassing, of course, barter effected through specie or money. In the following dispute, we see what is at issue:

MISHNAH-TRACTATE BABA BATRA 5:1

A. If one sold the wagon, he has not sold the mules. If he sold the mules, he has not sold the wagon. If he sold the yoke, he has not sold the oxen. If he sold the oxen, he has not sold the yoke.
B. R. Judah says, "The price tells all."
C. How so? If he said to him, "Sell me your yoke for two hundred zuz," the facts are perfectly clear, for there is no yoke worth two hundred zuz.
D. And sages say, "Price proves nothing."

The sages hold that the purchaser can have set a higher value on the yoke than people ordinarily do; perhaps he saw some special use or need for it. Judah's view is that there is an intrinsic value, against which the market does not operate. This notion of true value, though in the minority in the case at hand, in fact dominates in the sages' thought about the market mechanism. The notion that true value inheres in all transactions, so that each party remains exactly as he was prior to the engagement, comes to concrete expression in a variety of circumstances.

Not only price – for example, in relationship to supply and demand – but also services are so negotiated that ideally no one benefits or loses; a neat exchange of abstract value takes place. The point throughout is that one must so adjudicate disputes that no party emerges poorer or richer than he was when he entered the transaction. Here is another, extreme, example of keeping the measure equal:

MISHNAH-TRACTATE BABA QAMMA 10:6

A. He who stole something from his fellow or borrowed something from him or with whom the latter deposited something, in a settled area, may not return it to him in the wilderness.
B. If it was on the stipulation that he was going to go forth to the wilderness, he may return it to him in the wilderness.

The whole notion of preserving the status quo is expressed in many other ways, but the key is the insistence that the prevailing practice be followed:

MISHNAH-TRACTATE BABA MESIA 9:1

A. He who leases a field from his fellow, in a place in which they are accustomed to cut the crops, must cut them.
B. If the custom is to uproot the crops, he must uproot them.
C. If the custom is to plough after reaping and so to turn the soil, he must do so.
D. All is in accord with the prevailing custom of the province.

The market was not perceived as a price-setting mechanism, but rather as the setting in which distribution took place in such a way that the principle of equivalence was enforced. Both parties to an act of barter or sale must necessarily gain by it in the sense that they must prefer their economic situations after the act to the economic situations in which they found themselves before the act.

Since the sages maintain that there is a true value, as distinct from a market value, of an object, we may understand their acute interest in questions of fraud through not only misrepresentation but also overcharge. The *halakhah* maintains that, if a purchaser pays more than a sixth more than true value, or if a seller receives a sixth less than that amount, in the form of an overcharge, fraud has been committed. The sale is null. The defrauded party has the choice of getting his money back or of keeping the goods and receiving only the amount of the overcharge. The notion of true value logically belongs together with the conception of money as an item of barter or as something meant merely to facilitate barter, because both notions referred to the single underlying conception of the economy as a steady-state entity in which people

could not increase wealth but only exchange it. We take up both matters of
halakhah in the same discussion, therefore, just as the Mishnah presents them.

The governing conception is that money, by itself, does not effect an
exchange and acquisition of the purchased item. Only a symbolic act of barter does so, and that fact (not unique to the law of the Mishnah, to be sure)
tells us that, within this system, the theory of money is set aside by the theory
of barter, and the market is simply a mechanism for barter. The principles
that all transactions are really acts of barter, that money has no meaning other
than as an instrument of barter, and, consequently, that money (for example,
silver, gold) is merely another commodity – all these conceptions express in
detail the substitute, within distributive economics, for the notion of the
market as the mechanism of exchange.

MISHNAH-TRACTATE BABA MESIA 4:1–2

A. (1) Gold acquires silver, but silver does not acquire gold.

B. (2) Copper acquires silver, but silver does not acquire copper.

C. (3) Bad coins acquire good coins, but good coins do not acquire bad coins.

D. (4) A coin lacking a mint mark acquires a minted coin, and a minted coin does not
acquire a coin lacking a mint-mark.

E. (5) Movable goods acquire coins, and coins do not acquire movable goods.

F. This is the governing principle: All sorts of movable objects effect acquisition of
one another.

The commodity of lesser value effects acquisition of the commodity of
greater value. The mere transfer of funds does not effect transfer of ownership. The actual receipt of the item in trade by the purchaser marks the point
at which the exchange has taken place.

Barter of commodities, not exchange of (abstract) money, is what characterizes the exchange of things of value. Money is an abstraction. It does not
merely represent something of value nor is it something itself of value. The
entire notion of trade other than as an act of barter of materials or objects of
essentially equal worth is rejected. Trade now is merely a way of working out
imbalances when one party has too much of one thing but needs the other,
while the other party has too much of the other thing but needs what the
former has in excess. Since money does not effect a transaction, we have to
determine that sort of specie which is (functionally) deemed to constitute currency and that which is regarded as a commodity. In general, the more precious the metal, the more likely it is to be regarded not as money or ready
cash but as a commodity, subject to purchase or sale, just as much as is grain

or wine. This notion is expressed very simply: "Gold acquires silver," meaning, gold is a commodity, and when the purchaser has taken possession of the gold, the seller owns the silver paid as money for it. But if the exchange is in the reverse – someone paying in gold for silver – the transaction is effected when the seller has taken possession of the gold. In an exchange of copper and silver, copper is deemed money, silver is now the commodity.

The very fact that fraud is simply charging more for something than it is worth can only mean that object has intrinsic worth – hence the notion of true value. In accord with the notion of true value expressed in the next passage, an object has a true or intrinsic value which cannot be exceeded in payment or receipt by more than 18 per cent (but we do not know the time-frame involved, for example, per diem or per annum!).

MISHNAH-TRACTATE BABA MESIA 4:3

A. Fraud [overreaching] is an overcharge of four pieces of silver out of twenty four pieces of silver to the *sela* –

B. (one sixth of the purchase-price [=18%]).

C. For how long is it permitted to retract [in the case of fraud]?

D. So long as it takes to show [the article] to a merchant or a relative.

Now we have a case that illustrates the imprecision of the law just now set forth: how long a time is contemplated for checking with a friendly party? The sage allowed an "overcharge" of a third, so the merchants were pleased, but then a whole day to check out the deal, so they rejected the generous provision for profit:

E. R. Tarfon gave instructions in Lud:

F. "Fraud is an overcharge of eight pieces of silver to a *sela* –

G. "one third of the purchase price."

H. So the merchants of Lud rejoiced.

I. He said to them, "All day long it is permitted to retract."

J. They said to him, "Let R. Tarfon leave us where we were."

K. And they reverted to conduct themselves in accord with the ruling of sages.

The definition of fraud self-evidently rests on the conception of an intrinsic or true value; there is no conception of fraud as mere misrepresentation of the character of merchandise. That comes later and bears its own considerations. Fraud here is simply a charge higher than the intrinsic worth of the object permits. If an object has a true value of twenty-four and the seller pays twenty-eight, he has been defrauded and may retract. Tarfon gave and took, as in paragraphs E–K. Once we impute a true value to an object or commodity, we shall also dismiss from consideration all matters of worth extrinsic to the object or commodity; hence money is not an abstract symbol of worthy but itself a commodity, and, further, objects bear true value.

True value thus presupposes a steady state of what is of worth, and, so far as the sages are concerned, in this-worldly terms, wealth to the householder is ownership of land. Perhaps that definition of value sustained the notion of true value, since real estate does not increase or decrease, so, theoretically, the economy must remain in a steady state as to value. For the sages (and in this regard ancient economics concurred with them), any ownership of a piece of land, however small, constitutes "wealth." The result – the context – is important. The sages spoke of Israel in the Land of Israel. God and the farmer shared ownership of that holy, sanctified land. God's share of the crop fell due at the point at which, so far as the householder or farmer was concerned, the farmer deemed the crop to be of value, ready to harvest. God's intentions for the crop at that point are provoked by his partner's, the farmer's, counterpart intentions. In the present case, the crop of any piece of ground, however small, is liable for the designation of God's portion in the crop.

When the sages, as we shall see, compare the scarce resources of land with the unlimited resources of Torah-learning, they dealt with two media of sanctification, holy land, holy learning. That is the basis of equivalence, so far as I can discern. Accordingly, we must keep in mind, wealth and ownership of "land" speak of a very particular acreage, specifically, the territory known to the sages as the Land of Israel, that alone. And, in this same context, only Israel is subject to wealth, because it is only when an Israelite owns land in the Land of Israel that God shares in the ownership and cares about his share of the crop (to go, as we shall see, to his scheduled castes, the priests, Levites, and poor, or to the support of the city, Jerusalem). It follows that land in the Land of Israel that is liable to sacerdotal taxes must be owned by an Israelite. Gentiles are not expected to designate as holy portions of their crop, and, if they do so, those portions of the crop that they designate as holy nonetheless are deemed secular.

Let us dwell on the transcendent character of scarce resources (wealth) for which the sages legislated. We have an exceedingly specific set of conditions in hand, an economics of a remarkably particular, indeed, of an awry, character. Wealth for the *halakhah* is not ownership of land in general, for example, land held by Jews in Babylonia, Egypt, Italy, or Spain. It is ownership of land located in a very particular place. And wealth for that same system is not wealth in the hands of an undifferentiated owner. It is wealth in the domain of an Israelite owner in particular. Wealth is therefore ownership of land in the *Land of Israel* and by *Israel[ites]*, in two senses, both of them contained within the italicized words. "Israel" forms the key to the meaning of wealth, because it modifies persons and land alike: only an Israel[ite] can possess the domain that signifies wealth; only a domain within the land called by the name of "Israel" can constitute wealth. It is in the enchanted intersection of the two Israels, people and land, thus ownership of the land, ownership by the people, that wealth in the *halakhah* becomes, in a this-worldly sense, real and tangible.

Wealth is conceived as unchanging and not subject to increase or decrease, hence, by the way, the notion of true value imputed to commodities. For if we imagine a world in which, ideally, no one rises and no one falls, and in which wealth is essentially stable, then we want to know what people understand by money, on the one hand, and how they identify riches, on the other. The answer is simple. For the *halakhah*, wealth constitutes that which is of lasting value, and what lasts is real property in the land of Israel, that alone. As I said, real estate in the land of Israel does not increase in volume, it is not subject to the fluctuation of the market; it is permanent, reliable, and, however small, always useful for something. True enough, we find more spiritual definitions of wealth, for example, Mishnah-tractate Abot 4:2: "Who is rich? He who is happy in what he has." So, too, one can become rich through keeping or studying the Torah, for example: "He who keeps the Torah when poor will in the end keep it in wealth" (Mishnah-tractate Abot 4:9). We also find the following: "Keep your business to a minimum and make your business Torah" (Mishnah-tractate Abot 4:10). But these sayings have no bearing upon a single passage of the *halakhah* in which a concrete transaction in exchanges of material goods take place, nor does anyone invoke the notion of being satisfied with what one has when it comes to settling scores.

For the sages, since scarce resources are preserved in a steady state, profit or interest violate the norm; if I collect more than the true value of a piece of land or a cloak, I end up richer than before, and the buyer, poorer. And if, moving to the abstract, I treat money as subject to increase or decrease, I do the same. Hence, in the distributive economics of the Oral Torah, which sits squarely and symmetrically on the counterpart judgment of the Written Torah, profit making and usury cannot be tolerated. If I lend a *denar*, I should get back a *denar*; if I lend a *kor* of wheat, I should get back a *kor* of wheat. Waiting for my money yields no gain to me, the use by the other no charge to him. And if a kor of wheat costs more than I get it back than when I lent it, that makes no difference, wheat remains wheat.

Now, usury. By usury, the sages meant any payment for waiting on the return of something of value, but, as the matter was fully explicated, usury became equivalent to profit of any sort. Here is the classical definition of the matter:

MISHNAH-TRACTATE BABA MESIA 5:1

A. What is interest, and what is increase [which is tantamount to taking interest]?
B. What is interest?
C. He who lends a *sela* [which is four *denars*] for [a return of] five *denars*,
D. two *seahs* of wheat for [a return of] three –
E. because he bites [off too much].
F. And what is increase?
G. He who increases [profits] [in commerce] in kind.
H. How so?
I. [If] one purchases from another wheat at a price of a golden *denar* [25 *denars*] for a *kor*, which [was then] the prevailing price, and [then wheat] went up to thirty] *denars*.
J. [If] he said to him, "Give me my wheat, for I want to sell it and buy wine with the proceeds" –
K. [and] he said to him, "Lo, your wheat is reckoned against me for thirty *denars*, and lo, you have [a claim of] wine on me" –
L. but he has no wine.

The meaning of interest is clear as given. Usury involves a repayment of 25 per cent over what is lent in cash, or 50 per cent over what is lent in kind (once more, we have no definition of the span of time involved).

Increase is less clear. We clearly deal with a case of trading in futures. The purchaser agrees to pay at the current price of twenty-five *denars* for a *kor*; delivery is postponed until the harvest. Mishnah-tractate Baba Mesia 5:7 permits this procedure. When the purchaser calls his contract, the vendor concurs in revising the price of the contract. But he also revises the cost of wine upward to its then-prevailing price. In point of fact, the seller has no wine for sale. This would appear, in contemporary terms, to be trading in "naked" or uncovered futures. If that is at issue, the prohibition would be based upon the highly speculative character of the vendor's trading practices. But the "increase" is that the vendor now has to pay for the wine at a higher price than is coming to the purchaser.

Usury or profit encompasses, also, payment in kind, not only in cash, and payment in kind can take a variety of forms. Not only so, but discounts for paying in advance for purchased property are classified as usury as well. But one may discount a rental paid in advance:

MISHNAH-TRACTATE BABA MESIA 5:2

A. He who lends money to his fellow should not live in his courtyard for free.
B. Nor should he rent [a place] from him for less [than the prevailing rate],
C. for that is [tantamount to] usury.

Now, the distinction between sale and rental, the former imputing less than true value, the latter not pertinent to true value at all:

D. One may effect an increase in the rent-charge [not paid in advance], but not the purchase-price [not paid in advance].
E. How so?
F. [If] one rented his courtyard to him and said to him, "If you pay me now [in advance], lo, it's yours for ten *selas* a year,
G. "but if [you pay me] by the month, it's a *sela* a month" –
H. it is permitted.
I. [But if] he sold his field to him and said to him, "If you pay me the entire sum now, lo, it's yours for a thousand *zuz*.
J. "But if you pay me at the time of the harvest, it's twelve *maneh* [1,200 *zuz*]," –
K. it is forbidden.

A-C prohibit interest in kind. D is neatly explained at F-H versus I-K. The rent falls due month by month, so there is no fee for "waiting" on the payment, while at I-K there is a 20 per cent surcharge for postponing payment, tantamount to mortgage-interest. Since the rent falls due only month by month, it is not as if the tenant is gaining an undue advantage. The landlord is handing over two *selas* in exchange for the tenant's paying money which has not yet fallen due. But in the latter case, the seller of the field is owed the money as soon as the sale has been effected. By collecting 20 per cent extra some time later, he is receiving interest on money which, in fact, already is owing to him. This is not permitted.

From the specifics, let us turn to the theology that animates the details. The sages' distributive economics derives from the theory that the temple and its scheduled castes on earth exercise God's claim to the ownership of the holy land. It is, in fact, a theology that comes to expression in the details of material transactions. The theology derives from the conviction such as is expressed in the Psalm 24:1, "The earth is the Lord's." That conviction is a statement of ownership in a literal sense, and also, as we know, in a very particular sense. God owns the earth. But the particular earth that God owns consequentially is the Land of Israel, and, within that land, the particular earth is land in the Land of Israel that is owned by an Israelite. With that Israelite, a landowner in the land of Israel, God is co-owner. From that theological principle, spun out of the notion that when Israelites occupy the land that God has given to the Israelites, namely, the land of Israel, that land is transformed and so too are the principles of ownership and distribution of the land, all else flows.

Since God owns the Land of Israel, God – represented by, or embodied through, the temple and priesthood, the Levites and the poor – joins each householder who also owns land in the Land of Israel as an active partner, indeed, as senior partner, in possession of the landed domain. God not only demands a share of the crop, and hence comprises a householder. God also dictates rules and conditions concerning production, and therefore controls the householder's utilization of the means of production. Furthermore, it goes without saying, God additionally has provided as a lasting inheritance to Israel, the people, the enduring wealth of the country, which is to remain stable and stationary and not to change hands in ways that one grows richer, the other poorer. Every detail of the distributive economics restates that single point: *the earth is the Lord's*. That explains why the householder is partner of the Lord in ownership of the land, so that the Lord takes his share of the crop at the exact moment at which the householder asserts his ownership of his portion. All land was held in joint tenancy, with the householder as one partner, God as the other.

The householder, for the *halakhah*, therefore occupies an exalted position as God's partner. Consequently, the opinions, attitudes, plans, and intentions of the householder form the centrepiece of the system. Indeed, the will and intention of the householder, in matters of the disposition of scarce resources in particular, are what make the system work. Here is an instance in concrete terms of what is at stake:

MISHNAH-TRACTATE KILAYIM 7:6–7

A. The usurper who sowed a vineyard –
B. and it left his possession –
C. [the rightful owner] cuts down [the other kind],
D. even on a festival.

It is forbidden to sow grain in a vineyard. A squatter, not the owner, has done so. The rightful owner may then cut down the forbidden crop.

E. How much more does he pay the workers [for cutting down the other kind on the intermediate days of a festival]?

F. Up to a third [more than their usual wages].

G. [If they demand] more than this,

H. he continues to cut [it] down in his [usual] manner,

I. even [if he does not finish cutting it down until] after the festival.

J. At what point is [the vineyard] called [that of the] usurper?

K. At the point that [the vineyard] settles.

7:7 A. Wind which hurled vines on top of grain –

B. he should cut them [the vines] down at once.

C. If an unavoidable accident befell him [and he could not immediately cut down the vines], it is permitted [the grain is not sanctified].

The action and attitude of the householder set aside the violation of the taboo which, had the householder deliberately done the deed, would have rendered forfeit the entire vineyard. If a usurper sows a vineyard with mixed seeds and loses possession of the vineyard, the rightful owner who has recovered ownership must cut down the sown crop immediately. If he does so, however, there is no consequence to the prior presence of what should have been prohibited. The decision and action of the landowner make all the difference; for example, if a wind hurled vines on top of grain, the householder cuts the vines at once and there is no further penalty, since the householder bears no responsibility for the violation. The intentionality of the householder governs throughout, an important instance in which the *halakhah* bears a heavy burden of theological meaning.

Intervention of God – that is to say, the considerations of cult and taboo, not solely those of market and trade and value – into land ownership is total and complete. No householder can permanently sell his land received by inheritance. Lev. 25:10 has land revert after fifty years, in the Jubilee, to the original owner. What does not revert? The portion of the first-born, inheritance of one who inherits his wife's estate, inheritance of the one who enters into Levirate massage (Mishnah-tractate Bekhorot 8:10). Consequently, the householder cannot alienate his property and invest his capital in some other medium. The cultic rule imposes a valuation on the real estate that otherwise it cannot have enjoyed, and, at the same time, freezes in land the equity of the householder.

An other-than-market consideration overrides the market's valuation of the land. This consideration affects not only the householder's land but also his residence. Specifically, a house in a walled city cannot be permanently sold but reverts to the original owner (Lev. 25:25–34). Mishnah-tractate Arakhin in chapters 7 and 8 goes over this rule. When someone dedicates a field, and another person then buys it (redeems it) from the temple, he may not do so permanently. The field or the house reverts at the jubilee. At issue is only the field of possession, which is one that is received by inheritance (Lev. 27:16–25 and Mishnah-tractate Arakhin 7:1–8:3). The field received as an inheritance and the dwelling house in a walled city, which are to revert to the "original" owner, are treated at Lev. 25:25–34/Mishnah-tractate Arakhin 9:1–8. The sale here is assumed to be brought about because of need: "If your brother becomes poor and sells part of his property ..." (Lev. 25:25). The intervention of the law into the disposition of the capital of the household, that is, in the form of the herds and the flocks, derives from Ex. 13:2 and Num. 18:15–18. Invalidated holy things are sold in the marketplace, but the blemished firstling may not be sold in the marketplace (M. Bekh. 5:1). Here, too, the *halakhah* invents nothing but integrates into the larger statement rules of Scripture deemed systemically urgent.

One aspect of the steady-state economy of a world without change draws attention to the correct ordering and classification of all things. This takes the form of the application to production of scriptural taboos as to commingling different categories of plants, animals, or fibres (Lev. 19:19, Deut. 22:9–11). The Mishnah-tractate devoted to these taboos, Kilayim, established criteria for distinguishing among different classes, defined what constitutes the commingling of such classes, and determined how to keep each category separate and distinct from others. Mandelbaum defines the interest of the tractate as follows: "Although the Mishnah's regulations clearly depend upon their scriptural antecedents, the conception of the law which they express is distinctive to the Mishnah ... It is man, using his powers of observation, who determines what is orderly and what lies in confusion. Unlike Scripture, which takes for granted the existence of an established and immutable order, the Mishnah calls upon man to create order based upon his own perception of the world around him."[4] Man defines what constitutes a class and determines how to keep the different classes distinct from one another; man thus imposes upon an otherwise disorderly world limits and boundaries which accord with human perception of order and regularity.[5] The priestly conception of this matter, in Leviticus, is set forth by Mandelbaum as follows:

In the view of the priestly circles which stand behind the Priestly Code, order is a precondition of holiness. This notion is clearly reflected in the Priestly Code's account of the creation ... The Priestly Code describes the making of a well-ordered, hierarchical

---

4. Irving Mandelbaum, *A History of the Mishnaic Law of Agriculture: Kilayim. Translation and Exegesis* (Chicago: Scholars Press for Brown Judaic Studies 1982), ix.

5. *Ibid.*, 1.

world. Each type of creation is brought forth in order of ascending importance ... All living things furthermore were created each according to its kind ... Creation is thus an act of ordering, the purpose of which is to make the world perfect and thus prepare it to be made holy. The actual act of the sanctification of the world then takes place on the Sabbath. The point of the Priestly Code's laws in Leviticus is to prevent the confusion of those classes and categories which were established at the creation. The Priestly Code thus commands man to restore the world from its present condition of chaos to its original orderly state and so to make the world ready once again for sanctification ... The Mishnah claims that it is man, and not a sort of already established rules, who decides what is orderly and what is confused.[6]

The "man" whose judgment is decisive in these matters, of course, is the farmer, that is to say, the householder, and a human being becomes fully human through ownership of land: land "of Israel" in the ownership of a human being "of Israel," in partnership with God.

So much for the rational disposition of scarce resources, aimed, as we see, at the establishment of a steady-state economy, a world in perfect order and without change. But the sages treated as equal in standing real estate and Torah-learning. In that way they also took up the opposite of the notion of scarce resources, insusceptible of increase, such as real estate in the Land of Israel. They contemplated the conception of resources susceptible of infinite increase. In doing so, they accomplished the redefinition of scarce and valued resources in so radical a manner that the concept of value, while remaining material in consequence and character, nonetheless took on a quite different sense altogether. Issues such as the definition of wealth, the means of production and the meaning of control thereof, the disposition of wealth through distributive or other media, the role of money, the reward for labour, and the like – all these questions found their answers in systematic discussion of another "scarce resource," another currency. Specifically, the definition of wealth changes from land to Torah. Why was such a transvaluation of value found plausible? Land produced a living; so did Torah. Land formed the foundation of the social entity, so did Torah.

When Torah-learning was deemed counterpart to land ownership, an economics concerning the rational management and increase of scarce resources worked itself out in such a way as to answer, for quite different things of value from real property or capital, precisely the same questions that the received economics addressed in connection with wealth of a real character: land and its produce. The utter transvaluation of value finds expression in a jarring

6. *Ibid.*, 2–3.

juxtaposition, an utter shift of rationality, specifically, the substitution of Torah for real estate. In the following statement in a fifth-century document in the name of first-century authorities, Tarfon thinks wealth takes the form of land, while Aqiba explains to him that wealth takes the form of Torah-learning. That the sense is material and concrete is explicit: land for Torah, Torah for land. Thus, to repeat the matter of how Torah serves as an explicit symbol to convey the systemic world-view, let us note the main point of the now-familiar passage:

LEVITICUS RABBAH XXXIV:XVI

I. B. R. Tarfon gave to R. Aqiba six silver *centenarii*, saying to him, "Go, buy us a piece of land, so we can get a living from it and labor in the study of Torah together."
C. He took the money and handed it over to scribes, Mishnah-teachers, and those who study Torah.
D. After some time R. Tarfon met him and said to him, "Did you buy the land that I mentioned to you?"
E. He said to him, "Yes."
F. He said to him, "Is it any good?"
G. He said to him, "Yes."
H. He said to him, "And do you not want to show it to me?"
I. He took him and showed him the scribes, Mishnah teachers, and people who were studying Torah, and the Torah that they had acquired.
J. He said to him, "Is there anyone who works for nothing? Where is the deed covering the field?"
K. He said to him, "It is with King David, concerning whom it is written, 'He has scattered, he has given to the poor, his righteousness endures forever' " (Ps. 112:9).

If, as we have seen, the sages framed an economics to provide for a world without change, we must wonder how this shift in the meaning of value accomplishes their goal.

The stress in the story at hand is on the enduring character of righteousness, meaning, in this context, support of masters and their disciples. That establishes the stability of wealth, marking it for eternity. So the theory of the rational disposition of scarce resources now encompasses the rational increase of resources that, by an act of will, the Israelite can make infinitely abundant – an anti-economics. How does the theological goal, the formulation of a steady-state economy, follow? When it comes to land, a finite resource, one's gain marks another loss. But when it comes to Torah, a renewable resource, everyone gets richer when anyone acquires more: all Israel is enhanced. It follows that the sages' theory of a just society of permanent stability opens out onto a supernatural world of ever-increasing abundance. Only when we keep in mind, at every line of the discussion here, the supernatural character of holy Israel and the promise of the Torah as God's medium of self-revelation can we see how a single account of a perfect world at rest is set out. That comes when we grasp how both the distributive economics of the *hala-khah* and its counterpart-economics in the *aggadah* work together to form a coherent statement. That takes place when they are viewed in the larger theological context here under construction.

Ownership of land, even in the Land of Israel, contrasts with wealth in another form altogether, and the contrast that was drawn was material and concrete, not merely symbolic and spiritual. It was material and tangible and palpable because it produced this-worldly gains, for example, a life of security, comfort, ease, as these too found definition in the systemic context of the here and the now. It follows that it is an economics of scarce resources defined as something other than particular real estate. Whether thinking about real estate or Torah-learning, the sages deal with the rules or theory of the rational management of scarce resources, their preservation and increase. What the *aggadah* changes is the definition of resources of value, the rationality involved in the management of scarcity. In a word, while real estate cannot increase and by definition must always prove scarce, the value represented by Torah could expand without limit. Value could then increase indefinitely, resources that were desired and scarce be made ever more abundant, in the transformed economics of the successor system.

For at stake is not merely the spiritualization of wealth, that is to say, the representation of what "wealth" *really* consists of in other-than-material terms. That would represent not an economics but a theology. For example, the familiar saying in tractate Abot, "Who is rich? One who is happy in his lot," simply does not constitute a statement of economics at all. Like sayings in the Gospels that denigrate wealth, this one tells nothing about the rational management (for example, increase) of scarce resources, it merely tells about appropriate moral attitudes of a virtuous order: how life is worth living, not answering an economic question at all. On the other hand, the tale that contrasts wealth in the form of land and its produce with wealth in the form of Torah (whatever is meant by "Torah") does constitute a statement of economics. The reason is that the storyteller invokes precisely the category of wealth – real property – that conventional economics defines as wealth. Let me state with heavy emphasis what holds the two theories of wealth together and places both in the same category: *If I have land, I have wealth, and I can support myself; if I have Torah, I have wealth, and I can support myself.*

Those form the two components of the contrastive equation before us. But wealth is then "disenlandized," and the Torah substituted for real property of all kinds.

Take, for example, the following explicit statement that a sentence of the Torah is more valuable than a pearl:

YERUSHALMI-TRACTATE PEAH I:I XVII
(TRANS. BY ROGER BROOKS)

E. Ardaban [king of Parthia] sent our holy Rabbi [Judah the Patriarch, sponsor of the Mishnah] a priceless pearl and said to him, "Send me something as valuable as this."
F. He sent him a doorpost-scroll [mezuzah, containing words of Torah].
G. Ardaban said to him, "I sent you an item beyond price, but you send me something worth but a few cents."
H. Rabbi said to him, "Your precious things and my precious things are not equivalent. You sent me something I have to guard, but I sent something that guards you while you sleep: 'When you walk along, [the words of Torah] will lead you, when you lie down, they will watch over you'" (Prov. 6:22).

If I have words of the Torah in hand, there are scarce resources in my possession that I otherwise do not have: security, for example, against whatever demons may want to harm me in my sleep.

Why do I insist that these kinds of stories deal with scarce resources in a concrete sense? Because in both cases cited to this point the upshot of the possession of Torah is this-worldly, concrete, tangible, and palpable. The rewards are not described as "filling treasuries in the heart," nor do they "enrich the soul," nor are they postponed to the world to come (as would be the case in a kind of capitalistic theology of investment on earth for return in heaven). The tale concerning Aqiba and Tarfon, like the one involving Rabbi and Ardaban, insists upon precisely the same *results* of the possession of wealth of value in the form of "Torah" as characterize wealth or value in the form of real estate. The key-language is this: "Go, buy us a piece of land, *so we can get a living from it* and labor in the study of Torah together." Tarfon assumes owning land buys leisure for Torah-study; Aqiba does not contradict that assumption, he steps beyond it. In Tarfon's mind, therefore, real (in the theological sense) value is real (in the economic sense) wealth, that is, real estate, because if you own land, you can enjoy the leisure to do what you really want to do, which (as every philosopher understood) is to study (in the sages' case) the Torah. But to Aqiba, in the tale, that is beside the point, since the real (in the theological sense) value (in the economic sense, that is, what provides a living, food to eat for instance) is Torah (study), and that, in itself, suffices. The sense is, if I have land, I have a living, and if I have Torah, I have a living, which is no different from the living that I have from land – but which, as a matter of fact, is more secure.

Owning land involved control of the means of production, and so did knowing the Torah. But – more to the point – from land people derived a living, and from Torah people derived a living in *precisely* the same sense – that is to say, in the material and concrete sense – in which from land they could do so. That is alleged time and again, and so at stake is not the mere denigration of wealth but the transvaluation of value. The transvaluation consisted in, first, the "disenlandizement" of value, and, second, the transvaluation of (knowing or studying) the Torah, the imputation to Torah of the value formerly associated with land. And that is why it is valid to claim for Torah the status of a counterpart category: the system's economics, its theory of the way of life of the community and its account of the rational disposition of those scarce resources that made everyday material existence possible and even pleasant: an economics of wealth, but of wealth differently defined, while similarly valued and utilized. So the concept of scarce resources was linked to the conception of Torah and took on altogether fresh meanings, but in exactly the same context and producing exactly the same material consequences, for example, having food to eat and a dwelling for shelter, with the result that we have to redefine that which serves the very category, "economics," altogether.

It should be understood that this conception of Torah coexists with another, one in which knowledge of the Torah did not, was not meant to, guarantee one's living. In the Mishnah's *halakhah* it is not assumed that a disciple of a sage gets support on account of his Torah-study, and it also is not assumed that the sage makes his living through Torah-study or other Torah-activities. Knowledge of the Torah or the act of study enjoys no material value. For instance, an act of betrothal requires an exchange of something of value; among the examples of value the act of study or teaching of the Torah is never offered; for example, "Lo, thou art betrothed to me in exchange for my teaching you [or your brother or your father] a teaching of the Torah" is never suggested as a possibility. So Torah-learning is not material and produces no benefits of a material character. The sages' status may derive from knowledge of Torah, but that status is not confused with the material consideration involved in who may marry whom. In Mishnah-tractate Qiddushin 4:1 the sages do not form a caste. "Ten castes came up from Babylonia," but the "status" of sage has no bearing upon his caste status. Then what difference does Torah-study or Torah-knowledge make? It is one of status, but with no bearing whatsoever upon one's livelihood. Here are the important statements of the value of knowledge of the Torah for classifying things, and, in each of them, what is gained is not of a material or concrete order at all:

MISHNAH-TRACTATE BABA MESIA 2:11

A. [If he has to choose between seeking] what he has lost and what his father has lost,
B. his own takes precedence.
C. what he has lost and what his master has lost,
D. his own takes precedence.
E. what his father has lost and what his master has lost,
F. that of his master takes precedence.
G. For his father brought him into this world.
H. But his master, who taught him wisdom, will bring him into the life
I. But if his father is a sage, that of his father takes precedence.

The matter of status comes to the fore, first master, then father, once more:

J. [If] his father and his master were carrying heavy burdens, he removes that of his master, and afterward removes that of his father.
K. [If] his father and his master were taken captive,
L. he ransoms his master, and afterward he ransoms his father.
M. But if his father is a sage, he ransoms his father, and afterward he ransoms his master.

In this passage Torah-learning has not attained practical consequence. That is to say, there is no theory that, because the master has studied Torah, therefore the master does not have to earn a living ("carrying heavy burdens"). The same is so in the following set of indicators of proper classification:

MISHNAH-TRACTATE HORAYOT 3:6–8

3:6 A. Whatever is offered more regularly than its fellow takes precedence over its fellow, and whatever is more holy than its fellow takes precedence over its fellow.
B. [If] a bullock of an anointed priest and a bullock of the congregation [M. Hor. 1:5] are standing [awaiting sacrifice] –
C. the bullock of the anointed [high priest] takes precedence over the bullock of the congregation in all rites pertaining to it.
3:7 A. The man takes precedence over the woman in the matter of the saving of life and in the matter of returning lost property.

B. But a woman takes precedence over a man in the matter of [providing] clothing and redemption from captivity.

C. When both of them are standing in danger of defilement, the man takes precedence over the woman.

3:8 A. A priest takes precedence over a Levite, a Levite over an Israelite, an Israelite over a *mamzer* [the child of a man and woman who are not legally permitted to marry, e.g., a brother and sister or mother and son] or a married woman and someone not her husband], a *mamzer* over a *Netin,* a *Netin* over a proselyte, a proselyte over a freed slave.

B. Under what circumstances?

C. When all of them are equivalent.

D. But if the *mamzer* was a disciple of a sage and a high priest was an *am haares*, the *mamzer* who is a disciple of a sage takes precedence over a high priest who is an *am haares*.

What is explicit here is that knowledge of the Torah does not change one's caste status, for instance, priest or *mamzer* or *Netin*, and that caste status does govern whom one may marry, a matter of substantial economic consequence. But it does change one's status as to precedence of another order altogether – one that is curiously unspecific at Mishnah-tractate Horayot 3:8. Along these same lines, the premise of Mishnah-tractate Sanhedrin is that the sage is judge and administrator of the community; knowledge of the Torah qualifies him, but it does not provide a living or the equivalent of a living. No provision for supporting the sage as administrator, clerk, or judge is suggested in the tractate.

What about knowledge of Torah as a way of making one's living? In the list of professions by which men make a living, already noted in another connection, we find several positions. First is that of Meir and Simeon:

MISHNAH-TRACTATE QIDDUSHIN 4:14

E. R. Meir says, "A man should always teach his son a clean and easy trade. And let him pray to him to whom belong riches and possessions.

G. "For there is no trade which does not involve poverty or wealth.

H. "For poverty does not come from one's trade, nor does wealth come from one's trade.

I. "But all is in accord with a man's merit."

J. R. Simeon b. Eleazar says, "Have you ever seen a wild beast or a bird who has a trade? Yet they get along without difficulty. And were they not created only to serve me? And I was created to serve my Master. So is it not logical that I should get along without difficulty? But I have done evil and ruined my living."

One's merit makes the difference between poverty and wealth, or one's sinfulness. A more practical position is that which follows in the continuation of the passage:

K. Abba Gurion of Sidon says in the name of Abba Gurya, "A man should not teach his son to be an ass driver, a camel driver, a barber, a sailor, a herdsman, or a shopkeeper For their trade is the trade of thieves."

L. R. Judah says in his name, "Most ass drivers are evil, most camel drivers are decent, most sailors are saintly, the best among physicians is going to Gehenna, and the best of butchers is a partner of Amalek."

The third view is that of Nehorai, who holds that Torah suffices as a means for making a living:

M. R. Nehorai says, "I should lay aside every trade in the world and teach my son only Torah.

N. "For a man eats its fruits in this world, and the principal remains for the world to come.

O. "But other trades are not that way.

P. "When a man gets sick or old or has pains and cannot do his job, lo, he dies of starvation.

Q. "But with Torah it is not that way.

R. "But it keeps him from all evil when he is young, and it gives him a future and a hope when he is old.

S. "Concerning his youth, what does it say? 'They who wait upon the Lord shall renew their strength' (Is. 40:31). And concerning his old age what does it say? 'They shall still bring forth fruit in old age' (Ps. 92:14).

T. "And so it says with regard to the patriarch Abraham, may he rest in peace, 'And Abraham was old and well along in years, and the Lord blessed Abraham in all things' (Gen. 24:1).

U. "We find that the patriarch Abraham kept the entire Torah even before it was revealed, since it says, 'Since Abraham obeyed my voice and kept my charge, my commandments, my statutes, and my laws'" (Gen. 26:5).

Does Nehorai tell us that, if we study the Torah, we will have all our worldly needs met, as Aqiba tells Tarfon that Torah is the counterpart of real estate but a more secure investment? I think not. Precisely why Torah works as it does is made explicit at R: "It keeps him from evil when he is young." That is to say, the position of Meir and Simeon is repeated, only in a fresh way. If I know the Torah, I will not sin but will remain virtuous. The conception that,

if I study Torah, I automatically get the food I need to eat and the roof I need
for shelter is not at issue here, where our concern is with being kept from evil
in youth and enjoying God's blessing in old age on account of keeping the
Torah – a very different thing, as we shall see presently.

Tractate Abot takes the view that one should not make one's living through
study of the Torah. That is made explicit in Torah-sayings of tractate Abot,
where we find articulated the rejection of the theory of Torah-study as a means
of avoiding one's obligation to earn a living. Torah-study without a craft is
rejected, Torah-study along with labour at a craft is defined as the ideal way of
life. The following sayings make that point quite clearly:

TRACTATE ABOT 2:2 AND 3:17

2:2 A. Rabban Gamaliel, a son of Rabbi Judah the Patriarch says, "Fitting is learning in the Torah along with a craft, for the labour put into the two of them makes one
forget sin. And all learning of the Torah which is not joined with labour is destined to
be null and causes sin."

3:17 A. R. Eleazar b. Azariah says, "... If there is no sustenance [lit.: flour], there is
no Torah-learning. If there is no Torah-learning, there is no sustenance."

Here, there is no contrast between two forms of wealth, one less secure, the
other more. The way of virtue lies rather in economic activity in the conventional sense, joined to intellectual or philosophical activity in the sages'
sense. The labour in Torah is not an economic activity and produces no solutions to this-worldly problems of getting food, shelter, clothing. To the contrary, labour in Torah defines the purpose of human life; it is the goal; but it
is not the medium for maintaining life and avoiding starvation or exposure to
the elements. So, too, Tosefta's complement to the Mishnah is explicit in
connection with M. Gittin 1:7A, "a commandment pertaining to the father
concerning the son:"

TOSEFTA-TRACTATE QIDDUSHIN I:II

E. It is to circumcise him, redeem him [should he be kidnapped], teach him Torah,
teach him a trade, and marry him off to a girl

There clearly is no conception that, if one studies Torah, he need not work for
a living, nor in the Tosefta's complement to the Mishnah does anyone imagine that merit is gained by supporting those who study the Torah.

Yohanan ben Zakkai speaks of Torah-study as the goal of a human life, on
the one side, and a reward paid for Torah study, clearly in a theological sense

and context, on the other. That the context of Torah-study is intangible and not economic in any sense is shown by Hananiah's saying, which is explicit: if people talk about the Torah, the Presence of God joins them to participate:

TRACTATE ABOT 2:8, 2:16, 3:2

2:8 A. Rabban Yohanan ben Zakkai received [the Torah] from Hillel and Shammai. He would say: "If you have learned much Torah, do not puff yourself up on that account, for it was for that purpose that you were created."

2:16 A. He would say: "It's not your job to finish the work, but you are not free to walk away from it. If you have learned much Torah, they will give you a good reward. And your employer can be depended upon to pay your wages for what you do. And know what sort of reward is going to be given to the righteous in the coming time."

Now we turn to how the Presence of God is with those that study the Torah:

3:2 B. R. Hananiah b. Teradion says, "[If] two sit together and between them do not pass teachings of the Torah, lo, this is a seat of the scornful, as it is said, 'Nor sits in the seat of the scornful' (Ps. 1:1). But two who are sitting, and words of the Torah do pass between them – the Presence is with them, as it is said, 'Then they that feared the Lord spoke with one another, and the Lord hearkened and heard, and a book of remembrance was written before him, for them that feared the Lord and gave thought to his name' (Mal 3:16). I know that this applies to two. How do I know that even if a single person sits and works on the Torah, the Holy One, blessed be he, sets aside a reward for him? As it is said, 'Let him sit alone and keep silent, because he has laid it upon him' " (Lam. 3:28).

Do worldly benefits accrue to those who study the Torah? The rabbi cited in the following statement maintains that it is entirely inappropriate to utilize Torah-learning to gain either social standing or economic gain:

TRACTATE ABOT 4:5

B. R. Sadoq says, "Do not make [Torah-teachings] a crown in which to glorify yourself or a spade with which to dig.

C. "So did Hillel say, 'He who uses the crown perishes. Thus have you learned: Whoever derives worldly benefit from teachings of the Torah takes his life out of this world.' "

I cannot think of a statement more likely to startle the author of the story involving Aqiba and Tarfon than this one, since Aqiba's position is precisely the one rejected here. The following, however, draws us closer to the view that, indefining wealth, treats Torah-learning as superior to real estate. Here we find a statement that contrasts working for a living with studying Torah and that maintains that the latter will provide a living, without recourse to hard labour:

TRACTATE ABOT 3:15

A. R. Nehunia b. Haqqaneh says, "From whoever accepts upon himself the yoke of the Torah do they remove the yoke of the state and the yoke of hard labour. And upon whoever removes from himself the yoke of the Torah do they lay the yoke of the state and the yoke of hard labor."

But the competing view treats Torah-study as an activity that competes with economic venture and insists that Torah-study take precedence, even though it is not of economic value in any commonplace sense of the words. That is explicitly imputed to Meir and to Jonathan in the following:

TRACTATE ABOT 4:10

4:10 A. R. Meir says, "Keep your business to a minimum and make your business the Torah. And be humble before everybody. And if you treat the Torah as nothing, you will have many treating you as nothing. And if you have laboured in the Torah, [the Torah] has a great reward to give you."
4:9 A. R. Jonathan says, "Whoever keeps the Torah when poor will in the end keep it in wealth. And whoever treats the Torah as nothing when he is wealthy in the end will treat it as nothing in poverty."

Torah-study competes with, rather than replaces, economic activity. Here, the sages contrast their wealth, which is spiritual and intellectual, with material wealth; they do not deem the one to form the counterpart of the other, but only as the opposite.

A theological system that declares forbidden the practice of using the Torah as a spade with which to dig, as a means of making one's living, will have found proof for its position in the numerous allegations in Wisdom literature that the value of wisdom, understood of course as the Torah, is beyond price: "Happy is the man who finds wisdom ... for the gain from it is better than gain from silver, and its profit better than gold; she is more precious than jewels, and nothing you desire can compare with her" (Prov. 3:13–15). That and numerous parallels were not understood to mean that, if people devoted themselves to the study of the Torah and the teaching thereof, they would not have to work any more. Nor do the praises of wisdom specifically contrast Torah-learning with land ownership. But now, in the fully articulated theological system of the Oral Torah, that is precisely what is commonplace.

The issue of scarce resources in the context of a society that highly valued honour and despised and feared shame was phrased in terms not only of material wealth but also of worldly repute. Knowledge of the Torah served as did coins, that is, to circulate the name of the holy man or woman (Abraham or Sarah, in this context), all figures to whom, quite naturally, heroic deeds of Torah-learning and -teaching were attributed:

GENESIS RABBAH XXXIX:XI.5

A. R. Berekhiah in the name of R. Helbo: "[The promise that God will make Abram great] refers to the fact that his coinage had circulated in the world.
B. "There were four whose coinage circulated in the world."

Now the four cases are assembled, the facts of Scripture systematized to sustain the announced proposition:

C. "Abraham: 'And I will make you' (Gen. 12:2). And what image appeared on his coinage? An old man and an old woman on the obverse side, a boy and a girl on the reverse [Abraham, Sarah, Isaac and Rebekkah].
D. "Joshua: 'So the Lord was with Joshua and his fame was in all the land' (Josh. 6:27). That is, his coinage circulated in the world. And what image appeared on his coinage? An ox on the obverse, a wild-ox on the reverse: 'His firstling bullock, majesty is his, and his horns are the horns of a wild ox' (Deut. 33:17). [Joshua descended from Joseph.]
E. "David: 'And the fame of David went out into all lands' (1 Chr. 14:17). That is, his coinage circulated in the world. And what image appeared on his coinage? A staff and a wallet on the obverse, a tower on the reverse: 'Your neck is like the tower of David, built with turrets' (Song 4:4).
F. "Mordecai: 'For Mordecai was great in the king's house, and his fame went forth throughout all the provinces' (Est. 9:4). That is, his coinage circulated in the world. And what image appeared on his coinage? Sackcloth and ashes on the obverse, a golden crown on the reverse."

"Coinage" is meant to be jarring, to draw an ironic contrast between true currency, which is the repute that is gained through godly service, and worldly currency; kings use their coins to make their persons and policies known, so do the saints. But this is not, by itself, a saying that assigns to Torah the value equivalent to coins.

Of course, it cannot make such an assignment, since the value imputed to Torah-study and -teaching compares not to (mere) currency, which in the *halakhah* bore the merely contingent value of a commodity, but only to land. Here, however, the Torah serves as Israel's deed to the land, and, it must follow, knowledge of the Torah is what demonstrates one's right to possess the one material resource worth having:

GENESIS RABBAH I.II.I

1. A. R. Joshua of Sikhnin in the name of R. Levi commenced [discourse by citing the following verse]: " 'He has declared to his people the power of his works, in giving them the heritage of the nations' (Ps. 111:6).

B. "What is the reason that the Holy One, blessed be he, revealed to Israel what was created on the first day and what on the second?

C. "It was on account of the nations of the world. It was so that they should not ridicule the Israelites, saying to them, 'Are you not a nation of robbers [having stolen the land from the Canaanites]?'

D. "It allows the Israelites to answer them, 'And as to you, is there no spoil in your hands? For surely: "The Caphtorim, who came forth out of Caphtor, destroyed them and dwelled in their place" (Deut. 2:23)!

E. " 'The world and everything in it belongs to the Holy One, blessed be he. When he wanted, he gave it to you, and when he wanted, he took it from you and gave it to us.'

F. "That is in line with what is written, '... in giving them the heritage of the nations, he has declared to his people the power of his works' (Ps. 111:6) ... [So as to give them the land, he established his right to do so by informing them that he had created it.]

G. "He told them about the beginning: 'In the beginning God created ...' " (Gen. 1:1).

Here is the linkage of Torah to land, but for merely instrumental purposes. Not only so, but the conception of riches in the conventional philosophical sense certainly persisted. "Abram was very rich in cattle" is understood quite literally, interpreted in line with Ps. 105:37: "He brought them forth with silver with gold, and there was none that stumbled among his tribes" (Genesis Rabbah XLI:III.1.A-B). Along these same lines, "Jacob's riches" of Gen. 30:43 are understood to be material and concrete: sixty-thousand dogs, for example (Genesis Rabbah LXXIII:XI.1.D).

So, too, the allegation that "Torah" is represented by bread does not require, and perhaps does not even sustain, the interpretation that Torah-learning forms a scarce resource that provides bread and that is worth bread and that serves as does bread:

GENESIS RABBAH LXX:V.I

A. "... will give me bread to eat and clothing to wear":

B. Aqilas the proselyte came to R. Eliezer and said to him, "Is all the gain that is coming to the proselyte going to be contained in this verse: '... and loves the proselyte, giving him food and clothing'" (Deut. 10:18)?

C. He said to him, "And is something for which the old man [Jacob] beseeched going to be such a small thing in your view namely, '... will give me bread to eat and clothing to wear'? [God] comes and hands it over to [a proselyte] on a reed [and the proselyte does not have to beg for it]."

So much for the material reading of matters. Now to the metaphorical, for bread stands for Torah-learning:

D. He came to R. Joshua, who commenced by saying words to appease him: "'Bread' refers to Torah, as it is said, 'Come, eat of my bread' (Prov. 9:5). 'Clothing' refers to the cloak of a disciple of sages.

E. "When a person has the merit of studying the Torah, he has the merit of carrying out a religious duty. [So the proselyte receives a great deal when he gets bread and clothing, namely, entry into the estate of disciples.]

Torah-learning functions as does wealth, making the man's daughters desirable for marriage:

F. "And not only so, but his daughters may be chosen for marriage into the priesthood, so that their sons' sons will offer burnt-offerings on the altar. [So the proselyte may also look forward to entry into the priests' caste. That statement will now be spelled out.]

G. "'Bread' refers to the show-bread.'

H. "'Clothing' refers to the garments of the priesthood.'

I. "So lo, we deal with the sanctuary.

J. "How do we know that the same sort of blessing applies in the provinces? 'Bread' speaks of the dough-offering [that is separated in the provinces], 'while 'clothing' refers to the first fleece [handed over to the priest]."

Here, too, we may reasonably interpret the passage in a merely symbolic way: "bread" stands for Torah-learning, because just as bread sustains the body, so Torah-learning sustains the soul.

But there are passages that are quite explicit: land is wealth, or Torah is wealth, but not both; owning land is power and studying Torah permits (re)gaining power. In passages such as these we deal with what is concrete and material, not metaphorical, when we speak of Torah-learning and land or bread alike. To take the first of the two propositions in its most explicit formulation:

LEVITICUS RABBAH XXX:I.4.

A. R. Yohanan was going up from Tiberias to Sepphoris. R. Hiyya bar Abba was supporting him. They came to a field. He said, "This field once belonged to me, but I sold it in order to acquire merit in the Torah."

B. They came to a vineyard, and he said, "This vineyard once belonged to me, but I sold it in order to acquire merit in the Torah."

C. They came to an olive grove, and he said, "This olive grove once belonged to me, but I sold it in order to acquire merit in the Torah."

D. R. Hiyya began to cry.

E. Said R. Yohanan, "Why are you crying?"

F. He said to him, "It is because you left nothing over to support you in your old age."

G. He said to him, "Hiyya, my disciple, is what I did such a light thing in your view? I sold something which was given in a spell of six days [of creation] and in exchange I acquired something which was given in a spell of forty days [of revelation].

H. "The entire world and everything in it was created in only six days, as it is written, 'For in six days the Lord made heaven and earth' (Ex. 20:11).

I. "But the Torah was given over a period of forty days, as it was said, 'And he was there with the Lord for forty days and forty nights' (Ex. 34:28).

J. "And it is written, 'And I remained on the mountain for forty days and forty nights'" (Deut. 9:9).

Yohanan attained the reward of high repute, as the end of the tale shows:

5. A. When R. Yohanan died, his generation recited concerning him [the following verse of Scripture]: "If a man should give all the wealth of his house for the love" (Song 8:7), with which R. Yohanan loved the Torah, "he would be utterly destitute" (Song 8:7) ...

C. When R. Eleazar b. R. Simeon died, his generation recited concerning him [the following verse of Scripture]: "Who is this who comes up out of the wilderness like pillars of smoke, perfumed with myrrh and frankincense, with all the powders of the merchant?" (Song 3:6).

D. What is the meaning of the clause, "With all the powders of the merchant"?

E. [Like a merchant who carries all sorts of desired powders,] he was a master of Scripture, a repeater of Mishnah traditions, a writer of liturgical supplications, and a liturgical poet.

The sale of land for the acquisition of "merit in the Torah" introduces two principal systemic components, merit and Torah. For our purpose, the importance of the statement lies in the second of the two, which deems land the counterpart – and clearly the opposite – of the Torah.

Now one can sell a field and acquire "Torah," meaning, in the context established by the exchange between Tarfon and Aqiba, the opportunity to gain leisure for (acquire the merit gained by) the study of the Torah. That the sage has left himself nothing for his support in old age makes explicit the material meaning of the statement, and the comparison of the value of land, created in six days, and the Torah, created in forty days, is equally explicit. The comparison of knowledge of Torah to the merchandise of the merchant simply repeats the same point, but in a lower register. So, too, does the this-worldly power of study of the Torah make explicit in another framework the conviction that study of the Torah yields material and concrete benefit, not just spiritual renewal. Thus R. Huna states, "All of the exiles will be gathered together only on account of the study of Mishnah-teachings" (Pesiqta deRab Kahana VI:III.3.B).

Equating Torah-learning with real estate bore a more practical charge as well. The sage devoted to study of the Torah has to be supported because he can no longer perform physical work. Study of the Torah deprives him of physical strength, and that contrast and counterpart represented by land and working of the land as against Torah and the study of the Torah comes to symbolic expression in yet another way:

LEVITICUS RABBAH XI:XXII.I

A. R. Eleazar bar Simeon was appointed to impress men and beasts into forced labour [in the corvée]. One time Elijah, of blessed memory, appeared to him in the guise of an old man. Elijah said to him, "Get me a beast of burden."

B. Eleazar said to him, "What do you have as a cargo [to load on the beast]?"

C. He said to him, "This old skin-bottle of mine, my cloak, and me as rider."

D. He said, "Take a look at this old man! I [personally] can take him and carry him to the end of the world, and he says to me to get a beast ready!"

E. What did he do? He loaded him on his back and carried him up mountains and down valleys and over fields of thorns and fields of thistles.

F. In the end [Elijah] began to bear down on him. He said to him, "Old man, old man! Make yourself lighter, and if you don't, I'll toss you off."

G. [Elijah] said to him, "Now do you want to take a bit of a rest?"

H. He said to him, "Yes."

I. What did he do? [Elijah] took him to a field and set him down under a tree and gave him food and drink. When he had eaten and drunk, he [Elijah] said to him, "All this running about – what is in it for you? Would it not be better for you to take up the vocation of your fathers?"

Now the muscle-man takes up Torah-study, thereby losing all his strength:

J. He said to him, "And can you teach it to me?"

K. He said to him, "Yes."

L. And there are those who say that for thirteen years Elijah of blessed memory taught him until he could recite even Sifra [the exegesis of Leviticus, which is particularly difficult].

M. But once he could recite that document, [he had so lost his strength that] he could not lift up even a cloak.

The same story is now told in a this-worldly setting; the porter became a disciple of a Torah-master and lost his strength:

2. A. The household of Rabban Gamaliel had a member who could carry forty *seahs* [of grain] to the baker [on his back].

B. He said to him, "All this vast power do you possess, and you do not devote yourself to the study of Sifra."

C. When he could recite that document, they say that even a single *seah* of grain he was unable to bear.

D. There are those who say that if someone else did not take it off him, he would not have been able to take it off himself.

These stories about how a mark of the sage is physical weakness are included only because they form part of the (in this instance, secondary) composition on Eleazar b. Simeon. But they do form part of a larger program of contrasting Torah-study with land ownership, intellectual prowess with physical power, the superiority of the one over the other. No wonder that sages would in time claim that their power protected cities, which then needed neither police nor walls. These were concrete claims, affecting the rational utilization of scarce resources as much as the use and distribution of land constituted an expression of a rationality concerning scarce resources, their preservation and increase.

In alleging that the pertinent verses of Proverbs were assigned a quite this-worldly and material sense, so that study of the Torah really was worth more than silver, I say no more than the documents of the Oral Torah allege in so many words. Thus we find the following, which faces head-on the fact that masters of the Torah are paid for studying the Torah, so confirming the claim that the Torah now served as a spade with which to dig, the rationale having been set forth in the earlier accounts:

1. A. R. Abba bar Kahana commenced [discourse by citing the following verse]: "Take my instruction instead of silver, and knowledge rather than choice gold" (Prov. 8:10).

B. Said R. Abba bar Kahana, " 'Take the instruction of the Torah instead of silver.'

C. "Take the instruction of the Torah and not silver.

D. " 'Why do you weigh out money? [Because there is no bread]' " (Is. 55:2).

Now, however, we turn to the situation of all Israel, not the individual Israelite, and we ask why Israel is subordinate to Rome, why Israel must labour while the nations prosper. Failure to master the Torah is the logically required answer, since, as we recall, all that differentiates Israel from the gentiles is Torah-learning:

E. " 'Why do you weigh out money to the sons of Esau [Rome]? [It is because] 'there is no bread, 'because you did not sate yourselves with the bread of the Torah.

F. " 'And [why] do you labour? Because there is no satisfaction' (Is. 55:2).

G. " 'Why do you labour' while the nations of the world enjoy plenty? 'Because there is no satisfaction,' that is, because you have not sated yourselves with the bread of the Torah and with the wine of the Torah.

H. "For it is written, 'Come, eat of my bread, and drink of the wine I have mixed' " (Prov. 9:5).

Now we revert to the question, why do masters of Torah-learning collect a wage for their work?

2. A. R. Berekhiah and R. Hiyya, his father, in the name of R. Yosé b. Nehorai: "It is written, 'I shall punish all who oppress him' (Jer. 30:20), even those who collect funds for charity [and in doing so, treat people badly], except [for those who collect] the wages to be paid to teachers of Scripture and repeaters of Mishnah traditions.

B. "For they receive [as a salary] only compensation for the loss of their time, [which they devote to teaching and learning rather than to earning a living].

C. "But as to the wages [for carrying out] a single matter in the Torah, no creature can pay the [appropriate] fee in reward."

The homily at 1.E, surely stands against my claim that we deal with allegations of concrete and material value: the imputation to the learning of the Torah of the status of "scarce resources." But, as a matter of fact, the whole of No. 2 makes the contrary position explicit: wages are paid to Torah-teachers. The following makes the same point:

A. It is written, "Behold, I have taught you statutes and ordinances" (Deut. 4:5).

B. Just as I do so without pay, so you must do so without pay.

C. Is it possible that the same rule applies to teaching Scripture and translation [cf. Mishnah-tractate Nedarim 4:3D]?

D. Scripture says, "Statutes and ordinances."

E. Statutes and ordinances must you teach without pay, but you need not teach Scripture and translation without pay.

F. And yet we see that those who teach Mishnah collect their pay.

G. Said R. Judah b. R. Ishmael, "It is a fee for the use of their time [which they cannot utilize to earn a living for themselves] which they collect."

True, this transformation of Torah-study into something of real worth is rationalized as salary in compensation for loss of time. But the same rationalization clearly did not impress the many masters of the initial system who insisted that one must practise a craft in order to make a living and study the Torah only in one's leisure time. We see the contrast in the two positions quite explicitly in what follows.

D. It is forbidden to a person to teach his son a trade, in as much as it is written, "And you shall meditate therein day and night" (Joshua 1:8.)

E. But has not R. Ishmael taught, " 'You shall choose life" (Deut. 30:19) – this refers to learning [Torah] and practicing a trade as well. [One both studies the Torah and also a trade.]

There is no harmonizing the two views by appeal to the rationalization before us. In fact, study of the Torah substituted for practising a craft, and it was meant to do so, as A alleges explicitly. In all, therefore, the case in favour of the proposition that Torah has now become a material good, and, further, that Torah has now been transformed into the ultimate scarce resource – explicitly substituting for real estate, even in the Land of Israel – is firmly established.

That ultimate value – Torah-study – surely bears comparison with other foci of sanctification, such as prayer, using money for building synagogues, and the like. It is explicitly stated that spending money on synagogues is a waste of money, while spending money supporting Torah-masters is the right use of scarce resources. Further, we find the claim that synagogues and schoolhouses – communal real estate – in fact form the property of sages and their disciples, who may dispose of them just as they want, as any owner may dispose of his property according to his unfettered will. In Yerushalmi-tractate Sheqalim we find the former allegation, in Yerushalmi-tractate Megillah the latter:

YERUSHALMI-TRACTATE SHEQALIM 5:4.II.

A. R. Hama bar Haninah and R. Hoshaia the Elder were strolling in the synagogues in Lud. Said R. Hama bar Haninah to R. Hoshaia, "How much money did my forefathers invest here [in building these synagogues]!"
B. He said to him, "How many lives did your forefathers invest here! Were there not people who were labouring in Torah [who needed the money more]?"

The same point is made in a separate case:

C. R. Abun made the gates of the great hall [of study]. R. Mana came to him. He said to him, "See what I have made!"
D. He said to him, " 'For Israel has forgotten his Maker and built palaces'! (Hos. 8:14). Were there no people labouring in Torah [who needed the money more]?"

Time for Torah-study bears greater value than any other activity; all else will flow to the master of Torah-learning, in due course:

YERUSHALMI-TRACTATE SOTAH 9:13.VI.

C. A certain rabbi would teach Scripture to his brother in Tyre, and when they came and called him to do business, he would say, "I am not going to take away from my fixed time to study. If the profit is going to come to me, let it come in due course [after my fixed time for study has ended]."

By right, then, sages own the title to the buildings used for prayer and study, and stories indicate that this was not merely a fanciful, but a practical claim; sages may use the sacred spaces for their private convenience:

YERUSHALMI-TRACTATE MEGILLAH 3:3:V.

A. R. Joshua b. Levi said, "Synagogues and schoolhouses belong to sages and their disciples."
B. R. Hiyya bar Yosé received [guests] in the synagogue [and lodged them there].
C. R. Immi instructed the scribes, "If someone comes to you with some slight contact with Torah learning, receive him, his asses, and his belongings."

That the claim affects common behaviour is set forth in the continuation:

D. R. Berekhiah went to the synagogue in Beisan. He saw someone rinsing his hands and feet in a fountain [in the courtyard of the synagogue]. He said to him, "It is forbidden to you [to do this]."

E. The next day the man saw [Berekhiah] washing his hands and feet in the fountain.

F. He said to him, "Rabbi, is it permitted to you and forbidden to me?"

G. He said to him, "Yes."

H. He said to him, "Why?"

I. He said to him, "Because this is what R. Joshua b. Levi said: 'Synagogues and schoolhouses belong to sages and their disciples.'"

Not all acts of piety, we see, are equal, and the one that takes precedence over all others (just as was alleged at Mishnah-tractate Peah 1:1) is study of the Torah. But the point now is a much more concrete one, namely that, through study of the Torah, sages and their disciples gain possession, as a matter of fact, over communal real estate, which they may utilize in any way they wish; and that is a quite concrete claim indeed, as the same story alleges.

No wonder, then, that people in general are expected to contribute their scarce resources for the support of sages and their disciples. Moreover, society at large was obligated to support sages, and the sages' claim upon others was enforceable by Heaven. Those who gave sages' disciples money so that they would not have to work would get it back from Heaven, and those who did not would lose what they had:

YERUSHALMI-TRACTATE SOTAH 7:4.IV

F. R. Aha in the name of R. Tanhum b. R. Hiyya: "If one has learned, taught, kept, and carried out [the Torah], and has ample means in his possession to strengthen the Torah and has not done so, lo, such a one still is in the category of those who are cursed." [The meaning of "strengthen" here is to support the masters of the Torah.]

G. R. Jeremiah in the name of R. Hiyya bar Ba, "[If] one did not learn, teach, keep, and carry out [the teachings of the Torah], and did not have ample means to strengthen [the masters of the Torah] [but nonetheless did strengthen them], lo, such a one falls into the category of those who are blessed."

People who sustain sages share in the supernatural benefit attained by the sages in their Torah-study:

H. And R. Hannah, R. Jeremiah in the name of R. Hiyya: "The Holy One, blessed be he, is going to prepare a protection for those who carry out religious duties [of support for masters of Torah] through the protection afforded to the masters of Torah [themselves].

I. "What is the Scriptural basis for that statement? 'For the protection of wisdom is like the protection of money' (Qoh. 7:12).

J. "And it says, '[The Torah] is a tree of life to those who grasp it; those who hold it fast are called happy' "(Prov. 3:18).

Such contributions form the counterpart to taxes: scarce resources taken away from the owner by force for the purposes of the public good, the ultimate meeting point of economics and politics, the explicit formation of distributive, as against market, economics. What is distributed and to whom and by what force forms the centrepiece, and the answer is perfectly simple: all sorts of valued things are taken away from people and handed over for the support of sages:

PESIQTA DERAB KAHANA V:IV.2

A. "A man's gift makes room for him and brings him before great men" (Prov. 18:16).

B. M'SH B: R. Eliezer, R. Joshua, and R. Aqiba went to the harbor-side of Antioch to collect funds for the support of sages.

C. [In Aramaic:] A certain Abba Yudan lived there.

D. He would carry out his religious duty [of philanthropy] in a liberal spirit, but had lost his money. When he saw our masters, he went home with a sad face. His wife said to him, "What's wrong with you, that you look so sad?"

E. He repeated the tale to her: "Our masters are here, and I don't know what I shall be able to do for them."

F. His wife, who was a truly philanthropic woman – what did she say to him? "You only have one field left. Go, sell half of it and give them the proceeds."

G. He went and did just that. When he was giving them the money, they said to him, "May the Omnipresent make up all your losses."

H. Our masters went their way.

I. He went out to plough. While he was ploughing the half of the field that he had left, the Holy One, blessed be he, opened his eyes. The earth broke open before him, and his cow fell in and broke her leg. He went down to raise her up, and found a treasure beneath her. He said, "It was for my gain that my cow broke her leg."

J. When our masters came back, [in Aramaic:] they asked about a certain Abba Yudan and how he was doing. They said, "Who can gaze on the face of Abba Yudan [which glows with prosperity] – Abba Yudan, the owner of flocks of goats, Abba Yudan, the owner of herds of asses, Abba Yudan, the owner of herds of camels."

K. He came to them and said to them, "Your prayer in my favour has produced returns and returns on the returns."

L. They said to him, "Even though someone else gave more than you did, we wrote your name at the head of the list."

M. Then they took him and sat him next to themselves and recited in his regard the following verse of Scripture: "A man's gift makes room for him and brings him before great men" (Prov. 18:16).

What is at stake in the scarce resource represented by Torah-study? It cannot be a (merely) spiritual benefit, when, in consequence of giving money to sages so they will not have to work, I get rich. Not only so, but the matter of position is equally in play. I get rich and I also enjoy the standing of sages, sitting next to them. So far as social position intersects with wealth, we find in the Torah that wealth that, in this systemic context, serves to tells us what we mean by scarce resources: source of this-worldly gain in practical terms, source of public prestige in social terms, validation of the use of force – in context, psychological force – for taking away scarce (material) resources in favour of a superior value.

No wonder, then, that sages protect cities. So it is claimed that sages are the guardians of cities, and later on that would yield the further allegation that sages do not have to pay taxes to build walls around cities, since their Torah-study protects the cities, on which basis sages ought neither serve in the army nor pay taxes to support those who do:

PESIQTA DERAB KAHANA XV:V.I

A. R. Abba bar Kahana commenced discourse by citing the following verse: "Who is the man so wise that he may understand this? To whom has the mouth of the Lord spoken, that he may declare it? Why is the land ruined and laid waste like a wilderness, [so that no one passes through? The Lord said, It is because they forsook my Torah which I set before them; they neither obeyed me nor conformed to it. They followed the promptings of their own stubborn hearts, they followed the Baalim as their forefathers had taught them. Therefore these are the words of the Lord of Hosts the God of Israel: I will feed this people with wormwood and give them bitter poison to drink. I will scatter them among nations whom neither they nor their forefathers have known; I will harry them with the sword until I have made an end of them] (Jer. 9:16)."

B. It was taught in the name of R. Simeon b. Yohai, "If you see towns uprooted from their place in the land of Israel, know that [it is because] the people did not pay the salaries of teachers of children and Mishnah-instructors.

C. "What is the verse of Scripture that indicates it? 'Why is the land ruined and laid waste like a wilderness, [so that no one passes through?]' What is written just following? 'It is because they forsook my Torah [which I set before them; they neither obeyed me nor conformed to it.]' "

The principle at hand, that sages defend the city through the merit their learning attains, is translated into the sages' view of the social order. Teachers of children turn out to be the defence of the city:

2. A. Rabbi sent sent R. Yosé and R. Ammi to go and survey the towns of the Land of Israel. They would go into a town and say to the people, "Bring me the guardians of the town."

B. The people would bring out the head of the police and the local guard.

C. [The sages] would say, "These are not the guardians of the town, they are those who destroy the town. Who are the guardians of the town? They are the teachers of children and Mishnah-teachers, who keep watch by day and by night, in line with the verse, 'And you shall meditate in it day and night' " (Josh. 1:8).

D. "And so Scripture says, 'If the Lord does not build the house, in vain the builders labor' " (Ps. 127:1).

Once more, the sages represent matters in a practical, not in a fanciful, way; so long as Israel studies the Torah – children chirping the words in the school room – the nations cannot prevail over Israel, even though they may subjugate them. If Israel no longer studies the Torah, then the nations will prevail in the end. But that, again, reminds us of what makes Israel Israel and the gentiles God's enemies, which is that the one possesses, the other rejects, the Torah:

7. A. Said R. Abba bar Kahana, "No philosophers in the world ever arose of the quality of Balaam ben Beor and Abdymos of Gadara. The nations of the world came to Abdymos of Gadara. They said to him, 'Do you maintain that we can make war against this nation?'

B. "He said to them, 'Go and make the rounds of their synagogues and their study houses. So long as there are there children chirping out loud in their voices [and studying the Torah], then you cannot overcome them. If not, then you can conquer them, for so did their father promise them: "The voice is Jacob's voice" (Gen. 27:22), meaning that when Jacob's voice chirps in synagogues and study houses, "The hands are not the hands of Esau" [so Esau has no power].

C. "So long as there are no children chirping out loud in their voices [and studying the Torah] in synagogues and study houses, 'The hands are the hands of Esau' [so Esau has power].'"

The reference to Esau, that is, Rome, of course links the whole to the contemporary context and alleges that, if the Israelites will support those who study the Torah and teach it, then their cities will be safe, and, still more, the rule of Esau/Rome will come to an end; then the Messiah will come. The stakes are not trivial.

Economics deals with scarce resources, and the "disenlandizement" of economics in favour of Torah-learning has turned upon its head the very focus of economics: scarcity and the rational confrontation with scarcity. To land, rigid limits are set by nature; to the Holy Land, still more narrow ones apply. But to knowledge of the Torah, no limits pertain. So we find ourselves dealing with an economics that concerns not only the rational utilization of scarce resources, but also the opposite: the rational utilization and increase of what can and ought to be the opposite of scarce. In identifying knowledge and teaching of the Torah as the ultimate value, the sages have not simply found of value something other than had earlier been valued; it has redefined economics altogether. It has done so, as a matter of fact, in a manner that is entirely familiar, by setting forth in place of an economics of scarcity an economics of abundant productivity. In so doing, the sages take a position consistent with their generative conception about Torah as distinguishing Israel from the nations. Torah serves, then, to form the point of differentiation in every detail, inclusive of the matter of value: the nations value land, Israel values Torah-learning; the nations know scarcity and have to learn the rules of estate management we call economics; Israel knows only abundance, on the condition that it chooses abundance.

So much for the components of world order comprised by how people mark time and distribute wealth, both aimed at perfecting the just creation. But stasis in the distribution of scarce resources, and adhering to the unchanging present in keeping time – both stand for negative indicators of perfection. They say what must not happen, which is change. We now turn to the indicators of perfection that appeal to positive traits of creation: the complementarity of things and the correspondence, in a well-ordered world, of heaven and earth, such as the language of the Qaddish invokes: *He who makes peace in the heavens on high will bring peace for us and for all Israel.*

8 Complementarity

Complementarity characterizes the way in which God and man relate, correspondence, the way in which God and man reach ultimate definition. Here we reach the heart of world order: what is man, who is God, and how and why they need each other. Let me explain, accounting also for the position just here, just now, of these two modes of relationship, complementary, then correspondence, in my exposition of the theology of the Oral Torah. In this chapter and the next, the account of world order is complete, except for the story of chaos and the restoration of order, told in parts 3 and 4.

The negative dimensions of the sages' theology showed that world order exhibited no flaws. When, therefore, the sages insisted that time stands still in a steady-state social order, they explained that creation and society were unimpaired by change, whether marked by the passage of historical time or indicated by revisions in social relationships. So, in a negative mode, the sages demonstrated how world order attained stasis and therefore perfection. Chapters 6 and 7 stressed how world order bore no flaws, the absence of change indicating a world at perfect rest. In their doctrines of marking time and of economics, the sages emphasized what does not or should not happen, history, on the one side, inequitable exchange, on the other. Humanity lives in a timeless present, the past and future belonging to the here and now. And a command economics assured that no change in value or status would result from material transactions, while providing for an endless increase in values that counted. But these indicative traits of perfection, both in design and in execution of the just world order, while necessary, were insufficient. Two positive ones would have to complete the picture of the design and its execution.

In this analysis of the system and structure of the theology animating the documents of the Oral Torah, I discern four indicative qualities of mind and method, each of which precipitates sustained thought on the message and the doctrine of the system seen whole, two negative, two positive. We have now identified two of the four principal traits that characterize the whole. The two now-familiar, negative ones stress the absence of indications of flaws. God's plan for a just and perfect order involves a timeless world of lasting, rational traits of social organization, called here "paradigms." That aspect of perfection dictated the sages' doctrine of history, their denial of historical modes of thinking, such as Scripture afforded, in favour of the analytical modes that we today find common in social science. God's plan further is realized in a world of stasis, in which scarce resources of a worldly order, such as real estate, continue in enduring patterns, governing the holdings of households, for all time. At the same time, the sages made provision for an increase in wealth of a supernatural order, in which everyone participated in the benefits. In both components of the sages' theology, dealing with history and political economy, the sages framed doctrines, therefore, that declared the God's plan flawless by reason of the absence of traits deemed negative.

But the sages claimed much more in behalf of the perfection of God's ordering of creation. They set forth two further characteristics of perfection, characteristics involving other qualities of mind, which in turn shaped other fundamental components in the sages' larger structure. The two affirmative ones, considered in this chapter and the next, which highlight the presence of the positive marks of perfection, complete the sages' theology. Just as the principle of perfection attested by transcending time, balance shown by overcoming changes in the material relationships of the players in the social order, yielded a doctrine of history and of political economy, so we shall now examine two other principles of systemic perfection and the doctrines consequent upon them, traits of God (theology narrowly construed) and traits of man (theological anthropology), respectively.

What are those qualities of mind and message besides the traits of stasis in time and in resources? They involve considerations of balance, proportion, and coherence indicated by the prevalence of certain positive relationships. A single, simple logic, treating as self-evidently rational the relationship, between principal components, of complementarity, and the dynamics, between the major theological principals, God and man, of correspondence, governs throughout. Complementarity and correspondence form two sides of the same coin. Components of the social order – whether classes of persons or types of virtue or qualities of mind – fit together into a coherent whole, one class or type without the other being incomplete, unable to achieve its teleological task. The soul and the body present a principal theological case of complementarity; and that spills over into the matter of theological doctrine, God's relationship to the world being compared with the soul's relationship to the body. Some entities furthermore correspond with one another, not only matching static qualities but intersecting in dynamic ones. Among these, one relationship makes all the difference, the one between God and man, man in God's image. Once more, theological doctrine emerges from modes of thought and argument characteristic of a complete and governing system, a logic, a theology.

First, for the sake of clarity: correspondence identifies the meeting point of God and man, where and how they match ("in our image, after our likeness"). That relationship therefore forms the dynamic variation of the same principle of stasis, but now with reference to the conduct of ongoing transactions. The parties that correspond, specifically, are God and man – they alone. The task of revealing how they are alike, how different, derives from the Written Torah, with its message that man is like, or corresponds in some ways to, God. Specifically, because Scripture repeatedly insists, "for in his image did God make man" (Gen. 9:4–6), the sages determined to explain how God and man correspond. From their perspective, the Torah set forth God's image of man. Being revealed by God to Moses, the Torah provides God's account of man, the climax and goal of creation. The theological principle of correspondence then required the sages to show how man matches God, being like him. In Chapter 9 we shall follow the sages in their exposition of this dimension of theological anthropology.

To focus upon the matter of complementarity, we wonder, what are some of these necessary and also sufficient complementary relationships, public and private, that attest by their presence to the perfection of world order defined through justice? In public the logic of complementarity is discerned in the encounter of Heaven and earth, nature and super-nature, justice and mercy, and the one now in hand, soul and body. The Land, standing for the natural world, the transcendent God, and Israel come together to complement and complete the processes of sustaining life. All are necessary, none alone sufficient. God, Israel, and the Land meet, specifically, in the Temple, whence all of life is nourished and blessed. In private, in the inner lives of men, God's transactions of free grace respond to, are complemented by, man's actions of uncoerced generosity.

World order exhibits perfection because in any orderly, unflawed arrangement, whether of aesthetics, sociology, or architecture – flowers, social classes, or buildings – all things hold together in proportion, each with its sustaining counterpart and complement. That is what provides stability and strength. The principal systemic components or categories, then, do not stand in isolation, but require the balance of an other to form a coherent whole. Complementarity points to that same logic that seeks to show the match of matters. Indeed, it is a principle comparable to the logic that deems justice to require the meting out of measure for measure, this sin or crime, that compensating penalty; this act of obedience to the Torah, that beneficent response in the order of society or desired result in nature. But in place of exchange, this for that, complementarity speaks of coherence, this together with that, above all, *this impossible without that*.

A single example suffices. As we shall see in a moment, the sages insist that without mercy, justice cannot function. They also hold that categorically unrelated matters, such as creation and nature, Israel and society, and justice cannot endure in separation from one another, but that nature, Israel, and justice converge and work together. That is where the principle of complementarity is invoked, maintaining that, in world order, the one is necessary to the other. Accordingly, complementarity positively indicates the completion and perfection of world order, yet another mark of everything in place, with no loose ends to disrupt either the natural or the social order.

To identify what is at stake, then, in the logic of complementarity, we turn first to a simple example of how, for perfection to come about, two traits must join together with one another. That same insistence upon the just match that we have seen in chapter 2 leads to the quest for other points at which world order comes to completion through the same just match. If we can show how one matter complements and completes another – mercy, justice, for example, or sanctification, election – then we can reveal the architectonic perfection of categories viewed in their relationships, their ultimate balance. The principle of complementarity is best illustrated by the sages' insistence that justice without mercy is incomplete. God created the world with the attribute of mercy and also of justice, so that in complementary the balance, the world might endure:

GENESIS RABBAH XII:XV.I

A. "The Lord God [made earth and heaven]" (Gen. 2:4):

B. The matter [of referring to the divinity by both the names, Lord, which stands for mercy, and God, which stands for justice] may be compared to the case of a king who had empty cups. The king said, "If I fill them with hot water, they will split. If I fill them with cold water, they will contract [and snap]."

C. What did the king do? He mixed hot water and cold water and put it into them, and the cups withstood the liquid.

D. So said the Holy One, blessed be he, "If I create the world in accord with the attribute of mercy, sins will multiply. If I create it in accord with the attribute of justice, the world cannot endure.

E. "Lo, I shall create it with both the attribute of justice and the attribute of mercy, and may it endure!"

F. "Thus: The Lord [standing for the attribute of mercy] God [standing for the attribute of justice] [made the earth and heavens]" (Gen. 2:4).

Just as too much justice will destroy the world, but too much mercy, ruin its coherence, so each set of traits achieving complementarity must be shown, like dancers, to move in balance one with the other. Then, and only then, are excesses avoided, stasis in motion attained. That brings about the world of justice at rest that the sages deemed God to have created in the beginning, to have celebrated on the original Sabbath, and to intend to restore in the end. Success in that inquiry into how this complements that imparts integrity and coherence to the components of the theology, in the present case justice and mercy. That is why, when we can show complementarity, we identify the affirmative indicators of a well-crafted world. That is a world in which each component links in one way or another to others, one set to another, all parts holding together in a single coherent statement. In this instance, the statement declares the work of the Creator just and reliable. How, in specific details, does such a demonstration take place? Three cases, the first two brief, the third protracted, suffice.

The first, brief case goes over the familiar ground of the complementarity of mercy and justice and states simply that, when it comes to judgment, God cannot accomplish the work of justice without introducing the quality of mercy. Then, if all things are equal, the execution of justice is completed with God's intervention on the side of mercy. The case is cited at length in chapter 14, and so only a brief abstract is required here:

YERUSHALMI-TRACTATE PEAH I:I XXXII

A. "He who performs mostly good deeds inherits the Garden of Eden, but he who performs mostly transgression inherits Gehenna.

B. [But what if the scales] are balanced, [so that he has neither a majority of sins nor a majority of good deeds]?

C. Said R. Yosé b. Hanina, "[Consider Ex. 34:6–7's description of God's attributes] – 'Who forgives transgressions' [in the plural] is not written there, but rather, 'Who forgives transgression' [in the singular]. [This means that] the Holy One, blessed be he, will seize one document [bearing the record of one of] a person's transgressions, so that his good deeds will outweigh [his transgressions]."

God goes to any extreme to bestow mercy where it is possible, repaying each accord to his works but then tipping the scales of justice. That is the solution to the problem of strict justice's destroying the world.

The second brief case concerns the soul and the body, which exist in a complementary relationship and are so represented. How does this work? The sages raise the issue of which is responsible for man's fate, the soul or the body, and they maintain that the two are complementary. The soul and the body are reciprocally responsible for what a person does; the one cannot function without the other. The parable is a famous one, serving diverse cultures that wish to express the principle of complementarity:

LEVITICUS RABBAH IV:V.2:

A. R. Ishmael taught, "[The matter of the soul's and body's guilt for sin may be] compared to the case of a king, who had an orchard, in which were excellent early figs. So he set up two guards to keep watch [over the orchard], one lame, one blind. He told them, 'Keep watch over the early figs.' He left them there and went his way.

B. "The lame guard said to the blind one, 'I spy some wonderful figs.'

C. "The other said, 'Come on, let's eat.'

D. "The lame one said, 'Now can I walk around?'

E. "The blind one said, 'And can I see a thing?'

F. "What did they do? The lame one rode on the blind one and they picked the figs and ate them. Then they went back and each one took his original place.

G. "After a while the king came back and said to them, 'Where are my figs?'

H. "The blind one said to him, 'Can I see a thing?'

I. "The lame one said, 'And can I walk around?'

J. "Since the king was smart, what did he do? He had the lame one climb onto the blind one, and he judged the two of them as a single defendant. He said to them, 'This is how you did it when you went and ate the figs.'"

Now the parable is given force, embodied in the final judgment:

K. "So in time to come, the Holy One will say to the soul, 'Why did you sin before me?'

L. "And the soul will say before him, 'Lord of the age[s], am I the one that sinned before you? It is the body that sinned. From the day that I left it, have I committed a single sin?'

M. "So the [Holy One] will say to the body, 'Why did you sin?'

N. "And it will say before him, 'Lord of the ages, it is the soul that committed the sin. From the day on which it left me, have I not been cast down before you like a shard on a garbage dump?'

O. "What will the Holy One, blessed be he, do? He will put the soul back into the body and judge them as a single defendant."

Scriptural evidence now takes over, to validate the claim of self-evidence just now made by implication:

P. "That is in line with the following verse of Scripture: 'He calls to the earth above, heavens above, and to the earth, that he may judge his people' (Ps. 50:4).

Q. " 'He calls to the heaven' – to produce the soul.

R. " 'And to the earth' – to bring forth the body.

S. "And then: 'To judge with him' [all together, reading as if it read not *amo* but *imo*]."

Next, a homely case is produced for the same purpose. But here the soul, complemented by the body, still bears the heavier burden of responsibility:

3. A. R. Hiyya taught, "[The matter of the soul's guilt for sin may be compared] to the case of a priest who had two wives, one the daughter of a priest, the other the daughter of an Israelite.

B. "He gave them a piece of dough in the status of heave offering [which was to be kept in conditions of cultic cleanness], but they rendered it cultically unclean.

C. "He went and remonstrated with the daughter of the priest, but he left the daughter of the Israelite alone.

D. "She said to him, 'Our lord, priest, you gave it to both of us simultaneously. Why do you remonstrate with me and leave that one alone?'

E. "He said to her, 'You are a priest's daughter and experienced [on account of growing up] in your father's house [in dealing with the rules of cultic cleanness], but that one is an Israelite's daughter and not experienced from her upbringing in her father's house.

F. " 'Therefore I remonstrate with you.'

G. "So in time to come, the Holy One, blessed be he, will say to the soul, 'Why have you sinned before me?'

H. "And the soul will say before him, 'Lord of the age[s], the body and I sinned simultaneously. Why then are you remonstrating with me but leaving that one alone?'

I. "He will then say to the soul, 'You come from the upper world, a place in which people do not sin, while the body comes from the lower world, a place in which people sin. Therefore I remonstrate with you.' "

Here we have a familiar and uncomplicated example of a logic that holds together opposites in a relationship of complementarity.

Why the issue proves urgent becomes clear when we realize that the relationship of the body to the soul serves as a metaphor for the relationship of God to the world. God is the soul, the world, the body, and the one infuses the other. So moral questions fade, and those involving the theology of being take over:

LEVITICUS RABBAH IV:VIII.I

A. Why did the soul of David praise the Holy One, blessed be he (B. Ber. 10a)?

B. David said, "Just as the soul fills the body, so the Holy One, blessed be he, fills the whole world, as it is written, 'Do I not fill the entire heaven and earth? says the Lord' [Jer. 23:24]. So let the soul, which fills the body, come and praise the Holy One, blessed be he, who fills the world.

Then follows a sequence of applications of the principle that the soul complements and completes the body as a metaphor for how God complements the material world:

C. "The soul supports the body, the Holy One [blessed be he] supports the world, for it is written, 'Even to your old age I am he, and to gray hairs [I will carry you]' (Is. 46:4). So let the soul, which supports the body, come and praise the Holy One, blessed be he, who supports the world.

God will live when the world has died:

D. "The soul outlasts the body, and the Holy One, blessed be he, outlasts the world: 'They will perish, but you do endure, they will all wear out like a garment. [You change them like a garment and they pass away, but you are the same, and your years have no end]' (Ps. 102:26–27). So let the soul, which outlasts the body, come and praise the Holy One, blessed be he, who outlasts the world.

God is immaterial (a view we shall find challenged in Chapter 9), the world material:

E. "The soul in the body does not eat, and as to the Holy One, blessed be he, there is no eating so far as he is concerned, as it is written, 'If I were hungry, I would not tell you, for the world and all that is in it is mine' (Ps. 50:12). Let the soul in the body, which does not eat, come and praise the Holy One, blessed be he, before whom there is no eating.

F. "The soul is singular in the body, and the Holy One, blessed be he, is singular in his world, as it is said, 'Hear, O Israel, the Lord our God is a singular Lord' (Deut. 6:4). Let the soul, which is singular in the body, come and praise the Holy One, blessed be he, who is singular in his world.

The traits of God are to be discerned from the traits of the soul, purity, for example:

G. "The soul is pure in the body, and the Holy One, blessed be he, is pure in his world: 'You who are of eyes too pure to behold evil' (Hab 1:13). Let the soul, which is pure in the body, come and praise the Holy One, blessed be he, which is pure in his world.

H. "The soul sees but is not seen, and the Holy One, blessed be he, sees but is not seen, as it is written, '[Am I a God at hand says the Lord, and not a God afar off?] Can a man hide himself in secret places so that I cannot see him? says the Lord. Do I not fill heaven [and earth? says the Lord]' (Jer. 23:23–24). Let the soul, which sees but is not seen, come and praise the Holy One, blessed be he, who sees but is not seen ...

Here the relationship of complementarity conveys a deeper truth concerning the relationship of God to the world.

A much more complex instance of the same type of synergistic relationship among discrete categories emerges when we address the Temple and its sacrificial cult. This case forms the centrepiece and model of much thought about how things hold together. The sages maintained that, one, the world of nature came to concrete realization in the Temple and its cult, and that, two, the Temple and its cult embodied the principles of justice that infused nature as much as the realm of human activity. Here they found the meeting point of three categorically disparate entities, creation, man, and abstract principle, specifically, nature, Israel, and justice, and, in detail, they identified the way in which the three coalesce to form a unity. This, the principal focus of complementarity, identifies the Temple and its sacrifices as the point at which separate components of the larger structure meet and complete each other. These separate components that complement one another are creation and the natural world, Israel and the social world, and the just moral order.

The natural world without the embodiment of the just moral order, the moral order without full realization in Israel, and Israel divorced from nature and the nurture of justice – all three prove incomplete, indeed, if not chaotic then in any case inchoate. Only when joined before God do the three attain each its full realization in the others. And that takes place in the elect abode of Israel, in the Land of Israel, the chosen of all lands as we have seen, in Jerusalem, the chosen of all cities, and in the Temple, the highest of all mountains. All three form the setting for the perfect union of creation, Israel, and the moral order. Complementarity attests to perfection, then, in the conduct of the cult. The character of the offerings, the representation of the vestments of the priest, the very inanimate furniture of the Temple – all complete the union of man and nature in the service of God. These are the propositions we shall now see spelled out in so many words, the result of an interior logic that holds together creation, Israel, and justice.

First comes creation in relationship to the Temple cult. As we shall now see, creation reaches its climax in the cult, where the blessings of the natural world are offered up to God in Heaven. Second comes Israel, the complement and counterpart to the world of nature, and partner of God in creation. That brings us to the first match in the trilogy of mutually complementary components of world order, the natural order, the social order, embodied in Israel, and the cult. Here is the way that the sages show how creation is embodied in and celebrated by the offerings of the Temple in Jerusalem. The sacrificial cult is celebrated as a memorial to creation, and the Psalms that the Levites sing identify the particular aspect of creation that took place on a given day of the week. So the selected Psalm set the stage for the offering that celebrated what took place in creation on that day:

BAVLI-TRACTATE ROSH HASHANAH 4:4A-E I.2/31A

A. It is taught on Tannaite authority [at Mishnah-tractate Tamid 7:4]: R. Judah says in the name of R. Aqiba:

B. "On the first day what did they sing? [Ps. 24, which begins]: 'The earth is the Lord's and the fullness thereof, [the world and they who live therein].' [This psalm was used] because [on Sunday God] took possession and gave possession and was ruler over his world [without the heavenly hosts, who were created on the second day].

C. "On the second day what did they sing? [Ps. 48, beginning]: 'Great is the Lord and highly to be praised [in the city of our God, even upon his holy hill].' [This psalm was used] because [on Monday, God] divided that which he created [into the upper and lower worlds] and was sovereign over them.

D. "On the third day they did sing [Ps. 82, which begins]: 'God stands in the congregation of God, [he is a judge among the gods].' [This psalm was used] because [on Tuesday, God] revealed the dry land in his wisdom and prepared the earth for his congregation.

E. "On the fourth day they did sing [Ps. 94, which begins]: 'Lord God to whom vengeance belongs, [you God to whom vengeance belongs, show yourself].' [This psalm was used] because [on Wednesday, God] created the sun and moon and was destined to exact punishment from those who serve them.

F. "On the fifth day they did sing [Ps. 81, which begins], 'Sing aloud to God our strength, [make a joyful noise to the God of Jacob].' [This psalm was used] because [on Thursday, God] created birds and fish, which bring glory to his name.

G. "On the sixth day they did sing [Ps. 92, which begins], 'The Lord reigns; he is robed in majesty.' [This psalm was used] because [on Friday, God] finished his work and ruled over all [he created].

H. "On the seventh day they did sing [Ps. 92, which begins], 'A Psalm, a song for the Sabbath day' – [a psalm] for the day that is wholly Sabbath rest [for eternity]."

Now the entire set is recapitulated, with an explicit statement of how each day of the week corresponds to a moment of creation:

I. Said R. Nehemiah, "What was sages' understanding [that led them] to distinguish between these passages? [Why, that is, do they say that the first passages refer to God's acts in the past, at the time of creation, while the passage for the Sabbath, they say, refers to the future?]

J. "Rather [the passages should be explained as follows, in which only the interpretation of Ps. 92, for the Sabbath differs from what has preceded]: On the first day [Ps. 24 was used] because [on Sunday God] took possession and gave possession and was ruler over his world [without the heavenly hosts, who were created on the second day].

K. "On the second day [Ps. 48 was used] because [on Monday, God] divided that which he created [into the upper and lower worlds] and was sovereign over them.

L. "On the third day [Ps. 82 was used] because [on Tuesday, God] revealed the dry land in his wisdom and prepared the earth for his congregation.

M. "On the fourth [Ps. 94 was used] because [on Wednesday, God] created the sun and moon and was destined to exact punishment from those who serve them.

N. "On the fifth [Ps. 81 was used] because [on Thursday, God] created birds and fish, which bring glory to his name.

O. "On the sixth [Ps. 92 was used] because [on Friday, God] finished his work and ruled over all [he created].

P. "On the seventh [Ps. 92 was used] because [on the Sabbath, God] rested."

So the Temple cult celebrates the natural order. We shall presently note the correspondence between the priests' garments and the sins that are atoned for by the wearing of those garments, and that egregious match, in fact precipitated by substantive points of contact, will bring the social order too within the framework of complementarity and completion. Here the invocation of Psalms to be sung in the Temple that correspond to events in the creation of the world underscores that same sense of the integrity of all reality, natural and social.

If the correspondence of creation and cult presents no difficulty, the inclusion in the equation of Israel does. How, one must wonder, does Israel (outside the framework of the cult) complement creation, and creation Israel, so that Israel without creation or creation without Israel proves incomplete? In the following we see how the sages express the notion that creation takes cognizance of the second component of world order, Israel. Specifically, God made a stipulation with all of creation to accommodate the Israelites:

GENESIS RABBAH V:V.I

A. Said R. Jonathan, "The Holy One, blessed be he, made a stipulation with the sea to split open before the Israelites.
B. "That is in line with this verse of Scripture: 'And the sea returned to its former strength', which word may be read, 'in accord with the stipulation that it had given' " (Ex. 14:27).
C. Said R. Jeremiah b. Eleazar, "It was not with the sea alone that the Holy One, blessed be he made such a stipulation, but he made the same stipulation with everything that was created on the six days of creation.
D. "That is in line with this verse of Scripture: 'I, even my hands, have stretched out the heavens and all their host have I commanded' " (Is. 45:12).

Now the case is supported with the evidentiary details:

E. " 'I commanded' the sea to divide.
F. " 'I commanded' the heaven to be silent before Moses: "Give ear, heaven" (Deut. 32:1).
G. " 'I commanded' the sun and the moon to stand still before Joshua.
H. " 'I commanded' the ravens to bring food to Elijah.
I. " 'I commanded' the fire not to harm Hananiah, Mishael, and Azariah.
J. " 'I commanded' the lions not to harm Daniel, the heaven to open before Ezekiel, the fish to vomit up Jonah."

Listing these items can yield one consequence: all represent occasions on which God saved Israel, all are media through which God did so. Nature like Israel forms part of God's kingdom, subject to Heavenly dominion. Nature and Israel, then, form a single, integral whole. And it is at the cult, where creation is celebrated, that nature, Israel, and God meet.

Not only so, but the very narrative of creation links to the standing of Israel in the Land, so that Israel without creation has no claim upon the Land

– another, and most striking, exercise in postulating necessary complementarities. Here is how the sages frame matters:

GENESIS RABBAH I.II.I

A. R. Joshua of Sikhnin in the name of R. Levi commenced [discourse by citing the following verse]: " 'He has declared to his people the power of his works, in giving them the heritage of the nations' (Ps. 111:6).

B. "What is the reason that the Holy One, blessed be he, revealed to Israel what was created on the first day and what on the second?

C. "It was on account of the nations of the world. It was so that they should not ridicule the Israelites, saying to them, 'Are you not a nation of robbers [having stolen the land from the Canaanites]?'

D. "It allows the Israelites to answer them, 'And as to you, is there no spoil in your hands? For surely: "The Caphtorim, who came forth out of Caphtor, destroyed them and dwelled in their place" (Deut. 2:23)!

E. " 'The world and everything in it belongs to the Holy One, blessed be he. When he wanted, he gave it to you, and when he wanted, he took it from you and gave it to us.'

F. "That is in line with what is written, '... in giving them the heritage of the nations, he has declared to his people the power of his works' (Ps. 111:6) ... [So as to give them the land, he established his right to do so by informing them that he had created it.]

G. "He told them about the beginning: 'In the beginning God created ...' " (Gen. 1:1).

Israel without (the narrative of) creation is incomplete, and (the narrative of) creation without Israel loses its very purpose.

When we turn to the complementarity between the sacred and the profane, we come to the Temple and its offerings. There, this world meets the transcendent when Israel designates as holy and then, in conditions of sanctification, offers up what was profane but now is holy to God, the gifts of nature particular to the Land of Israel, wine, wheat, oil, meat of domesticated and other than carnivorous beasts. We here address an elect locus, locative sanctification.

To begin with, we deal with the realm of the sacred, where enchantment takes place automatically. For example, the mere entry within the walls of Jerusalem serves to impose the status of sanctification within Jerusalem upon produce that is brought there. Produce in the status of second tithe that is to be eaten in Jerusalem is automatically consecrated for that purpose once it comes within the walls. But coins in the status of second tithe enter Jerusalem. After they have been brought into Jerusalem they may be taken out again. But produce which is in the status of second tithe once in Jerusalem must remain in the city until it is consumed (Mishnah-tractate Maaser Sheni 3:5).

The Temple, where God and holy Israel meet, is the highest point in earth, where God receives his share of the natural gifts of the Holy Land, meat, grain, wine, and olive oil; and where, through the presentation of these gifts, the Israelite fulfils his obligations to God, inclusive of atoning for sin. Concomitantly, prayers are to be recited in the direction of the Temple, for instance, Mishnah-tractate Berakhot 4:6 A: If he was travelling in a ship or on a raft, he should direct his heart towards the Chamber of the Holy of Holies. The priority of the Land of Israel over all other lands, and Jerusalem over all other places, and the Temple over the rest of Jerusalem, is expressed in this language at Tosefta-tractate Berakhot 3:15. Those who are outside the Land turn towards the Land of Israel. Those who are in the Land of Israel turn towards Jerusalem. Those who are in Jerusalem turn towards the Temple. Those who are in the Temple turn towards the Chamber of the Holy of Holies and pray. "It turns out that those standing in the north face south, those in the south face north, those in the east face west, and those in the west face east. Thus all Israel turn out to be praying toward one place, the Temple mount."

The stakes in Temple worship prove cosmic, for the welfare of the natural world as well as of Israel rests upon the Temple service:

ABOT DERABBI NATAN IV:IV.I

B. So long as the Temple service of the house of the sanctuary went on, the world was blessed for its inhabitants and rain came down in the proper time.

C. For it is said, "To love the Lord your God and to serve him with all your heart and with all your soul that I will provide the rain of your land in its season, the former rain and the latter rain ... and I will provide grass in your fields for your cattle" (Deut. 11:13–14).

D. But when the Temple service of the house of the sanctuary ceased to go on, the world was not blessed for its inhabitants, and rain did not come down in the proper time,

E. as it is said, "Take heed to yourselves lest your heart be deceived ... and he shut up the heaven so that there shall be no rain" (Deut. 11:16–17).

The Temple cult sustained life, and its offerings of the gifts of creation to the Creator brought the response of renewed blessing of nature. But, in representing the world of creation, the Temple is incomplete. The Temple requires the complement of Israel.

What we already know about the doctrine of Israel – Israel stands for life, the gentiles for death – explains why the Temple, with its celebration of created life, finds in Israel its complement: gentiles do not have the right to bring sin-offerings, and they do not atone through the cult the way Israel does. The Temple sacrifices find their context and meaning only in the life of Israel, which is another way of saying, only among the living and not among the dead:

SIFRA XXXIV:I.1-2

1. A. ["And the Lord said to Moses, 'Say to the people of Israel, "If any one sins unwittingly in any of the things which the Lord has commanded not to be done"'" (Lev. 4:1-12):]
B. Israelites bring a sin-offering, but gentiles do not bring a sin-offering.
C. It is not necessary to say that [they do not have to bring a sin-offering for inadvertently violating] religious duties that were not assigned to the children of Noah, but even for violating religious duties concerning which the children of Noah were commanded, they do not have to bring a sin-offering on that account.
2. A. "Say to the people of Israel:" I know that the sin-offering is owing only from Israelites.
B. How do I know that it is owing also from proselytes and bondmen?
C. Scripture says, "If any one [sins unwittingly]."

Gentiles may present certain types of offerings to the altar, free-will and thanksgiving offerings in particular, but no offerings that distinguish Israel as pure or elect and legitimate beneficiaries of the cult of Israel may come from them. Thus, Mishnah-tractate Sheqalim 1:5: "A gentile and a Samaritan who paid the sheqel in support of the daily whole offering presented in behalf of Israel – they do not accept it from them. Nor do they accept from them bird offerings for male Zabs, bird offerings for female Zabs, bird offerings for women who have given birth, sin-offerings, or guilt offerings. But offerings brought by reason of vows and free-will offerings they accept from them. This is the governing principle: Anything which is vowed or given as a free-will offering do they accept from them. Anything which is not vowed or given as a free-will offering do they not accept from them. And so is the matter explained by Ezra, since it is said, 'You have nothing to do with us to build a house unto our God' (Ezra 4:3)." For nature to fulfil its purpose of serving God, for the gifts of nature – wine, grain, oil, meat – to reach Heaven, Israel located in the Land of Israel is required.

Not only Israel in general, but the particular saints of Israel stand for occasions for completion of the cult. Each of the following represents the equivalent of an offering: Abraham, Hananiah, Mishael, Azariah; Moriah and Sinai. All stand for a fire that produced a sweet savour for God, the one the fire of martyrdom, the other the fire of faith:

PESIQTA DER. KAHANA XII:III.1–2:

1. A. R. Isaac commenced his discourse by citing the following verse: "Refresh me with raisins, [he revived me with apricots, for I was faint with love. His left arm was under my head, his right arm was around me]" (Song 2:5).
B. "[Reading the letters for the word for raisins to yield the sound for the word for fire, we interpret as follows]: 'Refresh me with two fires, the fire of Abraham [whom Nimrod threw into the fiery furnace] and the fire of Hananiah, Mishael, and Azariah.' "

Two further instances are offered:

2. A. Another interpretation: "Refresh me with raisins, [he revived me with apricots, for I was faint with love. His left arm was under my head, his right arm was around me]" (Song 2:5).
B. "[Reading the letters for the word for raisins to yield the sound for the word for fire, we interpret as follows]: 'Refresh me with two fires, the fire of Moriah and the fire of Sinai.' "

Torah-study compares to sacrifices as well:

3. A. Another interpretation of the verse: "Refresh me with raisins, [he revived me with apricots, for I was faint with love. His left arm was under my head, his right arm was around me]" (Song 2:5).
B. "[Reading the letters for the word for raisins to yield the sound for the word for well construed, we interpret as follows]: 'Refresh me with laws that are well construed.'
C. " '… revived me with apricots': this refers to words of Torah, which have a fragrance as pleasant as apricots."

That martyrdom is the equivalent to faith is shown by the treatment as comparable of the stated items.

Israel's involvement in the cult begins with the founders. The animals selected for offerings stand for the virtues of the patriarchs. In this way, once again, Israel and the Temple, man and nature, join together to perfect creation by completing the transaction between Heaven and earth. The explicit joining of Abraham to the bull, Isaac to the sheep, and Jacob to the goat, the principal animal offerings of the Temple altar, proceeds in a now-familiar direction:

LEVITICUS RABBAH XXVII:IX:

1. A. "A bull, a sheep, or a goat" (Lev. 22:27):

B. "A bull" on account of the merit of Abraham, as it is said: "And Abraham ran to the herd and took a calf" (Gen. 18:7).

C. "A sheep" on account of the merit of Isaac, as it is written, "And he looked, and behold, a ram caught by its horns" (Gen. 22:13).

D. "A goat" on account of the merit of Jacob, as it is written in his regard, "Now go to the flock and get me two good kid goats" (Gen. 27:9).

2. A. What is the meaning of "good"?

B. R. Berekhiah in the name of R. Helbo: "Good for you, good for your children.

C. "Good for you, for on their account you will receive indications of blessing.

D. "Good for your children, for on their account you will have atonement on the Day of Atonement: 'For on this day atonement will be made for you' [Lev. 16:30], [including the atonement of the sacrifice of the goat]" (Lev. 16:9).

The theological logic, the quest for complementarity linking Israel to the cult, accounts for the hermeneutics that yields the particular exegesis at hand. But of equal importance is the mode of thought. It is the philosophical one that is explained in chapter 1, explaining things through comparison and contrast – here, matching complementary counterparts – that accounts for the effort to match the patriarchs with the chosen animals of offering. The proof-texts are integral, once the comparison has been undertaken. For Scripture's facts are required to validate a proposition. But the systemic origin of the impulse to integrate is fundamental to the formulation.

We recall in this same connection the explanation of why God chose for the altar the particular beasts that he preferred: they are the pursued, not the pursuer. I briefly record the source already examined above:

LEVITICUS RABBAH XXVII:V.I FF.:

1. A. "God seeks what has been driven away" (Qoh. 3:15).

B. R. Huna in the name of R. Joseph said, "It is always the case that 'God seeks what has been driven away' [favouring the victim].

J. "And the rule applies also to the matter of offerings. A bull is pursued by a lion, a sheep is pursued by a wolf, a goat is pursued by a leopard.

K. "Therefore the Holy One, blessed be he, has said, 'Do not make offerings before me from those animals that pursue, but from those that are pursued: 'When a bull, a sheep, or a goat is born' '" (Lev. 22:27).

Traits of Israel and of nature correspond and complement one another, meeting at the holy altar in the union of nature and transcendence.

What about justice, which I noted at the outset of this part of the argument as the third component of the complementary trio, besides creation and Israel? The moral order infuses the whole, and the presence of the rules of justice takes the form of the clothing of the priests. This systematic claim of connection and complementarity, on the surface nothing short of bizarre, is said in so many words:

BAVLI-TRACTATE YOMA 7: I.10/72A-B

11. A. R. Hama b. Hanina said, "What is the meaning of the verse, 'The plaited [72B] garments for ministering in the holy place' (Ex. 35:19)? Were it not for the priestly garments, there would not have remained of Israel a single remnant and survivor."

That general remark is amplified in vast detail in the following:

SONG OF SONGS RABBAH XLVIII:V

3. C. "Your teeth are like a flock of shorn ewes that have come up from the washing, all of which bear twins, and not one among them is bereaved" (Song of Songs 4:2): That is to say, things that are subject to a definite and fixed number, specifically, the garments of the high priesthood.

We now list the clothing of the high priest and link each piece of clothing with a counterpart sin, for which the priest's wearing of the garment in the conduct of the sacrificial rite atones:

4. A. For we have learned in the Mishnah:
B. The high priest serves in eight garments, and an ordinary priest in four:
C. tunic, underpants, head-covering, and girdle.
D. The high priest in addition wears the breastplate, apron, upper garment, and frontlet [M. Yoma 7:5A-C].

Item by item, we now link a garment with an appropriate verse, which then indicates how the wearing of the garment appropriately atones; thus the completion of the last two stages in the process of justice – sin, punishment, repentance, atonement, forgiveness:

E. The tunic would atone for bloodshed: "And they dipped the coat in the blood" (Gen. 37:31).
F. Some say, "It atoned for those who wear mixed varieties: 'And he made him a coat of many colors' " (Gen. 37:3).

The next items are self-explanatory, with or without proof-texts:

G. The underpants atone for fornication: "And you shall make them linen underpants to cover the flesh of their nakedness" (Ex. 27:42).
H. The head-covering atones for arrogance: "And he set the head-covering on his head" (Lev. 8:9).
I. For what did the girdle atone?
J. For the double-dealers.
K. Others say, "For thieves."

Now the composer shows on what basis he links one thing to the other:

L. The one who says that it was for thieves maintains that view because the garment was hollow, standing for thieves, who work in hiding.
M. The one who says that it was for the double-dealers is in accord with that which R. Levi said, "It was thirty-two cubits long, and he would twist it on either side."
N. The breastplate would atone for those who pervert justice: "And you shall put in the breastplate of judgment the Urim and the Thummim" (Ex. 28:30).
O. The apron [ephod] would atone for idolatry: "And without ephod or teraphim" (Hos. 3:4).
P. The upper garment [robe] would atone for slander.

A different result emerges from the same basic mode of thought:

5. A. R. Simon in the name of R. Jonathan of Bet Gubrin: "For two matters there was no atonement, but the Torah has provided atonement for them, and these are they:
B. "Gossip and involuntary manslaughter."

How do the priestly garments atone for these matters?

C. "For gossip there was no atonement, but the Torah has provided atonement for it, specifically through the bell of the robe: 'And it shall be upon Aaron to minister, and the sound thereof shall be heard' (Ex. 28:35).

D. "Let the sound that this makes come and atone for the sound of slander.

E. "For involuntary manslaughter there was no atonement, but the Torah has provided atonement for it, specifically through the death of the high priest: 'And he shall dwell therein until the death of the high priest'" (Num. 35:25).

Now we take up the interrupted flow of exposition:

6. A. [Resuming 4.P:] The frontlet would atone for impudence.

B. Some say, "It was for blasphemy."

C. The one who says it was for impudence cites the following verse of Scripture: "And it shall be upon Aaron's forehead" (Ex. 28:38), and also, "Yet you had a harlot's forehead" (Jer. 3:3).

D. The one who says it was for blasphemy cites the following verse of Scripture: "And it shall always be upon his forehead" (Ex. 28:38) alongside, "And the stone sank into his forehead" (1 Sam. 17:49).

So much for the garments of the priest and how they correspond with specific sins and complete the process of atonement. The sages go still another step further, dealing with the moral lessons that can derive from the Temple's furniture:

BAVLI-TRACTATE YOMA 7: I.10/72A-B

A. R. Hama b. Hanina said, "What is the meaning of the verse, 'You shall make the boards of the tabernacle of acacia wood, standing up' (Ex. 26:15) – 'Acacia wood standing up' (Ex. 26:15) means that the wood is arranged so that it stands up in the manner in which it grows [with the grain perpendicular to the ground].

B. Another interpretation: "Standing" in the sense that they had up[right] the golden plating [that is affixed to them].

C. Another interpretation of "Standing:"

D. Should you say, "Their hope is lost, their prospects null," Scripture to the contrary says, "Acacia wood standing up" (Ex. 26:15), meaning that they stand for ever and ever.

In context the garments are introduced:

11. A. R. Hama b. Hanina said, "What is the meaning of the verse, 'The plaited [72B] garments for ministering in the holy place' (Ex. 35:19)? Were it not for the priestly garments, there would not have remained of Israel a single remnant and survivor."

The crowns are assigned to those with sufficient merit to receive them:

13. A. Said R. Yohanan, "There were three crowns: the altar, the ark, and the table.

B. "the altar: Aaron enjoyed the grace to possess it and he took it;

C. "the table: David enjoyed the grace to possess it and took it;

D. "and the ark: it is still available. Whoever wants to take it may come and take it.

E. "Might you suppose it is trivial?

F. "Scripture states, 'By me kings rule' " (Prov. 8:15).

14. A. R. Yohanan contrasted these verses: "An alien" and we read the word as "crown" – yielding this lesson: if he deserves it, it is a wreath to him, if not, it is alien to him.

The question that is answered, how the Temple furniture contributes to the process of atonement, finds response in a familiar inquiry. Complementarity emerges in the resolution of the categorical confusion between things and persons, identified as the match of the activities and objects of the Temple building and its cult and the moral condition of Israel. So in these concrete ways we see how the theological principle of complementarity constitutes one positive indicator of the perfection of world order by showing how principal parts of the structure logically require one another, depend upon one another, complete one another.

The components on which we have concentrated, creation, the just moral order, and Israel, in no way match categorically, and that is the challenge to complementarity. The sages, for their part, claim more than that within the world order of justice that God thought up and made, principal parts coexist in harmony. They further allege a quality of complementary relationship that transcends mere harmony, the absence of conflict. The sages maintain that the parts fit *only* when they function in perfect union. That is not an easy claim to sustain. For the natural world and the social order define their own categories, respectively, but do not intersect: what has a lamb to do with a city? And how does the particular social entity, Israel (or its categorical equivalent, the gentiles), match a cloud, on the one side, and an abstract category of thought (whether philosophical or legal or theological), justice, on the other. And yet, in the quest for showing how the generative categories (creation, society, justice) complement one another, the theology of the Oral Torah finds its answer in that hierarchy established by Land of Israel, Jerusalem, Temple Mount, priesthood, sacrifice. Only within the intellectual framework defined by the principle of complementarity can the remarkable statements about the union of nature and supernature, the social order and Israel, attain their full significance.

For this theological statement to make sense within its givens and its logic, it must encompass the principals, not only the secondary players. And the principals are God and man (its being taken for granted that under discussion is Israelite man). As we have already noted, once the Torah has announced God's intent in making man, "Let us make man in our image, after our likeness," and further specified God's act in actually doing so, "And God created an in his image, in the image of God he created him, male and female he created them" (Gen. 1:26–27), from the perspective guiding this discussion an urgent question arises. It is, in what way are God and man complementary, meaning, how and why is the one completed in and by the other? Wherein – within the theory of complementary relationships that is meant to justify world order – does God need man as complement?[1]

The Oral Torah provides its distinctive answer. Since God has commanded love, "You will love the Lord your God with all your heart, and with all your soul, and with all your might" (Dt. 6:4), God has announced that aspect in which he is incomplete, identifying what he requires but does not possess. And that is the love of man. Thus, God, at the very moment of the declaration of his uniqueness, pronounces what he yet needs for completion, man's entire devotion. But, by its nature, that love cannot be commanded or coerced, only beseeched on God's part, freely given on man's. And reciprocally, it hardly need be added, what man requires but cannot gain through coercion or manipulation or fixed exchange is God's favour and love. So, in the ineffable exchange of love, in the transaction of the will, each party to the drama of creation seeks in the other its own complement, completion and wholeness. When that exchange takes place, Eden is regained, Israel restored to the Land of Israel. When it does not take place, man's intentionality takes the form of arrogance, which leads to sin, which disrupts world order. In the relationship of complementarity, love surpasses even justice. The exposition of how that relationship of complementarity is fully set forth in the Oral Torah will require a systematic exposition of how a single word encompasses a principal theological component of an entire system.

The Oral Torah finds in a very particular transaction the working out of this relationship of complementarity between God and man. That transaction it identifies in the performance of acts of will consisting of offerings of love to Heaven. Such acts take on a particular quality, which we shall see in a moment. But the principle they embody is this: What we cannot by will impose, we can by will evoke. What we cannot accomplish through coercion, we can achieve through submission. God will do for us what we cannot do for

---

1. In the next chapter we ask, in what way does the One correspond with the other?

ourselves, when we do for God what God cannot make us do. In a wholly concrete and tangible sense, that means to love God with all the heart, the soul, the might that we have. In that way, we enter a relationship of complementarity with God, freely and unconditionally contributing what we have and control, which is our capacity to love, and so completing that unity that God aspires to enjoy with us.

To define matters more concretely, we turn to stories that embody the ultimate and perfect transaction of complementarity: giving God what he cannot coerce, receiving from God what we cannot compel or inveigle. In all three instances that follow, the deeds of the heroes of the story make them worthy of having their prayers answered, which is a mark of the God's response. These are, in particular, deeds that transcend the strict requirements of the Torah and even the limits of the law altogether. The key word in some of the stories, *zekhut*, which may be translated "the heritage of supererogatory virtue and its consequent entitlements," stands for the empowerment, of a supernatural character, that derives from the virtue of one's ancestry or from one's own virtuous deeds of a very particular order. These are, concretely, deeds not commanded but impelled by utter generosity of the heart. These are deeds that make a difference only when they are done without hope let alone prospect of recompense and without pressure of any kind except the kind that wells up from within. It is, then, an indicator of one's inner quality and character. No single word in American English bears the same meaning, nor can I identify even a synonym for *zekhut* in usages of the canonical writings, only the antonym, which is sin. Sin represents an act of rebellion, *zekhut*, an act of humble and willing, gratuitous submission, so the two represent binary opposites, and complements of another order, as we shall see in due course.

To illustrate the transaction, or relationship, of *zekhut*,[2] we turn not to such familiar media as composites setting forth a systematic exposition in exegetical form, or even to compositions exposing an argument in propositional form enriched with the anticipated parables, but to some simple stories. Here the language of *zekhut* figures and the meaning of that language is then conveyed in context. In the opening text, when the beggar asks for money, he says, literally, "acquire *zekhut* through me," referring in context to the action he solicits. But the same word, as noun or verb, in other contexts takes on

---

2. The concept is systemically so particular as to make it difficult even to find appropriately precise language. Better here than "relationship of zekhut" might be "a transaction involving a relationship that in Heaven provokes the bestowal of uncoerced favor, thus zekhut," but such complicated formulations will leave still greater obscurity than what I hope permissible imprecision creates.

other meanings, always with the same deeper significance for the relationship of a relationship of grace, unearned, uncoerced love, that is besought. The difficulty of translating a word of systemic consequence with a single word in some other language (or in the language of the system's documents themselves) tells us that we deal with what is unique:

YERUSHALMI-TRACTATE TAANIT I:4.I

F. A certain man came before one of the relatives of R. Yannai. He said to him, "Rabbi, attain *zekhut* through me [by giving me charity]."

G. He said to him, "And didn't your father leave you money?"

H. He said to him, "No."

I. He said to him, "Go and collect what your father left in deposit with others."

J. He said to him, "I have heard concerning property my father deposited with others that it was gained by violence [so I don't want it]."

K. He said to him, "You are worthy of praying and having your prayers answered."

The point of K, of course, is self-evidently a reference to the possession of entitlement to supernatural favour, and it is gained through deeds that the law of the Torah cannot require but does favour: what one does on one's own volition, beyond the measure of the law. Here I see the opposite of sin. A sin is what one has done by one's own volition beyond all limits of the law. So an act that generates *zekhut* for the individual is the counterpart and opposite: what one does by one's own volition that also is beyond all requirements of the law.

L. A certain ass-driver appeared before the rabbis [the context requires: in a dream] and prayed, and rain came. The rabbis sent and brought him and said to him, "What is your trade?"

M. He said to them, "I am an ass driver."

N. They said to him, "And how do you conduct your business?"

O. He said to them, "One time I rented my ass to a certain woman, and she was weeping on the way, and I said to her, 'What's with you?' and she said to me, 'The husband of that woman [me] is in prison [for debt], and I wanted to see what I can do to free him.' So I sold my ass and I gave her the proceeds, and I said to her, 'Here is your money, free your husband, but do not sin [by becoming a prostitute to raise the necessary funds].'"

P. They said to him, "You are worthy of praying and having your prayers answered."

The ass-driver clearly has a powerful lien on Heaven, so that his prayers are answered even while those of others are not. What he did to get that entitlement? He did what no law could demand: impoverished himself to save the woman from a "fate worse than death."

Q. In a dream of R. Abbahu, Mr. Pentakaka ["Five sins"] appeared, who prayed that rain would come, and it rained. R. Abbahu sent and summoned him. He said to him, "What is your trade?"

R. He said to him, "Five sins does that man [I] do every day, [for I am a pimp:] hiring whores, cleaning up the theater, bringing home their garments for washing, dancing, and performing before them."

S. He said to him, "And what sort of decent thing have you ever done?"

T. He said to him, "One day that man [I] was cleaning the theater, and a woman came and stood behind a pillar and cried. I said to her, 'What's with you?' And she said to me, 'That woman's [my] husband is in prison, and I wanted to see what I can do to free him,' so I sold my bed and cover, and I gave the proceeds to her. I said to her, 'Here is your money, free your husband, but do not sin.' "

U. He said to him, "You are worthy of praying and having your prayers answered."

Q moves us still further, since the named man has done everything sinful that one can do, and, more to the point, he does it every day. So the singularity of the act of *zekhut*, which suffices if done only one time, encompasses its power to outweigh a life of sin – again, an act of *zekhut* as the mirror-image and opposite of sin. Here, too, the single act of saving a woman from a "fate worse than death" has sufficed.

V. A pious man from Kefar Imi appeared [in a dream] to the rabbis. He prayed for rain and it rained. The rabbis went up to him. His householders told them that he was sitting on a hill. They went out to him, saying to him, "Greetings," but he did not answer them.

W. He was sitting and eating, and he did not say to them, "You break bread too."

X. When he went back home, he made a bundle of faggots and put his cloak on top of the bundle [instead of on his shoulder].

Y. When he came home, he said to his household [wife], "These rabbis are here [because] they want me to pray for rain. If I pray and it rains, it is a disgrace for them, and if not, it is a profanation of the Name of Heaven. But come, you and I will go up [to the roof] and pray. If it rains, we shall tell them, 'We are not worthy to pray and have our prayers answered.' "

Z. They went up and prayed and it rained.

AA. They came down to them [and asked], "Why have the rabbis troubled themselves to come here today?"

BB. They said to him, "We wanted you to pray so that it would rain."

CC. He said to them, "Now do you really need my prayers? Heaven already has done its miracle."

DD. They said to him, "Why, when you were on the hill, did we say hello to you, and you did not reply?"

EE. He said to them, "I was then doing my job. Should I then interrupt my concentration [on my work]?"

FF. They said to him, "And why, when you sat down to eat, did you not say to us 'You break bread too?'"

GG. He said to them, "Because I had only my small ration of bread. Why would I have invited you to eat by way of mere flattery [when I knew I could not give you anything at all]?"

HH. They said to him, "And why when you came to go down, did you put your cloak on top of the bundle?"

II. He said to them, "Because the cloak was not mine. It was borrowed for use at prayer. I did not want to tear it."

JJ. They said to him, "And why, when you were on the hill, did your wife wear dirty clothes, but when you came down from the mountain, did she put on clean clothes?"

KK. He said to them, "When I was on the hill, she put on dirty clothes, so that no one would gaze at her. But when I came home from the hill, she put on clean clothes, so that I would not gaze on any other woman."

LL. They said to him, "It is well that you pray and have your prayers answered."

The pious man of V, finally, enjoys the recognition of the sages by reason of his lien upon Heaven, able as he is to pray and bring rain. What has so endowed him with *zekhut*? Acts of punctiliousness of a moral order: concentrating on his work, avoiding an act of dissimulation, integrity in the disposition of a borrowed object, his wife's concern not to attract other men and her equal concern to make herself attractive to her husband. None of these stories refers explicitly to *zekhut*; all of them tell us about what it means to enjoy not an entitlement by inheritance but a lien accomplished by one's own supererogatory acts of restraint.

The critical importance of the heritage of virtue together with its supernatural entitlements emerges in a striking claim. Even though a man was degraded, one action sufficed to win for him that heavenly glory to which rabbis in lives of Torah-study aspired. A single remarkable deed, exemplary for its deep humanity, sufficed to win for an ordinary person the *zekhut* that elicits the supernatural favour enjoyed by some rabbis on account of their Torah-study. *Zekhut* represents a power that only God can ultimately grasp: the power of weakness. It is what the weak and excluded and despised can do that outweighs what the great masters of the Torah – impressed with the power of the ass-driver to pray and get his prayers answered – have accomplished. *Zekhut* also forms the inheritance of the disinherited: what you receive as a heritage when you have nothing in the present and have gotten nothing in the past, that scarce resource that is free and unearned but much valued.

Thus far we have treated the relationship of complementarity – a transaction of reciprocal grace – between man and God. But the theology of the Oral Torah differentiates man into Israel[ites] and gentiles, those who know God and those who worship idols. Therefore, it follows, the relationship of complementarity through acts of uncoerced generosity and love has likewise to be defined in the particular context of Israel. That, quite predictably, takes place with the addition, to the word *zekhut*, of the Hebrew word for patriarchs, *abot*, thus *zekhut abot*. The phrase refers to the relationship of complementarity between God and Israel in particular. That relationship works itself out within the principle that God not only responds freely to what we do as an act of grace but remembers in our favour what our progenitors, the patriarchs, did to express selfless love and loyalty to God. We recall that the patriarchs form an abiding presence within Israel, so at stake is not an inheritance by reason of genealogy but a heritage by reason of shared virtue. When Israel does what the patriarchs do, they, too, enter into the relationship of complementarity with God that characterizes the patriarchs' link to God.

The conception of a heritage of grace to which Israel has access is entirely familiar. Scripture, for example, knows that God loves Israel because he loved the patriarchs (Dt. 4:37); the memory or deeds of the righteous patriarchs and matriarchs appear in a broad range of contexts, for instance, "Remember your servants, Abraham, Isaac, and Jacob" (Ex. 32:13), for Moses, and "Remember the good deeds of David, your servant" (II Chr. 6:42), for David. But more specific usages of the concept in the context of a heritage of unearned grace derive only from the documents of the Oral Torah. There, one finds a clear indication of the presence of a conception of an entitlement deriving from some source other than one's own deed of the moment:

MISHNAH-TRACTATE SOTAH 3:4–5

3:4. E. There is the possibility that *zekhut* suspends the curse for one year, and there is the possibility that *zekhut* suspends the curse for two years, and there is the possibility that *zekhut* suspends the curse for three years.

F. On this basis Ben Azzai says, "A man is required to teach Torah to his daughter.

G. "For if she should drink the water, she should know that [if nothing happens to her], *zekhut* is what suspends [the curse from taking effect]."

3:5 A. R. Simeon says, "*Zekhut* does not suspend the effects of the bitter water.

B. "And if you say, '*Zekhut* does suspend the effects of the bitter water,' you will weaken the effect of the water for all the women who have to drink it.

C. "And you give a bad name to all the women who drink it who turned out to be pure.

D. "For people will say, 'They are unclean, but *zekhut* suspended the effects of the water for them.' "

E. Rabbi says, "*Zekhut* does suspend the effects of the bitter water. But she will not bear children or continue to be pretty. And she will waste away, and in the end she will have the same [unpleasant] death."

Now, if we insert for *zekhut* at each point, "the heritage of virtue and its consequent entitlements" (thus: "For people will say, 'They are unclean, but *zekhut* suspended the effects of the water for them,' " then, "For people will say, 'They are unclean, but the [received, inherited] heritage of virtue and its consequent entitlements suspended the effects of the water for them),' " we have good sense. That is to say, the woman may not suffer the penalty to which she is presumably condemnable, not because her act or condition (for example, her innocence) has secured her acquittal or nullified the effects of the ordeal, but because she enjoys some advantage extrinsic to her own act or condition. She may be guilty, but she may also possess a benefice deriving by inheritance, hence, heritage of virtue, and so be entitled to a protection not because of her own but because of someone else's action or condition. A further instance is as follows:

TRACTATE ABOT 2:2

C. "And all who work with the community – let them work with them for the sake of Heaven.

D. "For the [1] *zekhut* of their fathers strengthens them, and their [fathers'] [2] righteousness stands forever.

E. "And as for you, I credit you with a great reward, as if you had done [all of the work required by the community on your own merit alone]."

Here, the only meaning possible is the one that I have given above: "the heritage of virtue and its consequent entitlements." The reference to an advantage that one gains by reason of inheritance out of one's fathers' righteousness is demanded by the parallel between *zekhut* of clause 1 and *righteousness* of clause 2. Whatever the conceivable ambiguity of the Mishnah, none is sustained by the context at hand, which is explicit in language and pellucid in message. That the sense is exactly the same as the one I have proposed is shown at the following passages, which seem to me to exhibit none of the possible ambiguity that characterized the usage of *zekhut* in the Mishnah.

Now, we find one antonym for *zekhut*, which, as I have just said, is sin. A person by his action brings about *zekhut* for the community, or he may by his action cause the community to sin:

TRACTATE ABOT 5:18

A. He who causes *zekhut* to the community never causes sin.

B. And he who causes the community to sin – they never give him a sufficient chance to attain penitence.

Here the contrast is between causing *zekhut* and causing sin, so *zekhut* is the opposite of sin. The continuation is equally clear that a person attained *zekhut* and endowed the community with *zekhut* – or sinned and made the community sin:

C. Moses attained *zekhut* and bestowed *zekhut* on the community.

D. So the *zekhut* of the community is assigned to his [credit],

E. as it is said, "He executed the justice of the Lord and his judgments with Israel" (Dt. 33:21).

F. Jeroboam sinned and caused the community to sin.

G. So the sin of the community is assigned to his [debit],

H. as it is said, "For the sins of Jeroboam which he committed and wherewith he made Israel to sin" (I Kings 15:30).

The appropriateness of interpreting the passage in the way I have proposed will now be shown to be self-evident. All that is required is to substitute for *zekhut* the proposed translation:

C. Moses attained the heritage of virtue and bestowed its consequent entitlements on the community.

D. So the heritage of virtue end its entitlements enjoyed by the community are assigned to his [credit],

The sense is simple. Moses through actions of his own (of an unspecified sort) acquired *zekhut*, which is the credit for such actions that accrued to him and bestowed upon him certain supernatural entitlements; and he for his part passed on as an inheritance that credit, a lien on Heaven for the performance of these same supernatural entitlements: *zekhut*, pure and simple. The upshot is to present *zekhut* as an action, as distinct from a (mere) attitude; an action that is precisely the opposite of a sinful one; an action that may be done by an individual or by the community at large; and an action that a leader may provoke the community to do (or not do).

How does complementarity as mode of thought and message of the system come into play? *Zekhut* completes and complements the category, sin. Just as sin forms an act of will, as we shall see in chapters 10 and 11, one of rebellion against God, so *zekhut* constitutes an act of will, one of uncoerced love for, submission to, God. The one is incomplete without the other, God and man, *zekhut* and sin. But *zekhut* and sin differ, for Scripture is explicit that the burden of sins cannot be passively inherited, willy-nilly, but, to form a heritage of guilt, must be actively accepted and renewed; the children cannot be made to suffer for the sins of the parents, unless they repeat them. Thus, *zekhut*, being a mirror-image, can be passively inherited, not by one's own merit, but by one's good fortune alone. But what constitute these *actions* that form mirror-images of sins? Here the principle of complementarity of relationship between God and man explains the concept at hand: the Israelite possesses a lien upon Heaven by reason of God's love for the patriarchs, his appreciation for certain things they did, and his response to those actions not only in favouring them but also in entitling their descendants to do or benefit from otherwise unattainable miracles.

Genesis Rabbah, where the sages set forth their doctrine of origins, creation, and Israel in particular, provides the best systematic account of the doctrine of *zekhut*. Here, *zekhut* draws in its wake the notion of the inheritance of an ongoing (historical) family, that of Abraham and Sarah, and *zekhut* works itself out in the moments of crisis of that family in its larger affairs. So the Israelites later on enjoy enormous *zekhut* through the deeds of the patriarchs and matriarchs. That conception comes to expression in what follows:

GENESIS RABBAH LXXVI:V.

2. A. "… for with only my staff I crossed this Jordan, and now I have become two companies":

B. R. Judah bar Simon in the name of R. Yohanan: "In the Torah, in the Prophets, and in the Writings we find proof that the Israelites were able to cross the Jordan only on account of the *zekhut* achieved by Jacob:

C. "In the Torah: '… for with only my staff I crossed this Jordan, and now I have become two companies.'

D. "In the prophets: 'Then you shall let your children know, saying, "Israel came over this Jordan on dry land"' (Josh. 4:22), meaning our father, Israel.

E. "In the Writings: 'What ails you, O you sea, that you flee? You Jordan, that you burn backward? At the presence of the God of Jacob'" (Ps. 114:5ff.).

Here is a perfect illustration of *zekhut* as an entitlement one will enjoy by reason of what someone else – an ancestor – has done; and that entitlement involves supernatural power. Jacob did not only leave *zekhut* as an estate to his heirs. The process is reciprocal and ongoing. *Zekhut* deriving from the ancestors had helped Jacob himself:

GENESIS RABBAH LXXVII:III.3.

A. "When the man saw that he did not prevail against Jacob, [he touched the hollow of his thigh, and Jacob's thigh was put out of joint as he wrestled with him]" (Gen. 32:25):

B. Said R. Hinena bar Isaac, "[God said to the angel,] 'He is coming against you with five "amulets" hung on his neck, that is, his own *zekhut*, the *zekhut* of his father and of his mother and of his grandfather and of his grandmother.

C. "'Check yourself out, can you stand up against even his own *zekhut* [let alone the *zekhut* of his parents and grandparents].'

D. "The matter may be compared to a king who had a savage dog and a tame lion. The king would take his son and sick him against the lion, and if the dog came to have a fight with the son, he would say to the dog, 'The lion cannot have a fight with him, are you going to make out in a fight with him?'

E. "So if the nations come to have a fight with Israel, the Holy One, blessed be he, says to them. 'Your angelic prince could not stand up to Israel, and as to you, how much the more so!'"

The collectivity of *zekhut*, not only its transferability, is illustrated here as well: what an individual does confers *zekhut* on the social entity. It is, moreover, a matter of the legitimate exercise of supernatural power. And the reciprocity of the process extended in all directions. Accordingly, what we have in hand is first and foremost a matter of the exercise of legitimate violence, hence a political power.

Zekhut might project not only backward, deriving from an ancestor and serving a descendant, but forward as well. Thus, Joseph accrued so much *zekhut* that the generations that came before him were credited with his *zekhut*:

GENESIS RABBAH LXXXIV:V.2.

A. "These are the generations of the family of Jacob. Joseph [being seventeen years old, was shepherding the flock with his brothers]" (Gen. 37:2):

B. These generations came along only on account of the *zekhut* of Joseph.

C. Did Jacob go to Laban for any reason other than for Rachel?

D. These generations thus waited until Joseph was born, in line with this verse: "And when Rachel had borne Joseph, Jacob said to Laban, 'Send me away' " (Gen. 30:215).

E. Who brought them down to Egypt? It was Joseph.

F. Who supported them in Egypt? It was Joseph.

G. The sea split open only on account of the *zekhut* of Joseph: "The waters saw you, O God" (Ps. 77:17). "You have with your arm redeemed your people, the sons of Jacob and Joseph" (Ps. 77:16).

H. R. Yudan said, "Also the Jordan was divided only on account of the *zekhut* of Joseph."

The passage at hand asks why only Joseph is mentioned as the family of Jacob. The inner polemic is that the *zekhut* of Jacob and Joseph would more than suffice to overcome Esau. Not only so, but Joseph survived because of the *zekhut* of his ancestors:

GENESIS RABBAH LXXXVII:VIII.I.

A. "She caught him by his garment ... but he left his garment in her hand and fled and got out of the house. [And when she saw that he had left his garment in her hand and had fled out of the house, she called to the men of her household and said to them, 'See he has brought among us a Hebrew to insult us; he came in to me to lie with me, and I cried out with a loud voice, and when he heard that I lifted up my voice and cried, he left his garment with me and fled and got out of the house']" (Gen. 39:13–15):

B. He escaped through the *zekhut* of the fathers, in line with this verse: "And he brought him forth outside" (Gen. 15:5).

C. Simeon of Qitron said, "It was on account of bringing up the bones of Joseph that the sea was split: 'The sea saw it and fled' (Ps. 114:3), on the *zekhut* of this: '... and fled and got out.' "

Zekhut, we see, is both personal and collective, involving the Israelite and Israel as a whole. B refers to Joseph's enjoying the *zekhut* he had inherited, while C refers to Israel's enjoying the *zekhut* that they gained through their supererogatory loyalty to that same *zekhut*-rich personality. How do we know that the *zekhut* left as a heritage by ancestors is in play? Here is an explicit answer:

GENESIS RABBAH LXXIV:XII.1.

A. "If the God of my father, the God of Abraham and the Fear of Isaac, had not been on my side, surely now you would have sent me away empty-handed. God saw my affliction and the labour of my hand and rebuked you last night" (Gen. 31:41–2):

B. Zebedee b. Levi and R. Joshua b. Levi:

C. Zebedee said, "Every passage in which reference is made to 'if' tells of an appeal to the *zekhut* accrued by the patriarchs."

D. Said to him R. Joshua, "But it is written, 'Except we had lingered' (Gen. 43:10) [a passage not related to the *zekhut* of the patriarchs]."

E. He said to him, "They themselves would not have come up except for the *zekhut* of the patriarchs, for if it were not for the *zekhut* of the patriarchs, they never would have been able to go up from there in peace."

The issue of the *zekhut* of the patriarchs comes up in the reference to the God of the fathers. The conception of the *zekhut* of the patriarchs is explicit, not general. It specifies what later benefit to the heir, Israel the family, derived from which particular action of a patriarch (rarely: matriarch):

GENESIS RABBAH XLIII:VIII.2

A. "And Abram gave him a tenth of everything" (Gen. 14:20):

B. R. Judah in the name of R. Nehorai: "On the strength of that blessing the three great pegs on which the world depends, Abraham, Isaac, and Jacob, derived sustenance.

C. "Abraham: 'And the Lord blessed Abraham in *all* things' (Gen. 24:1) on account of the *zekhut* that 'he gave him a tenth of *all* things' (Gen. 14:20).

D. "Isaac: 'And I have eaten of *all*' (Gen. 27:33), on account of the *zekhut* that 'he gave him a tenth of *all* things' (Gen. 14:20).

E. "Jacob: 'Because God has dealt graciously with me and because I have all' (Gen. 33:11) on account of the *zekhut* that 'he gave him a tenth of *all* things' (Gen. 14:20).

Now, we account for the *zekhut* that brings to Israel the grace involved in the priestly blessing:

GENESIS RABBAH XLIII:VIII.3

A. Whence did Israel gain the *zekhut* of receiving the blessing of the priests?

B. R. Judah said, "It was from Abraham: '*So* shall your seed be' (Gen. 15:5), while it is written in connection with the priestly blessing: '*So* shall you bless the children of Israel' " (Num. 6:23).

C. R. Nehemiah said, "It was from Isaac: 'And I and the lad will go *so* far' (Gen. 22:5), therefore said the Holy One, blessed be he, '*So* shall you bless the children of Israel' " (Num. 6:23).

D. And rabbis say, "It was from Jacob: 'So shall you say to the house of Jacob' (Ex. 19:3) (in line with the statement, '*So* shall you bless the children of Israel'" (Num. 6:23).

No. 2 links the blessing at hand with the history of Israel. The reference is to the word "all," which joins the tithe of Abram to the blessing of his descendants. Since the blessing of the priest is at hand, No. 3 treats the origins of the blessing.

The picture is clear. "Israel" constitutes a family as a genealogical and juridical fact. It inherits the estate of the ancestors. It hands on that estate. It lives by the example of the matriarchs and patriarchs, and its history exemplifies events in their lives. And *zekhut* forms the entitlement that one generation may transmit to the next, in a way in which the heritage of sin is not to be transmitted except by reason of the deeds of the successor-generation. The good that one does lives on, the evil is interred with the bones.

This statement appeals to the binding of Isaac as the source of the *zekhut*, deriving from the patriarchs and matriarchs, which will in the end lead to the salvation of Israel. What is important here is that the *zekhut* that is inherited joins together with the *zekhut* of one's own deeds; one inherits the *zekhut* of the past, and, moreover, if one does what the progenitors did, one not only receives an entitlement out of the past, one secures an entitlement on one's own account. So the categorical difference between *zekhut* and sin lies in the sole issue of transmissibility:

GENESIS RABBAH LVI:II.5

A. Said R. Isaac, "And all was on account of the *zekhut* attained by the act of prostration.

B. "Abraham returned in peace from Mount Moriah only on account of the *zekhut* owing to the act of prostration: '... and we will worship [through an act of prostration] and come [then, on that account] again to you' (Gen. 22:5).

C. "The Israelites were redeemed only on account of the *zekhut* owing to the act of prostration: And the people believed ... then they bowed their heads and prostrated themselves' (Ex. 4:31).

D. "The Torah was given only on account of the *zekhut* owing to the act of prostration: 'And worship [prostrate themselves] you afar off' (Ex. 24:1).

E. "Hannah was remembered only on account of the *zekhut* owing to the act of prostration: 'And they worshipped before the Lord' (1 Sam. 1:19).

F. "The exiles will be brought back only on account of the *zekhut* owing to the act of prostration: 'And it shall come to pass in that day that a great horn shall be blown and they shall come that were lost ... and that were dispersed ... and they shall worship the Lord in the holy mountain at Jerusalem' (Is. 27:13).

G. "The Temple was built only on account of the *zekhut* owing to the act of prostration: 'Exalt you the Lord our God and worship at his holy hill' (Ps. 99:9).

H. "The dead will live only on account of the *zekhut* owing to the act of prostration: 'Come let us worship and bend the knee, let us kneel before the Lord our maker'" (Ps. 95:6).

The entire history of Israel flows from its acts of worship ("prostration") beginning with that performed by Abraham at the binding of Isaac. Every sort of advantage Israel has ever gained came about through that act of worship done by Abraham and imitated thereafter. Israel constitutes a family and inherits the *zekhut* laid up as a treasure for the descendants by the ancestors. It draws upon that *zekhut* but, by doing the deeds they did, it also enhances its heritage of *zekhut* and leaves to the descendants greater entitlement than they would enjoy by reason of their own actions. And their own actions – here, prostration in worship – generate *zekhut* as well.

Still, one's own deeds can generate *zekhut* for oneself, with the simple result that *zekhut* is as much personal as it is collective. Specifically, Jacob reflects on the power that Esau's own *zekhut* had gained for Esau. He had gained that *zekhut* by living in the Land of Israel and also by paying honour and respect to Isaac. Jacob then feared that, because of the *zekhut* gained by Esau, he, Jacob, would not be able to overcome him. So *zekhut* worked on its own; it was a credit gained by proper action, which went to the credit of the person who had done that action. What made the action worthy of evoking Heaven's response with an act of supernatural favour? God could not coerce the action, only respond to and reward it. In Esau's case, it was the simple fact that he had remained in the holy land:

GENESIS RABBAH LXXVI:II.

2. A. "Then Jacob was greatly afraid and distressed" (Gen. 32:7): [This is Jacob's soliloquy:] "Because of all those years that Esau was living in the Land of Israel, perhaps he may come against me with the power of the *zekhut* he has now attained by dwelling in the Land of Israel.

B. "Because of all those years of paying honour to his father, perhaps he may come against me with the power of the *zekhut* he attained by honouring his father.

C. "So he said: 'Let the days of mourning for my father be at hand, then I will slay my brother Jacob' (Gen. 27:41).

D. "Now the old man is dead."

The important point, then, is that *zekhut* is not only inherited as part of a collective estate left by the patriarchs. It is also accomplished by an individual in his or her own behalf. By extension, we recognize, the successor-system opens a place for recognition of the individual, both man and woman as a matter of fact, within the system of *zekhut*. As we shall now see, what a man or a woman does may win for that person an entitlement upon Heaven for supernatural favour of some sort. So there is space, in the system, for a private person, and the individual is linked to the social order through the shared possibilities of generating or inheriting an entitlement upon Heaven.

For if we now ask, what are the sorts of deeds that generate *zekhut*, we realize that those deeds produce a common result of gaining for the actor, as much as for his heirs, an entitlement for Heavenly favour, grace, and support when needed. And that fact concerning gaining and benefiting from *zekhut* brings us to the systemic message to the living generation, its account of what now is to be done. That message proves acutely contemporary, for its stress is on the power of a single action to create sufficient *zekhut* to outweigh a life of sin. Then the contrast between sin and *zekhut* gains greater depth still. One sin of sufficient weight condemns, one act of *zekhut* of sufficient weight saves; the entire issue of entitlements out of the past gives way when we realize what is actually at stake.

Torah-study is one – but only one – means for an individual to gain access to that heritage, to get *zekhut*. There are other equally suitable means, and, not only so, but the merit gained by Torah-study is no different from the merit gained by acts of a supererogatory character. If one gets *zekhut* for studying the Torah, then we must suppose there is no holy deed that does not generate its share of *zekhut*. But when it comes to specifying the things one does to get *zekhut*, the documents before us speak of what the Torah does not require but does recommend: not what we are commanded to do in detail, but what the right attitude, formed within the Torah, leads us to do on our own volition:

YERUSHALMI-TRACTATE TAANIT 3:11.IV.

C. There was a house that was about to collapse over there [in Babylonia], and Rab set one of his disciples in the house, until they had cleared out everything from the house. When the disciple left the house, the house collapsed.

D. And there are those who say that it was R. Adda bar Ahwah.

E. Sages sent and said to him, "What sort of good deeds are to your credit [that you have that much merit]?"

F. He said to them, "In my whole life no man ever got to the synagogue in the morning before I did. I never left anybody there when I went out. I never walked four cubits without speaking words of Torah. Nor did I ever mention teachings of Torah in an inappropriate setting. I never laid out a bed and slept for a regular period of time. I never took great strides among the associates. I never called my fellow by a nickname. I never rejoiced in the embarrassment of my fellow. I never cursed my fellow when I was lying by myself in bed. In the marketplace I never walked over to someone who owed me money.

G. "In my entire life I never lost my temper in my household."

H. This was meant to carry out that which is stated as follows: "I will give heed to the way that is blameless. Oh when wilt thou come to me? I will walk with integrity of heart within my house" (Ps. 101:2).

What I find striking in this story is that mastery of the Torah is only one means of attaining the merit that enabled the sage to keep the house from collapsing. For what the sage did to gain such remarkable merit is not to master such-and-so many tractates of the Mishnah. Nor does the storyteller refer to carrying out the commandments of the Torah as specified. It was rather acts of that expressed courtesy, consideration, restraint. These acts, which no specification can encompass in detail, produced the right attitude, one of gentility, that led to gaining merit. Acts rewarded with an entitlement to supernatural power are those of self-abnegation or the avoidance of power over others – not taking great strides among the associates, not using a nickname, not rejoicing in the embarrassment of one's fellow, not singling out one's debtor – and the submission to the will of others.

What about what we have to do to secure an inheritance of *zekhut* for our heirs? Here is a concrete example of how acts of worth or *zekhut* accrue to the benefit of the heirs of those that do them. What makes it especially indicative is that gentiles – always represented, to be sure, in relationship to Israel, not on their own – have the power to acquire *zekhut* for their descendants, which is coherent with the system's larger interest in not only Israel (as against the faceless, undifferentiated outsider) but the gentiles as well.

GENESIS RABBAH C:VI.I

A. "When they came to the threshing floor of Atad, which is beyond the Jordan, they lamented there with a very great and sorrowful lamentation, and he made a mourning for his father seven days" (Gen. 50:10):

B. Said R. Samuel bar Nahman, "We have reviewed the entire Scripture and found no other place called Atad. And can there be a threshing floor for thorns [the Hebrew word for thorn being *atad*]?

C. "But this refers to the Canaanites. It teaches that they were worthy of being threshed like thorns. And on account of what *zekhut* were they saved? It was on account of the acts of kindness that they performed for our father, Jacob [on the occasion of the mourning for his death]."

D. And what were the acts of kindness that they performed for our father, Jacob?

E. R. Eleazar said, "[When the bier was brought up there,] they unloosened the girdle of their loins."

F. R. Simeon b. Laqish said, "They untied the shoulder-knots."

G. R. Judah b. R. Shalom said, "They pointed with their fingers and said, 'This is a grievous mourning to the Egyptians' (Gen. 50:11).

H. Rabbis said, "They stood upright."

I. Now is it not an argument *a fortiori*: now if these, who did not do a thing with their hands or feet, but only because they pointed their fingers, were saved from punishment, Israel, which performs an act of kindness [for the dead] whether they are adults or children, whether with their hands or with their feet, how much the more so [will they enjoy the *zekhut* of being saved from punishment]!

J. Said R. Abbahu, "Those seventy days that lapsed between the first letter and the second match the seventy days that the Egyptians paid respect to Jacob. [Seventy days elapsed from Haman's letter of destruction until Mordecai's letter announcing the repeal of the decree (cf. Est. 3:12, 8:9). The latter letter, which permitted the Jews to take vengeance on their would-be destroyers, should have come earlier, but it was delayed seventy days as a reward for the honour shown by the Egyptians to Jacob."

The Egyptians gained *zekhut* by honouring Jacob in his death, according to Abbahu. This same point then registers for the Canaanites. The connection is somewhat far-fetched, that is, through the reference to the threshing floor, but the point is a strong one. And the explanation of history extends not only to Israel's but also the Canaanites' history.

If the Egyptians and the Canaanites, how much the more so Israelites! What is it that Israelites as a nation do to gain a lien upon Heaven for themselves or entitlements of supernatural favour for their descendants? Here is one representative answer to that question:

GENESIS RABBAH LXXIV:XII.I.

A. "If the God of my father, the God of Abraham and the Fear of Isaac, had not been on my side, surely now you would have sent me away empty-handed. God saw my affliction and the labour of my hand and rebuked you last night" (Gen. 31:41–2):

B. Zebedee b. Levi and R. Joshua b. Levi:

C. Zebedee said, "Every passage in which reference is made to 'if' tells of an appeal to the *zekhut* accrued by the patriarchs."

D. Said to him R. Joshua, "But it is written, 'Except we had lingered' (Gen. 43:10) [a passage not related to the *zekhut* of the patriarchs]."

E. He said to him, "They themselves would not have come up except for the *zekhut* of the patriarchs, for it if it were not for the *zekhut* of the patriarchs, they never would have been able to go up from there in peace."

F. Said R. Tanhuma, "There are those who produce the matter in a different version." [It is given as follows:]

G. R. Joshua and Zebedee b. Levi:

H. R. Joshua said, "Every passage in which reference is made to 'if' tells of an appeal to the *zekhut* accrued by the patriarchs except for the present case."

I. He said to him, "This case too falls under the category of an appeal to the *zekhut* of the patriarchs."

So much for *zekhut* that is inherited from the patriarchs. But what about the deeds of Israel in the here and now?

J. R. Yohanan said, "It was on account of the *zekhut* achieved through sanctification of the divine name."

K. R. Levi said, "It was on account of the *zekhut* achieved through faith and the *zekhut* achieved through Torah."

Faith despite the here and now, study of the Torah – these are what Israel does in the here and now, with the result that they gain an entitlement for themselves or their heirs.

L. "The *zekhut* achieved through faith: 'If I had not believed ...' (Ps. 27:13).

M. "The *zekhut* achieved through Torah: 'Unless your Torah had been my delight' " (Ps. 119:92).

2. A. "God saw my affliction and the labour of my hand and rebuked you last night" (Gen. 31:41–2):

B. Said R. Jeremiah b. Eleazar, "More beloved is hard labour than the *zekhut* achieved by the patriarchs, for the *zekhut* achieved by the patriarchs served to afford protection for property only, while the *zekhut* achieved by hard labour served to afford protection for lives.

C. "The *zekhut* achieved by the patriarchs served to afford protection for property only: 'If the God of my father, the God of Abraham and the Fear of Isaac, had not been on my side, surely now you would have sent me away empty-handed.'

D. "The *zekhut* achieved by hard labour served to afford protection for lives: 'God saw my affliction and the labor of my hand and rebuked you last night.'"

Here is as good an account as any of the theology that finds a probative, exemplary detail in the category *zekhut*. The issue of the *zekhut* of the patriarchs comes up in the reference to the God of the fathers. The conception of the *zekhut* of the patriarchs is explicit, not general. It specifies what later benefit to the heir, Israel the family, derived from which particular action of a patriarch or matriarch. But acts of faith and Torah-study form only one medium; hard labour, that is, devotion to one's calling, defines that source of *zekhut* that is going to be accessible to those many Israelites unlikely to distinguish themselves either by Torah-study and acts of faith, encompassing the sanctification of God's name, or by acts of amazing gentility and restraint.

The systemic statements made by the usages of *zekhut* speak of relationship, function, the interplay of humanity and God. One's store of *zekhut* derives from a relationship, that is, from one's forebears. That is one dimension of the relationships in which one stands. *Zekhut* also forms a measure of one's own relationship with Heaven, as the power of one person, but not another, to pray and so bring rain attests. What sort of relationship does *zekhut*, as the opposite of sin, then posit? It is one of autonomous grace, for Heaven cannot force us to do those types of deeds that yield *zekhut*, and that, story after story suggests, is the definition of a deed that generates *zekhut*: doing what we ought to do but do not have to do. But then, we cannot coerce Heaven to do what we want done either, for example, by carrying out the commandments. These are obligatory, but do not obligate Heaven.

This exposition of a single concept through one source after another would prove tedious, were the materials themselves not so engaging on their own, and were the issues not so critical. Nonetheless, we may easily lose sight of the central position of this concept in the account of the sages' theology. Hence it is appropriate, now, to return to the starting point, the relationship of man to God that I have characterized as complementary. A simple answer is demanded to the question, why does *zekhut* form the centrepiece in the sages' doctrine of how God and man require one another? Whence – in mythic language – our lien on Heaven? A few words contain the response: God needs man's love, man needs God's grace, and neither can coerce the other to give what, by definition, cannot be coerced at all. The relationship of complementarity is realized through man's deeds of a supererogatory character – to which Heaven responds by deeds of a supererogatory character.

That defines the heart and soul of the sages' theology of man's relationship to God. Self-abnegation or restraint shown by man precipitates a counterpart attitude in Heaven, hence generating *zekhut*. The complementary relationship measured by *zekhut* – Heaven's response by an act of uncoerced favour to a person's uncoerced gift, for example, act of gentility, restraint, or self-abnegation – contains an element of unpredictability for which appeal to the *zekhut* inherited from ancestors accounts. So while one cannot coerce Heaven, he can through *zekhut* gain acts of favour from Heaven, and that is by doing what Heaven cannot require but only desire. Heaven then responds to man's attitude in carrying out what transcends his duties. The simple fact that rabbis cannot pray and bring rain, but a simple ass-driver can, tells the whole story. That act of pure disinterest – giving the woman his means of livelihood – is the one that gains for him Heaven's deepest interest. And we must not miss the starting point of the transaction, the woman's act of utter and tangible self-sacrifice in behalf of her husband, which wins the ass-driver's empathy and provokes the action to which Heaven responds.

"Make his wishes yours, so that he will make your wishes his ... From anyone from whom people take pleasure God takes pleasure" (tractate Abot 2:4). These two statements hold together the two principal elements of the conception of the relationship to God that the single word *zekhut* conveys. Give up, please others, do not impose your will but give way to the will of the other, and Heaven will respond by giving a lien that is not coerced but evoked. By the rationality of discipline within, man has the power to form rational relationships beyond ourselves, with Heaven; and that is how the system expands the boundaries of the social order to encompass not only the natural but also the supernatural world. The conviction that, by dint of special effort, a person may so conduct himself as to acquire an entitlement of supernatural power turns his commonplace circumstance into an arena encompassing Heaven and earth. God responds to holy Israel's virtue, filling the gap that one leaves when he forebears, withdraws, and gives up: his space, his self-hood. Then God responds; man's sacrifice evokes memories of Abraham's readiness to sacrifice Isaac.

We observe at the end that order is ultimately attained by transcending the very rules of order. In order to establish the moral order of justice, therefore, God breaks the rules, accords an entitlement to this one, who has done some one remarkable deed, but not to that one, who has done nothing wrong and everything right. So a life in accord with the rules – even a life spent in the study of the Torah – in Heaven's view is outweighed by a single moment, a gesture that violates the norm, extending the outer limits of the rule, for instance, of virtue. And who but a God who, like us, feels, not only thinks, responds to impulse and sentiment, can be portrayed in such a way as this?

So I sold my ass and I gave her the proceeds, and I said to her, 'Here is your money, free your husband, but do not sin [by becoming a prostitute to raise the necessary funds].' They said to him, "You are worthy of praying and having your prayers answered."

No rule exhaustively describes a world such as this. We are in God's image, after God's likeness, not only because we penetrate through right thinking the principles of creation, but because we replicate through right attitude the heart of the Creator. Humanity on earth, the Israelite family in particular, incarnates God on high, and, in consequence, earth and Heaven join.

This brings us back to the principle of complementarity. What is asked of Israel and of the Israelite is Godly restraint, supernatural generosity of soul that is "in our image, after our likeness": that is what sets aside all rules. The bounds of earth have now extended to Heaven. God dwells with Israel, in Israel: "today, if you will it," a phrase we shall meet when we ask when the Messiah is going to come. The sages portray a social order in which in relationship to God Israelites and Israel alike control their own destiny. This they do by ceasing to exercise control and submitting to God's will and purpose. Both the nation and the individual have in hand the power to shape the future. How is this to be done? It is not alone by keeping the Torah, studying the Torah, dressing, eating, making a living, marrying, procreating, raising a family, burying and being buried, all in accord with those rules. That life in conformity with the rule, obligatory but merely conventional, does not evoke the special interest of Heaven. Why should it? The rules describe the ordinary.

But "God wants the heart," and that is not an ordinary thing. Nor is the power to bring rain or hold up a tottering house gained through a life of merely ordinary sanctity. Special favour responded to extraordinary actions, in the analogy of special disfavour, misfortune deemed to punish sin. And just as culpable sin, as distinct from mere error, requires an act of will, specifically, arrogance, so an act of extraordinary character requires an act of will. But, as mirror image of sin, the act would reveal in a concrete way an attitude of restraint, forbearance, gentility, and self-abnegation. A sinful act, provoking Heaven, was one that deliberately defied Heaven. An act that would evoke Heaven's favour, so imposing upon Heaven a lien that Heaven freely gave, was one that, equally deliberately and concretely, displayed humility.

Now to look ahead to what must follow. Complementarity shades over into correspondence. For, in stressing the complementarity of God and man, we ought not to miss their correspondence at the deepest levels of sentiment and emotion and attitude. The one completes the other through common acts of humility, forbearance, accommodation, a spirit of conciliation. In the first place, Scripture itself is explicit that God shares and responds to the attitudes and intentionality of human beings. God cares what humanity feels – wanting love, for example – and so the conception that actions that express right attitudes of humility will evoke in Heaven a desired response will not have struck as novel the authors of the Pentateuch or the various prophetic writings, for example. The Written Torah's record of God's feelings and God's will concerning the feelings of humanity leaves no room for doubt.

Before turning from the relationship of complementarity to the closely similar relationship of correspondence between man and God, let us fix firmly in mind the two results of this inquiry: first, the conception that acts of omission or commission expressing an attitude of forbearance and self-abnegation generate *zekhut* in particular; and, second, the principle that *zekhut* functions in those very specific ways that the system deems critical: as the power to attest to human transformation and regeneration, affording that power inhering in weakness, that wealth inhering in giving up what one has, that in the end promise the attainment of our goals.

When we deem the attitude of affirmation and acceptance, rather than aggression, and the intentionality of self-abnegation and forbearance, to define the means for gaining *zekhut*, what we are saying is contrary and paradoxical. It is this: if you want to have, then give up. If you want to impose your judgment, then make the judgment of the other into your own. If you want to coerce Heaven, then evoke in Heaven attitudes of sympathy that will lead to the actions or events that you want, whether rain, whether long life, whether the salvation of Israel and its hegemony over the nations. So, too to rule, be ruled by Heaven; to show that Heaven rules, give up what you want to the other.

Embodying all of these views in a single, protean concept, *zekhut*, results: the lien upon Heaven, freely given by Heaven in response to one's free surrender to the will and wish of Heaven. And by means of *zekhut*, whether one's own, whether one's ancestors', the social order finds its shape and system, and the individual his or her place within its structure.

The ultimate statement of complementarity is left for the end: man, woman, and God, described in so many words as one: there is no possibility for the one to endure without the other:

GENESIS RABBAH VIII:IX.2

2. A. Said R. Simlai, "In any passage in which you find an answer that heretics may give, you find a remedy right alongside."

B. They went and asked him, "What is the sense of the verse of Scripture, 'And God said, "Let us make man"' (Gen. 1:26)?

C. He said to him, "Read the verse immediately following. What is written is not, 'And gods created man' [using the verb in the plural], but rather, 'And God created man' (Gen. 1:27) [using the singular form of the verb]."

D. His disciples asked him, after the others had gone out, "These you have pushed aside with a mere reed, but what are you going to answer us?"

E. He said to them, "To begin with, man was created from the dust, and Eve was created from man. [Man without woman is dirt, woman without man has no existence.] But from this point onward: 'In our image, after our likeness' (Gen. 1:26).

F. "There is no possibility for a man without a woman, nor for a woman without a man, nor for the two of them without the Presence of God."

So matters of complementarity shade over into the issue of correspondence: in what way is man like God? And the answer carries us to the Oral Torah's doctrine of theological anthropology.

9 Correspondence

Man not only complements God, he also is like God. When the sages read in the Torah that man is created in God's image, they understood that to mean that God and man correspond, bearing comparable traits. These have now to be examined. The theological anthropology of the Oral Torah, treating the study of man as a chapter in the knowledge of God, in whose image man is made, defined correspondence between God and man in three ways: intellectually, sharing a common rationality; emotionally, sharing common sentiments and attitudes; and physically, sharing common features. That is why, to begin with, God and Israel relate. They think alike. They feel the same sentiments. And they look alike. Like God, man is in command of, and responsible for, his own will and intentionality and consequent conduct. The very fact that God reveals himself through the Torah, which man is able to understand, there to be portrayed in terms and categories that man grasps, shows how the characteristics of God and man prove comparable. The first difference between man and God is that man sins, but the one and the just God, never; connecting "God" and "sin" yields an unintelligible result. And the second difference between creature and Creator, man and God, is that God is God. The former matter we take up in chapter 11, where theological anthropology addresses a very particular, and critical issue, sin on its own terms.

Let us start with the most startling point, that correspondence encompasses not only intangible but also material qualities. How do God and man compare in physical presence? Because theology in its later, philosophical mode has long insisted on the incorporeality of God, we take up in some detail the Oral

Torah's explicit claim that God and man look exactly alike, being distinguished only by actions performed by the one but not the other:

GENESIS RABBAH VIII:X.I

A. Said R. Hoshayya, "When the Holy One, blessed be he, came to create the first man, the ministering angels mistook him [for God, since man was in God's image,] and wanted to say before him, 'Holy, [holy, holy is the Lord of hosts].'

B. "To what may the matter be compared? To the case of a king and a governor who were set in a chariot, and the provincials wanted to greet the king, 'Sovereign!' But they did not know which one of them was which. What did the king do? He turned the governor out and put him away from the chariot, so that people would know who was king.

C. "So too when the Holy One, blessed be he, created the first man, the angels mistook him [for God]. What did the Holy One, blessed be he, do? He put him to sleep, so everyone knew that he was a mere man.

D. "That is in line with the following verse of Scripture: 'Cease you from man, in whose nostrils is a breath, for how little is he to be accounted'" (Is. 2:22).

Man – Adam – is in God's image, interpreted in a physical way, so the angels did not know man from God. Only the fact that man sleeps distinguishes him from God.

The theme derives from the verse that states, "in our image, after our likeness" (Gen. 1:26). While this passage is not cited in the present construction, Genesis Rabbah VIII:X simply carries forward the concluding entry of Genesis Rabbah VIII:IX, examined at the end of chapter 8, in which the relevant verse is cited. Accordingly, "in our image" yields two views, first, that the complete image of man is attained in a divine union between humanity – man and woman – and, further, that what makes man different from God is that man sleeps, and God does not sleep.

Here is another clear statement that represents God in the form of a man, now as seen in the interpretation of the vision of the prophet Zechariah:

BAVLI-TRACTATE SANHEDRIN I:I.XLII [93A

A. And said R. Yohanan, "What is the meaning of the verse of Scripture, 'I saw by night, and behold a man riding upon a red horse, and he stood among the myrtle trees that were in the bottom' (Zech. 1:8)?

B. What is the meaning of, 'I saw by night'?

C. "The Holy One blessed be he, sought to turn the entire world into night.

D.   "'And behold, a man riding' – 'man' refers only to the Holy One, blessed be he, as it is said, 'The Lord is a man of war, the Lord is his name' (Ex. 15:3).

E.   "'On a red horse' – the Holy One, blessed be he, sought to turn the entire world to blood.

F.   "When, however, he saw Hananiah, Mishael, and Azariah, he cooled off, as it is said, 'And he stood among the myrtle trees that were in the deep.'"

Scripture knows that God has a face, upon which human beings are not permitted to gaze. But was that face was understood in a physical way, and to God are other human, physical characteristics ascribed? An affirmative answer emerges entirely clearly in the following:

BAVLI-TRACTATE BERAKHOT I:2 III.39/7A

A.   "And he said, 'You cannot see my face'" (Ex. 33:20).

B.   It was taught on Tannaite authority in the name of R. Joshua b. Qorha, "This is what the Holy One, blessed be he, said to Moses:

C.   'When I wanted [you to see my face], you did not want to, now that you want to see my face, I do not want you to.'"

No one in the composition doubts that God has a face, which man may or may not see, and that God has physical traits is never called into question:

D.   This differs from what R. Samuel bar Nahmani said R. Jonathan said.

E.   For R. Samuel bar Nahmani said R. Jonathan said, "As a reward for three things he received the merit of three things.

F.   "As a reward for: 'And Moses hid his face,' (Ex. 3:6), he had the merit of having a glistening face.

G.   "As a reward for: 'Because he was afraid to' (Ex. 3:6), he had the merit that 'They were afraid to come near him' (Ex. 34:30).

H.   "As a reward for: 'To look upon God' (Ex. 3:6), he had the merit: 'The similitude of the Lord does he behold'" (Num. 12:8).

A.   "And I shall remove my hand and you shall see my back" (Ex. 33:23)

B.   Said R. Hana bar Bizna said R. Simeon the Pious, "This teaches that the Holy One, blessed be he, showed Moses [how to tie] the knot of the phylacteries."

That God is able to tie the knot indicates that (in the present context at least) God has fingers and other physical gifts. God furthermore is portrayed as wearing phylacteries as well. It follows that God has an arm and a forehead. There is no element of a figurative reading of the indicated traits, no defence or apology for invoking a mere metaphor. Quite the opposite, in passage after passage, without the slightest trace of embarrassment or reservation, the correspondence of God and man yields a variety of physical traits. Indeed, the entirety of the Song of Songs is read as an account of God's love for Israel, and Israel's for God, and for the sages the most suitable way of expressing that account required the physicalization of God and of Israel alike.

That is why, when God is further represented as having eyes and teeth, we have every reason to receive the account as a sustained representation of God in light of his own declaration about man in his image, after his likeness:

BAVLI-TRACTATE KETUBOT 13:11 III.31/111B

A. "His eyes shall be red with wine, and his teeth white with milk" (Gen. 49:12):
B. R. Dimi, when he came, interpreted the verse in this way: "The congregation of Israel said to the Holy One, blessed be he, 'Lord of the Universe, wink to me with your eyes, which gesture will be sweeter than wine, and show me your teeth, which gesture will be sweeter than milk.'"

The attribution of physical traits is explicit and no longer general or possibly figurative. Another such representation assigns to God cheeks:

BAVLI-TRACTATE SHABBAT 88B

A. R. Joshua b. Levi, "What is the meaning of the verse, 'His cheeks are as a bed of spices' (Song 5:13)?
B. "At every act of speech which went forth from the mouth of the Holy One, blessed be he, the entire world was filled with the fragrance of spices."
C. But since at the first first act of speech, the world was filled, where did the second act of speech go?
D. The Holy One, blessed be he, took from his treasures a strong wind, which removed the first draft of fragrance in sequence."

From eyes and teeth and cheeks, we move on to arms and hands:

BAVLI-TRACTATE TAANIT 4A

E. Further, [the congregation of Israel] made its request in an improper manner, "O God, set me as a seal on your heart, as a seal on your arm" (Song 8:6).
F. [But the Holy One, blessed be he, responded in a proper way.] Said the Holy One, blessed be he, to [the congregation of Israel,] "My daughter, now you are asking for

something which sometimes can be seen and sometimes cannot be seen. But I shall give you something which can always be seen.

G. "For it is said, 'Behold, I have graven you on the palms of my hands' (Is. 49:16) [and the palms are always visible, in a way in which the heart and arm are not]."

Hands are attached to arms, and it is implicit that God has arms as well. That God has arms again is shown by the claim that God puts on phylacteries just as Moses does:

BAVLI-TRACTATE BERAKHOT I:I III.21/6A

A. Said R. Abin bar Ada said R. Isaac, "How do we know on the basis of Scripture that the Holy One, blessed be he, puts on phylacteries? As it is said, 'The Lord has sworn by his right hand, and by the arm of his strength' (Is. 62:8).

B. " 'By his right hand' refers to Torah, as it is said, 'At his right hand was a fiery law for them' (Deut. 33:2).

C. " 'And by the arm of his strength' refers to phylacteries, as it is said, 'The Lord will give strength to his people' (Ps. 29:11).

D. "And how do we know that phylacteries are a strength for Israel? For it is written, 'And all the peoples of the earth shall see that the name of the Lord is called upon you and they shall be afraid of you' " (Deut. 28:10).

E. And it has been taught on Tannaite authority:

F. R. Eliezer the Great says, "This [Deut. 28:10] refers to the phylacteries that are put on the head."

Once more we find clear evidence of a corporeal conception of God. We have no basis on which to believe that the text at hand meant a (merely) poetic characterization, or, indeed, what such a more spiritual interpretation would have required. Assuming that the words mean precisely what they say, we have to conclude that God is here portrayed as incarnate. Later on we shall be told what passages of Scripture are written in the phylacteries that God puts onto his right arm and forehead. We recall the complementary relationship of God and man in the matter of actions involving uncoerced generosity and grace. In due course we shall also contemplate the correspondence in emotions and sentiments between God and man. That, in the end, turns out to be crucial to the entire theology of the Oral Torah, the point of conflict and tension between the loving God who commands and the churlish, rebellious man who disobeys. The reason is, the One understands the other – all too well.

Beyond the words of the Torah, God makes himself manifest to man in many ways, most of them corporeal. It is quite proper, in the sages' view, to imagine God in human form; God makes himself manifest in ways in which man can comprehend, and God becomes accessible to man by taking on forms that man can grasp:

PESIQTA DERAB KAHANA XII:XXV

1. A. Another interpretation of "I am the Lord your God [who brought you out of the land of Egypt"] (Ex. 20:2):

B. Said R. Hinena bar Papa, "The Holy One, blessed be he, had made his appearance to them with a stern face, with a neutral face, with a friendly face, with a happy face.

C. "with a stern face: in Scripture. When a man teaches his son Torah, he has to teach him in a spirit of awe.

D. "with a neutral face: in Mishnah.

E. "with a friendly face: in Talmud.

F. "with a happy face: in lore.

G. "Said to them the Holy One, blessed be he, 'Even though you may see all of these diverse faces of mine, nonetheless: "I am the Lord your God who brought you out of the land of Egypt" ' " (Ex. 20:2).

So far we deal with attitudes. As to the iconic representation of God, the following is explicit:

2. A. Said R. Levi, "The Holy One, blessed be he, had appeared to them like an icon that has faces in all directions, so that if a thousand people look at it, it appears to look at them as well.

B. "So too when the Holy One, blessed be he, when he was speaking, each and every Israelite would say, 'With me in particular the Word speaks.'

C. "What is written here is not, I am the Lord, your [plural] God, but rather, 'I am the Lord your [singular] God who brought you out of the land of Egypt' " (Ex. 20:2).

That God may show diverse faces to various people is now established. The reason for God's variety is made explicit. People differ, and God, in the image of whom all mortals are made, must therefore sustain diverse images – all of them formed in the model of human beings:

3. A. Said R. Yosé bar Hanina, "And it was in accord with the capacity of each one of them to listen and understand what the Word spoke with him.

B. And do not be surprised at this matter, for when the mana came down to Israel, each and every one would find its taste appropriate to his capacity, infants in accord with their capacity, young people in accord with their capacity, old people in accord with their capacity.

C. "infants in accord with their capacity: just as an infant sucks from the tit of his mother, so was its flavour, as it is said, 'Its taste was like the taste of rich cream' (Num. 11:8).

D. "young people in accord with their capacity: as it is said, 'My bread also which I gave you, bread and oil and honey' (Ez. 16:19)

E. "old people in accord with their capacity: as it is said 'the taste of it was like wafers made with honey' (Ex. 16:31).

F. "Now if in the case of mana, each and every one would find its taste appropriate to his capacity, so in the matter of the Word, each and every one understood in accord with capacity.

The same is so for God's voice:

G. "Said David, 'The voice of the Lord is [in accord with one's] in strength' (Ps. 29:4).

H. "What is written is not, 'in accord with his strength in particular, but rather, in accord with one's strength,' meaning, in accord with the capacity of each and every one.

I. "Said to them the Holy One, blessed be He, 'It is not in accord with the fact that you hear a great many voices, but you should know that it is I who [speaks to all of you individually]: 'I am the Lord your God who brought you out of the land of Egypt'" (Ex. 20:2).

The individuality and particularity of God rest upon the diversity of humanity. Yet, it must follow, the model of humanity – "in our image" – dictates how we are to envisage the face of God.

But first comes shared rules of intellect, which render God and man consubstantial. God and man intellectually correspond in the common logic and reason that they share. That is in two aspects. First, like Abraham at Sodom, the sages simply took for granted that the same rationality governs. God is compelled by arguments man finds persuasive, appeals to which man responds: "Will not the Judge of all the world ..." Second, meeting God through the study of the record of God's self-revelation, the Torah, the sages worked out their conviction that man's mind corresponded to God's, which is why man can receive the Torah to begin with. That man can study the Torah proves that man has the capacity to know God intellectually. That explains why they maintained that God is to be met in the study of the Torah, where his presence will come to rest. God's Presence, then, came to rest with those who, in an act of intellect, took up the labour of Torah-learning:

TRACTATE ABOT 3:6

A. R. Halafta of Kefar Hananiah says, "Among ten who sit and work hard on Torah the Presence comes to rest,

B. "as it is said, 'God stands in the congregation of God' (Ps. 82:1).

C. "And how do we know that the same is so even of five? For it is said, 'And he has founded his group upon the earth' (Am. 9:6).

D. "And how do we know that this is so even of three? Since it is said, 'And he judges among the judges' (Ps. 82:1).

E. "And how do we know that this is so even of two? Because it is said, 'Then they that feared the Lord spoke with one another, and the Lord hearkened and heard' (Mal. 3:16).

F. "And how do we know that this is so even of one? Since it is said, 'In every place where I record my name I will come to you and I will bless you' " (Ex. 20:24).

But there is more. The sages took as their task not only passive learning of the Torah but active and thoroughly critical participation in the inquiry into the meaning of the Torah. It is one thing to absorb the Torah, quite another to join in the processes of thought, the right way of thinking, that sustain the Torah.

Through their critical, analytical inquiry into the Torah and its law, the sages intended to gain access to the modes of thought that guided the formation of the Torah. Their strategy involved, for instance, dialectical argument concerning comparison and contrast in this way, not in that, identification of categories in one manner, not in another. Those were the modes of thought that, in the sages' conception, dictated the structure of intellect upon which the Torah rested. The sages could meet God in the Torah. In their analysis of the deepest structures of intellect of the Torah, they hoped to enter into the mind of God, showing how God's mind, expressed in God's words, worked when God formed the Torah. And there, in the intellect of God, man gained access to God. But in discerning how God's mind worked, the sages claimed for themselves a place in that very process of thought that had given birth to the Torah.

This view that God thinks like man and therefore man thinks like God, that God responds to man's argument and insight as much as man to God's logic portrayed by the Torah, is expressed in the following tale, which involves God and the saints in Heaven studying the Torah together. They came upon a problem that stymied them and required a great sage, then still alive, to help them solve it. So they called him up to the Heavenly academy, or *yeshiva* ("session" in the following translation) to join in the argument.

BAVLI-TRACTATE BABA MESIA 86A

A. [Rabbah bar Nahmani] was in session on the trunk of a palm and studying.

B. Now in the session in the firmament they were debating the following subject: If the bright spot preceded the white hair, he is unclean, and if the white hair preceded the bright spot, he is clean. [The Mishnah-paragraph continues: and if it is a matter of doubt, he is unclean.

C. And R. Joshua was in doubt] (M. Neg. 4:11F-H) –

D. the Holy One, blessed be he, says, "It is clean."

E. And the entire session in the firmament say, "Unclean." [We see, therefore, that in Heaven, Mishnah-study was going forward, with the Holy One participating and setting forth his ruling, as against the consensus of the other sages of the Torah in heaven.]

F. They said, "Who is going to settle the question? It is Rabbah b. Nahmani."

Here is an explicit statement of the correspondence of man's and God's intellects; they think alike. That makes all the more urgent the study of the Torah, where God sets forth his plan for creation and his will for man, since, in the words of the Torah, man penetrates into the modes of thought and rationality that yielded those words, that is to say, the very mind of God.

BAVLI BABA MESIA 86A

G. For said Rabbah b. Nahmani, "I am absolutely unique in my knowledge of the marks of skin-disease that is unclean and in the rules of uncleanness having to do with the corpse in the tent."

H. They sent an angel for him, but the angel of death could not draw near to him, since his mouth did not desist from repeating his learning. But in the meanwhile a wind blew and caused a rustling in the bushes, so he thought it was a troop of soldiers. He said, "Let me die but not be handed over to the kingdom."

I. When he was dying, he said, "It is clean, it is clean." An echo came forth and said, "Happy are you, Rabbah bar Nahmani, that your body is clean, and your soul has come forth in cleanness." [The body would not putrefy.]

J. A note fell down from heaven in Pumbedita: "Rabbah bar Nahmani has been invited to the session that is on high."

The critical point in this story comes at three turnings. First, God and the sages in heaven study the Torah in the same way as the Torah is studied on earth. Second, God is bound by the same rules of rationality as prevail down here. Third, the sage on earth studies the way God does in heaven, and God calls up to heaven sages whose exceptional acuity and perspicacity are required on the occasion. God is bound by the same rules of logical analysis and sound discourse that govern sages.

In their delineation of correct hierarchical logic, the sages maintained that they uncovered, within the Torah (hence by definition, written and oral components of The Torah alike) an adumbration of the working of the mind of God. That is because the premise of all discourse is that the Torah was written by God and dictated by God to Moses at Sinai. Here is the point at which the correspondence of man and God bears profound theological meaning. It is one thing to absorb the Torah, oral and written, and it is quite another to join in the processes of thought, the right way of thinking, that sustain the Torah. That is what the sages maintained that they did. In their study they proposed to gain access to the modes of thought that guided the formation of the Torah, oral and written alike. A simple conclusion is the sole possible one. For their minds, like God's, penetrated reality through the same paths. The sages, in insisting that man's and God's minds correspond, claimed for themselves a place in that very process of thought that had given birth to The Torah. They could debate about the Torah because, knowing how the Torah originally was written, they, too, could write (though not reveal) the Torah. That is, man is like God, but God is always god.

This view of man's capacity to join his mind with God's is not left merely implicit. God not only follows and joins in the argument of the laws of the Torah conducted by sages. God is party to the argument and subjects himself to the ruling formed by the consensus of sages – and says so. God not only participates in the debate but takes pride when his children win the argument over him. The miracles of nature cast God's ballot – which does not count over man's reason. God's judgment, as at Sodom, is outweighed by reason, which man exercises, and which takes priority in the reading of the Torah's laws even over God's judgment!

In the following story, we find an explicit affirmation of the priority of reasoned argument over all other forms of discovery of truth:

BAVLI-TRACTATE BABA MESIA 59A-B

A. There we have learned: If one cut [a clay oven] into parts [so denying it its normal form as an oven] but put sand between the parts, [so permitting it to function as an oven]

B. Eliezer declares the oven [broken-down and therefore] insusceptible to uncleanness. [A utensil that is broken and loses the form in which it is useful is deemed null, and so it cannot receive the uncleanness that pertains to whole and useful objects.]

C. And sages declare it susceptible [because while it is formally broken it is functionally useful, and therefore retains the status of an ordinary utensil].
D. And this is what is meant by the oven of Akhenai (Mishnah-tractate Kelim 5:10).

Up to this point we have examined only the statement of the issue, which, as we see, concerns in practical terms the theoretical problem of what defines an object, form or function. When an object loses its ordinary form, it ceases to belong to its category, so the one side. But so long as an object accomplishes that for which it is made, its teleology, it remains within its category, so the other side. No philosopher will have found the dispute a difficult problem to follow. But what has God to do with all this? Now comes the answer:

E. Why [is it called] the oven of Akhenai?
F. Said R. Judah said Samuel, "It is because they surrounded it with argument as with a snake and proved it was insusceptible to uncleanness."
G. It has been taught on Tannaite authority:

Here come God's ballots, the miracles, and the sages' rejection of them in favour of arguments devised by man:

H. On that day R. Eliezer produced all of the arguments in the world, but they did not accept them from him. So he said to them, "If the law accords with my position, this carob tree will prove it."
I. The carob was uprooted from its place by a hundred cubits – and some say, four hundred cubits.
J. They said to him, "There is no proof from a carob tree."
K. So he went and said to them, "If the law accords with my position, let the stream of water prove it."
L. The stream of water reversed flow.
M. They said to him, "There is no proof from a stream of water."
N. So he went and said to them, "If the law accords with my position, let the walls of the schoolhouse prove it."
O. The walls of the schoolhouse tilted toward falling.
P. Joshua rebuked them, saying to them, "If disciples of sages are contending with one another in matters of law, what business do you have?"
Q. They did not fall on account of the honour owing to R. Joshua, but they also did not straighten up on account of the honour owing to R. Eliezer, and to this day they are still tilted.
R. So he went and said to them, "If the law accords with my position, let the Heaven prove it!"

S. An echo came forth, saying, "What business have you [contending] with R. Eliezer, for the law accords with his position under all circumstances!"

T. Joshua stood up on his feet and said, " 'It is not in heaven' " (Deut. 30:12).

Next, we reach the point at which God is told the rules of engagement: the sages' reason rules, and miracles do not matter. How does God take it?

U. What is the sense of, " 'It is not in heaven' " (Deut. 30:12)?

V. Said R. Jeremiah, "[The sense of Joshua's statement is this:] For the Torah has already been given from Mount Sinai, so we do not pay attention to echoes, since you have already written in the Torah at Mount Sinai, 'After the majority you are to incline' " (Ex. 23:2).

W. Nathan came upon Elijah and said to him, "What did the Holy One, blessed be he, do at that moment?"

X. He said to him, "He laughed and said, 'My children have overcome me, my children have overcome me!' "

Here man is not only like God but, in context, equal to God because subject to the same logic. God is bound by the same rules of logical argument, of relevant evidence, of principled exchange, as is man. The mere declaration of fact or opinion – even God's – beyond the Torah must be measured against God's own reason, set forth, we see, within the written part of the Torah. That is why the (mere) declaration of matters by Heaven is dismissed. Why? Because God is bound by the rules of rationality that govern in human discourse, and because humanity in the person of the sage thinks like God, as God does; so right is right, and nature has no call to intervene, nor even God to reverse the course of rational argument.

How, then, are we to take the measure of man's and God's correspondence with one another? To answer that question, we have to systematize the place of God in the coherent theological system that animates the documents of the Oral Torah. These yield four categories that organize what in the Torah man is told about God. In the Oral Torah God takes up a position as premise, presence, person, and personality. It is at the fourth category, the representation of God as a personality, that man and God meet. In the first three, God takes up a position to which man does not aspire; for, as I said, God is always God.

By God as premise, I refer to passages in which an author reaches a particular decision because that author believes God created the world and has revealed the Torah to Israel. God as Presence stands for yet another consideration. It refers to God as part of a situation in the here and now. God's law governs, but, when present, God does not always participate; the law of the

Torah fully suffices. When an author speaks of an ox goring another ox, the law does not appeal to God to reach a decision for them and does not suggest that God in particular has witnessed the event and plans to intervene. But God may make his Presence known, especially when needed. For example, when the law speaks of a wife's being accused of unfaithfulness to her husband, by contrast, that law's authority expects that God will intervene in a particular case and so declare a decision. In the former instance, God is assuredly a premise of discourse, having revealed in the Torah the rule governing a goring ox. In the latter, God not only is premise but also is present in discourse and in making a decision. God furthermore constitutes a person in certain settings, not in others. But these do not form points of correspondence between God and man. It is when the sages envisage God as a "you," that is, as a Presence, that God enters into relationship with man. But in such settings God is not always represented in ways that correspond to traits of man.

The correspondence of God and man – the point when the image that they share in common registers – emerges when God is portrayed as a vivid and highly distinctive personality, actor, conversation-partner, hero. It is in references to God as a personality, for example, that God is given corporeal traits. God looks like God in particular, just as each person exhibits distinctive physical traits. Not only so, but in matters of heart and mind and spirit, well-limned individual traits of personality and action alike endow God with that particularity that identifies every individual human being. These correspondences present no surprise, since the Written Torah for its part portrays God in richly personal terms: God wants, cares, demands, regrets, says, and does – just like man. God is not merely a collection of abstract theological attributes and thus rules for governance of reality, nor a mere person to be revered and feared. God is not a mere composite of regularities, but a very specific, highly particular personality, whom people can know, envision, engage, persuade, impress.

When God is represented in human terms, it is commonly but not invariably as a king. For example, a great proportion of the parables in the Oral Torah proposing to capture and explain the relationship of God and man compare God to a king, man to a prince or princess. Thus, God mourned for the destruction of Jerusalem, adopting the customs of a mortal king, in a passage we examined briefly in chapter 1:

PESIQTA DERAB KAHANA XV:III:

1. A. Bar Qappara opened discourse by citing the following verse: "In that day the Lord God of hosts called to weeping and mourning, to baldness and girding with sackcloth; [and behold, joy and gladness, slaying oxen and killing sheep, eating meat

and drinking wine. 'Let us eat and drink for tomorrow we die.' The Lord of hosts has revealed himself in my ears: 'Surely this iniquity will not be forgiven you until you die,' says the Lord of hosts]" (Is. 15:12–14)

B. "Said the Holy One, blessed be He, to the ministering angels, 'When a mortal king mourns, what does he do?'

C. "They said to him, 'He puts sack over his door.'

D. "He said to them, 'I too shall do that. "I will clothe the heavens with blackness [and make sackcloth for their covering]" ' " (Is. 50:3).

E. "He further asked them, 'When a mortal king mourns, what does he do?'

F. "They said to him, 'He extinguishes the torches.'

G. "He said to them, 'I too shall do that. "The sun and moon will become black [and the stars stop shining]" ' " (Joel 4:15).

H. "He further asked them, 'When a mortal king mourns, what does he do?'

I. "They said to him, 'He goes barefooted.'

J. "He said to them, 'I too shall do that. "The Lord in the whirlwind and in the storm will be his way and the clouds [the dust of his feet]' ' " (Nahum 1:3).

K. "He further asked them, 'When a mortal king mourns, what does he do?'

L. "They said to him, 'He sits in silence.'

M. "He said to them, 'I too shall do that. "He will sit alone and keep silence because he has laid it upon himself" ' " (Lam. 3:28).

N. "He further asked them, 'When a mortal king mourns, what does he do?'

O. "They said to him, 'He overturns the beds.'

P. "He said to them, 'I too shall do that. "I beheld to the seats of thrones [having been overturned, now] were placed right side up" ' " (Dan. 7:9).

Q. "He further asked them, 'When a mortal king mourns, what does he do?'

R. "They said to him, 'He tears his [royal] purple garment.'

S. "He said to them, 'I too shall do that. "The Lord has done that which he devised, he tore his word" ' " (Lam. 2:17).

V. [Resuming the earlier account,] "He further asked them, 'When a mortal king mourns, what does he do?'

W. "They said to him, 'He sits and laments.'

X. "He said to them, 'I too shall do that. "How lonely sits the city [that was full of people! How like a widow has she become, she that was great among the nations! She that was a princess among the cities has become a vassal. She weeps bitterly in the night, tears on her cheeks, among all her lovers she has none to comfort her; all her friends have dealt treacherously with her, they have become her enemies]" ' " (Lamentations 1:1–2).

What is important in this story is the insistence that God takes on the traits of mortal kings; he wishes to be perceived in ways that correspond to the ways of man.

As the sages read the declaration of man "in our image, after our likeness," man has the capacity to imitate God. But that conviction freed the sages to represent God as doing the deeds that they themselves know characterize man. The God like whom, in whose image and likeness, man is made does what man does. Here we find how, by reason of that conviction, the sages impute to God profoundly human actions and concerns. God's deeds amply characterize the divinity as familiar by reason of man's image and likeness:

GENESIS RABBAH VIII:XIII.1

A. Said R. Abbahu, "The Holy One, blessed be he, took the cup of blessing [for the benediction of the marriage of Adam and Eve] and said the blessing for them."

B. Said R. Judah b. R Simon, "Michael and Gabriel were the best men of the first man."

C. Said R. Simlai, "We have found that the Holy One, blessed be he, says a blessing for bridegrooms, adorns brides, visits the sick, buries the dead, and says a blessing for mourners.

D. "What is the evidence for the fact that he says a blessing for bridegrooms? As it is said, 'And God blessed them' (Gen. 1:28).

E. "That he adorns bride? As it is written, 'And the Lord God built the rib ... into a woman' (Gen. 2:22).

F. "Visits the sick? As it is written, 'And the Lord appeared to him' (Gen. 18:1).

G. "Buries the dead? As it is written, 'And he buried him in the valley' " (Deut. 34:6).

H. R. Samuel bar Nahman said, "Also he concerns himself for the mourner. It is written, 'And God appeared to Jacob again, when he came from Paddan-aram, and blessed him' (Gen. 35:9).

I. "What was the blessing that he said for him? It was the blessing for mourners."

But it should be said, in the sages' own words, that the deeds that God does, like the deeds of man, should be seen in the opposite way: deeds man does in imitation of God. The particular ethical actions emphasized by the sages therefore follow the model that God has provided; hence, just as rites are (merely) natural, so acts of supererogatory virtue fostered by sages, acts that produce merit, are treated as divine. What is stunning is the clear notion that God does the things virtuous mortals do, and these things are spelled out in homely terms indeed. But matters go still further. God not only acts like a human being. God also takes the form of a human being. God is incarnate in that God and mortals look exactly alike. God and man correspond, the virtuous deeds that God values in man God himself carries out.

Accordingly, God not only looks like a human being but also does the acts that human beings do. For example, God spends the day much as does a mortal ruler of Israel, at least as the sages imagine such a figure. That is, he studies the Torah, makes practical decisions, and sustains the world (meaning, administers public funds for public needs) – just as (in the sages' picture of themselves) sages do. What gives us a deeply human God is that, for the final part of the day, God plays with his pet, Leviathan, as a master of the Torah might relax by playing with his dog. Some correct that view and hold that God spends the rest of the day teaching the Torah to children:

BAVLI-TRACTATE ABODAH ZARAH I:I I.2/3B

A. Said R. Judah said Rab, "The day is twelve hours long. During the first three, the Holy One, blessed be he, is engaged in the study of the Torah.

B. "During the next three God sits in judgment on the world and when he sees the world sufficiently guilty to deserve destruction, he moves from the seat of justice to the seat of mercy.

C. "During the third he feeds the whole world, from the horned buffalo to vermin.

D. "During the fourth he plays with the Leviathan, as it is said, 'There is Leviathan, whom you have made to play with'" (Ps. 104:26).

Now comes the point of correction. God teaches children:

E. [Another authority denies this final point and says,] 'What then does God do in the fourth quarter of the day?

F. "He sits and teaches school children, as it is said, 'Whom shall one teach knowledge, and whom shall one make to understand the message? Those who are weaned from milk'" (Is. 28:9).

G. 'And what does God do by night'?

H. "If you like, I shall propose that he does what he does in daytime.

I. "Or if you prefer: he rides a light cherub and floats in eighteen thousand worlds ...

J. "Or if you prefer: he sits and listens to the song of the heavenly creatures, as it is said, 'By the day the Lord will command his loving kindness and in the night his song shall be with me'" (Ps. 42:9).

It seems hardly necessary to note that the physicality of God forms a premise of all else. Other actions of God that presuppose a physical capacity are indicated in the following, although the picture is not so clearly one of concrete physical actions as in the earlier instances:

BAVLI BABA MESIA 7:1 IV.6/86B

A. Said R. Judah said Rab, "Everything that Abraham personally did for the ministering angels the Holy One, blessed be he, personally did for his children, and everything that Abraham did through servants the Holy One, blessed be he, carried out also through ministering angels.

B. "'And Abraham ran to the herd' (Gen. 18:7). 'And a wind went forth from the Lord' (Num. 11:31).

C. "'And he took butter and milk' (Gen. 18:8). 'Behold, I will rain bread from heaven for you' (Ex. 16:4).

D. "'And he stood by them under the tree' (Gen. 18:8). 'Behold, I will stand before you there upon the rock'" (Ex. 17:6).

The passage proceeds to point out further examples of the same parallels. The various actions of God in favour of Israel correspond to the concrete actions of Abraham for God or the angels. The comparison of Abraham's actions to those of God invites the notion that God is represented as incarnate. But in this instance we are not compelled to a reading of God as an essentially corporeal being. The actions God does can be accomplished in some less material or physical way. In the balance, however, we do find evidence to suggest that the Bavli understood that God looks like a human being, specifically, like a man, and that God does what human beings of a particular order or class do.

So much for the tangible correspondence in physical traits and in concrete actions. But our protracted encounter with the transaction that yields *zekhut* has already shown us the critical importance of attitude and emotion. What moves God, and moves God to action, are emotions that man also feels, attitudes that guide man's actions as much as God's. Uncoerced love matched by an act of grace – that transaction above all tells us what really matters, and it is precisely there that the correspondence of man and God extends to emotional or attitudinal traits. God emerges in the Oral Torah as a fully exposed personality. The common character of divinity and humanity, therefore, encompassed God's virtue, the specific traits of character and personality that God exhibited above and here below.

God's emotions correspond with man's. Like a parent faced with a recalcitrant child, he takes no pleasure in man's fall but mourns. Not only so, but even while he protects those who love him, Israel, from his, and their, enemies, he takes to heart that he made all man; he does not rejoice at the Sea when Israel is saved, because, even then, his enemies are perishing. This is said in so many words in the context of a discussion on whether God rejoices when the wicked perish:

BAVLI-TRACTATE SANHEDRIN 4:5 VI.1/39B

A. Therefore man was created alone (4:5J):

B. "And there went out a song throughout the host" (1 Kgs. 22:36) [at Ahab's death at Ramoth in Gilead].

C. Said R. Aha b. Hanina, " 'When the wicked perish, there is song' (Prov. 11:10).

D. "When Ahab, b. Omri, perished, there was song."

Does God sing and rejoice when the wicked perish? Not at all:

E. But does the Holy One, blessed be he, rejoice at the downfall of the wicked?

F. Is it not written, "That they should praise as they went out before the army and say, 'Give thanks to the Lord, for his mercy endures forever' (2 Chr. 20:21),

G. and said R. Jonathan, "On what account are the words in this psalm of praise omitted, 'Because he is good'? Because the Holy One, blessed be he, does not rejoice at the downfall of the wicked."

Now we revert to the conduct of God at the very moment of Israel's liberation, when Israel sings the Song at the Sea:

H. For R. Samuel bar Nahman said R. Jonathan said, "What is the meaning of the verse of Scripture [that speaks of Egypt and Israel at the sea], 'And one did not come near the other all night' (Ex. 14:20)?

I. "At that time, the ministering angels want to recite a song [of rejoicing] before the Holy One, blessed be he.

J. "Said to them the Holy One, blessed be he, 'The works of my hands are perishing in the sea, and do you want to sing a song before me?' "

Now the matter is resolved:

K. Said R. Yosé bar Hanina, "He does not rejoice, but others do rejoice. Note that it is written, '[And it shall come to pass, as the Lord rejoiced over you to do good, so the Lord] will cause rejoicing over you by destroying you' (Deut. 28:63) – and not 'so will the Lord [himself] rejoice'"

L. That proves the case.

God's emotions correspond, then, to those of a father or a mother, mourning at the downfall of their children, even though their children have rebelled against them. Even at the moment at which Israel first meets God, with God's act of liberation at the Sea, God cannot join them in their song. Only a parent could know why.

Among the virtuous emotions, which one did the sages impute to God? Above all, it was humility, the virtue the sages most often asked of themselves, that characterized the divinity. God wanted people to be humble, and God therefore showed humility:

BAVLI-TRACTATE SHABBAT 89A

A. Said R. Joshua b. Levi, "When Moses came down from before the Holy One, blessed be he, Satan came and asked [God], " 'Lord of the world, Where is the Torah?"

B. "He said to him, 'I have given it to the earth ...' [Satan ultimately was told by God to look for the Torah by finding the son of Amram.]

C. "He went to Moses and asked him, 'Where is the Torah which the Holy One, blessed be he, gave you?'

D. "He said to him, 'Who am I that the Holy One, blessed be he, should give me the Torah?'

E. "Said the Holy One, blessed be he, to Moses, 'Moses, you are a liar!'

F. "He said to him, 'Lord of the world, you have a treasure in store which you have enjoyed every day. Shall I keep it to myself?'

G. "He said to him, 'Moses, since you have acted with humility, it will bear your name: "Remember the Torah of Moses, my servant" ' " (Mal. 3:22).

God here is represented as favouring humility and rewarding the humble with honour. What is important is that God does not cite Scripture or merely paraphrase it; the conversation is an exchange between two vivid personalities. True enough, Moses, not God, is the hero. But the personality of God emerges in a vivid way. Arrogance – the opposite – is treated as denial of God, humility, the imitation of God. When in chapters 10 and 11, we take up the cause of sin, which disrupts the world order, we shall see why the opposite of humility, which is arrogance, takes so critical a role. It is because sin forms the action of which arrogance is the attitude, and catastrophe for man, on the one side, and for Israel, on the other, the result. So what provokes the calamitous transaction that is the story of mankind originates in the attitude of arrogance.

This, quite naturally, links itself to idolatry, the supreme act of arrogance, the quintessential sin:

BAVLI-TRACTATE SOTAH I:I V.5 /5B

P. And R. Yohanan said in the name of R. Simeon b. Yohai, "Whoever is arrogant is as if he worships idolatry.

Q. "Here it is written, 'Everyone who is arrogant in heart is an abomination to the Lord,' (Prov. 16:5), and elsewhere it is written, 'You will not bring an abomination into your house'" (Deut. 7:26).

Arrogance represents the rejection of God himself:

R. And R. Yohanan on his own account said, "He is as if he denied the very Principle [of the world],
S. "as it is said, 'Your heart will be lifted up and you will forget the Lord your God'" (Deut. 8:14).
T. R. Hama bar Hanina said, "He is as if he had sexual relations with all of those women forbidden to him on the laws of incest.
U. "Here it is written, 'Everyone who is arrogant in heart is an abomination to the Lord' (Prov. 16:5), and elsewhere it is written, 'For all these abominations ...'" (Lev. 18:27).
V. Ulla said, "It is as if he built a high place,
W. "as it is said, 'Cease you from man, whose breath is in his nostrils, for wherein is he to be accounted of' (Is. 2:22).
X. "Do not read, 'wherein,' but rather, 'high place.'"

Since God is offended by the arrogance of idolatry, God is capable of ridicule, when it comes to the gentiles and their idolatry:

BAVLI-TRACTATE ABODAH ZARAH I:I 1.2/3B

BBB. Said R. Yosé, "In the age to come idolators will come and convert [to Judaism] ... and will put phylacteries on their foreheads and arms, place show-fringes on their garments and a *mezuzah* on their doorposts. When, however, the battle of Gog and Magog takes place, they will be asked, 'Why have you come?'
CCC. "They will reply, 'Against God and his anointed ...' (Ps. 2:1).
DDD. "Then each of the converts will toss off the religious emblems and leave ... and the Holy One, blessed be he, will sit and laugh,
EEE. "as it is said, 'He who sits in heaven laughs ...'" (Ps. 2:4).

To return to the systematic exposition on the theme of arrogance versus humility, the composite now continues with a demonstration that arrogance is not only an act of idolatry but also violates the admonition of the Torah:

BAVLI-TRACTATE SOTAH I:I V.18/5B

A. Whence [in Scripture] do we derive an admonition against the arrogant?
B. Said Raba said Zeiri, "'Listen and give ear, do not be proud'" (Jer. 13:15).

C. R. Nahman bar Isaac said, "From the following: 'Your heart will be lifted up, and you will forget the Lord your God' (Deut. 8:14).

D. "And it is written, 'Beware, lest you forget the Lord your God'" (Deut. 8:11).

E. And that accords with what R. Abin said R. Ilaa said.

F. For R. Abin said R. Ilaa said, "In every place in which it is said, 'Beware lest … that you not …,' the meaning is only to lay down a negative commandment [so that one who does such a thing violates a negative admonition]."

The close identification of God with the virtue of contrition and humility underscores that correspondence between man and God that comes to fulfilment in shared attitudes and emotions:

BAVLI-TRACTATE SOTAH I:I V.20/5B

A. "With him also who is of a contrite and humble spirit" (Is. 57:15).

B. R. Huna and R. Hisda:

C. One said, "I [God] am with the contrite."

D. The other said, "I [God] am the contrite."

E. Logic favours the view of him who has said, "I [God] am with the contrite," for lo, the Holy One, blessed be he, neglected all mountains and heights and brought his Presence to rest on Mount Sinai,

F. and he did not raise Mount Sinai upward [to himself].

G. R. Joseph said, "A person should always learn from the attitude of his Creator, for lo, the Holy One, blessed be he, neglected all mountains and heights and brought his Presence to rest on Mount Sinai,

H. "and he neglected all valuable trees and brought his Presence to rest in the bush."

Once again, arrogance matches idolatry:

BAVLI-TRACTATE SOTAH I:I V.21/5B

A. Said R. Eleazar, "Whoever is arrogant is worthy of being cut down like an asherah [a tree that is worshipped].

B. "Here it is written, 'The high ones of stature shall be cut down' (Is. 10:33),

C. "and elsewhere it is written, 'And you shall hew down their Asherim'" (Deut. 7:5).

The inevitable result is death, without resurrection at the other side of the grave:

D. And R. Eleazar said, "Whoever is arrogant – his dust will not be stirred up [in the resurrection of the dead].

E. "For it is said, 'Awake and sing, you that dwell in the dust' (Is. 26:19).

F. "It is stated not 'you who lie in the dust' but 'you who dwell in the dust,' meaning, one who has become a neighbour to the dust [by constant humility] even in his lifetime."

G. And R. Eleazar said, "For whoever is arrogant the Presence of God laments,

H. "as it is said, 'But the haughty he knows from afar' " (Ps. 138:6).

If humility in man corresponds to humility in God, still it finds perfection in God but not in man:

BAVLI-TRACTATE SOTAH I:I V.22/5B

A. R. Avira expounded, and some say it was R. Eleazar, "Come and take note of the fact that not like the trait of the Holy One, blessed be he, is the trait of flesh and blood.

B. "The trait of flesh and blood is that those who are high take note of those who are high, but the one who is high does not take note of the one who is low.

C. "But the trait of the Holy One, blessed be he, is not that way. He is high, but he takes note of the low,

D. "as it is said, 'For though the Lord is high, yet he takes note of the low' " (Ps. 138:6).

That is why God cannot abide the arrogant:

BAVLI-TRACTATE SOTAH I:I V.23/5B

A. Said R. Hisda, and some say it was Mar Uqba, "Concerning whoever is arrogant said the Holy One, blessed be he, he and I cannot live in the same world,

B. "as it is said, 'Whoever slanders his neighbour in secret – him will I destroy; him who has a haughty look and a proud heart I will not endure' (Ps. 101:5).

C. "Do not read, 'him [I cannot endure]' but 'with him [I cannot endure].' "

D. There are those who apply the foregoing teaching to those who slander, as it is said, "Whoever slanders his neighbour in secret – him will I destroy" (Ps. 101:5).

The repertoire shows clearly that the sages impute to God those traits of personality that are recommended and claim that God favours personalities like God's own. The clear implication is that God and the human being are consubstantial as to attitudes, emotions, and other aspects of virtue.

God not only exhibits and favours humility and has the capacity to laugh out of both joy and ridicule. God also becomes angry and performs acts that express that anger. For, as in the Written Torah, God corresponds to man in his passion. God hates idolatry as an act of arrogance and rebellion against him, so God is capable of hatred; and, since God is made angry by idolatry, God possesses the quality of anger. These and other traits of emotion in God find their correspondence in man, who is to learn from God's emotions and attitudes and imitate them – even, or especially, the capacity for passion:

BAVLI-TRACTATE BERAKHOT I:I III.35/7A

A. And said R. Yohanan in the name of R. Yosé, "How do we know that one should not placate a person when he is angry?

B. "It is in line with the following verse of Scripture: 'My face will go and then I will give you rest' (Ex. 33:14).

C. "Said the Holy One, blessed be he, to Moses, 'Wait until my angry countenance passes, and then I shall give you rest.'"

D. But does the Holy One, blessed be he, get angry?

E. Indeed so.

F. For it has been taught on Tannaite authority:

G. "A God that is angry every day" (Ps. 7:12).

But God's anger and man's are not the same, for God is never angry for very long; he responds to what man feels and does, but he is always God:

H. And how long is this anger going to last?

I. A moment.

J. And how long is a moment?

K. It is one fifty-eight thousand eight hundred and eighty-eighth part of an hour.

Now the prophet of the gentiles enters the picture:

L. And no creature except for the wicked Balaam has ever been able to fix the moment exactly.

M. For concerning him it has been written, "He knows the knowledge of the Most High" (Num. 24:16).

N. Now if Balaam did not even know what his beast was thinking, was he likely to know what the Most High is thinking?

O. But this teaches that he knew exactly how to reckon the very moment that the Holy One, blessed be he, would be angry.

P. That is in line with what the prophet said to Israel, "O my people, remember now what Balak, king of Moab, devised, and what Balaam, son of Beor, answered him ... that you may know the righteous acts of the Lord" (Mic. 6:5).

The theme of Balaam is extended:

Q. Said R. Eleazar, "The Holy One, blessed be he, said to Israel, 'Know that I did any number of acts of righteousness with you, for I did not get angry in the time of the wicked Balaam. For had I gotten angry, not one of Israel would have survived, not a remnant.'

R. "That is in line with what Balaam said to Balak, 'How shall I curse whom God has not cursed, and how shall I execrate whom the Lord has not execrated?' (Num. 23:8).

S. "This teaches that for that entire time [God] did not get mad."

T. And how long is God's anger?

U. It is a moment.

Now we revert to the main point:

V. And how long is a moment?

W. Said R. Abin, and some say, R. Abina, "A moment lasts as long as it takes to say 'a moment.'"

X. And how do we know that a moment is how long God is angry?

Y. For it is said, "For his anger is but for a moment, his favour is for a lifetime" (Ps. 30:6).

Z. If you like, you may derive the lesson from the following: "Hide yourself for a little while until the anger be past" (Is. 26:20).

What is striking in this sizable account is the characterization of God's anger in entirely corporeal terms. God not only becomes angry, God also acts in anger. For one example, in anger God loses his temper:

BAVLI-TRACTATE BABA BATRA 5:1 IV.23/74B

A. Said R. Judah said Rab, "When the Holy One, blessed be he, proposed to create the world, he said to the angelic prince of the sea, 'Open your mouth and swallow all the water in the world.'

B. "He said to him, 'Lord of the world, it is quite sufficient if I stick with what I already have.'

C. "Forthwith he kicked him with his foot and killed him.

D. "For it is written, 'He stirs up the sea with his power, and by his understanding he smites through Rahab'" (Job 26:12).

Like a human being, God thus can lose his temper. God's anger derives not only from ill-temper but deeper causes. God is dissatisfied with the world as it is and so expresses anger with the present condition of humanity, on account of Israel. Here is a systematic composite on the theme of God's anger with the world, with Israel in the world, and with Israel for what it has done to make the world what it is:

BAVLI-TRACTATE BERAKHOT I:I II.1/3A

F. For it has been taught on Tannaite authority:
G. R. Eliezer says, "The night is divided into three watches, and [in heaven] over each watch the Holy One, blessed be he, sits and roars like a lion,
H. "as it is said, 'The Lord roars from on high and raises his voice from his holy habitation, roaring he does roar because of his fold' (Jer. 25:30).
I. "The indication of each watch is as follows: at the first watch, an ass brays, at the second, dogs yelp, at the third, an infant sucks at its mother's breast or a woman whispers to her husband."

Once again, we see that God is given the physical trait of a voice, and the emotional trait of anger and sorrow:

BAVLI-TRACTATE BERAKHOT I:I II.2/3A

A. Said R. Isaac bar Samuel in the name of Rab, "The night is divided into three watches, and over each watch, the Holy One, blessed be he, sits and roars like a lion.
B. "He says, 'Woe to the children, on account of whose sins I have wiped out my house and burned my palace, and whom I have exiled among the nations of the world.' "

The next composition goes over the same matter:

BAVLI-TRACTATE BERAKHOT I:I II.3/3A

A. It has been taught on Tannaite authority:
B. Said R. Yosé, "Once I was going along the way, and I went into one of the ruins of Jerusalem to pray. Elijah, of blessed memory, came and watched over me at the door until I had finished my prayer. After I had finished my prayer, he said to me, 'Peace be to you, my lord.'
C. "And I said to him, 'Peace be to you, my lord and teacher.'
D. "And he said to me, 'My son, on what account did you go into this ruin?'
E. "And I said to him, 'To pray.'

F. "And he said to me, 'You would have done better to pray on the road.'

J. "And he said to me, 'My son, what sound did you hear in this ruin?'

K. "I said to him, 'I heard the sound of an echo moaning like a pigeon and saying, "Woe to the children, on account of whose sins I have wiped out my house and burned my palace and whom I have exiled among the nations of the world."'

Now we see why we retell the story in a different framework:

L. "He said to me, 'By your life and the life of your head, it is not only at this moment that the echo speaks in such a way, but three times daily, it says the same thing.

M. "'And not only so, but when Israelites go into synagogues and schoolhouses and respond, "May the great name be blessed," the Holy One shakes his head and says, "Happy is the king, whom they praise in his house in such a way! What does a father have, who has exiled his children? And woe to the children who are exiled from their father's table!'"

God's anger and mourning form emotions identical to those of human beings, as is made explicit. Israel are God's children, and God mourns for them as a parent mourns for children who have suffered. God's attitudes correspond with the those of human beings, though of a cosmic order. God responds to Israel's prayer, their sanctification of his name comforting him. But God's anger derives from broader causes than Israel's current condition.

God enters into transactions with human beings and accords with the rules that govern those relationships. So God exhibits precisely the social attributes that human beings do. A number of stories, rather protracted and detailed, tell the story of God as a social being, living among and doing business with mortals. These stories provide extended portraits of God's relationships, in particular arguments, with important figures, such as angels as well as Moses, David, and Hosea. In them, God, like man, negotiates, persuades, teaches, argues, exchanges, reasons. God will engage in arguments with men and angels and so enters into the existence of ordinary people. These disputes, negotiations, transactions yield a portrait of God who is reasonable and capable of give and take, as in the following:

BAVLI-TRACTATE ARAKHIN 3:5/15A-B

F. Rabbah bar Mari said, "What is the meaning of this verse: 'But they were rebellious at the sea, even at the Red Sea; nonetheless he saved them for his name's sake' (Ps. 106:7)?

G. "This teaches that the Israelites were rebellious at that time, saying, 'Just as we will go up on this side, so the Egyptians will go up on the other side.' Said the Holy

One, blessed be he, to the angelic prince who reigns over the sea, 'Cast them [the Israelites] out on dry land.'

H. "He said before him, 'Lord of the world, is there any case of a slave [namely, myself] to whom his master [you] gives a gift [the Israelites], and then the master goes and takes [the gift] away again? [You gave me the Israelites, now you want to take them away and place them on dry land.]'

I. "He said to him, 'I'll give you one and a half times their number.'

J. "He said before him, 'Lord of the world, is there a possibility that a slave can claim anything against his master? [How do I know that you will really do it?]'

K. "He said to him, 'The Kishon brook will be my pledge [that I shall carry out my word. Nine hundred chariots at the brook were sunk, (Jud. 3:23) while Pharaoh at the sea had only six hundred, thus a pledge one and a half times greater than the sum at issue.]'

L. "Forthwith [the angelic prince of the sea] spit them out onto dry land, for it is written, 'And the Israelites saw the Egyptians dead on the sea shore'" (Ex. 14:30).

God is willing to give a pledge to guarantee his word. He furthermore sees the right claim of the counterpart actor in the story. Hence we see how God obeys precisely the same social laws of exchange and reason that govern other incarnate beings.

The Written Torah establishes that Abraham is prepared to contend with God through reasonable argument. The occasion was the destruction of Sodom. Matching God's contention over destroying the gentile city with his conduct in destroying Israel's Jerusalem, the Oral Torah constructs a counterpart dispute. God is represented as accepting accountability, by the standards of humanity, for what he does. And Abraham is represented as forcing this point in an implacable argument:

BAVLI-TRACTATE MENAHOT 5:1 I.4/53B

A. Said R. Isaac, "When the temple was destroyed, the Holy One, blessed be he, found Abraham standing in the Temple. He said to him, 'What is my beloved doing in my house?'

B. "He said to him, 'I have come because of what is going on with my children.'

C. "He said to him, 'Your children sinned and have been sent into exile."

D. "He said to him, 'But wasn't it by mistake that they sinned?'

E. "He said to him, 'She has wrought lewdness' (Jer. 11:15).

Now comes an echo of the exchange before the destruction of Sodom:

F. "He said to him, 'But wasn't it just a minority of them that did it?'

G. "He said to him, 'It was a majority' (Jer. 11:15).

H. "He said to him, 'You should at least have taken account of the covenant of circumcision [which should have secured forgiveness despite their sin]!'

I. "He said to him, 'The holy flesh is passed from you' (Jer. 11:15).

Why did God not wait for Israel to repent?

J. " 'And if you had waited for them, they might have repented!'

K. "He said to him, 'When you do evil, then you are happy' (Jer. 11:15).

L. "He said to him, 'He put his hands on his head, crying out and weeping, saying to them, 'God forbid! Perhaps they have no remedy at all!'

M. "A heavenly voice came forth and said, 'The Lord called you "a leafy olive tree, fair with excellent fruit" ' " (Jer. 11:16).

The matter is resolved only at the advent of the restoration, the world to come, with the return of the exiles to the Land, as we shall see at length in chapter 14:

N. "Just as in the case of an olive tree, its future comes only at the end [that is, it is only after a long while that it attains its best fruit], so in the case of Israel, their future comes at the end of their time."

God relates to Abraham as to an equal. That is shown by God's implicit agreement that he is answerable to Abraham for what has taken place with the destruction of the Temple. God does not impose on Abraham silence, saying that that is a decree not to be contested but only accepted. God as a social being accepts that he must provide sound reasons for his actions, as must any other reasonable person in a world governed by rules applicable to everyone. Abraham is a fine choice for the protagonist, since he engaged in the argument concerning Sodom. His complaint is expressed at B: God is now called to explain himself. At each point Abraham offers arguments in behalf of sinning Israel, and God responds, item by item. The climax, of course, has God promising Israel a future worth having. God emerges as both just and merciful, reasonable but sympathetic. The transaction attests to God's conformity to rules of reasoned transactions in a coherent society.

But God does not invariably play the role of Israel's prosecutor; he also serves as attorney for the defence. For the same picture is drawn in still greater detail when God engages Hosea in discussion. Here, however, Hosea complains against Israel, and God takes the part of Abraham in the earlier account. God's social role is defined in the model of the sage or master. God teaches Hosea by providing an analogy, for Hosea, of what Hosea proposes that God do.

BAVLI-TRACTATE PESAHIM 8:1 1.7/87A

I. A. Said the Holy One, blessed be he, to Hosea, "Your children have sinned."

B. He should have said to him, "They are your children, children of those to whom you have shown grace, children of Abraham, Isaac, and Jacob. Send your mercy to them."

C. It is not enough that he did not say the right thing, but he said to him, "Lord of the world, the entire world is yours. Trade them in for some other nation."

D. Said the Holy One, blessed be he, "What shall I then do with that elder? I shall tell him, 'Go, marry a whore and have children of prostitution.' Then I'll tell him, 'Divorce her.' If he can send her away, then I'll send away Israel.'

E. For it is said, "And the Lord said to Hosea, Go, take a whore and have children of prostitution" (Hos. 1:1).

Now God is able to communicate his message to Hosea only by asking Hosea to understand how God feels, which is, exactly as does Hosea, and for the same reason:

II. A. After he had two sons and a daughter, the Holy One, blessed be he, said to Hosea, "Should you not have learned the lesson of your master, Moses? Once I had entered into discourse with him, he separated from his wife. So you too, take your leave of her."

B. He said to him, "Lord of the world, I have children from her, and I simply cannot drive her out or divorce her."

C. Said to him the Holy One, blessed be he, "Now if you, married to a whore, with children of prostitution, and you don't even know whether they're yours or whether they come from some other fathers, are in such a state, as to Israel, who are my children, children of those whom I have tested, the children of Abraham, Isaac and Jacob ...

D. "... how can you say to me, 'Trade them in for some other nation?'"

E. When [Hosea] realized that he had sinned, he arose to seek mercy for himself. Said the Holy One, blessed be he, to him, "Instead of seeking mercy for yourself, seek mercy for Israel, against whom I have on your account issued three decrees [exile, rejection, and without compassion, reflecting the names of his children]."

F. He went and sought mercy and [God] annulled [the decrees] and gave them this blessing: "Yet the number of the children of Israel shall be as the sand of the sea ... and instead of being called 'You are not my people,' they will be called 'You are the children of the living God.' And the children of Judah and the children of Israel shall be gathered together ... And I will sow her to me in the land, and have compassion on her who was not treated with compassion and say to those who were not my people, 'You are my people'" (Hos. 2:1–2, 25).

So when Hosea negotiates with God, proposing that God reject Israel for some other nation, God invokes the correspondence of man and God, taking for granted that man bears the feelings that God does; then God can win the argument. God's reply is that of an experienced teacher. He puts the disciple through a concrete lesson, which imparts to the disciple the desired experience and leads to the disciple's drawing the right conclusion. The social transaction is worked out in accord with rules of reason. Just as experience teaches Hosea the lesson that one does not reject, but forgives, sinful relations, so Hosea draws the correct conclusion. The story, then, portrays God in a social transaction that is governed by accepted laws of orderly conduct. But once more, we realize the difference of perspective that separates the ages. Some will read the story as an account of God in the image of man. But from the perspective of the sages, the story depends upon the fact that man is in the image of God.

Abraham and Hosea are not the only ones who contend with God. The same possibilities of protracted, civil, reasonable argument with God are realized in a sizable account of God's relationships with David. A paramount theme in the story of David's sin with Bath Sheba yields the picture of how God responds in a reasonable way to a reasonable proposal. Then, to be sure, God teaches a lesson of right conduct. But, throughout, God's nature remains the same: a social and rational being, like mortals. What is important for my argument is the representation of God as engaged in negotiation in accord with rules that apply to heaven and earth alike. God enters into society as a full participant in the world of humanity and plays a role that forms the counterpart to that of any just person. Once again the correspondence of man and God is precise and material. In the following, for example, God is fully engaged in social transactions with counterparts on earth. We consider only those portions of the protracted story that pertain to our topic:

BAVLI-TRACTATE SANHEDRIN 11:2 XII.9/106B–107A

A. Said R. Judah said Rab, "One should never put himself to the test, for lo, David, king of Israel, put himself to the test and he stumbled.

B. "He said before him, 'Lord of the world, on what account do people say, "God of Abraham, God of Isaac, and God of Jacob," but they do not say, "God of David?' "

C. "He said to him, 'They endured a test for me, while you have not endured a test for me.'

D. "He said before him, 'Lord of the world, here I am. Test me.'

E. "For it is said, 'Examine me, O Lord, and try me' (Ps. 26:1).

F. "He said to him, 'I shall test you, and I shall do for you something that I did not do for them. I did not inform them [what I was doing], while I shall tell you what I am going to do. I shall try you with a matter having to do with sexual relations.'

G. "Forthwith: 'And it came to pass in an eventide that David arose from off his bed'" (2 Sam. 11:2).

The opening passage represents God in conversation with David and responsive to David's reasoning. This is more than the Presence of God familiar in the earliest strata of the canon, and God in conversation with David forms a personality, not the mere "you" of prayer familiar in the initial writings of the Judaism of the dual Torah. Where God cites Scripture, it is not merely to prove a point but to make a statement particular to the exchange at hand. So it is not a conventional portrait of God's serving as the voice of an established text. It is, to the contrary, the picture of God engaged in a social transaction with a sentient being.

Continuing in the same passage we skip the description of David's relationship with Bath Sheba and move directly to David's plea of forgiveness. In the passages that follow, God serves merely as audience for David's statements:

A. Raba interpreted Scripture, asking, "What is the meaning of the following verse: 'To the chief musician, a Psalm of David. In the Lord I put my trust, how do you say to my soul, Flee as a bird to your mountain?' (Ps. 11:1)?

B. "Said David before the Holy One, blessed be he, 'Lord of the world, Forgive me for that sin, so that people should not say, "The mountain that is among you [that is, your king] has been driven off by a bird."'"

The foregoing is now clarified:

C. Raba interpreted Scripture, asking, "What is the meaning of the following verse: 'Against you, you alone, have I sinned, and done this evil in your sight, that you might be justified when you speak and be clear when you judge' (Ps. 11:1)?

D. "Said David before the Holy One, blessed be he, 'Lord of the world. It is perfectly clear to you that if I had wanted to overcome my impulse to do evil, I should have done so. But I had in mind that people not say, "The slave has conquered the Master [God, and should then be included as 'God of David']."'"

The same process is repeated:

E. Raba interpreted Scripture, asking, "What is the meaning of the following verse: 'For I am ready to halt and my sorrow is continually before me' (Ps. 38:18)?

F. "Bath Sheba, daughter of Eliam, was designated for David from the six days of creation, but she came to him through anguish."

G. And so did a Tannaite authority of the house of R. Ishmael [teach], "Bath Sheba, daughter of Eliam, was designated for David, but he 'ate' her while she was yet unripe."

Yet again, the matter is amplified:

H. Raba interpreted Scripture, asking, "What is the meaning of the following verse: 'But in my adversity they rejoiced and gathered themselves together, yes, the abjects gathered themselves together against me and I did not know it, they tore me and did not cease' (Ps. 35:15)?

I. "Said David before the Holy One, blessed be he, 'Lord of the world, it is perfectly clear to you that if they had torn my flesh, my blood would not have flowed [because I was so embarrassed.

J. " 'Not only so, but when they take up the four modes of execution inflicted by a court, they interrupt their Mishnah-study and say to me, "David, he who has sexual relations with a married woman – how is he put to death?"

K. "I say to them, "He who has sexual relations with a married woman is put to death through strangulation, but he has a share in the world to come," while he who humiliates his fellow in public has no share in the world to come." ' "

Now God emerges once more and plays the role of antagonist to David's protagonist:

A. R. Dosetai of Biri interpreted Scripture, "To what may David be likened? To a gentile merchant.

B. "Said David before the Holy One, blessed be he, 'Lord of the world, "Who can understand his errors?" ' (Ps. 19:13).

C. "He said to him, 'They are remitted for you.'

D. " ' "Cleanse me of hidden faults" ' (Ps. 19:13).

E. " 'They are remitted to you.'

F. " ' "Keep back your servant also from presumptuous sins" ' (Ps. 19:13).

G. " 'They are remitted to you.'

H. " ' "Let them not have dominion over me, then I shall be upright" (Ps. 19:13), so that the rabbis will not hold me up as an example.'

I. " 'They are remitted to you.'

J. " ' "And I shall be innocent of great transgression" (Ps. 19:13), so that they will not write down my ruin.'

K. "He said to him, 'That is not possible. Now if the Y that I took away from the name of Sarah [changing it from Sarai, ending with a Y to Sarah, ending with an H] stood crying for so many years until Joshua came and I added the Y [removed from

Sarah's name] to his name, as it is said, "And Moses called Oshea, the son of Nun, Jehoshua" (Num. 13:16), how much the more will a complete passage of Scripture [cry out if I remove that passage from its rightful place]!' "

God once more emerges as a fully formed personality. For God's role here is not merely to cite Scripture. K forms the centrepiece. God can do just so much, but no more, and this detail is the contribution not of Scripture but of the storyteller. Corresponding to man, God is bound by rules of procedure and conduct. God enters into civil and rational transactions with human beings and conforms to the same rules. with the result that is expressed here, as the story of David proceeds:

A. "And I shall be innocent from great transgression: (Ps. 19:13):
B. He said before him, "Lord of the world, forgive me for the whole of that sin [as though I had never done it]."
C. He said to him, "Solomon, your son, even now is destined to say in his wisdom, 'Can a man take fire in his bosom, and his clothes not be burned? Can one go upon hot coals, and his feet not be burned? So he who goes in to his neighbour's wife, whoever touches her shall not be innocent'" (Prov. 6:27–29).
D. He said to him, "Will I be so deeply troubled?"
E. He said to him, "Accept suffering [as atonement]."
F. He accepted the suffering.

The transaction continues along these same lines, marked by David's affliction and repentance and God's response of forgiveness:

A. Said R. Judah said Rab, "For six months David was afflicted with *saraat* [the skin ailment described at Leviticus 13], and the Presence of God left him, and the sanhedrin abandoned him.

David is abandoned by God's presence:

B. "He was afflicted with *saraat*, as it is written, 'Purge me with hyssop and I shall be clean, wash me and I shall be whiter than snow' (Ps. 51:9).
C. "The Presence of God left him, as it is written, 'Restore to me the joy of your salvation and uphold me with your free spirit' (Ps. 51:14).

The sanhedrin leaves him:

D. "The sanhedrin abandoned him, as it is written, 'Let those who fear you turn to me and those who have known your testimonies' (Ps. 119:79).

E. "How do we know that this lasted for six months? As it is written, 'And the days that David rules over Israel were forty years: [107B] Seven years he reigned in Hebron, and thirty-three years he reigned in Jerusalem' (1 Kgs. 2:11).

F. "Elsewhere it is written, 'In Hebron he reigned over Judah seven years and six months' (2 Sam. 5:5).

G. "So the six months were not taken into account. Accordingly, he was afflicted with *saraat* [for such a one is regarded as a corpse].

David repents and pleads for forgiveness:

H. "He said before him, 'Lord of the world, forgive me for that sin.'

I. " 'It is forgiven to you.'

David asks for public vindication, ending his humiliation:

J. " 'Then show me a token for good, that they who hate me may see it and be ashamed, because you, Lord, have helped me and comforted me' " (Ps. 86:17).

K. "He said to him, 'While you are alive, I shall not reveal [the fact that you are forgiven], but I shall reveal it in the lifetime of your son, Solomon.' "

Only after his death was David publicly vindicated, with a miracle:

L. "When Solomon had built the house of the sanctuary, he tried to bring the ark into the house of the Holy of Holies. The gates cleaved to one another. He recited twenty-four prayers, but was not answered.

M. "He said, 'Lift up your head, O you gates, and be lifted up, you everlasting doors, and the King of glory shall come in. Who is this King of glory? The Lord strong and might, the Lord mighty in battle' (Ps. 24:7ff.).

N. "And it is further said, 'Lift up your heads, O you gates even lift them up, you everlasting doors' (Ps. 24:7).

O. "But he was not answered.

P. "When he said, 'Lord God, turn not away the face of your anointed, remember the mercies of David, your servant' (2 Chr. 6:42), forthwith he was answered.

Q. "At that moment the faces of David's enemies turned as black as the bottom of a pot, for all Israel knew that the Holy One, blessed be he, had forgiven him for that sin."

The story portrays God as consubstantial with humanity not only in physical and emotional traits but also, and especially, in the conformity to the social laws of correct transactions that, in theory at least, make society possible.

Among the available models for the comparing man to God – warrior, teacher, young man – the one that predominated entailed representation of God as sage. That is hardly surprising in the Oral Torah. The sage in the Oral Torah embodied the teachings of the Oral Torah, did the deeds that the Torah required, such as Torah-study, and so conformed to God's image of man as set forth in the Torah. In this connection we recall that God is represented as a schoolmaster: "He sits and teaches school children, as it is said, 'Whom shall one teach knowledge, and whom shall one make to understand the message? Those who are weaned from milk' " (Is. 28:9) (Bavli-tractate Abodah Zarah 3b). But this is not the same thing as God as a master-sage teaching mature disciples, that is, God as rabbi and sage.

God's personality is merged throughout with the personality of the ideal master or sage. That representation proves detailed and specific. A sage's life – Torah first learned through discipleship in the chain extending backward to Sinai, and then taught, through discipleship – encompassed the correct modes of discourse and ritual argument as well as the recasting of all relationships in accord with received convention of courtesy and subservience. God, then, is represented in both dimensions, as a master requiring correct conduct of his disciples, and as a teacher able to hold his own in arguments conducted in accord with the prevailing ritual. For one example, a master had the right to demand an appropriate greeting, and God, not receiving that greeting, asked why:

BAVLI-TRACTATE SHABBAT 9:3–4 I.43/89A

A. Said R. Joshua b. Levi, "When Moses came up on high, he found the Holy One, blessed be he, tying crowns onto the letters of the Torah. He said to him, 'Moses, don't people say hello in your town?'

B. "He said to him, 'Does a servant greet his master [first]?'

C. "He said to him, 'You should have helped me [at least by greeting me and wishing me success].'

D. "He said to him, 'Now I pray you let the power of the Lord be great, just as you have said' " (Num. 14:17).

Moses here plays the role of disciple to God the teacher, a persistent pattern throughout. Not having offered the appropriate greeting, the hapless disciple is instructed on the matter. Part of the ritual of "being a sage" thus comes to expression. Yet another detail of that same ritual taught how to make a request – and how not to do so. A request offered in humility is proper; one made in an arrogant or demanding spirit is not. Knowing what to ask is as important as knowing how. The congregation of Israel shows how not to do so, and God shows, nonetheless, the right mode of response, in the following:

BAVLI-TRACTATE TAANIT I:I/4A

A. The congregation of Israel made its request in an improper way, but the Holy One, blessed be he, responded in a proper way.

B. For it is said, [the congregation of Israel said to God,] "And let us know, eagerly strive to know, the Lord, the Lord's going forth is sure as the morning, and the Lord shall come to us as the rain" (Hos. 6:3).

C. Said the Holy One, blessed be he, to [the congregation of Israel,] "My daughter, now you are asking for something which sometimes is wanted and sometimes is not really wanted. But I shall give you something which is always wanted.

D. "For it is said, 'I will be as dew to Israel'" (Hos. 14:6).

Here the congregation of Israel acts improperly, but God responds with the wisdom of the sage that he is:

E. Further, [the congregation of Israel] made its request in an improper manner, "O God, set me as a seal on your heart, as a seal on your arm" (Song 8:6).

F. [But the Holy One, blessed be he, responded in a proper way.] Said the Holy One, blessed be he, to [the congregation of Israel,] "My daughter, now you are asking for something which sometimes can be seen and sometimes cannot be seen. But I shall give you something which can always be seen.

G. "For it is said, 'Behold, I have graven you on the palms of my hands' (Is. 49:16) [and the palms are always visible, in a way in which the heart and arm are not]."

Dew is always wanted, rain not. To be a seal on the heart or arm is to be displayed only occasionally. But the hands are always visible. Consequently, God as sage teaches Israel as disciple how to make a proper request.

We recall the division of humanity into two parts, Israel with the Torah, the nations with idolatry. We may hardly find surprising that, while God corresponds to man in general, the relationship of correspondence, shading over into intimacy and union, takes place with Israel in particular. Where there is love, there is true identification, such as takes place in Song of Songs Rabbah, so frequently cited in these pages. But, for the most part, in the Oral Torah's representation of matters God's person forms the counterpart to Israel's person, and the two correspond but also differ. The two, when equally hypostatized, are deemed counterparts, forming a relationship of deep love for one another. God indeed attains personhood in relationship to Israel, God's twin:

PESIQTA DERAB KAHANA V:VI.2

A. Said R. Hiyya bar Abba, "How do we know that the Holy One is called 'the heart of Israel'?
B. "On the basis of this verse: 'Rock of my heart and my portion is God forever'" (Ps. 73:26).

The amplification of the foregoing yields the picture of God as Israel's kin and lover, so both parties – the abstraction, "Israel," along with the abstraction, divinity – takes on the traits of personhood, personality in particular:

PESIQTA DERAB KAHANA V:VI.3

A. "... My beloved is knocking" refers to Moses: "And Moses said, Thus said the Lord, At about midnight I shall go out in the midst of Egypt" (Ex. 11:4).
B. "Open to me:"said R. Yosé, "Said the Holy One, blessed be he, 'Open to me [a hole] as small as the eye of a needle, and I shall open to you a gate so large that troops and siege-engines can go through it.'"
C. "... my sister": [God speaks:] "My sister – in Egypt, for they became my kin through two religious duties, the blood of the Passover-offering and the blood of circumcision."
D. "... my dearest" – at the sea, for they showed their love for me at the sea, "And they said, the Lord will reign forever and ever" (Ex. 15:19).
E. "... my dove" – my dove at Marah, where through receiving commandments they become distinguished for me like a dove.
F. "... my perfect one" – My perfect one at Sinai, for they became pure at Sinai: "And they said, all that the Lord has spoken we shall do and we shall hear" (Ex. 24:7).
G. R. Yannai said, "My twin, for I am not greater than they, nor they than I."
H. R. Joshua of Sikhnin said in the name of R. Levi, "Just as in the case of twins, if one of them gets a headache, the other one feels it, so said the Holy One, blessed be he, 'I am with him in trouble'" (Ps. 91:15).
I. "... for my head is drenched with dew." "The heavens dropped dew" (Judges 5:4).
J. "... my locks with the moisture of the night": "Yes, the clouds dropped water" (Judges 5:4).
K. When is this the case? In this month: "This month is for you the first of the months" (Ex. 12:2).

The notion of God and Israel as twins, the one formed as the counterpart of the other, thus involves the hypostatization of both parties to the transaction.

Accordingly, the final focus of correspondence between God and man concerns Israel, unique among nations and holy to God. How do God and, within humanity, Israel correspond? It is, first, that Israel forms on earth a society that corresponds to the retinue and court of God in Heaven. No surprise, then, that, just as Israel glorifies God, so God responds and celebrates Israel. Here, correspondence of man and God, now Israel and God, in physical, emotional, and social traits, comes to expression. God wears phylacteries, as does Israel, but while Israel's phylacteries contain verses of Scripture in praise of God, God's choice of Scripture praises Israel. God further forms the correct attitude towards Israel, which is one of love, an indication of an attitude on the part of divinity corresponding to right attitudes on the part of human beings. Finally, to close the circle, just as there is a "you" to whom humanity prays, so God, too, says prayers – to himself, to God – and the point of these prayers is that God should elicit from himself forgiveness for Israel. If there is sublimity in the Oral Torah, this is where it is:

BAVLI-TRACTATE BERAKHOT I:I III.23/6A-B

A. Said R. Nahman bar Isaac to R. Hiyya bar Abin, "As to the phylacteries of the Lord of the world, what is written in them?"

B. He said to him, " 'And who is like your people Israel, a singular nation on earth' (1 Chr. 17:21).

C. "And does the Holy One, blessed be he, sing praises for Israel?"

D. "Yes, for it is written, 'You have avouched the Lord this day ... and the Lord has avouched you this day' (Deut. 26:17, 18).

E. "Said the Holy One, blessed be he, to Israel, 'You have made me a singular entity in the world, and I shall make you a singular entity in the world.

F. " 'You have made me a singular entity in the world,' as it is said, 'Hear O Israel, the Lord, our God, the Lord is one' (Deut. 6:4).

G. " 'And I shall make you a singular entity in the world,' as it is said, 'And who is like your people, Israel, a singular nation in the earth' " (1 Chr. 17:21).

H. Said R. Aha, son of Raba to R. Ashi, "That takes care of one of the four subdivisions of the phylactery. What is written in the others?"

I. He said to him, " 'For what great nation is there ... And what great nation is there ...' (Deut. 4:7, 8), 'Happy are you, O Israel ...' (Deut. 33:29), 'Or has God tried ...,' (Deut. 4:34). And 'To make you high above all nations' " (Deut. 26:19).

J. "If so, there are too many boxes!

K. "But the verses, 'For what great nation is there' and 'And what great nation is there,' which are equivalent, are in one box, and 'Happy are you, O Israel' and 'Who is like your people Israel' are in one box, and 'Or has God tried ...,' in one box, and 'To make you high' in one box.

L. "And all of them are written in the phylactery that is on the arm."

We proceed to God's saying prayers, as does man, and the contents of those prayers:

BAVLI-TRACTATE BERAKHOT I:I III.32/7A

A. Said R. Yohanan in the name of R. Yosé, "How do we know that the Holy One, blessed be he, says prayers?

B. "Since it is said, 'Even them will I bring to my holy mountain and make them joyful in my house of prayer' (Is. 56:7).

C. " 'Their house of prayer' is not stated, but rather, 'my house of prayer.'

D. "On the basis of that usage we see that the Holy One, blessed be he, says prayers."

E. What prayers does he say?

F. Said R. Zutra bar Tobiah said Rab, " 'May it be my will that my mercy overcome my anger, and that my mercy prevail over my attributes, so that I may treat my children in accord with the trait of mercy and in their regard go beyond the strict measure of the law.' "

God seeks the blessing of the sage as well:

BAVLI-TRACTATE BERAKHOT I:I III.34/7A

A. It has been taught on Tannaite authority:

B. Said R. Ishmael b. Elisha, "One time I went in to offer up incense on the innermost altar, and I saw the crown of the Lord, enthroned on the highest throne, and he said to me, 'Ishmael, my son, bless me.'

C. "I said to him, 'May it be your will that your mercy overcome your anger, and that your mercy prevail over your attributes, so that you treat your children in accord with the trait of mercy and in their regard go beyond the strict measure of the law.'

D. "And he nodded his head to me."

E. And from that story we learn that the blessing of a common person should not be negligible in your view.

God's wearing phylacteries treats him as physically comparable to man; but the consubstantial traits of attitude and feeling – just as humanity feels joy, so does God, just as humanity celebrates God, so does God celebrate Israel – are the more urgent. Just as Israel declares God to be unique, so God declares Israel to be unique. And just as Israel prays to God, so God says prayers. What God asks of himself is that he transcend himself – which is what, in prayer, humanity asks for as well. It would be difficult to find more ample evidence of a theological system that deems God and Israelite man to correspond.

Among these, however, as in the Written Torah, the point of correspondence of greatest consequence concerns attitudes, feelings, and emotions. Our consideration of the matter of *zekhut* in chapter 8 has prepared us for that result, the point at which complementarity shades over into correspondence. God and man are consubstantial, above all, at heart. A systematic statement of the matter comes to us in tractate Abot, which presents the single most comprehensive account of religious affections. These turn out to pertain to God's as much as to man's feelings. The reason is that, in that document above all, how we feel defines a critical aspect of virtue. A simple catalogue of permissible feelings comprises humility, generosity, self-abnegation, love, a spirit of conciliation of the other, and eagerness to please. A list of impermissible emotions is made up of envy, ambition, jealousy, arrogance, sticking to one's opinion, self-centredness, a grudging spirit, vengefulness, and the like. People should aim at eliciting from others acceptance and good will and should avoid confrontation, rejection, and humiliation of the other. This they do through conciliation and giving up their own claims and rights. So both catalogues form a harmonious and uniform whole, aiming at the cultivation of the humble and malleable person, one who accepts everything and resents nothing.

Time and again, the compilation tractate Abot underscores, one who conciliates others is favoured by God, who respects and honours those who, as in the stores that convey the transaction that generates *zekhut*, give up what no one can demand:

TRACTATE ABOT 2:4

2:4 A. He would say, "Make his wishes into your own wishes, so that he will make your wishes into his wishes.

B. "Put aside your wishes on account of his wishes, so that he will put aside the wishes of other people in favour of your wishes."

If a man makes God's wishes his own, he will make the man's wishes his, and if one gives way to others, God will protect the man from the ill-will of others. God further favours those who seek to please others:

3:10 A. He would say, "Anyone from whom people take pleasure – the Omnipresent takes pleasure.

B. "And anyone from whom people do not take pleasure, the Omnipresent does not take pleasure."

Along these same lines, Mishnah-tractate Abot 3:10 advises that God is pleased by those who try to please others: "Anyone from whom people take pleasure – the Omnipresent takes pleasure. Aqiba at T. Berakhot 3:3 goes over the same ground: "One in whom mankind delights, God delights. One in whom mankind does not delight, God does not delight. One who is content with his own portion, it is a good sign for him. One who is not content with his own portion, it is a bad sign for him."

A sequence of paradoxes – strength is marked by weakness, wisdom by the capacity to learn, wealth by making do, honour by the power to honour others – yields the picture of traits that man should cultivate, to which God will respond:

4:1 A. Ben Zoma says, "Who is a sage? He who learns from everybody,

B. "as it is said, From all my teachers I have gotten understanding (Ps. 119:99).

C. "Who is strong? He who overcomes his desire,

D. "as it is said, He who is slow to anger is better than the mighty, and he who rules his spirit than he who takes a city (Prov. 16:32).

E. "Who is rich? He who is happy in what he has,

F. "as it is said, When you eat the labour of your hands, happy will you be, and it will go well with you (Ps. 128:2).

G. ("Happy will you be in this world, and it will go well with you in the world to come.")

H. "Who is honoured? He who honors everybody,

I. "as it is said, 'For those who honor me I shall honour, and they who despise me will be treated as of no account' " (I Sam. 2:30).

4:18 A. R. Simeon b. Eleazar says, "(1) Do not try to make amends with your fellow when he is angry,

B. "or (2) comfort him when the corpse of his beloved is lying before him,

C. "or (3) seek to find absolution for him at the moment at which he takes a vow,

D. "or (4) attempt to see him when he is humiliated."

4:19 A. Samuel the Small says, "Rejoice not when your enemy falls, and let not your heart be glad when he is overthrown, lest the Lord see it and it displease him, and he turn away his wrath from him" (Prov. 24:17).

True, these virtues, in this tractate as in the system as a whole, derive from knowledge of what really counts, which is what God wants. But God favours those who – like God – aspire to please others. The point of correspondence is clear: virtues appreciated by human beings prove identical to the ones to which God responds as well. And what single virtue of the heart encompasses the rest? Restraint, the source of self-abnegation, humility, serves as the antidote for ambition, vengefulness, and, above all, arrogance. It is restraint of our own interest that enables us to deal generously with others, humility about ourselves that generates a liberal spirit towards others.

So the emotions prescribed in tractate Abot turn out to provide variations of a single feeling, which is the sentiment of the disciplined heart, whatever affective form it may take. And where does the heart learn its lessons, if not in relationship to God? So: "Make his wishes yours, so that he will make your wishes his" (Abot 2:4). Applied to the relationships between human beings, this inner discipline of the emotional life will yield exactly those virtues of conciliation and self-abnegation, humility and generosity of spirit, that the framers of tractate Abot spell out in one example after another. Imputing to Heaven exactly those responses felt on earth, for example, "Anyone from whom people take pleasure, God takes pleasure" (Abot 3:10), makes the point at the most general level.

Do the sages mean that man and God correspond, or do we deal with some sort of figurative or poetic representing relationships of a less tangible character than I have suggested? I should claim that the entire system of theology, with its account of world order based on God's pervasive justice and rationality, means to portray exactly how things actually are – or, with man's correct engagement, can be made to be. For the sages, we deal with the true reality that this world's corruption obscures.

What we see, therefore, is an application of a large-scale, encompassing exercise in analogical thinking – something is like something else, stands for, evokes, or symbolizes that which is quite outside itself. It may be the opposite of something else, in which case it conforms to the exact opposite of the rules that govern that something else. The reasoning is analogical or it is contrastive, and the fundamental logic is taxonomic. The taxonomy rests on those comparisons and contrasts we should call parabolic. In that case what lies on the surface misleads, just as we saw how the sages deem superficial the challenges to God's justice that private lives set forth. Conceding the depth of human suffering, the sages also pointed out that, sometimes, suffering conveys its own blessing. And so throughout, what lies beneath or beyond the surface – there is the true reality. People who see things this way constitute the opposite of ones who call a thing as it is. Self-evidently, they have become accustomed to perceiving more – or less – than is at hand.

God and man correspond in the call from the One to the other for forbearance, patience, humiliation, self-abnegation. God, disappointed with creation, challenged by the gentiles with their idolatry, corresponded with Israel, defeated and subjugated, challenged by the worldly dominance of those who rejected the Torah. Both, the sages maintained, dealt with failure, and both had to survive the condition of defeat. But if, we cannot remind ourselves too often, God and man correspond, God is always God, man, man, Creator and creature.

We conclude the matter of theological anthropology exactly where we ended our account of the ultimate anomaly, man's condition in the world order of justice, with the insistence that, all things having been said, man's ultimate task is silence in the face of the tremendum:

BAVLI TRACTATE MENAHOT 3:7 II.5/29B

5. A. Said R. Judah said Rab, "At the time that Moses went up on high, he found the Holy One in session, affixing crowns to the letters [of the words of the Torah]. He said to him, 'Lord of the universe, who is stopping you [from regarding the document as perfect without these additional crowns on the letters]?'

B. "He said to him, 'There is a man who is going to arrive at the end of many generations, and Aqiba b. Joseph is his name, who is going to interpret on the basis of each point of the crowns heaps and heaps of laws.'

C. "He said to him, 'Lord of the Universe, show him to me.'

D. "He said to him, 'Turn around.'

E. "He went and took a seat at the end of eight rows, but he could not grasp what the people were saying. He felt faint. But when the discourse reached a certain matter, and the disciples said, 'My lord, how do you know this?' and he answered, 'It is a law given to Moses from Sinai,' he regained his composure.

F. "He went and came before the Holy One. He said before him, 'Lord of the Universe, How come you have someone like that and yet you give the Torah through me?'

G. "He said to him, 'Silence! That is how the thought came to me.'

H. "He said to him, 'Lord of the Universe, you have shown me his Torah, now show me his reward.'

I. "He said to him, 'Turn around.'

J. "He turned around and saw his flesh being weighed out at the butcher-stalls in the market.

K. "He said to him, 'Lord of the Universe, 'Such is Torah, such is the reward?'

L. "He said to him, 'Silence! That is how the thought came to me.' "

The sages had in mind to construct man in God's image, not God in man's.

So much for the doctrines that systematically and coherently set forth the theology of a world order regulated by God's justice, an order in which reward and punishment proportionately and exactly responded to man's deeds, an order in which God responded according to reliable rules to both Israel and the

Torah, gentiles and idolatry, and an order that encompassed both public affairs and private life. This perfect world, unchanging and beyond time, brought God together with man in relationships of a complementary character, endowing Israel and God with corresponding traits, so that the one could understand and rely upon the other. But if the Oral Torah's theology of a just world order could account for how things are and are supposed to be, how, in a manner coherent with their doctrines of justice and rationality and coherence, did the sages make sense of what ought not to happen, which is the way things have come about in the here and now? To the sources of disruption and the causes of chaos, the true challenges to the sages' theology of prevailing justice in the public order and private condition as well, we now turn.

PART III

Sources of World Disorder

10 Intentionality

The theology of the Oral Torah now realizes in its fullness the theological anthropology set forth in the relationships of complementarity and correspondence. Here that theology explains, at just this turning in the unfolding of the system, its logic that explains who is man. Complementary with God in some ways, corresponding in others, man bears a single trait that most accords with the likeness of God: it is his possession of free will and the power of the free exercise thereof. In his act of will God makes just rules, and in his, man wilfully breaks them.

Man matches God in possessing freedom of will. And therein the sages found the source of world disorder. Man's will was the sole power in the world that matched the power of God. And it is that variable in creation that accounts for the present imperfection of creation. To understand why, we recall that by his act of will God created the orderly world of justice, one that exhibits abundant, indicative marks of perfection. Then whence chaos embodied by disorder and dissonance? And when the rules that embody rationality – that guarantee measure for measure above all – cease to describe the everyday experience of mankind and the here and now of Israel, where shall we find the reason why? In the logic of a world order based on exact justice, in the Torah God accords to man a statement of his own will, a commandment, and one who issues a command both wants the command to be obeyed but also accords to the other the power to disobey. That is the very premise of commandments.

For the sages, therefore, it was man's rebellion, beyond God's control but within God's dominion, that explains change. And change, imperfection, the ephemerality of affairs – these signal the actualities of disorder in a world meant for perfection, stasis, balance throughout. God proposes, man disposes. Chaos begins not in God but in man, in that trait of man that endows man with the same power that the Creator has, to conceive and to do. Since God has made an orderly world, only his counterpart on earth, man, can account for the disruption of world order. For the sole player in the cosmic drama with the power to upset God's plans is man. He alone is like God, "in our image, after our likeness." In their penetrating reflection on the power of intentionality, the sages explain chaos, and that prepares the way for their investigation of sin and its remedy.

That is why, explaining the imperfection of change, the advent of time in the historical sense, the inequality of exchange, the theology of the Oral Torah finds in the opposite of the indicators of perfection the sources of disruption. And change comes about principally because man by an act of will corrupts perfection. Accordingly, the Oral Torah takes as its critical problem the generative tension between the word of God and the will of man, in full recognition that God judges what man does by reason of the exercise of free will. Set forth in many ways, this principle is stated on its simplest form when R. Aqiba says, "Everything is foreseen, and free choice is given; in goodness the world is judged; and all is in accord with the abundance of deeds" (Tractate Abot 3:15A).

Free will, moreover, reaches concrete expression in the deeds a man does by reason of the plans or intentions that he shapes on his own. The high value accorded by God to man's voluntary act of accepting God's dominion, the enthusiastic response made by God to man's supererogatory deeds of uncoerced love and uncompelled generosity, the heavy emphasis upon the virtues of self-abnegation and self-restraint – these emblematic traits of the coherent theology attest to the uncertainty of man's response that, from the beginning, God has built into creation. For the one power that lies beyond the rules of reason, that defies predicting, is man's power to make up his own mind.

How are we to show how these convictions form the center of the theological structure and system set forth in the Oral Torah? Commensurate with the claim just now set forth, that intentionality defines the centre of the system, the demonstration must adduce evidence of a systemic and systematic character. For that purpose, sayings, however demonstrably typical, and episodic stories or exegeses of verses of Scripture, however probative in character, do not match the task. Turning, rather, to norms of behaviour, we seek evidence in the authority of required, enforced law. This is of two kinds.

First, the Oral Torah designs enduring structures, institutions for the governance of Israel as a Godly realm. If I can show that, in its very doctrine of how holy Israel is governed, intentionality forms the critical point of differentiation even of institutional politics – the power legitimately to inflict violence – then my claim concerning the centrality of intentionality in explaining world order and its corruption will find commensurate demonstration.

Second, the Oral Torah makes its theological statement not only in apodictic sayings, such as the one of Aqiba cited just now, or in exegesis of Scripture, or in tales of the sages and exemplary stories. It speaks also, and especially, through specific norms of conduct. My task is to show how intentionality governs actualities of behaviour, not of mere belief. We shall see how the consideration of the will of man preoccupies the sages when they define the norms of everyday conduct.

To accomplish the task of showing the normative and paramount power of intentionality or the act of will, I have selected the sages' theoretical account[1] of the working of the enduring institutions of holy Israel, the theological politics of their system. When they describe the government of holy Israel, they carry out a labour of differentiation of power, indicating what agency or person has the power to precipitate the working of politics as legitimate violence at all. And, as we shall see through the provisions that they make for various institutional foci of power to carry out diverse tasks, it is at the point of intentionality, with the story of Eden in hand, that the sages accomplish their goal. Were we to ignore Eden, we could make no sense of their concrete provisions for holy Israel's government. When, therefore, we understand the differentiating force of intentionality at the most practical level of the sages' theory of the social order, the power of the human will that imparts to politics its activity and dynamism, we shall grasp what everywhere animates the structures of the politics and propels the system. That is why I have chosen as a principal part of my account of intentionality the sages' theological politics.

---

1. I see no point in speculating on the relationship between that theory and political actualities of this-worldly Israel, before, during, or after the composition of the documents of the Oral Torah. The theory of a tripartite government, in the hands of high priest and Temple, king and administration, and sage and court, does not pertain to how Israel actually was governed at any point, whether in the picture of the Written Torah of ancient Israelite times, the historical accounts of the Second Temple period, or the epoch after the destruction of political autonomy in 70 C.E. Not only so, but to imagine that the sages anticipated in Mishnah-tractate Sanhedrin-Makkot and other passages how Israel's government would constitute itself in the return to the Land of Israel at the time of the Messiah is to ignore the entirety of the sages' thought on what would and would not take place in the world to come. As we shall see in chapter 14, with the resurrection complete, the world to come fully realized, God in charge, there would be no need for the legitimate violence of high priest, king, or sage. Our account of the theology of the Oral Torah does not require an answer to the question, to what circumstance do the sages address their politics? This is just as well, since, in any case, I cannot answer the question.

Politics concerns legitimate violence, the functioning of sanctions. Specifically, we analyse the mythic foundations of sanctions that the sages assign to various authorities, on earth and in Heaven. And when we move from sanctions to the myth expressed and implicit in the application and legitimation of those sanctions, we see a complex but cogent politics sustained by a simple political theology. This survey of sanctions and their implications had best commence with a clear statement of what we shall now uncover. The encompassing political framework of rules, institutions, and sanctions is explained and validated by appeal to God's shared rule. That dominion, exercised by God and his surrogates on earth, is focused partly in the royal palace, the king, partly in the Temple, the priesthood, and partly in the court and its sages. For us, the issue here is, which part falls where and why? Helpfully, the political myth explains who exercises legitimate violence and under what conditions, and furthermore specifies the source for differentiation. The myth consequently serves a particular purpose – which is to answer that particular question. Indeed, the sages' political myth comes to expression in its details of differentiation, which permit us to identify, and of course to answer, the generative question of politics.

Moving from the application of power to the explanation thereof, we find that the system focuses upon finding answers to the question of who imposes which sanction, and why. And those answers contain the political myth, nowhere expressed, everywhere in full operation. Through the examination of sanctions, we identify the foci of power. At that point we ask how power is differentiated. In spelling out what the reader may now find somewhat enigmatic, I have skipped many stages in the argument and the examination of the evidence. So let us begin from the very beginning. How, exactly, do I propose to identify the political myth of the Dual Torah? And precisely what data are supposed to attest to that myth?

Institutions of political persuasion and coercion dominate not only through physical but also through mental force, through psychological coercion or appeal to good will. So my inquiry's premise is not far to seek. I take as a given that a political myth animates the structure of a politics. But the authorship of the Mishnah, upon the politics of which we concentrate for the present analysis, has chosen other media for thought and expression than narrative and teleological ones. It is a philosophical, not a historical (fictive) account; it is conveyed through masses of detailed rules about small things. While the Mishnah through its cases amply informs us on the institutions of politics, the mythic framework within which persuasion and inner compliance are supposed to bring about submission to legitimate power scarcely emerges, remaining only implicit throughout.

But it is readily discerned when we ask the right questions. If we were to bring to the authors of the Mishnah such questions as "who tells whom what to do?" (or "who can do what to whom, and for how long?"), they would point to the politics' imaginary king and its equally fictive high priest, and its court comprised by sages, all with associated authorities and functionaries. Here, they would tell us, are the institutions of politics – represented in personal rather than abstract form, to be sure. But if we were to say to them, "And tell us the story (in our language: the myth) that explains on what basis you persuade people to conform," they would find considerable difficulty in bringing to the fore the explicit mythic statements made by their writing.

How, then, are we to identify, on the basis of what the Mishnah does tell us, the generative myths to which the system is supposed to appeal? A myth explains the exercise of legitimate power. Now, we know, power comes to brutal expression when the state kills or maims someone or deprives a person of property through the imposition of legal sanctions for crime or sin.[2] In the absence of a myth of power, we therefore begin with power itself. We shall work our way back from the facts of power to the intimations, within the record of legitimately violent sanctions, of the intellectual and even mythic sources of legitimation for the exercise and use of that legitimate violence. For it is at the point of imposing sanctions, of killing, injuring, denying property, excluding from society, that power operates in its naked form. How these legitimate exercises of violence are validated will then set before us such concrete evidence of the myth. And, so far as there is such evidence, that will identify the political myth of the Dual Torah that commences with the Mishnah. The relevance to the centrality of intentionality in the theology of the Dual Torah will become transparent by the end, even though it is obscure at this point.

Since the analysis of sources will prove somewhat abstruse, let me signal in advance the main line of argument. Analysing myth by explaining sanctions draws our attention to the modes of legitimate violence that the system identifies. There we find four types of sanctions, each deriving from a distinct institution of political power, each bearing its own mythic explanation.

1) what God and the Heavenly court can do to people;
2) what the earthly court can do to people (the legitimate application of the worldly and physical kinds of violence of which political theory ordinarily speaks);

---

2. I do not distinguish crime from sin, since I do not think the system does. At the same time, our own world does make such a distinction, and it would be confusing not to preserve it. That accounts for the usage throughout.

3) what the cult can do to people (the cult through its requirements can deprive people of their property as legitimately as can a court); and

4) conformity with consensus – self-imposed sanctions (here the issue is, whose consensus, and defined by whom?).

Across these four types of sanction, four types of coercion are in play. They depend on violence of various kinds – psychological and social as much as physical. Clearly, then, the sanctions that are exercised by other than judicial-political agencies prove violent and legitimately coercive, even though the violence and coercion are not the same as those carried out by courts.

On this basis we can differentiate among types of sanctions – and hence trace evidences of how the differentiation is explained. Since our data focus upon who does what to whom, the myth of politics must explain why various types of sanctions are put into effect by diverse political agencies or institutions. As we shall see, the exercise of power, invariably and undifferentiatedly in the name and by the authority of God in Heaven to be sure, is kept distinct. And the distinctions in this case signal important differences which then require explanation. Concrete application of legitimate violence by Heaven covers different matters from parts of the political and social world governed by the policy and coercion of the this-worldly political classes. And both sorts of violence have to be kept distinct from the sanction effected by the community through the weight of attitude and public opinion. Here, again, we find a distinct set of penalties applied to a particular range of actions.

When we have seen the several separate kinds of sanction and where they apply, we shall have a full account of the workings of politics as the application of power, and from that concrete picture we may, I think, identify the range of power and the mythic framework that has accommodated and legitimized diverse kinds of power.

Our task, therefore, is to determine, on the basis of sanctions' distinct realms, Heaven, earth, and the mediating range of the Temple and sacrifice, which party imposes sanctions for (in modern parlance) what crimes or sins. Where Heaven intervenes, do other authorities participate, and if so, what tells me which party takes charge and imposes its sanction? Is the system differentiated so that where earth is in charge, there is no pretense of appeal to Heaven? Or do we find cooperation in coextensive jurisdiction, such that one party penalizes an act under one circumstance, the other the same act under a different circumstance? A survey of the sanctions enables us to differentiate the components of the power structure before us. So we wonder whether each of these three estates that enjoy power and inflict sanctions of one kind or another – Heaven, earth, Temple in-between – governs its own affairs, without the intervention of the others, or whether each takes charge in collaboration with the other, so that power is parcelled out and institutions simultaneously differentiate themselves from one another and also intersect. The survey of sanctions will allow us to answer these questions and so identify the myth of politics and the exercise of power that the Oral Torah promulgated through the institutional arrangements set forth by the law of the Mishnah.

Our authors represent the entire system as the realization of God's dominion over Israel. And this representation is specific and detailed. It thus justifies an inquiry, once we have identified the questions the myth must answer, into how, in Scripture, we find responses to just those questions. Here, then, is one instance of the way in which Scripture provides a detail of a myth accompanying a detail of legitimate coercion. The following lists the number of law-violations that one commits by making a profit, which is to say, as we recall from chapter 7, collecting interest:

MISHNAH-TRACTATE BABA MESIA 5:11

A. Those who participate in a loan on interest violate a negative commandment: these are the lender, borrower, guarantor, and witnesses.
B. Sages say, "Also the scribe."
C. They violate the negative commandment, "You will not give him your money upon usury" (Lev. 25:37); "You will not take usury from him" (Lev. 25:36); "You shall not be a creditor to him" (Ex. 22:25); "Nor shall you lay upon him usury" (Ex. 22:25); and they violate the negative command, "You shall not put a stumbling block before the blind, but you shall fear your God. I am the Lord" (Lev. 19:14).

We appeal to the Torah to justify law-obedience and to impose sanction for disobedience. But where is the myth that sustains obedience? Let me explain this question, which is critical to all that follows. On the basis of the passage just cited, we do not know what actually happens to me if I do participate in a loan on interest and so violate various rules of the Torah. More to the point, we do not know who enforces that penalty or effects it. That is to say, the generalized appeal to the law of the Torah and the assumed premise that one should obey that law and not violate it hardly tell me the morphology of the political myth at hand. They assume a myth that is not set forth, and they conceal those details in which the myth gains its sustaining vitality and power.

Clearly, simply knowing that everything is in accord with the Written Torah and that God wants Israel to keep the laws of the Torah does not reveal the systemically active component of the political myth. On the one hand, the propositions are too general; on the other hand, they do not address the critical question. The sequence of self-evident premises that runs, one, God revealed the Torah, two, the political institutions and rules carry out the Torah, and therefore, three, people should conform, hardly sustains a concrete theory of *just* where and how God's authority serves the systemic construction at hand. The appeal to Scripture, therefore, reveals no incisive information about the Oral Torah's validating myth as set forth in the laws of the Mishnah.

This conclusion is reinforced by the references we find here and there to "the kingdom of Heaven" that appeal to God's rule in an everyday framework. These form a mere allegation that, in general, what the political authorities tell people to do is what God wants them to do. For example, at Mishnahtractate Ber. 2:5, to Gamaliel is attributed the statement, "I cannot heed you to suspend from myself the kingdom of Heaven even for one hour." As a matter of fact, that is not a political context – there is no threat of legitimate violence, for instance – for the saying has to do with reciting the *Shema*. No political conclusions are drawn from that allegation. Quite to the contrary, Gamaliel, head of the collegium of sages, is not thereby represented as relinquishing power to Heaven, only as expressing his obedience to divine rule even when he does not have to. Indeed, as we recall from chapter 3, Israel, living in the kingdom of Heaven, does not form a political category, even though, as we shall see, in the theological politics of the sages, all power flows from God's will and law, expressed in the Torah.

In the Oral Torah the manipulation and application of power, allowing the impositions of drastic sanctions in support of the law, for instance, invariably flow through institutions, on earth and in Heaven, of a quite concrete and material character. "The kingdom of Heaven" may be within, but violate the law deliberately and wantonly and God will kill you sooner than you should otherwise have had to die. And, as a matter of fact, the Mishnah's framers rarely appeal in the context of politics and the legitimate exercise of violence to "the kingdom of Heaven." When we considered the same matter earlier, we noted that Israel's acceptance of the dominion of the kingdom of Heaven involved acts of worship and obedience but at no point invoked coercion in a this-worldly framework.

Indeed, from the Pentateuchal writings, we can hardly construct the *particular* politics, including the mythic component thereof, that operates. First of all, the Written Torah does not prepare us to make sense of the institutions that the politics of the sages designs – government by king and high priest, rather than, as in the Pentateuch, prophet. Second, and concomitantly, the Pentateuchal myth that legitimatizes coercion – rule by God's prophet, governance through explicitly revealed laws that God has dictated for the particular occasion! – plays no active and systemic role whatsoever in the formulation and presentation of the Mishnah's theological politics. Rather, of the types of political authority contained within the scriptural repertoire, the Mishnah's philosophers reject prophetic and charismatic authority and deem critical the authority exercised by the sage's disciple who has been carefully nurtured in rules, not in gifts of the spirit. The authority of sages in their theological politics does not derive from charisma (revelation by God to the sage who makes a ruling in a given case, or even from general access to God for the sage). The myth we shall presently explore in no way falls into the classification of a charismatic myth of politics.

True, everybody knows and believes that God has dictated the Torah to Moses. But the Mishnah's framers do not then satisfy themselves with a paraphrase of what God has said to Moses in the Torah. How might they have done so? The answer to that question provides perspective on what our authors have done. The following allows us to see how matters might have been phrased – but never were:

MISHNAH-TRACTATE ROSH HASHANAH 3:8

A. "Now it happened that when Moses held up his hand, Israel prevailed, and when he let his hand fall, Amalek prevailed" (Ex. 17:11).

B. Now do Moses's hands make war or stop it?

C. But the purpose is to say this to you:

D. So long as the Israelites would set their eyes upward and submit their hearts to their Father in Heaven, they would grow stronger. And if not, they fell.

E. In like wise, you may say the following:

F. "Make yourself a fiery serpent and set it on a standard, and it shall come to pass that every one who is bitten, when he sees it, shall live" (Num. 21:8).

G. Now does that serpent [on the standard] kill or give life? [Obviously not.]

H. But: So long as the Israelites would set their eyes upward and submit to their Father in Heaven, they would be healed. And if not, they would pine away.

The silence now becomes eloquent. We look in vain in the pages of our systemic writing for a *single* example in which authorities ask people to raise their eyes on high and so to obey what said authorities command. Such a political myth may, however, be implicit. But when made explicit and systemically active, not left in its inert condition, the myth we seek by definition precipitates not obedience in general but rather concrete decision-making processes, to be sure inclusive of obedience to those decisions once made. And we shall know the reason why.

More to the point, is God's direct intervention (for example, as portrayed in Scripture) represented as a preferred or even available sanction? Yes and no, but mostly no. For in our system what is important is that the myth of

God's intervention on an ad hoc and episodic basis in the life of the community hardly serves to explain obedience to the law in the here and now. What sort of evidence would indicate that God intervenes in such wise as to explain the obedience to the law on an everyday basis? Invoking God's immediate presence, a word said, a miracle performed, would suffice. But in the entirety of the more than five hundred chapters of the Mishnah, no one ever prays to have God supply a decision in a particular case. Furthermore, no judge appeals to God to put to death a convicted felon. If the judge wants the felon killed, he orders him killed. When God intervenes, it is on the jurisdiction assigned to God, not the court. And then the penalty is a different one from execution.

It follows that an undifferentiated myth explaining the working of undifferentiated power by appeal to God's will, while relevant, is not exact and does not explain this system in its rich detail. How the available mythic materials explain the principles of differentiation now requires attention. The explanation must be both general and specific. That is to say, while the court orders and carries out the execution, the politics works in such a way that all three political institutions, God, the court (sage) and the Temple (priest), the three agencies with the power to bestow or take away life and property and to inflict physical pain and suffering, work together in a single continuum and in important ways cooperate to deal with the same crimes or sins. The data to which we now turn will tell us who does what to whom and why, and, in the reason why, we shall uncover the political myth we seek. At the very heart of matters we shall uncover the determinative power of intentionality. But the process by which we reach that conclusion is what counts, since that requires us to sift the evidence meant by the sages to dictate the very governance of holy Israel, the institutions, procedures, and sanctions of government on earth and in Heaven. And out of the result we shall see a clear, powerful, and normative statement of the meaning of intentionality, how man's and God's acts of will bear equal weight.

Predictably, when we work our way through sanctions to recover the mythic premises thereof, we begin with God's place in the institutionalization and execution of legitimate violence. Of course, the repertoire of sanctions does encompass God's direct intervention, but that is hardly a preferred alternative or a common one. Still, God does commonly intervene when oaths are violated, for oaths are held to involve the person who invokes God's name and God. Further, whereas when faced with an insufficiency of valid evidence under strict rules of testimony, the earthly court cannot penalize serious crime, the Heavenly court can and does impose a penalty. Clearly, then, God serves to justify the politics and account for its origin. Although God is never asked to join in making specific decisions and effecting policy in the every-day politics of the state, deliberate violation of certain rules provokes God's or the Heavenly court's direct intervention. Thus, obedience to the law clearly represents submission to God in Heaven. Further, forms of Heavenly coercion such as we shall presently survey suggest a complex mythic situa-tion, with more subtle nuance than the claim that, overall, God rules, would indicate. A politics of rules and regulations cannot admit God's ad hoc partic-ipation, and this system did not do so. God joined in the system in a regular and routine way, and the rules took for granted God's part in the sages' theo-logical politics.

Precisely how does the intervention of God into the system come to con-crete expression? By appeal to the rules handed down at Sinai as an ultimate reference in legal questions, for instance. This is the case in the story about R. Simeon of Mispah, who sowed his field with two types of wheat. Simeon's problem is that he may have violated the law against sowing mixed seeds in a single patch. When the matter came before Rabban Gamaliel, the passage states:

MISHNAH-TRACTATE PEAH 2:6

C. They went up to the Chamber of Hewn Stone and asked [about the law regarding sowing two types of wheat in one field].

D. Said Nahum the Scribe, "I have received [the following ruling] from R. Miasha, who received it from his father, who received [it] from the pairs, who received [it] from the prophets, [who received] the law [given] to Moses on Sinai, regarding one who sows his field with two types of wheat ..."

Here, the law's legitimacy clearly depends on its descent by tradition from Sinai. But that general principle of descent from Sinai was invoked only rarely. Indeed, R. Simeon's case undermines the Mishnah's relation to God's intervention. R. Simeon's problem is minor. Nothing important requires so drastic a claim to be made explicit. That is to say, it is a mere commonplace that the system appeals to Sinai.

But this is not a politics of revelation, for a politics of revelation consis-tently and immediately appeals to the fact that God works in the here and now, all the time, in concrete cases. Such a politics would leave little space for the working of man's will. That appeal is not common in the Mishnah's statement of its system nor in the elaboration thereof in the Talmuds and related *halakhic* writings, and, consequently, that appeal to revelation does not bear important political tasks and is not implicit here. Indeed, I do not think it was present at all, except where Scripture made it so (for example, with the ordeal inflicted on the wife accused of adultery, which played so critical a role in our understanding, in chapter 1, of measure for measure). Why the persistent interest in legitimization other than through the revelation of the Torah for the immediate case? The answer to that question draws upon the traits of philosophers, who are interested in the prevailing rule governing all cases and the explanation for the exceptions, rather than upon those of historian-prophets, who are engaged by the exceptional case which is then represented as paradigmatic. Our philosophers appeal to a story to explain what is routine and orderly, and what they wish to explain is what is ordinary and everyday: nstitutions and rules, not cases and ad hoc decisions yielding no rule at all.

It is the regularity and order of God's participation in the politics that the character of the myth of the politics maintains we have to understand and account for. Mere allegations in general that the law originates with God's revelation to Moses at Sinai do not serve to identify that middle-range story that accounts for the structure and the system and above all the systematic sanctions. If God is not sitting at the shoulder of the judge and telling the judge what to do (as the writers of Exodus 21ff. seem to suppose), then what legitimacy attaches to the judge's decision to give Mr Smith's field over, or back, to Mr Jones? And why (within the imaginary state at hand) should people support, sustain, and submit to authority? The sages' abstract language contains no answers to these questions.

And yet the sages' system presupposes routine and everyday obedience to power, not merely the utilization of legitimate violence to secure conformity. That is partly because the systemic statement tells very few stories. Matters that the Pentateuchal writers expressed through narrating a specific story about how God said thus and so to Moses in this particular case, rewarding the ones who obeyed and punishing those who did not, in the Mishnah come to expression in language of an allusive and philosophical, generalizing character.

Here, too, we discern the character of the myth even before we determine its contents. While we scarcely expect that this sort of writing is apt to spell out a myth, even though a myth infuses the system, we certainly can identify the components of the philosophical and theological explanation of the state that have taken mythic form.

Even here, to be sure, the evidence proves sparse. First, of course, in the structure comes God, who commands and creates, laying out what humanity is to do, exercising the power to form the social world in which humanity is to obey. God then takes care of his particular concerns, and these focus upon *deliberate* violation of God's wishes. If a sin or crime is inadvertent, the penalties are of one order, if deliberate, of a different order. The most serious infraction of the law of the Torah is identified not by what is done but by the attitude of the sinner or criminal. If one has deliberately violated his rule, then God intervenes. If the violation is inadvertent, then the Temple imposes the sanction. And the difference is considerable. In the former case, God through the Heavenly court ends the felon's or sinner's life. Then a person who defies the laws – as these concern one's sexual conduct, attitude towards God, relationships within the family – will be penalized either (if necessary) by God or (if possible) by the earthly court. This means that the earthly court exercises God's power, and the myth of the system as a whole, so far as the earthly court forms the principal institutional form of the system, emerges not merely in a generality but in all its specificity. These particular judges, here and now, stand for God and exercise the power of God. In the latter case, the Temple takes over jurisdiction; a particular offering is called for, as the book of Leviticus specifies. But there is no need for God or the earthly court in God's name to take a position.

Now come the data of real power, the sanctions. We may divide sanctions just as the authorship of the Mishnah did, by simply reviewing the range of penalties for law-infraction as they occur. These penalties, as we mentioned above, fall into four classifications: what Heaven does, what political institutions do, what religious institutions do, and what is left to the coercion of public opinion, that is, consensus, with special attention to the definition of that "public" that has effective opinion to begin with. The final realm of power, conferring or withholding approval, proves constricted and, in this context, not very consequential.

Let us begin with the familiar, with sanctions exercised by the earthly court as they are fully described in Mishnah-tractates Sanhedrin and Makkot. Here is covered the imposition of sanctions as it is represented by the earthly court, the Temple, and by the Heavenly court, the sages. This review allows us to identify the actors in the system of politics – those with power to impose sanctions, and the sanctions they can inflict. Only from this perspective will the initial statement of the sages, the Mishnah, in its own odd idiom, be able to make its points in the way its authors have chosen. When we take up the myth to which that statement implicitly appeals, we shall have a clear notion of the character of the evidence, in rich detail, on which our judgment of the mythic substrate of the system has been composed.

The most impressive mode of legitimate violence is killing; it certainly focuses our attention. The earthly court may justly kill a sinner or felon. This death-dealing priority accorded to the earthly court derives from the character of the power entrusted to that court. The earthly court enjoys full power to dispose of the property and life of all subject to its authority – that is, in the context imagined by the sages, of all residing in territory that comes under the state's control. Imposing the death penalty is described in the following way:

MISHNAH-TRACTATE SANHEDRIN 7:1

A. Four modes of execution were given over to the court [in order of severity]:
B. (1) stoning, (2) burning, (3) decapitation, and (4) strangulation.
C. R Simeon says, "(2) Burning, (1) stoning, (4) strangulation, and (3) decapitation."

The passage leaves no doubt that the court could put people to death. Only the severity of suffering imposed by each mode of execution is in question. Thus, Simeon's hierarchy of punishments (C) differs from that of B in the degradation and suffering inflicted on the felon, not in the end result. The passage details four modes of execution, that is, four forms of legitimate violence. In the account, the following is of special interest. I have emphasized the key words.

MISHNAH-TRACTATE SAN. 7:3

A. The religious requirement of decapitation [is carried out as follows]:
B. They would cut off his head with a sword,
C. just as the government does.
D. *R Judah says, "This is disgusting.*
E. "But they put the head on a block and chop it off with an axe."
F. *They said to him, "There is no form of death more disgusting than this one."*
G. The religious requirement of strangulation [is carried out as follows:]
H. They would bury him in manure up to his armpits, and put a towel of hard material inside one of soft material, and wrap it around his neck.
I. This [witness] pulls it to him from one side, and that witness pulls it to him at the other side, until he perishes.

Among all the practical detail, Judah's intervention stands out. It leaves no doubt that carrying out the law ("way of life") realizes a particular world view. Specifically, his language implies that the felon remains a human being, in God's image. Clearly, then, at stake in the theoretical discussions at hand is how to execute someone in a manner appropriate to his or her standing after the likeness of God. This problem obviously presupposes that, in imposing the

penalty in the first place and in carrying it out, the court acts wholly in conformity with God's will. This being the case, a political myth of a dominion
belonging to God and carrying out God's plan and program certainly stands
behind the materials at hand.

But that observation still leaves us struggling with a mere commonplace.
On the strength of our knowledge that God stands behind the politics and that
the consideration that human beings are in God's image and after God's likeness applies even in inflicting the death penalty, we still cannot identify the
diverse media by which power is carried out. More to the point, we can
hardly distinguish one medium of power from another, which we must do if
we are to gain access to the myth that sustains what we shall soon see is the
fully differentiated political structure before us. We do well at this turning
point to remember the theoretical basis for the entire inquiry: a politics is a
theory of the ongoing exercise of the power of coercion, including legitimate
violence. Sanctions form the naked exercise of raw power – hence will
require the protection and disguise of a heavy cloak of myth.

How to proceed? By close attention to the facts of power and by sorting out
the implications of those facts. A protracted journey through details of the law
of sanctions leads us to classify the sanctions and the sins or crimes to which
they apply. What precisely do I think requires classification? Our project is to
see who does what to whom and, on the basis of the consequent perception, to
propose an explanation for that composition. For from these sanctions of
state, that is, the legitimate exercise of coercion, including violence, we may
work our way back to the reasons adduced for the legitimacy of the exercise
of coercion, which is to say, the political myth. The reason is that such a classification will permit us to see how in detail the foci of power are supposed to
intersect or to relate: autonomous powers, connected and related ones, or
utterly continuous ones, joining Heaven to earth, for instance, in the person of
this institutional representative or that one. What we shall see is a system that
treats Heaven, earth, and the mediating institution, the Temple, as interrelated,
thus, connected, but that insists, in vast detail, upon the distinct responsibilities and jurisdiction accorded to each. Once we have perceived that fundamental fact, we may compose for ourselves the myth, or, at least the point and
propositions of the myth, that accounted for the political structures contemplated by the Oral Torah and persuaded people to obey or conform even when
there was no immediate threat of penalty.

A survey of types of sanctions, the classifications of crimes or sins to
which they apply, and who imposes them, now yields these results. First
come the death penalty on earth and its counterpart, which is extirpation
(death before one's allotted time) imposed by Heaven:

Figure 1
For Deliberate Actions

Heaven Extirpation	Earth Death Penalty	Temple Death Penalty	Community
SEXUAL CRIMES incest violating sex taboos (bestiality, homosexuality)	SEXUAL CRIMES: in improper relationships: incest		
RELIGIOUS CRIMES AGAINST GOD blasphemy idolatry magic sorcery profaning Sabbath	RELIGIOUS CRIMES AGAINST GOD: blasphemy idolatry magic sorcery profaning Sabbath		
	RELIGIOUS SINS AGAINST FAMILY: cursing parents		
	SOCIAL CRIMES: murder communal apostasy kidnapping		
	SOCIAL SINS: public defiance of the court false prophecy		
RELIGIOUS SINS, DELIBERATELY COMMITTED, AGAINST GOD unclean person who ate a Holy Thing uncleanness in sanctuary violating food taboos making offering outside Temple violating taboos of holy seasons replicating Temple incense or oil outside			

Figure 2
For Inadvertent Action

Heaven	Earth	Temple	Community
	FLOGGING	OBLIGATORY OFFERING	SHUNNING
	EXILE	AND/OR FLOGGING	OR APPROBATION
	manslaughter	uncleanness	repay moral
	incest	eating Temple	obligation (debt
	violation of	food in violation	cancelled by
	menstrual	of the law	sabbatical year)
	taboo	replicating	stubbornly
	marriage in	Temple oil,	rejecting
	violation of	incense outside	majority view
	caste rules	violating	opposing
		Temple food	majority will
		taboos	opposing
		violating taboos	patriarch
		of holy days	obedience to
		(Passover,	majority
		atonement)	or patriarch
		uncleanness	
	violating food	(Zab, mesora, etc.)	
	taboos	Nazirite	
	removing dam	sex with bondwoman,	
	with offspring	unclean Nazirite	
	violating negative	false oath of testimony	
	commandments	false oath of deposit	

Next we deal with court-inflicted sanctions carried out against property or person (for example, fines against property, flogging, or other social or physical violence short of death for the felon or sinner).

The operative distinction between inflicting a flogging and requiring a sacrifice (Temple sanctions against person or property), and the sanction of extirpation (Heavenly death penalty), is made explicit as follows: "For those [transgressions] are people liable, for deliberately doing them, to the punishment of extirpation, and for accidentally doing them, to the bringing of a sin-offering, and for not being certain of whether or not one has done them, to a suspensive guilt-offering." Here is how the Mishnah sorts matters out:

MISHNAH-TRACTATE KERITOT I:I−2

A. Thirty-six transgressions subject to extirpation are in the Torah:
B. He who has sexual relations with (1) his mother, and (2) with his father's wife, and (3) with his daughter-in-law;

C. he who has sexual relations (4) with a male, and (5) with a beast; and (6) the woman who has sexual relations with a beast;

D. he who has sexual relations (7) with a woman and with her daughter, and (8) with a married woman;

E. he who has sexual relations (9) with his sister, and (10) with his father's sister, and (11) with his mother's sister, and (12) with his wife's sister, and (13) with his brother's wife, and (14) with his father's brother's wife, and (15) with a menstruating woman (Lev. 18:6ff.);

F. (16) he who blasphemes (Num, 15:30), and (17) he who performs an act of blasphemous worship (Num 15:31), and (18) he who gives his seed to Molekh (Lev. 18:21), and (19) one who has a familiar spirit (Lev. 20:6);

G. (20) he who profanes the Sabbath-day (Ex. 31:14);

H. and (21) an unclean person who ate a Holy Thing (Lev. 22:3), and (22) he who comes to the sanctuary when unclean (Num. 19:20);

I. he who eats (23) forbidden fat (Lev. 7:25), and (24) blood (Lev. 17:14), and (25) remnant (Lev. 19:6–8), and (26) refuse (Lev. 19:7–8);

J. he who (27) slaughters and who (28) offers up [a sacrifice] outside [the Temple court] (Lev. 17:9);

K. (29) he who eats leaven on Passover (Ex. 12:19); and he who (30) eats and he who (31) works on the Day of Atonement (Lev. 23:29–30);

L. he who (32) compounds anointing oil [like that made in the Temple (Ex. 30:23–33)], and he who (33) compounds incense [like that made in the Temple], and he who (34) anoints himself with anointing oil (Ex. 30–2);

M. [he who transgresses the laws of] (35) Passover (Num. 9:13) and (36) circumcision (Gen. 17:14), among the positive commandments.

A. For those [transgressions] are people liable, for deliberately doing them, to the punishment of extirpation,

B. and for accidentally doing them, to the bringing of a sin-offering,

C. and for not being certain of whether or not one has done them, to a suspensive guilt-offering [Lev. 5:17] –

D. "except for the one who imparts uncleanness to the sanctuary and its Holy Things,

E. "because he is subject to bringing a sliding-scale offering (Lev. 5:6–7, 11)," the words of R. Meir.

F. And sages say, "Also: [except for] the one who blasphemes, as it is said, 'You shall have one law for him that does anything unwittingly' (Num 15:29) – excluding the blasphemer, who does no concrete deed."

The points important to our argument are these: Scripture refers to thirty-six sorts of transgressions subject to the penalty of extirpation. If one deliberately does any of these transgressions, he is liable to extirpation; M. 1:2B-C add that if he does them inadvertently, he brings a sin-offering, and if he is not sure whether or not he has done them, he brings a suspensive guilt-offering, as noted above. If a person is in doubt about whether or not he has accidentally entered the Temple while in a state of uncleanness, or whether or not he has eaten Holy Things in a state of uncleanness, he brings a sliding-scale offering (Lev. 5:2).

What about penalties imposed by the Temple? These take the form of sanctions assessed against property. The Temple does not take an active role in imposing such sanctions. Rules apply, and the consequence of the rules in some instances is that the Temple is owed, and collects, property and passes it on to Heaven. The reason I regard the present sanction as distinct from those imposed by the Heavenly and the earthly courts is simple. Legitimate violence against the person or life of a felon, such as the earthly and Heavenly courts exercise, is precipitated by the consideration of a particular case, under appropriate rules, in the earthly court, and counterpart procedures involving the individual miscreant in the Heavenly venue as well. But in the case of the penalties administered by the Temple, there is no court action that a particular sinner or felon faces. The rules apply in general and no need to investigate particular cases is suggested in the systemic document. The penalty of loss of property means that one is automatically required to present to Heaven, through the Temple, something of value. The wealth to be given up must of course be given the form that the Temple can receive and transmit to Heaven, that is, an appropriate animal or vegetable product.

The above summary yields a simple and clear fact, and on the basis of that simple fact we may now reconstruct the entire political myth of the Oral Torah. This myth accounts for the differentiation among penalties and the institutions that impose them, and from the facts we reach backward to the myth that explains them. The basis for all conclusions, let me emphasize, is this: *some of the same crimes or sins for which the Heavenly court imposes the penalty of extirpation are also those for which, under appropriate circumstances (for example, sufficient evidence admissible in court), the earthly court imposes the death penalty.*

That is, the Heavenly court and the earthly court impose precisely the same sanctions for the same crimes or sins. The earthly court therefore forms down here the exact replica and counterpart, within a single system of power, of the Heavenly court up there. This no longer looms as an empty generalization; it is a concrete and systemically active and indicative detail, and the system speaks through its details.

But this is not the entire story. There is a second fact, equally indicative for our recovery of the substrate of myth. We note that there are crimes for which the earthly court imposes penalties, but for which the Heavenly court does not, as well as vice versa. The earthly and Heavenly courts share jurisdiction over sexual crimes and over what I classify as serious religious crimes against God. The Heavenly court penalizes, with its form of the death penalty, religious sins against God, in which instances a person deliberately violates the taboos of sanctification.

And that fact calls our attention to a third partner in the distribution and application of power, the Temple with its system of sanctions that cover precisely the same acts subject to the jurisdiction of the Heavenly and earthly courts. The counterpart on earth is now not the earthly court but the Temple. This is the institution that, in theory, automatically receives the appropriate offering from the person who inadvertently violates these same taboos of sanctification. The juxtaposition involves courts and Temple. In the theory at hand, then, the earthly court, for its part, penalizes social crimes against the community that the Heavenly court, on the one side, and the Temple rites, on the other, do not take into account at all. These are murder, apostasy, kidnapping, public defiance of the court, and false prophecy. The earthly court further imposes sanctions on matters of particular concern to the Heavenly court, with special reference to taboos of sanctification (for example, negative commandments). These three institutions, therefore, exercise concrete and material power, utilizing legitimate violence to kill someone, exacting penalties against property, and inflicting pain. The sages' modes of power, by contrast, stand quite apart, apply mainly to their own circle, and work through the intangible though no less effective means of inflicting shame or paying honour.

The facts we have in hand draw us back to the analysis of our differentiation of applied and practical power. In the nature of the facts before us, that differentiation tells us precisely for what the systemic myth will have to give its account. Power flows through three distinct but intersecting dominions, each with its own concern, all sharing some interests in common: the Heavenly court attends to deliberate defiance of Heaven; the Temple pays attention to inadvertent defiance of Heaven; and the earthly court attends to matters subject to its jurisdiction by reason of sufficient evidence, proper witnesses, and the like, and these same matters will come under Heavenly jurisdiction when the earthly court finds itself unable to act.

Accordingly, we have a tripartite system of sanctions – Heaven cooperating with the Temple in some matters, with the court in others, and, as noted, each bearing its own distinct media of enforcing the law as well. What, then, can we say concerning the systemic myth of politics? The forms of power and the modes of mediating legitimate violence draw our attention to a single political myth. The unity of that myth is underlined by the simple fact that the earthly court enters into the process right alongside the Heavenly court and the Temple; as to blasphemy, idolatry, and magic, its jurisdiction prevails. So a single myth must serve all three correlated institutions. It is the myth of God's authority infusing the institutions of Heaven and earth alike, an authority diffused among three principle foci or circles of power, Heaven's court, the earthly court, and the Temple in-between.

Each focus of power has its own jurisdiction and responsibility, Heaven above, earth beneath, the Temple in the position of mediation – transmitting as it does from earth to Heaven the penalties handed over as required. And all media of power in the matter of sanctions intersect at some points as well: a tripartite politics, a single myth drawing each component into relationship with a single source and origin of power, God's law set forth in the Torah. But the myth has not performed its task until it answers not only the question of why but also the question of how. Specifically, the details of myth must address questions of the details of power. Who tells whom to do what? And how are the relationships of dominion and dominance to compliance and obedience made permanent through myth?

We did not require this sustained survey to ascertain that God through the Torah has set forth laws and concerns. Nor on the surface did this considerable exercise claim a place in any account of the role of intentionality in the cosmic order. So God's place in transactions of power requires explanation, and the primacy of intentionality has now to be set out. Specifically, it is where power is differentiated and parcelled out that we see the workings of the political myth, and there we find the facts that we seek. So we ask, how do we know who tells whom to do, or suffer, what sanction or penalty? It is the power of myth to differentiate that defines the generative question. The key lies in the criterion by which each mode of power, earthly, mediating, and Heavenly, identifies the cases over which it exercises jurisdiction. The criterion lies in the attitude of the human being who has done what he or she should not: did he act deliberately or unintentionally?

I state the upshot with heavy emphasis, as we identify the point of relevance to our inquiry: *the point of differentiation within the political structures, supernatural and natural alike, lies in the attitude and intention of a human being.*

We differentiate among the application of power by reference to the attitude of the person who comes into relationship with that power. A person who comes into conflict with the system, rejecting the authority claimed by the powers that be, does so deliberately or inadvertently. The myth accounts in the end for the following hierarchization of action and penalty, infraction, and sanction: if the deed is deliberate, then one set of institutions exercises jurisdiction and utilizes supernatural power; if the deed is inadvertent, another institution exercises jurisdiction and utilizes the power made available by that same supernatural being.

A sinner or criminal who has deliberately violated the law has by his action challenged the world order of justice that God has wrought. Consequently, God or God's surrogate imposes sanctions – extirpation (by the court on high), or death or other appropriate penalty (by the court on earth). A sinner or criminal who has inadvertently violated the law is penalized by the imposition of Temple sanctions, losing valued goods. People obey because God wants them to and has told them what to do, and when they do not obey, a differentiated political structure appeals to that single hierarchizing myth. The components of the myth are two: first, God's will, expressed in the law of the Torah, second, the human being's will, carried out in obedience to the law of the Torah or in defiance of that law.

Since the political myth has to explain the differentiation of sins or crimes, with their associated penalties or punishments, and so sanctions of power, I have to find that story in the Torah that accomplishes that labour of differentiation. And given the foci and premises of the present study of the governing theology of the Oral Torah, that story must pertain to the nature of things and concern beginnings. And in Scripture there is a very precise answer to the question of how to differentiate among sins or crimes and why to do so. Not only so, but, in the framework of the present chapter of that theology, the point of differentiation must rest with one's attitude or intentionality And, indeed, I do have two stories of how the power of God – the power to command – conflicts with the power of humanity – the power to obey or to rebel – in such wise as to invoke the penalties and sanctions in precisely the differentiated modes we have before us. Where do I find such stories of the conflict of wills, God's and humanity's, captured by the words "will" or "intentionality"?

The first such story of power differentiated by the will of the human being in communion or conflict with the word of the commanding God comes to us from the Garden of Eden. We cannot too often reread the following astonishing words:

GENESIS 2:15FF.

The Lord God took the man and placed him in the garden of Eden ... and the Lord God commanded the man, saying, "Of every tree of the garden you are free to eat; but as for the tree of knowledge of good and bad, you must not eat of it; for as soon as you eat of it, you shall die."

... When the woman saw that the tree was good for eating and a delight to the eyes, and that the tree was desirable as a source of wisdom, she took of its fruit and ate; she also gave some to her husband, and he ate ...

The Lord God called out to the man and said to him, "Where are you?"

He replied, "I heard the sound of You in the garden, and I was afraid, because I was naked, so I hid."

Then He asked, "Who told you that you were naked? Did you eat of the tree from which I had forbidden you to eat?"

... And the Lord God said to the woman, "What is this you have done!"

The woman replied, "The serpent deceived me, and I ate."

Then the Lord said to the serpent, "Because you did this, more cursed shall you be than all cattle ..."

So the Lord God banished him from the garden of Eden ...

A reprise of the exchange between God, Adam, and Eve tells us that at stake was responsibility: not who has violated the law, but who bears responsibility for deliberately violating the law. Each blames the next, and God sorts things out, responding to each in accord with the facts of the case: whose intentionality matches the actual deed?

"The woman You put at my side – she gave me of the tree, and I ate."

"The serpent duped me, and I ate."

Then the Lord God said to the serpent, *"because you did this ..."*

The ultimate responsibility lies with the one who acted deliberately, not under constraint or on account of deception or misinformation, as did Adam because of Eve, and Eve because of the serpent.

True enough, all are punished, the serpent but also woman – "I will make most severe your pangs in childbearing" and Adam – "Because you did as your wife advised and ate of the tree about which I commanded you, 'you shall not eat of it,' cursed be the ground because of you." Yet the punishment is differentiated. Those who were duped are distinguished from the one who acted wholly on his own. The serpent himself is cursed; man has to go to work; the woman is subjected to pain in childbearing, which ought to have been pain-free; because of man, the earth is cursed – a diminishing scale of penalties, each in accord with the level of intentionality or free, uncoerced will, involved in the infraction. Then the sanction applies most severely to the one who by intention and an act of will has violated God's intention and will.

Adducing this story by itself poses several problems. First, the storyteller does not allege that Adam intended to violate the commandment; he followed his wife. Second, the penalty is not extirpation but banishment. That is why, to establish what I conceive to be the generative myth, I turn to a second story of disobedience and its consequences, the tale of Moses's hitting the rock:

NUMBERS 20:1-13

The community was without water, and they joined against Moses and Aaron ... Moses and Aaron came away from the congregation to the entrance of the Tent of Meeting and fell on their faces. The Presence of the Lord appeared to them, and the Lord spoke to Moses, saying, "You and your brother Aaron take the rod and assemble the community, and before their very eyes order the rock to yield its water. Thus you shall produce water for them from the rock and provide drink for the congregation and their beasts."

Moses took the rod from before the Lord as He had commanded him. Moses and Aaron assembled the congregation in front of the rock; and he said to them, "Listen, you rebels, shall we get water for you out of this rock?" And Moses raised his hand and struck the rock twice with his rod. Out came copious water, and the community and their beasts drank.

But the Lord said to Moses and Aaron, "Because you did not trust me enough to affirm My sanctity in the sight of the Israelite people, therefore you shall not lead this congregation into the land that I have given them."

Those are the waters of Meribah, meaning that the Israelites quarrelled with the Lord – through which He affirmed His sanctity.

Here we have not only intentional disobedience, but also the penalty of extirpation. Both this myth and the myth of the fall make the same point. They direct attention to the generative conception that at stake in power is the will of God over against the will of the human being, and in particular, the Israelite human being.

What we see is quite striking. The political myth of the Oral Torah emerges in the Mishnah in all of its tedious detail as a reprise – in now-consequential and necessary detail – of the story of God's commandment, humanity's disobedience, God's sanction for the sin or crime, and humanity's atonement and reconciliation. The Mishnah omits all explicit reference to myths that explain power and sanctions, but it invokes in its rich corpus of details the absolute given of the story of the distinction between what is deliberate and what is mitigated by an attitude that is not culpable, a distinction set forth in the tragedy of Adam and Eve, in the failure of Moses and Aaron, in the distinction between murder and manslaughter that the Written Torah works out, and in countless other passages in the Pentateuch, Prophetic Books, and Writings. Then the Mishnah's *halakhah* sets forth a politics of life after Eden and outside Eden. The upshot of the matter is that the political myth of the Oral Torah sets forth the constraints of freedom, the human will brought to full and unfettered expression, imposed by the constraints of revelation, God's will made known.

Since it is the freedom of humanity to make decisions and frame intentions that forms the point of differentiation among the political media of power, we are required, in my view, to return to the paradigmatic exercise of that same freedom, that is, to Eden, to the moment when Adam and Eve exercise their own will and defy God. Since the operative criterion in the differentiation of sanction – that is, the exercise of legitimate violence by Heaven or by earth or by the Temple – is the human attitude and intention in carrying out a culpable action, we must recognize that the politics before us rehearses the myth of Adam and Eve in Eden – it finds its dynamic in the correspondence between God's will and humanity's freedom to act however it chooses, thus freely incurring the risk of penalty or sanction for the wrong exercise of freedom.

At stake is what Adam and Eve, Moses and Aaron, and numerous others intend, propose, plan, for that is the point at which the politics intervenes, making its points of differentiation between and among its sanctions and the authorities that impose those penalties. For that power to explain difference, which is to say, the capacity to represent and account for hierarchy, we are required, in my opinion, to turn to the story of the fall of Adam and Eve from Eden and to counterpart stories. The reason is that the political myth derives from that same myth of origins its points of differentiation and explains by reference to the principal components of that myth – God's and humanity's will and power – the dynamics of the political system at hand. God commands, but humanity does what it then chooses, and in the interplay, each power in its own right, the sanctions and penalties of the system apply.

Power comes from two conflicting forces, the commanding will of God and the free will of the human being. Power expressed in immediate sanctions is also mediated through these same forces, Heaven above, human beings below, with the Temple mediating between the two. Power works its way in the interplay between what God has set forth in the law of the Torah and what human beings do, whether intentionally, whether inadvertently, whether obediently, whether defiantly. That is why the politics of the Oral Torah is a politics of Eden.[3] True, we listen in vain in the creation myth of Genesis for

3. Here we may claim that the Oral Torah understands the Written Torah in its full implications even better than do those who set forth the Authorized History that is conveyed by the sequence from Genesis through Kings. For that Authorized History does not identify creation and the fall as the governing paradigm of Israel's life, but the sages do. The Authorized History looks backward from the destruction in 586 and forward to the restoration. The sages' Oral Torah, by contrast, encompasses not only 586 but 70, not only a singular event but a series, and therefore defines the paradigm that the series realizes. And therein lies all the difference. Reading forward from Scripture, the sages followed what, in the nature of things, was simply a much longer narrative; but it was not one that they conceived either as linear or as cyclical. The one model led nowhere, the other defied all rationality. That is the foundation for paradigmatic thinking on their part. That is the argument of my *The Presence of the Past, the Pastness of the Present: History, Time, and Paradigm in Rabbinic Judaism* (Bethesda, Md.: CDL Press 1996).

echoes resounding in the shape of the institutions such as those the theology of politics actually invents. But the points of differentiation of one political institution from another will serve constantly to remind us of what, in the end, distinguishes this from that, rather than just setting out a generalized claim that God rules through whoever is around with a sword. At every point we are therefore reminded of the most formidable source of power, short of God, in all. That always is the will of the human being. And that is why only man has the power to disrupt that world order so painstakingly created and maintained by God. Only man is sufficiently like God to possess the utterly free will to corrupt perfection.

From this survey of how institutional arrangements embody the systemic centrality of intentionality in the Oral Torah's law, let us turn to details of some of the many laws that effect that same principle. By "intentionality" in the context of normative rules of law, the sages mean the attitude that motivates a given action, the intention of the person who performs the action: what he hopes to accomplish – effect, affect, or prevent. That intentionality, or expression of an attitude, governs the action's classification, for example, as to effect or lack of effect, as to acceptability or lack of acceptability, such as in recitation of prayer. While a single word, *kavvanah*, corresponds, the category, intentionality, is shown by context to pertain even where that particular word does not appear. And other words also serve to convey the same meaning, for instance, *leb*, heart.

Intentionality classifies actions, so that with one intention an action is cursed, but with the opposite, it is blessed. Hence T. Bik. 2:15: He who sells a Torah scroll never sees a sign of blessing. Scribes who copy Torah scrolls, tefillin-parchments, and mezuzah-parchments – they and their dealers who buy these items from scribes, and their dealers' dealers who buy them from other merchants, and all those who deal in sacred objects for the sake of making a profit will never see a sign of blessing. But if they were dealing with these objects for the sake of Heaven, lo, they shall be blessed. Dealing in holy objects for the sake of a profit is not acceptable, but for the sake of Heaven is.

One's intention affects the assessment of one's deed, whether it is for good or ill. Miriam criticized Moses and was punished, but her intention was honourable; had it been dishonourable, the punishment would have been greater, just as the sages' political theology has already shown us:

SIFRÉ TO NUMBERS XCIX:II.2

1. A. "Miriam and Aaron spoke against Moses [because of the Cushite woman whom he had married]:"

B. [It is now taken for granted that the criticism of Moses had to do with his ceasing to have sexual relations with his wife, Zipporah.] Now how did Miriam, know that Moses had ceased to have sexual relations with his wife? She realized that Zipporah was not making herself up with women's ornaments. She said to her, "How come you're not making up like other women?"

C. She said to her, "Your brother does not pay any attention to such things." Thus Miriam realized and told her brother, and both of them spoke against him.

D. R. Nathan says, "Miriam was standing alongside Zipporah when it was said, 'And the youth ran.' When Zipporah heard the message, she said, 'Woe for the wives of these men [who have become prophets, since they now will lose their husbands' attention].'

E. "On that basis Miriam realized the situation and told her brother and both of them spoke against them."

Now the issue of intentionality enters and affects the outcome:

2. A. Now it is an argument *a fortiori:* if Miriam, who intended to speak against her brother not to his detriment but to his credit, and not to lessen procreation but to increase it, and who spoke only in private, yet she was punished, if someone intends to speak ill of his fellow and not in praise, to diminish and not to increase procreation, and speaks not in private but among others – how much the more so [will such a one be punished]!

B. Now it is an argument *a fortiori:* if Uzziah the king, who had no intention of arrogating greatness to himself for his own honour but for the honour of his creator, was punished as he was, one who arrogates greatness to himself for his own honour and not for the honour of his creator – how much the more so [will such a one be punished]!

What is taken as premise here, once more, is the power of intentionality to differentiate among actions, even of the same classification, and to designate the one as the weightier, the other as the less consequential.

Concrete actions take on consequence only by reference to the intention with which they are carried out. For example, what matters in the offerings is intentionality; the size of the offering makes no difference, only the intent of the person who presents it:

B. MEN. 13:11 I.2/110A:

A. It is said of the burnt offering of a beast, "An offering by fire, a smell of sweet savour" (Lev. 1:9) and of the bird offering, "An offering by fire, a smell of sweet savour" (Lev. 1:17) and [even] of the meal offering, "An offering by fire, a smell of sweet savour" (Lev. 2:9) –

B. to teach that all the same are the one who offers much and the one who offers little, on condition that a man will direct his intention to Heaven.

The exegesis of the Mishnah's rule on the centrality of intentionality in determining God's response to an offering is set forth in the Talmud:

I.2. A. It has been taught on Tannaite authority:

B. Said R. Simeon b. Azzai, "Furthermore it is said: It is said of the burnt offering of a beast, 'An offering by fire, a smell of sweet savour' (Lev. 1:9) and of the bird offering, 'An offering by fire, a smell of sweet savour' (Lev. 1:17) and [even] of the meal offering, 'An offering by fire, a smell of sweet savour' (Lev. 2:9) – to teach that all the same are the one who offers much and the one who offers little, on condition that a man will direct his intention to Heaven.

D. "Now might you say, 'Then it is because God needs the food,' Scripture states, 'If I were hungry, I would not tell you, for the world is mine and the fulness thereof' (Ps. 50:12); 'For every beast of the forest is mine and the cattle upon a thousand hills; I know all the fowl of the mountains and wild beasts of the field are mine; do I eat the meat of bulls or drink the blood of goats' (Ps. 50:10, 11, 13). I did not order you to make sacrifices so you might say, 'I will do what he wants so he will do what I wants.' You do not make sacrifices for my sake but for your sake: 'you shall sacrifice at your own volition'" (Lev. 19:5).

The exegesis goes another step, namely, the entire cult represents an act of human volition and is evaluated solely on that basis, so that if a sacrifice were carried out without proper intentionality, it does not accomplish its purpose, for example, atonement:

3. A. Another reading of "... you shall sacrifice at your own volition" (Lev. 19:5):

B. "Sacrifice at your own volition! Slaughter at your own volition!"

C. That is in line with what Samuel asked R. Huna, "How on the basis of Scripture do we know that if an act of slaughter was done incidentally, the offering is invalid?"

D. He said to him, " 'And he shall slaughter the bullock' (Lev. 19:5) – the act of slaughter must be carried out with regard to that particular bullock."

E. He said to him, "That we have in hand. The issue is, how do we know that correct intentionality is indispensable?"

F. "Scripture states, 'you shall sacrifice at your own volition' (Lev. 19:5) – perform the act of sacrifice in accord with proper intentionality."

It would be difficult to find a more explicit statement of the taxonomic power of intentionality, which man exercises, as does God, to settle questions of a practical order.

What attitude, then does God favour, love or fear (reverence)? The answer is, reverence, a response to the *tremendum*, rather than love, a response to one's own inner feelings. That is the particular aspect of the actor's intention to which God responds in his evaluation of an action. The correct attitude in serving God is on account of reverence or fear, not as an entirely votive action, out of love:

MISHNAH-TRACTATE SOTAH 5:5

A. On that day did R. Joshua b. Hurqanos expound as follows: "Job served the Holy One, blessed be He, only out of love,

B. "since it is said, 'Though he slay me, yet will I wait for him' (Job. 13:15).

C. "But still the matter is in doubt [as to whether it means], 'I will wait for him,' or, 'I will not wait for him.'

D. "Scripture states, 'Until I die I will not put away mine integrity from me' (Job. 27:5).

E. "This teaches that he did what he did out of love."

F. Said R. Joshua, "Who will remove the dirt from your eyes, Rabban Yohanan b. Zakkai. For you used to expound for your entire life that Job served the Omnipresent only out of awe,

G. "since it is said, 'The man was perfect and upright and one who feared God and avoided evil' (Job. 1:8).

H. "And now has not Joshua, the disciple of your disciple, taught that he did what he did out of love."

But correct intentionality is subject to dispute. Yohanan ben Zakkai placed the highest value on fear, Joshua on love. Others hold that one is permitted to fear God alone, and that is the sole correct source of intentionality, as the following story indicates:

YERUSHALMI-TRACTATE BABA MESIA 2:5 I.2

R. R. Samuel bar Suseretai went to Rome. The queen had lost her jewellery. He found it. A proclamation went forth through the city: "Whoever returns her jewellery in thirty days will receive thus and so. [If he returns it] after thirty days, his head will be cut off."

S. He did not return the jewellery within thirty days. After thirty days, he returned it to her.

T. She said to him, "Weren't you in town?"

U. He said to her, "Yes [I was here]."

V. She said to him, "And didn't you hear the proclamation?"

W. He said to her, "Yes [I heard it]."

X. She said to him, "And what did it say?"

Y. He said to her. that it said, "Whoever returns her jewelry in thirty days will receive thus-and-so. [If he returns it] after thirty days. his head will be cut off."

Z. She said to him, "And why didn't you return it within thirty days?"

AA. "So that people should not say, 'It was because I was afraid of you that I did so.' But it was because I fear the All-Merciful."

BB. She said to him. "Blessed be the God of the Jews."

Here the right attitude in doing the right thing is exposed. To do the right thing for the wrong reason does not sanctify the Name of God, but doing so for the right reason does, and that is the implicit message of the conclusion, AA-BB. The upshot, hardly a surprise by this point, is that even in the classification of a meritorious action intentionality makes all the difference.

That correct intentionality, as the story at hand shows, involves submission to God's will, and that is what governs under all conditions; thus, as we have seen, Mishnah-tractate Rosh Hashanah 3:8 indicates, in commenting on Ex. 17:11: "Now do Moses's hands make war or stop it? But the purpose is to say this to you: So long as the Israelites would set their eyes upward and submit their hearts to their Father in heaven, they would grow stronger. And if not, they fell." God plays a role by responding to man's intentionality. Hence, as regards a good intention – the Omnipresent, blessed be He, refines it so that it produces a corresponding deed. As for an evil intention – the Omnipresent does not refine it, so that it does not produce a corresponding deed (Tosefta-tractate Peah 1:4).

Intentionality is critical in doing not only supererogatory acts, such as returning the Queen's jewellery, but also, and especially, the more commonplace ones. In carrying out religious duties, a man must not utilize the Torah and the commandments for an inappropriate purpose:

II.8 A. It has been taught on Tannaite authority:

B. "That you may love the Lord your God and that you may obey his voice and that you may cleave to him" (Deut. 30:20):

C. This means that someone shouldn't say, "I shall study Scripture, so as to be called a sage, I shall repeat Mishnah teachings, so as to be called 'my lord.' I shall reason critically, so that I may be an elder and take a seat at the session."

D. Rather: Learn out of love, and honor will come on its own: "Bind them on your fingers, write them on the table of your heart" (Prov. 7:3); "Her ways are ways of pleasantness" (Prov. 3:17); "She is a tree of life to those that hold onto her, and happy is everyone who keeps her" (Prov. 3:18).

The same view is articulated through a different case:

II.9 A. R. Eliezer b. R. Sadoq says, "Do things for the sake of the One who has made them and speak of them for their own sake, and don't turn them into a crown for self-glorification or make them into a spade with which to dig.

B. "It derives from an argument a fortiori in the case of Belshazzar, namely, if Belshazzar – who used the holy utensils that were removed from their status of sanctification, in line with the statement, 'for the robbers shall enter into it and profane it' (Ezek. 7:22), since they had broken in, the utensils were profaned – was removed from the world – 'in that night was Belshazzar slain' (Dan. 5:30) – one who makes selfish use of the crown of the Torah, which lives and endures forever, all the more so will be uprooted from this world!"

Even when it comes to doing religious deeds, intentionality dictates the value of what is done; while one may well carry out one's obligation to Heaven through correct action, without matching intentionality, still, to study the Torah to achieve honour negates the action. Purity of heart, desire to serve God and not to aggrandize oneself – these govern the effect of the act.

What about doing the commandments? The correct intentionality is to carry out the requirements of the Torah for their own sake, not for the sake of a reward. This is expressed, first of all, in terms of Torah-study itself, and, further, in the setting of carrying out the commandments. One must study the Torah for an appropriate motive, which is not to gain prestige and honour but to love God. Sincerity means doing the deed for its own sake, in all contexts, as an act of willing, uncoerced obedience to the kingdom of Heaven. The sages go so far, as we shall see in the next chapter, as to say, "A transgression committed for its own sake, in a sincere spirit, is greater in value than a religious duty carried out not for its own sake, but in a spirit of insincerity."

Fulfilling the teachings of the Torah likewise should be motivated by the correct attitude of faith, not improper motivation:

SIFRÉ DEUTERONOMY CCCVI:XXII.I

1. A. Another teaching concerning the phrase, "May my discourse come down as the rain, [my speech distill as the dew, like showers on young growths, like droplets on the grass. For the name of the Lord I proclaim]":

B. R. Benaiah would say, "If you carry out the teachings of the Torah for their own sake, the teachings of the Torah will live for you.

C. "For it is said, 'For they are life to those that find them' (Prov. 4:22).

D. "But if you do not carry out teachings of the Torah for their own sake, they will kill you.

E. "For it is said, 'My doctrine shall drop as the rain.'

F. "And the word for 'drop' yields the sense of 'killing,' in line with its usage in the following verse: 'And he shall break the heifer's neck there in the valley' (Dt. 21:4).

G. "'For she has cast down many wounded, yes, a mighty host are all those she has slain'" (Prov. 7:26).

The right attitude furthermore involves sincerity, a total commitment to the action for its own sake, which means, for the sake of Heaven.

This instruction then carries us to the matter of faith, where intentionality shades over into the more generalized matter of attitude. It is a subtle matter, but the sages treat as a cluster of virtues proper intentionality, good faith, and faith as an act and attitude of trust. That is why faith forms another chapter in the story of intentionality. It represents an act of confidence in the good faith, in the true and benevolent, intentionality of God. In the sages' view, acting in good faith, in complete sincerity, makes a person worthy of encountering the Holy Spirit, because one thereby imputes to the Holy Spirit or to God that same attitude of correct and honest intention that God values:

MEKHILTA ATTRIBUTED TO R. ISHMAEL XXV:I.26

26. A. R. Nehemiah says, "How do you know that whoever takes upon himself the obligation to carry out a single religious duty in faith is worth that the Holy Spirit should rest upon him?

B. "For so we find in the case of our ancestors that as a reward for the act of faith that they made, they achieved merit, so that the Holy Spirit rested on them, as it is said, 'and they believed in the Lord and in his servant Moses. Then Moses and the people of Israel sang this song [to the Lord, saying, 'I will sing to the Lord, for he has triumphed gloriously; the horse and his rider he has thrown into the sea'].'"

Here "in faith" means, "in good faith," that is, with sincerity – proper intentionality. But the passage forthwith shifts over from "in faith" to "faith," and that speaks, as I said, of confidence in the correct intentionality of the other, in this case, God:

MEKHILTA ATTRIBUTED TO R. ISHMAEL XXV:I.27–30

27. A. So you find that Abraham our father inherited this world and the world to come only as a reward for the faith that he believed, as it is said, "And he believed in the Lord" (Gen. 15:6).

B. So you find that the Israelites were redeemed from Egypt only as a reward for the faith that they believed, as it is said, "And the people believed" (Ex. 4:31).

C. "The Lord preserves the faithful" (Ps. 31:25). He calls to mind the faith of the fathers.

D. "And Aaron and Hur held up his hands" (Ex. 17:12).

28. A. "This is the gate of the Lord. The righteous shall enter into it" (Ps. 118:20).

B. What does Scripture say of the faithful?

C. "Open the gates, that the righteous nation that keeps the faith may enter in" (Is. 26:2).

D. Through this gate all the faithful enter.

Evidence of Scripture is assembled in the following:

29. A. So Scripture says, "It is a good thing to give thanks to the Lord and to sing praises to your name, O Most High; to declare your loving kindness in the morning and your faithfulness in the night" (Ps. 92:2–3). "For you, Lord, have made me glad through your work" (Ps. 92:5).

B. What brought us to this joy?

C. It is as a reward for the faith with which our ancestors believed in this world, which is wholly night.

D. That is the point of the statement, "to declare your loving kindness in the morning and your faithfulness in the night" [that is, "because of faith in you through the night"] (Ps. 92:3).

Now comes a particular case to illustrate the point:

E. So Jehoshaphat says to the people, "Believe in the Lord your God, so you shall be established, believe in his prophets, so you shall prosper" (2 Chr. 20:20).

F. "O Lord, are your eyes not upon faith' (Jer. 5:3).

G. "But the righteous shall live by his faith" (Hab. 2:4).

H. "They are renewed every morning, great is your faithfulness" (Lam. 3:23).

We turn towards the ingathering of the exiles by the Messiah. That, too, takes place by reason of an act of faith:

30. A. So you find that the exiles are destined to be gathered together only as a reward for faith:

B. "Come with me from Lebanon, my bride, with me from Lebanon; look from the perspective of faith ["Hebrew: from the top of Amana," and the Hebrew letters of the word, Amana, can stand for 'faith']" (Song 4:8).

C. "And I will betroth you to me forever … and I will betroth you to me because of faith" (Hos. 2:21–22).

God's presence, to be realized at the world to come, finally marks the climax; God brought his Presence to rest on Israel by reason of Israel's act of faith in singing the Song at the Sea (Exodus 15):

D. Lo, great is faith before the One who spoke and brought the world into being.

E. For as a reward for the act of faith that the Israelites made in the Lord, the Holy Spirit rested upon them and they sang the song, as it is said, "and they believed in the Lord and in his servant Moses. Then Moses and the people of Israel sang this song [to the Lord, saying, 'I will sing to the Lord, for he has triumphed gloriously; the horse and his rider he has thrown into the sea']."

F. So too: "Then they believed what he said, they sang his praises" (Ps. 106:12).

What we see is how easily a discussion of intentionality shades over into an account of the faith required of Israel in trusting in God's own good intentions.

What governs the relationship between intentionality and action? Here the critical importance of classification in the mode of thought of the sages – natural historians of transcendence, we might call them – accounts for much, as we saw in chapter 2. Intentionality governs, we already anticipate, because it has the power to classify actions, one sort of action being valid, another, invalid. This we have already seen in a variety of practical, legal contexts. It is the intentionality of the actor, then, that defines the effect of an action; the same action, performed in the same way, may then produce diverse results, based on the will that one brings to bear upon the action. In religious duties, the effect of intentionality proves especially critical. That is to say, the intention to carry out one's obligation must accompany the act that effects that obligation; otherwise, the act bears no effect. Thus, Mishnah-tractate Ber. 2:1A-C: One who was reading the verses of the *Shema* in the Torah and the time for the recitation of the *Shema* arrived: If he directed his heart towards fulfilling the obligation to recite the *Shema*, he fulfilled his obligation to recite. And if he did not direct his heart, he did not fulfill his obligation. Whether or not the recitation of the prayer of supplication requires intentionality is subject to discussion, for example, Mishnah-tractate Ber. 4:4 A. R. Eliezer says, "One who makes his prayers a fixed task – his prayers are not valid supplications of God."

Intentionality may take precedence over actual activity, as at Mishnah-tractate Berakhot 4:5 A-C: If he was riding on an ass, he should dismount to recite the prayer. But if he cannot dismount, he should turn his face towards the east. And if he cannot turn his face, he should direct his heart towards the Chamber of the Holy of Holies. When one prays, he is to direct his heart to God; hence, Mishnah-tractate Ber. 5:1 A-E: One may stand to pray only in a solemn frame of mind. The early pious ones used to tarry one hour before they would pray, so that they could direct their hearts to the Omnipresent. While one is praying, even if the king greets him, he may not respond. And even if a serpent is entwined around his heel, he may not interrupt his prayer. Intentionality governs the effect of all rites. Mishnah-tractate Rosh Hashanah 3:7D-J: He who was going along behind a synagogue, or whose house was near a synagogue, and who heard the sound of the shofar or the sound of the reading of the Scroll of Esther, if he paid attention, thereby intending to carry out his obligation, he has fulfilled his obligation. But if not, he has not fulfilled his obligation. That is the rule even if this one heard and that one heard, for this one paid attention and that one did not pay attention to what he heard.

Intentionality may also prevent a negative result. That we know from the distinction between involuntary manslaughter and murder, which Scripture makes explicit. Along these same lines, in the view of the sages, the intentional violation of the law always invalidates the consequent action. What is done in violation of the law but not by intention, by contrast, may well be accepted, since it was not an act of rebellion against the Torah. For example, Mishnah-tractate Ter. 2:3: One who immerses unclean utensils on the Sabbath – if he does so unintentionally, he may use them; but if he does so intentionally, he may not use them. One who tithes his produce, or who cooks on the Sabbath – if he does so unintentionally, he may eat the food he has prepared; but if he does so intentionally, he may not eat the food. One who plants a tree on the Sabbath – if he does so unintentionally, he may leave it to grow; but if he does so intentionally, he must uproot it. But in the Seventh Year of the Sabbatical cycle, whether he has planted the tree unintentionally or intentionally, he must uproot it.

Similarly, intentionality forms the principal criterion for effecting atonement through repentance, a matter that will return in its own, still more critical, context in chapter 12. If one manifests the inappropriate intentionality, then the rite is null. Thus Mishnah-tractate Yoma 8:9 A.: He who says, "I shall sin and repent, sin and repent" – they give him no chance to do repentance. "I will sin and the Day of Atonement will atone" – the Day of Atonement does not atone. So, too, the law distinguishes inadvertence from deliberation in action, with appropriately diverse penalties, T. Shab. 2:17–18: He who slaughters an animal on the Sabbath – if he did so inadvertently – it may be eaten at the end of the Sabbath. If he did so deliberately, it may not be eaten. Produce that one gathered on the Sabbath – if he did so inadvertently, it may be eaten at the end of the Sabbath. If he did so deliberately, it may not be eaten.

It follows that intentionality overrides action. Thus, for example, a mere accident of speech is not binding; one must say exactly what he intended to say for the act of speech to be binding, whether in regard to oaths or offerings:

MISHNAH-TRACTATE TERUMOT 3:8
[TRANS. ALAN J. AVERY-PECK]

A. (1) One who [in designating agricultural gifts] intends to say, "heave offering," but says, "tithe," "tithe," but says "heave offering,"

B. (2) [or who, in designating a sacrifice, intends to say,] "burnt offering," but says, "peace offering," "peace offering," but says, "burnt offering";

C. (3) [or who, in making a vow, intends to say], "that I will not enter this house," but says, "that house," "that I will not derive benefit from this one," but says, "from that one,"

D. has not said anything,

E. until his mouth and heart agree.

The very status of the produce that has been designated for God is dictated by the match of intentionality and deed; the person must say what he means; if he does, his intentionality takes over and transforms the produce, sanctifying it. An act of sanctification effects the will and intention of the actor – or is null.

One's intentionality further governs the effect of one's deeds when it comes to dealing with consecrated produce. For example, Mishnah-tractate Maaser

Sheni 1:5 rules: One who buys outside Jerusalem with money in the status of second tithe, which is to be eaten only in Jerusalem pieces of fruit, if he did so 1) unintentionally, not realizing the coins were consecrated, let their payment be returned to its former place to the purchaser who bought them by mistake; if he did so 2) on purpose – let the pieces of fruit be brought up and eaten in the holy place Jerusalem. And if the Temple does not exist, let the pieces of fruit rot.

Here is another case in which the intentionality of the actor arouses God's response, which is commensurate. When the farmer has decided that he wishes to benefit from the crop, for example, to take it to market for sale, then God's rights of ownership are activated and the crop must be tithed. That is, God as co-owner of the land wants his share of the crop exactly when the farmer's intentionality to harvest the crop classifies the crop as ready. But random nibbling is not the same thing as harvesting the crop, though the action – plucking the produce – superficially is the same. It follows that the crop may be subjected to random nibbling and not become liable to tithing. The actions of the farmer convey his attitude and intention vis à vis the crop, for example, once he has covered a basket, once he has filled a vessel.

MISHNAH-TRACTATE MAASEROT 1:5
[TRANSLATION BY MARTIN JAFFEE]

A. At what point after the harvest must tithes be removed from produce?

B. (1) Cucumbers and gourds-after he removes the fuzz [from them].

C. But if he does not remove the fuzz, [tithes need not be removed] until he stacks them up.

D. (2) Chatemelons – after he scalds [them in order to remove the fuzz].

E. But if he does not scald [them], [tithes need not be removed] until he makes a store [of melons].

F. (3) Green vegetables which are [normally] tied in bunches-after he ties [them].

G. But if he does not tie them, [tithes need not be removed] until the vessel [into which he places the picked greens] is filled.

H. But if he does not fill the vessel, [tithes need not be removed] until he collects all he needs.

I. (4) [The contents of] a basket [need not be tithed] until he covers [the basket].

J. But if he does not cover [it, tithes need not be removed] until he fills the vessel.

K. But if he does not fill the vessel, [tithes need not be removed] until he collects all he needs [in that basket] –

L. Under what circumstances [do these criteria apply]? If he is bringing the produce to market.

M. But if he is bringing it home, [it is not liable to the removal of tithes, and) he eats some of it as a random snack until he reaches home.

It follows that, once more, intentionality classifies a set of similar actions into diverse categories, each governed by its own rule as to tithing.

Along these same lines, to incur guilt, one must intend the action that one has carried out. And that intention must cover the details of the action, not only its main purpose. So the law takes account of subtleties involving the interplay of partially realized intention in slightly incongruous action. If he acted in a manner different from his intended action, he is not as culpable as he would have been had he accomplished his purpose. So Mishnah-tractate Sanhedrin 9:4:

MISHNAH-TRACTATE SANHEDRIN 9:4

A. [If] he intended to kill a beast and killed a man,
B. a gentile and killed an Israelite,
C. an untimely birth and killed an offspring that was viable,
D. he is exempt.

Here the intention was not realized. But what about variations in the gray area between fully accomplishing one's intention through the actualities of what he has concretely done? Now the complexities enter in:

E. [If] he intended to hit him on his loins with a blow that was not sufficient to kill him when it struck his loins, but it hit his heart, and there was sufficient force in that blow to kill him when it struck his heart, and he died, he is exempt.
F. [If] he intended to hit him on his heart, and there was in that blow sufficient force to kill when it struck his heart, and it hit him on his loins, and there was not sufficient force in that blow to kill him when it struck his loins, but he died,
G. he is exempt.

To make the point clear through a sequence of matched examples, as the Mishnah's style requires, further illustrations proceed to recapitulate the unstated generalization (leading the Talmud commonly to ask why each illustration is required, what special qualification it contributes):

H. [If I he intended to hit a large person, and there was not sufficient force in that blow to kill a large person, but it hit a small person, and there was sufficient force in that blow to kill a small person, and he died,
I. he is exempt.

J. [If] he intended to hit a small person, and there was in that blow sufficient force to kill a small person, and it struck the large person, and there was not sufficient force in that blow to kill the large person, but he died,
K. he is exempt.

Now, once more, an important qualification is introduced. If one's intention and action coincide, though not as anticipated, the result is that the man has accomplished his goal and he bears responsibility:

L. But: [if] he intended to hit him on his loins, and there was sufficient force in the blow to kill him when it struck his loins, and it hit him on his heart and he died,
M. he is liable.
N. [If] he intended to hit a large person, and there was in that blow sufficient force to kill the large person, and it hit a small person and he died,
O. he is liable.
P. R. Simeon says, "Even if he intended to kill this party, and he actually killed some other party, he is exempt."

The system of criminal justice thus vastly expands on the distinction between manslaughter and murder. Once we take account, as Scripture does, of intentionality in the matter of killing a person, we amplify and elaborate the issue to accommodate the exact correspondence between what one proposed to do and what he has actually done.

Still more: the entire system of animal sacrifices in atonement of sin rests on the distinction between an intentional and an unintentional action. Indeed, that fact will loom large in our examination of the matter of repentance, which matches the correct intention against the improper intention then and so rights the balance between God's and man's will by bringing man's will back into synchronicity with God's. Take the matter of the sin-offering, for example. A sin is atoned for by a sin-offering – but that is only when the act is inadvertent. A deliberate action is not covered; so Mishnah-tractate Shab. 11:6J-K: "This is the general principle: All those who may be liable to sin-offerings in fact are not liable unless at the beginning and the end, their sin is done inadvertently."

But if the beginning of their sin is inadvertent and the end is deliberate, or the beginning deliberate and the end inadvertent, they are exempt – unless at the beginning and at the end their sin is inadvertent. The matter of intentionality governs the penalty to be paid by means of an animal sacrifice or some other form of sanction, for example, extirpation (premature death), death at the hands of Heaven, death at the hands of an earthly court. Thus, Mishnah-tractate Keritot 1:2, cited earlier: "For those transgressions are people liable,

for deliberately doing them, to the punishment of extirpation, and for accidentally doing them, to the bringing of a sin-offering, and for not being certain of
whether or not one has done them, to a suspensive guilt offering" (Lev. 5:17).

Intentionality governs the acceptability of some classes of animal offerings
but not others. Specifically, if an animal is designated for use as a Passover
offering or as a sin-offering, but then the officiating priest offers the animal
up under some other designation, that is, in a classification other than that
specified by the donor's intent, the offering is null. Hence, Mishnah-tractate
Zebahim 1:1 = Mishnah-tractate Menahot 1:1 for meal offerings: "All animal
offerings which were slaughtered not for their own name are valid so that the
blood is tossed, the entrails burned, etc., but they do not go to the owner's
credit in fulfillment of an obligation, except for the Passover and the sin
offering – the Passover at its appointed time the afternoon of the fourteenth of
Nisan." So, too, we find the following generalization:

MISHNAH-TRACTATE ZEBAHIM 2:3

A. This is the general rule:

B. Whoever slaughters, or receives [the blood], or conveys [the blood], or sprinkles
[the blood] [intending]

C. to eat something which is usually eaten [meat], [or] to burn something which is
usually burned [entrails],

D. outside its proper place [which is, the Temple court for Most Holy Things, the
walled city of Jerusalem for Lesser Holy Things] –

E. it is invalid [and the meat may not be eaten]. And extirpation does not apply to it.

F. [Supply: Whoever slaughters, or receives the blood, or conveys the blood, or sprinkles (the blood), intending to eat something which is usually eaten, to burn something
which is usually burned]

G. outside its proper time –

H. it is refuse.

I. And they are liable on its account to extirpation [even if despite their declared
intention, they actually eat the meat within the time limit].

Few actions in the Temple cult are entirely divorced from the intentionality of
the priest who sacrifices the beast or the farmer who supplies it and benefits
from the offering. The matter of intentionality, moreover, is differentiated;
diverse components of the procedure of sacrifice are singled out, and each
must be performed with the right purpose in mind. Specifically, the intentionality of the animal offering covers six matters, and for each of these matters,
the animal must be offered up under the donor's correct intentionality:

MISHNAH-TRACTATE ZEB. 4:6

A. For the sake of six things is the animal offering sacrificed: (1) for the sake of the animal offering, (2) for the sake of the one who sacrifices it, (3) for the sake of the Lord, (4) for the sake of the altar fires, (5) for the sake of the odour, (6) for the sake of the pleasing smell.

B. And as to the sin offering and the guilt offering, for the sake of the sin [expiated thereby].

C. Said R. Yosé, "Even if one who was not [mindful] in his heart [that he performed the various rites] for the sake of any one of all of these correct points of intentionality, [but slaughtered without specifying that he did so with these things properly in mind] – it is valid. For it is a condition imposed by the court, that intentionality follows only [the mind and will and attitude of] the one who carries out the act [not the owner; and the officiant does not have to specify the six considerations at all. If he acts in commendable silence, that suffices]."

Ideally, therefore, the priest will perform the rites in silence, rather than proclaiming the intentionality that governs his action, since in the latter case he may announce an error, and all will be lost.

We not only assess intentionality, we take account of the probability that someone will have acted in accord with the proper intentionality even in avoiding the cultic contamination of objects:

BAVLI-TRACTATE HAGIGAH 2:7 II.3–4/18B

3. A. Said R. Jonathan b. Eleazar, "If someone's head-band fell from him and he said to his fellow, 'Give it to me,' and he gave it to him, the headband is unclean" [Abraham: for we cannot assume that he took it upon himself to guard it from uncleanness while he handled it, since the owner did not ask whether he was clean or not, nor can we say that the owner guarded it against defilement while it was not in his possession].

4. A. Said R. Jonathan b. Amram, "If one's garments for the Sabbath were mixed up with his garments for everyday and he put them on, they are made unclean." [If someone protects something assuming it is one thing and finds it to be another, it is unclean.]

Here, once more, intentionality serves to classify an action and its consequence. The practical consequences should not be missed. If the garments are unclean and one wears them to the Temple or while wearing them eats food that is to be kept in a condition of cultic cleanness, one violates the laws of cleanness that protect the status of sanctification of Holy Things, a considerable concern.

Intentionality extends to other matters besides concrete issues of the law and its practice. Intentionality shades over into attitude, the abstract becoming concrete through feelings or emotions. As we have seen many times, the right attitude is one of accommodation of one's own will to the will of others, self-abnegation, restraint, prudence. The most prized virtue is humility, on account of which Judah merited that the monarchy be assigned to his tribe, as did Saul (T. Ber. 4:18). A person should conform to the prevailing practice of the community and not stand out; so Hillel the Elder says at T. Ber. 2:21: "Do not appear naked where others go clothed, and do not appear clothed where others go naked, and do not appear standing where others sit, and do not appear sitting where others stand, and do not appear laughing where others weep, and do not appear weeping where others laugh, because Scripture states, 'a time to weep, a time to laugh, a time to embrace, a time to refrain from embracing' (Qoh. 3:4, 5)." And altruism is the right attitude:

MISHNAH-TRACTATE ABOT 5:16–17

5:16 A. [In] any loving relationship which depends upon something, [when] that thing is gone, the love is gone.

B. But any which does not depend upon something will never come to an end.

C. What is a loving relationship which depends upon something? That is the love of Amnon and Tamar (11 Sam. 13:15).

D. And one which does not depend upon something? That is the love of David and Jonathan.

So, too, the right intention is what validates contention, praiseworthy when properly motivated, disgraceful when not:

5:17 A. Any dispute which is for the sake of Heaven will in the end yield results, and any which is not for the sake of Heaven will in the end not yield results.

B. What is a dispute for the sake of Heaven? This is the sort of dispute between Hillel and Shammai.

C. And what is one which is not for the sake of Heaven? h is the dispute of Korach and all his party.

Intentionality transcends the individual; the entire community of Israel forms a single intention and is responsible therefor. For example, God's response to prayer depends upon the attitude of the community. He cannot be coerced through mere recitation of the right words. Miracles respond to intentionality, a careful amplification of the doctrine of *zekhut*:

YERUSHALMI-TRACTATE TAANIT 3:4 I.I

A. There was a pestilence in Sepphoris, but it did not come into the neighbourhood in which R. Haninah was living. And the Sepphoreans said, "How is it possible that that elder lives among you, he and his entire neighbourhood, in peace, while the town goes to ruin?"

B. [Haninah] went in and said before them, "There was only a single Zimri in his generation, but on his account, 24,000 people died. And in our time, how many Zimris are there in our generation? And yet you are raising a clamor!"

Now the comparison of the power of the several sages to pray for rain and attain a response from Heaven is undertaken:

C. One time they had to call a fast, but it did not rain. R. Joshua carried out a fast in the South, and it rained. The Sepphoreans said, "R. Joshua b. Levi brings down rain for the people in the South, but R. Haninah holds back rain for us in Sepphoris."

D. They found it necessary to declare a second time of fasting and sent and summoned R. Joshua b. Levi. [Haninah] said to him, "Let my lord go forth with us to fast." The two of them went out to fast, but it did not rain.

The difference lies with the intentionality of the communities. The one is pure of heart, the other not:

E. He went in and preached to them as follows: "It was not R. Joshua b. Levi who brought down rain for the people of the south, nor was it R. Haninah who held back rain from the people of Sepphoris. But as to the Israelites in the south, their hearts are open, and when they listen to a teaching of Torah they submit [to accept it], while as to the Sepphoreans, their hearts are hard, and when they hear a teaching of Torah, they do not submit [or accept it]."

F. When he went in, he looked up and saw that the [cloudless] air was pure. He said, "Is this how it still is? [Is there no change in the weather?"] Forthwith, it rained. He took a vow for himself that he would never do the same thing again. He said, "How shall I say to the creditor [God] not to collect what is owing to him."

The variable, then, is the matter of intention, and it governs relationships with Heaven as much as those in the marketplace. That is because it is the one power that man totally exercises, like God.

It is the possibility of a minor's forming a valid intention in respect to religious obligations that determines the point at which the minor may begin to carry out those obligations. In T. Hag. 1:2, for example. Here we deal with a normative ruling governing actions. We want to know when the minor exercises sufficient power of will to accept responsibility to Heaven. It is when his understanding has sufficiently matured so that he may be held responsible for what he does: to know is to incur responsibility. Thus, in the case at hand, we emphasize the correspondence of knowledge and will:

TOSEFTA-TRACTATE HAGIGAH I:2

A. A minor goes forth in reliance upon the *'erub* put out by his mother [not by his father].

B. And he is liable to observe the commandment of dwelling in a *sukkah*.

C. And they prepare for him an *'erub* consisting of food sufficient for two meals, in connection with the commingling of Sabbath-boundaries.

D. [If] he knows how to shake [an object], he is liable to observe the commandment of the *lulab*.

E. [If] he knows how to cloak himself, he is liable for the commandment of fringes.

F. [If] he knows how to speak, his father teaches him the *Shema'*, Torah, and the Holy Language [Hebrew].

G. And if not, it would have been better had he not come into the world.

H. [If] he knows how to take care of his phylacteries, his father purchases phylacteries for him.

I. [If] he knows how to take care of his person, they eat food preserved in a state of cultic cleanness depending upon the cleanness of his person.

J. [If he knows how to take care of his] hands, they eat food preserved in a state of cultic cleanness depending upon the cleanness of his hands.

K. How do they examine him [to see whether he is able to take care of himself]?

L. They immerse him and give him unconsecrated food as if it were heave-offering.

M. [If] he knows how to fold over the corner of his garment [to receive heave-offering therein], they give him a share [of the heave-offering and tithes] at the threshing floor.

N. [If] he has sufficient intelligence to answer a question, then a doubt involving him in private domain is resolved as unclean, [and] one involving him in public domain is resolved as clean.

O. [If] he knows how to effect proper slaughter of an animal, then an act of slaughter on his part is valid.

P. [If] he can eat an olive's bulk of grain, they dispose of his excrement and urine at a distance of four cubits [from a settlement].

Q. [If he can eat] an olive's bulk of roast meat, they slaughter a Passover-sacrifice on his account.

Here we discern the components of intention, which are three: knowledge, action, and attitude. If one possesses knowledge, he can form an intelligent act of will. If he performs the action on the basis of knowledge. it is a valid act of will. But both statements contain the further qualification: that is the case only if, to begin with, the act of will corresponds to the proper one in the stated context.

And this leads us to the final point on the power of intentionality. It governs not only affirmative but negative action. The intention to do evil, even if the action is not done, is culpable and to be repented. So an improper intentionality, not carried out, is blameworthy; I cannot conceive of a more extreme statement of the centrality of intentionality in the theology of the Oral Torah than the following:

BAVLI-TRACTATE QIDDUSHIN 4:13/II.13/81B

A. R. Hiyya bar Ashi was accustomed, whenever he prostrated himself to his face, to say, "May the All-Merciful save us from the Evil Impulse."

But the rabbi was not wanton, his wife knew full well, and required no such prayer:

B. Once his wife heard this. She said, "Now how many years he has kept away from me, so how come he says this?"
C. One day he was studying in his garden, and she dressed up [in disguise] and walked back and forth before him. He said to him, "How are you?"
D. She said to him, "I'm Haruta [the famous whore], and I've come back today."
E. He lusted after her. She said to him, "Bring me that pomegranate from the top bough."
F. He climbed up and got it for her.

The rabbi went so far as to get the pomegranate, gave the woman what she asked, and did what he wanted. Then he went home and met his wife there:

When he went back inside his house, his wife was heating the oven, so he climbed up and sat down in it. She said to him, "So what's going on?"
G. He told her what had happened. She said to him, "So it was really me." But he wouldn't believe her until she gave him the pomegranate.

The act was perfectly acceptable to Heaven, but the intention transformed it into a sin:

H. He said to her, "Well, anyhow, my intention was to do what is prohibited."

Guilt took over, and the sage repented and fasted:

I. For the rest of the life of that righteous man he fasted [in penitence] until he died on that account.

The Oral Torah contains a multitude of such stories about the power of intention to classify an action, for instance, eating acceptable food in the impression that it is not suitable, violating the Sabbath only to discover it was an ordinary day, and the like. Other examples, such as we have noted, assign to intention an act of sanctification or an act of secularization. Indeed, much of the practiced law set forth by sages operates within the dynamics of intentionality.

So it would be difficult to assemble a more uniform set of diverse formulations of a single principle. Intentionality forms the systemic dynamics of the entire structure of sanctification and morality that the Oral Torah constructs. It is the principal variable, because it is the one thing that God has created that is possessed of its own autonomy. That is why, also, it is intentionality that explains sin, and it is sin that, we already anticipate, accounts for the imperfect condition of the world and of Israel therein.

The theology of the Oral Torah, like its law, therefore identifies free will as the principal point of correspondence between God and man, the point at which God's image makes its deepest mark upon man's visage. Just as God freely chooses, so does man. In man God has made and therefore has met his match. Man has the power to violate the rules of order, the rationality of justice then dictates the result. Chapter 11 will explain that, when man rebels against God, rejecting God's dominion instead of loving God, that sin disrupts world order. Punishment "with the proper fruit of his deeds" follows. But, as we shall see in Chapter 12, man's free will in response may inaugurate the process by which world order is restored, creation renewed. And that process leads to the last things of all, eternal life embodied in the resurrection of the dead and the world to come. So the theology of the Oral Torah accounts for life, death, and life restored. Now to the critical chapters in the system: what a man can do, with what result.

11 Sin

Sin explains the condition of Israel. The governing theory of Israel, that had Israel kept the Torah from the beginning, the Holy People would never have had any history at all but would have lived in a perfect world at rest and balance and order, is now invoked. There would have been nothing to write down, no history, had Israel kept the Torah. I can imagine no more explicit statement of how the world order is disrupted by sin, and, specifically, sinful attitudes, than this:

BAVLI-TRACTATE NEDARIM 3:1 I.14FF./22A-B

I.18 A. Said R. Ada b. R. Hanina, "If the Israelites had not sinned, to them would have been given only the Five Books of the Torah and the book of Joshua alone, which involves the division of the Land of Israel. How come? 'For much wisdom proceeds from much anger'" (Qoh. 1:18).

Adam ought to have stayed in Eden. With the Torah in hand, Israel, the new Adam, ought to have remained in the Land, beyond the reach of time and change, exempt from the events of interesting times. Sin ruined everything, for Adam, for Israel, bringing about the history recorded in Scripture – not a very complicated theodicy.

That the theology of the Oral Torah spins out a simple but encompassing logic makes the character of its treatment of sin entirely predictable. First, the system must account for imperfection in the world order of justice; sin supplies the reason. Second, it must explain how God remains omnipotent even in the face of imperfection. The cause of sin, man's free will corresponding to God's, tells why. Third, it must allow for systemic remission. Sin is so defined as to accommodate the possibility of regeneration and restoration. And, finally, sin must be so presented as to fit into the story of the creation of the perfect world. It is.

Defined in the model of the first sin, the one committed by man in Eden, sin is an act of rebellion against God. Rebellion takes two forms. As a gesture of omission, sin embodies the failure to carry out one's obligation to God set forth in the Torah. As one of commission, it constitutes an act of defiance. In both cases sin comes about by reason of man's intentionality to reject the will of God, set forth in the Torah. However accomplished, whether through omission or commission, an act becomes sinful because of the attitude that accompanies it. That is why man is responsible for sin, answerable to God in particular, who may be said to take the matter personally, just as it is meant. The consequence of sin is death for the individual, exile and estrangement for holy Israel, and disruption for the world. That is why sin accounts for much of the flaw of creation.

Since sin represents an act of rebellion against God, God has a heavy stake in the matter. It follows that sin in public is worse than sin in private, since in public one's sin profanes God's name:

BAVLI-TRACTATE QIDDUSHIN 1:10 1.10/40A

A. Said R. Abbahu in the name of R. Hanina, "It is better for someone to transgress in private but not profane the Name of Heaven in public: 'As for you, house of Israel, thus says the Lord God: Go, serve every one his idols, and hereafter also, if you will not obey me; but my holy name you shall not profane'" (Ezek. 20:39).
B. Said R. Ilai the Elder, "If someone sees that his impulse to sin is overpowering him, he should go somewhere where nobody knows him and put on ordinary clothing and cloak himself in ordinary clothing and do what he wants, but let him not profane the Name of Heaven by a public scandal."

Sin therefore defines one important point at which God and man meet and world order is affected. The just arrangement of matters that God has brought about in creation can be upset by man's intervention, for man alone has the will and freedom to stand against God's plan and intention for creation.

It follows, as we now realize, that the consequences of the correspondence of God and man account for all else. If the one power in all of creation that can and does stand against the will of God is man's will or intentionality, then man bears responsibility for the flawed condition of creation, and God's justice comes to its fullest expression in the very imperfection of existence, a circularity that once more marks a well-crafted, severely logical system. But free will also forms the source of remission; God's mercy, as we shall see in Chapter 12, intervenes when man's will warrants. Specifically, God restores the perfection of creation through his provision of means of atonement through repentance. But that presents no anomaly but conforms to the encompassing theory of matters. For repentance represents yet another act of human will that, like the transaction that yields *zekhut*, is countered with a commensurate act of God's will. The entire story of the world, start to finish, therefore records the cosmic confrontation of God's will and man's freedom to form and carry out an intention contrary to God's will. The universe is not animate but animated by the encounter of God and, in his image, after his likeness, man – the story, the only story, that the Oral Torah recapitulates from, and in completion of, the Written Torah.

The moral order, we have seen, encompasses exactly commensurate penalties for sin, the logic of a perfectly precise recompense forming the foundation of the theory of world order set forth by the Oral Torah. But knowing the just penalty tells us little about the larger theory of how sin disrupts the perfection of the world created by the one, just God. Since sin is deemed not personal alone but social and even cosmic, explaining sin carries us to the very center of the theology that animates the Oral Torah. What is at stake in sin is succinctly stated: it accounts for the deplorable condition of the world, defined by the situation of Israel. But sin is not a permanent feature of world order. It is a detail of an orderly progression, as God to begin with had planned, from chaos, which gave way to creation, to the Torah, which after the Flood through Israel restored order to the world, and onward to the age of perfection and stasis. To understand that doctrine, we have first to examine the place of sin in the unfolding of creation. In the Oral Torah the history of the world is divided into these three periods, indicated by Israel's relationship with God:

BAVLI-TRACTATE ABODAH ZARAH I:I II.5/9A
[=BAVLI-TRACTATE SANHEDRIN. I:I I.89/97A]

A. The Tannaite authority of the household of Elijah [stated], "The world will last for six thousand years: two thousand years of chaos, two thousand years of Torah, two thousand years of the time of the Messiah. But because of the abundance of our sins, what has passed [of the foreordained time] has passed."

The "two thousand years of chaos" mark the period prior to the giving of the Torah at Sinai, as God recognized the result of creating man in his image and the consequence of the contest between man's will and God's. Then come the two thousand years of Torah, which is intended to educate man's will and endow man with the knowledge to want what God wants. Then comes the time of the Messiah, of which we shall hear more in Chapter 12. Now the persistence of sin has lengthened the time of the Torah and postponed the advent of the Messiah. It follows that, to understand how the sages account for the situation of the world in this age, revealing God's justice out of the elements of chaos in the here and now, we have to pay close attention to the character of the sages' doctrine of sin.

What has already been said about sin as an act of rebellion bears the implication that an act may or may not be sinful, depending upon the attitude of the actor, a view that our inquiry into intentionality has adumbrated. In fact, only a few actions are treated as sinful in and of themselves. Chief among them are, specifically, murder, fornication, and idolatry. Under all circumstances a man must refrain from committing such actions, even at the cost of his own life. These represent absolute sins:

GENESIS RABBAH XXXI:VI.I

A. Another matter: "For the earth is filled with violence" (Gen. 6:13):
B. Said R. Levi, "The word for violence refers to idolatry, fornication, and murder.
C. "Idolatry: 'For the earth is filled with violence' (Gen. 6:13).
D. "Fornication: 'The violence done to me and to my flesh be upon Babylonia' (Jer. 51:35). [And the word for 'flesh' refers to incest, as at Lev. 18:6].
E. "Murder: 'For the violence against the children of Judah, because they have shed innocent blood' (Joel 4:19).
F. "Further, the word for 'violence' stands for its ordinary meaning as well."

Since these were the deeds of the men of the generation of the Flood that so outraged God as to bring about mass destruction, they form a class of sin by themselves. The children of Noah, not only the children of Israel, must avoid these sins at all costs. But there is a sin that Israel may commit that exceeds even the cardinal sins. Even those three are forgivable, but rejection of the Torah is not:

YERUSHALMI-TRACTATE HAGIGAH I:7/I:3

A. R. Huna, R. Jeremiah in the name of R. Samuel bar R. Isaac: "We find that the Holy One, blessed be he, forgave Israel for idolatry, fornication, and murder. [But] for their rejection of the Torah he never forgave them."
B. What is the scriptural basis for that view?

C. It is not written, "Because they practiced idolatry, fornication, and murder," but rather, "And the Lord said, 'Because they have forsaken my Torah.'"

D. Said R. Hiyya bar Ba, "'If they were to forsake me, I should forgive them, for they may yet keep my Torah. For if they should forsake me but keep my Torah, the leaven that is in [the Torah] will bring them closer to me.'"

E. R. Huna said, "Study Torah [even if it is] not for its own sake, for, out of [doing so] not for its own sake, you will come [to study it] for its own sake."

Still, that the classification of an action, even of the most severe character, depends upon the intentionality or attitude of the actor governs even here.

An Israelite's rejection of not God but the Torah is forthwith set into the context of will or intentionality. God does not object to insincerity when it comes to study of the Torah, because the Torah itself contains the power to reshape the will of man (as framed succinctly by the sages elsewhere, "The commandments were given only to purify the heart of man," "God craves the heart," and similar formulations). The very jarring intrusion at D, developing C but making its own point, underscores that conviction. God can forgive Israel for forsaking him, because if they hold on to the Torah, they will find their way back. The Torah will reshape Israel's heart. And then, amplifying that point but moving still further from the main proposition, comes Huna's sentiment, E, that studying the Torah does not require proper intentionality, because the Torah in due course will effect the proper intentionality. Two critical points emerge. First, intentionality plays a central role in the discussion of principal sins. Second, sin ordinarily does not form an absolute but only a relative category, which is to say, an action that is sinful under one set of circumstances, when the intent is wicked, is not sinful but even subject to forgiveness under another set of circumstances.

This point is spelled out explicitly, and in matters of *halakhah*, where – as we saw in chapter 10 – theological norms are realized. The same action in one setting is prohibited, in another, permitted, and, as I have underscored, that shows that the sinfulness of an action is relative to the circumstance, for example, of the sinner, and his intentionality. The Torah then sets up situations that contrast circumstance with action; then obeying the law in one situation involves refraining from what, in another, is entirely permitted. Obedience to the law in the two similar settings, therefore, forms the crux of matters, not the detail of the law itself, for while God has under some circumstances prohibited a given action, under other circumstances he has permitted the same matter:

LEVITICUS RABBAH XXII:X.I

C. "The Lord permits what is forbidden" (Ps. 146:7): "What I forbade to you, I have permitted to you."

We begin with laws governing foods:

D. "I forbade the abdominal fat in the case of domesticated cattle but permitted it in the case of wild beasts.

E. "I forbade you to eat the sciatic nerve in a wild beast, but I permitted it to you in fowl.

F. "I forbade you beasts not killed through proper slaughter in the case of fowl, but I permitted the same in the case of fish."

We now move to sexual activities, making the point that God's leniency vastly outweighs his stringency:

2. A. R. Aha, R. Bisna, and R. Jonathan in the name of R. Meir: "More that I prohibited to you, I permitted to you.

B. "I forbade you to have sexual relations in the presence of menstrual blood, but I permitted you to have sexual relations despite the presence of hymeneal blood.

C. "I forbade you to have sexual relations with a married woman but I permitted you to have sexual relations with a captive woman regardless of her marital status.

D. "I forbade you to have sexual relations with a brother's wife or widow, but I permitted you to marry the deceased childless brother's widow.

E. "I forbade you to marry a woman along with her sister, but I permitted you to do so after the sister you married had died.

The same trait of leniency extends to other matters as well:

F. "I forbade you to wear a garment made of mixed species wool and linen, but I permitted you to wear a linen cloak with show fringes made of wool.

G. "I forbade you to eat the meat of a pig, but I permitted you to eat the tongue of a fish which tastes like pork.

H. "I forbade you to eat abdominal fat of a beast, but I permitted you to eat ordinary fat.

I. "I forbade you to eat blood, but I permitted you to eat liver.

J. "I forbade you to eat meat with milk, but I permitted you to eat the cow's udder."

We take one step further: not only does God permit more than he prohibits, but he even provides something to replace each item that is forbidden:

3. A. R. Menahama, R. Aha, R. Yohanan in the name of R. Jonathan: "In place of whatever I forbade to you, I permitted something to you.

B. "In place of the prohibition of certain kinds of fish you may eat the Leviathan, a clean fish.

C. "In place of the prohibition of certain kinds of fowl you may eat *ziz*, [a clean bird].

D. "That is in line with the following verse of Scripture: 'I know all the fowl of the mountains, and the *ziz* of the fields is mine' " (Ps. 50:11).

E. Said R. Judah b. R. Simon, "When it spreads its wings, it darkens the orb of the sun.

F. "That is in line with the following verse of Scripture: 'Does the *nes* soar by your wisdom, and spread its wings toward the south' " (Job 39:26).

G. And why is it called a *ziz*? Because it has many kinds of tastes, a taste on this side (MZH), a taste on that side (MZH).

The passage recalls my comparison, in the prologue, of sages' and philosophers' modes of thought and analysis. Here is a fine example of systematic sifting of data, with a proposition emerging out of repeated instances thereof. The proposition comes at the outset: what I forbade I also permitted. This is then systematically illustrated. Then comes the next version, more than what I forbade, I have permitted, and then in place of what I forbade I permitted – and a sequence of compelling examples show the rationality and order of the divine commandments, each balanced or outweighed by the corresponding one. The systemic interest in rationalizing and organizing diverse data into patterns comes to rich expression here.

A single action, therefore, cannot be classified in its own framework, but only within the framework of the attitude with which the action is carried out. The act on its own is neutral. Here we have the case of saddling an ass, which may represent an act of devotion to God or of hatred of man. Love and hatred disrupt the natural order of things:

GENESIS RABBAH LV:VIII.1–2

1. A. "And Abraham rose early in the morning, [saddled his ass, and took two of his young men with him, and his son Isaac, and he cut the wood for the burnt offering and arose and went to the place which God had told him]" (Gen. 22:3):

B. Said R. Simeon b. Yohai, "Love disrupts the natural order of things, and hatred disrupts the natural order of things.

First comes love, with its exemplary case:

C. "Love disrupts the natural order of things we learn from the case of Abraham: '... he saddled his ass.' But did he not have any number of servants? [Why then did a slave not saddle the ass for him? Out of his dedication to his son, Abraham performed that menial task.] That proves love disrupts the natural order of things.

Then comes the instance of hatred and its power to corrupt the normal order:

D. "Hatred disrupts the natural order of things we learn from the case of Balaam: 'And Balaam rose up early in the morning and saddled his ass' (Num. 22:21). But did he not have any number of servants? That proves hatred disrupts the natural order of things.

Another set shows the regularity of the rule:

E. "Love disrupts the natural order of things we learn from the case of Joseph: 'And Joseph made his chariot ready' (Gen. 46:29). But did he not have any number of servants? But that proves love disrupts the natural order of things.
F. "Hatred disrupts the natural order of things we learn from the case of Pharaoh: 'And he made his chariot ready' (Ex. 14:6). But did he not have any number of servants? But that proves hatred disrupts the natural order of things."

God enters the equation in a manner we should by now anticipate: he responds to the attitude of the man who does the action – and he remembers the action in the account of the actor:

2. A. Said R. Simeon b. Yohai, "Let one act of saddling an ass come and counteract another act of saddling the ass. May the act of saddling the ass done by our father Abraham, so as to go and carry out the will of him who spoke and brought the world into being, counteract the act of saddling that was carried out by Balaam when he went to curse Israel.
B. "Let one act of preparing counteract another act of preparing. Let Joseph's act of preparing his chariot so as to meet his father serve to counteract Pharaoh's act of preparing to go and pursue Israel."

The two incidents are compared and contrasted, yielding a common principle and opposed concrete results.

That the variable of sin is man's intentionality in carrying out the action, not the intrinsic quality of most sinful actions (though, as we saw, not all), emerges in a striking formulation of matters. Here we find a position that is quite remarkable, yet entirely coherent with the principal stresses of the theology of the Oral Torah. The sages maintain that it is better sincerely to sin than hypocritically to perform a religious duty; to "sin bravely," the sages would respond, "No, rather, sincerely!" It would be difficult to state in more extreme language the view that all things are relative to attitude or intentionality than to recommend sincere sin over hypocritical virtue:

11. A. Said R. Nahman bar Isaac, "A transgression committed for its own sake, in a sincere spirit, is greater in value than a religious duty carried out not for its own sake, but in a spirit of insincerity.

B. "For it is said, 'May Yael, wife of Hever the Kenite, be blessed above women, above women in the tent may she be blessed' (Judges 5:24).

C. "Now who are these women in the tent? They are none other than Sarah, Rebecca, Rachel, and Leah." [The murder she committed gained more merit than the matriarchs great deeds.]

The saying shocks and is immediately challenged:

D. But is this really true that a transgression committed for its own sake, in a sincere spirit, is greater in value than a religious duty carried out not for its own sake, but in a spirit of insincerity. And did not R. Judah say Rab said, "A person should always be occupied in study of the Torah and in practice of the commandments, even if this is not for its own sake [but in a spirit of insincerity], for out of doing these things not for their own sake, a proper spirit of doing them for their own sake will emerge"?

E. Say: it is equivalent to doing them not for their own sake.

Now we revert to the view that insincere Torah-study and practice of the commandments still have the power to transform a man:

12. A. Said R. Judah said Rab, "A person should always be occupied in study of the Torah and in practice of the commandments, even if this is not for its own sake [but in a spirit of insincerity], for out of doing these things not for their own sake, a proper spirit of doing them for their own sake will emerge."

Then comes a concrete case of blatant insincerity's producing a reward; the Messiah himself is the offspring of an act of hypocrisy on the part of Balak, the king of Moab, the ancestor of Ruth, from whom the scion of David, the Messiah, descends:

B. For as a reward for the forty-two offerings that were presented by the wicked Balak to force Balaam to curse Israel, he was deemed worthy that Ruth should descend from him.

C. For said R. Yosé b. R. Hanina, "Ruth was the grand-daughter of Eglon, the grandson of Balak, king of Moab."

The upshot is that, as we already realize, intentionality is everything; sin is rarely absolute but ordinarily conditioned upon the attitude of the actor; and sincerity in sin exceeds in merit hypocrisy in virtue.

Our examination of the theological anthropology of the Oral Torah in chapter 9 has prepared us for the main point. It is that, thinking along lines of analogy and contrast, the sages find the origins of sin in the attitude of arrogance, the beginnings of virtue in that of humility. Arrogance leads to rebellion against God, humility, to submission to him. Israel, therefore, is in command of its own fate. Redemption depends upon righteousness, just as the present age comes about by reason of arrogance:

B. SHAB. 20:1 III.10–12/139A

A. It has been taught on Tannaite authority:
B. R. Yosé b. Elisha says, "If you see a generation on which great troubles break, go and examine the judges of Israel, for any punishment that comes into the world comes only on account of the judges of Israel, as it is said, 'Hear this, please you heads of the house of Jacob and rulers of the house of Israel, who abhor judgment and pervert all equity. They build up Zion with blood and Jerusalem with iniquity. The heads thereof judge for reward, and the priests thereof teach for hire, and the prophets thereof divine for money, yet will they lean upon the Lord?' (Mic. 3:9–11). They are wicked, yet they put their trust in him who by speaking brought the world into being. Therefore the Holy One, blessed be He, will bring upon them three punishments for three transgressions for which they bear responsibility, as it is said, 'Therefore shall Zion for your sake be ploughed as a field, and Jerusalem shall become heaps, and the mountain of the house as the high places of a forest' (Mic. 3:12).
C. "And the Holy One, blessed be He, will bring his Presence to rest on Israel only when the wicked judges and rulers will come to an end in Israel, as it is said, 'And I will turn my hand upon you and thoroughly purge away your dross and will take away all your tin, and I will restore your judges as at the first and your counsellors as at the beginning'" (Isa. 1:25–26).

The sages contrast righteousness and arrogance, the one effecting redemption, the other forming an obstacle to it:

III.11 A. Said Ulla, "Jerusalem will be redeemed only through righteousness, as it is written, 'Zion shall be redeemed with judgment and her converts with righteousness'" (Isa. 1:27).
B. Said R. Pappa, "If the arrogant end [in Israel], the Magi will end [in Iran], if the judges end [in Israel], the rulers of thousands will come to an end [in Iran]. If the arro-

gant end [in Israel], the magi will end [in Iran], as it is written, 'And I will purely purge away your haughty ones and take away all your sin' (Isa. 1:25). If judges end [in Israel], the rulers of thousands will come to an end [in Iran], as it is written, 'The Lord has taken away your judgments, he has cast out your enemy' (Zeph. 3:15)."

The theology, therefore, finds in arrogance the secret of Israel's subjugation, and in humility, of its redemption.

Given the sages' focus upon intentionality, it is not surprising that the matched traits of arrogance and humility should take priority in their systematic thinking about the imperfections of the world order. We recall the view cited in chapter 9 that arrogance embodies the bad attitude, and reason leads to the expectation that the arrogant will be cut down to size. If the arrogant person repents, however, then he abandons the bad attitude and adopts the good one, of humility, which is the condition of repentance. God is the model of humility, so too is Moses. The resurrection of the dead involves the exaltation of the humble – dust itself. Scripture and parable serve to convey these points, but the system at its core insists upon them. God favours the humble and accepts humility as equivalent to offerings in the Temple, responding to prayers of the humble just as the stories about *zekhut* have already shown us. The Bavli's systematic composite on the subject, which we have already examined, yields a brief and still-fresh statement for the present context:

BAVLI-TRACTATE SOTAH I:1–2 V.25/5B

A. Said R. Joshua b. Levi, "Come and take note of how great are the humble in the sight of the Holy One, blessed be he.

B. "For when the sanctuary stood, a person would bring a burnt-offering, gaining thereby the reward for bringing a burnt-offering, or a meal-offering, and gaining the reward for a meal offering.

C. "But a person who is genuinely humble does Scripture treat as if he had made offerings of all the sacrifices,

D. "as it is said, 'The sacrifices [plural] of God are a broken spirit' (Ps. 51:19).

E. "And not only so, but his prayer is not rejected, as it is said, 'A broken and contrite heart, O God, you will not despise' " (Ps. 51:19).

In a system that works out dialectics by matching opposites in a theory of ultimate complementarity, no explanation of sin can stand on its own, any more than any definition of sin can ignore the context in which sin takes place. All things are relative to one relationship: humility versus arrogance. Specific sins, such as adultery, are placed into that larger context of a failure of right attitude.

Adultery is an expression of arrogance, and so too is jealousy. A larger theory of sin and virtue, then, takes over this topic, among many others: sin is an expression of arrogance, and virtue, of humility. The marital bond expresses that same faithfulness that is required of Israel in relationship to God. Sin contrasts with faithfulness, since the opposite of faithfulness is arrogance, the opposite of sin, humility.

Then the question presses, why do people rebel against God? The answer is, by reason of arrogance, and that has to be accounted for. Specifically, they become arrogant when they are prosperous; then they trust in themselves and take for granted that their own power has secured abundance. They forget that it is God who, by his act of will, has given them what they have gotten. Prosperity and success bear their own threatening consequence in the change of man's attitude that they may well bring about. So arrogance comes from an excess of good fortune, but it is the absence of humility that accounts for the wrong attitude:

SIFRÉ TO DEUTERONOMY CCCXVIII:I.IFF.

1. A. ["So Jeshurun grew fat and kicked – you grew fat and gross and coarse – he forsook the God who made him and spurned the rock of his support. They incensed him with alien things, vexed him with abominations. They sacrificed to demons, no-gods, gods they had never known, new ones, who came but lately, who stirred not your fathers' fears. You neglected the rock that begot you, forgot the God who brought you forth" (Dt. 32:15–18).]

B. "So Jeshurun grew fat and kicked":

C. Out of satiety people rebel.

Now comes a standard trilogy of probative cases, the archetypal sinners: the Generation of the Flood, the Generation of the Dispersion from the Tower of Babel, and the Generation of Sodom and Gomorrah. They will exhibit the same trait in common and therefore prove the point at hand. In each case, we shall now note, people misunderstood their own prosperity and arrogantly claimed to control their own destiny. First comes the Generation of the Flood:

2. A. So you find in connection with the people of the generation of the flood, that they rebelled against the Holy One, blessed be He, only from an abundance of food, drink, prosperity.

B. What is said in their regard?

C. "Their houses are safe, without fear" (Job 21:9).

D. And so for the rest of the matter, as stated in connection with Deuteronomy.

Next is the generation of the dispersion from the Tower of Babel:

3. A. So you find in connection with the people of the generation of the tower, that they rebelled against the Holy One, blessed be He, only from prosperity.

B. What is said in their regard?

C. "And the whole earth was of one language" (Gen. 11:1).

Finally we come to Sodom:

4. A. So you find in connection with the people of Sodom, that they rebelled against the Holy One, blessed be He, only from abundance of food.

B. What is said in their regard?

C. "As for the earth, it produces bread" (Job 28:5).

D. And so for the rest.

E. And thus Scripture says, "As I live, says the Lord God, Sodom, your sister, has not done ..." (Ez. 16:48f.).

Next we move from the gentiles to Israel, showing that the Israelites, too, rebel by reason of prosperity:

6. A. So you find in connection with the people of the wilderness, that they rebelled only out of an abundance of food.

B. For it is said, "And the people sat down to eat and drink and rose up to make merry" (Ex. 32:6).

C. What then is stated in their regard? "They have turned aside quickly out of the way ..." (Ex. 32:8).

Then, from Israel in general the discussion reaches Israel in the Land itself:

7. A. Said the Holy One, blessed be He, to Moses, "Say to Israel, 'When you enter the land, you are going to rebel only out of abundance of food, drink, and prosperity.'"

B. For it is said, "For when I shall have brought them into the land which I swore to their fathers, flowing with milk and honey, and they shall have eaten their fill and gotten fat and turned to other gods and served them ..." (Deut. 31:20).

C. Said Moses to Israel, "When you enter the land, you are going to rebel only out of abundance of food, drink, and prosperity."

D. For it is said, "lest when you have eaten and are satisfied ... and when your herds and flocks multiply ... when your heart is lifted up and you forget the Lord your God" (Deut. 8:12ff.).

Then comes Job, who, for the Oral Torah, presents no intractable challenge; his complaint is readily addressed:

8. A. So you find concerning the sons and daughters of Job, that punishment came upon them only out of eating and drinking.
B. For it is said, "While he was yet speaking, another came and said, 'Your sons and your daughters were eating and drinking wine in their eldest brother's house and behold, there came a great wind'" (Job 12:18–19).

Then we turn to the Ten Tribes, who end the list of those who have suffered severe penalties for their arrogance, therefore embodying Israel in exile by reason of sin:

9. A. So you find in the case of the ten tribes, that they went into exile only out of an abundance of eating, drinking, and prosperity.
B. For it is said, "That lie on beds of ivory, that drink wine in bowls ... therefore now shall they go captive at the head of them who go captive" (Amos 6:4, 6, 7).

Israel when the Messiah comes is the last case in the sequence from the beginning of the story of man to the end:

10. A. So you find in connection [even] with the days of the Messiah, that [the Israelites] are going to rebel only out of an abundance of eating and drinking.
B. For it is said, "So Jeshurun grew fat and kicked – you grew fat and gross and coarse – he forsook the God who made him and spurned the rock of his support."

Given the high stakes in obedience to God's will – both nature and history respond to Israel's conduct, with dire results – why in the world would anyone rebel anyhow? The answer is, people forget the precariousness of their existence, and, in times of prosperity, they rebel. The rest follows.

We turn from entire generations to individuals, for the Oral Torah never distinguishes Israel from Israelites but endeavours throughout to explain the one in the same way as the other. So we ask, How shall we know that an improper attitude characterizes a given personality? A few indicators serve. A mark of arrogance is boastfulness, a sin that is attributed to the Generation of the Flood, the Sodomites, Pharaoh, Sisera, Sennacherib, Nebuchadnezzar, and the Fourth Kingdom (Rome). Whoever is boastful before the Omnipresent is punished only by fire:

LEVITICUS RABBAH VII:VI.I

A. Said R. Levi, "It is an ordinance and a decree that whoever is boastful before the Omnipresent is punished only by fire, [just as the fire offering, *olah*, meaning, that which goes up, goes up on the fire and is burned up].

We start before the gentiles on their own, the Generation of the Flood, the Sodomites:

B. "As to the generation of the flood, because they were boastful and said, 'Who is the Almighty, that we should serve him' (Job 21:15), they were punished only by fire, as it is said, 'In time of heat they disappear, when it is hot, they vanish from their place' " (Job 6:17).

F. [Levi resumes,] "As to the Sodomites, because they were boastful and said, 'Let us go and cause the laws of hospitality to be forgotten from our midst,' they were punished only by fire.

G. "That is in line with the following verse of Scripture: 'And he made to rain on Sodom and Gomorrah brimstone and fire' (Gen. 19:24).

Now we reach the gentiles in relationship to Israel; they reject God in their boasting: thus Pharaoh and Sennacherib and Nebuchadnezzar:

H. "As to Pharaoh, because he was boastful and said, 'And who is the Lord, that I should listen to his voice' (Ex. 5:2), he was punished only in fire, as it is written, 'So there was hail and fire flashing up amidst the hail' (Ex. 9:24).

I. "As to Sisera, because he was boastful and oppressed the Israelites, as it is written, 'And he oppressed the children of Israel forcefully' (Jud. 4:3) –

J. (what does "forcefully" mean? Said R. Isaac, "It means with blasphemy and cursing")

K. " 'he was punished only with fire.'

L. "That is in line with the following verse of Scripture: 'From heaven they fought [against Sisera]' (Jud. 5:20).

M. "As to Sennacherib, because he was boastful and said, 'Who are among the gods of these countries, who have delivered their country out of my hand' (Is. 36:20), he was punished only by fire.

N. "That is in line with the following verse of Scripture: 'And under his glory there shall be kindled a burning like the burning of fire' (Is. 10:16).

O. "As to Nebuchadnezzar, because he was boastful and said, 'And who is God, that he will deliver you out of my hands?' (Dan. 3:15), he was punished only by fire.

P. "That is in line with the following verse of Scripture: 'The flame of the fire slew those men that took up Shadrach, Meshach, and Abed-nego' (Dan. 3:22).

As is commonly the case, the gentiles of times past give way to the wicked empire, which is Rome, the last in the line before the Messiah's advent and Israel's restoration:

Q. "As to the wicked empire, because it is boastful and arrogant, saying, 'Whom have I in heaven, and Whom have I in heaven but you? And there is nothing on earth that I want besides you' (Ps. 73:25), it is destined to be punished by fire.

R. "That is in line with the following verse of Scripture: '[As to the fourth beast], as I looked, the beast was slain, and its body destroyed and given over to be burned with fire' (Dan. 7:11).

S. "But as to Israel, because they are despised and humble in this world, they will be comforted only with fire.

T. "That is in line with the following verse of Scripture: 'For I [Jerusalem shall be inhabited as villages without walls ...], for I will be to her a wall of fire round about' " (Zech. 2:9 [RSV: 2:5]).

Adding Nebuchadnezzar to the list invites the specific proposition to join the general one, that is, sinners are punished, and the particular sin at hand, boasting, is the focus. Here the inclusion of Nebuchadnezzar as the archetypal boaster serves, so it seems to me. But the evidence concerning the others is equally probative, and perhaps knowledge of the particular data associated with each category suffice, without special attention to the famous reference of Nebuchadnezzar.

Rejecting God's will as set forth in the Torah involves arrogance towards sages, who not only teach but also embody the Torah. It follows that sinfulness extends to disrespect for sages, and not listening to the exposition of sages is tantamount to rebellion against God. And rebellion against God involves those who know that God is lord but rebel against his dominion.

SIFRA CCLXIV:I.1FF.

1. A. "But if you will not hearken to me:"

B. "But if you will not hearken to me" means, if you will not listen to the exposition of sages.

Now we ask the obvious question: what makes us suppose that rejection of the sages is the same as rejection of the Torah, when the Torah is explicit that God speaks therein:

C. Might one suppose that reference is made to Scripture [rather than the sages' teachings]?
D. When Scripture says, "and will not do all these commandments," lo, reference clearly is made to what is written in the Torah.
E. Then how shall I interpret, "But if you will not hearken to me"?
F. It means, if you will not listen to the exposition of sages.

Israel is especially subject to sin and rebellion, because Israel knows the Torah and rejects it, while the gentiles reject what they do not even acknowledge:

2. A. "But if you will not hearken":
B. What is the point of Scripture here?
C. This refers to one who knows God's lordship and intentionally rebels against it.
D. And so Scripture says, "Like Nimrod, a mighty hunter [before the Lord]" (Gen. 10:9).
E. Now what is the point of saying "before the Lord"?
F. [It really means, rebellion, for the letters of the name for Nimrod can spell out "rebel," so that] this refers to one who knows God's lordship and intentionally rebels against it.

The same trait occurs once more, sustaining the generalization:

3. A. And so Scripture says, "The men of Sodom were evil and sinful against the Lord greatly" (Gen. 13:13).
B. Now why does Scripture say, "against the Lord"?
C. It is because they knew God's lordship and intentionally rebelled against it.

The basic proposition is that, to rebel, one must know that against which he rebels; mere disobedience of the law does not constitute rebellion, which requires an act of intentionality. In other contexts, knowing and rejecting the Torah characterize Jewish sectarians, possibly including Christians, but that polemic need not be adduced in the statement at hand.

The particular sin that Israel uniquely commits, then, comes about by reason of Israel's singular access to the Torah. Knowledge of the Torah creates possibilities for sin that ignorance denies, as other Israelite theologians recognized too. Rebellion can involve studying the Torah but not carrying out its commandments, yielding a variety of necessary corollaries:

SIFRA CCLXIV:I.4FF.

4. A. "But if you will not hearken to me [and will not do all these commandments]":

B. What is the point of Scripture in saying, "will not do"?

C. You have someone who does not learn but who carries out [the teachings of the Torah].

D. In that connection, Scripture says, "But if you will not hearken to me and will not do."

The first requirement is to study the Torah; without knowledge of the Torah, action is uninformed by the right intention; it is a mere accident, not a palpable gesture of acceptance of God's rule in the Torah. Not knowing the Torah not only insulates man from sin but also denies man the opportunity to serve God with proper intention. So ignorance not only is no excuse, it is no defence and no advantage. Now, we see, a generalized good will does not suffice either:

E. Lo, whoever does not learn [the Torah] also does not carry it out.

F. And you have someone who does not learn [the Torah] and also does not carry it out, but he does not despise others [who do so].

G. In that connection, Scripture says, "if you spurn my statutes."

H. Lo, whoever does not learn the Torah and does not carry it out in the end will despise others who do so.

The sages re-enter the equation; good will towards the sages is no protection against sin:

I. And you furthermore have someone who does not learn [the Torah], and also does not carry it out, and he does despise others [who do so], but he does not hate the sages.

M. In that connection, Scripture says, "and if your soul abhors my ordinances" –

N. Lo, whoever does not learn [the Torah], also does not carry it out, and does despise others [who do so], in the end will hate the sages.

Nor does tolerance protect the outsider to the Torah:

O. And you furthermore have someone who does not learn [the Torah], does not carry it out, despises others [who do so], and hates the sages, but who lets others carry out [the Torah].

P. Scripture says, "so that you will not do [all my commandments but break my covenant]" –

Q. lo, whoever does not learn [the Torah], does not carry it out, despises others [who do so], and hates the sages, in the end will not let others carry out [the Torah].

Now, moving in a different direction, we ask about one who acknowledges that God reveals the Torah and commands that the religious duties be carried out. Faith on its own is insufficient too:

R. Or you may have someone who does not learn [the Torah], does not carry it out, despises others [who do so], hates the sages, does not let others carry out [the Torah], but he confesses that the religious duties were spoken from Sinai.
S. Scripture says, "all my commandments" –
T. lo, whoever does not learn [the Torah], does not carry it out, despises others [who do so], hates the sages, does not let others carry out [the Torah], in the end will deny that the religious duties were spoken from Sinai.

In the end comes the acceptance of the principle of God's rule. But that alone does not serve:

U. Or you may have someone who exhibits all these traits but does not deny the very principle [of God's existence and rule].
V. Scripture says, "but break my covenant" –
W. lo, whoever exhibits all these traits in the end will deny the very Principle [of God's existence and rule].

The second proposition, flowing from the first, treats knowledge as tantamount to intentionality; if one has studied the Torah and does not act upon the knowledge he has acquired, this is a wilful act of rebellion, and it leads to a variety of inevitable consequences, ultimately involving utter denial of God.

Since the sages identify emotions and feelings, attitudes and intention, as the source of both virtue and sin, we may hardly find surprising their explanation of sin as the result of emotions that generate wrong attitudes. For the sages do not suppose that man is a creature only of reasoned reflection; rebellion comes about not only after intellection but by reason of wrong emotions, which yield sin. Chief among these is losing one's temper, on the one side, and losing composure, on the other. The discussion on losing one's temper sets forth the basic theory that people who lose their temper take vows. That is regarded as a sin.

BAVLI-TRACTATE NEDARIM 3:1 I.14FF./22A-B

I.14 A. Said R. Samuel bar Nahman said R. Yohanan, "Whoever loses his temper – all the torments of Hell rule over him: 'Therefore remove anger from your heart, thus will you put away evil from your flesh' (Qoh. 11:10), and the meaning of 'evil' is only Hell: 'The Lord has made all things for himself, yes, even the wicked for the day of evil' (Prov. 16:4). Moreover, he will get a belly ache: 'But the Lord shall give you there a trembling heart and failing of eyes and sorrow of mind' (Deut. 28:65). And what causes weak eyes and depression? Stomach aches."

The explicit involvement of God's presence in the situation is stated as follows:

I.16 A. Said Rabbah bar R. Huna, "Whoever loses his temper – even the Presence of God is not important to him: 'The wicked, through the pride of his countenance, will not seek God; God is not in all his thoughts' " (Ps. 10:4).

Sages lose their knowledge of the Torah by reason of ill-temper:

I.17 A. R. Jeremiah of Difti said, "[Whoever loses his temper] – he forgets what he has learned and increases foolishness: 'For anger rests in the heart of fools' (Qoh. 7:9), and 'But the fool lays open his folly' " (Prov. 13:16).
B. R. Nahman bar Isaac said, "One may be sure that his sins outnumber his merits: 'And a furious man abounds in transgressions' " (Prov. 29:22).

Losing one's temper marks a man as unlettered, an indication that, if he knew the Torah, he has forgotten it. But, we should not find surprising, the sages deemed even ill-temper to be subject to remissions. Losing composure in general is deplorable, but doing so when a sage dies is praiseworthy. This position is accomplished through the juxtaposition of a sequence of compositions.

Here the principle of coherence shows us what the sages deem self-evident. Specifically, Bavli Shabbat LXXVIII to Mishnah-Tractate Shabbat 13:3–4 concerns him who tears his clothing because of his anger or on account of his bereavement. The opening proposition, I:1, maintains that he who tears his clothing because of his anger or on account of his bereavement or for his deceased is liable, has violated the Sabbath, but, even so, he has carried out his obligation to tear his clothing as a mark of mourning. Juxtaposed is a composition, I:2, that qualifies the foregoing: "But if it was a sage, he would be obligated to mourn for him, as has been taught on Tannaite authority." This leads to a topical composite on mourning for a sage:

I:4: Said R. Simeon b. Pazzi said R. Joshua b. Levi in the name of Bar Qappara, "Whoever sheds tears for a good man – the Holy One, blessed be He, counts them up and puts them away in his treasure house: 'You count my grieving, put my tears into your bottle, are they not in your book' " (Ps. 56:9).
I:5: Said R. Judah said Rab, "Whoever is dilatory in lamenting a sage is worthy of being buried alive: 'And they buried him in the border of his inheritance in Timnath-

serah, which is in the hill country of Ephraim, on the north of the mountain of Gaash'
(Josh. 24:30) – since the word Gaash shares consonants with the root for rage this
teaches that the mountain raged against them to kill them." Said R. Hiyya bar Abba
said R. Yohanan, "Whoever is dilatory in lamenting a sage won't live a long time:
measure for measure: 'In measure when you send her away you contend with her' "
(Isa. 27:8).

The intersection – the point of self-evident connection, yielding a theological
principle – is at losing one's composure in general, which is deplorable, and
losing one's composure at the death of a sage, which is praiseworthy.

So much for the sages' general theory of sin and its causes. But, chapter 10
has already shown us, they formulate the theology of sin within a larger theory of the character of man. Responding to the question, if man is like God,
how is it that man's will does not correspond with, but rebels against, the will
of God? Here man's free will requires clarification. Man and God are possessed of free will. But man's free will encompasses the capacity to rebel
against God, as we know, and that comes about because innate in man's will
is the impulse to do evil, *yeser hara* in Hebrew. So here we extend theological
anthropology to encompass a more complex theory of man than that set out in
chapter 10: man corresponds to God but is comprised of conflicting impulses,
whereas God is one and unconflicted.

That impulse within man to do evil struggles with man's impulse to do
good, *yeser hattob*. The struggle between the two impulses in man corresponds with the cosmic struggle between man's will and God's word. But
creation bears within itself the forces that ultimately will resolve the struggle.
That struggle will come to an end in the world to come, which itself comes
about by an act of divine response to human regeneration, as we shall see in
due course. Chapter 12 will spell out the foundation for renewal of creation.
The main point is, the impulse to do evil having perished in the regeneration
brought about by man, that impulse to do evil in the world to come will be
slain by God, a topic that will return to the fore in chapter 13:

BAVLI-TRACTATE SUKKAH 5:ID II.3–4/52A

G. [The answer] is in accord with the exposition of R. Judah: "In the world to come,
the Holy One, blessed be he, will bring the evil inclination and slay it before the righteous and before the wicked.
H. "To the righteous the evil inclination will look like a high hill, and to the wicked it
will appear like a hair-thin thread.
I. "These will weep, and those will weep.

J. "The righteous will weep, saying, 'How could we ever have overcome a hill so high as this one!'

K. "The wicked will weep, saying, 'How could we not have overcome a hair-thin thread like this one!'

L. "And so too the Holy One, blessed be he, will share their amazement, as it is said, "Thus says the Lord of Hosts. If it be marvellous in the eyes of the remnant of this people in those days, it shall also be marvellous in my eyes' " (Zech. 8:6).

The stress on the relative, not absolute, character of sin finds its counterpart here.

4. A. Said R. Assi, "The inclination to do evil to begin with is like a spider's thread and in the end like cart ropes.

B. "For it is said, 'Woe to them who draw iniquity with cords of vanity and sin as with cart ropes' " (Is. 5:18).

Everything, therefore, depends upon man himself. Since the sages encompass within their theology, explaining in the same way large and small things, both the condition of Israel and the character of the individual Israelite, we may not find surprising the dimensions of the impulse to do evil on the part of individual persons (the sages in particular) and Israel in general.

What about the gentiles – why do they sin? What is striking in the following is that the impulse to do evil does not attack the nations of the world but only Israel, and, within Israel, predictably, the sages of the Torah are a prime target, or, in other language, are possessed of a greater *yeser hara* than ordinary folk:

BAVLI-TRACTATE SUKKAH 5:1D II.7/52A

7. A. Our rabbis have taught on Tannaite authority:

B. "But I will remove far away from you the hidden one" (Joel 2:20) speaks of the impulse to do evil, which is ready and hidden away in a man's heart.

C. "And I will drive it into a land barren and desolate" (Joel 2:20) speaks of a place in which are found no men against whom it may make an attack.

D. "With his face towards the eastern sea" (Joel 2:20): For it set its eyes against the first sanctuary and destroyed it and killed the disciples of sages who were there.

E. "And his hind part toward the western sea" (Joel 2:20): For it set its eyes against the second sanctuary and destroyed it and killed the disciples of sages who were there.

F. "That its foulness may come up and its ill-savour may come up" (Joel 2:20): For he neglects the nations of the world and attacks only Israel.

That is not to say the nations do not sin; but when they sin against God, it is through idolatry; their sins are scarcely differentiated, except in relationship to Israel.

Now we turn to the individual Israelite and his struggle with the impulse to do evil, which, with God's help, through application to Torah-study, man overcomes:

BAVLI-TRACTATE SUKKAH 5:1D II.9–13/52B

9. A. Said R. Isaac, "A man's inclination [to do evil] overcomes him every day.

B. "For it is said, 'Only [52B] evil all day long'" (Gen. 6:5).

C. Said R. Simeon b. Laqish, "A man's inclination [to do evil] prevails over him every day and seeks to kill him.

D. "For it is said, 'The wicked watches the righteous and seeks to slay him' (Ps. 37:32).

E. "And if the Holy One, blessed be he, were not there to help him, he could not withstand it.

F. "For it is said, 'The Lord will not leave him in his hand nor suffer him to be condemned when he is judged'" (Ps. 37:32).

God's help will be found, in particular, in the Torah, so when one is subject to the impulse to do evil, he should repair to the study-house:

10. A. It was taught on Tannaite authority in the house of R. Ishmael, "If that vile one meets you, drag it to the house of study.

B. "If it is a stone, it will dissolve. If it is iron, it will be pulverized."

C. "If it is a stone, it will dissolve," as it is written, "Ho, everyone who is thirsty, come to water" (Is. 55:1). And it is written, "The water wears down stones" (Job. 14:19).

D. "If it is iron, it will be pulverized," as it is written, "Is not my word like fire, says the Lord, and like a hammer that breaks the rock into pieces" (Jer. 23:29).

11. A. Said R. Samuel bar Nahmani said R. Jonathan, "The evil inclination entices a man in this world and then gives testimony against him in the world to come."

Does the impulse to do evil function within or without, a formulation that recalls the debate between nature and nurture? The answer is that it begins outside but is rapidly domesticated:

12. A. R. Huna contrasted the following verses of Scripture: "It is written, 'For the spirit of harlotry has caused them to err' (Hos. 4:12) [thus the cause is external to the person].

B. "But it also is written, '[For the spirit of harlotry] is within them' (Hos. 5:4).

C. "In the beginning, it caused them to err, but in the end, it is within them."

D. Said Raba, "In the beginning one calls it a passer-by, then a guest, and finally, a man [of the household].

E. "For it is said, 'And there came a passer-by to the rich man, and he spared to take of his own flock and of his own herd, to dress for the guest [no longer passer-by],' and [at the end] the verse states, 'But he took, the poor man's lamb and dressed it for the man [now a household member] who had come to him'" (2 Sam. 12:4).

That the impulse to do evil is localized in sexuality is expressed in the attached composition, which leaves no doubt of the sages' definition of the prime venue of the impulse:

13. A. Said R. Yohanan, "There is in man a small organ, which makes him feel hungry when he is sated,

B. "and makes him feel sated when he is hungry,

C. "as it is said, 'When they were starved, they became full'" (Hos. 13:6).

This account, a systematic and well-constructed statement, is only one of several definitive presentations of the matter.

In a variety of ways, the impulse to do evil finds its opposite and complement in Torah-study. The impulse to do evil can be overcome, specifically through Torah-study:

GENESIS RABBAH LIV:I.I

1. A. "At that time Abimelech and Phicol the commander of his army said to Abraham, 'God is with you in all that you do'" (Gen. 21:22).

I. R. Joshua b. Levi said, "The cited verse refers to the impulse to do evil.

J. "Under ordinary circumstances if someone grows up with a fellow for two or three years, he develops a close tie to him. But the impulse to do evil grows with someone from youth to old age, and, if one can, someone strikes down the impulse to do evil even when he is seventy or eighty.

K. "So did David say, 'All my bones shall say, "Lord, who is like unto you, who delivers the poor from him who is too strong for him, yes, the poor and the needy from him who spoils him"'" (Ps. 35:10).

Now the antidote is made explicit:

L. Said R. Aha, "And is there a greater thief than this one? And Solomon said, 'If your enemy be hungry, give him bread to eat' (Prov. 25:21). The meaning is, the bread of the Torah [which will help a person resist the enemy that is the impulse to do evil], as it is said, 'Come, eat of my bread' (Prov. 9:5).

M.   " 'If he is thirsty give him water to drink' (Prov. 25:21), that is, the water of the Torah, as it is said, 'Ho, everyone who is thirsty come for water' (Is. 55:1)."

N.   R. Berekhiah said, "The verse says, '... *also* his enemies' (Prov 16:7), with the word 'also' encompassing the insects of the house, vermin, flies and the like.' "

Sometimes Torah-study is treated in concrete terms, with an explanation of precisely how the Torah serves as antidote to sin, and sometimes, as here, in symbolic terms. The result is the same, a coherent system that explains many things in a few simple ways.

What, precisely, Torah-study will yield is expressed in terms of knowledge deemed salvific. What keeps man from sin is knowledge of who he is, and before Whom he is judged. Here knowledge of the Torah takes on a gnostic character, that is to say, it is knowledge that brings about salvation:

TRACTATE ABOT 3:1

A.   Aqabiah b. Mehallalel says, "Reflect upon three things and you will not fall into the clutches of transgression: Know (1) from whence you come, (2) whither you are going, and before whom you are going to have to give a full account of yourself. From whence do you come? From a putrid drop. Whither are you going? To a place of dust, worms, and maggots. And before whom are you going to give a full account of yourself? Before the King of kings of kings, the Holy One, blessed be he."

Torah-study will teach the lesson of humility, the powerful antidote to the cause of sin, which is arrogance. This is how Torah-study brings about victory over sin: what one learns, in specific terms, persuades man not to sin but to exercise humility in light of what he knows about himself.

Throughout, the emphasis is upon how the impulse to do evil begins in small things but gradually expands and takes over the entire personality. This matter of sexuality is broadened and set into context. For Israel, the impulse to do evil encompasses two of the three absolute sins we have noted, idolatry, fornication, and murder. The two that are eliminated are idolatry and murder. The impulse to do evil that exercises greatest power is sexual, which is why the language, *yeser hara*, often bears a specifically sexual connotation:

SONG OF SONGS RABBAH XCVI:I.I

A.   "You are stately as a palm tree" (Song 7:7):

B.   R. Hunia in the name of R. Dosa b. R. Tebet: "Two impulses to do evil did the Holy One, blessed be He, create in his world, the impulse to worship idols, and the impulse to fornicate. The impulse to worship idols has already been eliminated, but the impulse to fornicate still endures.

C. "Said the Holy One, blessed be He, 'Whoever can withstand the impulse to fornicate do I credit as though he had withstood them both.'"

Now comes the anticipated parable:

D. Said R. Judah, "The matter may be compared to the case of a snake-charmer who had [two] snakes. He charmed the larger and left the smaller, saying, 'Whoever can withstand this one is certainly credited as though he had withstood them both.'

E. "So the Holy One, blessed be He, eliminated the impulse to worship idols but left the impulse to fornicate. He said, 'Whoever can withstand the impulse to fornicate do I credit as though he had withstood them both.'"

Israel, then, is freed by the Torah from the impulse to commit idolatry; the sages cannot imagine that Israel is subject to the impulse to murder. But the impulse to do evil through inappropriate sexual activity remains powerful.

How, exactly, does the the impulse to do evil work? It tries to insinuate itself and bring about sin; it is not to be trusted. Even God's help should not be taken for granted:

BAVLI-TRACTATE HAGIGAH 2:1–2 VI.3/16A:

A. Expounded R. Judah b. R. Nahmani, R. Simeon b. Laqish's public representative, "What is the meaning of the verse, 'Don't trust a friend, and don't put confidence in a buddy' (Mic. 7:5)?

B. "If the impulse to do evil tells you, 'Sin, and the Holy One, blessed be he, will forgive you,' don't you believe it! 'Don't trust a friend ...' [since the word for friend and evil use the same consonants, this yields the conclusion:] the meaning of 'wicked' here is only, 'the impulse to do evil,' in line with the verse, 'For the inclination of man's heart is evil' (Gen. 8:21).

C. "And the meaning of 'buddy' here is only the Holy One, blessed be he, in line with the verse, 'You are the buddy of my youth'" (Jer. 3:4).

Nor does the impulse to do evil do its work in secret; the consequences always become public:

D. "Now perhaps you might imagine, 'Who will testify against me?' Well, the very stones of the house and the beams of the house of a person are the witnesses against him, as it is said, 'For the stone shall dry out of the wall and the beam out of the timber shall answer it'" (Hab. 2:11).

E. And sages say, "A man's own soul testifies against him: 'Keep the doors of your mouth from her who lies in your bosom' (Mic. 7:5). Now what is that which lies in a man's bosom? You have to say, it is the spirit."

F. R. Zeriqa said, "Two ministering angels who keep someone company are the ones who will testify against him: 'For he will give his angels charge over you, to keep you in all your ways' " (Ps. 91:11).

G. And sages say, "A man's own limbs will testify against him: 'Therefore you are my witnesses, says the Lord, and I am God' " (Is. 43:12).

The upshot is that the realms of nature and supernature conspire to testify against the man who gives in to the impulse to do evil. Along these same lines, we note the following:

BAVLI-TRACTATE NEDARIM 3:11G-R I.16/32B

A. And said R. Ammi bar Abba, " 'There is a little city, with a few men in it, and there came a great king against it and besieged it, and built great bulwarks against it. Now there was found in it a poor wise man, and he by his wisdom delivered the city, and yet no man remembered that poor man' (Qoh. 9:14-15):

B. " 'There is a little city': this is the body;

C. " 'With a few men in it': these are the limbs;

D. " 'And there came a great king against it and besieged it': this refers to the urge to do evil."

Now in the unfolding exposition we turn to the remedies against the impulse to do evil. These are, first, the innate impulse to do good; second, repentance and good deeds. In due course, we shall examine the prevailing theory of restoration in its own terms. Here we see how details of that theory enter into the account of the working of sin:

E. " 'And built great bulwarks against it': this refers to sin;

F. " 'Now there was found in it a poor wise man': this refers to the urge to do good;

G. " 'And he by his wisdom delivered the city': this refers to repentance and good deeds;

H. " 'And yet no man remembered that poor man': For when the urge to do evil rules, no body remembers the urge to do good."

I.17 A. "Wisdom strengthens the wise more than ten mighty ones that are in the city" (Qoh. 7:19):

B. "Wisdom strengthens the wise": This refers to repentance and good deeds.

C. "More than ten mighty ones that are in the city": This refers to the two eyes, ears, hands, feet, penis, and mouth.

So much for the impulse to do evil and its workings. What about the competing impulse, the one to do good – is that also innate in man? The answer,
hardly surprising in light of what has already been said, is negative. The
impulse to do good is not innate, man is innately sinful, but changed to do
good only through the study of the Torah. That is what brings about that
regeneration that overcomes man's rebellion from the beginning.

Here is the crux of the matter: man by nature is sinful, but only by encounter with the Torah knows how to do good. That explains why the gentiles,
with idolatry in place of the Torah, in the end cannot overcome their condition but perish, while Israel, with Torah as the source of life, will stand in
judgment and enter eternal life, as we shall see fully spelled out in chapters
12, 13, and 14. The key to man's regeneration lies in that fact, that Israel,
while part of humanity and by nature sinful, possesses the Torah. That is how
and where Israel may overcome its natural condition. Herein lies the source
of hope. Gentiles enjoy this world but have no hope of regeneration in the
world to come. Here three distinct components of the theology of the Oral
Torah – theological anthropology, the doctrine of sin, and eschatology –
intersect to make a single coherent statement accounting for the destiny of the
whole of humanity, all in accord with the account of world order set forth at
the very outset, in chapters 2 through 5. At the outset of this book I alleged
that, when we examine the theology of sin, we see that the Oral Torah spins
out a simple but encompassing logic, so framing a single, coherent theology. I
did not exaggerate.

That position on man's nature is set forth in terms of the individual life.
The impulse to do evil grows from the womb, but the impulse to do good is
born only at thirteen years of age. Here is where the Torah intervenes. Since
age thirteen marks the point at which the child enters the state of responsibility for his own deeds and is subject to the law of the Torah, the point is
clear. When the Torah takes over, then the impulse to do good gains entry;
before that time, without the Torah, man is wholly subject to the impulse to
do evil, lacking all remedy. This critical doctrine is set forth in so many
words:

THE FATHERS ACCORDING TO RABBI NATHAN XVI:III.I

B. The impulse to do evil is thirteen years older than the impulse to do good.

C. From the mother's womb it grows and develops with a person.

D. If one began to profane the Sabbath, it does not stop him. If he wanted to kill, it
does not stop him. If he goes to commit a transgression [of a sexual character], it does
not stop him.

E. After thirteen years the impulse to do good is born. When the man then violates the Sabbath, it says to him, "Empty head, lo, Scripture says, 'Those who profane it will surely die' " (Ex. 31:11).

F. When the man then kills, it says to him, "Empty head, lo, Scripture says, 'One who sheds man's blood by man his blood will be shed' " (Gen. 9:6).

G. When he goes to commit a transgression, it says to him, "Empty head, lo, Scripture says, 'The adulterer and the adulteress will surely die' " (Lev. 20:10).

Still more: the impulse to do evil, being intrinsic, though not limited, to the sex-act, is present from conception:

THE FATHERS ACCORDING TO RABBI NATHAN XVI:V.I

A. R. Reuben b. Astrobuli says, "How can someone escape from the evil impulse in his guts, for the very first drop [of semen] that a man puts into a woman is the evil impulse.

B. "And the impulse to do evil is located only at the gates of the heart. For it is said, 'Sin couches at the door' (Gen. 4:7).

Now we see the innate wickedness of the infant:

C. "It says to a person while still an infant in the cradle, 'Someone wants to kill you,' [and] the infant wants to pull out his hair.

D. "When an infant in the cradle puts its hand on a snake or a scorpion and gets bitten, is it not the impulse to do evil that is the cause?

E. "[If the infant] puts its hand on coals and is burned, is it not the evil impulse in his guts that is the cause?

F. "For the evil impulse is what drives him headlong.

G. "But come and see the case of a kid or a lamb: when it sees a well, it jumps backward, because there is no evil impulse in a beast."

The same matter is stated in other ways as well. That the impulse to do evil is innate from conception itself is further expressed as a colloquy between Rabbi Judah the Patriarch and Antoninus:

GENESIS RABBAH XXXIV:X.4

A. Antoninus asked our rabbi, "At what point is the impulse to do evil placed in the human being?"

B. He said to him, "From the moment that the human being is formed."

C. He said to him, "If that were so, then the foetus would dig through the walls of the womb and come forth right away. Rather, it must be at the moment that the foetus comes forth."

D. Then Rabbi concurred with him, for what he said conformed to the statement of Scripture: "For the imagination of man's heart is evil from his youth" (Gen. 8:21).

E. R. Yudan said, " 'From his youth' is written, 'from his awakening, that is, 'when he awakes to the world.' "

The same problem is given a new formulation:

F. He further asked him, "At what point is the soul placed in the human being?"

G. He said to him, "At the point at which the human being emerges from his mother's womb."

H. He said to him, "Put meat out without salt for three days. Will it not rot? Rather, it must be at that moment at which the human being is remembered [and God determines the life-story of the person, which is while the person is still in the womb]."

I. Then Rabbi concurred with him, for what he said conformed to the statement of Scripture: "All the while my soul is in me, and the spirit of God is in my nostrils" (Job 27:3), and it is written, "And your providence has preserved my spirit" (Job 10:12). "At what point did you put the soul in me? It is when you remembered me."

Rabbi must concur that the soul germinates while the body is still in the womb. God then remembers the infant when it is still a foetus, and the struggle against the impulse to do evil commences in the womb, with God's help but without the *paideia* of the Torah. So, to summarize, innate in man, the impulse to do evil expresses man's will and embodies his freedom. This is explained by appeal to metaphors and narratives (parabolic or otherwise) and exegeses, but, in the main, it is through the narrative that the working of the impulse to do evil is explained.

As we have seen time and again, the sages formulate a single doctrine of the consequences of sin, to deal both with Holy Israel and with the individual Israelite. They say the same thing in ways appropriate to the respective settings. That is why, while the impulse to do evil, embodied in sexuality but not at all exhausted thereby, focuses on the private person, the sages identify sins of another dimension altogether that characterize the community, the public sins. These counterparts to the sexuality of the impulse to do evil encompass the social sins of slander and common gossip. A major sin is gossip, and all forms of wicked speech fall within that same category. Perhaps the reason that gossip for the community mirrors sexual desire for the individual is that both are deemed natural to the human condition. In any event, in the principle of measure for measure, gossip, which disrupts community harmony, finds its penalty in ostracism, inflicted on the person who gossips through the medium of the skin ailment that is treated by excluding the afflicted from the common life:

LEVITICUS RABBAH XVI:VI.I

1. A. Said R. Joshua b. Levi, "The word 'torah' [law] occurs with regard to the leper on five different occasions:
B. "'This is the Torah governing a spot of leprosy' (Lev. 13:59).
C. "'This is the Torah governing him on whom is a spot of leprosy' (Lev. 14:32).
D. "'This is the Torah governing every spot of leprosy and itch' (Lev. 14:54).
E. "'This is the Torah governing leprosy' (Lev. 14:57).
F. "And the encompassing reference: 'This will be the Torah governing the leper' (Lev. 14:2) – the Torah governing the common gossip.
G. "This teaches you that whoever repeats gossip violates all five scrolls of the Torah."
2. A. Therefore Moses admonished the Israelites, saying to them, "This will be the Torah governing the leper (mesora)" (Lev. 14:2) – the Torah governing the gossip.

The sages' familiar interest in showing the match between an offering and the sin for which it atones is followed up once more:

LEVITICUS RABBAH XVI:VII

1. A. "The priest shall command them to take for him who is to be cleansed two living clean birds [and cedar-wood and scarlet stuff and hyssop]" (Lev. 14:4).
B. Said R. Judah b. R. Simon, "Birds chirp a lot. This one who speaks gossip.
C. "Said the Holy One, blessed be he, 'Let the one with a voice [the bird] come and effect atonement for what the voice [of the gossip has done].'"

This reference to atonement through an appropriate medium recalls the careful match between sin and punishment that captured our attention in chapters 2 and 5, and will occupy us once again when in chapter 12 we investigate the dynamics of repentance and concomitant atonement. The main point is that what the sages say about public sin they repeat about personal acts of sinfulness.

The sages simply take for granted that speech, like sexuality, may embody virtue or bring about sin, and they make a systematic statement about the sin committed by public speech through their juxtaposition of virtuous as against sinful speech. This they do at Bavli-tractate Arakhin, on verbal pledges to contribute to the Temple the value of a person; at that point the act of slander is introduced. Here we see how the principle of self-evident connections, introduced in chapter 1, serves to identify normative views. What the sages deem obvious, requiring no detailed validation, reveals the consensus that governs throughout. In the present case, the topic of valuations naturally, automatically, brings up the topic of gossip.

Here is how the connections are made. For a statement of pledge of one's own, or another party's, valuation for the purposes of the Temple and the service of God therein does not demand that we also discuss the very opposite of the use of speech for God's purpose. But once we do consider how an act of speech may destroy, as much as build, the sacred community, our appreciation for the matter of valuations deepens, and its moral meaning comes to the surface. What the sages in the Talmud add to the Mishnah-tractate, therefore, is the profound statement indeed: through an act of speech, one may sanctify, but through an act of speech one may also destroy, the holy community of Israel. The one – the act of sanctification through an act of speech – devotes to God through the Temple the results of good will. The other – the act of slander through an act of speech – diminishes God's people through the expression of ill will.

Let us consider the detailed outline of the inserted composites, The passage commences at Mishnah-tractate Arakhin 3:5B: "For so we find that the decree against our forefathers in the wilderness was sealed only on account of evil speech [Num. 13:32], as it is said, 'And they tempted me these ten times and have not hearkened to my voice'" (Num. 14:22). This then yields compositions that set forth the following propositions, signified by their positions in an outline of the whole:

II:1: On what account [do we reach the conclusion just now stated]? Perhaps it was because the measure [of their guilt] was not yet full?

II:2: Come and see how great is the power of slander [evil speech]. From whence do we learn that lesson? From the case of the spies.

II:4: Whoever repeats slander is as if he denied the very principle of God's rule.

II:5: Slander is the cause of leprosy, as in the case of Miriam.

II:6: Whoever speaks slander is worthy of being stoned.

II:7: What remedy is there for those who speak slander? If it is a disciple of a sage, let him keep busy in Torah.

II:8: Whoever speaks slander inflates his sins [so that they are as great] as the three cardinal sins of idolatry, fornication, and bloodshed.

II:9: "What is the meaning of the verse of Scripture, 'Death and life are in the hands of the tongue' (Prov. 18:21)? Now does the tongue have a hand? Rather it is to indicate to you that just as the hand can commit murder, so the tongue can commit murder."

II:10: How shall we define slander?

II:11: "What is the meaning of the verse of Scripture, 'He who blesses his friend with a loud voice, rising early in the morning, it shall be regarded as a curse to him' (Prov. 27:14)?

II:12: On account of seven causes plagues come [upon someone]: slander, bloodshed, a vain oath, incest, arrogance, theft, and envy.

II:15: "You shall not hate your brother in your heart" (Lev. 19:17). Is it possible to suppose that all one should not do is not smite, slap, or curse him, and that is what is at issue only? Scripture says, "... in your heart," thus speaking of the sort of hatred that is in the heart as much as hatred expressed through physical means.

What the Talmud's compilers do is make a connection of opposites: sanctification through speech as against sin through speech.

In this context we call to mind that the principal mode of thought is the familiar philosophical one of comparison and contrast. Something is like something else, therefore follows its rule; or unlike, therefore follows the opposite of the rule governing that something else. So the sages made connections between things that were alike, on the one side, or things that were opposite, on the other. Speech that consecrates and speech that demolishes stand on the single plane of social being: the community of Israel is sanctified through holy speech or it is diminished through evil speech (the exact equivalent in English to the Hebrew words translated as gossip or (assumed to be the same thing) slander (*lashon hara*). Tractate Arakhin sets forth how through an act of speech one carries out a deed of sanctification; the Talmud's important and fresh compositions explain how through an act of speech one does a deed that is the opposite of sanctification, which is a deed that is unclean in that it contaminates the holy community.

From the definition of sin, both public and personal, we turn to its consequences, once more noting the correspondence between the costs of sin to the individual and those exacted from holy Israel all together. In both cases sin exacts a two-sided penalty. The sinner, acting out of arrogance, is diminished; the sinner, defying God, is cut off from God. That applies, in so many words, to both the private person and all Israel. So, as in declarations and even exact language familiar from Chapters 2 and 5, what the person sought – aggrandizement through rebellion against God's will – he does not gain, but what he did not want – diminution – is what he gets. Thus, when it comes to seeking to feed one's arrogance, before someone sins, people pay reverence and awe to that person, but once the person sins, reverence and awe are imposed on that person:

PESIQTA DERAB KAHANA V:III.3FF.

3. A. R. Ishmael taught on Tannaite authority, "Before a man has sinned, people pay him reverence and awe. Once he has sinned, they impose on him reverence and awe.

This is spelled out in the case of Adam:

B. "Thus, before the first man had sinned, he would hear [God's] voice in a workaday way. After he had sinned, he heard the same voice as something strange. Before he had sinned, the first man heard God's voice and would stand on his feet: 'And they heard the sound of God walking in the garden in the heat of the day' (Gen. 3:8). After he had sinned, he heard the voice of God and hid: 'And man and his wife hid'" (Gen. 3:8).

C. Said R. Aibu, "At that moment the height of the first Man was cut down and he became a hundred cubits high."

Now we turn to Israel, which found itself diminished:

D. [Ishmael continues:] "Before the Israelites sinned, what is written in their regard? 'And the appearance of the glory of the Lord was like a consuming fire on the top of the mountain before the eyes of the children of Israel'" (Ex. 24:17).

E. Said R. Abba bar Kahana, "There were seven veils of fire, one covering the next, and the Israelites gazed and did not fear or take fright."

F. "But when they had sinned, even on the face of the intercessor [Moses] they could not look: 'And Aaron and all the children of Israel feared ... to come near'" (Ex. 34:40).

We turn next to David, then Solomon, and finally Saul:

5. A. "Before the deed of David [with Bath Sheba] took place, what is written? 'For David: The Lord is my light and my salvation, of whom shall I be afraid?' (Ps. 27:1).

B. "But after that deed took place, what is written? 'I will come upon him while he is weary and weak-handed' (2 Sam. 17:2).

6. A. "Before Solomon sinned, he could rule over demons and demonesses: 'I got for myself ... Adam's progeny, demons and demonesses' (Qoh. 2:8).

B. "What is the sense of 'demons and demonesses'? For he ruled over demons and demonesses.

C. "But after he had sinned, he brought sixty mighty men to guard his bed: 'Lo, the bed of Solomon, with sixty mighty men around it, all of them holding a sword and veterans of war' (Song 3:7–8).

7. A. "Before Saul had sinned, what is written concerning him? 'And when Saul had taken dominion over Israel, he fought against all his enemies on every side, against Moab, against the Ammonites, against Edom, against the kings of Zobah, and against the Philistines; wherever he turned he put them to the worse' (1 Sam. 14:47).

B. 'After he had sinned what is written concerning him? 'And Saul saw the camp of the Philistines and was afraid'" (1 Sam. 28:5).

The cases validate the proposition that sin weakens the sinner; prior to sin, various figures are shown to have been strong, but afterward, weak. The composition of the list – Adam, Israel, David, Solomon, Saul – on its own does not suggest that the point common to the entries is the one that is made. But a second look shows that joining these particular names yields the proposition at hand.

We recall what we noted in chapter 5 about how the sages systematically linked specific ailments or misfortunes to concrete actions of sin. Here is a recapitulation of that same view, placing into the present context an already-familiar notion, that sin exercises such power that on account of sin, various ailments commenced in Israel, beginning with the advent of people afflicted with the skin ailment of Leviticus 13:

SIFRÉ TO NUMBERS I:X.2

2. A. R. Yosé the Galilean says, "Come and take note of how great is the power of sin. For before the people had laid hands on transgression, people afflicted with flux and people afflicted with the skin ailment were not located among them, but after they had laid hands on transgression, people afflicted with flux and with the skin ailment did find a place among them.

B. "Accordingly, we learn that these three events took place on one and the same day: [transgression, the presence of those afflicted with flux, the development of the skin ailment among the people]."

The same point is made in more general terms. Before sin, people could face God. Afterward, they could not even approach Moses:

3. A. R. Simeon b. Yohai says, "Come and take note of how great is the power of sin. For before the people had laid hands on transgression, what is stated in their regard?

B. " 'Now the appearance of the glory of the Lord was like a devouring fire on the top of the mountain in the sight of the people of Israel' (Ex. 24:17).

C. "Nonetheless, the people did not fear nor were they afraid.

D. "But once they had laid hands on transgression, what is said in their regard?

E. " 'And when Aaron and all the people of Israel saw Moses, behold, the skin of his face shone, and they were afraid to come near.' "

A different formulation of the same matter broadens the range of penalty, encompassing the public ailments exhibited not only by flux and the skin ailment but other infirmities and deformities:

LEVITICUS RABBAH XVIII:IV.I

A. R. Simeon b. Yohai taught, "When the Israelites stood before Mount Sinai and said, 'All that the Lord has spoken we shall do and we shall hear' (Ex. 24:7), among them there were no people afflicted with flux, no people suffering from the skin ailment of Leviticus 13, no cripples, no blind, no dumb, no deaf, no idiots, no imbeciles, no fools.

B. "Concerning that hour Scripture says, 'You are wholly fair, my beloved, and there is no blemish in you' (Song 4:7).

C. "When they had sinned, not many days passed before there were found among them people afflicted with flux, people suffering from the skin ailment of Leviticus 13, cripples, blind, dumb, deaf, idiots, imbeciles, and fools.

D. "Concerning that hour what does Scripture then state? 'And they shall send out of the camp every leper and everyone afflicted with flux' " (Num. 5:2).

So much for individuals and the price they pay for their arrogance towards God. In the end, what they devise to dominate they cannot even approach. In a moment, we shall see the other side of this same circumstance, God's response.

But first, we ask about the costs of sin to holy Israel all together. The sages' view of the costs of sin fits tightly with their larger theory of the world order of justice that God has established. Because Israel has sinned, it has lost everything. Exile forms a particularly appropriate mode of punishing the entirety of holy Israel; Israel suffers in exile in the way in which gentiles do not, because their religious duties isolate them, and their poverty degrades them and weakens them:

LAMENTATIONS RABBAH XXXVII.I.I F.

1. A. "Judah has gone into exile":

B. Do not the nations of the world go into exile?

C. Even though they go into exile, their exile is not really an exile at all.

D. But for Israel, their exile really is an exile.

E. The nations of the world, who eat the bread and drink the wine of others, do not really experience exile.

F. But the Israelites, who do not eat the bread and drink the wine of others, really do experience exile.

G. The nations of the world, who travel in litters, do not really experience exile.

H. But the Israelites, who [in poverty] go barefoot – their exile really is an exile.

I. That is why it is said, "Judah has gone into exile."

2. A. Here Scripture states, "Judah has gone into exile,"

B. and elsewhere, "So Judah was carried away captive out of his land" (Jer. 52:27).

C. When they went into exile, they grew weak like a woman,

D. so it is said, "Judah has gone into exile."

The Torah, which defines Israel and sanctifies the people, also accounts for Israel's isolation among the gentiles. Israel is not suited to exile, because it cannot assimilate with the gentiles. Exile weakens Israel and tries the people.

Beyond exile, the sages go so far as to attribute to Israel's own failings the fall of Jerusalem and the cessation of the animal offerings of atonement to God. Just what these failures were is subject to the sort of dispute at which the sages excel, that is to say, dispute that underscores the iron consensus on the main principle. Once the sages concur that sin explains the fall of Jerusalem, they are free to differ to their hearts' content on the identity of that sin; then they do not even have to state the generative principle at all, it is simply taken as self-evident:

BAVLI-TRACTATE SHABBAT 16:2 II.42FF./119B-120A

II.42 A. Said Abbayye, "Jerusalem was ruined only because they violated the Sabbath therein: 'And they have hidden their eyes from my Sabbaths, therefore I am profaned among them'" (Ezek. 22:26).

From the Sabbath, we turn to the rejection of the yoke of the Kingdom of Heaven, signified by the failure to recite the *Shema*:

B. Said R. Abbahu, "Jerusalem was ruined only because they stopped reciting the *Shema* morning and evening: 'Woe to them that rise up early in the morning, that they may follow strong drink ... and the harp and the lute, the tabret and the pipe and wine are in their feasts, but they do not regard the works of the Lord,' 'Therefore my people have gone into captivity for lack of knowledge'" (Isa. 5:11–13).

Now comes neglect of Torah-study:

C. Said R. Hamnuna, "Jerusalem was ruined only because they neglected the children in the schoolmaster's household: 'pour out ... because of the children in the street' (Jer. 6:211). Why pour out? Because the children are in the streets."

A general collapse of public morals follows, encompassing both the lapse of shame and the failure to honour Torah-sages:

D. Said Ulla, "Jerusalem was ruined only because they were not ashamed on account of one another: 'Were they ashamed when they committed abomination? No, they were not at all ashamed, therefore they shall fall'" (Jer. 6:15).

E. Said R. Isaac, "Jerusalem was ruined only because they treated equally the small and the great: 'And it shall be, like people like priest' and then, 'the earth shall be utterly emptied'" (Isa. 24:2–3).

F. Said R. Amram b. R. Simeon bar Abba said R. Simeon bar Abba said R. Hanina, "Jerusalem was ruined only because they did not correct one another: 'Her princes are become like harts that find no pasture' (Lam. 1:6) – just as the hart's head is at the side of the other's tail, so Israel of that generation hid their faces in the earth and didn't correct one another."

G. Said R. Judah, "Jerusalem was ruined only because they humiliated disciples of sages therein: 'But they mocked the messengers of God and despised his words and scoffed at his prophets, until the wrath of the Lord arose against his people till there was no remedy'" (2 Chr. 36:16).

II.44 A. And said Raba, "Jerusalem was destroyed only once faithful people had disappeared from among them, as it is said, 'Run you to and fro through the streets of Jerusalem and see now and know and look in the spacious piazzas there, see if you can find a man, if there be any who does justly, who seeks truth, and I will pardon him'" (Jer. 5:1).

The specific sins review religious obligations – Sabbath, recitation of the *Shema*, Torah-study, improper social mores, and, inevitably in the Oral Torah, humiliation of sages. The details hardly matter. Later on, in chapter 12, we shall find out why the false Messiah lost out and how he marked himself as a deceiver, and there again, the answer focuses upon the sin that he committed; that, predictably, is arrogance. So the costs of sin are heavy indeed. But we should not miss the upside of the doctrine at hand. Israel controls its own destiny, as proven by the fact that it bears complete responsibility for its greatest disaster. Not only so, but specific sins can be identified, and though these failures are diverse – violation of the Sabbath, failure to recite the *Shema*, neglect of education, immodesty, disgrace, failure to reform, dishonour of disciples of sages – the main point stands.

The heaviest cost exacted by sin, however, is neither individual nor communal but cosmic. Sin separated God from man. Man's arrogance, his exercise of his will to confront the will of God, brings about sin and ultimately exiled Israel from the Land of Israel. That same act of attitude estranges God from Israel. If sin cuts the individual off from God and diminishes him in the world, then the sin of all Israel produces the same result. The costs of sin to Israel have proved catastrophic. Just as Israel was given every advantage by reason of accepting the Torah, so by rejecting the Torah, death, exile, and suffering took over. When Israel accepted the Torah, death, exile, and suffering and illness no longer ruled them. When they sinned, they incurred all of them. That is because God himself went into exile from the Temple, the City, the Land. We begin with the penalty of alienation from God, marked by the advent of death:

LEVITICUS RABBAH XVIII:III.2FF.

2. A. "Yet the harvest will flee away (ND)" (Is. 17:11).

B. You have brought on yourselves the harvest of the foreign governments, the harvest of violating prohibitions, the harvest of the angel of death.

C. For R. Yohanan in the name of R. Eliezer, son of R. Yosé the Galilean, said, "When the Israelites stood before Mount Sinai and said, 'All that the Lord has said we shall do and we shall hear' [Ex. 24:7]. At that very moment the Holy One, blessed be he, called the angel of death and said to him, 'Even though I have made you world ruler over all of my creatures, you have no business with this nation. Why? For they are my children.' That is in line with the following verse of Scripture: 'You are the children of the Lord your God'" (Deut. 14:1).

D. And it says, "And it happened that when you heard the voice out of the midst of the darkness" (Deut. 5:20).

E. Now was there darkness above? And is it not written, "And the light dwells with Him" (Dan. 2:22)?

F. That (D) refers to the angel who is called, "Darkness."

At Sinai, for the brief moment when Israel declared "We shall do and we shall obey," death died. But when Israel rebelled as Moses tarried on the mountain, sin took over, and the process of alienation from God got under way. Later on, we shall learn when and how death again will die, marking the end of time and change that commenced with Adam's sin. But the main point is clear. Death, exile, suffering, and illness do not belong to the order of nature; they have come about by reason of sin. Israel was exempt from them all when they accepted the Torah. But when they sinned, they returned to the natural condition of unredeemed man. A basic rationality, then, explains the human condition: people bring about their own fate. They possess the power to dictate their own destiny – by giving up the power to dictate to God.[1]

But there is more to the costs of sin, the cosmic charge. Since God now finds himself alienated, he has abandoned not only Israel but the Temple, the City, the Land – the world altogether. The estrangement of God from Israel is portrayed in concrete terms, as a series of departures. This is expressed in a set of remarkably powerful statements, narratives of profound theological

---

1. No one is moved to compare this view of matters with the one that assigns to the patriarchs the origin of death, suffering, and illness, and deems them to form divine gifts. The systemic principle produces disjunctive results.

consequence. In one version, God's Presence departed in ten stages, as God abandoned the people of Israel and they were estranged from him, and the sanhedrin was banished in ten stages as well.

BAVLI-TRACTATE ROSH HASHANAH 4:4A-E I.6/31A-B

[A] Said R. Judah bar Idi said R. Yohanan, "The divine presence [Shekhinah] made ten journeys [in leaving the land and people of Israel prior to the destruction of the first Temple]. [That is, "The Divine Presence left Israel by ten stages." This we know from] Scripture. And corresponding to these [stages], the Sanhedrin was exiled [successively to ten places of banishment]. [This we know from] tradition."

[B] The divine presence [Shekhinah] made ten journeys [in leaving the people, Israel, prior to the destruction of the first Temple]. [This we know from] Scripture: [It went]

(1) from the ark-cover to the cherub;

(2) and from the cherub to the threshold [of the Holy-of-Holies];

(3) and from the threshold to the [Temple-] court;

(4) and from the court to the altar;

(5) and from the altar to [Temple-] roof;

(6) and from the roof to wall;

(7) and from the wall to the city;

(8) and from the city to the mountain;

(9) and from the mountain to the wilderness;

(10) and from the wilderness it ascended and dwelled in its place [in heaven] – as it is said (Hos. 5:15): "I will return again to my place, [until they acknowledge their guilt and seek my face]."

We are now given the facts of Scripture to sustain the point at hand:

[C] From the ark-cover to the cherub;

(2) and from the cherub to the threshold [of the Holy-of-Holies] – as it is written [Ex. 25:22, proving that the original location of the divine presence was above the ark-cover]: "There I will meet with you, and [from above the ark-cover, from between the two cherubim that are upon the ark of the testimony], I will speak with you." And [showing that, later, the divine presence had moved to the cherub] it is written (II Sam. 22:11): "He rode on a cherub and flew." And [proving that the divine presence then moved to the threshold] it is written (Ez. 9:3): "Now the glory of the God of Israel had gone up from the cherubim on which it rested to the threshold of the house."

(3) And from the threshold to the [Temple-] court – as it is written (Ez. 10:4): "And the house was filled with the cloud, and the court was full of the brightness of the glory of the Lord."

(4) And from the court to the altar – as it is written (Am. 9:1): "I saw the Lord standing beside the altar."

(5) And from the altar to [Temple-] roof – as it is written (Prov. 21:9): "It is better to live in a corner of the roof [than in a house shared with a contentious woman]."

(6) And from the roof to wall – as it is written (Am. 7:1): "He showed me: behold, the Lord was standing beside a wall built with a plumb line."

(7) And from the wall to the city – as it is written (Micah 6:9): "The voice of the Lord cries to the city."

(8) And from the city to the mountain – as it is written (Ez. 11:23): "And the glory of the Lord went up from the midst of the city and stood upon the mountain which is on the east side of the city."

(9) And from the mountain to the wilderness – as it is written (Prov. 21:19): "It is better to live in a land of wilderness [than with a contentious and fretful woman]."

(10) And from the wilderness it ascended and dwelled in its place [in heaven] – as it is said (Hos. 5:15): 'I will return again to my place, [until they acknowledge their guilt and seek my face].'

The systematic proof, deriving from Scripture, shows how God moved by stages from the inner sanctum of the Temple; but the climax comes at C.10, pointing towards the next stage in the unfolding of the theology of the Oral Torah: the possibility of reconciliation and how this will take place. The language that I have supplied contains the key.

The next phase in the statement before us expands on that point: God hopes for the repentance of Israel, meaning, as we shall see, its freely given act of acceptance of God's will by a statement of a change in attitude, specifically, regret for its act of arrogance. This is articulated in what follows:

[D] Said R. Yohanan, "For sixth months, the divine presence waited on Israel [the people] in the wilderness, hoping lest they might repent. When they did not repent, it said, 'May their souls expire.' [We know this] as it says (Job 11:2): 'But the eyes of the wicked will fail, all means of escape will elude them, and their [only] hope will be for their souls to expire.' "

God's progressive estrangement in Heaven finds its counterpart in the sequence of exiles that Israel's political institution suffered, embodying therein the exile of all Israel from the Land:

[E] "And corresponding to these [stages through which the divine presence left Israel], the Sanhedrin was exiled [successively to ten places of banishment; this we know from] tradition." [The Sanhedrin was banished] (1) from the Chamber of Hewn

Stone [in the inner court of the Temple] to the market; and (2) from the market into Jerusalem [proper], and (3) from Jerusalem to Yabneh, [31b] and (4) from Yabneh to Usha, and (5) from Usha [back] to Yabneh, and (6) from Yabneh [back] to Usha, (7) and from Usha to Shefar, and (8) from Shefar to Beth Shearim, and (9) from Beth Shearim to Sepphoris, and (10) from Sepphoris to Tiberias.

[F] And Tiberias is the lowest of them all [below sea-level at the Sea of Galilee, symbolic of the complete abasement of the Sanhedrin's authority]. [We know of the lowered physical location and reduced status of the Sanhedrin] as it is said (Is. 29:4): "And deep from the earth you shall speak."

A different reading of the matter uses more general terms to account for the exile of the sanhedrin, that is to say, the end of Israel's political existence:

[G] [Proposing a different description of the banishment of the Sanhedrin] R. Eleazar says, "There were [only] six [places of] banishment, as it says (Is. 26:5): 'For (1) he has brought low the inhabitants of the height, the lofty city. (2) He lays it low, (3) lays it low (4) to the ground, (5) he casts it (6) to the dust.' "

[H] Said R. Yohanan, "And from there are destined to be redeemed, as it says (Is. 52:2): 'Shake yourself from the dust; arise!' "

In the interim, God has abandoned the holy place to accept Israel's fate, and that means that God endures even in a condition of uncleanness, a point made as follows:

SIFRÉ TO NUMBERS CLXI:III.2:

A. "in the midst of which I dwell":

B. So precious is Israel that even though the people suffer uncleanness, the Presence of God is among them, as it is said, "Thus he shall make atonement for the holy place, because of the uncleanness of the people of Israel ... and so he shall do for the tent of meeting, which abides with them in the midst of their uncleannesses" (Lev. 16:16).

C. And Scripture says, "Through their imparting uncleanness to my tabernacle, which is in their midst" (Lev. 15:31).

D. And Scripture says, "That they not make their camp unclean" (Num. 5:3).

E. And Scripture says, "You shall not defile the land in which you live."

This same intimate relationship continues in the exile:

F. R. Nathan says, "So precious is Israel that, wherever they have been carried away into exile, the Presence of God is with them."

The exiles now are Babylonia, Elam, and Edom, followed by the return to Zion:

G. "They were carried into exile to Egypt, the Presence of Gd was with them, as it is said, 'Thus the Lord has said, I exiled myself with the house of your father when they were in Egypt subject to the house of Pharaoh' (1 Sam. 2:27).

H. "When they went into exile to Babylonia, the Presence of God was with them, as it is said, 'On Your account I was sent to Babylonia' (Is. 43:14).

I. "When they went into exile to Elam, the Presence of God was with them, as it is said, 'And I will set my throne in Elam and destroy their king and princes' " (Jer. 49:38).

Now comes the final exile, the one in which sages now find themselves, Rome's:

J. "When they went into exile to Edom, the Presence of God was with them, as it is said, 'Who is this that comes from Edom, in crimsoned garments from Bozrah, he that is glorious in his apparel, marching in the greatness of his strength' " (Is. 63:1).

The return from exile, to take place when the Messiah brings back the Israelites to the Land of Israel as part of the cosmic restoration to Eden, will encompass God as well:

K. "And when they return, the Presence of God will return with them, as it is said, 'Then the Lord your God will restore your fortunes and have compassion upon you, and he will gather you again from all the peoples where the Lord your God has scattered you. If your outcasts are in the uttermost parts of heaven, from there the Lord your God will gather you, and from there he will fetch you; and the Lord your God will bring you into the land which your fathers possessed, that you may possess it' (Deut. 30:4–5). The word that is used is not, 'restore,' but 'the Lord your God will return.' "

More than a single metaphor portrays God's relationship to Israel. Israel is God's bride, Israel is God's chosen son, and that is why God is always with Israel:

L. "And Scripture says, 'Come with me from Lebanon, my bride; come with me from Lebanon; depart from the peak of Amana, from the peak of Senir and Hermon, from the dens of lions, from the mountains of leopards' " (Song 4:7–8).

The parable completes the picture, along with a set of facts of Scripture, of how God's and Israel's lives intertwine:

M. Rabbi says, "There is a parable: to what is the matter to be compared? To the case of a king who said to his servant, 'If you seek me, lo, I shall be with my son. Whenever you seek me, lo, I shall be with my son.'

N. "And so Scripture says, 'Who dwells with them in the midst of their uncleanness' (Lev. 17:16).

O. "And it says, 'Through their imparting uncleanness to my tabernacle, which is in their midst' (Lev. 15:31).

P. "And it says, 'That they not make their camp unclean, where I dwell in their midst' (Num. 5:3).

Q. "And it says, 'You shall not defile the land in which you live, in the midst of which I dwell; for I the Lord dwell in the midst of the people of Israel.' "

So much for estrangement from Israel in particular.

But this same mode of thinking about God and man in the context of man's sin yields a quite separate account. The same matter of God's progressive alienation is stated in relationship to humanity at large, rather than the Temple, City, and Land. Though the alienation from sinning humanity still forms the motif, Israel takes a different position in the journey; Israel in this account forms the medium for bringing God back into the world. That stands to reason, for it is through Israel that God relates to all humanity, and only to Israel that God has given the Torah; indeed, Israel is defined as those who have accepted the Torah. Hence, if God abandons Israel, it is not to take up a location in some other place of humanity, but to give up humanity. This finds its localization in movement through the Heavens, rather than through the Temple (the counterpart to Heaven, as we noted in chapter 8).

God's progress out of the created world is therefore set forth with seven movements, corresponding to the fixed stars (the visible planets) of the seven firmaments, out of, and back into, the world; the implication is that the present condition of Israel also comes about by reason of sin and will be remedied through attainment of *zekhut*:

PESIQTA DERAB KAHANA I:I.3, 6

3. A. R. Tanhum, son-in-law of R. Eleazar b. Abina, in the name of R. Simeon b. Yosni: "What is written is not, 'I have come into the garden,' but rather, 'I have come back to my garden.' That is, 'to my canopy.'

B. "That is to say, to the place in which the the principal [Presence of God] had been located to begin with.

C. "The principal locale of God's presence had been among the lower creatures, in line with this verse: 'And they heard the sound of the Lord God walking about' " (Gen. 3:8).

6. A. [Reverting to 3.C,] the principal locale of God's presence had been among the lower creatures, but when the first man sinned, it went up to the first firmament.

B. The generation of Enosh came along and sinned, and it went up from the first to the second.

C. The generation of the flood [came along and sinned], and it went up from the second to the third.

D. The generation of the dispersion [came along] and sinned, and it went up from the third to the fourth.

E. The Egyptians in the time of Abraham our father [came along] and sinned, and it went up from the fourth to the fifth.

F. The Sodomites [came along], and sinned ... from the fifth to the sixth.

G. The Egyptians in the time of Moses ... from the sixth to the seventh.

God returns to the world through the founders of Israel:

H. And, corresponding to them, seven righteous men came along and brought it back down to earth:

I. Abraham our father came along and acquired merit, and brought it down from the seventh to the sixth.

J. Isaac came along and acquired merit and brought it down from the sixth to the fifth.

K. Jacob came along and acquired merit and brought it down from the fifth to the fourth.

L. Levi came along and acquired merit and brought it down from the fourth to the third.

M. Kahath came along and acquired merit and brought it down from the third to the second.

N. Amram came along and acquired merit and brought it down from the second to the first.

O. Moses came along and acquired merit and brought it down to earth.

P. Therefore it is said, "On the day that Moses completed the setting up of the Tabernacle, he anointed and consecrated it" (Num. 7:1).

God yearns for Israel, but Israel is estranged – why is that the case? The explanation appeals to Israel's sin. The same explanation, in more explicit language, emerges in the account of how God departed from the world. The estrangement took place by reason of the sins of one generation after another. Then the merit of successive generations of Israel brought God back to the world.

Both the question and the answer derive from the sustaining system. The two accounts – God leaves the world by reason of man's sin, is brought back through Israel's saints, God leaves the world by reason of Israel's sin but can be restored to the world by Israel's act of repentance – match. They conform to the theory, already spelled out in chapter 3, of Israel as the counterpart to Man, the other Adam, the Land as counterpart to Eden, and, now we see, the exile of Israel as counterpart to the fall of Man. The first set – God abandons the Temple – without the second story would leave an imbalance; only when the one story is told in the setting of the other does the theology make its complete statement.

But estrangement finds embodiment in the loss of the Temple, the catastrophe that is the mark of Israel's condition and emblem of its sin. Another formulation – now as a given – of God's estrangement from Israel is spelled out in the Bavli's treatment of Mishnah-tractate Hagigah Chapter One. Here again, as in the case of vows of valuation intersecting with gossip, we see how one topic triggers the introduction of another, superficially quite distinct topic. When the two are made to intersect, a point is made that neither topic on its own can register. It is yet another instance in which a self-evident connection reveals what the sages deem normative, a matter of universal consensus. Given the remarkable character of the statements just now reviewed concerning God's cosmic exile, I find it urgent to demonstrate that that position characterizes the system as a whole, not simply a few named sages. Hence I offer a demonstration of the self-evidence, the givenness, of the conception of God's estrangement from the world by reason of Israel's alienation from the Torah – the ultimate cost of sin.

Specifically, Mishnah-tractate Hagigah Chapter One deals with the festal and appearance offerings. The Talmud imparts to those offerings a profound message: they signal the character of Israel's relationship with God. When Israel can make the pilgrimage to see and be seen by God, as the offering's very name indicates, that is a mark of Israel's relationship with God. That Israel cannot make the pilgrimage at this time evokes weeping not only among the sages but also in God; the condition of Israel, the slave whose master yearns for him, is marked by the tragic flaw of estrangement. Study of the rules of who makes the pilgrimage is then made into an occasion for reflection upon the condition of Israel and what is required to correct that condition, which is, study of the Torah under the guidance of the sages. The sages' weeping for Israel, like God's, marks the point of commensurability; the sages' mastery and teaching of the Torah form the measure of Israel's hope; and God's weeping for Israel's condition brings assurance that the estrangement is only for the moment, but reconciliation will be forever. These are the connections that are drawn in the treatment of the subject of the appearance-offerings.

First let us consider the basic outline and then explain the point of intersection: Mishnah-tractate Hagigah 1:1E states that (8) the lame, (9) the blind, (10) the sick, (11) the old are not required to present an appearance-offering in Jerusalem on the occasion of a pilgrim-festival. The next major entry deals with various sages who wept upon reading verses that indicate the estrangement of Israel from God:

VI:4: The same proof-text is repeated, now in the context of a sage's weeping when he read said verse. Then comes a set of other verses that prompted weeping on the part of named sages, a passage that we briefly examined just now: When R. Huna came to this verse, "he will see, being seen," he wept, saying, "A slave whose master yearns to see him is estranged from him."

VI:5: When R. Huna came to this verse, he wept: "And you shall sacrifice peace offerings and shall eat there' (Deut. 27:7). A slave whose master yearns to see him is estranged from him."

VI:6: When R. Eleazar came to this verse, he wept: " 'And his brothers couldn't answer him, because they were frightened in his presence' " (Gen. 45:3).

VI:7: When R. Eleazar came to this verse, he wept: " 'And Samuel said to Saul, why have you disturbed me to bring me up' " (1 Sam. 28:15).

VI:8: When R. Ammi came to this verse, he wept: "Let him put his mouth in the dust, perhaps there may be hope."

VI:9: When R. Ammi came to this verse, he wept: "Seek righteousness, seek humility, perhaps shall you be hid in the day of the Lord's anger."

VI:10: When R. Assi came to this verse, he wept: "Hate the evil and love the good and establish justice in the gate, perhaps the Lord, the God of hosts, will be gracious."

VI:11: When R. Joseph came to this verse, he wept: "But there is he who is swept away without judgment" (Prov. 13:23).

VI:12: When R. Yohanan came to this verse, he wept: "And you did incite me against him, to destroy him without a cause" (Job 2:3).

VI:13: When R. Yohanan came to this verse, he wept: "Behold, he puts no trust in his holy ones" (Job 15:15).

VI:14: When R. Yohanan came to this verse, he wept: "And I will come near to you to judgment and I will be a swift witness against the sorcerers and against the adulterers and against false swearers and against those who oppress the employee in his wages" (Mal. 3:5).

VI:18: When R. Yohanan came to this verse, he wept: "For God shall bring every work into the judgment concerning every hidden thing [whether it be good or whether it be evil]" (Qoh. 12:14).

VI:21: When R. Yohanan came to this verse, he wept: "And it shall come to pass, when many evils and troubles have come upon them" (Deut. 31:21).

VI:28: For lo, he who forms the mountains and creates the wind and declares to man what his conversation was" (Amos 4:13). He said, "A slave whose master tells him what his conversation was – has he any remedy?"

[Then comes a new unit: Does God weep? With an exegeses of Jer. 13:17, these are the pertinent units]:

VI:30: [Gloss on foregoing. Introduces the theme of: God's weeping.]

VI:34: For three persons does the Holy One, blessed be he, weep every single day: for him who has the opportunity to study the Torah but does not engage in it, for him who does not have the opportunity to engage in study of the Torah but does so, and for a community leader who lords it over the community. [Finally comes a unit on seeing and being seen by God.]

VI:36: "You have greeted me, who can be seen but cannot see; may you enjoy the Heavenly response of greeting him who sees but is not seen."

VI:37: The analogy in the study of Torah: R. Idi father of R. Jacob bar Idi was accustomed to go for three months on the trip and spend one day at the school.

A vast insertion then adds a stunning and jarring point, reverting to the Mishnah rule to establish the fact: Israel as a whole cannot now present the appearance offering, since making an appearance in Jerusalem at the Temple is rendered moot by the destruction of the Temple. So added to the list of those who do not make the pilgrimage is the entire people of Israel. Not only the lame, blind, sick, and old, but all Israel are now exempt – and what an exemption!

The inclusion of the composite, formed around the theme of the sages' weeping upon encountering various verses of Scripture, is accomplished in a simple way. A proof-text vital for the exposition of a Mishnah rule is now treated in its own context, which is a formal one. But the formal construction turns out remarkably, since this and the other verses that provoked tears make the same point, which is that Israel is estranged from God and cannot make the pilgrimage to greet him. This is spelled out in so many words. Women, slaves, the lame, and so on, are excluded from the pilgrimage; then the slave is made to stand for Israel: a slave whose master yearns to see him is estranged from him. The profound irony of the sentence cannot be missed: the master owns the slave and the slave possesses no independent power of will for that reason. Yet the master yearns for the slave but is estranged from him. Beyond that one scarcely need to go. The inclusion of the entire formal set imparts to the tractate a depth that, on its own, the Mishnah-tractate simply lacks; the Mishnah's rule for an aspect of the pilgrimage festival is now recast into that one context that in the Mishnah's presentation the topic lacks, which is the historical one.

The Mishnah's framers of the tractate on the pilgrimage simply ignore the context in which the tractate is set forth; the Talmud's commentators' intrusion of the proposition at hand, at this very point, imparts to the Mishnah's presentation an irony and a message of tragedy but also hope – God yearns for a reconciliation, the study of the pilgrim offering then underscoring the coming reward for penitence – that the Mishnah-tractate simply lacks. The sages weep at Israel's condition. But so does God. The message of the tragedy of estrangement now finds its completion: God weeps too. The juxtaposition of VI:34 and VI:35 is jarring, since the one speaks of the domestic condition of Israel, which is measured by study of the Torah and the character of the community's leadership, and the other focuses on the public condition of Israel, signalled by the book of Lamentations. It would be difficult to miss the point expressed through that juxtaposition of otherwise unrelated compositions. And for reasons of a shared hero, Rabbi, VI:36 is tightly linked to the foregoing, yielding a message that transcends the formal point of intersection. That is to bring us back to the topic of our tractate, the pilgrimage to see and by seen by God. Nor can VI:37 be dismissed as tacked on, since the analogy is then drawn between Temple and Torah-study, and that analogy is specific and not merely generic: one goes to the Temple for a day, makes the offering, and goes home; one may do the same, making a pilgrimage for three months to an academy, spending a day, and going home.

And this – that God yearns for Israel, misses Israel, weeps for Israel – carries us to the final point in the sages' doctrine of sin, a point that, at this stage in the exposition, comes as no surprise. It is that God shares Israel's exile. That is the step beyond what equity requires, what is owing in the principle of measure for measure. It is how God attains *zekhut*: by giving of his own free will what Israel cannot reasonably have asked, let alone coerced: God's sharing of the fate that Israel has brought upon itself. God, clearly, is affected by Israel's sin. That is shown by his strong, negative response, the actions that he takes to respond to sin with appropriate penalties. But God is affected in another way as well. He responds to Israel's sin by sending Israel into exile, but he himself also goes into exile, as we have now seen in two striking, complementary formulations. But, the sages add, God goes into exile where Israelites are exiled.

God's fate is bound up with Israel's, just as God's inner life of affections and emotions is lived in response to Israel's feelings and attitudes:

YERUSHALMI-TRACTATE TAANIT I:I II:5

A. It has been taught by R. Simeon b. Yohai, "To every place to which the Israelites went into exile, the presence of God went with them into exile."

First comes the archetypal exile, to Egypt.

B. "They were sent into exile to Egypt, and the presence of God went into exile with them. What is the scriptural basis for this claim? '[And there came a man of God to Eli, and said to him, Thus the Lord has said], I revealed myself to the house of your father when they were in Egypt subject to the house of Pharaoh'" (I Sam. 2:27).

Now follows the familiar pattern of the four kingdoms, Babylonia, Media, Greece, and Rome.

C. "They were sent into exile to Babylonia, and the presence of God went into exile with them. What is the scriptural basis for this claim? '[Thus says the Lord, your Redeemer, the Holy One of Israel]: For your sake I will send to Babylon [and break down all the bars, and the shouting of the Chaldeans will be turned to lamentations]' (Is. 43:14).
D. "They were sent into exile into Media, and the presence of God went into exile with them. What is the scriptural basis for this claim? 'And I will set my throne in Elam [and destroy their king and princes, says the Lord]' (Jer. 49:38). And Elam means only Media, as it is said, '[And I saw in the vision; and when I saw], I was in Susa the capital, which is in the province of Elam; [and I saw in the vision, and I was at the river Ulai]' (Dan. 8:2).
E. "They went into exile to Greece, and the presence of God went into exile with them. What is the scriptural basis for this claim? '[For I have bent Judah as my bow; I have made Ephraim its arrow]. I will brandish your sons, O Zion, over your sons, O Greece, [and wield you like a warrior's sword]' (Zech. 9:13).
F. "They went into exile to Rome, and the presence of God went into exile with them. What is the scriptural basis for this claim? '[The oracle concerning Dumah]. One is calling to me from Seir, "Watchman, what of the night? Watchman, what of the night?"'" (Is. 21:11).

In this systematic statement, what should not be missed is not only God's exile but also what will bring God back to the Land, which is Israel's return at the end of the reign of the fourth and final empire, Rome. Then Israel will govern, because all mankind will accept God and give up idolatry. So cosmic dimensions take the measure of what is at stake in sin.

If the sages' theology builds upon the foundation of God's justice in creating a perfect world and accounts for the imperfections of the world by appeal to the conflict of man's will and God's plan, then, we must ask ourselves, what is the logical remedy for the impasse at which, in the present age, Israel and the world find themselves? Their explanation for flaws and transience in creation, sin brought about by the free exercise of man's will, contains within itself the systemic remission – that required, logical remedy for the human condition and creation's as well. It is an act of will to bring about reconciliation between God and Israel, God and the world. And that act of will on man's part will evoke an equal and commensurate act of will on God's part. When man repents, God forgives, and Israel and the world will attain the perfection that prevailed at Eden. And that is why death will die. So we come to the account of restoring world order. Here we begin to follow the unfolding of the restorationist theology of eschatology that completes and perfects the sages' theology set forth in the documents of the Oral Torah.

PART IV

Restoring World Order

12 Repentance and Atonement

The logic of repentance is simple and familiar. It is a logic that appeals to the balance and proportion of all things. If sin is what introduces rebellion and change, and the will of man is what constitutes the variable in disrupting creation, then the theology of the Oral Torah makes provision for restoration through the free exercise of man's will. That requires an attitude of remorse, a resolve not to repeat the act of rebellion, and a good-faith effort at reparation, in all, transformation from rebellion against to obedience to God's will. So with repentance we come once more to an exact application of the principle of measure for measure, here, will for will, each comparable to, corresponding with, the other. World order, disrupted by an act of will, regains perfection through an act of will that complements and corresponds to the initial, rebellious one. That is realized in an act of wilful repentance (Hebrew: *teshubah*).

Repentance, a statement of regret and remorse for the sin one has committed and hence an act of will, in the Oral Torah effects the required transformation of man and inaugurates reconciliation with God. Through a matched act of will, now in conformity with God's design for creation, repentance therefore restores the balance upset by man's act of will. So the act of repentance, and with it atonement, takes its place within the theology of perfection, disruption, and restoration which all together organizes – shows the order of – the world of creation.

Apology does not suffice; an atoning act also is required. That is why repentance is closely related to the categories, atonement and Day of Atonement, and integral to them. The one in the cult, the other in the passage of time, respond to the change of will with an act of confirmation, on God's part, that the change is accepted, recognized, and deemed effective. That is because, through the act of repentance, a person who has sinned leaves the status of sinner but must also atone for the sin and gain forgiveness, so that such a person is no longer deemed a sinner. Self-evidently, within a system built on the dialectics of competing wills, God's and man's, repentance comes first in the path to reconciliation. That is because the act of will involves a statement of regret or remorse, resolve never to repeat the act, and, finally, the test of this change of heart or will (where feasible). Specifically, it is a trial of entering a situation in which the original sin is possible but is not repeated. Then the statement of remorse and voluntary change of will is confirmed by an act of omission or commission, as the case requires.

Followed by atonement, therefore, repentance commences the work of closing off the effects of sin: history, time, change, inequity. It marks the beginning of the labour of restoring creation to Eden: the perfect world as God wants it and creates it. Since the Hebrew word *teshubah* is built out of the root for return, the concept is generally understood to mean returning to God from a situation of estrangement. The turning is not only from sin but towards God, for sin serves as an indicator of a deeper pathology, utter estrangement from God – man's will alienated from God's.

Teshubah, then, involves not humiliation but reaffirmation of the self in God's image, after God's likeness. It follows that repentance forms a theological category encompassing moral issues of action and attitude, wrong action, arrogant attitude, in particular. Repentance forms a step in the path to God that starts with the estrangement represented by sin: doing what I want, instead of what God wants, thus rebellion and arrogance. Sin precipitates punishment, whether personal for individuals or historical for nations; punishment brings about repentance for sin, which, in turn, leads to atonement for sin and, it follows, reconciliation with God. That sequence of stages in the moral regeneration of sinful humanity, individual or collective, defines the context in which repentance finds its natural home.

True, the penitent corrects damage one has actually carried out to his fellow man. But, apart from reparations, the act of repentance involves only the attitude, specifically, substituting feelings of regret and remorse for the arrogant intention that led to the commission of the sin. If the person declares regret and undertakes not to repeat the action, the process of repentance gets under way. When the occasion to repeat the sinful act arises and the penitent refrains from doing it again, the process comes to a conclusion. So it is through the will and attitude of the sinner that the act of repentance is realized; the entire process is carried on beyond the framework of religious actions, rites, or rituals. The power of repentance overcomes sins of the most heinous and otherwise unforgiveable character. The following is explicit that no sin overwhelms the transformative power of repentance:

BAVLI GITTIN 5:6 I.26/57B

A. A Tannaite statement:
B. Naaman was a resident proselyte.
C. Nebuzaradan was a righteous proselyte.
D. Grandsons of Haman studied Torah in Bene Beraq.
E. Grandsons of Sisera taught children in Jerusalem.
F. Grandsons of Sennacherib taught Torah in public.
G. And who were they? Shemaiah and Abtalion.

Shemaiah and Abtalion are represented as the masters of Hillel and Shammai, who founded the houses dominant in many areas of the *halakhah* set forth in the Mishnah and related writings. The act of repentance transforms the heirs of the destroyers of Israel and the Temple into the framers of the redemptive Oral Torah. A more extreme statement of the power of any attitude or action defies imagining – even the fact of our own day that a distant cousin of Adolph Hitler has converted to Judaism and serves in the Israeli army reserves.

That to such a remarkable extent God responds to man's will, which time and again has defined the dynamics of complementarity characteristic of the Oral Torah's theology, accounts for the possibility of repentance. As much as mercy completes the principle of justice, so repentance forms the complement to sin; without mercy, represented here by the possibility of repentance, justice as God defines justice cannot endure. For were man to regret sin and see things in God's way without a corresponding response from God, God would execute justice but not mercy, and, from the sages' perspective, the world would fall out of balance. To them, therefore, it is urgent that God have his own distinctive message to the sinner, separate from the voices of Wisdom, Prophecy, and even the Pentateuch (the Torah narrowly defined) of the Written Torah:

YERUSHALMI-TRACTATE MAKKOT 2:6 I:4/10A

A. Said R. Phineas: " 'Good and upright [is the Lord; therefore he instructs sinners in the way]' (Ps. 25:8).
B. "Why is he good? Because he is upright.
C. "And why is he upright? Because he is good.

D. "Therefore he instructs sinners in the way – that is, he teaches them the way to repentance."

Now we interrogate the great compendia of God's will, Wisdom and Prophecy, and then turn to God himself and ask how to treat the sinner:

E. They asked wisdom, "As to a sinner, what is his punishment?"
F. She said to them, "Evil pursues the evil" (Prov. 13:21).
G. They asked prophecy, "As to a sinner, what is his punishment?"
H. She said to them, "The soul that sins shall die" (Ez. 18:20).
I. They asked the Holy One, blessed be he, "As to a sinner, what is his punishment?"
J. He said to them, "Let the sinner repent, and his sin will be forgiven for him."
K. This is in line with the following verse of Scripture: "Therefore he instructs sinners in the way" (Ps. 25:8).
L. "He shows the sinners the way to repentance."

The response of wisdom presents no surprise; it is the familiar principle of measure for measure, and prophecy concurs, but God has something more to say. Accordingly, the proposition concerns the distinctive mercy of God, above even the Torah. The data for the composition E-L respond to the question that is addressed to the components of the Torah, that is, what does prophecy say about the punishment of the sinner? But the question is prior and forms part of the systemic plan: to demonstrate the uniquely merciful character of God, the way in which God is God.

But, as we shall see, the power of repentance is disproportionate, out of all balance with sin in a way in which the penalty for sin never exceeds the gravity of the sin. We may say that, while, when it comes to sin, God effects exact justice, when it comes to repentance, God accords mercy out of all proportion to the arrogance of the act of rebellion, an idea already familiar from chapter 8. The act of will that is represented by repentance vastly outweighs in effect the act of will that brings about sin. That is because one may commit many sins, but a single act of repentance encompasses them all and restores the balance that those sins all together have upset. So repentance makes sense, in its remarkable power, only in the context of God's mercy. It follows that any account of repentance and atonement must commence with a clear statement of God's mercy, the logical precondition for the act of repentance.

Now as to the matter of divine mercy, God's mercy vastly exceeds his justice, so when God metes out reward he does so very lavishly: as we recall from chapter 2, citing T. Sotah 4:1: "I know only with regard to the measure of retribution that by that same measure by which a man metes out, they mete out to him (M. Sot. 1:7A). How do I know that the same is so with the measure of goodness?" God's power to forgive sin, however formidable, and to reward virtue, however slight, is expressed in his acts of mercy. And the mercy of God comes to expression in his deeds:

GENESIS RABBAH XXXIII:III.1F.

1. A. "The Lord is good to all, and his tender mercies are over all his works" (Ps. 145:9):
B. Said R. Joshua b. Levi, "The Lord is good to all, and his tender mercies are over all, for they are his works."
C. Said R. Samuel bar Nahman, "The Lord is good to all, and his tender mercies are over all, for lo, by his very nature, he extends mercy."
D. R. Joshua in the name of R. Levi: "The Lord is good to all, and out of his store of tender mercy he gives [mercy] to his creatures."
E. R. Abba said, "Tomorrow a year of scarcity will come, and people will show mercy to one another, on account of which the Holy One, blessed be he, is filled with mercy for them." [This point will now be illustrated.]

The attitude of mercy that characterizes God must shape man's will, and that comes about when man needs mercy from Heaven and learns out of necessity to show mercy to other men. When God sees men treating one another mercifully, then God responds with an act of mercy of his own – a replay of the dynamics that produces *zekhut*. Here is a case in which what is at stake is shown:

2. A. In the time of R. Tanhuma Israel had need of a fast [on account of the lack of rain]. People came to him. They said to him, "Our master, decree a fast." He decreed a fast for one day, then for a second day, then for a third day, but it did not rain.
B. He went up and preached to them, saying to them, "My children, show mercy for one another, and the Holy One, blessed be he, will show mercy to you."

The lesson is spelled out in so many words, and now we come to a remarkable act of uncoerced mercy, indeed one that contradicts human nature:

C. While they were passing out charity, they saw a man giving money to a woman whom he had divorced. They came to [Tanhuma] and said to him, "How can we sit here while someone is doing such a thing!"
D. He said to them, "What did you see?"

E. They said to him, "We saw Mr. So-and-so paying off the woman he had divorced [so we assumed he was buying her sexual services]."

F. He sent the people to the man, and they brought him to the sage. He said to him, "Why did you give money to the woman you divorced?"

G. He said to him, "I saw her in great need and I felt pity for her."

The lesson is drawn from that remarkable act of self-abnegation and generosity, a lesson that pertains to Heaven and invokes the relationship captured by the word *zekhut*:

H. R. Tanhuma raised his face upward and said, "Lord of all ages, Now if this man, who was under absolutely no obligation to provide food for the woman, could see her in need and be filled with mercy for her, you, concerning whom it is written, 'The Lord is full of compassion and gracious' (Ps. 103:8), and whose children we are, that is, the children of those who are precious to you, children of Abraham, Isaac, and Jacob, how much the more so should you be filled with mercy for us!"

I. Forthwith the rain came and the world returned to prosperity.

The natural animal will not have shown mercy; the man had divorced the woman and, having compensated her properly, owed nothing; but if he had divorced her, then reason suggests he bore her no good will. That is when the act of mercy takes place: it is to those to whom we owe nothing that an act of mercy must be offered, and the rest follows. So, while God does not owe man the merciful act of responding to repentance, God shows man the right way by giving what he does not owe, and what man cannot demand or coerce – once more, the transaction that yields *zekhut*.

God takes an active role in bringing about the restoration of the perfection of the world. This he does by goading man into an act of repentance – the purpose of punishment of sin being not so much retributive as redemptive. Aiming at bringing about repentance, God first penalizes property, then the person, in the theory that the first will arouse the man to reflect on what he has done, so a penalty exacted from the person himself will not be necessary, repentance having intervened:

RUTH RABBAH IX:I.IFF.

B. R. Huniah in the name of R. Joshua b. R. Abin and R. Zechariah son-in-law of R. Levi in the name of R. Levi: "The merciful Lord does not do injury to human beings first. [First he exacts a penalty from property, aiming at the sinner's repentance.]

C. From whom do you derive that lesson? From the case of Job: 'The oxen were plowing and the asses feeding beside them [and the Sabaeans fell upon them and took them and slew the servants with the edge of the sword; and I alone have escaped to tell you' (Job 1:14). Afterward: 'Your sons and daughters were eating and drinking wine in their eldest brother's house, and behold, a great wind came across the wilderness and struck the four corners of the house, and it fell upon the young people, and they are dead' " (Job 1:19).]

D. Now were the oxen plowing and the asses feeding beside them? Said R. Hama b. R. Hanina, "This teaches that the Holy One, blessed be He, showed him a paradigm of the world to come.

E. "That is in line with the following verse of Scripture: 'The plowman shall overtake the reaper' " (Amos 9:13).

In the manner of philosophers assembling data from nature, the sages gather further facts from Scripture, now in the case of Egypt:

2. A. So too it was in Egypt [that God punished the Egyptians herds before he punished the people themselves]: "He gave over their cattle to the hail and their flocks to thunderbolts" (Ps. 78:48).

B. And then: "He smote their vines and fig trees and shattered the trees of their country" (Ps. 105:33).

C. And finally: "He smote all the firstborn in their land, the first issue of all their strength" (Ps. 105:36).

History having made its contribution to the process of proof, we turn to nature, which conforms:

3. A. So when leprous plagues afflict a person, first they afflict his house. If he repents the house requires only the dismantling of the affected stones. If not, the whole house requires demolishing.

B. Lo, when they hit his clothing, if he repents, the clothing has only to be torn. If he did not repent, the clothing has to be burned.

C. Lo, if one's body is affected, if he repents, he may be purified.

D. If the affliction comes back, and if he does not repent, "He shall dwell alone in a habitation outside the camp."

4. A. So too in the case of Mahlon and Chilion:

B. first their horses and asses and camels died, and then: Elimelech, and finally the two sons.

God warns before inflicting punishment, preferring repentance to imposing penalties for sin. It is a mark of his mercy. The proposition is demonstrated by four probative cases; these cases do not form a natural list but coalesce only in the matter at hand. The second, third, and fourth cases are presented in an unadorned way. No other point in common draws them together.

Repentance never stands alone but shares traits of two other actions and works with them to elicit God's mercy and avert harsh decrees from Heaven. Integral to the process of repentance, these are acts of prayer and of charity, both of them, like repentance, expressions of attitude and will. The act of prayer is a statement of dependence upon Heaven, a submission of man's will before God's mercy, and the act of charity, as we have already noted, embodies that attitude of will that man seeks to evoke from God. In like manner repentance belongs with charity and prayer; these three actions nullify the evil decree:

YERUSHALMI-TRACTATE TAANIT 2:1/III:5

A. Said R. Eleazar, "Three acts nullify the harsh decree, and these are they: prayer, charity, and repentance."

The facts of Scripture are adduced to validate that statement:

B. And all three of them are to be derived from a single verse of Scripture:
C. "If my people who are called by my name humble themselves, [pray and seek my face, and turn from their wicked ways, then I will hear from heaven and will forgive their sin and heal their land]" (2 Chron. 7:14).
D. "Pray" – this refers to prayer.
E. "And seek my face" – this refers to charity,
F. as you say, "As for me, I shall behold thy face in righteousness; when I awake, I shall be satisfied with beholding thy form" (Ps. 17:15).
G. "And turn from their wicked ways" – this refers to repentance.
H. Now if they do these things, what is written concerning them there?
I. "Then I will hear from heaven and will forgive their sin and heal their land."

To shape one's own future, one can take action to overcome the effects of past sin. Through prayer, acts of charity, and repentance, one may so express a change of attitude as to persuade Heaven to respond and change its attitude as well. The message is concrete, having to do with declaring a fast in response to the withholding of rain by Heaven.

As we noted at the very outset, repentance itself is complemented by yet another act of reconciliation, which is atonement. Just as repentance, prayer, and charity form a natural cluster, so repentance and atonement form another. That is because repentance cannot be fully understood outside the context of atonement; repentance forms a stage in the quest for atonement for, and complements the process that results in, the forgiveness of sin. While, as we have seen, the relationship of repentance and atonement is integral, atonement receives an exposition in its own terms as well. Here we shall see how repentance relates to atonement, and, presently, we shall take up atonement on its own as the goal of the entire transaction.

Repentance is the precondition of atonement; there is no atonement without the statement of remorse and appropriate, confirming action. If one rebels against God's rule and does not repent, no atonement is possible. But if he does repent, then the Day of Atonement effects atonement for him, so

BAVLI-TRACTATE SHEBUOT I:IFF. XVI.2/13A

D. Rabbi says, "For all of the transgressions that are listed in the Torah, whether one has repented or not repented, the Day of Atonement attains atonement, except for one who breaks the yoke [of the kingdom of heaven from himself, meaning, denies God] and one who treats the Torah impudently, and the one who violates the physical mark of the covenant. In these cases if one has repented, the Day of Atonement attains atonement, and if not, the Day of Atonement does not attain atonement."

Now come the facts to validate the proposition:

E. What is the scriptural basis for the position of Rabbi?

F. It is in line with that which has been taught on Tannaite authority:

G. "Because he has despised the word of the Lord": This refers to one who is without shame in interpreting the Torah.

H. "And broken his commandment": This refers to one who removes the mark fleshly arks of the covenant.

I. "That soul shatter utterly be cut of "Be cut off" – before the Day of Atonement. "Utterly" – after the day of atonement.

J. Might one suppose that that is the case even if he has repented?

K. Scripture says, "his iniquity shall be upon him" (Num. 15:31) – I say that the Day of Atonement does not effect atonement only when his iniquity is still upon him.

The contrary view invokes the same facts but interprets them differently:

L. And rabbis?

M. "That soul shatter utterly be cut of "Be cut off"– in this world. "Utterly"– in the world to come.

N. "his iniquity shall be upon him" (Num. 15:31) – if he repented and died, death wipes away the sin.

What is reconciled is the atoning power of the Day of Atonement with the intransigence of the sinner. How to explain the limits of the one in the face of the other? The answer lies in the power of repentance or of failure to repent, which explains when the Day of Atonement atones or fails. When faced with the possible conflict between the power of the Day of Atonement and the enormity of sins against Heaven itself, the resolution lies in invoking the matter of intentionality, expressed through the act of repentance or the failure to perform that act.

While repentance is required, in a system of hierarchical classification such as this one, the other components of the process, prayer in this case, have to be situated in relationship to one another. Whether or not repentance accomplishes the whole of atonement is subject to some uncertainty, since prayer retains a critical role in the process:

LEVITICUS RABBAH X:V.I

I. A. Judah b. Rabbi and R. Joshua b. Levi:

B. Judah b. Rabbi said, "Repentance achieves [only] part, while prayer achieves the complete [atonement]."

C. R. Joshua b. Levi said, "Repentance achieves the whole [of atonement], while prayer achieves only part [of atonement]."

The two views now have to be sustained by fact, and the facts of Scripture serve. But both parties are clear that repentance forms a stage in the path to atonement, with or without the necessity of prayer.

D. In the view of R. Judah b. Rabbi, who has said that repentance achieves [only] part [of the needed atonement], from whom do you derive proof?

E. It is from Cain, against whom a harsh decree was issued, as it is written, "A fugitive and a wanderer will you be on the earth" (Gen. 4:12). But when Cain repented, part of the harsh decree was removed from him.

F. That is in line with the following verse of Scripture: "Then Cain went away from the presence of the Lord and dwelt in the land of the wanderer [Nod], east of Eden" (Gen. 4:16). "In the land of a fugitive *and* a wanderer" is not written here, but rather, only "in the land of the wanderer." [The matter of being a fugitive is thus annulled.]

M. When he had left [God], the first man met him, saying to him, What happened at your trial?

N. He said to him, "I repented and copped a plea."

Here Cain illustrates the total power of repentance, meaning, confession and a statement of remorse:

O. When the first man heard this, he began to slap his own face, saying, "So that's how strong repentance is, and I never knew!"

P. At that moment, the first man pronounced [this Psalm], "A Psalm, the song for the Sabbath day" (Ps. 92:1) [which says, "It is a good thing to make a confession to the Lord" (Ps. 92:2)].

Q. Said R. Levi, "It was the first man who made up that psalm."

Contrary facts are adduced for the opposed position:

2. A. In the view of Judah b. Rabbi, who said that prayer accomplishes the whole of the necessary atonement? From whence do you derive proof? It is from Hezekiah.

B. The allotted time for Hezekiah's rule was only fourteen years. That is in line with the following verse of Scripture: "And it happened in the fourteenth year of King Hezekiah [Sennacherib, king of Assyria came up against all the fortified cities of Judah and took them]" (Is. 36:1).

C. But when Hezekiah prayed, fifteen more years were added to his rule.

D. That is in line with the following verse of Scripture: "Behold, I will add fifteen years to your life" (Is. 38:5).

Another exemplary case is introduced:

3. A. In the view of R. Joshua b. Levi, who has said that repentance effects the whole of the required atonement, from whom do you derive evidence? From the inhabitants of Anathoth:

B. "Therefore thus says the Lord concerning the men of Anathoth, who seek your life and say, Do not prophecy ... Behold, I will punish them; the young men shall die by the sword; [their sons and their daughters shall die by famine; and none of them shall be left. For I will bring evil upon the men of Anathoth, the year of their punishment]" (Jer. 11:21–3).

C. But because they repented, they enjoyed the merit of being listed in the honourable genealogies: "The men of Anathoth were one hundred twenty-eight" (Ezra 2:23; Neh. 7:27).

We revert to the position that prayer accomplishes only part of atonement:

7. A. In the view of R. Joshua b. Levi, who has said that prayer only accomplishes part of the required atonement, from whom do you derive proof?

B. It is from Aaron, against whom a decree was issued.

C. That is in line with the following verse: "Moreover the Lord was very angry with Aaron, to have destroyed him" (Deut. 9:20).

D. R. Joshua of Sikhnin said in the name of R. Levi, "The meaning of the word 'destruction' used here is only the utter extinction of all offspring, sons and daughters alike.

E. "That is in line with the following usage: 'And I destroyed his fruit from above and his roots from beneath'" (Amos 2:9).

F. Yet when Moses prayed on behalf of Aaron, only two of his sons died [Nadab and Abihu], while the other two survived.

G. "Take Aaron and his sons with him" (Lev. 8:2).

This protracted exercise shows how the sages sifted facts of Scripture so as to test hypothesis. The exposition of the complex interplay of repentance and atonement takes the form of not only narratives, exegesis of Scripture, and apodictic statements, however, but also – and especially – normative law. In the statement of law, the focus is on atonement, of the process of which repentance is a component. But there are other components as well. One is an offering at the Temple, a sin-offering in particular, which is accepted as atonement for an inadvertent act. One cannot deliberately sin and trade off with an animal sacrifice; God wants the heart, and an act of rebellion not followed by a change of heart is indelible. But if a sinful act is not deliberate, then a sin-offering suffices, along with an unconditional guilt offering.

Two other media of atonement for sin are death, on the one side, and the advent of the Day of Atonement, which accomplishes atonement: "For on this day atonement shall be made for you to cleanse you of all your sins" (Lev. 16:30). Death marks the final atonement for sin, which bears its implication for the condition of man at the resurrection, as we shall see in chapter 13. Because one has atoned through sin (accompanied at the hour of death by a statement of repentance, "May my death be atonement for all my sins," in the liturgy in due course), when he is raised from the dead, his atonement for all his sins is complete. The judgment after resurrection becomes for most a formality. That is why "all Israel has a portion in the world to come," with the exception of a few whose sins are not atoned for by death, and that is by their own word. The Day of Atonement provides atonement, as the Written Torah makes explicit, for the sins of the year for which one has repented, and that accounts for the elaborate rites of confession that fill the day. Here is how the media of atonement of death, for a lifetime, and the Day of Atonement, for the year just past, are sorted out:

MISHNAH-TRACTATE YOMA 8:8–9

8:8

A. A sin offering and an unconditional guilt offering atone.

B. Death and the Day of Atonement atone when joined with repentance.

C. Repentance atones for minor transgressions of positive and negative commandments.

D. And as to serious transgressions, [repentance] suspends the punishment until the Day of Atonement comes along and atones.

8:9

A. He who says, "I shall sin and repent, sin and repent" –

B. they give him no chance to do repentance.

C. [If he said,] "I will sin and the Day of Atonement will atone" – the Day of Atonement does not atone.

D. For transgressions done between man and the Omnipresent, the Day of Atonement atones.

E. For transgressions between man and man, the Day of Atonement atones, only if the man will regain the good will of his friend.

The first statement sorts out the workings of repentance, death, the Day of Atonement, and atonement. We see that repentance on its own serves for the violation of commandments, for that involves God; when another man is involved in a man's sin, then the this-worldly counterpart to repentance, which is reparation and reconciliation, is required. The formulation underscores the tight weaving of the several components of a single tapestry.

First comes inadvertent sin, acts that violate God's will but are not done intentionally. A sin-offering in the Temple in Jerusalem, presented for unintentional sins, atones, and therein we find the beginning of the definition of repentance. It lies in the contrast between the sin-offering at A, that is, atonement for unintentional sin, and those things that atone for intentional sin, which are two events, on the one side, and the expression of right attitude, *teshubah*, returning to God, on the other. The role of repentance emerges in the contrast with the sin-offering; what atones for what is inadvertent has no bearing upon what is deliberate. The wilful sin can be atoned for only if repentance has taken place, that is to say, genuine regret, a turning away from the sin, after the fact, therefore transforming the sin from one that is deliberate to one that is, if not unintentional beforehand, then at least, unintentional afterward. Then death, on the one side, or the Day of Atonement, on the other, work their enchantment.

The process of reconciliation with God – at-one-ment so to speak – encompasses a number of steps and components, not only repentance; and repentance, for its part, does not reach concrete definition in the formulation of the process. This is how the Bavli deals with precisely the problem of intransigence on the part of the victim:

VI.1 A. [Citing the Mishnah-rule:] For transgressions done between man and the Omnipresent, the Day of Atonement atones. For transgressions between man and man, the Day of Atonement atones, only if the man will regain the good will of his friend:

The matter of reconciling the other is now spelled out:

2. A. Said R. Isaac, "Whoever offends his fellow, even if through what he says, has to reconcile with him, as it is said, 'My son, if you have become surety for your neighbour, if you have struck your hands for a stranger, you are snared by the words of your mouth ... do this now, my son, and deliver yourself, seeing you have come into the power of your neighbour, go, humble yourself, and urge your neighbour' (Prov. 6:1–3). If it is a money-claim against you, open the palm of your hand to him [and pay him off], and if not, send a lot of intermediaries to him."

B. Said R. Hisda, "He has to reconcile with him through three sets of three people each: 'He comes before men and says, I have sinned and perverted that which was right and it did not profit me' " (Job 33:27).

C. Said R. Yosé bar Hanina, "Whoever seeks reconciliation with his neighbour has to do so only three times: 'Forgive I pray you now ... and now we pray you' (Gen. 50:17).

D. "And if he has died, he brings ten people and sets them up at his grave and says, 'I have sinned against the Lord the God of Israel and against this one, whom I have hurt."

Specific cases exemplifying the working of the law now are set forth:

3. A. R. Abba had a complaint against R. Jeremiah, [Jeremiah] went and sat at the door of R. Abba. In the interval his serving girl threw out slops. Some drops fell on his head. He said, "They've made a dung heap out of me," and about himself he cited the verse, "He raises up the poor out of the dust" (1 Sam. 2:8).

B. R. Abba heard and came out to him, saying, "Now I must come out to seek reconciliation with you: 'Go, humble yourself and urge your neighbour' " (Prov. 6:1).

Here is how a sage gave the offending man an opportunity of reconciliation:

4. A. When R. Zira had a quarrel with someone, he would pass by him repeatedly, so as to show himself to him, so that the other might come forth to seek reconciliation with him.

But reconciliation is not always wanted, and the result is catastrophic for the recalcitrant:

B. Rab had a fight with a certain butcher. The butcher did not come to him on the eve of the Day of Atonement, so he said, "I shall go and seek reconciliation with him."

C. R. Huna met him. He said to him, "Where is the master going?"

D. He said to him, "To seek reconciliation with Mr. So-and-so."

E. He thought, "Abba [Rab] is going to bring about the other's death."

F. [Rab] went and stood by the man. The other was sitting and chopping up a beast's head. He raised his eyes and saw him. He said to him, "You're Abba, go away, I have no business to do with you." While he was chopping the head, a bone flew off, struck his throat, and killed him.

The matter has its own limits. Beyond the specified point, the penitent has carried out his obligation as best he can, and nothing more is to be done.

But that provision for reconciliation even after the fact raises the question of deliberate and wilful violation of the law, encompassing repentance – before the fact. And that is the point at which repentance loses its power. If one has insinuated repentance into the sinful act itself, declaring at the outset that afterward one will repent, the power of repentance is lost, the act of will denying the *post facto* possibility altogether. That is the point of Mishnah-tractate Yoma 8:9A-C, which is now amplified. For, we now observe, the issue of attitude takes over, and it is in the end the fundamental attitude that governs: if, at the beginning, the wilful act is joined to an act of will affecting the *post facto* circumstance, all is lost; one's attitude nullifies all further possibilities.

FATHERS ACCORDING TO RABBI NATHAN XL:V.I

A. He who says, "I shall sin and repent" will never suffice to carry out repentance.

B. "I will sin and the Day of Atonement will accomplish atonement" – the Day of Atonement will not accomplish atonement.

C. "I shall sin and the day of death will wipe away the sin" – the day of death will not wipe away the sin.

D. R. Eliezer b. R. Yosé says, "He who sins and repents and then proceeds in an unblemished life does not move from his place before he is forgiven.

E. "He who says, 'I shall sin and repent' is forgiven three times but no more."

That is why there is no such thing as pre-emptive repentance, that is, planning in advance to atone for a sin. We shall presently take up atonement in its own terms; at this point it suffices to register that repentance leads to atonement, at which point God and man reconcile.

We recall from chapter 1 that the normative view of the Oral Torah is signalled by the proposition of a large-scale composite devoted to a topic; the shape of that composite and its thrust will then signal the self-evidently valid proposition on the topic and so form the theological counterpart to a legal decision, one that is given the form of a systematic compilation of statements into a coherent account. A sizable abstract allows the Talmud of Babylonia in its usual, systematic way to state the normative view of repentance. For, organizing topical presentations on such theological themes, the Talmud makes its definitive statement of the norms of the subject in the following terms, a sequence of sayings expressing the main components of the concept:

BABYLONIAN TALMUD TRACTATE YOMA
8:8–9 III.1/86A-B

6. A. Said R. Hama bar Hanina, "Great is repentance, which brings healing to the world: 'I will heal their backsliding, I will love them freely' " (Hos. 14:5).
B. R. Hama bar Hanina contrasted verses: " 'Return you backsliding children' – who to begin with were backsliding. Vs. 'I will heal your backsliding' (Jer. 3:22). There is no contradiction, in the one case, the repentance is out of love, in the other, out of fear."

Now the matter of right motivation enters, love or fear. As we shall see presently, repentance is something that God, too, can precipitate, by bringing the penalty of suffering upon the sinner, so alerting him to the consequences of his act of rebellion:

C. R. Judah contrasted verses: " 'Return you backsliding children, I will heal your backsliding' (Jer. 3:22). Vs. 'For I am lord to you, and I will take you one of a city and two of a family' (Jer. 3:14). There is no contradiction, in the one case, the repentance is out of love or fear, in the other, repentance comes as a consequence of suffering."

Repentance is placed into the context of other data supplied by the Torah. First, the Written Torah's references to "return" all are taken to pertain to repentance, and this yields a variety of insights into the power of repentance:

7. A. Said R. Levi, "Great is repentance, which reaches up to the throne of glory: 'Return, Israel, to the Lord your God' " (Hos. 14:2).
8. A. [86B] Said R. Yohanan, "Great is repentance, for it overrides a negative commandment that is in the Torah: 'If a man put away his wife and she go from him and become another man's wife, may he return to her again? Will not that land be greatly polluted? But you have played the harlot with many lovers, and would you then return to me, says the Lord' " (Jer. 3:1).

The next statement, consistent with many others we shall examine in chapters 13 and 14, finds in repentance the key to redemption, the restoration of Israel to the Land of Israel, counterpart to the restoration of Man to Eden:

9. A. Said R. Jonathan, "Great is repentance, for it brings redemption near: 'And a redeemer shall come to Zion and to those who return from transgression in Jacob' (Is. 59:20) – how come 'a redeemer shall come to Zion'? Because of 'those who return from transgression in Jacob.' "

Repentance proves retroactive, transforming the very weight of sins already done:

10. A. Said R. Simeon b. Laqish, "Great is repentance, for by it sins that were done deliberately are transformed into those that were done inadvertently: 'And when the wicked turns from his wickedness and does that which is lawful and right, he shall live thereby' (Ez. 33:19) – now 'wickedness' is done deliberately, and yet the prophet calls it stumbling!"
11. A. Said R. Samuel bar Nahmani said R. Jonathan, "Great is repentance, for it lengthens the years of a person: 'And when the wicked turns from his wickedness ... he shall live thereby' " (Ez. 33:19).

The power of repentance proves absolute, God's response disproportionate, as we already realize, because of the logic of justice that entails the attitude of mercy in response to the attitude of remorse:

12. A. Said R. Isaac, [or they say in the West in the name of Rabbah bar Mari,] "Come and take note of how the characteristic of the Holy One, blessed be he, is not like the characteristic of mortals. If a mortal insults his fellow by something that he has said, the other may or may not be reconciled with him. And if you say that he is reconciled with him, he may or may not be reconciled by mere words. But with the Holy One, blessed be he, if someone commits a transgression in private, he will be reconciled with him in mere words, as it is said, 'Take with you words and return to the Lord' (Hos. 14:3). And not only so, but [God] credits it to him as goodness: 'and accept that which is good' (Hos. 14:5); and not only so, but Scripture credits it to him as if he had offered up bullocks: 'So will we render for bullocks the offerings of our lips' (Hos. 14:5). Not you might say that reference is made to obligatory bullocks, but Scripture says, 'I will heal their backsliding, I love them freely' " (Hos. 14:5).

The claim for the power of repentance rises to a new height. One man's repentance can save the world:

13. A. It has been taught on Tannaite authority:

B. R. Meir would say, "Great is repentance, for on account of a single individual who repents, the whole world is forgiven in its entirety: 'I will heal their backsliding, I will love them freely, for my anger has turned away from him' (Hos. 14:5). What is said is not 'from them' but 'from him.'"

We come now to the concrete definition of what seals the transaction of repentance, namely, the opportunity to perform the same action, which, on the second go-around, is rejected:

14. A. How is a person who has repented to be recognized?

B. Said R. Judah, "For example, if a transgression of the same sort comes to hand once, and second time, and the one does not repeat what he had done."

The sinful act of rebellion, we recall, commonly involves sexuality, so we cannot be surprised at the character of the illustration of the authentic act of repentance:

C. R. Judah defined matters more closely: "With the same woman, at the same season, in the same place."

In this way the sinner shows the true regeneration of will: he has the opportunity to commit exactly the same sin under the same circumstances but responds with the proper attitude and consequent deed, this time, one of restraint and forbearance.

The act of repentance commences with the sinner but then compels divine response; the attitude of the penitent governs, the motive – love, fear – making the difference. The power of repentance to win God over, even after recurring sin, forms the leading theme – the leitmotif – of the composite. Israel's own redemption depends upon Israel's repentance. The concluding statement proves most concrete. Repentance takes place when the one who has sinned and declares his regret ("in words") faces the opportunity of repeating the sinful action but this time refrains (No. 14). That we deal with the critical nexus in the relationship between God and humanity emerges in one composition after another, for example, repentance overrides negative commandments of the Torah (the more important kind); brings redemption; changes the character of the already committed sins; lengthens the life of the penitent. Not only so, but the power of repentance before the loving God of grace is such that mere words suffice. The upshot is that we deal with a matter of attitude that comes to the surface in concrete statements; but as to deeds, the penitent cannot repeat the sin, so no deed can be required; the penitent has a more difficult task: not to do again what he has done before.

Yet repentance is a far cry from loving and forgiving one's unrepentant enemy. God forgives sinners who atone and repent and asks of humanity that same act of grace – but no greater. For forgiveness without a prior act of repentance violates the rule of justice and also humiliates the law of mercy, cheapening and trivializing the superhuman act of forgiveness by treating as compulsive what is an act of human, and divine, grace. Sin is to be punished, but repentance is to be responded to with forgiveness, as the written Torah states explicitly: "You shall not bear a grudge nor pursue a dispute beyond reason, nor hate your brother in your heart, but you shall love your neighbor as yourself" (Lev. 19:18). The role of the sinful other is to repent, the task of the sinned-against is to respond to and accept repentance, at which point loving one's neighbour as oneself becomes the just person's duty. Repentance forms the critical center of the moral transaction in a contentious and wilful world.

The perfect balance between sin and repentance, mercy and forgiveness, emerges when we ask about the children of sinners. In the context of the Oral Torah, the question finds its meaning when we recall that, when the founders of Israel, Abraham, Isaac, and Jacob, performed acts of supererogatory love for God and exemplary service, the *zekhut* with which God responded to their attitude accrued to the advantage of their heirs, Israel in time to come. For the sages, the antonym of *zekhut* is sin, and the causative, to cause others *zekhut* (to endow others with zekhut), finds its opposite in the causative, to cause others to sin. So, in their language-world, even without the explicit statement of Exodus 20:5, "visiting the sins of the parents upon the children, upon the third and fourth generations of those who reject me," it was natural to wonder about a heritage of not *zekhut* but guilt, unmerited favour matched by unearned penalty. This, the sages found it easy to re-frame in terms of their prevailing logic. They did so when they maintained that God punishes the sons who continue the sins of the father, but not those who repent of the fathers' sins:

MEKHILTA ATTRIBUTED TO R. ISHMAEL LII:I.8:

A. "visiting the iniquity of the fathers upon the children":
B. That is when there is no break in the chain, but not when there is a break in the chain.
C. How so?
D. In the case of a wicked person, son of a wicked person, son of a wicked person.

This is now instantiated and confirmed: in Israel son such sequence of wicked generations is to be imagined:

E. R. Nathan says, "It is one who cuts down [the plantings], son of one who cuts down [the plantings], son of one who cuts down [the plantings]."

F. When Moses heard this matter, "Moses made haste and bowed his head toward the earth and worshipped" (Ex. 34:8).

G. He said, "God forbid, there cannot be among all the Israelites a wicked person, son of a wicked person, son of a wicked person."

9. A. Might one suppose that, just as the measure of punishment covers four generations, so the measure of goodness covers the same span of four generations?

B. Scripture says, "to thousands."

C. If "to thousands," might I understand that the minimum plural of "thousands" is two?

D. Scripture says, "to a thousand generations" (Deut. 7:9), that is to say, to generations beyond all discover and all counting.

The question of fairness is implicit: if the father has sinned, what has the son done to merit punishment? The question finds its answer in a revision of the facts of the matter: if the son continues the father's tradition, he will be punished as the father was. This turns matters around.

That formulation accounts for the statements concerning the heirs of Israel's worst enemies, Haman and Sennacherib and the rest, cited earlier, and alerts us to the remarkable power of repentance. Indeed, the power of repentance overcomes all else:

PESIQTA DERAB KAHANA XXIV:XII.I

1. A. R. Judah the Patriarch in the name of R. Judah bar Simon: "Under ordinary circumstances if someone shoots an arrow, it may go a distance of a kor or two. But so great is the power of repentance that [the act of repentance] reaches the throne of glory."

B. Said R. Yosé, "It is written, 'Open to me' (Song 5:2). Said the Holy One, blessed be He, 'Open to me an opening as small as a hole of a needle and I shall open for you a space through which military camps and siege engines can enter.' "

C. R. Tanhuma in the name of R. Haninah, R. Aibu in the name of R. Simeon b. Laqish: "Repent for a brief moment and 'know that I am the Lord' " (Ps. 46:11).

Repentance is not only personal but public, as we should expect in a system that treats the private person and the community in accord with the same principles. Therefore, just as Israelites repent and are forgiven, so all Israel will do the same. That is why repentance emerges as the precondition of redemption:

D. Said R. Levi, "If the Israelites repented for a single day, they would be redeemed.
E. "What verse of Scripture makes that point? '[He tends one flock in his care.] Today if you listen to his voice' " (Ps. 95:7).

All Israel in the end must do is confess God as the one true God:

F. Said R. Judah bar Simon, " 'Return, Israel, to the Lord your God' (Hosea 14:2), even if you have denied the very principle [of the faith]."

And that may be done in circumstances that avoid humiliating the sinner, even in private for a public action:

G. Said R. Eleazar, "Under ordinary circumstances, if someone humiliates his fellow in public and after a while wants to conciliate him, the other says, 'Are you going to humiliate me in public and then conciliate me in private? Go and bring those people before whom you humiliated me and in their presence I shall be conciliated with you.'
H. "But the Holy One, blessed be He, is not that way. Rather, a person may go and blaspheme and curse in the marketplace, but the Holy One, blessed be He, says to him to repent 'even between you and me and I shall accept you.' "

The sinner, therefore, finds every reason to tame his will and accept God's word, giving up arrogance and ceasing rebellion. God's mercy accomplishes the rest of the process of reconciliation, once man has taken the smallest step.

So much for repentance, testimony to the deep logic of a theology that aims at the perfection of creation, as God originally made it, and that finds in man's intentionality the cause for the imperfections in creation. Earlier we noted that repentance marked only one stage on the path toward the restoration, but that atonement defined the next step. We now consider atonement in its own terms.

As we now realize, by atonement, the sages understand an act or event (death or the Day of Atonement in particular) that removes the effects of sin by bringing about God's forgiveness of sin. The forms of the Hebrew based on the root KPR do not exhaust the category, for any action that produces the result of removing the effect of a sin will fit into that category, whether or not labelled an act of *kapparah*. The written Torah speaks of atoning offerings in the Temple. Atonement in this age, without the Temple and its offerings, is accomplished through charity; so b. B.B. 1:5 IV.23/9a: And said R. Eleazar, "When the Temple stood, someone would pay off his sheqel-offering and achieve atonement. Now that the Temple is not standing, if people give to charity, well and good, but if not, the gentiles will come and take it by force.

And even so, that is still regarded for them as an act of righteousness: 'I will make your exactors righteousness' " (Isa. 60:17).

The principal categorical component is the atonement brought about by the advent of the Day of Atonement. So, for instance, on that day the high priest, representing all Israel, brings about atonement through the rites of the Day of Atonement, beginning with the confession. Scripture presents diverse facts on a given sin, the penalty thereof, and the media of remission of the penalty, and reason and exegesis then make possible the classification of those facts into a coherent whole:

TOSEFTA-TRACTATE KIPPURIM 4:6–8

T. Kip. 4:6 A. R. lshmael says, "There are four kinds of atonement.

B. "[If] one has violated a positive commandment but repented, he hardly moves from his place before they forgive him,

C. "since it is said, 'Return, backsliding children. I will heal your backsliding' (Jer. 3:22).

4:7 A. "[If] he has violated a negative commandment but repented, repentance suspends the punishment, and the Day of Atonement effects atonement,

B. "since it is said, 'For that day will effect atonement for you (Lev. 16:30).

4:8 A. "[If] he has violated [a rule for which the punishment is] extirpation or death at the hands of an earthly court, but repented, repentance and the Day of Atonement suspend [the punishment], and suffering on the other days of the year will wipe away [the sin],

B. "since it says, 'Then will I visit their transgression with a rod' (Ps. 89:32).

C. "But he through whom the Name of Heaven is profaned deliberately but who repented – repentance does not have power to suspend [the punishment], nor the Day of Atonement to atone,

D. "but repentance and the Day of Atonement atone for a third, suffering atones for a third, and death wipes away the sin, with suffering,

E. "and on such a matter it is said, 'Surely this iniquity shall not be purged from you until you die' " (Is. 22:14).

The four kinds of atonement are worked out in their own systematic and logical terms, but the verses of Scripture contribute to the validation of the classification-scheme. There is a grid established by positive and negative commandments, intersecting with the matter of repentance; then there is the grid established by the kind of penalty – extirpation or the earthly court's death sentence (here repentance and the Day of Atonement form the intersecting grid); and then there is the matter of the profanation of the divine name, in which case repentance and the Day of Atonement come into play along with suffering and death. So the point of differentiation is established by appeal to the type of sin, on the one side, and the pertinent penalties and the effects of media of atonement – repentance, death, Day of Atonement, suffering – on the other. The entire complex exhibits the traits of mind that we have met many times: systematic classification by indicative traits, an interest in balance, order, complementarity, and commensurate proportionality.

But here we come to an unanticipated fact, a moment in man's relationship to God at which man's intentionality is null. God's mercy so exceeds man's just deserts that one's intention as to atonement may or may not affect the actuality of atonement. In the case of one's violation of a positive commandment, even if one did not repent and so conform to the correct intentionality, the Day of Atonement – on its own, by divine decree, as an act of supererogatory mercy utterly unrelated to considerations of justice, accomplishes the atonement. But as to negative commandments that one has deliberately violated, the Day of Atonement atones only if the sinner repents:

YERUSHALMI-TRACTATE YOMA 8:7 I:I

A. As to violation of a positive commandment, [the Day of Atonement effects atonement] even if the person did not repent.
B. As to violation of a negative commandment –
C. R. Samuel in the name of R. Zeira: "[The Day of Atonement effects atonement] only if the person repented [of violating the negative commandment]."

If one denies the power of the burnt-offering to effect atonement, nonetheless, his attitude is null, and the offering effects atonement *ex opere operato*:

I:2 A. He who states, "The burnt-offering does not effect atonement, the burnt-offering does not effect atonement for me" –
B. the burnt-offering effects atonement for him.

But if he declared that he did not want the burnt offering to effect atonement for him in particular, then the offering is null:

C. [If he said,] "I do not want [the burnt-offering] to effect atonement for me," it does not effect atonement for him against his will.

The same pattern is repeated for other media of atonement, beginning with the Day of Atonement:

D. [If he said,] "The Day of Atonement does not effect atonement," the Day of Atonement effects atonement.

E. [If he said,] "I do not want it to effect atonement for me," it effects atonement for him against his will.

F. [Y. Shebu. 1:6 adds:] As to an offering, whether he said, "I do not believe that this offering effects atonement," or, "that it effects atonement for me," or if he said, "I know it does effect atonement, but I do not want it to effect atonement for me," in all of these cases, it does not effect atonement against his will.

The analysis of these positions shows what is at stake: the power of the Day of Atonement to accomplish atonement without regard to the intentionality of those affected by it:

G. Said R. Haninah b. R. Hillel, "Is it not logical that the rule should be just the opposite? [In the case of an offering, whatever the man said, he did indeed bring an offering. But as to the Day of Atonement, if he said that he did not want it to effect atonement for him, it should not effect atonement for him.]"

H. Does someone say to a king, "You are not a king"? [Surely not. So whatever the man says, the Day of Atonement does effect atonement.]

Why the burnt-offering does not prove effective if one rejects its effects upon his situation is now spelled out:

I:3 A. The burnt-offering effects atonement for the murmurings of one's heart.

B. What is the scriptural basis for that statement?

C. "What is in your mind shall never happen" (Ezek. 20:32).

D. Said R. Levi, "The burnt-offering effects atonement for what is in your mind, and so Job states, 'And when the days of the feast had run their course, Job would send and sanctify them, and he would rise early in the morning and offer burnt-offerings according to the number of them all; for Job said, "It may be that my sons have sinned, and cursed God in their hearts." Thus Job did continually' (Job 1:5). This indicates that the burnt-offering effects atonement for the murmurings of the heart."

A further qualification now affects what has already been said, namely, the power of the Day of Atonement to work *ex opere operato*. That is nearly total:

I:4 A Rabbi says, "For all transgressions which are listed in the Torah the Day of Atonement effects atonement, except for the one who totally breaks the yoke [of Heaven] off of him, who removes the signs of the covenant, or who behaves presumptuously against the Torah.

B. "For if such a person does repent, then atonement is effected for him, but if not, it is not effected for him."

C. R. Zebida said R. Yosé raised the question: "Does Rabbi truly maintain that [except for the specified cases] the Day of Atonement [otherwise] effects atonement without [the sinner's] repenting?"

D. R. Asian, R. Jonah, R. Ba, R. Hiyya in the name of R. Yohanan: "Rabbi concurs that the Day of Atonement does not effect atonement without an act of repentance. But one's death washes away sin without an act of repentance."

E. And so it has been taught: The day of one's death is tantamount to an act of repentance.

F. Who taught that statement? It was Rabbi.

G. Is this in line with that which we have learned there:

H. Death and the Day of Atonement effect atonement [only] with an act of repentance?

I. That teaching is not in accord with the position of Rabbi.

Facts do not effect outcomes, but what one wills – intentionality – does.

However, the Day of Atonement has its own autonomous power, unaffected by an individual's intentionality. An argument a fortiori suggests the opposite. When that view is challenged, the mode of argument is to appeal to a metaphor, in this case, the king. If one tells the king he is not king, he is still king. There are facts that stand in the face of the argument a fortiori. But when it comes to suspending the effects of the Day of Atonement, the condition of one's heart makes a difference, since the Day of Atonement serves only with repentance. So intentionality in general is null, but intentionality specifically with reference to the Day of Atonement is effective. Rabbi imposes a special rule having to do with someone outside the framework of the faith, who rejects the covenant and the Torah. Such a person is untouched by the Day of Atonement and its power, unless he repents and gives effect to that Day. The logic is, one who rejects the entire system gains no benefit, *ex opere operato*, from the system. He is bound by the logic of his own position. So, too, death is a universal solvent for the stain of sin.

The sages do recognize limits to the power of repentance and atonement. They recognize that, in the world order, atonement does not always accomplish its goals. for with genuinely evil persons repentance on its own may not suffice to accomplish atonement. Specifically, they recognize that genuinely wicked people may repent but not for long, or their repentance in the end proves incommensurate to the affront against God that they have committed. The process of repentance and atonement therefore works only in a limited way. In this doctrine they are able in yet another way to to account for the prosperity of the wicked.

THE FATHERS ACCORDING TO R. NATHAN XXXIX:V.I

XXXIX:V.I A. The repentance of genuinely wicked people suspends [their punishment], but the decree against them has been sealed.
B. The prosperity of the wicked in the end will go sour.
C. Dominion buries those that hold it.
D. Repentance suspends [punishment] and the Day of Atonement achieves atonement.
E. Repentance suspends [punishment] until the day of death, and the day of death atones, along with repentance.

The doctrine proves familiar from chapter 5. The wicked enjoy this world, getting their reward now, but they do not gain the life eternal of the world to come. The righteous suffer now, atoning for their sins through suffering, but they will have a still more abundant life in the world to come:

THE FATHERS ACCORDING TO R. NATHAN XXXIX:VII.I

A. They [immediately, in this world] pay off the reward owing to the wicked [for such good as they may do], while they credit to the righteous [the reward that is coming to them, but do not pay it off, rather paying them off in the world to come].
B. They pay off the reward owing to the wicked [in this world] as though they were people who had carried out the Torah ungrudgingly, in whom no fault had ever been found.
C. They credit to the righteous [the reward that is coming to them, but do not pay it off, rather paying them off in the world to come], as though they were people lacking all good traits.
D. They thus give a little bit to each party, with the bulk of the remainder laid up for them.

In these ways, the complementary doctrines of repentance and atonement are given nuance, fitting together with comparable doctrines to account for the condition of individuals in the here and now.

In theory, there ought to be no atonement for gossip and involuntary manslaughter, but the Torah has provided means of atonement, in a statement that we have already noted in another connection:

SONG OF SONGS RABBAH XLVIII:V.5

5. A. R. Simon in the name of R. Jonathan of Bet Gubrin: "For two matters there was no atonement, but the Torah has provided atonement for them, and these are they:
B. "Gossip and involuntary manslaughter."

The Torah, then, provides in the cult for even those who disrupt the community of Israel through slander and gossip. The community has to be protected from those who disturb its just order, but those who do so can atone for their sin in a process commencing with repentance.

So much for the individual Israelite. What about the community of Israel viewed whole? That all Israel may and should engage in acts of repentance and atonement hardly requires articulation; it is taken for granted in every discussion of the Day of Atonement, which speaks of the community as much as of the private person. So from the individual sinner, the Israelite, we take up that other category of world order, the whole of holy Israel. If God's mercy for the individual sinner vastly outweighs the guilt of the sinner, then all the more so does God treat Israel with abundant mercy. God forgives Israel sins that vastly exceed those of the gentiles.

Adam found no fault with God, even though he paid for his sin; Adam accepted the justice of God's decree. But, as we shall see, Israel found fault with God. Yet God forgave them. That pattern, repeatedly embodied in cases, shows the full extent of God's capacity to forgive Israel and promises the result of Israel's repentance, when it comes about:

PESIQTA DERAB KAHANA XIV:V.I

A. It is written, "Thus said the Lord, What wrong did your fathers find in me that they went far from me and went after worthlessness and became worthless?" (Jer. 2:5)

B. Said R. Isaac, "This refers to one who leaves the scroll of the Torah and departs. Concerning him, Scripture says, "What wrong did your fathers find in me that they went far from me?"

C. "Said the Holy One, blessed be He, to the Israelites, 'My children, your fathers found no wrong with me, but you have found wrong with me.'"

Adam comes first:

D. "'The first Man found no wrong with me, but you have found wrong with me.'

E. "To what may the first Man be compared?

F. "To a sick man, to whom the physician came. The physician said to him, 'Eat this, don't eat that.'

G. "When the man violated the instructions of the physician, he brought about his own death.

H. "[As he lay dying,] his relatives came to him and said to him, 'Is it possible that the physician is imposing on you the divine attribute of justice?'

I. "He said to them, 'God forbid. I am the one who brought about my own death. This is what he instructed me, saying to me, 'Eat this, don't eat that,' but when I violated his instructions, I brought about my own death.'"

Adam bears responsibility for Adam but also serves as model for mankind:

J. "So too all the generations came to the first Man, saying to him, 'Is it possible that the Holy One, blessed be He, is imposing the attribute of justice on you?'

L. "He said to them, 'God forbid. I am the one who has brought about my own death. Thus did he command me, saying to me, 'Of all the trees of the garden you may eat, but of the tree of the knowledge of good and evil you may not eat' (Gen. 2:17). When I violated his instructions, I brought about my own death, for it is written, 'On the day on which you eat it, you will surely die'" (Gen. 2:17).

Pharaoh, Israel's enemy, affirmed the justice of God's decree, a model for Israel:

M. "[God's speech now continues:] 'Pharaoh found no wrong with me, but you have found wrong with me.'"

A parable realizes the allegation:

N. "To what may Pharaoh be likened?

O. "To the case of a king who went overseas and went and deposited all his possessions with a member of his household. After some time the king returned from overseas and said to the man, 'Return what I deposited with you.'

P. "He said to him, 'I did not such thing with you, and you left me nothing.'

Q. "What did he do to him? He took him and put him in prison.

R. "He said to him, 'I am your slave. Whatever you left with me I shall make up to you.'

S. "So, at the outset, said the Holy One, blessed be He, to Moses, 'Now go and I shall send you to Pharaoh' (Ex. 3:10).

T. "That wicked man said to him, 'Who is the Lord that I should listen to his voice? I do not know the Lord' (Ex. 2:5).

U. "But when he brought the ten plagues on him, 'The Lord is righteous and I and my people are wicked'" (Ex. 9:27).

So, too, Pharaoh's opposite and nemesis, Moses, accepted the justice of God's decree:

V. "[God's speech now continues:] 'Moses found no wrong with me, but you have found wrong with me.' "

Once more, a parable serves to embody the proposition:

W. "To what may Moses be compared?
X. "To a king who handed his son over to a teacher, saying to him, 'Do not call my son a moron.'
AA. [Resuming the discourse:] "One time the teacher belittled the boy and called him a moron. Said the king to him, 'With all my authority I instructed you, saying to you, Do not call my son a fool,' and yet you have called my son a fool. It is not the calling of a smart fellow to go along with fools. ['You're fired!']
BB. "Thus it is written, 'And the Lord spoke to Moses and to Aaron and commanded them concerning the children of Israel' (Ex. 6:13).
CC. "What did he command them? He said to them, 'Do not call my sons morons.' But when they rebelled them at the waters of rebellion, Moses said to them, 'Listen, I ask, you morons' (Num. 20:10).
DD. "Said the Holy One, blessed be He, to them, 'With all my authority I instructed you, saying to you, Do not call my sons fools,' and yet you have called my sons fools. It is not the calling of a smart fellow to go along with fools. ['You're fired!']
EE. "Therefore, what is written is not 'You [singular] therefore shall not bring, but you [plural] therefore shall not bring' (Num. 20:12). [For God said,] 'Neither you nor your brother nor your sister will enter the Land of Israel.' "

So no one found fault with God, but Israel has found fault with God, and, nonetheless, God forgave them:

FF. "[God's speech now continues:] Said the Holy One, blessed be He, to Israel, 'Your fathers in the wilderness found no wrong with me, but you have found wrong with me.'
GG. "I said to them, 'One who makes an offering to other gods will be utterly destroyed' (Ex. 22:19), but they did not do so, but rather, 'They prostrated themselves to it and worshipped it' (Ex. 32:8).
HH. "After all the wicked things that they did, what is written, 'And the Lord regretted the evil that he had considered doing to his people' " (Ex. 32:14).

The proposition concerning Israel – only Israel found fault with God – yields a still more consequential one, concerning God's mercy. If we juxtapose Adam, Pharaoh, and Moses, with no further explanation, we are not compelled to reach the conclusion at hand, and the elaborate amplification of each entry underscores that only by selecting appropriate details of the repertoire associated with each category do we attain our goal. This means that the juxtaposition of native categories on its own does not supply the rule that yields the (systemically) intelligible proposition at hand.

Now, to move forward: any discussion involving the community of Israel draws in its wake Israel's antonym, the gentiles, that is, the other component of humanity viewed whole. Surely, the nations of the world lay claim to a place in the process of reconciliation! But their condition is defined not by particular acts of rebellion against God, for example, gossip or transgression of other laws of the Torah, but rather by the condition of idolatry, an act of rebellion that transcends all details. And to overcome their condition, the gentiles have to give up idolatry and accept the Torah, the statement of God's will. Short of doing so, no repentance is possible, no atonement even relevant. That basic definition of the gentiles, which we examined in chapters 3 and 4, explains why, in being accorded the opportunity for repentance, Israel gains a role in shaping the destiny of the cosmos; in being denied that opportunity (except so far as they give up their idols and become Israel), the nations remain bystanders to the drama of creation.

Quite naturally, therefore, the nations raise the question of why Israel should be forgiven by the Day of Atonement when they do not enjoy the same advantage. The nations of the world indict Israel for committing the same sins that the nations practise and then escaping the consequences through the Day of Atonement:

LEVITICUS RABBAH XXI:IV.I

A. Rabbis interpret [the intersecting] verse ["The Lord is my light and my salvation; whom shall I fear? [The Lord is the stronghold of my life; of whom shall I be afraid?]" (Ps. 27:1) to speak of the New Year and Day of Atonement:

B. " 'My light' (Ps. 27:1) is on the New Year.

C. " 'And my salvation' (Ps. 27:1) is on the Day of Atonement.

D. " 'Whom shall I fear' (Ps. 27:1): 'The Lord is my strength and my song' [Ex. 15:2].

E. " 'When evildoers come near me' (Ps. 27:2) refers to the princes [of heaven] who represent the nations of the world."

As a matter of fact, Israel in ordinary life is neither better than nor different from the nations. In committing the cardinal, absolute sins of murder, fornication, and idolatry, Israel rebels against God. But Israel repents and atones through the act of repentance and the Day of Atonement, so these affect atonement for Israel, while the gentiles are excluded. Why is this so?

F. " 'To eat my flesh' (Ps. 27:2): For the princes representing the nations of the world come and draw an indictment against Israel before the Holy One, blessed be he, saying before him, 'Lord of the world, these [nations] practise idolatry and those [Jews] practise idolatry. These practise fornication and those practise fornication. These shed blood and those shed blood. Why then do these [nations of the world] go down to Gehenna and those do not go down?

G. " 'My adversaries and foes' (Ps. 27:2): You find that the number of days in the solar year are three hundred sixty-five, but the number of names of Satan are three hundred and sixty-four.

H. "For on all the days of the year, Satan is able to draw up an indictment, but on the Day of Atonement, Satan is not able to draw up an indictment.

I. "Said the Israelites before the Holy One, blessed be he, 'Though a host encamp against me' – the host of the nations of the world,

J. " 'My heart shall not fear' (Ps. 27:3).

K. " 'Though war arise against me' – the war of the nations of the world.

L. " 'In this I shall trust' (Ps. 27:3).

M. "In this which you have promised me: 'With this will Aaron come' (Lev. 16:3) [on the Day of Atonement]."

The Day of Atonement is transformed into the occasion for an act of trust, so that, with the Day of Atonement, Israel is accorded atonement despite its actions during the rest of the year. The nations of the world, enemies of Israel, on that day cannot send their paraclete against Israel.

Gentiles, estranged from God by idolatry, gain no benefit from the heritage of unearned grace that the saints of Israel leave to Israel. We already have noted that there are other means of repentance and atonement besides the Day of Atonement. Deemed comparable to sacrifices, for example, is the death of the righteous or of sages, and these, too, accrue to Israel's advantage. But again, gentiles with their idolatry cannot participate, and so they have no role in the coming restoration, no task to perform:

YERUSHALMI-TRACTATE YOMA I:I I:2

[FF] In the view of R. Yohanan, why is the death of the sons of Aaron called to mind in this context, for they died only in the setting of the rite of consecration?

[GG] Said R. Hiyya bar Ba, "The sons of Aaron died on the first day of Nisan. And why is their death called to mind in connection with the Day of Atonement?

[HH] "It is to indicate to you that just as the Day of Atonement effects expiation for Israel, so the death of the righteous effects atonement for Israel."

The same pertains to the death of Miriam and the death of Aaron:

[II] Said R. Ba bar Binah, "Why did the Scripture place the story of the death of Miriam side by side with the story of the burning of the red cow?

[JJ] "It is to teach you that just as the dirt of the red cow [mixed with water] effects atonement for Israel, so the death of the righteous effects atonement for Israel."

[KK] Said R. Yudan b. Shalom, "Why did the Scripture set the story of the death of Aaron side by side with the story of the breaking of the tablets?

[LL] "It is to teach you that the death of the righteous is as grievous before the Holy One, blessed be he, as the breaking of the tablets."

None of this pertains to gentiles, excluded as they are by their own decision to reject the Torah.

The Temple, uniquely Israel's in the process of repentance and atonement, figures in yet another way. Song too constitutes a form of atonement, and the Song takes place in the Temple, once more omitting reference to the gentiles:

YERUSHALMI-TRACTATE TAANIT 4:2 II.3

[L] How do we know that the song [in the Temple] is called a form of atonement?

[M] Hinena. father of Bar Netah, in the name of R. Benaiah: " 'To make atonement for the people of Israel' – this refers to the song.

[N] How do we know that the song is indispensable [to the cult]?

[O] R. Jacob bar Aha, R. Bulatah in the name of R. Hinena: " 'To make atonement for the people of Israel' – this refers to the song.' "

We recall that the garments that the high priest wears on the Day of Atonement also signify, and effect, atonement, as we noted in chapter 8 (at Leviticus Rabbah X:VI.1). The upshot is, just as the will of man, initially of Adam but then localized in Israel, disrupts the world order and stands against the will of God, so God responds to the regeneration of that will in acts of repentance and atonement only as these are carried out by Israel.

Clearly, then, what is at stake in repentance and atonement vastly transcends issues of this world. Time and again we have noted that repentance, along with atonement, forms the condition of the restoration of world order. Even in the here and now, Israel is able through repentance to reconcile itself with God, and in God's own time, the reconciliation – Israel's will now voluntarily conforming to God's word – will mark the end of the world as man knows it and the beginning of the time of restoration. That is why repentance forms the bridge between the analysis of the imperfection of world order and the account of the restoration of world order at the last. In so many words repentance is linked to the salvation of the individual Israelite and the redemption of Israel, for these mark the return to Eden.

And so we find, as I surmised earlier, that repentance is required if one is to be resurrected at the end of time and gain a portion in the world to come:

Y. SHEBBIIT 4:10 VI

[TRANSLATION BY ALAN J. AVERY-PECK]

A. Said R. Jonah in the name of R. Hama bar Hanina, "One who dies during the seven year [battle of] Gog [Ezekiel 38–9] [so as not to suffer fully the troubles of the nation] does not have a portion in the coming world.

B. "The mnemonic sign for this is: 'One who takes part in the wedding preliminaries will [also] have a share in the wedding feast.' " [But whoever is not involved in the preliminaries does not have a part in the feast.]

C. R. Yosé heard [this] and said, "Now, is this really true?

D. "[For] there is always repentance [as a method of earning a place in] the world to come." [This applies even if the individual has not suffered along with the Israelite nation.]

The act of repentance, then, serves to secure the victory over death represented by resurrection and consequent entry into the world to come – a considerable result.

Once we ask about how repentance forms a principal requirement for the restoration of life over death, in resurrection, and the restoration of Israel over its condition of exile and alienation, we turn to the place of repentance in the end of the world as it now is. We begin with the figure of the Messiah, an important motif in all discussions of matters of eschatology: the resurrection of the dead, the advent of the world or age to come. We already realize that Israel's repentance is a precondition for salvation, hence for the coming of the Messiah. We should not find surprising, then, that the characterization of the Messiah should stress his humility, as much as claim that the promise of his coming to raise the dead should rest upon Israel's conduct as well.

For the theology of the Oral Torah delivers in diverse ways its single, fundamental messages concerning world order attained through humility before God. In the present instance, the theology takes up the Messiah-theme to make its statement. It says that the true Messiah will be humble and the false

Messiah will be marked as false by his arrogance towards God. What we already have learned about repentance in the Oral Torah has made inevitable – indeed urgent – that very odd juxtaposition, the contrapuntal relationship of arrogance and repentance, sinfulness and reconciliation. Here is how the false Messiah shows why he cannot save Israel, and, in so many words, it is because of his blasphemous arrogance:

LAMENTATIONS RABBAH LVIII:II.8FF.

4. A. Rabbi would interpret the verse, "There shall come forth a star out of Jacob" (Num. 24:17) in this way: "Do not read the letters of the word for 'star' as 'star' but as 'deceit.'"

5. A. When R. Aqiba saw Bar Koziba, he said, "This is the royal messiah."

B. R. Yohanan b. Torta said to him, "Aqiba, grass will grow from your cheeks and he will still not have come."

We are now told why Aqiba is wrong. He accepted as Messiah the general who led the Jewish rebellion against Rome in 132–35 C.E.:

7. A. Eighty thousand trumpeters besieged Betar. There Bar Koziba was encamped, with two hundred thousand men with an amputated finger.

B. Sages sent word to him, saying, "How long are you going to produce blemished men in Israel?"

C. He said to them, "And what shall I do to examine them [to see whether or not they are brave]?"

D. They said to him, "Whoever cannot uproot a cedar of Lebanon do not enroll in your army."

E. He had two hundred thousand men of each sort [half with an amputated finger, half proved by uprooting a cedar].

Now comes the explicit statement of the false Messiah's arrogance towards Heaven:

8. A. When they went out to battle, he would say, "Lord of all ages, don't help us and don't hinder us!"

B. That is in line with this verse: "Have you not, O God, cast us off? And do not go forth, O God, with our hosts" (Ps. 60:12).

It would be difficult to find a passage more directly opposed to the sages' fundamental theological convictions than Bar Kokhba's explicit rejection of God's help in favour of his own strength.

A separate story underscores the unsuitable character of this particular Messiah, namely, the mark of arrogance represented by temper. Losing one's temper is a mark of arrogance towards Heaven, and here Bar Kokhba does just that:

10. A. For three and a half years Hadrian besieged Betar.

B. R. Eleazar the Modiite was sitting in sack cloth and ashes, praying, and saying, "Lord of all the ages, do not sit in judgment today, do not sit in judgment today."

C. Since [Hadrian] could not conquer the place, he considered going home.

D. There was with him a Samaritan, who said to him, "My lord, as long as that old cock wallows in ashes, you will not conquer the city.

E. "But be patient, and I shall do something so you can conquer it today."

The first act is one of gossip:

F. He went into the gate of the city and found R. Eleazar standing in prayer.

G. He pretended to whisper something into his ear, but the other paid no attention to him.

From slander the conspiracy turns to false witness, taking God's name in vain:

H. People went and told Bar Koziba, "Your friend wants to betray the city."

I. He sent and summoned the Samaritan and said to him, "What did you say to him?"

J. He said to him, "If I say, Caesar will kill me, and if not, you will kill me. Best that I kill myself and not betray state secrets."

The false Messiah proved a false judge as well, rejecting even the testimony in his hands and the plea of the honest sage:

K. Nonetheless, Bar Koziba reached the conclusion that he wanted to betray the city.

L. When R. Eleazar had finished his prayer, he sent and summoned him, saying to him, "What did this one say to you?"

M. He said to him, "I never saw that man."

N. He kicked him and killed him.

O. At that moment an echo proclaimed: "Woe to the worthless shepherd who leaves the flock, the sword shall be upon his arm and upon his right eye" (Zech. 11:17).

P. Said the Holy One, blessed be He, "You have broken the right army of Israel and blinded their right eye. Therefore your arm will wither and your eye grow dark."

Q. Forthwith Betar was conquered and Ben Koziba was killed.

That God has responded to the arrogance of the Messiah is now underscored. On his own, Hadrian could have accomplished nothing. It was God who killed the Messiah, not Hadrian:

R. They went, carrying his head to Hadrian. He said, "Who killed this one?"

S. They said, "One of the Goths killed him," but he did not believe them.

T. He said to them, "Go and bring me his body."

U. They went to bring his body and found a snake around the neck.

V. He said, "If the God of this one had not killed him, who could have vanquished him?"

W. That illustrates the following verse of Scripture: "If their Rock had not given them over" (Deut. 32:30).

The same attitude is set forth in a further story of the arrogance of the army of the Messiah, which repeated the Messiah's plea to heaven, Let him not help us nor hinder us, and which was defeated not by Hadrian's army but by God:

19. A. There were two brothers in Kefar Haruba, and no Roman could pass by there, for they killed him.

B. They decided, "The whole point of the thing is that we must take the crown and put it on our head and make ourselves kings."

C. They heard that the Romans were coming to fight them.

D. They went out to do battle, and an old man met them and said, "May the Creator be your help against them."

E. They said, "Let him not help us nor hinder us!"

F. Because of their sins, they went forth and were killed.

G. They went, carrying his head to Hadrian. He said, "Who killed this one?"

H. They said, "One of the Goths killed him," but he did not believe them.

I. He said to them, "Go and bring me his body."

J. They went to bring his body and found a snake around the neck.

K. He said, "If the God of this one had not killed him, who could have vanquished him?"

L. That illustrates the following verse of Scripture: "If their Rock had not given them over" (Deut. 32:30).

Arrogance towards God, rather than repentance and remorse, thus characterizes the false Messiah. If Israel wants to bring about the restoration, whether the individual to life or Israel to the Land, it must accomplish repentance.

That view is expressed in the statement that, when Israel really wants the Messiah to come, he will come. But we are now aware of the special weight attached to the words "want" or "will." What Israel must want is only what God wants. What Israel must do is give up any notion of accomplishing on its own, by its own act of will, the work of redemption. It is only through the self-abnegation of repentance that Israel can accomplish its goal. Specifically, when Israel's will conforms to the will of God, then God will respond to the act of repentance by bringing about the time of restoration and eternal life. This is expressed in a colloquy that announces that the Messiah will come when all Israel keeps a single Sabbath. And that will take place when Israel wants it to take place. It requires only an act of will on the part of Israel to accept one of the Ten Commandments. Then, in a broader restatement of matters, the entire redemptive process is made to depend upon Israel's repentance:

YERUSHALMI-TRACTATE TAANIT I:I II:5

G. The Israelites said to Isaiah, "O our Rabbi, Isaiah, What will come for us out of this night?"

H. He said to them, "Wait for me, until I can present the question."

I. Once he had asked the question, he came back to them.

J. They said to him, "Watchman, what of the night? What did the Guardian of the ages say [a play on 'of the night' and 'say']?"

K. He said to them, "The watchman says: 'Morning comes; and also the night. [If you will inquire, inquire; come back again]' " (Is. 21:12).

L. They said to him, "Also the night?"

M. He said to them, "It is not what you are thinking. But there will be morning for the righteous, and night for the wicked, morning for Israel, and night for idolaters."

Now comes the main point in the exchange: when will this happen? It will happen when Israel wants. And what is standing in the way is Israel's arrogance, to be atoned for by Israel's remorseful repentance:

N. They said to him, "When?"

O. He said to them, "Whenever you want, He too wants [it to be] – if you want it, he wants it."

P. They said to him, "What is standing in the way?"

Q. He said to them, "Repentance: 'come back again' " (Is. 21:12).

This is stated in the clearest possible way: one day will do it.

R. R. Aha in the name of R. Tanhum b. R. Hiyya, "If Israel repents for one day, forthwith the son of David will come.

S. "What is the scriptural basis? 'O that today you would hearken to his voice!' "
(Ps. 95:7).

Now comes the introduction of the Sabbath as a test case:

T. Said R Levi, "If Israel would keep a single Sabbath in the proper way, forthwith the son of David will come.
U. "What is the scriptural basis for this view? 'Moses said, Eat it today, for today is a Sabbath to the Lord; [today you will not find it in the field]' (Ex. 16:25).
V. "And it says, '[For thus said the Lord God, the Holy One of Israel], 'In returning and rest you shall be saved; [in quietness and in trust shall be your strength.' And you would not]' " (Is. 30:15). By means of returning and [Sabbath] rest you will be redeemed.

The main point, then, is the linkage of repentance to the coming restoration of Israel to the Land, the dead to life, by the Messiah. But the advent of the Messiah depends wholly upon Israel's will. If Israel will subordinate its will to God's, all else will follow. The Sabbath is the key to Eden.

We recall that, to hasten Israel's repentance, God promises to abrogate those conditions of prosperity that bring about excessive confidence in one's own power and therefore nurture arrogance. The Messiah will come when all Israel will keep a single Sabbath. The matter therefore depends upon Israel's own conduct, which expresses Israel's attitude and will. What is required is repentance, an act of humility that removes the consequences of arrogance. The tribulations that accompany the Messiah are placed into the context of Israel's conduct, rather than world history, and the point appears to be, if Israel suffers, it will repent, and when it repents, God will respond with love and bring the age to come. Accordingly, the Messiah will come at the right time, which is when Israel is in greatest need of his advent. The pre-conditions for the coming of the Messiah, God's response to Israel's repentance, are described variously, and the calculations to decipher events prove even more diverse. But the generative conviction that repentance and that alone will bring about the restoration accounts for the systematic speculation on the tribulations that will accompany the advent of the Messiah:

BAVLI-TRACTATE SANHEDRIN 11:1 1.81–2,
87, 90–2, 97/96B–97A

I.81 A. Said R. Nahman to R. Isaac, "Have you heard when the son of 'the fallen one' will come?"
B. He said to him, "Who is the son of 'the fallen one'?"
C. He said to him, "It is the Messiah."

D. "Do you call the Messiah 'the son of the fallen one'?"

E. He said to him, "Yes, for it is written, 'On that day I will raise up [97A] the tabernacle of David, the fallen one'" (Amos 9:11).

A mark of tribulation will be the suffering of the sages, among all Israel.

F. He said to him, "This is what R. Yohanan said, 'The generation to which the son of David will come will be one in which disciples of sages grow fewer,

G. "'and, as to the others, their eyes will wear out through suffering and sighing,

H. "'and troubles will be many, and laws harsh, forever renewing themselves so that the new one will hasten onward before the old one has come to an end.'"

The world of nature will conspire to bring Israelite repentance:

I.82 A. Our rabbis have taught on Tannaite authority:

B. The seven-year cycle in which the son of David will come:

C. As to the first one, the following verse of Scripture will be fulfilled: "And I will cause it to rain upon one city and not upon another" (Amos 4:7).

D. As to the second year, the arrows of famine will be sent forth.

E. As to the third, there will be a great famine, in which men, women, and children will die, pious men and wonder-workers alike, and the Torah will be forgotten by those that study it.

F. As to the fourth year, there will be plenty which is no plenty.

G. As to the fifth year, there will be great prosperity, and people will eat, drink, and rejoice, and the Torah will be restored to those that study it.

H. As to the sixth year, there will be rumours.

I. As to the seventh year, there will be wars.

J. As to the end of the seventh year [the eighth year], the son of David will come.

K. Said R. Joseph, "Lo, how many seven-year cycles have passed like that one, and yet he has not come."

L. Said Abbayye, "Were there rumours in the sixth year and wars in the seventh year? And furthermore, did they come in the right order?"

Israel's own situation will reach the nadir, with few disciples, no cash, and many traitors; people will give up hope of redemption. Then, in a state of desperation, they may repent:

I.87 A. Our rabbis have taught on Tannaite authority:

B. "For the Lord shall judge his people and repent himself of his servants, when he sees that their power has gone, and there is none shut up or left" (Deut. 32:36).

C. The son of David will come only when traitors are many.

D. Another matter: Only when disciples are few.

E. Another matter: Only when a penny will not be found in anyone's pocket.

F. Another matter: Only when people will have given up hope of redemption, as it is said, "There is none shut up or left" (Deut. 32:36), as it were, when there is none [God being absent] who supports and helps Israel.

G. That accords with the statement of R. Zira, who, when he would find rabbis involved in [figuring out when the Messiah would come], would say to them, "By your leave, I ask you not to put it off.

H. "For we have learned on Tannaite authority: Three things come on the spur of the moment, and these are they: the Messiah, a lost object, and a scorpion."

Above all, the arrogant will die out in Israel, and that is the point at which repentance can take place for the entire community of Israel:

I.97 A. Said R. Hanina, "The son of David will come only when a fish will be sought for a sick person and not be found, as it is said, 'Then I will make their waters deep and cause their rivers to run like oil' (Ez. 32:14), and it is written, 'In that day I will cause the horn of the house of Israel to sprout forth' " (Ez. 29:21).

B. Said R. Hama bar Hanina, "The son of David will come only when the rule over Israel by the least of the kingdoms will come to an end, as it is said, 'He shall both cut off the springs with pruning hooks and take away and cut down the branches' (Is. 18:5), and further: 'In that time shall the present be brought o the Lord of hosts of a people that is scattered and peeled' " (Is. 18:7).

In constructions on when the Messiah comes, the issue of arrogance arises quite regularly, and in the next two entries it is explicit:

C. Said Zeiri said R. Hanina, "The son of David will come only when arrogant people will no longer be [found] in Israel, as it is said, 'For then I will take away out of the midst of you those who rejoice in your pride' (Zeph. 8:11), followed by: 'I will also leave in the midst of you an afflicted and poor people, and they shall take refuge in the name of the Lord' " (Zeph. 3:12).

D. Said R. Simlai in the name of R. Eliezer b. R. Simeon, "The son of David will come only when all judges and rulers come to an end in Israel, as it is said, 'And I will turn my hand upon you and purely purge away your dross and take away all your tin, and I will restore your judges as at the first' " (Is. 1:25–6).

Clearly, little thought about the resolution of the crisis in which Israel finds itself takes place without addressing the issue of repentance, and that issue is commonly framed in terms of arrogance. These formulations express in detail the principal theological doctrine that relates world order to the struggle of God's and Israel's conflicting wills.

But God's other paramount trait, mercy, complementing his justice, will then make its entry. Consistent with the emphasis on the tribulations that will bring about repentance and consequent redemption, a necessary doctrine of God's mercy is restated in this very context. It is that God will ultimately forgive Israel when Israel throws itself on God's mercy. Israel's repentance will assuredly evoke God's response of mercy and forbearance, which is to say, an equal and balanced response:

BAVLI-TRACTATE SHABBAT 9:3–4 II.2–3

II.2 A. Raba expounded, "What is the meaning of this verse of Scripture: 'Go now and let us reason together, shall the Lord say' (Isa. 1:18)? Instead of 'go' what is required is 'come.'

B. "In the time to come the Holy One, blessed be He, will say to Israel, 'Go to your fathers and they will rebuke you.'

C. "And they shall say to him, 'Lord of the world, to whom shall we go? Should it be to Abraham, to whom you said, "Know for sure that your seed shall be a stranger ... and they shall afflict them" (Gen. 15:23) – and he didn't seek mercy for us? To Isaac, who blessed Esau, "And it shall come to pass that when you shall have dominion" (Gen. 27:40), and yet he did not seek mercy for us? To Jacob, to whom you said, "I will go down with you to Egypt" (Gen. 46:4), and he didn't ask for mercy for us? So to whom shall we go now? Rather let the Lord say!'

D. "The Holy One, blessed be He, will say to them, 'Since you have thrown yourselves on me, "though your sins be as scarlet, they shall be as white as snow"'" (Isa. 1:18).

In the end, even the grace accruing to the patriarchs will not suffice to save Israel, only their return to God will redeem them. But trusting in God will surely serve. We now go over the same matter in a more elaborate statement:

II.3 A. Said R. Samuel bar Nahmani said R. Jonathan, "What is the meaning of the verse of Scripture: 'For you are our father, though Abraham doesn't know us, and Israel doesn't acknowledge us, you Lord are our father, our redeemer, from everlasting is your name'" (Isa. 63:16)?

The formulation, recalling how the saints live in a single plane of time and communicate with one another over eternity, has a dialogue between God, Abraham, Isaac, and Jacob:

B. "In the time to come the Holy One, blessed be He, will say to Abraham, 'Your children have sinned against me.' He will answer him, 'Lord of the world, let them be wiped out for the sake of the sanctification of your name.'"

So implacable an answer cannot serve, and God cannot accept it:

C. "And he will say, 'So I'll go and say this to Jacob, who went through the pain in raising children, maybe he'll ask for mercy for them.' So he will say to Jacob, 'Your children have sinned against me.' He will answer him, 'Lord of the world, let them be wiped out for the sake of the sanctification of your name.'"

Jacob does not improve upon Abraham. Isaac then intervenes:

D. "He will say, 'There's no good sense in old men and no good counsel in young ones.' I'll go tell Isaac, 'Your children have sinned against me.' He will answer him, 'Lord of the world, are they my children and not your children? At the moment when they said to you first " 'we will do" and then "we will hearken," you called them "Israel, my son my firstborn" (Ex. 4:22). Now you're calling them my sons, not your sons! And furthermore, how much have they sinned, how many years does a man live? Seventy. Take off twenty for which you don't impose punishment [Num. 14:29: Those who rejected the gift of the land were punished from twenty years of age and upward], leaving fifty. Take off twenty-five that cover the nights, when people don't sin. Take off twelve and a half for praying, eating, and shitting – and all you've got is twelve and a half. So if you can take it, well and good, and if not, then let half be on me and half on you And if you should say, they all have to be on me, well, now, I offered myself up to you as a sacrifice.'
E. "They therefore open prayers saying, 'For you are our father.'"

Isaac now gives up the honour owing to him in favour of the honour owing to God, and Israel responds, turning to God:

F. "Then will Isaac say to them, 'Instead of praising me, praise the Holy One, blessed be He,' and Isaac will show them the Holy One, blessed be He, with their own eyes.
G. "On the spot they will raise up their eyes to the heavens and say, 'You Lord are our father our redeemer, from everlasting is your name'" (Isa. 63:16).

This statement presents in a somewhat odd way quite commonplace sentiments. By this point in our review of complex and disparate materials, we recognize the recurrence of the few and simple propositions concerning repentance, encompassing atonement that begins with repentance.

The theology delivers a few, simple messages, repeating them with great power of intricate variation but with little substantive change. That is because, as we have already noted, the sages adopt as their mode of thought the paradigmatic way of organizing and interpreting experience. They look for patterns that are simple but capable of sustaining endless applications, and they find in narrative and exegesis of narrative (whether of their own or more commonly of Scripture's stories) the ideal mode of making their statement. In this case, it is the story of how God created an orderly world but at the climax of creation made man, in his image, after his likeness.

Man both complemented and corresponded with God, and it was man's freedom, meaning his effective will and power of intentionality, that matched God's will. When these conflict, man's arrogance leads him to rebel against God, sin resulting. And from sin comes the imperfection of world order, change, inequity, imbalance. Punished and remorseful, man gives up his arrogant attitude and conforms his will to God's. God responds with mercy, freely accepting the reformation that is freely offered. Then world order is restored, that perfection effected at the outset is regained for Israel, which means, for God's part of mankind. Eden, now the Land of Israel, is recovered, Adam, now embodied in Israel, is restored to his place. For the Israelite, death dies, man rises from the grave to life eternal. For Israel, the gentiles' rule comes to an end, and Israel regains the Land. Repentance marks the recovery of the world as God wanted it to be, which is to say, the world in which Israel regains its promised place.

13 Restoring Private Lives: Resurrection

Throughout the Oral Torah the main point of the theological eschatology – the theory of last things – registers both negatively and affirmatively. Death does not mark the end of the individual human life, nor exile the last stop in the journey of holy Israel. Israelites will live in the age or the world to come, all Israel in the Land of Israel; and Israel will comprehend all who know the one true God. The restoration of world order that completes the demonstration of God's justice encompasses both private life and the domain of all Israel. For both, restorationist theology provides eternal life; to be Israel means to live. So far as the individual is concerned, beyond the grave, at a determinate moment, man rises from the grave in resurrection, is judged, and enjoys the world to come. For the entirety of Israel, congruently: all Israel participates in the resurrection, which takes place in the Land of Israel, and enters the world to come.

Restorationist eschatology flows from the same cogent logic that has dictated theological doctrine from the beginning of this systematic account. The last things are to be known from the first. In the just plan of creation, man was meant to live in Eden, and Israel in the Land of Israel in time without end. The restoration will bring about that long and tragically postponed perfection of the world order, sealing the demonstration of the justice of God's plan for creation. Risen from the dead, having atoned through death, as we just saw in chapter 12, man will be judged in accord with his deeds. Israel, for its part, when it repents and conforms its will to God's, recovers its Eden. So the consequences of rebellion and sin having been overcome, the struggle of man's will and God's word having been resolved, God's original plan will be realized at the last. The simple, global logic of the system, with its focus on the world order of justice established by God but disrupted by man, leads inexorably to this eschatology of restoration, the restoration of balance, order, proportion – eternity.

The two principal components of the Oral Torah's theology of last things – resurrection and judgment, the world to come and eternal life – as laid out in the several documents do not fit together seamlessly. In general, it would appear, the theology arranges matters in categorical sequence, individual, then community. First comes the resurrection of individuals, and, with it, judgment of individuals one by one. Then, those chosen for life having been identified, "the world to come" takes place, and that final restoration of perfection, involving all Israel in place of Adam, lasts forever. Israel forms the cohort of those chosen for life, and Israelites are restored to life in the Land of Israel. That sequence suggests a single, uninterrupted narrative of last things, while, in general, passages that concern themselves with resurrection do not ordinarily join together with composites that deal with the world to come. While mutually complementary, each of the two components of eschatology in the Oral Torah bears its distinctive focus. Before we proceed, let us consider a cogent statement of what is at stake in all eschatological thinking in the Oral Torah.

The absolute given, a logical necessity of a theology revealing God's justice, maintains that individual life goes forward from this world, past the grave, to the world to come, and people are both judged and promised eternal life. That is a necessary doctrine for a system that insists upon the rationality and order of the universe under God's rule. Chapter 5 has already adumbrated the urgency of resurrection; without judgment and eternal life for the righteous, this world's imbalance cannot be righted, nor can God's justice be revealed. Monotheism without an eschatology of judgment and the world to come leaves unresolved the tensions inherent in the starting point: God is one, God is just. That is why the starting point of the theology dictates its conclusion: the deeds one does in this world bear consequences for his situation in the world to come, and the merit attained through this-worldly-deeds, for example, of generosity, persists; individuals retain their status as such through all time to come.

We shall return to this matter in chapter 14, when we examine in its own terms the theology of the world to come. Here it suffices to note that the basic logic of the system requires the doctrine of personal resurrection, so that the life of this world may go onward to the next. Indeed, without the conception of life beyond the grave, the system as a whole yields a mass of contradictions and anomalies: injustice to the righteous, prosperity to the wicked, never recompensed. That explains why, at one point after another, the path to the future passes through, and beyond, the grave to – for all Israel with few exceptions – eternity. The principal continues and yields interest, or punishment may take place in this world, while eternal punishment goes onward as well, especially for the trilogy of absolute sins, idolatry, incest (or fornication), and murder, capped by gossip. But how all of this squares with the conception of "all Israel" that transcends individual Israelites remains to be seen.

A simple approach may address the logical relationship of the two components, the personal (Israel) and the public (Israelite). It derives from a duality on the reference-point of "Israel" that characterizes the organization of the theology of the Oral Torah and that already has served to clarify otherwise confused issues. We earlier have sorted matters out by noting that the word "Israel," sometimes refers to the entire community, the holy people, and other times speaks of the individual Israelite. That point of differentiation helped us to deal in an orderly way with the demonstration of God's justice: in chapter 3, with respect to Israel and the Torah; and in chapter 5, with respect to the private life of the Israelite.[1] True, the same principle, perfect justice, governs both components of the category Israel (as all components of the system throughout).

But each component requires articulation within its own framework. Indeed, what validated the subdivision of "Israel" was that when "Israel" in a composition stood for the individual Israelite, "Israel" as the holy people rarely intervened. But when a passage clearly referred to the entirety of "Israel," the people, the individual Israelite (except for saints such as Abraham), rarely played a role. So, too, sin characterizes the attitude of all Israel and of individual Israelites, and while sin bears a single meaning in both settings, rebellion, its specific valence requires articulation and definition particular to each. Similarly with repentance: a turning towards God would mark true remorse for the individual sinner and also for all Israel, and the requirement of collective, not only individual, repentance is explicit in the passages just now considered.

The two distinct foci of discourse tend to a certain concentricity. When the theology of the Dual Torah explains the imperfections of creation, the lapse of justice, it says the same thing about the two distinct categorical foci of discourse: the private and the public life. Recognizing that fact brings considerable clarity to the analysis of the evidence pertinent to the principal categories

---

1. Gentile individuals form part of the undifferentiated mass of idolators and only in special cases are judged otherwise, for example, the Generation of the Flood, the Generation of the Dispersion, the Men of Sodom, or truly wicked figures like Balaam, Amalek, Haman, and the like.

of theological discourse, whether justice or repentance. But this work has shown that the single, unitary message requires two quite separate modes of articulation, as a review of chapters 11 and 12 will quickly reveal. And that prepares the way for the work of the present chapter and the one to follow. Here we treat resurrection as a dimension of restoration to Eden in the private lives of Israelites, and in the next chapter we focus on the world to come as a dimension of restoration to Eden in the public life of Israel. So, when we examine the principal components of the doctrine of eschatology, which, in my reading, means the account of the ultimate restoration of creation to its initial perfection, we deal first with Israel meaning the Israelite and then with Israel meaning the people.

But why that order and, logically, no other? Built into the eschatological doctrine and its logic of a world ordered by justice is even the detail at hand: this sequence, no other. To explain why, we recall how God's justice governs even in the chaos of private life, despite the clear disruption brought about by dreadful actualities: the prosperous wicked, the penurious righteous, in all the many variations that the imperfect world presents. In Chapter 5 we addressed the theodicy that promises resurrection and eternal life in the world to come to those who live out their years in accord with God's will, even suffering here to expiate sin, so as to enjoy a sinless eternity. The doctrine of resurrection proved integral to, an absolute necessity for, the account of the world's justice as the sages recorded matters. Without the doctrine of resurrection for eternal life, the theology can have found no solution to the crisis of everyday life, which hardly confirms the logic of a system of a just order.

Now, within that framework, the righteous, who will stand in judgment and enter the world to come, must by definition encompass in their number not only those alive at the final moment of humanity's life beyond Eden but also all those who have ever lived. Otherwise, where is the order, the justice for the unnumbered ranks of the humble and virtuous who perished in poverty, knowing full well that the arrogant and wicked died after enjoying a long, satisfying, and nasty life? The promise of renewed life, forever, systematically accounted for the ultimate justice of existence, even for private lives. By definition, the world to come cannot commence without the presence of all who belong to the party of life. And that requirement explains why we follow the logical sequence, first, resurrection and judgment, then the world or the age to come and life eternal. There is no reversing the order, for obvious reasons built into the logic of the theology's basic premise and purpose. Let me state the matter negatively. Only with a complete loss of sense – omission of all those who have died before the end of days – can the world to come and life eternal take place prior to the resurrection of the dead. But in that case world order proves manifestly unjust. So the very explanation of the justice of world order dictates that matters be just so.

The identification of "Israel" as the Israelite as the focus of the eschatology in the chapter involving resurrection and judgment proves equally logical. "Israel" the holy people, by contrast, never dies. It is an enduring component of humanity, the part of humanity that knows God through God's own self-manifestation in the Torah, the sector of mankind that accepts the law of the Torah as the will of God. This Israel, integral to the perfection of creation, cannot die any more than God can. Thus, to Israel the people, resurrection categorically does not pertain.

True, judgment does. But, for Israel the people, judgment is not left to the end of days, when the dead will rise from their graves. For holy Israel, judgment takes place in this world and in this age. The Written Torah laid down the principle that Israel suffers for its sins, and everything that has happened since the closure of the Written Torah only confirms that principle. The very continuation of Scripture beyond the Pentateuch and the account of the inheritance of the Land makes that point, as we noted earlier. Not only so, but the very heart of the doctrine of paradigm against against historical time – the explanation of Israel's subjugation to the gentiles and their idolatry – carries within itself a profound statement about Israel's identity, its enduring presence, from this age to the world to come, without interruption. Israel is judged and suffers its punishment in the here and now. That conviction animates the entire theological system before us. Then that same Israel, the never-dying people, emerges in the world to come fully at one with God. Indeed, that is the meaning of the advent of the world to come: "today if all Israel will it," "today if all Israel keeps a single Sabbath." To Israel the holy people, the resurrection of the dead therefore bears no categorical relevance. The advent of the world to come and eternal life bears its own meaning for Israel the holy people, as we shall see in Chapter 14. To Israel the Israelite, the resurrection of the dead forms the beginning of the restoration of Eden, now meaning the restoration of Israel to the Land of Israel, as we have noted many times. In this way the somewhat confusing components of the theory of last things sort themselves out.

As it happens, the documents of the Oral Torah tend to sustain the distinction just now set forth. The sources that deal with resurrection rarely refer to the world to come, except as an ordinal consequence of resurrection. And when it comes to speak of resurrection, the Oral Torah rarely speaks of holy Israel, but nearly always addresses Israel the Israelite. Along these same lines, gentiles occur only as a collectivity, non-Israel, and rarely as individuals, except in a special case of a gentile who had a special relationship with

Israel, such as Balaam. Nearly all proofs in the Talmud, for example, for the facticity of resurrection invoke the metaphor of individual, not collective life; even with the opportunity near at hand, in the very hermeneutics of the discourse, not a single one in the sizable exercise in Bavli-tractate Sanhedrin Chapter Eleven, which we shall examine below, points to the eternity of holy Israel as evidence, in Scripture, for the resurrection of the dead. Most cases, most analogies, most arguments appeal to the private person. And, concomitantly, the sources that address the world to come ordinarily refer to all Israel, speaking of the Israelite only in the setting of the beginning of the age that will not end. The Israelite is subsumed within, though never obliterated by, all Israel. To be sure, we shall note that the promise of "the life of the world to come" addresses individual Israelites, whose conduct dictates their ultimate destination; but implicit there is the intervention of the last judgment, which assures the correct reward or punishment. In any event, overall, the theoretical logic just now spelled out conforms to the character of the bulk of the evidence in the Oral Torah. It is on that basis that I maintain we deal with normative doctrine, necessary to the theology as a whole, and not with a mass of confused details. So much for the two principal components of the eschatological theology of the Oral Torah, resurrection and judgment, the world to come and eternal life.

Let us now address the resurrection of the dead in its own terms. That conviction is stated in so many words: in the end of days, death will die. The certainty of resurrection derives from a simple fact of restorationist theology: God has already shown that he can do it; so Genesis Rabbah LXXVII:I.1: "You find that everything that the Holy One, blessed be he, is destined to do in the age to come he has already gone ahead and done through the righteous in this world. The Holy One, blessed be he, will raise the dead, and Elijah raised the dead."

The paramount composite on the subject derives its facts, demonstrating the coming resurrection of the dead, from the Written Torah, which, as we realize, serves as counterpart to nature for philosophy, the source of actualities. The sages deem urgent the task of reading outward and forward from Scripture, and at the critical conclusion of their theological system the Oral Torah focuses upon Scripture's evidence, the regularization of Scripture's facts. But the doctrine of resurrection as defined by the principal (and huge) composite of the Talmud of Babylonia contains a number of components: origin of the doctrine in the Written Torah; the gentiles and the resurrection of the dead; the distinction between the days of the Messiah and the world to come; the restoration of Israel to the Land of Israel. Here is the systematic exposition:

I.22 A. R. Simeon b. Laqish contrasted [these two verses]: "It is written, 'I will gather them ... with the blind and the lame, the woman with child and her that trail travails with child together' (Jer. 31:8), and it is written, 'Then shall the lame man leap as a hart and the tongue of the dumb sing, for in the wilderness shall waters break out and streams in the desert' (Is. 35:6). How so [will the dead both retain their defects and also be healed]?

B. "They will rise [from the grave] bearing their defects and then be healed."

The first inquiry deals with the problem of the condition of the body upon resurrection and finds its resolution in the contrast of verses, yielding the stated doctrine: the dead rise in the condition in which they died and then are healed. Next comes the question of what happens to the gentiles, and the answer is given:

I.23 A. Ulla contrasted [these two verses]: "It is written, 'He will destroy death forever and the Lord God will wipe away tears from all faces' (Is. 25:9), and it is written, 'For the child shall die a hundred years old ... there shall no more thence an infant of days' (Is. 65:20).

B. "There is no contradiction. The one speaks of Israel, the other of idolators."

But then after the resurrection, the gentiles have no role except in relationship to Israel:

C. But what do idolators want there [after the resurrection]?

D. It is to those concerning whom it is written, "And strangers shall stand and feed your flocks, and the sons of the alien shall be your plowmen and your vine-dressers" (Is. 61:5).

The clear distinction between the days of the Messiah, involving, as we have seen, the resurrection of the dead, and the world to come is now drawn:

I.24 A. R. Hisda contrasted [these two verses]: "It is written, 'Then the moon shall be confounded and the sun ashamed, when the Lord of hosts shall reign' (Is 24:23), and it is written, 'Moreover the light of the moon shall be as the light of seven days' (Is 30:26).

B. "There is no contradiction. The one refers to the days of the Messiah, the other to the world to come."

The world to come demands attention in its own terms. Samuel's doctrine, that the world to come is marked solely by Israel's return to the Land of Israel – that is, the restoration of man to Eden – requires attention in its own terms:

C. And in the view of Samuel, who has said, "There is no difference between the world to come and the days of the Messiah, except the end of the subjugation of the exilic communities of Israel"?
D. There still is no contradiction. The one speaks of the camp of the righteous, the other the camp of the Presence of God.
I.25 A. Raba contrasted [these two verses]: "It is written, 'I kill and I make alive' (Deut. 32:39) and it is written, 'I wound and I heal' (Deut. 32:39). [The former implies that one is resurrected just as he was at death, thus with blemishes, and the other implies that at the resurrection all wounds are healed].
B. "Said the Holy One, blessed be he, 'What I kill I bring to life,' and then, 'What I have wounded I heal.'"

Since people will enjoy individual existence beyond death, at the resurrection, death itself must be fated to die. We simply complete the exposition of the principle by encompassing an important detail.

A sequence of virtues, properly carried out, will lead to the resurrection of the dead, which forms a natural next step beyond this world's life. No radical caesura interrupts the course of affairs, but this-worldly traits, for example, cleanness, abstinence, holiness, modesty, and the like, carry directly to other-worldly events, the encounter with the Holy Spirit, the resurrection of the dead, and onward:

MISHNAH-TRACTATE SOTAH 9:15

MM. R. Pinhas b. Yair says, "Heedfulness leads to cleanliness, cleanliness leads to cleanness, cleanness leads to abstinence, abstinence leads to holiness, holiness leads to modesty, modesty leads to the fear of sin, the fear of sin leads to piety, piety leads to the Holy Spirit, the Holy Spirit leads to the resurrection of the dead, and the resurrection of the dead comes through Elijah, blessed be his memory, Amen."

The passage is amplified with the provision of data from the Written Torah in the following extension, which links to Scripture each rung in the ladder upward to the resurrection of the dead:

V:3 A. On this basis, R. Phineas b. Yair says, "Heedfulness leads to cleanliness, cleanliness leads to cultic purity, cultic purity leads to holiness, holiness leads to modesty, modesty leads to the fear of sin, the fear of sin leads to the Holy Spirit, the Holy Spirit leads to the piety, the piety leads to the resurrection of the dead, and the resurrection of the dead 'leads to Elijah, blessed be his memory' " (M. Sot. 9:15).

B. Heedfulness leads to cleanliness: "And when he has made an end of atoning [for the holy place and the tent of meeting and the altar, he shall present the live goat" (Lev. 16:20).

C. Cleanliness leads to cultic purity: "And the priest shall make atonement for it, and it will be clean" (Lev. 12:7).

D. Cultic purity leads to holiness: "[And he shall sprinkle some of the blood upon it with his finger seven times,] and purify it and hallow it [from the uncleannesses of the people of Israel]" (Lev. 16:19).

E. Holiness leads to modesty: "For thus says the high and lofty One who inhabits eternity, whose name is Holy: 'I dwell in the high and holy place, and also with him who is of a contrite and humble spirit, to revive the heart of the contrite' " (Is. 57:15).

F. Modesty leads to fear of sin: "The reward for modesty and fear of the Lord is riches and honour and life" (Prov. 22:4).

J. The fear of sin leads to the Holy Spirit as it is written: "Then you will understand the fear of the Lord and find the knowledge of God" (Prov. 2:5).

K. The Holy Spirit leads to piety as it is written: "Of old thou didst speak in a vision to thy faithful ones" (Ps. 89:19).

L. Piety leads to the resurrection of the dead as it is written:

M. "[Thus says the Lord God to these bones: Behold], I will cause breath to enter you, and you shall live" (Ezek. 37:5).

N. The resurrection of the dead leads to Elijah, of blessed memory as it is written: "Behold, I will send you Elijah the prophet before the great and terrible day of the Lord comes, and he will turn the hearts of fathers to their children, and the hearts of children to their fathers, [lest I come and smite the land with a curse]" (Mal. 4:5).

O. It has been taught in the name of R. Meir, "Whoever lives permanently in the Land of Israel, eats his unconsecrated produce in a state of cultic cleanness, speaks in the Holy Language [of Hebrew], and recites the Shema morning and night may be certain that he belongs among those who will live in the world to come."

The ladder of virtue reaches the perfection of man, who, perfect in form in life ("in our image, after our likeness"), will be resurrected in the same form beyond the grave. That seems to me to form the restorationist logic of the composition. That explains why there are stages in the road to resurrection, leading through the virtues of cultic cleanness to holiness to the fear of sin to piety, and then the Holy Spirit and the resurrection of the dead, a straight path for those who take it.

The first component of the doctrine of the resurrection of the dead – belief both that the resurrection of the dead will take place and that it is the Torah that reveals that the dead will rise are fundamental to the Oral Torah – is fully exposed in a fundamental composition devoted by the framers of the Mishnah to that subject. The components of the doctrine fit together, in that statement, in a logical order. First, in a predictable application of the governing principle of measure for measure, those who do not believe in the resurrection of the dead will be punished by being denied what they do not accept. Some few others bear the same fate. Second, but to be Israel means to rise from the grave, and that applies to all Israelites. That is to say, the given of the condition of Israel is that the entire holy people will enter the world to come, which is to say, will enjoy the resurrection of the dead and eternal life. "Israel," then, is anticipated to be the people of eternity. Third, excluded from the category of resurrection and the world to come are only those who by their own sins have denied themselves that benefit. These are those who deny that the teaching of the world to come derives from the Torah, or who deny that the Torah comes from God, or hedonists. Exegesis of Scripture also yields the names of three kings who will not be resurrected, as well as four commoners; also specified generations: the Flood, the Dispersion, and Sodom, the Generation of the wilderness, the Party of Korah, and the Ten Tribes:

MISHNAH-TRACTATE SANHEDRIN 10:1
[BAVLI-TRACTATE SANHEDRIN 11:1]

A. All Israelites have a share in the world to come,
B. as it is said, "Your people also shall be all righteous, they shall inherit the land forever; the branch of my planting, the work of my hands, that I may be glorified" (Is. 60:21).

That single statement serves better than any other to define Israel in the Oral Torah. Now we take up exceptions:

C. And these are the ones who have no portion in the world to come:
D. He who says, the resurrection of the dead is a teaching which does not derive from the Torah, and the Torah does not come from Heaven; and an Epicurean.

E. R. Aqiba says, "Also: He who reads in heretical books,

F. "and he who whispers over a wound and says, 'I will put none of the diseases upon you which I have put on the Egyptians, for I am the Lord who heals you'" (Ex. 15:26).

G. Abba Saul says, "Also: He who pronounces the divine Name as it is spelled out."

From classes of persons we turn to specified individuals who are denied a place within Israel and entry in the world to come; all but one are Israelites, and the exception, Balaam, has a special relation to Israel, as the gentile prophet who came to curse but ended with a blessing:

MISHNAH-TRACTATE SANHEDRIN 10:2

A. Three kings and four ordinary folk have no portion in the world to come.

B. Three kings: Jeroboam, Ahab, and Manasseh.

C. R. Judah says, "Manasseh has a portion in the world to come,

D. "since it is said, 'And he prayed to him and he was entreated of him and heard his supplication and brought him again to Jerusalem into his kingdom'" (2 Chr. 33:13).

E. They said to him, "To his kingdom he brought him back, but to the life of the world to come he did not bring him back."

F. Four ordinary folk: Balaam, Doeg, Ahitophel, and Gehazi.

Then come entire generations of gentiles before Abraham, who might have been considered for eternal life outside of the framework of God's self-manifestation, first to Abraham, then in the Torah. These are the standard sets, the Generation of the Flood, the Generation of the Dispersion, and the Men of Sodom:

MISHNAH-TRACTATE SANHEDRIN 10:3

A. The Generation of the Flood has no share in the world to come,

B. and they shall not stand in the judgment,

C. since it is written, "My spirit shall not judge with man forever" (Gen. 6:3)

D. neither judgment nor spirit.

E. The Generation of the Dispersion has no share in the world to come,

F. since it is said, "So the Lord scattered them abroad from there upon the face of the whole earth" (Gen. 11:8).

G. "So the Lord scattered them abroad" – in this world,

H. "and the Lord scattered them from there" – in the world to come.

I. The Men of Sodom have no portion in the world to come,

J. since it is said, "Now the Men of Sodom were wicked and sinners against the Lord exceedingly" (Gen. 13:13)

K. "Wicked" – in this world,

L. "And sinners" – in the world to come.

M. But they will stand in judgment.

N. R. Nehemiah says, "Both these and those will not stand in judgment,

O. "for it is said, 'Therefore the wicked shall not stand in judgment [108A], nor sinners in the congregation of the righteous' (Ps. 1:5)

P. 'Therefore the wicked shall not stand in judgment' – this refers to the Generation of the Flood.

Q. 'Nor sinners in the congregation of the righteous' – this refers to the Men of Sodom."

R. They said to him, "They will not stand in the congregation of the righteous, but they will stand in the congregation of the sinners."

S. The spies have no portion in the world to come,

T. as it is said, "Even those men who brought up an evil report of the land died by the plague before the Lord" (Num. 14:37)

U. "Died" – in this world.

V. "By the plague" – in the world to come.

What about counterparts in Israel, from the Torah forward? The issue concerns the Generation of the Wilderness, which rejected the Land; the Party of Korah; and the Ten Tribes. These match the gentile contingents. But here there is a dispute, and no normative judgment emerges from the Mishnah's treatment of the matter:

MISHNAH-TRACTATE SANHEDRIN 10:4

A. "The Generation of the Wilderness has no portion in the world to come and will not stand in judgment,

B. "for it is written, 'In this wilderness they shall be consumed and there they shall die' " (Num. 14:35), the words of R. Aqiba.

C. R. Eliezer says, "Concerning them it says, 'Gather my saints together to me, those that have made a covenant with me by sacrifice' " (Ps. 50:5).

D. "The Party of Korah is not destined to rise up,

E. "for it is written, 'And the earth closed upon them' – in this world.

F. " 'And they perished from among the assembly' – in the world to come," the words of R. Aqiba.

G. And R. Eliezer says, "Concerning them it says, 'The Lord kills and resurrects, brings down to Sheol and brings up again' " (1 Sam. 2:6).

MISHNAH-TRACTATE SANHEDRIN 10:5

A. "The Ten Tribes [of northern Israel, exiled by the Assyrians] are not destined to return [with Israel at the time of the resurrection of the dead],

B. "since it is said, 'And he cast them into another land, as on this day' (Deut. 29:28). Just as the day passes and does not return, so they have gone their way and will not return," the words of R. Aqiba.

C. R. Eliezer says, "Just as this day is dark and then grows light, so the Ten Tribes for whom it now is dark – thus in the future it is destined to grow light for them."

Scripture contributes the details that refine the basic proposition; the framer has found the appropriate exclusions. But the prophet, in Scripture, also has provided the basic allegation on which all else rests, that is, "Israel will be entirely righteous and inherit the land forever." Denying the stated dogmas removes a person from the status of "Israel," in line with the opening statement, so to be Israel means to rise from the dead, and Israel as a collectivity is defined as those persons in humanity who are destined to eternal life, a supernatural community, as we saw in chapter 3. So much for the initial statement of the eschatological doctrine in the Oral Torah.

Among the components of that doctrine, that resurrection of the dead is a doctrine set forth by the Written Torah and demonstrable within the framework of the Torah, occupies a principal place in the Oral Torah's exposition of the topic. That proposition is demonstrated over and over again. Evidence from the Torah concerning the resurrection of the dead is ubiquitous:

SIFRÉ TO DEUTERONOMY CCCVI:XXVIII.3:

A. And so did R. Simai say, "There is no passage [in the Torah] which does not contain [clear evidence concerning] the resurrection of the dead, but we have not got the power of exegesis [sufficient to find the pertinent indication].

B. "For it is said, 'He will call to the heaven above and to the earth, that he may judge his people' (Ps. 50:4).

C. "'He will call to the heaven above': this refers to the soul.

D. "'and to the earth': this refers to the body.

E. "'that he may judge his people': who judges with him?

F. "And how on the basis of Scripture do we know that Scripture speaks only of the resurrection of the dead?

G. "As it is said, 'Come from the four winds, O breath, and breathe upon these slain, that they may live'" (Ez. 37:9).

Further proofs of the same proposition are abundant, with the following instances representative of the larger corpus. First, we note the recurrent formula, "how on the basis of the Torah do we know…?" Then we are given a sequence of cases, each one of them, as noted earlier, deriving from an individual, none of them appealing to the eternity of the collectivity of Israel. We start with the case of Aaron:

BAVLI SANHEDRIN 11:1/1.2−14/90B-91B

I.2 A. How, on the basis of the Torah, do we know about the resurrection of the dead?
B. As it is said, "And you shall give thereof the Lord's heave-offering to Aaron the priest" (Num. 18:28).
C. And will Aaron live forever? And is it not the case that he did not even get to enter the Land of Israel, from the produce of which heave-offering is given? [So there is no point in Aaron's life at which he would receive the priestly rations.]
D. Rather, this teaches that he is destined once more to live, and the Israelites will give him heave-offering.
E. On the basis of this verse, therefore, we see that the resurrection of the dead is a teaching of the Torah.

Now come the patriarchs, who also will rise from the dead:

I.4 A. It has been taught on Tannaite authority:
B. R. Simai says, "How on the basis of the Torah do we know about the resurrection of the dead?
C. "As it is said, 'And I also have established my covenant with [the patriarchs] to give them the land of Canaan' (Ex. 6:4).
D. "'With you' is not stated, but rather, 'with them,' indicating on the basis of the Torah that there is the resurrection of the dead."

The question is then reframed, no longer in terms of proof based on the facts of Scripture, but now in more general terms. Sectarians ask how we know that God will do this thing:

I.5 A. Minim asked Rabban Gamaliel, "How do we know that the Holy One, blessed be he, will resurrect the dead?"

Proofs from Scripture will not serve when dealing with outsiders to the community of the Torah:

B. He said to them, "It is proved from the Torah, from the Prophets, and from the Writings." But they did not accept his proofs.

In each of the three matched demonstrations, a verse is adduced but interpreted in some way other than the proposed one:

C. "From the Torah: for it is written, 'And the Lord said to Moses, Behold, you shall sleep with your fathers and rise up'" (Deut. 31:16).
D. They said to him, "But perhaps the sense of the passage is, 'And the people will rise up'" (Deut. 31:16)?
E. "From the Prophets: as it is written, 'Thy dead men shall live, together with my dead body they shall arise. Awake and sing, you that live in the dust, for your dew is as the dew of herbs, and the earth shall cast out its dead'" (Is. 26:19).
F. "But perhaps that refers to the dead whom Ezekiel raised up."
G. "From the Writings, as it is written, 'And the roof of your mouth, like the best wine of my beloved, that goes down sweetly, causing the lips of those who are asleep to speak'" (Song 7:9).
H. "But perhaps this means that the dead will move their lips?"
I. That would accord with the view of R. Yohanan.
J. For R. Yohanan said in the name of R. Simeon b. Yehosedeq, "Any authority in whose name a law is stated in this world moves his lips in the grave,
K. "as it is said, 'Causing the lips of those that are asleep to speak.'"

Finally, Gamaliel is able to find a pertinent verse that the sectarians could accept; why this proof served and the prior ones did not yields insight into the sages' characterization of their critics:

L. [The Jewish heretics, called minim, would not concur in Gamaliel's view] until he cited for them the following verse: "'Which the Lord swore to your fathers to give to them' (Deut. 11:21) – to them and not to you, so proving from the Torah that the dead will live."
M. And there are those who say that it was the following verse that he cited to them: "'But you who cleaved to the Lord you God are alive, everyone of you this day' (Deut. 4:4). Just as on this day all of you are alive, so in the world to come all of you will live."

The successful proof involves little more than a dismissal of the others, at L, or a reaffirmation of the faith – Israel cleaves to the Lord – at M.

From the sectarians, we take a step still farther outside the circle of faith and deal with "Romans" (which in some MSS becomes Aramaeans). Now the discussion is broadened to God's knowledge of the future as well as his power to raise the dead:

I.6 A. Romans asked R. Joshua b. Hananiah, "How do we know that the Holy One will bring the dead to life and also that he knows what is going to happen in the future?"

B. He said to them, "Both propositions derive from the following verse of Scripture:

C. "As it is said, 'And the Lord said to Moses, Behold you shall sleep with you fathers and rise up again, and this people shall go awhoring ...' " (Deut. 31:16).

D. "But perhaps the sense is, '[the people] will rise up and go awhoring'

E. He said to them, "Then you have gained half of the matter, that God knows what is going to happen in the future."

Another composition goes over the same matter, now not with sectarians in view:

I.7 A. It has also been stated on Amoraic authority:

B. Said R. Yohanan in the name of R. Simeon b. Yohai, "How do we know that the Holy One, blessed be he, will bring the dead to life and knows what is going to happen in the future?

C. "As it is said, 'Behold, you shall sleep with you fathers, and ... rise again ...'" (Deut. 31:16).

The sectarians now deny that the Torah teaches the principle of resurrection:

I.8 A. It has been taught on Tannaite authority:

B. Said R. Eliezer b. R. Yosé, "In this matter I proved false the books of the minim.

C. "For they would say, 'The principle of the resurrection of the dead does not derive from the Torah.'

D. "I said to them, 'You have forged your Torah and have gained nothing on that account.

E. " 'For you say, "The principle of the resurrection of the dead does not derive from the Torah."

F. " 'Lo, Scripture says, "[Because he has despised the Lord of the Lord ...] that soul shall be cut off completely, his iniquity shall be upon him" (Num. 15:31).

G. " ' "... shall be utterly cut off ...," in this world, in which case, at what point will "... his iniquity be upon him ..."?

H. " 'Will it not be in the world to come?' "

I. Said R. Pappa to Abbayye, "And might one not have replied to them that the words 'utterly ...' '... cut off ...,' signify the two worlds [this and the next]?"

J. [He said to him,] "They would have answered, 'The Torah speaks in human language [and the doubling of the verb carries no meaning beyond its normal sense].' "

The sages pursue the same dispute:

I.9 A. This accords with the following Tannaite dispute:
B. " 'That soul shall be utterly cut off' – 'shall be cut off' – in this world, 'utterly' – in the world to come," the words of R. Aqiba.
C. Said R. Ishmael to him, "And has it not been said, 'He reproaches the Lord, and that soul shall be cut off' (Num. 15:31). Does this mean that there are three worlds?
D. "Rather: '… it will be cut off …,' in this world, '… utterly …,' in the world to come, and 'utterly cut off …,' indicates that the Torah speaks in ordinary human language."

Subsidiary questions now arise: what will the dead be wearing?

I.10 A. Queen Cleopatra asked R. Meir, saying, "I know that the dead will live, for it is written, 'And [the righteous] shall blossom forth out of your city like the grass of the earth' (Ps. 72:16).
B. "But when they rise, will they rise naked or in their clothing?"
C. He said to her, "It is an argument a fortiori based on the grain of wheat.
D. "Now if a grain of wheat, which is buried naked, comes forth in many garments, the righteous, who are buried in their garments, all the more so [will rise in many garments]!"

From one royal figure we move on to another, and the colloquy leaves the framework of Scripture's facts and proceeds to arguments built on analogies drawn from nature. How can the dead be reconstituted out of the dirt?

I.11 A. Caesar said to Rabban Gamaliel, "You maintain that the dead will live. But they are dust, and can the dust live?"
B. [91A] His daughter said to him, "Allow me to answer him:
C. "There are two potters in our town, one who works with water, the other who works with clay. Which is the more impressive?"
D. He said to her, "The one who works with water."
E. She said to him, "If he works with water, will he not create even more out of clay?"

Yet another argument based on analogy is set forth:

I.12 A. A Tannaite authority of the house of R. Ishmael [taught], "[Resurrection] is a matter of an argument a fortiori based on the case of a glass utensil.

B. "Now if glassware, which is the work of the breath of a mortal man, when broken, can be repaired,

C. "A mortal man, who is made by the breath of the Holy One, blessed be he, how much the more so [that he can be repaired, in the resurrection of the dead]."

Dealing with a sectarian, a sage appeals to yet another analogy, now in the narrative form of a parable:

I.13 A. A min said to R. Ammi, "You say that the dead will live. But they are dust, and will the dust live?"

B. He said to him, "I shall draw a parable for you. To what may the matter be compared?

C. "It may be compared to the case of a mortal king, who said to his staff, 'Go and build a great palace for me, in a place in which there is no water or dirt [for bricks].

D. "They went and built it, but after a while it collapsed.

E. "He said to them, 'Go and rebuild it in a place in which there are dirt and water [for bricks].'

F. "They said to him, 'We cannot do so.'

G. "He became angry with them and said to them, 'In a place in which there is neither water nor dirt you were able to build, and now in a place in which there are water and dirt, how much the more so [should you be able to build it]!'

H. "And if you [the minim] do not believe it, go to a valley and look at a rat, which today is half-flesh and half-dirt and tomorrow will turn into a creeping thing, made all of flesh. Will you say that it takes much time? Then go up to a mountain and see that today there is only one snail, but tomorrow it will rain and the whole of it will be filled with snails."

Further proofs from the Written Torah that the dead will be resurrected include the following systematic statements.

In this protracted demonstration, certainly the Bavli's single most ambitious composite, the first proof appeals to the formulation of Scripture, its language bearing the implication that Moses and the children of Israel who sang the Song at the Sea will rise from the dead:

BAVLI-TRACTATE SANHEDRIN 11:1 1.27FF./91BFF

I.27 A. It has been taught on Tannaite authority:

B. R. Meir says, "How on the basis of the Torah do we know about the resurrection of the dead?

C. "As it is said, 'Then shall Moses and the children of Israel sing this song to the Lord' (Ex. 15:1).

D. "What is said is not 'sang' but 'will sing,' on the basis of which there is proof from the Torah of the resurrection of the dead.

E. "Along these same lines: 'Then shall Joshua build an altar to the Lord God of Israel' (Josh. 8:30).

F. "What is said is not 'built' but 'will build,' on the basis of which there is proof from the Torah of the resurrection of the dead.

G. Then what about this verse: "Then will Solomon build a high place for Chemosh, abomination of Moab" (1 Kgs. 11:7)? Does it mean that he will build it? Rather, the Scripture treats him as though he had built it [even though he had merely thought about doing so].

From proof of that kind, numerous extensions emerge, all of them appealing to the use of the future tense:

I.28 A. Said R. Joshua b. Levi, "How on the basis of Scripture may we prove the resurrection of the dead?

B. "As it is said, 'Blessed are those who dwell in your house, they shall ever praise you, selah' (Ps. 84:5).

C. "What is said is not 'praised you' but 'shall praise you,' on the basis of which there is proof from the Torah of the resurrection of the dead."

D. And R. Joshua b. Levi said, "Whoever recites the song [of praise] in this world will have the merit of saying it in the world to come,

E. "as it is said, 'Happy are those who dwell in you house, they shall ever praise you, selah' " (Ps. 84:5).

The same kind of proof follows:

F. Said R. Hiyya b. Abba said R. Yohanan, "On what basis do we know about the resurrection of the dead from Scripture."

G. "As it says, 'Your watchman shall lift up the voice, with the voice together they shall sing' " (Is. 52:8).

H. What is said is not 'sang' but 'will sing' on the basis of which there is proof from the Torah of the resurrection of the dead.

I. Said R. Yohanan, "In the future all the prophets will sing in unison, as it is written, 'Your watchman shall lift up the voice, with the voice together they shall sing' " (Is. 57:8).

Now we turn to individuals and how they are represented in Scripture. Here, the fact that Reuben will live bears the implication of resurrection, since we know he died:

I.31 A. Said Raba, "How on the basis of the Torah do we find evidence for the resurrection of the dead?

B. "As it is said, 'Let Reuben live and not die' (Deut. 33:6).

C. " 'Let Reuben live' in this world, and 'not die,' in the world to come."

The book of Daniel contains more explicit evidence:

D. Rabina said, "Proof derives from here: 'And many of them that sleep in the dust of the earth shall awake, some to everlasting life, and some to shame and everlasting contempt' " (Dan. 12:2).

E. R. Ashi said, "Proof derives from here: 'But go your way till the end be, for you shall rest and stand in your lot at the end of days' " (Dan. 12:13).

Wisdom literature likewise serves, an analogy deriving from a statement in Proverbs:

I.33 A. Said R. Tabi said R. Josiah, "What is the meaning of this verse of Scripture: 'The grave and the barren womb and the earth that is not filled by water' (Prov. 30:16).

B. "What has the grave to do with the womb?

C. "It is to say to you, just as the womb takes in and gives forth, so Sheol takes in and gives forth.

D. "And is it not an argument a fortiori? If in the case of the womb, in which they insert [something] in secret, the womb brings forth in loud cries, Sheol, into which [bodies] are placed with loud cries, is it not reasonable to suppose that from the grave people will be brought forth with great cries?

E. "On the basis of this argument there is an answer to those who say that the doctrine of the resurrection of the dead does not derive from the Torah."

The final proof of interest concerns the fate of those who are resurrected. When they are restored to life, it is in a condition of perfection, so they will never (again) die, an important point for a restorationist theology:

I.34 A. A Tannaite authority of the house of Elisha [taught], "The righteous whom the Holy One, blessed be he, is going to resurrect will not revert to dust,

B. "for it is said, 'And it shall come to pass that he that is left in Zion and he that remains in Jerusalem shall be called holy, even everyone that is written among the living in Jerusalem' (Is. 4:3).

C. "Just as the Holy One lives forever, so they shall live forever.

D. [92B] "And if you want to ask, as to those years in which the Holy One, blessed be he, will renew his world, as it is said, 'And the Lord alone shall be exalted in that day' (Is. 2:11), during that time what will the righteous do?

E. "The answer is that the Holy One, blessed be he, will make them wings like eagles, and they will flutter above the water, as it is said, 'Therefore will not fear, when the earth be moved and the mountains be carried in the midst of the sea' (Ps. 44:3).

F. "And if you should say that they will have pain [in all this], Scripture says, 'But those who wait upon the Lord shall renew their strength, they shall mount up with wings as eagles, they shall run and not be weary, they shall walk and not be faint'" (Is. 40:31).

The details of what happens in the age or world to come trail off; here we have the notion that the world will be renewed, yielding the question asked at D. When, earlier, I referred to the somewhat unclear account of eschatological matters, it is a detail such as this one that I had in mind; we can generalize only out of the main beams of the structure at hand: the dead will rise; God will do it; the dead then are judged; those who are justified will inherit the age or world to come; and the Messiah will come to mark the advent of the final drama, though his exact role and tasks beyond that basic function as signifier do not attain much clarity, or, at least, do not coalesce as a consensus I can identify.

That is not the only formulation of the resurrection of the dead. Scripture forms only one source for truth, though it is the main one. Nature also dictates its own, complementary logic. That accounts for the more general framing of the same matter, outside the setting of Scripture. Here Eliezer Haqqappar establishes that the complementary logic of birth is death, and of death, resurrection:

TRACTATE ABOT 4:21

A. R. Eliezer Haqqappar says, "Those who are born are destined to die, and those who die are destined for resurrection.

B. "And the living are destined to be judged so as to know, to make known, and to confirm that (1) he is God, (2) he is the one who forms, (3) he is the one who creates, (4) he is the one who understands, (5) he is the one who judges, (6) he is the one who gives evidence, (7) he is the one who brings suit, (8) and he is the one who is going to make the ultimate judgment.

C. "Blessed be he, for before him are not (1) guile, (2) forgetfulness, respect for persons, (4) bribe taking, for everything is his.

D. "And know that everything is subject to reckoning.

E. "And do not let your evil impulse persuade you that Sheol is a place of refuge for you.

F. "For (1) despite your wishes were you formed, (2) despite your wishes were you born, (3) despite your wishes do you live, (4) despite your wishes do you die King of kings of kings, the Holy One, blessed be he."

Nothing in this passage limits resurrection to Israel, but the context of the saying, in tractate Abot, defines Israel as the frame of discourse. Elsewhere, the view that Israel alone will be resurrected is stated explicitly. Those who die in the Land of Israel, and the righteous overseas, will enjoy the resurrection of the dead at the end of days, but gentiles are explicitly excluded, just as the theological logic that distinguishes Israel and the Torah from the gentiles and idolatry requires:

PESIQTA RABBATI I:VI.4

A. Thus you have learned that [1] those who die in the Land of Israel will live in the days of the Messiah, and [2] the righteous who die overseas come to it and live in it.

Those overseas – not being righteous – are explicitly excluded, but what about gentiles in the Land of Israel?

B. If that is the case, then will the gentiles who are buried in the Land also live?
C. No, Isaiah has said, "The neighbor shall not say, I too have suffered pain. The people who dwell therein shall be forgiven their sin" (Is. 33:24).
D. The sense is, "My evil neighbors are not going to say, 'We have been mixed up [with Israel and will share their fate, so] we too shall live with them.'"

Now comes the explicit identification of Israel as those who are forgiven their sin, having repented in accord with the vocation of the Torah:

E. But that one that was the people dwelling therein [is the one that will live, and what is that people? It is the people that has been forgiven its sin, namely, those concerning whom it is said, "Who is God like you, who forgives sin and passes over transgression for the remnant of his inheritance" (Mic. 7:18) [which can only be Israel].

The theology of the gentiles certainly points towards the conclusion set forth here, that only Israel will be resurrected from the dead. So, too, as we shall see at greater length in chapter 14, Israel in particular heads towards the world to come, by reason of its loyalty to God in this world:

TOSEFTA-TRACTATE SOTAH 7:10

A. "You have declared this day concerning the Lord that he is your God, and that you will walk in his ways and keep his statutes and his commandments and his ordinances and will obey his voice; and the Lord has declared this day concerning you that you are a people for his own possession" (Deut. 26:17–18).

B. "Said the Holy One blessed be He to them, 'Just as you have made me the only object of your love in the world, so I shall make you the only object of my love in the world to come.'"

The weight of opinion, the formulation of authoritative composites, all point to the exclusion of gentiles from the resurrection of the dead and consequently also from the world to come.

The passage at hand is explicit that the dead in the Land of Israel will rise. Israelites overseas will be transported to the Land for the resurrection. I have many times alluded to the inner logic of the restorationist theology, which views the Land of Israel as the coming Eden. That is why living and dying in the Land contain the promise of resurrection, among other advantages. Burial in the Land therefore forms a statement of faith in what is to come later on:

YERUSHALMI-TRACTATE KETUBOT 12:3 I:8

A. It is written, "You shall carry me out of Egypt and bury me in their burial ground" (Gen. 47:30): as to Jacob, wherever he was located [in death] – what loss would he sustain? [Granted that sinners benefit from burial in the Land of Israel, which atones for sin, since Jacob was entirely righteous, what difference did it make to him to be buried there rather than in Egypt]?

B. R. Eleazar said, "There is something hidden here."

C. Hanina said, "There is something hidden here."

That enigmatic statement is now clarified:

D. What is the meaning of "There is something hidden here"?

E. R. Simeon b. Laqish said, " 'I shall walk before the Lord in the lands of the living' (Ps. 116:9) – and is it not the fact that the lands of the living are only Tyre and Caesarea and their surroundings [so reference cannot be made to this world, since in this world life is most abundant in the cities that are named, and places like them]. There is everything, there is abundance."

F. [Rather,] R. Simeon b. Laqish in the name of Bar Qappara [said], "It is the land where the dead will be the first to return to life in the time of the Messiah. What is the scriptural foundation for that view? 'Thus says God, the Lord, who created the heaven and stretched them out, who spread forth the earth and what comes from it, who gives breath to the people upon it, and spirit to those who walk in it' " (Is. 42:5).

In this framework the righteous buried overseas have to be brought back, and that will take place through a miracle at the end of time; when they reach the Land, their souls are restored to their bodies:

G. If that is the case [that in the land of Israel the dead rise first,] then our masters who are located in Babylonia lose out!

H. Said R. Simai, "The Holy One, blessed be he, opens the ground before them, and they roll to the land like leather bottles, and once they get there, their soul comes back to them."

I. What is the Scriptural basis for that view?

J. "And I will place you on the land of Israel and I will put my spirit within you and you shall live" (Ez. 37:14).

The priority of the Land is aligned with the conception of the resurrection of the dead, and the result is that the latter must take place in the designated holy space. The same position is taken in the following composite:

BAVLI-TRACTATE KETUBOT 13:11 III.16FF./111A

III.17 A. Said R. Eleazar, "The dead that are abroad will not come back to life: 'And I will set glory in the land of the living' (Ezek. 26:20) – the dead buried in the land where I have my desire will live, but the dead of the land in which I have no desire won't live."

B. Objected R. Abba bar Mammal, "'Your dead shall live, my dead bodies shall arise' (Isa. 26:19) – doesn't 'your dead shall live' mean, they will live among the dead that are in the Land of Israel, and doesn't 'my dead bodies shall arise' mean, to the dead outside of the Land; and doesn't 'and I will give glory in the Land of Israel' refer to Nebuchadnezzar, concerning whom the All-Merciful has said, 'I will bring against them a king who is as swift as a stag'?"

C. He said to him, "My lord, I expound another verse of Scripture: 'He who gives breath to the people upon it, and spirit to them that walk therein'" (Isa. 42:5).

D. But isn't it written, "My dead bodies shall arise"?

E. That refers to abortions.

The same view is expressed in a different way:

III.18 A. "And spirit to them that walk therein":

B. Said R. Jeremiah bar Abbah said R. Yohanan, "Whoever walks four cubits in the Land of Israel is certain that he will belong to the world to come."

The problem finds its now-familiar solution:

III.19 A. Then according to R. Eleazar, won't the righteous who are outside of the Land live [at the end of time]?

B. Said R. Ilaa, "It will come about through rolling [to the Land]."

C. Objected R. Abba Sala the Elder, "Won't the rolling hurt the righteous?"

D. Said Abbayye, "Underground passages will be made for them."

So, too, the Land of Israel is where one will want to be buried, and that fully accords with the system's conception of the special sanctity of the Land of Israel when it is occupied by Israel:

THE FATHERS ACCORDING TO RABBI NATHAN XXVI:III.I

A. He would say, "Whoever is buried in other lands is as though he were buried in Babylonia. Whoever is buried in Babylonia is as if he were buried in the Land of Israel. Whoever is buried in the Land of Israel is as if he were buried under the altar.

B. "For the whole of the Land of Israel is suitable as a location for the altar.

C. "And whoever is buried under the altar is as if he were buried under the throne of glory.

D. "As it is said, You throne of glory, on high from the beginning, you place of our sanctuary" (Jer. 17:12).

The corollary of the doctrine that the dead will be raised at the last judgment, which will take place in the Land of Israel, is that one is best off to be buried in the Land of Israel. The righteous buried abroad will be brought back there for resurrection. Once the matters of the priority of the Land and the last judgment are juxtaposed, the doctrines set forth here become predictable.[2]

The details of judgment that follow resurrection prove less ample. The basic account stresses that God will judge with great mercy. But the Oral Torah presents no fully articulated story of judgment. Within the documents of the Oral Torah, we have little narrative to tell us how the judgment will be carried on. Even the detail that through repentance death man has already atoned, which is stated in so many words in the context of repentance and atonement, plays no role that I can discern in discussions of the last judgment. What we do know concerns two matters, When does the judgment take place? And by what criteria does God decide who inherits the world to come? As to the former: the judgment is comparable to the annual judgment for man's fate in the following year. It will happen either at the beginning of the New Year on the first of Tishré, when, annually, man is judged, or on the

2. We shall presently note that, at the advent of the age or world to come, the exiles will be ushered back to the Land of Israel by the Messiah. In context, this presumably pertains to those exiles who are alive at the moment of the advent of the age to come, the dead having been raised in the Land.

fifteenth of Nisan, when Israel celebrates its freedom from Egyptian bondage and begins its pilgrimage to Sinai. The detail is subject to dispute, leaving the main point to stand as normative doctrine:

BAVLI-TRACTATE TAANIT 1:2 I

A. It is taught on Tannaite authority:

B. R. Eliezer says, "In Tishré, the world was created; in Tishré, the patriarchs Abraham and Jacob were born; in Tishré, the patriarchs died; on Passover, Isaac was born; on New Year, Sarah, Rachel, and Hannah were visited; on New Year, Joseph left prison; on New Year, bondage was removed from our ancestors in Egypt; in Nisan, they were redeemed; in Tishré, they are destined to be redeemed again."

C. R. Joshua says, "In Nisan, the world was created; in Nisan, the patriarchs Abraham and Jacob were born; in Nisan, the patriarchs died; on Passover, Isaac was born; on New Year, Sarah, Rachel, and Hannah were visited; on New Year, Joseph left prison; on New Year, bondage was removed from our ancestors in Egypt; in Nisan, they were redeemed; in Nisan, they are destined to be redeemed again."

The final judgment lasts for a period of time, not forever, and at that point the resurrected who have endured in judgment pass to the world to come or eternal life. When the judgment comes, it will last for twelve (or six) months; this we know because Scripture is explicit. We have only to identify the correct verse of Scripture:

MISHNAH-TRACTATE EDUYYOT 2:10

A. Also he [Aqiba] would list five things which [last for] twelve months:

B. (1) the judgment of the Generation of the Flood is twelve months;

C. (2) the judgment of Job is twelve months;

D. (3) the judgment of the Egyptians is twelve months;

E. (4) the judgment of Gog and Magog in the time to come is twelve months;

E and (5) the judgment of the wicked in Gehenna is twelve months,

G. as it is said, "It will be from one month until the same month [a year later]" (Is. 66:23).

H. R. Yohanan b. Nuri says, "From Passover to Pentecost, as it is said, 'From one Sabbath until the next Sabbath'" (Is. 66:23).

The point is established by identifying five classes of persons that come under judgment and assigning them all to the term of judgment specified by the prophet. What about the others, who, when judged, are rejected? Those who do not pass judgment then are condemned and do not pass on to eternal life, and these are Israelites or gentiles who have a special relation to Israel. Other gentiles do not even figure in judgment at all as we saw at Mishnah-tractate Sanhedrin 10:2.

How to stand in judgment, meaning, go through the process of divine review of one's life and actions and emerge in the world to come, restored to the Land that is Eden? Proper conduct and study of Torah lead to standing in judgment and consequent enjoyment of the life of the world to come, and not keeping the one and studying the other deny entry into that life. What is striking is the appeal to Eden for just this message about re-entry into the Land.

LEVITICUS RABBAH XXXV:VI:I F.:

1. A. Said R. Abba b. Eliashib, "[The reference at Lev. 26:3 to statutes is to] statutes which bring a person into the life of the world to come.
B. "That is in line with the following verse of Scripture: 'And he who is left in Zion and remains in Jerusalem will be called holy, everyone who has been recorded for life in Jerusalem' (Is. 4:3) – for he is devoted to [study of] Torah, which is called the tree of life."

Now comes the reference to Eden in the context of the world to come, a matter to which we shall return in chapter 14:

2. A. It has been taught in the name of R. Eliezer, "A sword and a scroll wrapped together were handed down from heaven, as if to say to them, 'If you keep what is written in this [scroll], you will be saved from the sword,
B. " 'and if not, in the end [the sword] will kill you.' "
C. "Whence is that proposition to be inferred? 'He drove out the man, and at the east of the Garden of Eden he placed the cherubim, and a flaming sword which turned every way, to guard the way to the tree of life' (Gen. 3:4).
D. "The [first] reference to 'the way' refers to the rules of proper conduct, and the second reference, '[the way to] the tree of life' refers to the Torah."

The same message is given in a different framework:

3. A. It was taught in the name of R. Simeon b. Yohai, "A loaf and a rod wrapped together were given from heaven.
B. "It was as if to say to them, 'If you keep the Torah, lo, here is bread to eat, and if not, lo, here is a staff with which to be smitten.'

C. "Whence is that proposition to be inferred? 'If you are willing and obedient, you shall eat the good of the land; but if you refuse and rebel, you shall be devoured by the sword' " (Is. 15:19–20).

The world to come, involving resurrection and judgment, will be attained through the Torah, which teaches proper conduct. That simple doctrine yields the proposition here.

When it comes to the last judgment, we need hardly be reminded that God judges in a merciful manner. If the balance is equal, then God inclines the scale to forgiveness. Given that mercy complements justice, so that justice is not possible without mercy, that trait of God's judgment conforms to the logic that pervades the entire system. We deal first with the quality of justice, which, we know from chapter 2, involves measure for measure; and much of the judgment is worked out in this life, so that the world to come awaits those who suffer, a point critical to the discussion of chapter 5:

YERUSHALMI-TRACTATE SANHEDRIN IO:I I:2

H. If the greater part of his record consisted of honourable deeds, and the smaller part, transgressions, they exact punishment from him [in this world].

I. If the smaller part of the transgressions which he has done are of the lesser character, [he is punished] in this world so as to pay him his full and complete reward in the world to come.

J. If the greater part of his record consisted of transgressions and the lesser part of honourable deeds, they pay him off with the reward of the religious deeds which he has done entirely in this world, so as to exact punishment from him in a whole and complete way in the world to come.

K. If the greater part of his record consisted of honourable deeds, he will inherit the Garden of Eden. If the greater part consisted of transgressions, he will inherit Gehenna.

Now we reach the critical point at which mercy enters in:

L. [If the record] was evenly balanced –

M. Said R. Yosé b. Haninah, " '... forgives sins ...,' is not written here, but rather, '... forgives [a] sin' (Num 14:18). That is to say, the Holy One, blessed be he, tears up one bond [recorded] among the transgressions, so that the honourable deeds then will outweigh the others."

N. Said R. Eleazar, " 'And that to thee, O Lord, belongs steadfast love. For thou dost requite a man according to his work' (Ps. 62:13). 'His deed' is not written here, but 'like his deed' – if he has none, you give him one of yours."

Others concur in this same view, and I have identified no contrary opinion in the entire Oral Torah:

O. That is the view of R. Eleazar. R. Eleazar, who said, " '[The Lord passed before him, and proclaimed, The Lord, the Lord, a God merciful and gracious, slow to anger,] and abounding in steadfast love [and faithfulness]' (Ex. 34:6). He tips the scale in favour of mercy."

P. R. Jeremiah said R. Samuel bar R. Isaac asked about the following: " 'Righteous-ness guards him whose way is upright, but sin overthrows the wicked' (Prov. 3:6). 'Mis-fortune pursues sinners, but prosperity rewards the righteous' (Prov. 13:21). 'Toward the scorner he is scornful, but to the humble he shows favour' (Prov. 3:34). 'He will guard the feet of his faithful ones; but the wicked shall be cut off in darkness; [for not by might shall a man prevail]' (1 Sam. 2:9). 'The wise will inherit honour, but fools get disgrace' (Prov. 3:35).

Q. "Now do they build a fence and lock the doors? And thus indeed is the way, that they do build a fence and lock the doors, [as we shall now see that God makes it possible for the righteous to do righteous deeds and confirms the wicked in their way too]."

Man has a role in eliciting divine assistance in the matter:

R. R. Jeremiah in the name of R. Samuel bar R. Isaac: "[If] a man keeps himself from transgression once, twice, and three times, from that time forth, the Holy One, blessed be he, keeps him from it."

S. What is the Scriptural basis for this statement?

T. " 'Behold, God does all these things, twice, three times, with a man' " (Job 33:29).

Here is a further statement of the systemic realization of the future: the righ-teous will ultimately triumph, the wicked will ultimately suffer, in the age to come if not in this age. This age is the time in which the righteous atone for their sins, and in which the wicked do not. Then, in the world to come, the wicked will be punished, not having prepared and atoned. The systemic vari-able now allows God to intervene and help the righteous to attain the merit that they require.

All theologies deal with extreme cases and anomalies, each in terms of its system. For the Oral Torah, since merit derives from study of the Torah, it remains to ask about those who never have the opportunity to study the Torah or otherwise acquire merit, for instance, infants? Being born into Israel the holy people guarantees participation in the resurrection of the dead. Circum-cision of males is introduced as a *sine qua non* of their belonging to Israel only as one position among many. But in its own terms the issue is raised, at what point is an infant deemed an Israelite? The answers appeal to either the form – the very birth into Israel – or function – the capacity to form an intention, respectively:

YERUSHALMI-TRACTATE SHEBIIT 4:10 IX
[TRANSLATED BY ALAN J. AVERY-PECK]

A. Israelite children [who die] will live [again after the resurrection of the dead if they had attained] what age?
B. R. Hiyya the elder and R. Simeon b. Rabbi [disputed this question].
C. One said, "As soon as they are born [they are guaranteed resurrection]."
D. But the other said, "Only once they speak [are they guaranteed resurrection]."

Scripture's evidence now intervenes:

E. The one who says, "As soon as they are born [they are guaranteed resurrection," depends upon Ps. 22:31, which states]: "And proclaim his deliverance to a people yet unborn, that he has wrought it."
F. And the one who says, "Once they speak [they are guaranteed resurrection," depends upon Ps. 22:30, which states]: "Posterity shall serve him; men shall tell of the Lord to the coming generation."

Other views register as well:

G. It is taught on Tannaitic authority in the name of R. Meir, "[An Israelite child is guaranteed resurrection if he dies anytime] after he knows how to answer 'Amen' [to the prayers recited] in the synagogue."
H. What is the [Scriptural] basis [for this view]?
I. [Is. 26:2 states:] "Open the gates that the righteous nation which keeps faith may enter in." [The word translated here as "faith" has the same root as the term "Amen," G.]

Circumcision is introduced by schismatic opinion:

J. There [in Babylonia] they state: "[An Israelite child is guaranteed resurrection if he dies anytime] after he is circumcised."
K. [This is based on Ps. 88:15, which states: "Afflicted and close to death from my youth up] I suffer your terrors and I arise." [The word "terrors" is understood to refer to the pain of circumcision.]

The normative view takes the most inclusive position, that of "the rabbis":

L. But the rabbis from here [in the land of Israel] say, "[An Israelite child is guaranteed resurrection if he dies anytime] after he is born."
M. [This is based on Ps. 87:5, which states:] "And of Zion it shall be said, 'This one and that one were born in her, for the Most High himself will establish her.'"

From birth, we move backward to life in the womb. As to the status of the unborn infant, here, too, an inclusive view registers:

N. R. Eleazar said, "Even miscarried fetuses [are guaranteed resurrection]."
O. What is the [Scriptural] basis [for this view]?
P. [Is. 49:6 states:] "To restore the preserved [New Revised Standard] of Israel."
Q. [This means that] those of Israel who were created [NRS] [but not born] are to be restored [to life at the time of the resurrection].

So, too, Israelites living in the Land of Israel are sure to enter the world to come; thus Y. Shab. 1:3 V.3: It has been taught in the name of R. Meir, "Whoever lives permanently in the Land of Israel, eats his unconsecrated produce in a state of cultic cleanness, speaks in the Holy Language of Hebrew, and recites the Shema morning and night may be certain that he belongs among those who will live in the world to come."

At the outset we stressed that the resurrection of the dead focuses upon Israel as Israelite. Therefore the resurrection comes to mind whenever death takes an Israelite life, and the monument to the resurrection is the burial ground, the locus of eternity. That is why the coming resurrection of the dead is called to mind whenever one is located in a cemetery:

YERUSHALMI-TRACTATE BERAKHOT 9:1 III:8

A. One who passes between graves [in a cemetery], what does he recite? "Blessed [art Thou, O Lord, our God, King of the Universe,] who resurrects the dead." (Cf. Tosefta Berakhot 6:6.)
B. R. Hiyya in the name of R. Yohanan [says he recites], "Blessed [art Thou, O Lord, our God, King of the Universe] who is true to his word to resurrect the dead."
C. R. Hiyya in the name of R. Yohanan [says he recites], "He who knows your numbers, He shall awaken you, He shall remove the dust from your eyes. Blessed [art Thou, O Lord, our God, King of the Universe,] who resurrects the dead."
D. R. Eliezer in the name of R. Hanina [says he recites], "He who created you with justice, and sustained you with justice, and removed you [from the world] with justice,

and will resurrect you with justice; He who knows your numbers, He shall remove the dust from your eyes. Blessed [art Thou, O Lord, our God, King of the Universe,] who resurrects the dead."

Gentiles once more find no place in the matter:

E. This is the case [that one recites this blessing only if he passes among the graves of] the Israelite dead. But concerning [one who passes among the graves of] the gentile dead, he says, "Your mother shall be utterly shamed, and she who bore you shall be disgraced. Lo, she shall be the last of the nations, a wilderness dry and desert" (Jer. 50:12).

The resurrection of the dead of Israel marks the beginning of that process of restoration in response to Israelite repentance that God built into the very creation of the world. It also brings the final punishment to the gentiles, that is, those who do not know God.

The final subtopic of the theme of resurrection as of the world to come, already encountered, now has systematically to be addressed: what of the Messiah? The Messiah figures at every point in the categorical structure of the Oral Torah's eschatological thinking: troubles attendant upon the coming of the Messiah, which either do or do not bring about Israelite repentance, as we have already seen, leading to resurrection, as we shall see here, and a task then to be performed at the world to come, as the next chapter will show. But, important in two free-standing categories (resurrection, world to come) and a presence in the third (repentance), on its own account the Messiah-theme simply does not coalesce into an autonomous category. That theme certainly does not define a categorical imperative in the way that Israel and the gentiles, complementarity and correspondence, and the eschatological categories, sin and atonement, resurrection and the world to come, all do. By contrast, to take a specific case, the gentiles and idolatry encompass a broad range of data, interact with other categories, form a focus of thought and a logical centre; but they cannot then be reduced to some other categories, for example, Israel and the Torah, private life, repentance. For its part, the Messiah-theme forms a subset of several categories and by itself does not take up an autonomous presence in the theology of the Oral Torah. The Messiah-theme fits into the primary categories but is itself divisible among them.

So, if the principal components of the Oral Torah's eschatological theology turn out to be Israel in its two dimensions, private and public, what of that individual who figures prominently, but not consistently or in a single coherent role, in all eschatological discourse? We have already addressed the

Messiah-theme when, in considering the power of repentance (chapter 12), we found the figure of the Messiah an important but hardly ubiquitous theme. If Israel repents, the Messiah will come. A Messiah who exhibits inappropriate characteristics – arrogance in place of the humility that is the requirement of salvation – embodies the anti-Messiah. So the Messiah exemplifies what is required. But what the Messiah actually does, as distinct from what his advent signifies, is hardly clear in the setting of repentance. When it comes to resurrection, on the one side, and the world to come, on the other, the figure of the Messiah again plays its part. But while the doctrine of resurrection and the one of the world to come encompass in each case a few simple and coherent principles, the Messiah-theme does not.

Not only is there no categorical imperative identified with the Messiah-theme. There also is no logic that affords structure and system to that theme, no Rabbinic Messiology, in the way in which, as we have seen, there certainly is a Rabbinic theological anthropology (for one example). Further, as the structure of the theology of the Oral Torah has gradually taken shape in these pages, we have recognized that each category – Israel and the Torah, gentiles and idolatry, for instance – claims its place in the larger system, and, as we have seen time and again, denied a place, and a particular order in the larger sequence of categories, a necessary category can render the entire system null. To make the point in the simplest possible way: we cannot imagine a Christianity without Christology. Here we have a Judaism in which the Messiah-theme in the eschatological framework takes on significance only in contexts defined by other categories altogether. That he comes and goes, appears and then passes from the scene, is not a single figure but two (or more) marks his systemic subordination, the Messiah-theme's categorical inadequacy.

That fact is born out by the first and most important element of theological thinking about the Messiah-theme: the multiplicity of Messiahs, even in the eschatological setting – the multiplicity and also the transience. Like Elijah, the Messiah is forerunner and precursor, but he is hardly an enduring player in the eschatological drama. Only God is. Time and again we shall see that the Messiah refers back to God for instructions on what he is to do. A mark of categorical subordination of the Messiah-theme is the diversity of Messiahs, each with his own story. One Messiah comes out of the line of Joseph, another out of the line of David. Both Messiahs (and others in that same classification, for example, the Messiah who is anointed to be high priest in charge of the army [Dt. 20:2–7, Mishnah-tractate Sotah Chapter Eight]), are mortal and subject to the human condition. One Messiah is murdered, replaced by another. The Messiah, moreover, is subject to the impulse to do evil, like any other man. The Messiah plays a transient role in the eschatological drama. People want the Messiah to come – that is the premise of the stories told in connection with repentance – but that is only because he will inaugurate the eschatological drama, not because, on his own, he will bring the drama to its conclusion. Only God will.

Most strikingly, the Messiah-theme plays itself out not only in the eschatological categories but in those that concern sin and the evil inclination. This presentation of the theme is accomplished through a complex composite at Bavli-tractate Sukkah 5:1D-5:4, which we considered in chapter 11 and to fresh parts of which we now turn. The Mishnah-passage there invites from the framers of the Talmud's composite some comments on the "evil inclination," which in this context refers to libido in particular. Then we have a rather substantial discussion of sexuality. But a second look shows us that the composite concerns not sexual misbehaviour or desire therefor, so much as the Messiah-theme. Here we find the allegation that the Messiah son of Joseph was killed because of the evil inclination; the Messiah son of David will be saved by God; the evil inclination, then, is made the counterweight to the Messiah and a threat to his survival. It is overcome, however, by study of the Torah. The composite is hardly coherent in detail, but its thematic program – Torah, Messiah, in the context of the Festival of Tabernacles – imposes upon the topic of the Mishnah-paragraph a quite different perspective from that set forth in the Mishnah itself.

The pertinent part of the composite, other parts of which we have already examined, is as follows:

M. SUK. 5:1D–5:4 II.3FF./52A–B

3. A. [With regard to "And the land shall mourn, every family apart; the family of the house of David apart, and their wives apart" (Zech. 12:12),] What was the reason for the mourning [to which reference is made in Zechariah's statement]?
B. R. Dosa and rabbis differed on this matter.
C. One said, "It is on account of the Messiah, the son of Joseph, who was killed."
D. And the other said, "It is on account of the evil inclination, which was killed."

The dispute balances the death of the Messiah against the death of the inclination to do evil, though these surely are opposites, and that leads to the inquiry, why should the land mourn at the death of the latter?

E. Now in the view of him who said, "It is on account of the Messiah, the son of Joseph, who was killed," we can make sense of the following verse of Scripture: "And they shall look on me because they have thrust him through, and they shall mourn for him as one mourns for his only son" (Zech. 12:10).

F. But in the view of him who has said, "It is on account of the evil inclination, which was killed," should this be an occasion for mourning? It should be an occasion for rejoicing. Why then should [the people] have wept?

The eschatological drama now comes into play: the disposition of the inclination to do evil at the end of days, which is to say, the key action in the restoration of Eden, God's own intervention in securing for man the capacity to carry out God's will without obstacle:

G. [The answer] is in accord with the exposition of R. Judah: "In the time to come, the Holy One, blessed be he, will bring the evil inclination and slay it before the righteous and before the wicked.

L. "And so too the Holy One, blessed be he, will share their amazement, as it is said, 'Thus says the Lord of Hosts. If it be marvelous in the eyes of the remnant of this people in those days, it shall also be marvelous in my eyes'" (Zech. 8:6).

So much for the Messiah son of Joseph. Now what of the Messiah son of David, and how does he relate to the events just portrayed?

5. A. Our rabbis have taught on Tannaite authority:

B. To the Messiah, son of David, who is destined to be revealed – speedily, in our days! – the Holy One, blessed be he, will say, "Ask something from me, and I shall give it to you."

C. So it is said, "I will tell of the decree ... this day have I begotten you, ask of me and I will give the nations for your inheritance" (Ps. 2:7–8).

D. When [the Messiah, son of David] sees the Messiah, son of Joseph, killed, he will say before [God], "Lord of the Age, I ask of you only life."

E. He will say to him, "Life? Before you spoke of it, David your father had already prophesied about you, as it is said, 'He asked life of you, you gave it to him, [even length of days forever and ever']" (Ps. 21:5).

Here the Messiah-theme works itself out in the story of two Messiahs, one who was killed, the other not. This latter Messiah is the one who will participate in the process of the end of time, beginning with the resurrection – a matter more clearly expressed in sources we shall consider in a moment.

First, let us ask about the place, within the composite to which reference has just now been made, of the Messiah and the message that is conveyed by introducing that figure. A rapid recapitulation of the propositions in the large composite tells us what the Talmud has added to the Mishnah's topic, which is, the Festival of Tabernacles. None of them has any bearing at all on the topic at hand, but by introducing the set of propositions into the present context, the topic before us is recast, the first two and fourth components being familiar from chapter 11 but necessary to establish the whole picture here:

1. God created the impulse to do evil but regrets it: there are four things that the Holy One, blessed be he, regrets he created, and these are they: Exile, the Chaldeans, the Ishmaelites, and the inclination to do evil.
2. The impulse to do evil is weak at the outset but powerful when it becomes habitual. The inclination to do evil to begin with is like a spider's thread and in the end like cart ropes. In the beginning one calls the evil inclination a passer-by, then a guest, and finally, a man of the household. The impulse to do evil affects one's status in the world to come.

Now the integral character of the insertion about the Messiah becomes clear:

3. The Messiah was killed on account of the impulse to do evil. That is why the Messiah, son of David, asked God to spare his life and not allow him to be killed the way the Messiah son of Joseph was killed.
4. The impulse to do evil is stronger for sages than for others. But they possess the antidote in the Torah: "For it has done great things" (Joel 2:20): "And against disciples of sages more than against all the others." A man's inclination [to do evil] overcomes him every day. A man's inclination to do evil prevails over him every day and seeks to kill him. If that vile one meets you, drag it to the house of study. If it is a stone, it will dissolve. If it is iron, it will be pulverized.

Here is where the self-evident connection proves revealing. If we did not know that the Festival of Tabernacles was associated with an autumnal celebration of the advent of rain and the fructifying of the fields, on the one side, and also identified as the occasion for the coming of the Messiah, on the other, then, on the strength of this extrinsic composite, we should have formed the theory that those two protean conceptions governed.

So the self-evident connections reveal an entire cluster of connected categories and subsets. As is common in Rabbinic sources, we treat in one and the same setting private life and public affairs, this world and its concerns and the world to come as well. The private life – the role of the sexual impulse in one's personal affairs and fate – and the destiny of Israel in the world to come and the Messianic future correspond. God governs in both dimensions, the personal and the political. And the sages then represent the realm of affairs: suffering more than others from the desires to sin, but better able than others to resist those desires. The upshot is that the Messiah-theme is subordinate to the purpose of the compiler of the composite, who wishes to underscore the link between overcoming the evil impulse and the advent of the world to come, beginning with the appearance of a (not *the*) Messiah.

Apart from the definitive composite just now examined, we find other statements on the subject that enjoy normative standing. A well-documented component of the Messiah-theme introduces the motif of tribulations to attend the coming of the Messiah. That may or may not involve the war of Gog and Magog prophesied by Ezekiel Chapters Thirty-Seven and Thirty-Eight. It also may or may not be intended to bring about repentance, to lead to the resurrection of the dead. Matters are somewhat confused. The sages do not much expand on the war of Gog and Magog, only insisting that God will be with Israel at that time. I have not identified systematic expositions of the details of that war, only allusions invited by the context of repentance at the last:

SIFRA CCLXIX:II.12

A. "[Yet for all that, when they are in the land of their enemies,] I will not spurn them, neither will I abhor them so as to destroy them utterly":

D. But "I will not spurn them": – in the time of Vespasian.

E. "... neither will I abhor them": – in the time of Greece.

F. "... so as to destroy them utterly and break my covenant with them": – in the time of Haman.

G. "... for I am the Lord their God": – in the time of Gog.

Here is a statement that, in the age of the coming of the Messiah, the war of Gog and Magog will be so terrifying as to make people forget prior troubles:

TOSEFTA-TRACTATE BERAKHOT I:11:

J. Similarly, "Remember not the former things, nor consider the things of old" (Is. 43:18). Remember not the former things – these are [God's mighty acts in saving Israel] from the [various] kingdoms; nor consider things of old – these are [God's mighty acts in saving Israel] from Egypt.

K. "Behold, I am doing a new thing; now it springs forth" (Isa. 43:19) – this refers to the war of Gog and Magog [at the end of time].

L. They drew a parable, to what may the matter be compared? To one who was walking in the way and a wolf attacked him, but he was saved from it. He would continually relate the incident of the wolf. Later a lion attacked him, but he was saved from it.

He forgot the incident of the wolf and would relate the incident of the lion. Later still a serpent attacked him, but he was saved from it. He forgot the other two incidents and would continually relate the incident of the serpent.

M. So, too, are Israel: the recent travails make them forget about the earlier ones.

The same point is made at greater length at the next statement:

PESIQTA RABBATI XV:XV:I=PESIQTA
DERAB KAHANA V:X.13.

13. A. And rabbis say, "In the septennate in which the son of David comes, in the first of the seven year spell, 'I shall cause it to rain on one town and not on another' (Amos 4:7).

B. "In the second, the arrows of famine will be sent forth.

C. "In the third there will be a great famine, and men, women, and children will die in it, and the Torah will be forgotten in Israel.

D. "In the fourth, there will be a famine which is not really a famine, and plenty which is not plentiful.

E. "In the fifth year, there will be great plenty, and people will eat and drink and rejoice, and the Torah will again be renewed.

F. "In the sixth there will be great thunders.

G. "In the seventh there will be wars.

H. "And at the end of the seventh year of that septennate, the son of David will come."

I. Said R. Abbuha/Abbayye, "How many seven-year-cycles have there been like this one, and yet he has not come."

Another doctrine simply links the coming of the Messiah to trials in general, not connected with the great war of Gog and Magog:

J. But matters accord with what R. Yohanan said, "In the generation in which the son of David comes, disciples of sages will perish, and those that remain will have faint vision, with suffering and sighing, and terrible troubles will come on the people, and harsh decrees will be renewed. Before the first such decree is carried out, another will be brought along and joined to it."

K. Said R. Abun, "In the generation in which the son of David comes, the meeting place will be turned over to prostitution, the Galilee will be destroyed, Gablan will be desolate, and the Galileans will make the rounds from town to town and find no comfort.

L. "Truthful men will be gathered up, and the truth will be fenced in and go its way."

M. Where will it go?

N. A member of the household of R. Yannai said, "It will go and dwell in small flocks in the wilderness, in line with this verse of Scripture: Truth shall be among bands" (Is. 59:15).

But it is not only the dreadful war that will accompany the Messiah's advent. It also is the end of the social order altogether, the violation of all the rules of hierarchical classification that signify that order:

O. Said R. Nehorai, "In the generation in which the son of David comes, youths will humiliate old men, sages will rise before youths, a slave girl will abuse her mistress, a daughter-in-law her mother-in-law, a man's enemies will be his own householders, a son will not be ashamed for his father, the wisdom of scribes will turn rotten, the vine will give its fruit but wine will be expensive."

P. Said R. Abba bar Kahana, "The son of David will come only to a generation which is liable to be subject to total extermination."

Q. Said R. Yannai, "The son of David will come only to a generation the principal leaders of which are like dogs."

R. Said R. Levi, "If you see one generation after another blaspheming, look for the footsteps of the messiah-king.

S. "What verse of Scripture indicates it? 'Remember Lord the taunts hurled at your servant, how I have borne in my heart the calumnies of the nations; so have your enemies taunted us, O Lord, taunted the successors of your anointed king' (Ps. 89:51).

T. "What follows? 'Blessed is the Lord for ever, amen, amen'" (Ps. 89:52).

The tribulations of the end time thus may or may not involve the war of Gog and Magog, precipitated at the coming of the Messiah. A variety of troubles will mark that same event. But these motivate Israel to repent, and that repentance will bring the Messiah. Still, that is not consistently alleged in the main statements on the subject. The Messiah need not do more than signal a variety of events, political and social, that he neither brings about nor calls to a conclusion.

Whatever the other uses of the Messiah-theme, one fact is clear: the Messiah is linked to the resurrection of the dead, which inaugurates the period culminating in the world to come. But even here the Messiah – the one who descends from David – whose advent will mark the resurrection will not play an ongoing, enduring role in the eschatological process; he is a subordinated figure. That fact underscores what we have noticed about the Messiah-theme's not forming a category unto itself but serving to fill out details in autonomous categories. For one thing, his role is limited, a determinate stage in the coming age. But how long will the Messiah's period last?

Within the doctrine that that period is finite and determinate, ending with the resurrection of the dead or coincident with it, a number of positions, each within the logic of the exegesis of selected verses, are worked out. The first has three generations:

SIFRÉ TO DEUTERONOMY CCCX:V.1

A. "... consider the years of ages past":
B. This refers to the generation in which the Messiah will be, which encompasses, in time, three generations, as it is said, "They shall fear you while the sun endures and so long as the moon, throughout all generations" (Ps. 72:5).

Another view maintains that the time of the Messiah is limited to forty years, or four hundred, or some determinate period. Then the dead will be raised.

PESIQTA RABBATI I:VII.1

A. How long are the days of the Messiah?
B. R. Aqiba says, "Forty years, in line with this verse: "And he afflicted you and allowed you to hunger (Deut. 8:3), and it is written, Make us glad according to the days in which you afflicted us" (Ps. 90:15). Just as the affliction lasted forty years in the wilderness, so the affliction here is forty years [with the result that the glad time is the same forty years]."
C. Said R. Abin, "What verse of Scripture further supports the position of R. Aqiba? 'As in the days of your coming forth from the land of Egypt I will show him marvelous things' " (Mic. 7:15).

Aqiba's brief period is now extended by Eliezer, then others expand it still further, all concurring that the Messiah's place in the resurrection of the dead is determinate, his role contingent on the unfolding of a process of which he forms only a chapter:

D. R. Eliezer says, "Four hundred years, as it is written, 'And they shall enslave them and torment them for four hundred years' (Gen. 15:13), and further it is written, 'Make us glad according to the days in which you afflicted us' " (Ps. 90:15).

Now we move from the record of history to the facts of nature, invoking a different analogy, with strikingly different consequences:

E. R. Berekhiah in the name of R. Dosa the Elder says, "Six hundred years, as it is written, 'As the days of a tree shall be the days of my people' (Is. 65:22).
F. "How long are the days of a tree? A sycamore lasts for six hundred years."

From the world of nature we progress to the world of time, a day and its length:

G. R. Eliezer b. R. Yosé the Galilean says, "A thousand years, as it is written, 'For a thousand years in your sight as are but as yesterday when it has passed' (Ps. 90:40), and it is written, 'The day of vengeance as in my heart but now my year of redemption is come' (Is. 63:4).
H. "The day of the Holy One, blessed be he, is the same as a thousand years for a mortal."

Once the metaphor of the day takes over, then meanings imputed to "day" are sorted out as well:

I. R. Joshua says, "Two thousand years, 'according to the days in which you afflicted us' (Ps. 90:15).
J. "For there are no fewer days [as in the cited verse] than two, and the day of the Holy One, blessed be he, is the same as a thousand years for a mortal."
K. R. Abbahu says, "Seven thousand years, as it is said, As a bride groom rejoices over his bride will your God rejoice over you (Is. 62:5), and how long does a groom rejoice over his bride? It is seven days,
L. "and the day of the Holy One, blessed be he, is the same as a thousand years for a mortal."

We move from "day" to "year," and the discussion trails off:

M. Rabbi says, "You cannot count it: 'For the day of vengeance that was in my heart and my year of redemption have come' " (Is. 63:4).
N. How long are the days of the Messiah? Three hundred and sixty-five thousand years will be the length of the days of the Messiah.

The details being left unclear, the main claim stands: the Messiah functions for a finite period. But what does he do in that time?

This is the point at which the Messiah-theme's subordination to other categories becomes clear. In the present context, the advent of the Messiah plays a role in the raising of the dead. Indeed, I have several times taken as fact the presence of the doctrine that, at the end of the Messiah's period, the dead are raised. This is now explicitly stated, the resurrection being joined to the restoration of those who are raised from the grave to the Land of Israel. But at no point do I identify the claim that the Messiah is the one who raises the dead; the language used always simply says that, when he has come, the dead will rise or live but that God is the one who gives them breath:

2. A. Then the dead of the Land of Israel who are Israelites will live and derive benefit from them, and all the righteous who are overseas will come through tunnels.

B. And when they reach the land, the Holy One, blessed be he, will restore their breath, and they will rise and derive benefit from the days of the Messiah along with them [already in the land].

C. For it is said, "He who spread forth the the earth and its offspring gives breath to the people on it" (Is. 42:5).

But does the Messiah bear responsibility for raising the dead? I do not identify that claim in so many words. And then, who bears responsibility for doing so? It is Israel – that point is made time and again when pertinent. Israel's own repentance will provide the occasion, and God will do the rest. It is when Israel has repented, as we noted in chapter 12, that the Messiah will come. It follows that the Messiah's advent and activity depend upon Israel, not on the Messiah's own autonomous decision, character, and behaviour. Israel decides issues of its own attitude towards God and repents, God decides to respond to the change in will. But not a comparable, categorical imperative, the Messiah only responds to Israel's decision on when he should make his appearance to signal the change in the condition of mankind, and the Messiah responds to God's decision, taking a part within that sequence that comes to an end with Elijah.

That accounts for the heavy emphasis upon not the Messiah's intervention but Israel's own responsibility. We already have noted the tendency to assign the coming of the Messiah to times of suffering, which will have brought Israel to repent, and that is once more stated in the present context as well:

3. A. When will the royal Messiah come?

B. Said R. Eleazar, "Near to the Messiah's days, ten places will be swallowed up, ten places will be overturned, ten places will be wiped out."

C. And R. Hiyya bar Abba said, "The royal Messiah will come only to a generation the leaders of which are like dogs."

D. R. Eleazar says, "It will be in the time of a generation that is worthy of annihilation that the royal Messiah will come."

E. R. Levi said, "Near the time of the days of the Messiah a great event will take place in the world."

The time of the Messiah is compared to the period of redemption, and it is held to serve as a preparatory period, leading to the resurrection of the dead (systemic equivalent to the entry into the Land/Eden, which, by rights, ought to have marked the end of time). That inquiry into the correct analogy explains the definitions that are given, forty years, as with the Generation of the Wilderness, of four hundred years, as in the torment prior to redemption from Egypt, and so on down. The divisions of time do not come to an end with the end of history as written by the pagan kingdoms. From the time that their rule comes to an end, with the coming of the Messiah and the restoration of Israelite government, a sequence of further, differentiated periods commences; the time of the Messiah is only the first of these. Then comes the resurrection of the dead, along with the last judgment. Only at that point does the world to come get under way and time is no longer be differentiated.

This conviction that the Messiah's period is determinate has, moreover, to be set into the context of the three periods of the history of creation: those marked by chaos, Torah, and Messiah. Specifically, the history of the world is divided into three units of two thousand years each, the age of chaos, Torah, and Messiah: with the Torah succeeding the age of chaos, and the Messiah, the age of the Torah, as we already have noted in chapter 6:

B. A.Z. I:I II.5/9A

A. The Tannaite authority of the household of Elijah [stated], "The world will last for six thousand years: two thousand years of chaos, two thousand years of Torah, two thousand years of the time of the Messiah. But because of the abundance of our sins, what has passed [of the foreordained time] has passed."

Israel now lives in the period of the Torah, which succeeds upon the chaos brought about by man and educates the heart of the people of the Torah:

B. As to the two thousand years of Torah, from what point do they commence? If one should say that it is from the actual giving of the Torah [at Mount Sinai], then up to this time there has not been so long a span of time. For if you look into the matter, you find that, from the creation to the giving of the Torah, the years comprise two thousand and part of the third thousand [specifically, 2448; from Adam to Noah, 1056; from Noah to Abraham, 891; from Abraham to the Exodus, 500, from the Creation to Exodus and the giving of the law at Sinai, 2448 years]. Therefore the period is to be calculated from the time that Abraham and Sarah 'had gotten souls in Haran,' for we have learned by tradition that Abraham at that time was fifty-two years old. Now to what measure does the Tannaite calculation deduct? Since the Tannaite teaching is

448 years, you find that from the time that Abraham and Sarah 'had gotten souls in Haran,' to the giving of the Torah were 448 years."

The advent of the Messiah marks a stage in the unfolding of periods (not "history") within the logic of creation: chaos, sin; Torah, repentance; Messiah, restoration – and then, as the other calculations have indicated, comes the world to come or eternal life, an age beyond time and change.

What about the gentiles in all this? Naturally, as soon as the category, Israel and the Torah, is invoked, its counterpart and opposite, the gentiles and idolatry, complements and balances the discussion. So too, when it comes to the Messiah, the gentiles are given a role. Specifically, the nations will bring gifts to the Messiah, and it will be a great honour to them that they are permitted to do so. But, like the judgment of the nations set forth in chapter 4 ("In the age to come the Holy One, blessed be He, will bring a scroll of the Torah and hold it in his bosom and say, 'Let him who has kept himself busy with it come and take his reward' " – leading to the exclusion of the gentiles from the world to come), their participation in the Messiah's activities only underscores Israel's centrality to the human drama:

BAVLI-TRACTATE PESAHIM 10:7 II.22/118B

A. Said R. Kahana, "When R. Ishmael b. R. Yosé fell ill, Rabbi sent word to him: 'Tell us two or three of the things that you said to us in the name of your father.'

B. "He sent word to him, 'This is what father said: "What is the meaning of the verse of Scripture, 'Praise the Lord all you nations' (Ps. 117:1)? What are the nations of the world doing in this setting? This is the sense of the statement, 'Praise the Lord all you nations' (Ps. 117:1) for the acts of might and wonder that he has done with them; all the more so us, since 'his mercy is great toward us.' "

Now the nations take a more specific role in relationship to the Messiah, each claiming a relationship to the Messiah on account of its dealings with Israel:

C. " 'And further: "Egypt is destined to bring a gift to the Messiah. He will think that he should not accept it from them. The Holy One, blessed be He, will say to the Messiah, 'Accept it from them, they provided shelter for my children in Egypt.' Forthwith: 'Nobles shall come out of Egypt, bringing gifts' (Ps. 68:32).

D. "The Ethiopians will propose an argument a fortiori concerning themselves, namely: 'If these, who subjugated them, do this, we, who never subjugated them, all the more so!' The Holy One, blessed be He, will say to the Messiah, 'Accept it from them.' Forthwith: 'Ethiopia shall hasten to stretch out her hands to God' " (Ps. 68:32).

Rome always comes at the climax, and, in any sequence of the nations, will always mark the end of the discussion. Here Rome evokes its descent from Esau, a given for the Oral Torah, or from Edom, thus part of the extended family of Israel:

E. "Wicked Rome will then propose the same argument a fortiori in her own regard: 'If these, who are not their brethren, are such, then we, who are their brethren, all the more so!' The Holy One, blessed be He, will say to Gabriel, 'Rebuke the wild beast of the reeds, the multitude of the bulls' (Ps. 68:32) – 'rebuke the wild beast and take possession of the congregation.'

F. "Another interpretation: 'Rebuke the wild beast of the reeds' – who dwells among the reeds, 'the boar out of the wood ravages it, that which moves in the field feeds on it' " (Ps. 80:14).

Here the Messiah accords honour to the nations, except for Rome, the empire that will fall at the redemption of Israel now at hand. The governing concern – the nations relate to the Messiah only through Israel – registers. The Messiah plays a part in the resurrection of the dead, on the one side, and the restoration of Israel, on the other. But the Messiah-doctrine clearly encompasses the view that the Messiah will not endure for the world to come but himself carries out the task assigned to him and then passes from the scene, a doctrine clearly indicated by the specification of the period of time assigned to the Messiah. How the Messiah figures in discussions of the age or world to come remains to be seen.

14 Restoring the Public Order: The World to Come

For us it is not easy to imagine a thought-world in which patterns, rather than sequences of events treated as cause and effect, are asked to organize experience. Yet the theology of the Oral Torah sets forth a thought world in which what is at stake are not beginnings and endings in an ordinal or (other) temporal sense. At issue, rather, are balances and proportions, the match of this to that, start to finish, Eden and world to come. True, that mode of thought is not commonplace outside the rule-seeking sciences of nature and society. These worlds of intellect do not tell the teleologically framed story of a molecule or the history of a law of economics but seek to formulate in abstract terms the concrete facts of molecules and enduring rules of economics that describe secular facts whatever the temporal context. But, I think it is now clear, that is precisely how the sages think, which is to say, in the manner of the natural philosophers of antiquity in general, as I pointed out in chapter 1. And they have in mind, as I said, paradigms of relationship.

Specifically, when the sages speak of the world to come, their language signifies a final change in relationship between God and man, a model of how God and man relate that marks the utter restoration of the world order originally contemplated. That is the way man and God conduct their cosmic transaction that God had intended from the beginning and for eternity – time having no place in his category-formation for ordering creation. The point, specifically, is that Israel enjoys a set of relationships with God that are not differentiated temporally and certainly not organized in causal patterns of sequence, in ordered, causative sequence through time, but in other ways.

How then are these relationships are classified in this governing model? They are either rebellious or obedient, selfish and arrogant or selfless and humble, and so on, as we have seen at great length. Since at issue are patterns of relationship, the circumstance and context, whether temporal or singular in some other way, make no impact. That is because they make no difference, the relationship transcending circumstance. Therefore, it is entirely reasonable that the world to come match the world that has been – why not? The one, like the other, will find its definition in how God and man relate. That is what I mean when I claim that we deal with modes of thought of an other-than-historical and temporal character. As I shall explain, that kind of thinking makes difficult the use of the word eschatology in reference to the world to come. The restorationist character of the theology of the Oral Torah explains what the sages mean. That theology, by reason of the modes of thought that define its logic of making connections and drawing conclusions, requires that endings match beginnings, the relationships of God and man at the one point matching those at the other.

We should err if we invoked in this connection the word "cyclical" and supposed that the sages contemplate a recurring cycle of existence, beginnings and endings and new beginnings, such as nature presents. Cyclical thinking is as alien to the sages as historical thinking, because it presupposes an eternal return, an endless recapitulation of the pattern. But that is not what the sages have in mind. They anticipate a one-time return, then an eternity of perfection, as we shall see later in this chapter. The perfection of world order leaves no alternative. Once man has repented and conformed his will to God's, that relationship, embodying measure for measure in a most just and merciful realization, attains perfection and, man's will and God's meeting, finality, complementarity, utter correspondence. That is why there is no room in the sages' system for an endless cycle of sin, punishment, atonement, reconciliation. I see, within the system, three embodiments: Adam loses Eden, Israel, the new Adam, loses the Land – two times – then Israel repents, the dead are raised, Israel is restored to the Land, and eternal life follows; in that model, with its stress on eternal life with God, there is no logical place for the cyclical replay of the pattern. Paradigmatic thinking, then, finds its position between the historical-linear and ahistorical-cyclical kinds.

So here the story that commences with God's creation of a perfect world defined by a just order comes full circle. That world exhibits flaws, it is not perfect by reason of the character of man. But the world will be restored to perfection (requiring, then, eternity), man to Eden, Israel to the Land of Israel, through man's, and Israel's, act of repentance and reconciliation with God. That act of reconciliation, prepared for in countless lives of virtue and acts of merit, is realized in the world or age to come. Through its account of that world or age, therefore, that theology writes the last, but unending, chapter in the story of how God's justice establishes and ultimately restores the world order of perfection and equity.

The world to come concludes the eschatological series that is comprised by sequenced paradigms that cover past, present, Israel's collective repentance, the age (days) of the Messiah, the days of the war of Gog and Magog, the resurrection of the dead, the judgment, and onward to the last things at the world to come. If resurrection concerns the individual Israelite, with some further implications for the whole of Israel, the world to come that follows encompasses all Israel. The one embodies salvation for the private person, the other, redemption for the entire holy people, now at the end encompassing all of mankind within Israel. But what, exactly, when the sages set forth their theological eschatology, do they mean by *'olam habba,* the world or the age that is coming? The world or the age to come (the Hebrew, *'olam,* may sustain either the locative, world, or the temporal-ordinal, age) completes, and necessarily forms the final chapter, of the theology of the Oral Torah. The age that is coming will find Adam's successor in Eden's replacement, that is, resurrected, judged, and justified Israel – comprising nearly all Israelites who ever lived – now eternally rooted in the Land of Israel.

As we have seen, the governing theology sets out its main components in a simple narrative, and often a single sentence captures the story. Here is such a version of the complete tale of the world to come in one short sentence: *When Israel returns to God, God will restore their fortunes.* The sentence remains brief enough with the added adjectival clause, *in the model of Adam and Eve in Eden.* Everything else amplifies details. That simple sentence is explicitly built on the verb-root for return, encompassing restore, *shub,* yielding *teshubah,* repentance as well as the causative form of the verb, *hashib,* thus return or restore. It thereby defines the condition, (intransitive) return or repentance, for the advent of the age to come, which encompasses the action, (transitively) to return matters to their original condition.

How, exactly, do the sages envisage restoration? Predictably, because they think paradigmatically and not in historical (let alone cyclical) sequences, the sages find models of the end in beginnings. That is why in this context they cluster, and systematically review, the two principal ones, liberation, restoration. First is the account of Israel's liberation from Egypt, the initial act of redemption, which will be recapitulated in the end. Second, as we have seen many times now, comes the story of Adam and Eden for their picture of the world to come, the return of Adam to Eden, now in the form of Israel to Zion. (A secondary motif in the latter paradigm contains the complementary category, Gehenna, to which gentiles – meaning, those who deny God – and Israelites who sufficiently sin are consigned when they are denied life.) In the latter case the important point for paradigmatic thinking is that there is no meaningful difference between the world to come and "the Garden of Eden." We go over, once more in so many words, an explicit statement that the two are not to be distinguished, here in a formulation we shall more fully see again later on in a different context:

YERUSHALMI-TRACTATE PEAH I:I XXXII.I

A. "He who performs mostly good deeds inherits the Garden of Eden, but he who performs mostly transgression inherits Gehenna.

The Garden of Eden is the opposite of Gehenna, and the context – Mishnah-tractate Peah's picture of how good deeds store up merit for the world to come – explains the rest. Since Mishnah-tractate Peah at the outset speaks of the world to come, inheriting the Garden of Eden in context bears precisely the meaning of inheriting the world to come; there is no difference, and the two, Eden and world to come, are interchangeable when the sages speak of what happens after death, on the one side, or after resurrection and judgment, on the other. For man entering the world to come, on the other side of resurrection and judgment, marks a homecoming. At the moment of return to Eden, entry into the world to come, man returns to his original condition, in God's image, after God's likeness, complement and conclusion of creation. Here is the ultimate complementarity, the final point of correspondence.

Whatever model serves out of Scripture, that restorationist eschatology (a word that in the context now established can be used only a loose way, as I shall explain) is stated in so many words in the following, which appeals to the rhetoric of return, restoration, and renewal:

LAMENTATIONS RABBATI CXLIII:I.IFF.

A. "Restore us to yourself, O Lord, that we may be restored!":
B. Said the Community of Israel before the Holy One, blessed be He, "Lord of the world, it all depends on you: 'Restore us to yourself, O Lord.' "
C. Said to them the Holy One, blessed be He, "It all depends on you: 'Return to me and I will return to you, says the Lord of hosts' " (Mal. 3:7).
D. Said the Community of Israel before the Holy One, blessed be He, "Lord of the world, it all depends on you: 'Restore us, O God of our salvation' " (Ps. 85:5).
E. Thus it says, "Restore us to yourself, O Lord, that we may be restored!"

Israel insists that restoration depends on God, but God repays the compliment, and the exchange then is equal: God restores Israel when Israel returns to God, just as we learned when we examined the category of repentance and atonement.

Now we see a sequence of models of redemption. First, as anticipated, comes the explicit comparison of Adam's Eden with the coming restoration, part of a sequence of recapitulated paradigms:

2. A. "Renew our days as of old":
B. As in the days of the first Adam: "So he drove out the man and he placed at the east of the garden of Eden the cherubim" (Gen. 3:24). [The word for "east" and the word for "of old" using the same letters, the sense, is this: "Renew our days like those of him in connection with whom *kedem* is stated." After being driven out, Adam repented of his sin.]

The restoration involves the Temple offerings as well, which later on are defined in particular; this is here too "as in the days of old":

3. A. Another interpretation of the phrase, "Renew our days as of old":
B. That is in line with this verse: "Then shall the offering of Judah and Jerusalem be pleasant to the Lord as in the days of old and as in ancient years" (Mal. 3:4).

But the restoration is multidimensional, since it involves, also, the figures of Moses and Solomon:

C. "as in the days of old:" this refers to Moses: "Then his people remembered the days of old, the days of Moses" (Isa. 63:11).
D. "and as in ancient years:" this refers to the time of Solomon.

Noah and Abel, for reasons that are specified, now are introduced; they are necessary for the reason given at the end:

4. A. [Another interpretation of the phrase, "Renew our days as of old":]
B. Rabbi says, "'as in the days of old' refers to the time of Noah: 'For this is as the waters of Noah unto me' (Isa. 54:9).
C. "'and as in ancient years' refers to the time of Abel, prior to whose time there was no idolatry in the world."

Noah represents the moment at which God made his peace with man, even in man's flawed condition. Of intense interest for my analysis, within the restorationist pattern, Abel stands for the time before idolatry, so explicitly excluding idolators from the world to come. While Noah, representing all of humanity, and Abel, standing even for antediluvian humanity, make their appearance, the upshot remains exclusionary. The restoration to perfection involves the exclusion of imperfection, and so idolators cannot enter the new Eden. But, later on, we shall see other, inclusionary dimensions that logically complete the doctrine of the gentiles in the world to come.

As the reference to the Exodus has already alerted us, the pattern that is adumbrated in these statements encompasses not only restoration but the recapitulation of the paradigm of oppression, repentance, and reconciliation. For restoration cannot stand by itself but must be placed into that context in which the restoration takes on heavy weight. So not only Adam and Eden but the entire past of suffering and finally of salvation is reviewed in the same context. Many salvations, not only one, are recorded for Israel, all of them conforming to a single pattern, which imparts its definition upon the final act of salvation as well, the one that comes with personal resurrection and all-Israel's entry into the world to come. That is the claim explicitly set forth in the following composition:

YERUSHALMI TRACTATE BERAKHOT 1:6 1:7

A. Ben Zoma says, "Israel is destined not to mention the exodus from Egypt in the future age."
B. What is the basis for this statement? "And thus the days are coming says the Lord, you shall no longer say, 'God lives, who took us out of the Land of Egypt'; but 'God lives, who took out and who brought the seed of the House of Israel from the Land in the North' " (Jeremiah 23:7–8).

The point that is argued is that a pattern of salvation is established, and it is incremental, one salvation being added to the record already written of its predecessor:

C. This does not mean that the exodus from Egypt will be removed [and no longer mentioned]. Rather [mention of the redemption from] Egypt will be added to the [mention of] the redemption from the Kingdom [of the North]. The [mention of the redemption from the] Kingdom [of the North] will be primary and [the mention of the redemption from] Egypt will be secondary."
D. And so it says, "Your name shall no longer be called Jacob. Israel shall be your name."
E. They said, "That does not mean that the name Jacob will be removed. Rather Jacob will be added to Israel. Israel will be the primary name and Jacob will be secondary."

Now the war of Gog and Magog recurs, a detail of the eschatological program that is neither bypassed nor much developed in the Oral Torah:

F. And so its says, "Do not mention the first [redemption]" – this refers to [the redemption from] Egypt. "And pay no heed to the early [redemption]" – this refers to [the redemption from] the Kingdom of the North. "Lo, I am making a new [redemption]" – this refers to [the redemption to come in the time of] Gog.

Where a paradigm is rehearsed, a parable serves to realize the matter in a clear way, because it moves from the particular to the general:

G. They gave a parable. To what case is this matter similar? To the case of a person who was walking by the way and he met up with a wolf and was saved from it. He began to tell the story of [his salvation from] the wolf.
H. Afterwards he met up with a lion and was saved from it. He forgot the story of [his salvation from] the wolf and began to tell the story of [his salvation from] the lion.
I. Afterwards he met up with a serpent and was saved from it. He forgot both the previous incidents and began to tell the story of [his salvation from] the serpent.

Now comes the explicit application of the parable:

J. Just so was the case for Israel. Their [salvation from] the later troubles caused them to forget [to mention the story of their salvation from] the earlier troubles.

So the paradigm of trouble but salvation for Israel works itself out, and it gives reassurance that God will redeem Israel in the future, as he did in the past; a pattern governs throughout. Indeed, the surest evidence of the coming redemption is the oppression that now takes place.

This point is stated in a variety of ways, taking an important place in the set of doctrines set forth around the theme of the world to come. Here is the simplest statement of why suffering and oppression present cause for renewed hope:

LAMENTATIONS RABBATI CXXII:I.I

I. A. "The punishment of your iniquity, O daughter of Zion, is accomplished, he will keep you in exile no longer."

Now comes the point that the very condition of Israel, its life in exile, serves as guarantee of the redemption that God is going to bring about. That relationship of complementarity – oppression, redemption – is why the act of oppression, now realized, validates the hope for the Messiah to signal the advent of the redemption fulfilled in the world to come. The theology not only accommodates the dissonant fact of Israel's subjugation but finds reassurance in it, as is stated in so many words:

B. R. Helbo in the name of R. Yohanan said, "Better was the removing of the ring by Pharaoh [for the sealing of decrees to oppress the Israelites] than the forty years during which Moses prophesied concerning them, because it was through this [oppression] that the redemption came about, while through that [prophesying] the redemption did not come about."

C. R. Simeon b. Laqish said, "Better was the removing of the ring by Ahasuerus decreeing persecution of Israel in Media than the sixty myriads of prophets who prophesied in the days of Elijah, because it was through this [oppression] that the redemption came about, while through that [prophesying] the redemption did not come about."

D. Rabbis said, "Better was the Book of Lamentations than the forty years in which Jeremiah prophesied over them, because in it the Israelites received full settlement of their iniquities on the day the temple was destroyed.

E. "That is in line with the following verse: 'The punishment of your iniquity, O daughter of Zion, is accomplished.'"

In narrative form the statement sets forth the proposition that Israel's future is already clear from its present. Here the prophets provide the key to interpreting the one and anticipating the other. Just as the prophetic prediction of the ruin of Jerusalem has been realized, so the same prophets' promises of ultimate salvation will also come about. That yields a certainty about what is going to happen. The whole then forms a coherent pattern, one that reveals what will happen through what has happened.

At several points in this account of the final component of the sages' theology I have introduced the word "eschatology," which ordinarily is used to refer to not the theory of last things but rather the theory of the end of history in particular. And because of the precise meaning assigned to the word "teleology" in chapter 1, I have not employed that word in the present context, though others might reasonably do so. But in fact what we deal with is a teleology without an eschatology, that is to say, a doctrine of last things outside the context of history. That is because, as I announced at the head of this chapter, the sages do not think historically, and that means I have used the word "eschatology" without requisite precision.

For, as is already quite clear from chapter 6, we do not deal with a theology that tells time through history. At hand is something other than the eschatological type of teleology such as is always set forth by people who organize experience in terms of a linear sequence of singular events, deemed each to cause the next. Nor do the sages conceive of a sequence rigidly differentiated by the temporal categories, past, present, and future. And with no conception of singular, unique, and sequential events but rather exemplary ones, the sages do not imagine that events are linked so that that sequence, past through future, accounts for the beginning, middle, and end of time. That is why, while we deal with a teleology that speaks of last things, so that the category eschatology serves, in fact we should not confuse the sages' theological teleology with a historically grounded theological eschatology at all.

The reason, on the affirmative side, is that, for the Oral Torah, "last" does not define a temporal category or even an ordinal one in the exact sense. By "last things," the sages' theology means the model of things that applies at the last, from now on, for eternity. And by that, they mean to say *the last, the final realization or recapitulation of the ever-present and enduring paradigm(s)*, creation and Exodus, for instance, as we just noticed.[1] I cannot sufficiently stress that this is a paradigm that organizes and classifies relationships, treats concrete events as merely exemplary. So the actualities of this one's conduct with, and attitude towards, that One are restated in generalizations, laws, or rules. "Love God" defines a relationship, and actions and attitudes that express that relationship then may be exemplified by incidents that show what happens when Israel loves God, or what happens when Israel does not love God. These further may be captured, in many cases by a single pattern.

In concrete terms, that means that intense interest will focus on the way in which the redemption of Israel from Egypt compares with the advent of the world to come. This point is made explicitly. The fall of the oppressor at the start of Israel's history and the fall of the nations at the end match. So the two periods correspond. To see how this is made concrete is to enter into the theological workshop of the sages. No passage more clearly exposes the character of their thought – both its method and its message – than the one that requires them to select paradigmatic moments out of the detritus of history:

---

1. When we consider the longer list of paradigms that we have examined in these pages, we notice a number of paradigms that do not serve in the teleological context, not to mention exemplary figures that are given no assignment in that setting. In manipulating the persons and events of Scripture as components of a paradigm, the sages clearly choose those appropriate for a given purpose; symbolic speech, then, goes forward as much through choices of paradigmatic media as through the formulation of propositions illustrated or embodied in those paradigms, that is to say, through silences as much as through statements.

2. A. R. Levi, son-in-law of R. Zechariah, in the name of R. Berekhiah said, "As at the news concerning Egypt, so they shall be startled at the fall of the adversary" (Is. 23:5).
B. Said R. Eliezer, "Whenever the name of Tyre is written in Scripture, if it is written out [with all of the letters], then it refers to the province of Tyre. Where it is written without all of its letters [and so appears identical to the word for enemy], the reference of Scripture is to Rome. [So the sense of the verse is that Rome will receive its appropriate reward.]"

The fall of Egypt is matched by the fall of Rome, which, we surely should anticipate, is a precondition for the advent of the world to come, at which point, at a minimum, the subjugation of Israel to the pagan empire ceases:

3. A. R. Levi in the name of R. Hama bar Hanina: "He who exacted vengeance from the former [oppressor] will exact vengeance from the latter."

The first redemption, from Egypt, is shown to match point by point the final redemption, from Edom/Rome. Each detail finds its counterpart in an amazing selection of consequential facts, properly aligned – ten in all:

B. "Just as, in Egypt, it was with blood, so with Edom [=Rome] it will be the same: 'I will show wonders in the heavens and in the earth, blood, and fire, and pillars of smoke' (Job 3:3).
C. "Just as, in Egypt, it was with frogs, so with Edom it will be the same: 'The sound of an uproar from the city, an uproar because of the palace, an uproar of the Lord who renders recompense to his enemies' (Is. 66:6).
D. "Just as, in Egypt, it was with lice, so with Edom it will be the same: 'The streams of Bosrah will be turned into pitch, and the dust thereof into brimstone, and the land thereof shall become burning pitch (Is. 34:9). Smite the dust of the earth that it may become lice' (Ex. 8:12).
E. "Just as, in Egypt, it was with swarms of wild beasts, so with Edom it will be the same: 'The pelican and the bittern shall possess it' (Is. 34:11).
F. "Just as, in Egypt, it was with pestilence, so with Edom it will be the same: 'I will plead against Gog with pestilence and with blood' (Ez. 38:22).
G. "Just as, in Egypt, it was with boils, so with Edom it will be the same: 'This shall be the plague wherewith the Lord will smite all the peoples that have warred against Jerusalem: their flesh shall consume away while they stand upon their feet' (Zech. 14:12).
H. "Just as, in Egypt, it was with great stones, so with Edom it will be the same: 'I will cause to rain upon Gog ... an overflowing shower and great hailstones' (Ez. 38:22).

I. "Just as, in Egypt, it was with locusts, so with Edom it will be the same: 'And you, son of man, thus says the Lord God: Speak to birds of every sort ... the flesh of the mighty shall you eat ... blood shall you drink ... you shall eat fat until you are full and drink blood until you are drunk' (Ez. 39:17–19).

J. "Just as, in Egypt, it was with darkness, so with Edom it will be the same: 'He shall stretch over Edom the line of chaos and the plummet of emptiness' (Is. 34:11).

K. "Just as, in Egypt, he took out their greatest figure and killed him, so with Edom it will be the same: 'A great slaughter in the land of Edom, among them to come down shall be the wild oxen' " (Is. 34:6–7).

Merely juxtaposing "Egypt" and "Edom" suffices to establish that we shall compare the one and the other, and the paradigm of redemption emerges. The known, Egypt, bears the distinguishing trait of marking Israel's initial redemption; then the unknown can be illuminated. Therefore, say "Edom" (=Rome) and no one can miss the point. The stakes are sufficiently identified through the combination of the native categories, and all the rest spells out what is clear at the very outset. I do not think that the method of paradigmatic thinking finds more lucid expression than in this articulate statement that the redemption that is coming replicates the redemption that is past in a world that conforms to enduring paradigms. And that must encompass, also, the return to Eden that we have many times considered.

Within the theory of paradigmatic thinking about the received facts of Scripture that is set forth here, a given paradigm should come to expression in a broad variety of exemplary cases (matched events, arrangements of symbols whether verbal or actual). In theory, therefore, once we fix upon a restorationist paradigm to account for the sages' classification of data and interpretation thereof, we should find more than a single case that embodies the paradigm. In fact, as we shall now see, a number of patterns is adduced to explain how the world to come will come about and to define its character. Our next case is a pattern that once more involves the liberation of Israel from Egypt, this time as the liberation is celebrated at the Passover Seder by the drinking of four cups of wine. These four cups drunk at the Passover Seder correspond to the redemption of Israel, four instances of the same pattern: the retribution carried out against Pharaoh, the retribution to be carried out against the Four Kingdoms, and the nations of the world generally, and the consolation of Israel; there is, then, a balance between Israel's and the nations' fate.

All of these events represent embodiments of a single pattern, as much as the drinking of the four cups at the celebration of the liberation from Egypt marks a single event that recurs as a pattern over the ages:

A. Whence [did they derive the requirement] for four cups?

B. R. Yohanan [said] in the name of R. Benaiah, "[They] correspond to the four redemptions [or acts of redemption, mentioned in reference to Egypt]: 'Say, therefore, to the Israelite people: I am the Lord. I will take you out' ['from under the burdens of the Egyptians and deliver you from their bondage. I will redeem you with an outstretched arm and through extraordinary chastisements']. 'And I will take you to be my people' (Exod. 6:6–7). [These verses contain the four terms:] 'I will take out,' 'I will deliver,' 'I will redeem,' 'I will take.' "

Here is an explicit treatment of the rite as paradigmatic, and the purpose of the pattern is to go over the acts of redemption that God carried out in bringing Israel out of Egypt. But, as we should expect, others read the same symbols, in the same context of liberation, in a different way, each version going over the same basic pattern and saying the same thing, all versions distinct and enriching. Here we deal with how the cups of wine form the precondition of redemption of Israel or salvation for an Israelite, in this case, Joseph:

C. R. Joshua b. Levi said, "[They] correspond to the four cups of [wine mentioned in reference to] Pharaoh: 'Pharaoh's cup was in my hand, [and I took the grapes,] and I pressed them into Pharaoh's cup, and placed the cup in Pharaoh's hand' (Gen. 40:11) ... 'and you will place Pharaoh's cup in his hand' (Gen. 40:13). ['But think of me when all is well with you again ... so as to free me from this place' (Gen. 40:14).]" [The four cups in the dream and its interpretation brought or preceded a redemption, in this instance that of Joseph.].

The four cups further correspond to the four kingdoms that have ruled Israel and that Israel will succeed in the age to come:

D. R. Levi said, "[They] correspond to the four [world] kingdoms [that have oppressed Israel and that precede the kingdom of God – Babylonia, Media, Greece, and Rome, with each cup perhaps marking the release of Israel from a different oppressor]."

Rabbis at the end take a position entirely in harmony with the preceding ones, but they state the whole in its fulness by matching retribution for the nations of the world with consolation for Israel, thus encompassing all the other matters set forth in individual names. The introduction of the gentiles into the eschatological theology presents no surprise, since, in the theory of complementarity, the gentiles will make an appearance in any paradigm in which Israel plays the principal part. Here is one account of the gentiles at the advent of the world to come:

E. And rabbis say, "[They] correspond to the four cups of retribution that the Holy One Praised be He will give the nations of the world to drink: 'For thus said the Lord, the God of Israel, to me: "Take from my hand this cup of wine – of wrath [– and make all the nations to whom I send you drink of it]" ' (Jer. 25:15); '[Flee from the midst of Babylon ... for this is a time of vengeance for the Lord, He will deal retribution to her]. Babylon was a golden cup in the Lord's hand[, it made the whole earth drunk' (Jer. 51:[6–]7); 'For in the Lord's hand there is a cup [with foaming wine fully mixed; from this He pours; all the wicked of the earth drink, draining it to the very dregs]' (Ps. 75:9); 'He will rain down upon the wicked blazing coals and sulfur, a scorching wind shall be the portion of their cup' " (Ps. 11:6).

F. [Continuing the words of the Rabbis in E:] "And corresponding to them [to the four cups of retribution], the Holy One, Praised be He, will give Israel four cups of consolation to drink: 'The Lord is my allotted share and cup' (Ps. 16:5); '[You spread a table for me in full view of my enemies;] You anoint my head with oil; my drink is abundant' (Ps. 23:5); and this [verse:] 'I raise the cup of deliverances' (Ps. 116:13) [provides an additional] two [cups (as "deliverances" is plural), each of which represents a separate act of deliverance]."

So we see how the symbolic system evoked by the restorationist paradigm encompasses the received organization of the coming ages, matching past and future. The opinions complement one another. We begin with the redemption in Egypt, as is appropriate at the commemoration of that event; then comes the role of Pharaoh. This introduces the world kingdoms that correspond at the end of time to Pharaoh, Babylonia, Media, Greece, and Rome, and, in more general terms, the retribution that will overtake the nations. Here we have the working of a paradigm, a single action repeated, the meaning always the same, the moments alone differentiated one from the other by reason of a teleology completely incompatible with the linear sequence, past to future, that forms the foundation of the historical understanding.

In this set of checks and balances that forms the architectonics of the governing theology, what at the outset matches the act of redemption at the end can only be the initial act of creation. Creation reaches its complement and completion in redemption, a somewhat jarring match. When the sages speak of "the world to come" they refer to the realization of a paradigm that is, established "of old," meaning, that is, redemption of Israel that is built into the very structure of creation, a presence in the past, as much as the past of creation is present in redemption and the world to come. That is why God himself not only participated in Israel's affairs, going into exile, as we noted in connection with God's abandoning the Temple, but also participates in the return to the Land:

BAVLI-TRACTATE MEGILLAH 4:4/I.IO/29A

B. R. Simeon ben Yohai says, "Come and see how dear [the nation of] Israel is before The Holy One, Blessed Be He, for wherever they were exiled, the Divine Presence was with them.

C. "[When] they were exiled to Egypt, the Divine Presence was with them, as is said, 'was I not exiled to your father's house when they were in Egypt (I Sam. 2:27).

D. "[When] they were exiled to Babylonia, the Divine Presence was with them, as is said, 'for your sake I sent to Babylonia' (Is. 43:14).

E. 'And also when they will be redeemed [in the future], the Divine Presence will be with them, as is said, 'and the Lord your God will return your return' (Deut. 30:3).

F. "It does not say 'and He will cause to return' (ve-heshib) but 'and He will return' (ve-shab). This teaches that The Holy One, Blessed Be He, will return with them from among the places of exile.' "

Specifically, God redeems Israel and saves the individual Israelite, and *when* that act of redemption or salvation takes place bears no consequence for the meaning of the act or the consequences thereof. It is an act that embodies a relationship, and relationships take place unmediated by time or circumstance. That, sum and substance, embodies the result of paradigmatic thinking, extending beginnings to endings, creation to the world to come.

The salvation of Israel, finally in the world to come, represents the final instance of a recurrent pattern. This is portrayed through an account of the variety of occasions of redemption celebrated by the recitation of the Hallel Psalms, Psalms 113–18, which are sung on celebratory occasions. This account follows the patterns of thought set forth in chapter 1, for it homogenizes the like and distinguishes like from unlike:

BAVLI-TRACTATE PESAHIM IO:5–6 II.6/II6A

A. Our rabbis have taught on Tannaite authority:

B. Who recited this Hallel [Ps. 113–18]?

The answer to that question indicates that the attitude of supplication and thanks transcends all considerations of time and circumstance. The same pattern, supplication and divine response, may impose itself upon any and all contexts, which is another way of saying that considerations of time and sequence play no role in the Torah. Thus, the paradigm is realized by Moses and Israel, Joshua and Israel, Deborah and Barak, Hezekiah, and onward.

C. R. Eliezer says, "Moses and Israel said it at the time that they stood at the sea. They said, 'Not unto us, not unto us' (Ps. 115:1), and the Holy Spirit responded, 'For my own sake will I do it' " (Isa. 48:11).

D. R. Judah says, "Joshua and Israel said it when the kings of Canaan attacked them. They said, 'Not unto us, not unto us' (Ps. 115:1), and the Holy Spirit responded, 'For my own sake will I do it' " (Isa. 48:11).

E. R. Eleazar the Modiite says, "Deborah and Barak said it when Sisera attacked them. They said, 'Not unto us, not unto us' (Ps. 115:1), and the Holy Spirit responded, 'For my own sake will I do it' " (Isa. 48:11).

F. R. Eleazar b. Azariah says, "Hezekiah and his allies said it when Sennacherib attacked them. They said, 'Not unto us, not unto us' (Ps. 115:1), and the Holy Spirit responded, 'For my own sake will I do it' " (Isa. 48:11).

G. R. Aqiba says, "Hananiah, Mishael, and Azariah said it when Nebuchadnezzar the wicked attacked them. They said, 'Not unto us, not unto us' (Ps. 115:1), and the Holy Spirit responded, 'For my own sake will I do it' " (Isa. 48:11).

H. R. Yosé the Galilean says, "Mordecai and Esther said it when Haman the wicked attacked them. They said, 'Not unto us, not unto us' (Ps. 115:1), and the Holy Spirit responded, 'For my own sake will I do it' " (Isa. 48:11).

I. And sages say, "The prophets among them ordained that the Israelites should say it at every turning point and on the occasion of every sorrow – may such not come upon them, and when they are redeemed, they are to recite it in thanks for their redemption."

So much for "all Israel," as distinct from the Israelite. If what happens to the holy people bears no relationship to time or change but recapitulates a single pattern through eternity, all the more so the affairs of the private person, Israel the Israelite. It follows that Israel is saved from Egypt, the exiles from the rule of the pagan kingdoms, the righteous from the fiery furnace, or the souls of the righteous from Gehenna, one paradigm ordering all events and encounters. In that last detail the resurrection and the judgment are placed into alignment with the world to come, in the manner proposed in chapter 13. A further formulation now carries matters forward:

II.12 A. Now that there is the great Hallel, how come we recite this one [Ps. 113–18]?
B. It is because it contains these five references: the exodus from Egypt, dividing the Reed Sea, giving of the Torah, resurrection of the dead, and the anguish of the Messiah.

C. The exodus from Egypt: "When Israel came forth out of Egypt" (Ps. 114:1);

D. dividing the Reed Sea: "the sea saw it and fled" (Ps. 114:3);

E. giving of the Torah: "the mountains skipped like rams" (Ps. 114:4);

F. resurrection of the dead: "I shall walk before the Lord in the land of the living" (Ps. 116:9);

G. and the anguish of the Messiah: "not to us, Lord, not to us" (Ps. 115:1).

II.13 A. And said R. Yohanan, " 'The phrase, 'not to us, Lord, not to us' refers to the subjugation to the kingdoms."

B. There are those who say, said R. Yohanan, " 'The phrase, 'not to us, Lord, not to us' refers to the war of Gog and Magog."

Israel the Israelite, as distinct from Israel the people, is fully subjected to the same paradigm that governs the community. That carries us to the matter of Gehenna:

II.14 A. [Reverting to II.12.A], R. Nahman bar Isaac said, "It is because it alludes to the deliverance of the souls of the righteous from Gehenna: 'I beseech you, Lord, deliver my soul' " (Ps. 116:4).

B. Hezekiah said, "It is because it contains a reference to the descent of the righteous into the fiery furnace and their ascent from it. Their descent: 'not unto us, Lord, not to us' was said by Hananiah; 'but to your name give glory' was said by Mishael; 'for your mercy and for truth's sake' was said by Azariah; 'wherefore should the nations say' was said by all of them. It refers to their ascent: 'praise the Lord all you nations' was said by Hananiah; 'laud him all you peoples' was said by Mishael; 'for his mercy is great toward us' was said by Azariah; 'and the truth of the Lord endures forever' was said by all of them."

C. And there are those who say, " 'And the truth of the Lord endures forever' was said by Gabriel. When wicked Nimrod threw our father Abraham into the fiery furnace, said Gabriel before the Holy One, blessed be He, 'Lord of the world, let me go down and cool it off and save that righteous man from the fiery furnace.' Said to him the Holy One, blessed be He, 'I am unique in my world and he is unique in his world. It is worthy for the unique to save the unique.' And since the Holy One, blessed be He, doesn't withhold a reward from any creature, he said to him, 'You will have the merit of saving three of his descendents.' "

Salvation of the individual, redemption of the whole people – each takes many forms but elicits only a single response to what is, in the end, a uniform relationship, the encounter with God's love. And to that love, time and change, history and destiny, are monumentally irrelevant, as much as are intentionality and teleology to the laws of gravity.

So much for the definition of the world to come in the other-than-temporal-historical terms that are required. The world to come marks the final condition of world order. It signifies the realization of correct and perfect relationships between God and man, God and Israel in particular. Those who reject God having been disposed of, we realize, the age to come finds its definition in the time of total reconciliation between God and man. It is the age when man loves God and accepts his dominion and completes the work of repentance and atonement for acts of rebellion. While, clearly, that reconciliation of God and man takes place in individual life, in which case, as already instantiated, we may use the language of salvation, it also governs the public life of Israel, in which case we may speak of redemption. That leads us to wonder what is at stake in the location of the theology's final chapter in what is clearly not a historical-eschatological setting but one that finds definition in intangibles of relationship: reconciliation, return, renewal, right attitude.

So we reasonably ask, what indeed do the sages have in mind when they speak of the world to come – concrete actualities, or intangible feelings and attitudes, impalpable matters of the spirit? May we suppose that we deal with a mere narration, in mythic form, of what in fact represents an inner, other-worldly, intangible, and spiritual encounter? That is to say, if all that is at stake is abstract patterns of relationships that happen to come to expression in tales of the eschaton, one might suppose that the conception, "the world to come," simply serves as another way of saying, "man reconciled with God." Then, through paradigmatic thinking, the sages should be represented as finding in the myth a vivid and palpable way of speaking of the inner life of intentionality and attitude. That is a possible reading of the character of the discourse at hand. But I think that that would drastically misrepresent the worldly reality, the concrete actuality, of the sages' account of matters, their intent to speak to the here and now – "today, if you will it"! We contemplate what is palpable and real in an ordinary, everyday sense, not what is intangible or merely "spiritual" in the vulgar sense.

First, while their Israel is the holy people, living in the plane of transcendence, their Israel truly lives in the trenchant world of marketplace and farm and engages in the material and physical transactions of farming and love. Not a single line in the entire Oral Torah would sustain the reading of "Israel" as other than (in a different theology's language) "after the flesh." The sages found no cause to differentiate an "Israel after the spirit" from their "Israel after the flesh," since, when they referred to Israel, they meant all those who know God as God made himself manifest, meaning, in the Torah, and at the end, that Israel, shorn of the handful of aliens (those who deny God, the resurrection of the dead, the resurrection of the dead as a fact set forth by God in the Torah, and so on), all together, in the flesh, sees God and enters into eternal life.

Second, their Israel does constitute a political entity – this world's embodiment of the locus of God's rule – and, as we have already noted, God's intervention at the very least will bring about a radical change in the politics of world order, Rome giving way to Israel. We have already found it possible, in chapter 10, to state the theology of a governing intentionality by appealing to the theoretical politics that the sages put forth as medium for their statement. Sages, like philosophers, were public intellectuals, undertaking the work of the community of holy Israel (sages) or the *polis* (philosophers). They thought about concrete, practical things, and at no point can we identify an area of the law or lore of the Oral Torah that has no bearing upon the everyday world of the here and now. That, indeed, is the very upshot of the point-by-point match of *halakhah* and *aggadah*, law and lore, that we have had occasion to review here and there.

Third, when they speak of the world to come, the sages mean a world that is public and shared, not private and inner-facing, and, as I have underscored many times, certainly not personal as distinct from public. It is not a world of relativities and relationships as these intangibles are concretely symbolized, but a world of real encounter. The sages know a palpable God who punishes arrogance and rewards humility, in both instances in worldly ways. Prayers are answered with rain or healing, virtue responded to with grace bearing material benefit, acts of generosity with miracles. Heaven intervenes in matters of health and sickness, in the abundance or scarcity of crops, in good fortune and ill. The sages insist upon an exact correspondence between practicalities and transcendent relationships.

To give one simple example, if a writ of divorce is improperly drawn, a woman is deemed still married to her former husband, and should she remarry on the strength of the writ, she will incur the most drastic this-worldly penalties, including huge property losses – because of (in the sages' conviction) Heaven's intense interest in material details. Her relationship to the former husband, one of sanctification by Heaven, still engages Heaven until the conclusion of the writ of divorce with all of the t's crossed and the i's dotted. Any representation of the sages as thinkers in a merely spiritual realm misses the very heart of their program for holy Israel. In abstract language, the sages maintain that a substantive change in the life of this world will match and correspond to the change in the condition of Israel in relationship to God.

Accordingly, since man corresponds to God and in important ways serves God's purpose, the spiritualization of matters earthly would seriously misinterpret what is at stake here. When the sages see the world to come as the climax and conclusion of the processes of creation that commenced with Eden, they envisage the world that comes within their everyday gaze, the people they see out there, in the street, not only imagine in here, in the heart. Take the resurrection, for instance. When the dead are raised from the grave, they will stink and need new clothes:

BAVLI-TRACTATE SANHEDRIN 11:1-2 1.25.91B

A. Raba contrasted [these two verses]: "It is written, 'I kill and I make alive' (Deut. 32:39) and it is written, 'I wound and I heal' (Deut. 32:39). [The former implies that one is resurrected just as he was at death, thus with blemishes, and the other implies that at the resurrection all wounds are healed].
B. "Said the Holy One, blessed be he, 'What I kill I bring to life,' and then, 'What I have wounded I heal.' "

That humble fact captures the dialectic of paradigmatic, as against historical, thinking. History produces the dialectic of past against present, resolved in the future (thesis, antithesis, synthesis). Paradigms set the past within the present, Abraham or Moses consorting with the here and now and Jacob shaping public policy today – a considerable tension not to be resolved at all. On the one hand, the advent of the world to come is represented as part of an ordinal sequence, though, for reasons fully exposed, that sequence should not be treated as identical with temporal, historical happenings. On the other hand, the paradigm is fully as palpable in its shaping of the everyday world and workaday experience as history. So, as I said, at the resurrection, the corpse will need a bath.

And yet – and yet what is tangible is relationship, not the singular and exemplary event, as I have amply explained earlier. Paradigmatic thinking transforms the concrete into evocative symbol, the unique into the exemplary. But the sages' mode of paradigmatic thinking insists upon the here-and-now quality of relationships and events, the actuality of transactions with God as much as with man. And why think otherwise, when, after all, Scripture is clear and rich in instances. Both in the Written and in the Oral Torah God and man correspond, and man is in God's image, after God's likeness. So a theology that does not "spiritualize," that is, that does not represent as intangible God in heaven any more than man on earth, will insist upon the material and physical character of resurrection and the life of the Garden of Eden that is the world to come. That theology will have no motive to treat the transformation of relationships represented by the resurrection of the dead and the judgment and the world or age to come as other than consubstantial with the experienced world of the moment – if marvellously different.

Thinking paradigmatically, rather than historically, the sages envisaged matters not temporally but through epochs divided by the indicative traits of Israel's relationship with God, as we noted at Yerushalmi-tractate Megillah 2:1 I:2, cited in chapter 6. There, we saw, "past" is marked by Israel's exodus from Egypt; "present" by God's mercy as a mark not of Israel's desserts but of God's own love; the days of the Messiah as God's responding to Israel's supplication; the days of Gog and Magog as the embodiment of the verse, "[The Lord is God, and he has given us light.] Bind the festal offering with cords [up to the horns of the altar!]" (Ps. 118:27), and the age to come as the age of thanks to God for being God. The same matter is made still more explicit. Egypt, Sinai, Gog and Magog, and Messiah – locations, events, moments, persons – mark the four epiphanies of God to Israel:

SIFRÉ TO DEUTERONOMY CCCXLIII:VII.I

A. "He appeared from Mount Paran [and approached from Ribeboth-kodesh, lightning flashing at them from his right, lover, indeed, of the people, their hallowed are all in your hand]":

B. There are four epiphanies.

C. The first was in Egypt: "Give ear, O Shepherd of Israel, you who leads Joseph like a flock, you who are enthroned on the cherubim, shine forth" (Ps. 80:2).

D. The second at the time of the giving of the Torah: "he shone upon them from Seir."

E. The third in the days of Gog and Magog: "O Lord, you God to whom vengeances belongs, you God to whom vengeance belongs, shine forth" (Ps. 94:1).

F. And the fourth in the days of the Messiah: "Out of Zion the perfection of beauty, God has shown forth" (Ps. 50:2).

The list of these native categories on its own suffices to register the intent, which is to identify, compare and contrast, the epiphanies. Just as God was at Egypt and Sinai, with Israel, so God will be at the eschatological war and at the climactic moment of the Messiah as well. And, it goes without saying, in the age or world to come, the final epiphany will find God and Israel at one, as we shall see, celebrating the beneficence of God, studying the Torah, enjoying dance and song and feasting, for all eternity. Thinking paradigmatically, these "events" represent relationships with God. Israel in the here and now and Israel at the age to come differ only in relationship with God.

So much for the theory of matters. Now, after elaborately justifying the asking, we turn to a set of practical questions. With the advent of the world or age to come, exactly what happens, in the process of restoration of world order to the condition of Eden, and of Israel to the Land of Israel? Samuel's minimalist view, Bavli-tractate Sanhedrin 91b, cited above, "There is no difference between the world to come and the days of the Messiah, except the end of the subjugation of the exilic communities of Israel," alerts us to the breadth of opinion on how the days of the Messiah will differ from the world to come. But it is clear that, as stressed in Chapter 13, a clear sequence governs. First comes salvation in the aspect of resurrection and judgment pertains to individuals, and then, immediately following judgment, the world or age to come marks the time of redemption for the holy people, Israel. And the bulk of the evidence supports the view that the age to come differs from this age, as well as from the time of the Messiah, in more ways than the political one that Samuel (within the theory of the regnant theology set forth here) rightly selects as primary.

The Messiah, whose advent marks the period before the resurrection of individuals, takes on a public task in the age to come, one already adumbrated. It is the reunion of Israel with the Land of Israel, such as brings about the resurrection of the dead, but now with attention to living Israel when the age to come dawns. For the task of the king-messiah is to gather the exiles and restore Israel to the Land of Israel. That is why the Messiah has an important task to perform not only in his own age, in raising the dead, but in the last age as well, though so far as I can discern, beyond that one action of restoring the exiles to the holy land, the Messiah plays no consequential part in the life of the age to come:

GENESIS RABBAH XCVIII:IX.2

2. A. Said R. Hanin, "Israel does not require the learning of the king-messiah in the age to come, as it is said, 'Unto him shall the nations seek' (Is. 11:1) – but not Israel.
B. "If so, why will the king-messiah come? And what will he come to do? It is to gather together the exiles of Israel and to give them thirty religious duties: 'And I said to them, If you think good, give me my hire, and if not, forbear. So they weighed for my hire thirty pieces of silver' " (Zech. 11:12).

The same point, that when the Messiah comes he will gather the exiles back to the land, occurs at Song of Songs Rabbah LII:ii.1ff.: Said R. Hunia in the name of R. Justus, "When the exiles returning to Zion when the Messiah brings them back reach Taurus Munus, they are going to say a Song."

This brings us to the actualities of the world to come, what people are supposed to be doing then. What is going to happen in the age to come? Israel will eat and drink, sing and dance, and enjoy God, who will be lord of the dance. What about the restored Temple? The war of Gog and Magog having concluded, the dead having been returned to the Land and raised, the next stage in the restoration of world order requires the reconstruction of the Temple, where, as we recall, God and man, Heaven and earth, meet.

GENESIS RABBAH XCVIII:II.7

A. "Then Jacob called his sons and said, 'Gather yourselves together, that I may tell you what shall befall you in days to come'":

B. R. Simon said, "He showed them the fall of Gog, in line with this usage: 'It shall be in the end of days ... when I shall be sanctified through you, O Gog' (Ez. 38:165). 'Behold, it shall come upon Edom' " (Is. 34:5).

C. R. Judah said, "He showed them the building of the house of the sanctuary: 'And it shall come to pass in the end of days that the mountain of the Lord's house shall be established' " (Is. 2:2).

D. Rabbis say, "He came to reveal the time of the end to them, but it was hidden from him."

So, in the now-familiar sequence of restoration, final war, advent of the Messiah and the resurrection and judgment, and the age to come, next in sequence must be the restoration of Israel to the Land and the rebuilding of the Temple, destroyed by reason of Israel's sin.

But what purpose would now be fulfilled by the restoration of the Temple cult – the priesthood to the altar, the Levites to the platform, and all Israel to their courtyards, men's and women's respectively? Since the bulk of offerings in the Temple set forth by Moses in the written Torah had focused upon atonement for sin and guilt, what purpose would the Temple, and its surrogate, the synagogue, now serve? There is only a single one. In the age to come, responding to redemption, all offerings but the thanksgiving offering, appropriately, will cease, all prayers but thanksgiving prayers will cease. So it stands to reason:

LEVITICUS RABBAH IX:VII.I

A. R. Phineas and R. Levi and R. Yohanan in the name of R. Menahem of Gallia: "In time to come all offerings will come to an end, but the thanksgiving offering will not come to an end.

B. "All forms of prayer will come to an end, but the thanksgiving prayer will not come to an end.

C. "That is in line with that which is written, 'The voice of joy and the voice of gladness, the voice of the bridegroom and the voice of the bride,

D. " 'the voice of them that say, "Give thanks to the Lord of hosts" ' (Jer. 33:11). This refers to the thanksgiving prayer.

E. " 'Who bring a thanksgiving offering to the house of the Lord' (Jer. 33:11). This refers to the offering of thanksgiving sacrifice.

F. "And so did David say, 'Your vows are incumbent upon me, O God [I will render thanksgivings to you]' (Ps. 56:13).

G. "'I shall render thanksgiving to you' is not written here, but rather, 'I shall render thanksgivings [plural] to you' (Ps. 56:13).

H. "The reference [of the plural usage], then, is to both the thanksgiving prayer and the thanksgiving offering."

Predicting the character of the Temple offerings in the future presents no difficulty when we recall that, at that time, judgment will have taken place, sin removed, and atonement completed. Much of the work of the cult will have been accomplished, leaving only the one thing that remains: to give thanks.

In the sages' vision, the world to come will mark an age of illumination, celebration, eating, drinking, and dancing – bliss forever. Take lavish lighting, for example. Living in a time long before street lighting, when the stars and the moon alone illuminated the darkness, when the sages promised that in the world to come people will go out at night by the light of God, it meant something:

PESIQTA DERAB KAHANA XXI:V.2

A. R. Samuel bar Nahman: "While in this age people go by day in the light of the sun and by night in the light of the moon, in the coming age, they will undertake to go only by the light of the sun by day, and not by the light of the moon by night.

B. "What verse of Scripture indicates it? 'The sun shall no longer be your light by day, nor the moon shine on you when evening falls; [the Lord shall be your everlasting light, your God shall be your glory. Never again shall your sun set, nor your moon withdraw her light; but the Lord shall be your everlasting light and the days of your mourning shall be ended]' (Is. 60:19–20).

C. "By what light will they walk? By the light of the Holy One, blessed be He, in line with the passage: 'the Lord shall be your everlasting light.' "

In a moment we shall see that other sources of supernatural light will defeat the darkness.

Not only so, but the rebuilt Temple itself will bring illumination to the world. Further, in the world to come or the time of the Messiah, there will be celebrations for the righteous. God will preside over a banquet for the righteous; he will lead the dancing; he will prepare a tabernacle for the righteous to provide shade by day:

BAVLI-TRACTATE BABA BATRA 5:1A-D IV.28FF./75A

A. Rabbah said R. Yohanan said, "The Holy One, blessed be He, is destined to make a banquet for the righteous out of the meat of Leviathan: 'Companions will make a banquet of it' (Job 40:30). The meaning of 'banquet' derives from the usage of the same word in the verse, 'And he prepared for them a great banquet and they ate and drank'" (2 Kgs. 6:23).

The banquet will be for the disciples of sages in particular:

B. "'Companions' can refer only to disciples of sages, in line with this usage: 'You that dwells in the gardens, the companions hearken for your voice, cause me to hear it' (Song 8:13). The rest of the creature will be cut up and sold in the markets of Jerusalem: 'They will part him among the Canaanites' (Job 40:30), and 'Canaanites' must be merchants, in line with this usage: 'As for the Canaanite, the balances of deceit are in his hand, he loves to oppress' (Hos. 12:8). If you prefer: 'Whose merchants are princes, whose traffickers are the honourable of the earth'" (Isa. 23:8).

How "all Israel" relates is left somewhat obscure. I should hope that all Israel now will be classed as "companions," but I have not found any explicit statement to that effect. Perhaps the sages' concrete reading of matters led them to include in the on-going session of Torah-study only those of intellect. That too I have not located. But the paramount category of the world to come is "the righteous," and the division of Israel into disciples of sages and everybody else seems to me not to retain its normative status for eternity.

The main point, then, is that the righteous, in general, will be given shelter from the sun and rain, constructed out of the hide of Leviathan. God had done no less for Adam: "Said R. Hama bar Hanina, 'Ten canopies did the Holy One, blessed be He, make for the First Man in the garden of Eden: "You were in Eden, the garden of God; every precious stone was your covering, the cornelian, the topaz, the emerald, the beryl, the onyx, the jasper, the sapphire, the carbuncle, and the emerald and gold"'" (Ezek. 28:13) (Bavli-tractate Baba Batra 5:1 IV.35/71a). Here is the sages' counterpart account:

IV.29 A. Rabbah said R. Yohanan said, "The Holy One, blessed be He, is destined to make a tabernacle for the righteous out of the hide of Leviathan: 'Can you fill tabernacles with his skin' (Job 40:31). If someone has sufficient merit, a tabernacle is made for him; if he does not have sufficient merit, a mere shade is made for him: 'And his head with a fish covering' (Job 40:31). If someone has sufficient merit, a shade is made for him, if not, then a mere necklace is made for him: 'And necklaces about your neck' (Prov. 1:9). If someone has sufficient merit, a necklace is made for him; if not, then an amulet: 'And you will bind him for your maidens' (Job 40:29).

B.   "And the rest of the beast will the Holy One, blessed be He, spread over the walls of Jerusalem, and the glow will illuminate the world from one end to the other: 'And nations shall walk at your light, and kings at the brightness of your rising'" (Isa. 60:3).

The lot of each person will match his deeds during life, with those who are righteous receiving greater honour than others:

IV.33 A.   And said Rabbah said R. Yohanan, "The Holy One, blessed be He, is destined to make seven canopies for every righteous person: 'And the Lord will create over the whole habitation of Mount Zion and over her assemblies a cloud of smoke by day and the shining of a flaming fire by night, for over all the glory shall be a canopy' (Isa. 4:5). This teaches that for every one will the Holy One create a canopy in accord with the honour that is due him."

So much for housing and the comforts of eternity.

Now comes a point on which we shall dwell in a moment: nearly everybody gets to the world to come, but, when there, some are treated better than others, once more in response to their conduct in life. So, even beyond resurrection and judgment, what people did in life determines how they will spend even the joys of eternity. This point is critical in the ultimate balancing of the scales of justice, and we shall dwell on the matter:

IV.38 A.   And said Rabbah said R. Yohanan, "The righteous are destined to be called by the name of the Holy One, blessed be He: 'Every one that is called by my name, and whom I have created for my glory, I have formed him, yes, I have made him'" (Isa. 43:7).

IV.39 A.   Said R. Samuel bar Nahmani said R. Yohanan, "There are three who are called by the name of the Holy One, blessed be He, and these are they: the righteous, the Messiah, and Jerusalem.

B.   "The righteous, as we have just said.

C.   "The Messiah: 'And this is the name whereby he shall be called, the Lord is our righteousness' (Jer. 23:6).

D.   "Jerusalem: 'It shall be eighteen thousand reeds round about, and the name of the city from that day shall be, "the Lord is there"' (Ezek. 48:35). Do not read 'there' but 'its name.'"

The righteous then will be called holy, and Jerusalem will be exalted as well:

IV.40 A.   Said R. Eleazar, "The time will come when 'holy' will be said before the name of the righteous as it is said before the name of the Holy One, blessed be He: 'And it shall come to pass that he that is left in Zion and he that remains in Jerusalem shall be called holy' " (Isa. 4:3).

IV.41 A. And said Rabbah said R. Yohanan, "The Holy One, blessed be He, is destined to lift up Jerusalem to a height of three parasangs: 'And she shall be lifted up and be settled in her place' (Isa. 4:3). '... In her place' means 'like her place' [Slotki: Jerusalem will be lifted up to a height equal to the extent of the space it occupies]."

The righteous, the Messiah, and Jerusalem now form a single category of complements, united by the common trait that all will be called "holy" as God now is called holy. The model of anticipation then reaches a daring position, which is that, in time to come, the righteous, the Messiah, and Jerusalem all enter into the category of God himself. That explains why the righteous will have a banquet that God will make for them, why God will make a tabernacle for the righteous much as Moses made a tabernacle for the Lord in the wilderness, and why Jerusalem will enlighten the world. And, at the banquet, there will be dancing, led by God himself:

YERUSHALMI-TRACTATE MEGILLAH 2:4 I:3

A. R. Berekhiah, R. Helbo, Ulla Biriyyah, R. Eleazar in the name of R. Haninah: "In time to come the Holy One, blessed be he, will be made into the head of the dance of the righteous in time to come."

B. What is the scriptural basis for this view?

C. "Consider well her ramparts" (HYLH) – "Her dance" is what is written.

And what, in context, are the righteous going to do?

D. And the righteous will point to him in a gesture of respect with their finger and say, "That this is God, our God for ever and ever. He will be our guide for ever" (Ps. 48:14).

E. "He is our guide almuth" – with youthfulness, with liveliness.

F. Aqila translated [the word almut] as athanasia, that is, immortality: a world in which there is no death.

G. And the righteous will point to him in a gesture of respect with their finger and say, " 'That this is our God, our God for ever and ever. He will be our guide for ever' (Ps. 48:14).

H. "He will be our guide in this world, he will be our guide in the world to come."

So much for the life of the world to come. The age of restoration, the world to come, affords to the righteous the joys that Adam missed the first time around, beginning with the pleasure of loving God.

But, as we have noted, the pleasures of eternity are not spread about equally. Rather, people enjoy a continuous existence in both this world, past the grave, and in the world to come, so that what they do in this world affects their situation in the world to come. We need not review what has already been said in chapter 5 and in chapter 13 about the logical necessity of resurrection and judgment. We recall how resurrection solves the problem of inequity in private life, the imbalance of virtue and prosperity such as a fully realized, this-worldly justice would effect. It suffices to note that, once judgment has taken place, and the balance is righted, then the world to come defines the place and time for the reward of virtue to come to realization. Acts of loving kindness bear their own reward, and for certain actions of that kind, there is no limit to the reward in both this world and the next. Transgressions also bear their punishments, if not here, then there. These are familiar ideas, predictable in a system of stasis and balance.

At this point, we need to deal only with the relationship between this world and the world to come as the sages complete their account of the perfect justice of world order. The most important point comes first. Suffering in this world for the Torah brings reward in the world to come. Here we clearly refer to disciples of sages, but that is only right, in context, for we want to know how, in the world to come, they will receive recompense for the sacrifices that, in this world, they make for Torah-study:

BAVLI-TRACTATE SANHEDRIN 11:1–2 III.5/100A

III.5 A. R. Judah b. R. Simon interpreted, "Whoever blackens his face [in fasting] on account of teachings of Torah in this world will find that the Holy One, blessed be he, polishes his luster in the world to come.

B. "For it is said, 'His countenance shall be as the Lebanon, excellent as the cedars' " (Song 5:15).

Now we proceed to the reward for accepting poverty:

C. R. Tanhum bar Hanilai said, "Whoever starves himself for words of Torah in his world will the Holy One, blessed be he, feed to satisfaction in the world to come,

D. "as it is said, 'They shall be abundantly satisfied with the fatness of your house, and you shall make them drink of the river of your pleasures' " (Ps. 36:9).

From disciples, we turn to every righteous person:

E. When R. Dimi came, he said, "The Holy One, blessed be he, is destined to give to every righteous person his full pack-load, as it is said, 'Blessed be the Lord, day by day, who loads us with benefits, even the God of our salvation, Selah' " (Ps. 68:20).

F. Said Abbayye to him, "And is it possible to say so? Is it not said, 'Who has measured the waters in the hollow of his hand and measured out heaven with the span'" (Is. 40:12)?

G. He said to him, "What is the reason that you are not at home in matters of lore [but only in matters of law and legal analysis]. They say in the West in the name of Raba bar Mari, 'The Holy One, blessed be he, is destined to give each righteous person three hundred and ten worlds, as it is said, "That I may cause those who love me to inherit substance and I will fill their treasures" (Prov. 8:21), and the numerical value of the word for substance is three hundred ten.'"

The position throughout is the familiar one that a balance governs all things, so that if one suffers now, in this world, then one will rejoice in a reward in the world to come. That principle of balance, proportion, and commensurability comes to expression in diverse ways. People mourn now but will rejoice later on. Mourning now is appropriate, but must be kept in due proportion; it must not descend into sheer despair. This same conception applies to Torah-study. One sacrifices for Torah-study in this world, but one will get a reward in the world to come.

In concrete terms, exactly how does the eternal life of the world to come form that complement and recompense for life in the here and now, to which we made reference in chapter 5? By their deeds the righteous define themselves now and gain their reward then. This conviction, absolutely inevitable within the logic of a theology of world order defined by God's justice, comes to expression in a simple way. Since life continues beyond the grave, what we do in the initial life goes to our account, one way or the other, upon which we draw when we rise from death to eternal life. Scripture itself is explicit that benefits accrue both now and in the age to come:

TOSEFTA-TRACTATE HULLIN 10:16

A. A man should not take a dam with the young, and even to purify a person afflicted with the skin ailment [as is required at Lev. 14] [M. Hul. 12:5A] therewith,

B. because a transgression will have been committed therewith.

C. R. Jacob says, "You find no [other] commandment in the Torah, the specification of the reward for which is (not) located by its side,

D. "and the [promise of the] resurrection of the dead is written alongside it [as well],

E. "as it is said, 'If along the road you find a bird's nest ... with fledglings or eggs and the mother sitting over the fledglings or on the eggs, to not take the mother together with her young. Let the mother go and take only the young, in order that you may be well and have a long life' (Deut. 22:6–7).

F. "If this one went up to the top of a tree and fell and died, or to the top of a building and fell and died, where has the good of this one gone, and where is the prolonging of his life?

G. "One must therefore conclude: 'So that it will be good for you' – in this world. 'And so that your days may be prolonged' – in the world of endless time."

Here, as in many other settings of the Written Torah, the sages of the Oral Torah identify a case in which one's conduct in this age affects his standing in the age to come.

But there is a very particular way in which the sages work out that relationship. Within the theory of unlimited abundance of the scarcest resources, such as Torah and virtue, that we noted in chapter 7, we identify certain acts of virtue that yield benefits in this life but remain as principal upon which to draw in the age to come. That is the one genuinely important idea within the cluster of doctrines of theological theodicy that we have considered. It is expressed in terms of virtue beyond measure, the rational disposition of which is such that reward is unlimited and surpasses even the grave:

MISHNAH-TRACTATE PEAH I:I
[TRANSLATED BY ROGER BROOKS]

A. These are things which have no [specified] measure:
B. (1) [the quantity of produce designated as] peah, (2) [the quantity of produce given as] firstfruits, (3) [the value of] the appearance offering, (4) [the performance of] righteous deeds, (5) and [time spent in] study of Torah.
C. These are things the benefit of which a person enjoys in this world, while the principal remains for him in the world to come:

Now comes the list of selected deeds, the gilt-edged investments of the moral economy:

D. (1) [deeds in] honour of father and mother, (2) [performance of] righteous deeds, (3) and [acts which] bring peace between a man and his fellow.

And, predictably, the best of them all is Torah-study:

E. But the study of Torah is as important as all of them together.

So too, while virtue is rewarded, sin is punished as well, and that may take place both now and then. The principle remains the same but is extended, now, to the enduring recompense for vice or sin:

TOSEFTA-TRACTATE PEAH I:I
[TRANSLATED BY ROGER BROOKS]

T. Peah 1:1 A. These are things that have no [specified] measure: (1) [the quantity of produce designated as] peah (Lev. 19:9, 23:22), (2) [the quantity of produce designated as] first fruits (Deut. 26:1–11), (3) [the value of] the appearance-offering (Deut. 16:16–17), (4) [the quantity of] righteous deeds [performed], (5) and [time spent in] study of Torah (M. Peah 1:1A-B).

First comes the negative, punishment through eternity for sins of the weightiest sort, those actions that are absolutely sinful no matter the circumstance or intent:

1:2 A. For these things they punish a person in this world, while the principal [i.e., eternal punishment] remains for the world-to-come:
B. (1) for [acts of] idolatrous worship, (2) for incest, (3) for murder, (4) and for gossip, [which is] worse than all of them together.

Then comes eternal reward, especially in the setting of *zekhut*, as we should expect:

C. Acts of uncoerced generosity or merit [*zekhut*] create a principal [for the world to come] and bear interest [pyrwt, fruit] [in this world],
D. as it is stated [in Scripture], "Tell the righteous that it shall be well with them, for they shall enjoy the benefits [*pyrwt*] [of their deeds]" (Is. 3:10).

As merit works, so does sin, the familiar match of antonyms under a single rule:

1:3 A. A transgression creates a principal [i.e., eternal punishment, in the world-to-come] but bears no interest [pyrwt] [in this world],
B. as it is stated [in Scripture], "Woe to the wicked! It shall be ill with him, for what his hands have done shall be done to him" (Is. 3:11).
C. If so, how shall I interpret [the following verse]: "Because they hated knowledge and did not choose the way of the Lord, would have none of my counsel and despised all my reproof], therefore they shall suffer the consequences [*pry*] of their way" (Prov. 1:29–31)?
D. [The verse should be interpreted to mean:] A transgression that bears fruit [i.e., causes other transgressions] brings a penalty [in this world],
E. [but] one that does not bear fruit [i.e., does not cause other transgressions] brings no penalty [in this world].

The world to come it is to last forever, and in it one's fate is determined by his conduct in this world.

By this point we need hardly ask about what happens to the wicked in the world to come. Only a handful of the wicked are totally eliminated and do not stand in judgment. For the others, they may enjoy resurrection, with the rest of Israel, and they may even endure in judgment. But that is not the end of the story. If a good deed serves now and also in the world to come, a transgression brings punishment in the world to come but no advantage in this world. So the world to come involves penance for the wicked, who get eternal life but do not enjoy it the way the righteous do. This is worked out in the following language:

YERUSHALMI-TRACTATE PEAH 1:1 XXIX

A. A good deed creates a principal [for the world to come] and bears interest [in this world]. A transgression creates a principal [i.e., eternal punishment in the world to come], but bears no interest [in this world].

B. [The foregoing accords with the Tosefta:] A good deed creates a principal [for the world to come] and bears interest [in this world], as it is stated [in Scripture], "Hail the just man, for he shall fare well; he shall eat the fruit of his works" (Is. 3:10) (cf. T. Peah 1:2C-D).

C. A transgression creates a principal [i.e., eternal punishment in the world to come], but bears no interest [in this world], as it is stated [in Scripture], "Woe to the wicked man, for he shall fare ill; As his hands have dealt, so shall it be done to him" (Is. 3:11). (cf. T. Peah 1:2E-F).

D. If so, how shall I interpret [the following verse], "[Because they hated knowledge, and did not choose fear of the Lord; they refused my advice and disdained all my rebukes], they shall eat the fruit of their ways" (Prov. 1:29–31)? [The verse should be interpreted to mean] any transgression that bears fruit, [i.e., that causes other transgressions] brings a penalty [in this world]. But one that does not bear fruit, [i.e., that does not cause other transgressions], brings no penalty [in this world] (cf. T. Peah 1:2 G).

Given the importance of intentionality in driving the entire system, we should not find surprising the issue of how a good intention, not acted upon, registers in the calculus:

E. [As regards] a good intention – the Omnipresent converts it to a corresponding deed. [As for] an evil intention – the Omnipresent does not convert it to a corresponding deed.

F. [The foregoing corresponds to the Tosefta:] [As regards] a good intention – the Omnipresent, blessed be he, converts it to a a corresponding deed, as it is written [in Scripture], "In this vein have those who revere the Lord been talking to one another. [The Lord has heard and noted it, and a scroll of remembrance has been written at his behest]" (Mal. 3:16) (cf. T. Peah 1:2H). [The point is that their thoughts were counted in the record as deeds.]

But God, being merciful because he is just, addresses an evil intention in his own way as well:

G. [As for] an evil intention – the Omnipresent does not convert it to a corresponding deed, as it is stated [in Scripture], "Had I an evil thought in my mind, the Lord would not have listened" (Ps. 66:18) (cf. T. Peah 1:2 I).

The general match is left without systematic demonstration, but some verses of Scripture serve, if not in a systematic way. And when it comes to a case in which the scales are balanced, God's mercy makes the difference not only in judgment but even in the ongoing life of the world to come:

YERUSHALMI-TRACTATE PEAH I:I XXXII

A. "He who performs mostly good deeds inherits the Garden of Eden, but he who performs mostly transgression inherits Gehenna.
B. [But what if the scales] are balanced, [so that he has neither a majority of sins nor a majority of good deeds]?
C. Said R. Yosé b. Hanina, "[Consider Ex. 34:6–7's description of God's attributes] – 'Who forgives transgressions' [in the plural] is not written there, but rather, 'Who forgives transgression' [in the singular]. [This means that] the Holy One, blessed be he, will seize one document [bearing the record of one of] a person's transgressions, so that his good deeds will outweigh [his transgressions]."
D. Said R. Eleazar, "And unto you, O Lord, belongs mercy, for you pay each person according to his works. But if a person has no good deeds, you give him one of your own."
E. This is the opinion of R. Eleazar. For R. Eleazar said, "[Ex. 34:6–7 describes God as having] 'much mercy' – that is, he tips the scale toward mercy, [even to the point of giving evil-doers credit for good deeds they never performed]."

Transgressions also bear their punishments, if not here, then there. These are familiar ideas, predictable in a system of stasis and balance such as the present one.

So much for Israelites and for all Israel. As we realize full well, gentiles with their idolatry simply will cease to exist; some will perish, just as Israelites will perish, just as the Generation of the Flood, the Generation of the Dispersion, the Men of Sodom, and certain Israelites will perish. But some – a great many – will give up idolatry and become part of Israel. The gentiles as such are not subject to redemption; they have no choice at the advent of the world to come but to accept God or become extinct. But that is not the precise formulation that the system as I see it will set forth. Rather, the correct language is not, the gentiles will cease to exist, but rather, the category, "gentiles with their idolatry," will cease to function. Idolatry having come to an end, God having been recognized by all mankind, everyone will enter the category, "Israel."

Predictably, the sages seek analogies and patterns to work out in concrete terms the result of their compelling logic. In the present matter, the future of gentiles is worked out by analogy to Holy Things – the opposite, and the match in context, of gentiles. Some can be redeemed, some not.

MEKHILTA ATTRIBUTED TO R. ISHMAEL LXVII:I.31

B. As to Holy Things, there are those that are subject to redemption and there are those that are not subject to redemption;

C. as to things that may not be eaten, there are those that are subject to redemption and there are those that are not subject to redemption;

D. as to things that may not be used for any sort of benefit, there are those that are subject to redemption and there are those that are not subject to redemption;

E. as to fields and vineyards, there are those that are subject to redemption and there are those that are not subject to redemption;

F. as to bondmen and bondwomen, there are those that are subject to redemption and there are those that are not subject to redemption;

G. as to those subject to the death penalty by a court, there are those that are subject to redemption and there are those that are not subject to redemption;

The paradigm having established the possibilities, we come to the critical point.

H. so in the age to come, there are those that are subject to redemption and there are those that are not subject to redemption.

The nations cannot be redeemed. That is by definition: their idolatry in the end does them in:

I. The nations of the world are not subject to redemption: "No man can by any means redeem his brother nor give to God a ransom for him, for too costly is the redemption of their soul" (Ps. 49:8–9).

J. Precious are the Israelites, for the ransom of whose lives the Holy One, blessed be he, has given the nations of the world:

K. "I have given Egypt as your ransom" (Is. 43:4).

L. Why so?

M. "Since you are precious in my sight and honourable, and I have loved you, therefore I will give men for you and peoples for your life" (Is. 43:3–4).

Once more the past forms a presence in the immediate age, as much as the present participates in the past. Here the future of the gentiles realizes their present. They are idolators – that is why – we recall from chapter 4 – they are classified as gentiles – and therefore they will not be redeemed, meaning, they will not stand in judgment or enjoy the eternal life of the world to come. But that is not the whole story.

Second, Israel's enemies will finally receive their come-uppance, and the scourge with which the Israelites are smitten in the end will smite others:

MEKHILTA ATTRIBUTED TO R. ISHMAEL XLIV:I.I

A. "And the Lord said to Moses, 'Write this as a memorial in a book'":

B. The earlier elders say, "This is the measure that runs through all generations:

C. "The scourge with which the Israelites are smitten in the end will smite [others].

D. "Let everyone learn the rule of the world from the case of Amalek [Amalek embodies Israel's enemies; he will not live in the world to come]:

E. "who came to do injury to the Israelites, so the Omnipresent destroyed him from the life of this world and from the life of the world to come: 'that I will utterly blot out the remembrance of Amalek from under heaven.'

F. "So in the case of Pharaoh, who came to do injury to the Israelites, so the Holy One, blessed be he, drowned him in the Red Sea: 'But he overthrew Pharaoh and his host in the Red Sea' (Ps. 136:15).

G. "So in the case of every nation and empire that comes to do harm to Israel will God always judge in accord with this rule: 'Now I know that the Lord is greater than all gods, because he delivered the people from under the hand of the Egyptians when they dealt arrogantly with them'" (Ex. 18:11).

Comparing Amalek to Pharaoh rests on the policy towards Israel common to them both. Then they are shown to share a common fate.

Third and most important, what of gentiles in general, apart from those self-selected for eternal Gehenna by their conduct towards Israel? In the age to come gentiles will renounce idolatry and accept the one God. There simply will be no more gentiles, everyone will serve God and come under the wings of his Presence, within Israel.

MEKHILTA ATTRIBUTED TO R. ISHMAEL XXXIII:I.I

A. "Who is like you, O Lord, among gods? [Who is like you, majestic in holiness, terrible in glorious deeds, doing wonders?]":
B. When the Israelites saw that Pharaoh and his host had perished at the Red Sea, the dominion of the Egyptians was over, and judgments were executed on their idolatry, they all opened their mouths and said, "Who is like you, O Lord, among gods? [Who is like you, majestic in holiness, terrible in glorious deeds, doing wonders?]"

Now the nations participate in praising the one, true God of all creation:

C. And not the Israelites alone said the song, but also the nations of the world said the song.
D. When the nations of the world saw that Pharaoh and his host had perished at the Red Sea, the dominion of the Egyptians was over, and judgments were executed on their idolatry, they all renounced their idolatry and opened their mouths and confessed their faith in the Lord and said, "Who is like you, O Lord, among gods? [Who is like you, majestic in holiness, terrible in glorious deeds, doing wonders?]"

Once more the selected paradigm finds the future in the past, the pattern that governs in the quality of the relationship:

E. So, too, you find that at the age to come the nations of the world will renounce their idolatry: "O Lord, my strength and my stronghold and my refuge, in the day of affliction to you the nations shall come ... shall a man make himself gods" (Jer. 16:19–20); "In that day a man shall cast away his idols of silver ... to go into the clefts of the rocks" (Is. 2:20–21); "And the idols shall utterly perish" (Is. 20:18).

The final step in the unfolding of creation according to plan will be the redemption of the nations of the world, their renunciation of idolatry and acceptance of God's rule. That will bring to perfect closure the drama that began with Adam. The nations' response to Israel's Exodus and redemption from Egypt prefigures what is to come about at the end.

A great intellectual construction responds in a simple way to a fundamental question. We have spent fourteen long chapters spelling out the answer. Now let me articulate the question, though I should claim it has been asked on every page of this book. The urgent question, given a self-evidently valid answer, is how long, O Lord? The question embodies three parts: what are we to make of Israel, if God is just, and what will be with Israel, since God is just? and how do we know? The dialectics formed by the confrontation of God, Torah, and Israel therefore comes to expression in a system aimed at revealing God's justice, by the criteria of the Torah, for those who know God in the Torah, that is, Israel.

The theology of the Oral Torah accordingly reaches its climactic statement as it turns from the transcendent situation of Israel in the age to come to Israel at this time, and there finds grounds for sublime hope. The theology contains the promise that while now Israel grieves, in the end of days God will give them grounds for rejoicing, and that will be in a measure commensurate to the loyalty and patience of shown in the interim. How do we know, and how long? The perfect justice of the one God comes to realization in the promises that have been kept, surety and guarantee of the promises that will be kept. A homely story captures the promise:

TOSEFTA-TRACTATE KIPPURIM 2:7

A. Said R. 'Aqiba, "Simeon b. Luga told me, 'A certain child of the sons of their sons and I were gathering grass in the field. Then I saw him laugh and cry.

B. " 'I said to him, 'Why did you cry?'

C. " 'He said to me, 'Because of the glory of father's house, which has gone into exile.'

D. " 'I said to him, 'Then why did you laugh?'

E. " 'He said, 'At the end of it all, in time to come, the Holy One, blessed be He, is going to make his descendants rejoice.'

The exile guarantees the return: one promise kept, another is sure to be carried out. The story winds its way onward:

F. " 'I said to him, 'Why?' [What did you see to make you think of this?]

G. " 'He said to me, 'A smoke-raiser' in front of me [made me laugh].'

H. " 'I said to him, 'Show it to me.'

I. " 'He said to me, 'We are subject to an oath not to show it to anyone at all.' "

J. Said R. Yohanan b. Nuri, "One time I was going along the way and an old man came across me and said to me, 'I am a member of the house of Abtinas.

K. "'At the beginning, when the house of father was discreet, they would give their scrolls [containing the prescriptions for frankincense only] to one another.

L. "'Now take it, but be careful about it, since it is a scroll containing a recipe for spices.'

M. "And when I came and reported the matter before R. 'Aqiba, he said to me, 'From now on it is forbidden to speak ill of these people again.' "

N. On the basis of this story, Ben 'Azzai said, "Yours will they give you,

O. "by your own name will they call you,

P. "in your place will they seat you.

Q. "There is no forgetfulness before the Omnipresent.

R. "No man can touch what is designated for his fellow."

Israel finds itself subjugated to the gentiles in a world flawed by the prosperity of the wicked and the suffering of the righteous. So it is a time of mourning – but one of remembrance of the future, which the past promises out of the pathos of the present. Given the condition of the world and of Israel in it, it is right to mourn – beginning with mourning for Israel's own failures. But those who mourn properly now will rejoice in time to come, the one serving as an act of faith for what is to be. Whoever mourns for Jerusalem now will merit rejoicing with her in the world to come.

Not only so, but the mourning now should not be excessive; common sense should govern:

TOSEFTA-TRACTATE SOTAH 15:11

A. After the last Temple was destroyed, abstainers became many in Israel, who would not eat meat or drink wine.

The sage has now to transform mourning into the occasion for hope. This he does by defining the limits of mourning and also underscoring that which the mourning adumbrates, the restoration in the world to come of what today lies in ruins, whether the Temple, whether creation, and both are at issue in the following, with its reference to the gifts of nature, meat, wine, bread, water, fruit:

B. R. Joshua engaged them in discourse, saying to them, "My children, on what account do you not eat meat?"

C. They said to him, "Shall we eat meat, for every day a continual burnt-offering [of meat] was offered on the altar, and now it is no more?"

D. He said to them, "Then let us not eat it. And then why are you not drinking wine?"

E. They said to him, "Shall we drink wine, for every day wine was poured out as a drink-offering on the altar, and now it is no more."

F. He said to them, "Then let us not drink it."

G. He said to them, "But if so, we also should not eat bread, for from it did they bring the Two Loaves and the Show-Bread. We also should not drink water, for they did pour out a water-offering on the Festival. We also should not eat figs and grapes, for they would bring them as First Fruits on the festival of Weeks."

H. They fell silent.

15:12 A. He said to them, "My children, to mourn too much is not possible.

B. "But thus have the sages said: A man puts on plaster on his house but he leaves open a small area, as a memorial to Jerusalem.

15:13 A. "A man prepares what is needed for a meal but leaves out some small things, as a memorial to Jerusalem.

15:14 A. "A woman prepares her ornaments, but leaves out some small thing, as a memorial to Jerusalem,

B. "since it is said, 'If I forget you, O Jerusalem, let my right hand wither! Let my tongue cleave to the roof of my mouth, if I do not remember you, if I do not set Jerusalem above my highest joy!' " (Ps. 137:5–6).

15:15 A. And whoever mourns for her in this world will rejoice with her in the world to come,

B. as it is said, "Rejoice with Jerusalem and be glad for her, all you who love her; rejoice with her in joy, all you who mourn over her" (Is. 66:10).

The correct mode of mourning takes account of the Temple cult's character. It offered meat and wine to God, so the mourners gave up what had graced the altar. The decision thus represented a judgment of a symbolic character. This proves flawed, since water, grain, figs and grapes, and other staples likewise were offered. So the correct form of mourning is personal and symbolic, too: provision of some small memorial out of the materials of ordinary life. This then leads to the match of mourning now, rejoicing in the world to come.

What makes the sages so sure of themselves? To them, what gives Israel hope even now is that the prophetic warnings about punishment for sin have come true, so the prophetic consolation about God's response to Israel's repentance also will come true. That is, for them, a natural result of a theology that finds perfection in balance, order, proportion, above all complementarity. Just as the prophets warned that Israel would be punished for its rebellion against God, so they insisted that Israel would attain reconciliation through its repentance to God. Now that the first of the two elements of the equation, punishment for arrogant sin, has been realized, the sages find solid grounds for certainty in the ultimate fulfilment also of the promise of reconciliation in consequence of repentance in humility. The condition of the world today, the sages held, contains within itself not only the past and its consequence but, as a matter of certainty, also the future and its consolation. All are present in the here and now. As the Oral Torah says, "Today, if you want."

It is appropriate that this account of the theology of the Oral Torah should conclude with not my but the sages' voice:

LAMENTATIONS RABBATI CXL:I.I-2

1. A. "for Mount Zion which lies desolate; jackals prowl over it":
B. Rabban Gamaliel, R. Joshua, R. Eleazar b. Azariah, and R. Aqiba went to Rome. They heard the din of the city of Rome from a distance of a hundred and twenty miles.
C. They all begin to cry, but R. Aqiba began to laugh.
D. They said to him, "Aqiba, we are crying and you laugh?"
E. He said to them, "Why are you crying?"
F. They said to him, "Should we not cry, that idolators and those who sacrifice to idols and bow down to images live securely and prosperously, while the footstool of our God has been burned down by fire and become a dwelling place for the beasts of the field? So shouldn't we cry?"
G. He said to them, "That is precisely the reason that I was laughing. For if those who outrage him he treats in such a way, those who do his will all the more so!"
2. A. There was the further case of when they were going up to Jerusalem. When they came to the Mount of Olives they tore their clothing. When they came to the Temple mount and a fox came out of the house of the Holy of Holies, they began to cry. But R. Aqiba began to laugh.
B. "Aqiba, you are always surprising us. Now we are crying and you laugh?"
C. He said to them, "Why are you crying?"
D. They said to him, "Should we not cry, that from the place of which it is written, 'And the ordinary person that comes near shall be put to death' (Num. 1:51) a fox comes out? So the verse of Scripture is carried out: 'for Mount Zion which lies desolate; jackals prowl over it.'"
E. He said to them, "That is precisely the reason that I was laughing. For Scripture says, 'And I will take for myself faithful witnesses to record, Uriah the priest and Zechariah the son of Jeberechiah' (Isa. 8:2).
F. "Now what is the relationship between Uriah and Zechariah? Uriah lived in the time of the first temple, Zechariah in the time of the second!
G. "But Uriah said, 'Thus says the Lord of hosts: Zion shall be plowed as a field, and Jerusalem shall become heaps' (Jer. 26:18).
H. "And Zechariah said, 'There shall yet be old men and old women sitting in the piazzas of Jerusalem, every man with his staff in his hand for old age' (Zech. 8:4).

I. "And further: 'And the piazzas of the city shall be full of boys and girls playing in the piazzas thereof' (Zech. 8:5).

J. "Said the Holy One, blessed be He, 'Now lo, I have these two witnesses. So if the words of Uriah are carried out, the words of Zechariah will be carried out, while if the words of Uriah prove false, then the words of Zechariah will not be true either.'

K. "I was laughing with pleasure because the words of Uriah have been carried out, and that means that the words of Zechariah in the future will be carried out."

L. They said to him, "Aqiba, you have given us consolation. May you be comforted among those who are comforted."

And that is exactly what the sages intended, to console and hearten Israel, for God's sake. That has remained the task of sages in age succeeding age. Bearing this compelling theology of one, just God to account for all things through the ages, the sages have sustained Israel with a sufficiency of reasoned hope. And they still do, even – I should say, *especially* – in the aftermath of the Holocaust.

EPILOGUE

15 Before and After

The theology of the Oral Torah in its union with the Written Torah, on the one side, and with the liturgy of synagogue and home life, on the other, defines Judaism's world view, the details in context of its way of life, its explanation of what, and who, is Israel. In their distinctive language and idiom, which in no way copied the language or reproduced the modes of discourse of Scripture, the sages of the Oral Torah retold the story of the Written Torah. The liturgy of the synagogue and home, for its part, would rework modes of thought characteristic of the sages of the Oral Torah and reframe clusters of categories that the sages had formed to make their statement. That is why anyone who wishes to describe the principal characteristics of the religious world-view of that Judaism, in proportion and balance, will find the prescription here.

This theological structure and system hold together both received teaching and contemporary and future liturgical expression and elaboration alike. The sages claimed through the oral tradition formulated in the documents of the Oral Torah to complement the written tradition and so to set forth for all time the one whole Torah of Moses, our rabbi, and past and future join to prove them right. That claim to state the Torah – in secular language, "here is Judaism, pure and simple" – constitutes the sages' theological apologetics, an integral, logical component of their entire statement. And that fact shows us where – by their word, at least – to situate the Oral Torah in the cartography of Judaism. On that map all roads but dead ends coming from one side lead into the Oral Torah; all roads indicated for public use coming from the other side emerge from the Oral Torah.

Speaking descriptively, standing back and seeing things whole, can we concur? Two questions therefore remain to complete this reading of the Oral Torah whole and complete. The answers to them – answers the reader will find self-evidently sound – place that theology into the context of the history of the Judaism continuous with the Oral Torah fore and aft and validate the sages' claim to stand at the vital centre of the Torah.

Before: Are the sages right about the written part of the Torah, meaning, is what they say the Written Torah says actually what the ancient Israelite Scriptures say? Will those who put forth the books of Genesis through Kings as a sustained narrative and those who in that same context selected and organized the writings of the prophets, Isaiah, Jeremiah, Ezekiel, and the twelve, in the aggregate have concurred in the sages' structure and system? Certainly others who lay claim to these same Scriptures did not concur. At the time the sages did their greatest theological work, in the fourth and fifth centuries C.E., their Christian counterparts, in the Latin-, Greek- and Syriac-speaking sectors of Christianity alike, not only read Scripture in a very different way but also accused the rabbis of falsifying the Torah. How would the sages have responded to the charge?

After: In the ages that have passed since the conclusion of the documents of the Oral Torah, has holy Israel's encounter with God in synagogue worship found its shape and principal expression in the sages' re-presentation of the one whole Torah of Moses? How – on the basis of what evidence – do we know that it was, in particular, the sages' theology that animated the soul of faithful Israel in the prayerful encounter with God?

Accordingly, the question, framed merely descriptively, presses: did the sages get the past right, and did they effectively define the future? These two questions, the one concerning the Written Torah or Scripture, therefore the *before* of the Oral Torah, the other, the one concerning synagogue liturgy and piety that flow around and from the Oral Torah, therefore its *after*, respond to the mediating situation of the Oral Torah. But what is that situation, meaning, where and how, in what context, do I propose to situate or locate (borrowing the Spanish, *localizar*) the Oral Torah?

My answer must appeal not to sequence ("history") and circumstance (the sages' legislation concerning, and well-attested participation in, synagogue life) but to the persistent point of insistence. Nor, in the light of chapter 6, can the question concern what came first and what then followed, purporting to account for matters by appeal to temporal-causative sequences.[1] And

---

1. But it is the fact that the sages discuss liturgy, whether the Shema, or The Prayer, or other rules of synagogue worship and conduct. But only a few liturgical compositions are attributed in the Oral Torah to the authorship of the sages, and these always take their place around the fringes of the worship service, never at the centre. So, while the Siddur and Mahzor in their principal parts speak with the sages' approval, we require evidence that, in addition, they speak in behalf of the sages in particular. Only with the evidence of that very particular kind can I claim that the Oral Torah takes up that mediating position that I impute to it.

the question, further, is raised not for the merely adventitious fact that, in temporal sequence, the Oral Torah reached written form in documents that came together after the Written Torah had reached its ultimate statement but before the closure and systematization of the liturgy, from the ninth century C.E. Any of these approaches to explanation would provide a plausible answer to the question of the future: why did the course of the Torah take the route that it did? The sequential facts of history – first came this, then that, and finally, the other thing – do not explain the realities of faith.

My exposition claims to set forth normative theology; what represents the sages' views is an integrating logic, on the one side, and a ubiquitous principle, on the other. Consistent with the intellectual discipline that governs in these pages, I maintain that these realities, too – the integral relationship between the two Torahs, on the one side, and between the Torah and synagogue liturgy, on the other – unfold in accord with their own inner logic, their own dialectic and its tensions. That is to say, relationships fore and aft spin out their potentialities in the dialectic defined by the deep logic of theology that is built into the most profound levels of structure; the dynamics find motivation in the system's inexorable inertial forces. So I frame the question in my terms in this language: crossroads and meeting place, the Oral Torah forms the gateway to Scripture, in the one direction, the highway opening outward into the long future of practised piety, in the other – by what logic, by what admissible evidence?

Let me therefore spell out the localizing circumstances in which we address the matter. The faithful of Judaism through the ages reach Scripture through the oral tradition recorded here, never encountering an unmediated Scripture (whether historically or philologically or archaeologically, for example). Moses is always *rabbenu*, "our rabbi," and Isaiah, "Rabbi Isaiah." Jacob looked into the present and described the future, and Abraham, Moses, and the prophets met God on the afternoon of the ninth of Ab in the year we now number as 70 and rebuked him for what he had done through the Romans. These realizations do not draw upon easy sentimentality or resort to figurative conceits. People acted upon them every day, built their lives around them, met God in them. Their concrete actions, the deprivations they accepted and humiliations they turned into validation – these attest to the palpable reality, for holy Israel, of the vision of the Dual Torah. Have they been, and are they today, right in reaching the Written Torah through the path set out by the Oral one?

For their part, those who practise Judaism found their liturgy upon the theology set forth in that same oral tradition of Sinai. When holy Israel prays, people assume, they express in practical terms of "we" and "you" the relationship that is posited by the theology of the Oral Torah. That liturgy, moreover, takes place within the timeless world of enduring paradigms formulated by the Oral Torah. How people situated themselves to face, to speak to God uncovers the deepest corners of their soul. So the theology of the Oral Torah, further encompassing its realization in normative law, for Judaism compares with the brain and heart of man. For holy Israel, the Oral Torah defines the point of consciousness and cognition, the source of life, respectively. Is that so?

That is certainly how the sages want us to see matters, for that is how they present them. Implicit in the apologetics that forms an integral part of the theology of the Oral Torah are two judgments which take up a constant presence.

First – so this apologetics goes – the sages are right about Scripture. That is to say, nearly every proposition they set forth, the main beams of the structure of faith they construct – all are set securely and symmetrically upon the Written Torah. Proof-texts constantly take the measure of the structure. That is why the sages speak of the one whole Torah, in two media, correlative and complementary.

Second, the sages' formulation of the Torah, the one whole Torah of Moses, our rabbi, defines holy Israel's relationship with God for all time to come. The very character of the prayers that holy Israel offers up in place of Temple sacrifices attests to that fact: the theology of the Oral Torah is recapitulated in the liturgy of the synagogue. The sages teach Israel how to pray and what to say.

Accordingly – that is now the sages' view – if we take up the Oral Torah and explore its theological structure and system, we meet Judaism, pure and simple. There we find its learning and its piety, what it knows about and hears from God, what it has to say to God. So much for the claim of theological apologetics.

The facts support it. The sages have not only history – the pivotal position of their writings in the sequence from *before* to *after* – but also hermeneutics on their side. In their reading of the Written Torah whole, in canonical context, as a record of life with God, they are right to say that their story goes over the Written Torah's story. Start to finish, creation through Sinai to the fall of Jerusalem, all perceived in the light of the prophets' rebuke, consolation, and hope for restoration, Scripture's account is rehearsed in the Oral Torah. All is in proportion and balance. Viewed as a systematic hermeneutics, the sages' theology accurately sets forth the principal possibility of the theology that is implicit in the written part of the Torah – to be sure, in a more systematic and cogent manner than does Scripture.[2]

And, at the other end of the story, piety has certainly proved the sages correct in their claim to define holy Israel's encounter with God for all time. The character of the liturgical life of the synagogue proves that the sages' theology in particular – which is Scripture's theology – in important indicative traits of mind and of message defines holy Israel's approach to God in prayer. So, as I said, when Israel hears God's message in the Oral Torah, it is listening to God's message in the Written Torah. And when Israel speaks to God in the liturgy of the synagogue and the private life as well, Israel addresses God as the Oral Torah's theology shapes that address, to be sure in language that accommodates the circumstance of worship.

First, why do I maintain that the sages are right about Scripture? It is because, start to finish, the Oral Torah builds its structure out of a reading of the Written Torah. The sages read from the Written Torah forward to the Oral Torah. That is not only attested by the superficial character of proof-texting, but by the profound congruence of the theology of the Oral Torah with the course of the Scriptural exposition. Any outline of Scripture's account begins with creation and tells about the passage from Eden via Sinai and Jerusalem to Babylon – and back. It speaks of the patriarchal founders of Israel, the Exodus, Sinai, the Torah, covenants, Israel, the people of God, the priesthood and the tabernacle, the possession of the Land, exile and restoration. And so, too, has this outline of the Oral Torah's theology focused upon all of these same matters. True, the sages proportion matters within their own logic,

---

2. If I were engaged in constructive systematic theology, not just the historical kind, I should further claim that the sages' is the only possible system that the Hebrew Scriptures sustain. Whether or not other theologies built upon the Hebrew Scriptures may be deemed congruent with those Scriptures is not at issue here, only the claim that the sages' is. But I think a powerful case can be made in behalf of the congruity with Scripture, in proportion, balance, and also detail, of the sages' retelling of the Scriptural tale. Even here, in the mere description of the theological system of the Oral Torah, it should be said that how the sages diverge from Scripture in their basic theological structure and system I simply cannot discern. In my view, transcending the promiscuous use of proof-texts is the evidence on the surface of matters. At no point can I find important differences between the sages' and Scripture's respective theological systems and structures. In that sense, I should want in the right setting to argue that the sages are right about the Written Torah (Christianity's Old Testament) and everyone else is wrong. That is because the sages read outward and forward from Scripture, and the other, competing heirs of Scripture read backward to Scripture. So, in that simple sense, the sages say what Scripture means, and no one else does.

laying heaviest emphasis upon perfection, imperfection, and restoration of perfection to creation, focusing upon Israel, God's stake in humanity.

The theological structure and system appeal to the perfection of creation and account for imperfection by reference to the fall of man into sin by reason of arrogant rebellion and into death in consequence. They tell the story of the formation of holy Israel as God's party in humanity, signified by access to knowledge of God through God's self-manifestation in the Torah. They then present the exile of Israel from the Land of Israel as the counterpart to the exile of Adam from Eden. Therefore, main beams of the Hebrew Scripture's account of matters define the structure of the Oral Torah's theology. The generative tensions of the Hebrew Scripture's narrative empower the dynamics of that theology.

A few obvious facts suffice. Take the principal propositions of Scripture read in sequence and systematically, meaning, as exemplary, from Genesis through Kings. Consider the story of the exile from Eden and the counterpart exile of Israel from the Land. The sages did not invent that paradigm. Scripture's framers did. Translate into propositional form the prophetic messages of admonition, rebuke, and consolation, the promise that as punishment follows sin, so consolation will come in consequence of repentance. The sages did not fabricate those categories and make up the rules that govern the sequence of events. The prophets said them all. The sages only recapitulated the prophetic propositions with little variation except in formulation. All the sages did was to interpret within the received paradigm the exemplary events of their own day, the destruction of Jerusalem and Israel's subjugation in particular. But even at that they simply asked Scripture's question of events that conformed to Scripture's pattern. Identify as the dynamics of human history the engagement of God with man, especially through Israel, and what do you have if not the heart of the sages' doctrine of the origins and destiny of man. Review what Scripture intimates about the meaning and end of time, and how much do you miss of the sages' eschatology of restoration? Details, amplifications, clarifications, an unsuccessful effort at systematization – these do not obscure the basic confluence of the sages' and Scripture's account of last things (even though, as I said, the word "last" has its own meaning for the sages).

Nor do I have to stress the form that the sages impart to their propositions, nearly everything they say being joined to a verse of Scripture. That is not a formality. Constant citations of scriptural texts cited as authority serve merely to signal the presence of a profound identity of viewpoint. The cited verses are not solely pretexts or formal proof-texts. A hermeneutics governs, dictating the course of exegesis. In concrete terms, the theology I have outlined generates the exegesis we have encountered on nearly every page of this book. The sages cite and interpret verses of Scripture to show where and how the Written Torah guides the Oral one, supplying the specificities of the process of recapitulation. And what the sages say about those verses originates not in the small details of those verses (such as Aqiba was able to interpret to Moses's stupefaction) but in the large theological structure and system that the sages framed.

That is why I insist that the hermeneutics defined the exegesis, the exegesis did not define the hermeneutics – as I have shown many times in my systematic analysis of the various Midrash-compilations.[3] In most of the Midrash-compilations of the Oral Torah it is a simple fact that the sages read from the whole to the parts, from the Written part of the Torah outward to the Oral part, as we shall observe in a moment. That explains why nothing arbitrary or merely occasional, nothing ad hoc or episodic or notional characterized the sages' reading of Scripture, but a theology, formed whole in response to the whole. That explains why the sages did not think they imputed to Scripture meanings not actually there, and this account of their theology proves that they are right.

The sages read Scripture as a letter written that morning to them in particular about the world they encountered. That is because for them the past was forever integral to the present. So they looked into the Written part of the Torah to construct the picture of reality that is explained by the world-view set forth in the Oral part of the Torah. They found their questions in Scripture; they identified the answers to those questions in Scripture; and they then organized and interpreted the contemporary situation of holy Israel in light of those questions and answers. To that process the narrow focus of atomistic exegesis proves monumentally irrelevant, indeed, even incongruous. For the very category, proof-text, reduces that elegant theology of the here and now to the trivialities of grammar or spelling or other nonsense-details. It demeans the sages' intellectual honesty, such as, on every page of the Talmud of Babylonia among many documents, is affirmed and attested by the very character of discourse. And it misses the fact that Scripture's corpus of facts, like nature's, was deemed to transcend the bonds of time. That explains why the sages found in Scripture the main lines of structure and system that formed the architecture of their theology.

3. To give a single example, I point to *Judaism and Scripture: The Evidence of Leviticus Rabbah* (Chicago: The University of Chicago Press 1986). I have dealt systematically with the atomistic reading of the Midrash-compilations in *The Documentary Foundation of Rabbinic Culture. Mopping Up after Debates with Gerald L. Bruns, S. J. D. Cohen, Arnold Maria Goldberg, Susan Handelman, Christine Hayes, James Kugel, Peter Schaefer, Eliezer Segal, E. P. Sanders, and Lawrence H. Schiffman* (Atlanta: Scholars Press for South Florida Studies in the History of Judaism, 1995).

And it accounts for the fact that, in the Heavenly academy to which imagination carried them, the great sages could amiably conduct arguments with God and with Moses. Not only so, but they engage in ongoing dialogue with the prophets and psalmists and the other saints of the Written Torah as well as with those of their masters and teachers in the oral tradition who reached Eden earlier (much as entire legions of participants in the Oral Torah in recent centuries aspire to spend an afternoon in Eden with Moses Maimonides). A common language joined them all, for, in their entire engagement with the written part of the Torah, the sages mastered every line, every word, every letter, sorting matters of the day out in response to what they learned in the written tradition.

That explains why we may justifiably say that on every page of the writings of the Oral Torah we encounter the sages' encompassing judgment of, and response to, the heritage of ancient Israel's Scripture. There they met God, there they found God's plan for the world of perfect justice, the flawless, eternal world in stasis, and there in detail they learned what became of that teaching in ancient times and in their own day, everything seen in the same way. The result is spread out in the pages of this book: the sages' account of the Torah revealed by God to Moses at Sinai and handed on in tradition through the ages.

So if we ask, what if, in the timeless world of the Torah studied in the same Heavenly academy, Moses and the prophets, sages, and scribes of Scripture were to take up the results of oral tradition produced by their heirs and successors in the oral part of the Torah? The answer is clear. They would have found themselves hearing familiar words, their own words, used by honest, faithful men, in familiar, wholly legitimate ways. When, for example, Moses heard in the tradition of the Oral Torah that a given law was a law revealed by God to Moses at Sinai, he may have kept his peace, though puzzled, or he may have remembered that, indeed, that is how it was, just so. In very concrete, explicit language the sages themselves laid their claim to possess the Torah of Moses. We recall how impressed Moses is by Aqiba, when he observed, from the rear of the study hall, how Aqiba was able to interpret on the basis of each point of the crowns heaps and heaps of laws. But he could not follow the debate and felt faint until he heard the later master declare, "It is a law given to Moses from Sinai," and then he regained his composure (Bavli tractate Menahot 3:7 II.5/29, cited in chapter 5).

So it is entirely within the imaginative capacity of the Oral Torah to raise the question: what came before in relationship to what we have in hand? To state the matter more directly, are the rabbis of the Oral Torah right in maintaining that they have provided the originally Oral part of the one whole Torah of Moses our rabbi? To answer that question in the affirmative, the sages would have only to point to their theology in the setting of Scripture's as they grasped it. The theology of the Oral Torah tells a simple, sublime story:

1) God created a perfect, just world and in it made man in his image, equal to God in the power of will;
2) Man in his arrogance sinned and was expelled from the perfect world and given over to death. God gave man the Torah to purify his heart of sin;
3) Man educated by the Torah in humility can repent, accepting God's will of his own free will. When he does, man will be restored to Eden and eternal life.

In our terms, we should call it a story with a beginning, middle, and end. In the sages' framework, we realize, the story embodies an enduring and timeless paradigm of humanity in the encounter with God: man's powerful will, God's powerful word, in conflict, and the resolution thereof.

But if I claim that the sages were right about the Written Torah, then what about the hermeneutics of others? If the sages claimed fully to spell out the message of the Written Torah, as they do explicitly in nearly every document and on nearly every page of the Oral Torah, so too did others. And those others, who, like the sages, added to the received Scripture other writings of a (to-them) authoritative character, set forth not only the story of the fall from grace that occupied the sages but, in addition, different stories from those the sages told. They drew different consequences from the heritage of ancient Israel. The sages' critics will find their account not implausible but incomplete, a truncated reading of Scripture. They will wonder about leaving out nearly the entire apocalyptic tradition.[4] But, in the balance, the sages' critics err. For no one can reasonably doubt that the sages' reading of Scripture recovers, in proportion and accurate stress and balance, the main lines of Scripture's principal story, the one about creation, the fall of man, and God's salvation of man through Israel and the Torah. In familiar, though somewhat gauche, language, "Judaism" really is what common opinion thinks it is, which is, "the religion of the Old Testament." If, as Brevard Childs states, "The evangelists read from the New [Testament] backward to the Old,"[5] we may say very simply that this is what I claim to have shown

---

4. That is with two exceptions, for, so far as that tradition can be naturalized into the framework established by the sages' structure and system, sages do so, as in the case of Daniel. Second, they take over as fact and accept apocalyptic expectations, as with the war of Gog and Magog.

5. *Biblical Theology of the Old and New Testaments* (Philadelphia: Fortress Press 1989), 720.

in this theology: *the sages read from the Written Torah forward to the Oral one.*

So much for the *before* part of the Oral Torah. What about the *after* defined by synagogue piety? If the sages were right about the past, they assuredly commanded the future. In every synagogue in the world that addresses God in the words of the classical prayer-book, the *Siddur* (and associated liturgies of synagogue and home), that cherishes the Pentateuch and aspires to live by its law, the theology of the Oral Torah imparts shape and structure to holy Israel's address to God. We know that that is so, because the sages' distinctive modes of thought and the connections that they made, the clusters of categories they formed and the connections they drew between one thing and another, would account for the character of Israel's liturgy. That is why I claim that, in the practised piety of worship, not only is the Written Torah mediated through the Oral, but the act and attitude of prayer are given theological substance in modes of thought particular to the sages and in symbolic formulations distinctive to their account of God and the world. Accordingly, I am justified in claiming (in the language of history) that the sages shaped the future of Judaism as much as they mediated its past.[6]

At every point in my theological exposition readers familiar with the principal parts of the synagogue's order of worship ought to have found themselves on familiar ground. For the order of prayer (*matbe'a shel tefillah*),

6. But whether or not the same sages who formed the Oral Torah bear principal responsibility, also, for the character of synagogue liturgy as we know it has no bearing upon my argument. Many take for granted that they do. For reasons spelled out in this part of the chapter, I concur. But when I claim that the theology of the Oral Torah is realized in the liturgy of the synagogue, that is not a historical-temporal but a theological judgment. Why do I think it also is a historical fact? Certainly, the sages in the Oral Torah evinced the ambition to define the liturgy. Their *halakhah* extends to the order of common worship, defining its principal parts. The *aggadah* contains compositions of prayers in the name of various sages, and some of these are incorporated in the liturgy – the Siddur and Mahzor, the prayer-books for everyday, Sabbath, and festivals, on the one side, and for the Days of Awe, on the other. But whether or not the sages of the Oral Torah bear responsibility for the liturgy as it is first attested in detail is another question, and one that, as I said, has no bearing upon my claim in behalf of the sages' theology and its impact. In line with the character of this book, that claim forms an intellectual judgment about the power of ideas, not a historical one about the politics of public worship and who was in control thereof. The detailed wording of both the Siddur and the Mahzor is first attested centuries after the close of the Talmud of Babylonia, but the fixed order of prayer, as we know that order of prayer in the earliest written Siddurim, conforms to the law of the Talmud. Some prayers in both documents are assigned in the Talmud to named sages; others are merely alluded to, without a clear claim of the sages' authorship in particular. But my point of insistence, that the liturgy responds to the sages' theology, is to be evaluated in its own framework, which is phenomenological, not historical.

with recitation of the *Shema* ("Hear O Israel") with blessings fore and aft, of the Eighteen Benedictions of The Prayer, and the exit-prayer, *Alenu* ("It is incumbent upon us ..."), rehearse in ways appropriate to the circumstance of prayer principal propositions about creation, revelation, and redemption, God, Torah, and Israel that, in their theology, the sages worked out. But that allegation is far too general to suffice. As already adumbrated, in fact I identify as the definitive contribution of the Oral Torah very particular traits of mind, on the one side, and formations of distinctive clusters of ideas, on the other. These recapitulate the theology of the Oral Torah and impart to the liturgy the sages' indicative marker; intellectual traits of particular liturgies match modes of thought uniquely characteristic of the Oral Torah. Motifs or symbols or myths join together in conformity to the patterns established by the Oral Torah but (by definition) not by the Written Torah. These two traits prominent in the liturgy of synagogue and home point towards the conclusion offered at the outset, that the Oral Torah exercised a particular and highly distinctive – and therefore the formative – influence upon the encounter between Israel and God that acts of faith and piety bring about.[7]

As to the dominance of modes of thought characteristic of the sages in particular: in the liturgy, a timeless world of past, present, and future meet. That is how the sages recast history into paradigm, such as we examined in chapter 6. We recall how the sages reframed Scripture's history into laws governing the social order, turning events from singular, sequential, one-time, and unique happenings into exemplary patterns. These, we recall, encompass the past within the present and join future, present and the past onto a single plane of eternity. It is that mode of thought that brings about the formation of liturgies that have all the ages met in one place, the great themes of existence coming together to reshape a very particular moment. It is that same mode of thought, moreover, that insists on the union of the public and the private, the communal and the individual, all things subject to the same principle, explained in the same way. Liturgies that form the intersection of events out of widely separated periods in the Scriptural narrative, the gathering of persons who in Scripture do not meet, realize the sages' way of seeing Scripture.[8]

7. It seems to me self-evident that, when it comes to generative modes of thought and distinctive clusters of motifs, we do well to limit our inquiry into formative influences to the Dual Torah.

8. A fair test of this allegation of the particularity of the sages' reading will address the liturgies found in the library at Qumran and compare those of the synagogue with the prayers that the group represented by that library offered. Other such tests are readily to be imagined.

Two private liturgies exemplify the paradigmatic, as against the historical, formulation of matters. First, the particularly rabbinic mode of thought characterizes the prayer for the wedding of an Israelite man and woman, joining in one statement the motifs of creation, Adam, Eve, and Eden, the fall of Israel from the Land of Israel, and the hoped-for restoration of man to Eden and Israel to Jerusalem and the Land. The whole takes place out of time, in that "dream-time" characteristic of the theology of the Oral Torah. At a single moment the ages meet, discrete events intersect. Here we find fully exposed the matter of life in that timeless world of an ever-present past. So, too, the private and the public meet as well when a new family begins. Individual lover and beloved celebrate the uniqueness, the privacy of their love. They turn out to stand for Adam and Eve and to represent the very public hope for the restoration of Israel to the perfection of Eden in the Land. That imposes upon their love a heavy burden for the young, infatuated couple.

Here is where the liturgy takes theological modes of thought and casts them into moments of realization and reprise. What is striking is how the theme of Eden and alienation, Land of Israel and exile, so typical of the theology of the Oral Torah, is reworked into a new pattern: from the loneliness and exile of the single life to the Eden and Jerusalem of the wedding canopy. So while theme of exile and return is recapitulated, now it is reshaped by message that the joy of the bride and groom – standing, after all, for Israel and God – is a foretaste of what is last, that final reprise of creation, now in eternal perfection. Adam at the end time, the Temple restored, Jerusalem rebuilt – that peculiar tableau certainly stands for the sages' conception in particular. The personal and the public join, the individuals before us embody and re-enact the entirety of Israel's holy life, past to future:

Praised are You, O Lord our God, King of the universe, Creator of the fruit of the vine.

Praised are You, O Lord our God, King of the universe, who created all things for Your glory.

Praised are You, O Lord our God, King of the universe, Creator of Adam.

Praised are You, O Lord our God, King of the universe, who created man and woman in his image, fashioning woman from man as his mate, that together they might perpetuate life. Praised are You, O Lord, Creator of man.

May Zion rejoice as her children are restored to her in joy. Praised are You, O Lord, who causes Zion to rejoice at her children's return.

Grant perfect joy to these loving companions, as You did to the first man and woman in the Garden of Eden. Praised are You, O Lord, who grants the joy of bride and groom.

Praised are You, O Lord our God, King of the universe, who created joy and gladness, bride and groom, mirth, song, delight and rejoicing, love and harmony, peace and companionship. O Lord our God, may there ever be heard in the cities of Judah and in the streets of Jerusalem voices of joy and gladness, voices of bride and groom, the jubilant voices of those joined in marriage under the bridal canopy, the voices of young people feasting and signing. Praised are You, O Lord, who causes the groom to rejoice with his bride.[9]

The blessings speak of archetypical Israel, represented here and now by the bride and groom. They cover the great themes of the theology of the Oral Torah, excluding only one that does not fit. We find creation, Adam, man and woman in his image, after his likeness; then comes the restoration of Israel to Zion; then the joy of Zion in her children and the loving companions in one another; then the evocation of the joy of the restoration – past, present, future, all in the here and now. The sole critical component of the theology of the Oral Torah omitted here concerns justice, on the one side, sin, repentance, and atonement, on the other. That omission attests once more to the sages' fine sense of what fits and what does not.

The theme of ancient paradise is introduced by the simple choice of the word *Adam*, just as we should expect. The myth of man's creation is rehearsed: man and woman are in God's image, together complete and whole, creators of life, "like God." Woman was fashioned from man together with him to perpetuate life. But this Adam and this Eve – as we should expect in a Rabbinic document! – also are Israel, children of Zion the mother, as expressed in the fifth blessing. Israel is in exile, Zion lies in ruins. It is at that appropriate point that the restorationist motif enters: "Grant perfect joy to the loving companions," for they are creators of a new line in mankind – the new Adam, the new Eve – and their home – May it be the garden of Eden. And if joy is there, then "praised are you for the joy of bride and groom."

The concluding blessing returns to the theme of Jerusalem. Given the focus of the system as a whole, that hardly presents a surprise. For the union of bridegroom and bride provides a foretaste of the new Eden that is coming. But that is only at the right moment, in the right setting, when Israel will have repented, atoned, and attained resurrection and therefore restoration to Eden/the world to come. How is all this invoked? The liturgy conveys these motifs when it calls up the tragic hour of Jerusalem's first destruction. When

9. Jules Harlow, ed., *A Rabbi's Manual* (New York: Rabbinical Assembly 1965), 45. The "seven blessings" said at a wedding are printed in traditional Jewish prayer-books. All of the translations of liturgies set forth here derive from Rabbi Harlow's superlative translations.

everyone had given up hope, supposing with the end of Jerusalem had come the end of time, exile, the anti-Eden, only Jeremiah counselled renewed hope. With the enemy at the gate, he sang of coming gladness:

JEREMIAH 33:10–11

Thus says the Lord:
In this place of which you say, "It is a waste, without man or beast," in the cities of Judah and the streets of Jerusalem that are desolate, without man or inhabitant or beast,
There shall be heard again the voice of mirth and the voice of gladness, the voice of the bridegroom and the voice of the bride, the voice of those who sing as they bring thank-offerings to the house of the Lord ... For I shall restore the fortunes of the land as at first, says the Lord.

The intersection of characteristic motifs creates a timeless tableau. Just as here and now there stand before us Adam and Eve, so here and now in this wedding, the olden sorrow having been rehearsed, we listen to the voice of gladness that is coming. The joy of this new creation prefigures the joy of the Messiah's coming, inaugurating the resurrection and judgment and the final restoration. The joy then will echo the joy of bride and groom before us. So the small space covered by the marriage-canopy is crowded indeed with persons and events. People who think historically and not paradigmatically can commemorate and celebrate. But they cannot embody, or even exemplify, eternity in the here and now, the presence and past and future all at once. In this context, only the sages of the Oral Torah have formed a mode of thought that is capable of imagining such a convocation of persons and concatenation of events.

The same mode of thought marks other liturgies that celebrate events of the life cycle. The entry of the male child into the covenant of Abraham through the rite of circumcision, yet another moment that is intensely personal (to the infant) and massively public (to all Israel), forms another moment of timeless eternity. Specifically, in the case of a boy child, a minor surgical rite becomes the mark of the renewal of the agreement between God and Israel, the covenant carved into the flesh of the penis of every Jewish male – and nothing less. The beginning of a new life renews the rule that governs Israel's relationship to God. So the private joy is reworked through words of enchantment – once more, sanctification – and so transformed into renewal of the community of Israel and God. Those present find themselves in another time, another

place. Specific moments out of the past are recapitulated, and specific personalities called to attendance. In the present instant, eternity is invoked at the
moment of cutting off the foreskin of the penis. Calling the rite, *berit milah*,
the covenant effected through the rite of circumcision invites Abraham to
attend. *Berit milah* seals with the blood of the infant son the contract between
Israel and God, generation by generation, son by son.

The words that are said evoke in the intimacy of the private life the being
that all share together: Israel, its covenant with God, its origin in Abraham,
Isaac, Jacob. In the rite God sees the family beyond time, joined by blood of
not pedigree but circumcision, genealogy framed by fifty generations of
loyalty to the covenant in blood and birth from the union of the womb of the
Israelite woman with the circumcised penis of her Israelite husband: this is
the holy fruit of the womb. There are four aspects in which the operation is
turned into a rite. When the rite begins, the assembly and the *mohel* (the one
who performs the circumcision) together recite the following:

The Lord spoke to Moses saying, Phineas, son of Eleazar, son of Aaron, the priest,
has turned my wrath from the Israelites by displaying among them his passion for me,
so that I did not wipe out the Israelite people in my passion. Say therefore I grant him
my covenant of peace.

Commenting on this passage, Lifsa Schachter states, "Phineas is identified
with zealously opposing the … sins of sexual licentiousness and idolatry. He
is best known for an event which occurred when the Israelites, whoring with
Moabite women in the desert, were drawn to the worship of Baal-Peor …
Phineas leaped into the fray and through an act of double murder … quieted
God's terrible wrath."[10]

Second, a chair is set called "the chair of Elijah," so that the rite takes place
in the presence of a chair for Elijah, the prophet. The newborn son is set on
that chair, and the congregation says, "This is the chair of Elijah, of blessed
memory." Elijah had complained to God that Israel neglected the covenant
(I Kings 19:10–14). So he comes to bear witness that Israel observes the covenant of circumcision. Then, before the surgical operation, a blessing is said.
Third, after the operation, a blessing is said over a cup of wine. To understand
the invocation of Elijah, for whom we set a chair, we first recall the pertinent
biblical passage:

10. Lifsa Schachter, "Reflections on the Brit Mila Ceremony," *Conservative Judaism*,
vol. 38 (1986), 38–41.

I KINGS 19:10–14

Suddenly the word of the Lord came to him: "Why are you here, Elijah?"

"Because of my great zeal for the Lord the God of hosts," he said. "The people of Israel have forsaken your covenant, torn down your altars, and put your prophets to death with the sword. I alone am left, and they seek to take my life."

The answer came: "Go and stand on the mount before the Lord."

For the Lord was passing by: a great and strong wind came rending mountains and shattering rocks before him, but the Lord was not in the wind; and after the wind there was an earthquake, but the Lord was not in the earthquake; and after the earthquake fire; but the Lord was not in the fire; and after the fire a still small voice.

When Elijah heard it, he muffled his face in his cloak and went out and stood at the entrance of the cave. Then there came a voice: "Why are you here, Elijah?"

"Because of my great zeal for the Lord God of hosts," he said. "The people of Israel have forsaken your covenant, torn down your altars, and put your prophets to death with the sword. I alone am left, and they seek to take my life."

This passage stands behind the story told in a medieval document, *Pirke de-Rabbi Eliezer*, that Elijah attends the rite of circumcision of every Jewish baby boy[11]:

The Israelites were wont to circumcise until they were divided into two kingdoms. The kingdom of Ephraim cast off from themselves the covenant of circumcision. Elijah, may he be remembered for good, arose and was zealous with a mighty passion, and he adjured the heavens to send down neither dew nor rain upon the earth. Jezebel heard about it and sought to slay him.

Elijah arose and prayed before the Holy One, blessed be he. The Holy One, blessed be he, said to him, "'Are you better than your fathers' (1 Kgs. 19:4)? Esau sought to slay Jacob, but he fled before him, as it is said, 'And Jacob fled into the field of Aram' (Hos. 12:12).

"Pharaoh sought to slay Moses, who fled before him and he was saved, as it is said, Now when Pharaoh heard this thing, he sought to slay Moses. 'And Moses fled from the face of Pharaoh' (Ex. 2:15).

"Saul sought to slay David, who fled before him and was saved, as it is said, 'If you save not your life tonight, tomorrow you will be killed' " (1 Sam. 19:11).

Another text says, "And David fled and escaped" (1 Sam. 19:18). Learn that everyone who flees is said."

11. *Pirke deRabbi Eliezer*, trans. Gerald Friedlander (London, 1916), 212–14.

Elijah, may he be remembered for good, arose and fled from the land of Israel, and he betook himself to Mount Horeb, as it is said, 'and he arose and ate and drank' (1 Kings 19:8).

Then the Holy One, blessed be he, was revealed to him and said to him, "What you you doing here, Elijah"?

He answered him saying, "I have been very zealous."

The Holy One, blessed be he, said to him, "You are always zealous. You were zealous in Shittim on account of the immorality. For it is said, 'Phineas, the son of Eleazar, the son of Aaron the priest, turned my wrath away from the children of Israel, in that he was zealous with my zeal among them' (Num. 25:11).

"Here you are also zealous, By your life! They shall not observe the covenant of circumcision until you see it done with your own eyes."

Hence the sages have instituted the custom that people should have a seat of honour for the messenger of the covenant, for Elijah, may he be remembered for good, is called the messenger of the covenant, as it is said, 'And the messenger of the covenant, whom you delight in, behold he comes' (Mal. 3:1).

So, too, the "messenger of the covenant" (Malachi 1:23) is the prophet Elijah, and he is present whenever a Jewish son enters the *covenant* of Abraham, which is circumcision. God therefore ordered him to come to every circumcision so as to witness the loyalty of the Jews to the covenant. Elijah then serves as the guardian for the newborn, just as he raised the child of the widow from the dead (1 Kgs. 17:17–24). Along these same lines, on the Seder table of Passover, a cup of wine is poured for Elijah, and the door is opened for Elijah to join in the rite. Setting a seat for Elijah serves to invoke the presence of the guardian of the newborn and the zealous advocate of the rite of the circumcision of the covenant. Celebrating with the family of the newborn are not "all Israel" in general, but a very specific personage indeed. The gesture of setting the chair silent sets the stage for an event in the life of the family not of the child alone but of all Israel. The chair of Elijah, filled by the one who holds the child, sets the newborn baby into Elijah's lap. The enchantment extends through the furnishing of the room; what is not ordinarily present is introduced, and that makes all the difference.

We move, third, from gesture to formula, for there is a blessing said before the rite itself, that is, as the *mohel* takes the knife to cut the foreskin, these words are said:

Praised are You ... who sanctified us with Your commandments and commanded us to bring the son into the covenant of Abraham our father.

The explicit invocation of Abraham's covenant turns the concrete action in the here and now into a simile of the paradigm and archetype. The operation done, fourth, the wine is blessed, introducing yet a further occasion of enchantment:

Praised are You, Lord our God, who sanctified the beloved from the womb and set a statute into his very flesh, and his parts sealed with the sign of the holy covenant. On this account, Living God, our portion and rock, save the beloved of our flesh from destruction, for the sake of his covenant placed in our flesh. Blessed are You ... who makes the covenant.

The covenant is not a generality; it is specific, concrete, fleshly. It is, moreover, meant to accomplish a very specific goal – as all religion means to attain concrete purposes – and that is to secure a place for the child, a blessing for the child. By virtue of the rite, the child enters the covenant, meaning that he joins that unseen "Israel" that through blood enters an agreement with God. Then the blessing of the covenant is owing to the child. For covenants or contracts cut both ways.

After the father has recited the blessing, "... who has sanctified us by his commandments and has commanded us to induct him into the covenant of our father, Abraham," the community responds: "just as he has entered the covenant, so may he be introduced to Torah, the *huppah* [marriage canopy] and good deeds." Schachter interprets those who are present as follows:

In the presence of Elijah ... Torah – as against idolatry; in the presence of Phineas ... huppah, as against sexual licentiousness; in the presence of Abraham ... to good deeds: "For I have singled him out that he may instruct his children and his posterity to keep the way of the Lord by doing what is just and right" (Gen. 18:18).[12]

In the transformation of the *now* of the birth of the son into the *then* of Abraham's covenant with God, people make a public event of a private joy. Many join the occasion: Elijah complaining to God, Abraham obediently circumcising his sons, Phineas calming God's wrath by an act of violence, with whom a covenant of peace then is made.

So much for the way in which the sages' mode of thought shapes the liturgy, imposing in concrete and personal form the pattern of an ever-present past upon the present and turning present-tense time into paradigm of what will be. What of those distinctive clusters of themes that the theology of the Oral Torah

---

12. "Reflections on the Brit Mila Ceremony," 41.

calls together?[13] A glance at the *huppah*-liturgy defines what we should expect: Adam/Creation/Israel/Zion (=Land of Israel); or joy/Jerusalem; or image of God/image of man. Other such clusters will encompass Israel/gentile, this age/world to come, Eden/world to come, and so on. But the Oral Torah yields a limited number of archetypal clusters, allowing for a nearly unlimited number of recombinations thereof. Within this theory of the character of the Oral Torah's theology, a certain few clusters should suffice to animate the liturgy. A determinate list ought to supply reference-points, that is, to encompass the liturgy within the boundaries of the Oral Torah in particular.

Let us begin with a simple test. Within the theory of Israel set forth in chapter 3 and of the gentiles in chapter 4, we may offer the following hypothesis. If the Oral Torah imparts shape and structure to the liturgy, then, whenever Israel the holy people forms the focus of prayer, the gentiles must figure as well – and the same theory that defines the one has also to explain the other. To test that theory, we turn to the prayer *Alenu*, recited at the conclusion of every act of public worship, three times daily, when the congregation, having embodied holy Israel, prayers to depart. At the conclusion of worship, Israel thanks God for making Israel what it is: unlike the gentiles, following a unique destiny. This prayer, celebrating Israel's difference as destiny but looking forward to the end of that difference, simply restates in terms of "you" the theology of Israel and the gentiles that we have examined in the sources assembled in chapters 3 and 4:

Let us praise Him, Lord over all the world;
Let us acclaim Him, Author of all creation.
He made our lot unlike that of other peoples;
He assigned to us a unique destiny.
We bend the knee, worship, and acknowledge
The King of kings, the Holy One, praised is He.
He unrolled the heavens and established the earth;
His throne of glory is in the heavens above;
His majestic Presence is in the loftiest heights.
He and no other is God and faithful King,
Even as we are told in His Torah:
Remember now and always, that the Lord is God;
Remember, no other is Lord of heaven and earth.

13. In *The Theological Grammar of the Oral Torah* (Binghamton, N.Y.: State University of New York Press 1997), vol. 2, *Syntax: Connections and Constructions*, I have catalogued 150 of them.

So much for Israel, thanking God for making it what it is, God's assembly. Then, predictably, gentiles must follow. Here Israel prays for the end of idolatry, at which point the gentiles will cease to be gentile and become no other than Israel, living in God's kingdom. Integral to the same prayer is the next paragraph:

We, therefore, hope in You, O Lord our God,
That we shall soon see the triumph of Your might,
That idolatry shall be removed from the earth,
And false gods shall be utterly destroyed.
Then will the world be a true kingdom of God,
When all mankind will invoke Your name,
And all the earth's wicked will return to You.
Then all the inhabitants of the world will surely know
That to You every knee must bend,
Every tongue must pledge loyalty.
Before You, O Lord, let them bow in worship,
Let them give honour to Your glory.
May they all accept the rule of Your kingdom.
May You reign over them soon through all time.
Sovereignty is Yours in glory, now and forever.
So it is written in Your Torah:
The Lord shall reign for ever and ever.[14]

The unique, the particular, the private become testimonies of divine sovereignty, pertinent to all people. When God's will is to be done, then all people will recognize that the unique destiny of Israel is intended for everyone. Israel will be no more, because everyone will be Israel. Here, then, the complementary antonym, Israel/gentile, recapitulates the sages' theory of the gentiles and idolatry within their theology of Israel and the Torah. And, as we see, it is in so many words: "false gods ... utterly destroyed ... kingdom of God ... all mankind invoke ...," and the like.

Such is a cluster that fits naturally its two opposed components. But in the main the theology of the Oral Torah exhibits no sustained preference for antonymic or binary constructions. Rather, its intellectual ambition encompasses the power to combine many components into a single narrative statement. Creation, revelation, redemption form one such paramount cluster, land, liber-

14. *Weekday Prayer Book*, ed. the Rabbinical Assembly of America Prayerbook Committee, Rabbi Jules Harlow, secretary (New York: Rabbinical Assembly 1962), 97–8.

ation, covenant, Torah, another; Israel, Land of Israel, Jerusalem, restoration, a third; and so on. Above all, we must wonder, how do the several salvific symbols fit together in the larger mythic structure of creation, revelation, and redemption? In the Grace after Meals, recited whenever pious Jews eat bread, we see their interplay. To understand the setting, we must recall that in classical Judaism the table at which meals were eaten was regarded as the equivalent of the sacred altar in the Temple. Judaism taught that each Jew before eating had to attain the same state of ritual purity as the priest in the sacred act of making a sacrifice. So in the classic tradition the Grace after Meals is recited in a sacerdotal circumstance. That is why the entire theology of the Oral Torah comes to realization in this single, simple liturgy. I mark off its principal parts.

[1] Blessed art Thou, Lord our God, King of the Universe, who nourishes all the world by His goodness, in grace, in mercy, and in compassion: He gives bread to all flesh, for His mercy is everlasting. And because of His great goodness we have never lacked, and so may we never lack, sustenance – for the sake of His great Name. For He nourishes and feeds everyone, is good to all, and provides food for each one of the creatures He created.

Blessed art Thou, O Lord, who feeds everyone.

[2] We thank Thee, Lord our God, for having given our fathers as a heritage a pleasant, a good and spacious land; for having taken us out of the land of Egypt, for having redeemed us from the house of bondage; for Thy covenant, which Thou hast set as a seal in our flesh, for Thy Torah which Thou has taught us, for Thy statutes which Thou hast made known to us, for the life of grace and mercy Thou hast graciously bestowed upon us, and for the nourishment with which Thou dost nourish us and feed us always, every day, in every season, and every hour.

For all these things, Lord our God, we thank and praise Thee; may Thy praises continually be in the mouth of every living thing, as it is written, And thou shalt eat and be satisfied, and bless the Lord thy God for the good land which He hath given thee.

Blessed art Thou, O Lord, for the land and its food.

[3] O Lord our God, have pity on Thy people Israel, on Thy city Jerusalem, on Zion the place of Thy glory, on the royal house of David Thy Messiah, and on the great and holy house which is called by Thy Name. Our God, our Father, feed us and speed us, nourish us and make us flourish, unstintingly, O Lord our God, speedily free us from all distress.

And let us not, O Lord our God, find ourselves in need of gifts from flesh and blood, or of a loan from anyone save from Thy full, generous, abundant, wide-open hand; so we may never be humiliated, or put to shame.

O rebuild Jerusalem, the holy city, speedily in our day. Blessed art Thou, Lord, who in mercy will rebuild Jerusalem. Amen.
[4] Blessed art Thou, Lord our God, King of the Universe, Thou God, who art our Father, our powerful king, our creator and redeemer, who made us, our holy one, the holy one of Jacob, our shepherd, shepherd of Israel, the good king, who visits His goodness upon all; for every single day He has brought good, He does bring good, He will bring good upon us; He has rewarded us, does regard, and will always reward us, with grace, mercy and compassion, amplitude, deliverance and prosperity, blessing and salvation, comfort, and a living, sustenance, pity and peace, and all good – let us not want any manner of good whatever.[15]

The context of grace is enjoyment of creation, the arena for creation is the land. The land lay at the end of redemption from Egyptian bondage. Holding it, enjoying it is a sign that the covenant is intact and in force and that Israel is loyal to its part of the contract and God to his. The land, the Exodus, the covenant – these all depend upon the Torah, statutes, and a life of grace and mercy, here embodied in and evoked by the nourishment of the meal. Thanksgiving wells up, and the paragraph ends with praises for the land and its food.

This cluster on its own does not demand identification with the Oral Torah. The restorationist dynamic is what (in the present context) reveals the hand of the sages. Here we have not merely a messianic prayer for the end of days, but a specific framing of the end in terms of the beginning, the restoration of Israel to the Land of Israel, that the liturgy bespeaks. The restorationist theme recurs throughout, redemption and hope for return, and then future prosperity in the land: May God pity the people, the city, Zion, the royal house of the Messiah, the Holy Temple." The nourishment of this meal is but a foretaste of the nourishment of the messianic time, just as the joy of the wedding is a foretaste of the messianic rejoicing. Creation and re-creation, exile and return – these are the particular clusters that point to the substrate of the sages' theology.

Thus far, the first two clusters, dealing with Israel and the gentiles, creation, revelation, redemption, and restoration, go over secondary matters. The primary claim of the Oral Torah concerns God's creation of a world order over chaos, and specifically, a world ordered by justice, a world ruled by God himself, and a world that would recover its original perfection. Here, in the third cluster of particular concerns, we find the Judaic creed exactly as the

15. Judah Goldin, trans., *The Grace after Meals* (New York: Jewish Theological Seminary of America 1955), 9, 15*ff.*

sages would have defined it. That is to say, the themes that converge here and the way in which they are articulated respond to the distinctive theological structure and system put forth by the sages. When I maintain that the Oral Torah imparted its imprint upon all that came afterward, and that that is a matter of not historical influence based on political sponsorship but inner logic, I point to formations such as the one before us here, the creed contained in the twice-daily recitation of the *Shema*.

Evening and morning, the pious Jew proclaims the unity and uniqueness of God. The proclamation is preceded and followed by blessings, two at the beginning, then the recitation of the *Shema*, then one at the end, in the sequence, creation, revelation, proclamation of God's unity and dominion, then redemption. The recital of the *Shema* is introduced by a celebration of God as Creator of the world. God daily creates an orderly world, a world ordered in goodness. That is what is important about creation – as we have seen in chapter 2. The *Shema* is recited morning and night, and the prayer varies for the occasion, though the message, the creation of world order, does not. In the morning, one says,

Praised are You, O Lord our God, King of the universe.
You fix the cycles of light and darkness;
You ordain the order of all creation
You cause light to shine over the earth;
Your radiant mercy is upon its inhabitants.
In Your goodness the work of creation
Is continually renewed day by day ...
O cause a new light to shine on Zion;
May we all soon be worthy to behold its radiance.
Praised are You, O Lord, Creator of the heavenly bodies.[16]

The blessing in the morning celebrates light, ending with the new light when creation is renewed. The corresponding prayer in the evening refers to the setting of the sun:

Praised are You ...
Your command brings on the dusk of evening.
Your wisdom opens the gates of heaven to a new day.
With understanding You order the cycles of time;
Your will determines the succession of seasons;

16. *Weekday Prayer Book*, 42.

You order the stars in their heavenly courses.
You create day, and You create night,
Rolling away light before darkness ...
Praised are You, O Lord, for the evening dusk.[17]

The natural order of the world in the liturgical setting elicits thanks and praise of God who created the world and who actively guides the daily events of nature. Whatever happens in nature gives testimony to the sovereignty of the Creator. And that testimony takes place in the most ordinary events: the orderly regularity of sunrise and sunset.

It is through the Torah that Israel knows God as not merely Creator but purposeful Creator. There Israel encounters God as just, world order as a formulation of the benevolent, beneficent laws of life. Torah is the mark not merely of divine sovereignty and justice, but of divine grace and love, just as, in our account of complementarity, we saw mercy as the complement of justice. So goes the second blessing:

Deep is Your love for us, O Lord our God;
Bounteous is Your compassion and tenderness.

Now comes the pronouncement of the character of world order: reliable, guided by compassion, to be learned through God's self-manifestation in the Torah:

You taught our fathers the laws of life,
And they trusted in You, Father and king,
For their sake be gracious to us, and teach us,
That we may learn Your laws and trust in You.
Father, merciful Father, have compassion upon us:
Endow us with discernment and understanding.
Grant us the will to study Your Torah,
To heed its words and to teach its precepts ...
Enlighten our eyes in Your Torah,
Open our hearts to Your commandments ...
Unite our thoughts with singleness of purpose
To hold You in reverence and in love ...
You have drawn us close to You;

17. Ibid., 141.

We praise You and thank You in truth.
With love do we thankfully proclaim Your unity.
And praise You who chose Your people Israel in love.[18]

God, the Creator, revealed his will for creation through the Torah, given to Israel his people. That Torah contains the "laws of life." In identifying the world order of justice as the foundation-stone of the sages' theology, I simply recapitulated the liturgical creed.

In the *Shema*, Torah – instruction through revelation – leads to the chief teaching of revelation, the premise of world order, the dominion of the one and only God. In proclaiming the following words, Israel accepts, one, the rule of God, two, the yoke of the dominion of Heaven, and three, the yoke of the Torah and commandments:

Hear, O Israel, the Lord Our God, the Lord is One.

This proclamation is followed by three Scriptural passages. The first is Deuteronomy 6:5–9:

You shall love the Lord your God with all your heart, with all your soul, with all your might.

And further, one must diligently teach one's children these words and talk of them everywhere and always, and place them on one's forehead, doorposts, and gates. The second Scripture is Deuteronomy 11:13–21, which emphasizes that if Jews keep the commandments, they will enjoy worldly blessings; but that if they do not, they will be punished and disappear from the good land God gives them. The third is Numbers 15:37–41, the commandment to wear fringes on the corners of one's garments.

Then comes the address to God, not as Creator or Revealer, but God as Redeemer. This prayer, predictably within the sages' framework, treats as comparable the redemption from Egypt and the redemption at the last, the one as the embodiment of the other, just as we have seen in Chapter 14 in so many words:

You are our King and our father's King,
Our redeemer and our father's redeemer.

18. Ibid., 45–56.

You are our creator …
You have ever been our redeemer and deliverer
There can be no God but You …

Now we turn to the initial formation of the paradigm of redemption, the liberation from Egypt, through the passage through the sea:

You, O Lord our God, rescued us from Egypt;
You redeemed us from the house of bondage …
You split apart the waters of the Red Sea,
The faithful you rescued, the wicked drowned …
Then Your beloved sang hymns of thanksgiving …
They acclaimed the King, God on high,
Great and awesome source of all blessings,
The ever-living God, exalted in his majesty.

As soon as redemption makes its appearance, the theme of arrogance and humility appears alongside, since, for the sages, we need hardly remind ourselves, arrogance is the cause of sin and exile, whereas humility elicits God's favour and brings about restoration:

He humbles the proud and raises the lowly;
He helps the needy and answers His people's call …
Then Moses and all the children of Israel
Sang with great joy this song to the Lord:
Who is like You O Lord among the mighty?
Who is like You, so glorious in holiness?
So wondrous your deeds, so worthy of praise!
The redeemed sang a new song to You;
They sang in chorus at the sore of the sea,
Acclaiming Your sovereignty with thanksgiving:
The Lord shall reign for ever and ever.
Rock of Israel, arise to Israel's defence!
Fulfil Your promise to deliver Judah and Israel.
Our redeemer is the Holy One of Israel,
The Lord of hosts is His name.
Praised are You, O Lord, redeemer of Israel.[19]

19. Ibid., 50*ff.*

That God not only creates but also redeems is embodied in the redemption from Egyptian bondage. The congregation repeats the exultant song of Moses and the people at the Red Sea as participants in the salvation of old and of time to come. The stories of creation, the Exodus from Egypt, and the revelation of Torah at Sinai are repeated, not merely to recount what once happened but rather to recreate out of the reworked materials of everyday life the "true being" – life as it was, always is, and will be forever.

The final and most important liturgical exercise in reworking the sages' theology brings us to the main principle of world order, God's just rule over creation. No more eloquent and powerful statement of that principle occurs than in the liturgy of the New Year, Rosh Hashanah, and the Day of Atonement, Yom Kippur, which together mark the Days of Awe, of solemn penitence, at the start of the autumn festival season. These occasions work out in concrete terms how the world order of justice extends to the here and now of patterned, orderly, everyday life. For on the first of these occasions, the New Year, each person is inscribed for life or death in the Heavenly books for the coming year, and on the Day of Atonement the books are sealed. The synagogues on that day are filled with penitents. The New Year is called the birthday of the world: "This day the world was born." It is likewise a day of remembrance on which the deeds of all creatures are reviewed. On it God asserts his sovereignty, as in the New Year Prayer:

Our God and God of our Fathers, Rule over the whole world in Your honor ... and appear in Your glorious might to all those who dwell in the civilization of Your world, so that everything made will know that You made it, and every creature discern that You have created him, so that all in whose nostrils is breath may say, "The Lord, the God of Israel is king, and His kingdom extends over all."[20]

The themes of the liturgy are divine sovereignty, divine memory, and divine disclosure. These correspond to creation, revelation, and redemption. Sovereignty is established by creation of the world. Judgment depends upon law: "From the beginning You made this, Your purpose known ..." And therefore, since people have been told what God requires of them, they are judged:

On this day sentence is passed upon countries, which to the sword and which to peace, which to famine and which to plenty, and each creature is judged today for life or death. Who is not judged on this day? For the remembrance of every creature comes before You, each man's deeds and destiny, words and way ...

20. Traditional prayer; author's translation from the Hebrew.

The theme of revelation is further combined with redemption; the ram's horn, or *shofar*, which is sounded in the synagogue during daily worship for a month before the *Rosh Hashanah* festival, serves to unite the two:

You did reveal yourself in a cloud of glory ... Out of heaven you made them [Israel] hear Your voice ... Amid thunder and lightning You revealed yourself to them, and while the shofar sounded You shined forth upon them ... Our God and God of our fathers, sound the great shofar for our freedom. Lift up the ensign to gather our exiles ... Lead us happily to Zion Your city, Jerusalem the place of Your sanctuary.

The complex themes of the New Year, the most "theological" of Jewish holy occasions, thus recapitulate a familiar cluster of themes.

The most personal, solemn, and moving of the Days of Awe is the Day of Atonement, Yom Kippur, the Sabbath of Sabbaths. It is marked by fasting and continuous prayer. On it, Israel makes confession:

Our God and God of our fathers, may our prayer come before You. Do not hide yourself from our supplication, for we are not so arrogant or stiff-necked as to say before You ... We are righteous and have not sinned. But we have sinned.
We are guilt laden, we have been faithless, we have robbed ...
We have committed iniquity, caused unrighteousness, have been presumptuous. We have counselled evil, scoffed, revolted, blasphemed ...[21]

The Hebrew confession is built upon an alphabetical acrostic following the letters of the Hebrew alphabet, as if by making certain every letter is represented, God, who knows human secrets, will combine them into appropriate words. The very alphabet bears witness against us before God. Then:

What shall we say before You who dwell on high? What shall we tell You who live in heaven? Do You not know all things, both the hidden and the revealed? You know the secrets of eternity, the most hidden mysteries of life. You search the innermost recesses, testing men's feelings and heart. Nothing is concealed from You or hidden from Your eyes. May it therefore be Your will to forgive us our sins, to pardon us for our iniquities, to grant remission for our transgressions.[22]

A further list of sins follows, built on alphabetical lines. Prayers to be spoken by the congregation are all in the plural: "For the sin which we have sinned

---

21. *Mahzor*, Jules Harlow, trans. (New York: Rabbinical Assembly 1995).
22. Ibid.

against You with the utterance of the lips ... For the sin which we have sinned before You openly and secretly ..." The community takes upon itself responsibility for what is done in it. All Israel is part of one community, one body, and all are responsible for the acts of each. The sins confessed are mostly against society, against one's fellow men; few pertain to ritual laws. At the end comes a final word:

O my God, before I was formed, I was nothing. Not that I have been formed, it is as though I had not been formed, for I am dust in my life, more so after death. Behold I am before You like a vessel filled with shame and confusion. May it be Your will ... that I may no more sin, and forgive the sins I have already committed in Your abundant compassion.[23]

Israelites, within all Israel, see themselves before the just and merciful God: possessing no merits, yet hopeful of God's love and compassion. Where, then, shall we look for an address to God that is not framed within the theology of the Oral Torah?

Now, readers ought rightly to object, is this corpus of liturgy not a mere reprise of Scripture? Why invoke the Oral part of the Torah to make sense of the synagogue worship, when that liturgy simply reworks the main lines of thought of the Written part of the Torah, indeed constantly recites verses of Scripture within the act of worship? And I hasten to concede, as would the sages in whose behalf I have claimed so much, readers do not err. A liturgy that recapitulates the themes of creation, revelation, and redemption, that speaks of exile from and return to the Land in a plan of restoration, that celebrates God's sovereignty and invokes God's justice in judgment, surely reworks the themes of Scripture. And one that constantly makes reference to the Torah as the emblem of God's love and to Israel as the people of the Torah, that perpetually invokes the correspondence of world order in the heavens with peace on earth (as in the Qaddish-prayer) – such a liturgy surely rests squarely upon the Written Torah, which from its opening lines says no less.

A single, seamless statement, the *Siddur* and *Mahzor*, the Oral Torah, and the Written Torah, severally and jointly say the same few things. That is why the worship of the synagogue, in the *Siddur* and the *Mahzor*, with its enchanted and timeless world of ever-present eternity, is beyond all comprehending except within the framework of the Oral part of the Torah. But so too, the sages would have insisted, the Oral part of the Torah for its part restates precisely the message, in exact balance and proportion, of the

23. Ibid.

Written part. It too makes sense only within the framework of the Written part of the Torah. So, in sequence, the sages read from the Written Torah to the Oral one. And, reflecting on that reading, the theologians of the liturgy composed prayer to reframe, in the second-person "you" of prayer personally addressed to the person of God, precisely the result of that same reading: what the Torah teaches about God that Israel may bring in prayer to God.

So that is why, as I claimed at the outset, when we define the theology of the Oral Torah, we state Judaism pure and simple, no more, no less. Here we encounter the one, the only, the unique God, who to Israel makes himself known in the Torah, creates a world ordered by justice, and sustains and restores that world order, every day, making peace, as the Qaddish says, both in heaven and on earth. That is what revealing the justice of God in the world order requires: God's rule in the chaos of the here and now. So in the words of the Qaddish, invoking heaven and earth at once:

Magnified and sanctified be the great Name in the world that he created as he willed, and may his dominion come in your life and in your days and in the life of the whole house of Israel, speedily and soon ... May he who makes things whole on high make things whole for us ...

Index of Subjects

Index of References to Ancient Texts

MISHNAH

SIFRA

SIFRE

PESIQTA DERAB KAHANA

MEKHILTA ATTRIBUTED TO R. ISHMAEL

THE FATHERS ACCORDING TO RABBI